AF538633

PROCESS INSTRUMENTATION AND CONTROL

REVISED EDITION

FOR

THIRD YEAR DEGREE COURSE IN CHEMICAL AND ALLIED ENGINEERING COURSES

A. P. KULKARNI

B.Sc. (Physics), M.E. (Chemical Engineering)

Assistant Professor in Chemical Engineering,

Sinhgad College of Engineering,

Vadgaon (bk), Pune – 411041.

N0904

PROCESS INSTRUMENTATION AND CONTROL **ISBN 978-93-81237-06-9**

Eighteenth Edition : February 2017

Published By :
NIRALI PRAKASHAN
Abhyudaya Pragati, 1312, Shivaji Nagar,
Off J.M. Road, PUNE – 411005
Tel - (020) 25512336/37/39, Fax - (020) 25511379
Email : niralipune@pragationline.com

Printed By :
RACHANA OFFSETS
S. No. 15, Arihant Marg,
Sukhsagar Nagar, Katraj,
Pune – 411 0 46
Tel – (020) 26963220

☞ DISTRIBUTION CENTRES

PUNE

Nirali Prakashan : 119, Budhwar Peth, Jogeshwari Mandir Lane, Pune 411002, Maharashtra
Tel : (020) 2445 2044, 66022708, Fax : (020) 2445 1538
Email : bookorder@pragationline.com, niralilocal@pragationline.com

Nirali Prakashan : S. No. 28/27, Dhyari, Near Pari Company, Pune 411041
Tel : (020) 24690204 Fax : (020) 24690316
Email : dhyari@pragationline.com, bookorder@pragationline.com

MUMBAI

Nirali Prakashan : 385, S.V.P. Road, Rasdhara Co-op. Hsg. Society Ltd.,
Girgaum, Mumbai 400004, Maharashtra
Tel : (022) 2385 6339 / 2386 9976, Fax : (022) 2386 9976
Email : niralimumbai@pragationline.com

☞ DISTRIBUTION BRANCHES

JALGAON

Nirali Prakashan : 34, V. V. Golani Market, Navi Peth, Jalgaon 425001,
Maharashtra, Tel : (0257) 222 0395, Mob : 94234 91860

KOLHAPUR

Nirali Prakashan : New Mahadvar Road, Kedar Plaza, 1st Floor Opp. IDBI Bank
Kolhapur 416 012, Maharashtra. Mob : 9850046155

NAGPUR

Pratibha Book Distributors : Above Maratha Mandir, Shop No. 3, First Floor,
Rani Jhanshi Square, Sitabuldi, Nagpur 440012, Maharashtra
Tel : (0712) 254 7129

DELHI

Nirali Prakashan : 4593/21, Basement, Aggarwal Lane 15, Ansari Road, Daryaganj
Near Times of India Building, New Delhi 110002, Mob : 08505972553

BENGALURU

Pragati Book House : [illegible] 1, Sanjeevappa Lane, Avenue Road Cross,
Opp. Rice Church, Bengaluru – 560002.
Tel : (080) 64513344, 64513355,Mob : 9880582331, 9845021552
Email:bharatsavla@yahoo.com

CHENNAI

Pragati Books : 9/1, Montieth Road, Behind Taas Mahal, Egmore,
Chennai 600008 Tamil Nadu, Tel : (044) 6518 3535,
Mob : 94440 01782 / 98450 21552 / 98805 82331,
Email : bharatsavla@yahoo.com

niralipune@pragationline.com | www.pragationline.com

Also find us on f www.facebook.com/niralibooks

PREFACE

It gives me great pleasure in presenting this book titled **"Process Instrumentation and Control"**. The book combines the contents on diversified-but-related areas – **Process Instrumentation and Process Control**.

Part I of the book covers the topics on Process Instrumentation.

Chapter 1 explains the basic concepts of Process Instrumentation alongwith the modern techniques of measurement using μP, μC, PC and VI softwares. In this chapter the topics on electronics of the measurement systems are also discussed.

Chapter 2 deals with temperature measuring instruments along with calibration methods for temperature sensors.

Chapter 3 deals with pressure sensors used for measurement of absolute, gauge and vacuum pressures.

Chapter 4 describes the working of level measurement instruments.

Chapter 5 covers the methods of flow measurement.

Chapter 6 discusses the methods used for chemical analysis of materials. The methods explained in this chapter will be useful for researchers to analyze the mixtures of chemical species.

Part II of the book is devoted to Process Dynamics and Control.

In Chapter 7, basic concepts of Process Dynamics are explained in detail. The dynamic behaviour of first and second-order system is explained in detail alongwith the physical candidate processes. The mathematical tools required for studying process control are elaborated, which will be helpful for readers to understand the mathematical aspects of the subject.

Chapter 8 covers the basic feedback control systems used for controlling the performance of process system such as surge tank, heat exchanger, distillation column, CSTR, pumps and compressors. In this chapter, the control system for polymer processing operations, oil well drilling and production operations are explained in brief.

This book will be useful for students taking courses on process instrumentation and control. Also the book will serve as the reference guide for practicing professionals.

I am very much thankful to Mr. Dineshbhai Furia, Mr. Jignesh Furia, Mr. Kiran Velankar, Mr. Munde, Mr. Santosh Bare, Miss. Chaitali Takale and staff of Nirali Prakashan for publishing this book in short span. I am also thankful to my colleagues in Sinhgad College of Engineering for helping me in executing numerical calculations alongwith graphical presentations.

Finally thanks to my family members to bear with inconvenience due to extended hours of book writing.

Although efforts are made to present contents in correct form, author do not claim originality and correctness of the matter. If the reader finds any mistakes, errors, omissions in the text, feel free to communicate the suggestions to the author or publisher.

A. P. Kulkarni

T.E. Chemical Engineering
PROCESS INSTRUMENTATION AND CONTROL
SYLLABUS

Unit 1 : Fundamentals of Process Instrumentation (PI) : (06)

Need and scope of process instrumentation, classification of process variables, measurement problem analysis, basic measurement terms.

Functional elements of instruments, static and dynamic characteristics of measuring instruments (zeroth, first, and second-order instruments/systems), measurement system configuration, transducer elements (types and classification).

Intermediate elements : Instrument amplifiers, compensators, differential and integrator elements, signal conditioners (signal generation and processing), filtering and signal analysis, data acquisition and conversion (ADC, DAC), digital signal transmission and processing (serial communication, telemetry).

Indicating and recording elements, Microprocessors, microcontrollers, personal computer (PC)-based instrumentation systems (virtual instrumentation using softwares like Lab view), input-output (I/O) devices and displays, calibration of instruments.

Unit 2 : Temperature, Pressure, and Strain Measuring Instruments : (06)

Temperature measuring instruments : Introduction, classification, temperature scales (units), mechanical temperature sensors (filled-system thermometers, expansion thermometers), electrical temperature sensors (RTD, thermistors, thermocouples), radiation sensors (optical and radiation), solid-state sensors, quartz sensors, calibration methods (comparison and fixed point).

Pressure and strain measuring instruments : Introduction, classification, low, medium, and high pressure measuring instruments, pressure scales (units), manometers, elastic element pressure gauges with pressure equations (using Bourdon tube, diaphragms, capsule, and bellows), transduction/electrical sensors with pressure equations (based on variable capacitance, resistance, and inductance/reluctance-LVDT), force-balance transducers along with mathematical equations, solid-state devices, thin-film transducers, digital transducers, piezoelectric transducers, vibrating element sensors, pressure multiplexer, calibration of pressure sensors using dead-weight tester.

Mechanical, optical, and electrical strain gauges.

Unit 3 : Level and Flow Measuring Instruments : (06)

Level measuring instruments : Introduction, classification, direct methods (point contact methods, sight or gauge glass methods, buoyancy methods using floats and displacers), indirect methods (hydrostatic pressure methods, capacitance methods, radiation methods, ultrasonic methods, weighing method, sonic methods), solid level measurement.

Flow measuring instruments : Introduction, classification (rate of flow and total flow meters), pressure head-type flow meters (orifice plate, venturi tube, flow nozzle, pitot tube), variable-area flowmeters (rotameters), electromagnetic, mechanical (positive displacement and turbine-type), anemometer, ultrasonic-type, vortex-flow type, thermal-type, laser anemometers, mass flow meters (cover mathematical treatment for all the sensors).

Unit 4 : Instrumental Methods of Chemical Analysis : (06)

Introduction, classification, basic components of analytical instruments, measurements used. Absorption and emission spectrometric methods : ultraviolet (UV), visible, and infrared (IR) spectroscopy, atomic absorption spectroscopy (AAS), mass spectroscopy, refractometry. Chromatographic methods : Gas chromatography (GC), liquid chromatography (LC), high performance liquid chromatography (HPLC). Electrochemical methods : Measurement of pH, colorimetric, conductometric, potentiometric.

Process instruments and automatic on-line analysis.

Unit 5 : Fundamentals of Process Dynamics (P.D.) : (08)

Introduction to process dynamics (P.D.), mathematical tools for process control (Laplace transform, complex numbers), ideal forcing functions, control-relevant theoretical process modeling, transfer function and state-space models, poles and zeros of transfer function and their effect on dynamic response, block diagram representation, studying dynamic behavior of linear time invariant (LTI) systems, dynamic behavior of pure gain, pure capacitive, first-order, second-order systems, dead-time systems (derive differential equation model, transfer function, response to standard test signals and response characteristics along with physical examples), process identification using step response data.

Unit 6 : Feedback Control Systems : (08)

Introduction to feedback control system (FBCS), classification of process variables, selection of controlled variables (CV), manipulated variables (MV), disturbance or load variables (DV), block diagram with essential variables and instrument elements, derivation of closed-loop transfer function for servo and regulator operations, classical feedback controllers - ON-OFF, P, PI, PD, PID (control equation/law/algorithm, tuning parameters, open-loop response characteristics along with effect of tuning parameters), simple control performance measures (rise time, overshoot, decay ratio, offset), closed-loop response characteristics of first-and second-order processes with classical controllers.

Industrial Process Control Systems :

Control system symbols used in process and instrumentation (P and ID) diagrams and drawings, basic regulatory control loops for controlling temperature of liquid heated in stirred-tank heater using electrical (or steam) heating, pressure of air/gas in pressure vessel, level of liquid inside surge vessel, flow of liquid in pipe line. Single-loop controllers for surge vessel level control, reactors (batch and CSTR), heat exchangers, distillation columns, pumps, compressors.

❑❑❑

T.E. Petroleum Engineering

PETROLEUM FIELD INSTRUMENTATION AND CONTROL

SYLLABUS

Section – I

Unit I : Introduction : **(03 Lect.)**

Classification of instruments, metrological terms, definitions, units and standards, performance characteristics, calibration requirement, Hierarchy of standards and traceability, measurement of uncertainty codes and symbols etc.

Unit II : Process Instrumentation : **(03 Lect.)**

Instruments for indicating, recording and control of pressure (including mud pressure), flow, temperature, viscosity, level, pH, density, weight, penetration, torque, RPM, magnetic flux.

Unit III : Petroleum Field Instrumentation : **(03 Lect.)**

Instrumentation at drilling site, separation, transportation and storage of oil and gas operations. Aspects of process safety and reliability related to instrumentation, pipeline monitoring.

Section – II

Unit IV : Elements of Process Control : **(03 Lect.)**

Introduction to Process Control, Basic principles. Applications of Process Control. Control loop and its components. Concept of transfer function and transient response of first and second order elements.

Unit V : Introduction to Controllers : **(03 Lect.)**

Working mechanism of pneumatic, hydraulic and electronic controllers, Alarm systems, On-off controller. Limit switches. Solenoid valves. Characteristics of control valves.

Unit VI : Process Control of Petroleum Field Operations : **(03 Lect.)**

Applications of controls for drilling, separation, transportation and storage of oil and gas operations.

DCS. SCADA. Introduction to Ladder Logic. Logics for safe shutdown and startup.

❑❑❑

T.E. Petrochemical Engineering

INSTRUMENTATION AND INSTRUMENTAL ANALYSIS

SYLLABUS

Section - I

Unit I : Introduction to Instruments, Characteristics and Signal conditioning (8 Lect.)

Introduction to Instruments and their representation : Introduction, Elements, Classification, Standards, Calibration procedures. Static and Dynamic Characteristics of Instruments, Specification of static characteristics, Selection of instruments, Forcing functions, Formulation of First order and Second order system equations, Dynamic response. Principles of Analog signal conditioning, converters, guidelines for analog signal conditioning design, Principles of digital signal conditioning, computer interface, DACs, ADCs, DAS hardware, DAS software, characteristics of digital data.

Unit II : Temperature, Pressure, Level measurements (8 Lect.)

Temperature measurement : Temperature scales, Non-electrical methods, Electrical methods, Radiation methods. **Pressure measurement :** Moderate pressure measurement, High pressure measurement, vacuum measurement. **Level measurement :** Measurement techniques for liquids and slurries, advance measurement techniques.

Unit III : Flow Measurements and Study of Valves (8 Lect.)

Flow measurement : Introduction, Review of venturimeter, orifice meters, rotameters, pitot tube, working of turbine, vortex shedding, electromagnetic flow meters. **Introduction to Advanced flow measurement techniques :** Hot wire anemometer, Laser Doppler anemometer, Ultrasound, Particle image velocimetry. **Study of Valves :** Types of Valves, Actuators, Positioners, Valve characteristics, Controllability and Rangeability, Cavitation, Flashing, Choking, Valve sizing for incompressible fluids, compressible fluids, two-phase flows.

Section - II

Unit IV : Introduction to Quality Control and Analytical Techniques (8 Lect.)

Need for Chemical analysis in Petroleum industry. Crude Assay. Standard Test Methods. Introduction to principles of Analytical Techniques: Spectroscopic techniques, Chromatographic techniques, Crystallography, Electrochemical analysis, Thermal analysis, Electrophoresis, colorimetry, Hybrid techniques.

Unit V : Working and Interpretation of Instrumental analytical methods : (I) (8 Lect.)

Spectroscopic techniques : Atomic Absorption, X-ray, inductively coupled argon plasma (ICAP), ultraviolet – visible (UV-VIS), fluorescence, infrared (IR), Raman spectroscopy, mass spectrometry (MS), nuclear magnetic resonance (NMR). **Chromatographic Techniques :** Gas chromatography (GC), high pressure liquid chromatography, gel permeation chromatography (GPC), thin layer chromatography (TLC), supercritical fluid chromatography (SFC). Classification of spectroscopic and chromatographic techniques for analysis of fuels.

UNIT VI : Working and Interpretation of Instrumental Analytical Methods : (II) (8 Lect.)

Lubricant Analysis : Constituents of lubricants, characterization of lubricants by analytical techniques, importance of elemental analysis in lubricants. **Miscellaneous measurements and analysis :** Density, viscosity, Refractometer, pH and redox potential measurements. Thermal conductivity gas analyzers. Oxygen determination. Orsat analysis.

❑❑❑

T.E. Polymer Engineering

INSTRUMENTATION AND PROCESS CONTROL

SYLLABUS

Section - I

Unit I : Introduction to Measurement System (7 Hrs.)

Measurement system elements, Classification of Instruments, Static and Dynamic Characteristics of instruments, Calibration, Sources of error with measuring instruments, Designing of measuring system, Basics of sensing elements, Signal conditioning, Data display with some examples.

Unit II : Temperature and Pressure Measurements (8 Hrs.)

Temperature Measurement Instruments such as Expansion Thermometers, Filled System Thermometers, Thermoelectricity Based: Industrial thermocouple, response of thermocouples and other Electrical Temperature based sensors, Radiation and optical pyrometers. Pressure Measurement Instruments such as Liquid Column Elements, Elastic Element Gauges, Electrical Transducer, Forced Balanced Devices.

Unit III : Level, Flow, Viscosity and Density Measurements (7 Hrs.)

Direct and Indirect measurement of Liquid Level, Different Head flow meters, area flow meters, Total flow measuring instruments, Viscosity measurements of polymer solutions and polymer melt, and density measurement systems.

Section - II

Unit IV : Introduction to Process Control (7 Hrs.)

Introduction to process control, Designing aspects of process control system, control system performance, mathematical modeling principles used for process control, Dynamic response of linear open-loop systems such as first-order system, second-order system, first-order system in series with physical examples.

Unit V : Feedback Control Loop (8 Hrs.)

Introduction to control loop, open-loop and closed-loop, basic elements of closed-loop control system, feedback control system, closed-loop transfer function, open-loop transfer function, multiple closed loop transfer function, effect of disturbances, modes of control action and control valve, transient response of simple control system, controller tuning.

Unit VI : Advanced Process Control (7 Hrs.)

Introduction to Advanced process control system, Feed forward, cascade, ratio control with different applications, Introduction to Digital control, introduction to discrete-time system, Introduction to Programmable Logic Control, Supervisory control and data acquisition systems. Distributed control systems, Different examples of Microprocessor-based control system used for chemical and polymer manufacturing such as control of continuous and batch polymerization processes.

❑❑❑

CONTENTS

PART-I : PROCESS INSTRUMENTATION

❑❑❑

PART – I

PROCESS INSTRUMENTATION

1

CHAPTER

FUNDAMENTALS OF PROCESS INSTRUMENTATION

1.1 INTRODUCTION

In this chapter the basic concepts of Process Instrumentation (PI) are discussed. The need and scope of PI are explained in detailed. The basic measurement problem analysis is discussed along with the functional elements and operating characteristics (static and dynamic) of the measuring instruments. The construction and working of various types of transducers, intermediate elements, indicating and recording elements are explained in detail. To be in pace with the latest developments in the field of PI, use of microprocessors (μP), microcontrollers (μC) based instrumentation system are introduced at the end of the chapter.

1.2 NEED AND SCOPE OF PI

Instrumentation refers to the technology of using instruments for the purpose of observation, measurement and or control of the physical and chemical properties of the material.

Process Instrumentation (PI) covers the measurement of variables involved in process industries such as chemical, petroleum, power generation, air conditioning, metallurgical, food, textile, paper and many other industries.

Instrumentation encompasses the areas of detection, acquisition, control, and analysis of data. Application of instrumentation systems result in savings in time and labour involved, better quality control, higher plant utilization, better manpower productivity, material and energy savings.

Typical applications of instrument systems are :

1. Measurement of system or process parameters.
2. Control of a process or operation.
3. To simulate experimentally the actual conditions of complex systems, which help to study the true behavior of the system under different operating conditions. This information is obtained from a scale model which is then translated into the design and development of the prototype.

4. Instruments are used to perform operations on measurement signal such as addition, subtraction, multiplication, linearization, etc.
5. Instrumentation systems are used for conducting experimental design studies to supplement design and development studies.
6. Experimental measurements are used for verifying physical phenomena and scientific theories.
7. Quality control of products.
8. Manufacturing of products as per the national/international standards and specifications. This ensures that the products function as per the expectations.

1.3 MEASUREMENT SYSTEM

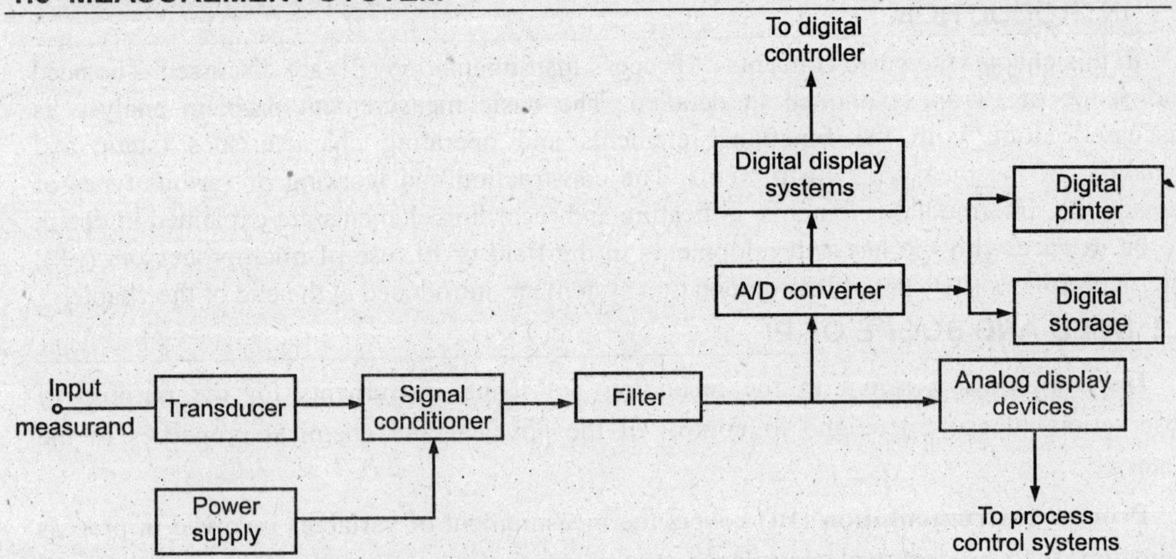

Fig. 1.1 : Generalized measurement system

Fig. 1.1 shows a generalized measurement system which consists of the following elements.

1. **Transducer :**

   Transducer is a device which converts the **measurand** (i.e. the quantity, property or condition to be measured) into a usable output form such as displacement, current, voltage, resistance change, capacitance change, etc. Therefore a transducer may be mechanical, electrical, magnetic, optical, chemical, acoustic, thermal, nuclear in construction. Many applications use electrical transducers which convert a physical, mechanical or optical quantity to be measured into an electrical voltage, current or resistance change proportional to the input measurand. The electrical output signals can be amplified, transmitted over longer distance with some modifications to meet the requirements of the indicating or controlling element.

2. **Signal Conditioner :**

   Usually, the output of the transducer element is too small (in magnitude) or weak (in strength) to operate an indicator or a recorder. Therefore, the signal conditioner is used to modify and process the output of transducer by amplification of magnitude, filtering the unwanted noise signals, linearization, differentiating, integration, sampling and A/D conversion. The output of a conditioner may be an analog or digital quantity.

3. **Display Devices :**

   The display or readout devices display the required information about the measurand to be seen or read by the experimenter. This element may be either of the visual display type, graphic recorder, oscilloscopes or a magnetic tape. The output of digital transducers are displayed on digital display devices.

4. **Power Supply :**

   The electrical power supply provides the required energy (excitation) to the transducer, signal conditioner and display devices.

1.4 MEASUREMENT PROBLEM ANALYSIS

Measurement problem involves choice of suitable electrical transducer, associated signal conditioner, display and recording instruments which will facilitate to determine the value of measurand in the form suitable for display and control purposes. Therefore, it is necessary to draw complete specifications of the devices and systems which will help in detailed design of the total measurement system. The important steps followed in measurement problem analysis are given below :

1. Define instrumentation problem precisely.
2. Determine the primary and secondary goals of the system.
3. Establish the minimum performance standards to be achieved by the instrumentation system in terms of the desired accuracy and reliability.
4. The physical dimensions and cost of the system along with test procedure and schedule.
5. Conduct component testing to collect the technical data about the effect of parameters on the overall performance of the system.
6. Establish design specifications based on engineering judgement.
7. Fabricate the instrumentation devices and systems with quality control measures and good workmanship at reasonable cost.
8. Perform calibration tests to ensure the required accuracy and precision under the given operating conditions. From the test results prepare error report in graphical or numerical data format.
9. The calibration data must be supplied with desired accuracy in a usable form which will be used to solve the original problem.

1.5 FUNCTIONAL ELEMENTS OF A MEASUREMENT SYSTEM

A generalized measurement system essentially comprise of the following functional elements.

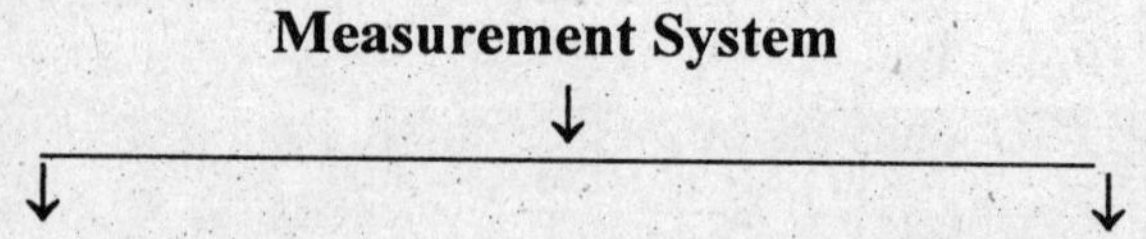

(A) Basic Functional Elements

1. Transducers
2. Signal conditioners
3. Data presentation elements

(B) Auxiliary Functional Elements

1. Calibration element
2. External power source
3. Feedback element
4. Microprocessor element.

(A) Basic Functional Elements

The basic functional elements are the integral parts of the measurement system which are represented by thick lines in the schematic diagram. Following are the basic functional elements of the system :

1. Transducer :

Transducer is the primary element which first receives the energy from the measured medium and converts it into a condition which is in convenient and practicable form. Thus, transducer senses the value of the measurand in one physical form (temperature, pressure) and converts it into some other convenient physical form such as displacement, voltage, current or resistance change which is useful for functioning of the instrument. The transducer element may be mechanical, electrical, magnetic, optical, acoustic, thermal or chemical in nature. Table 1.1 shows various types of transducer elements used for measuring common process variables.

Table 1.1 : Transducer Elements

Process variable (input)	Transducer	Output variable
Temperature	Liquid in glass thermometer	Displacement
Temperature	Pressure spring thermometer	Pressure
Temperature	Thermocouple	e.m.f.
Temperature	Resistance temperature detector (RTD)	Resistance change
Temperature	Pyrometer	Radiant intensity
Pressure	Manometer	Movement of a liquid column

... *Contd.*

Pressure	Bourdon, bellows, diaphragm, capsule gauges	Displacement of elastic elements
Pressure	Pirani gauge	Change in electrical resistance
Force or strain	Resistance strain gauge	Change in resistance
Liquid level	Dielectric gauge	Change in capacitance
Flow rate	Venturimeter/Orifice meter	Pressure
Flow velocity	Hot wire anemometer (for gas flow)	Resistance change
Flow velocity	Hot film anemometer (for liquid flow)	Resistance change
Displacement	LVDT	Inductance change
Humidity	Resistance hygrometer	Resistance change
Gas-liquid or any two-phase flow	Doppler frequency shift ultrasonic flow meter	Frequency shift

The transduction of input measurand signal into output signal may take place in single or multiple stages, namely, primary, secondary, tertiary, etc. transduction. For example, in pressure spring thermometer the bulb acts as a primary transducer which convert temperature change (input) into pressure change (output). A long capillary tube is connected to the bulb, at the other end of which a Bourdon spring is attached which acts as a secondary transducer as it converts pressure change into displacement of pointer attached at the free end of the spring. Thus, a combined effect of primary and secondary transducers convert the temperature signal into displacement of the pointer.

Desirable characteristics of a transducer :

(i) The transducer should respond or sense the desired input signal for which it is designed and should be insensitive to other signals simultaneously in the measurand. For example, the RTD sensor element should respond to change in temperature of the medium around it, and not to the pressure of the medium.

(ii) **Linearity :**

The input-output variables should be linear and symmetric.

(iii) **Accuracy :**

It should have good accuracy and should not alter the quantity to be measured.

(iv) **Good Reproducibility :**

It should be able to reproduce the same output signal when the same input signal is applied frequently under same operating conditions.

(v) **Ruggedness :**

It should have ability to withstand overloads and operating conditions.

(vi) Stability and reliability

(vii) Good dynamic response

(viii) Good mechanical strength

(ix) The transducer element should preferably give electrical output which is suitable for modern computing and display devices.

(x) Low cost.

Advantages and Limitations of Electrical Transducers over other types :

Mechanical transducers possess high accuracy, ruggedness, low cost and self-operated. But the output signal (i.e. displacement) is not suitable for modern process control instrumentation due to poor frequency response, lack of remote indication at longer distance. To overcome these limitations, electrical transducers convert physical, mechanical or optical quantity into proportional electrical voltage or current signal. The electrical transducers fulfil most of the desirable characteristics mentioned above. The advantages of electrical transducers are as follows :

(i) The electrical output can be amplified to any level for operating indicator, recorder and control devices.

(ii) Electrical signals can be transmitted over comparatively longer distance without attenuation for remote indication and further control action.

(iii) The output can be modified by converting analog signals into digital or frequency signals which can operate digital displays and controllers.

(iv) The output signals from different transducers can be multiplexed or mixed..

(v) The size, shape and contour of the transducer can be suitably designed for the desired application.

Inspite of the above advantages of the electrical transducers, they have the following disadvantages :

(i) Due to ageing of active components, sometimes electrical transducers are less reliable than mechanical ones.

(ii) Costly

(iii) Sometimes less accurate than mechanical elements.

Classification of Electrical Transducers :

Electrical transducers are classified as active and passive based on the requirement of external energy for their operation. The **active transducers** are self-generating or self-operated devices which generate energy required for their operation themselves from the measured medium. On the other hand, the **passive transducers** require external electrical energy for operation. Various types of active and passive transducers are given below.

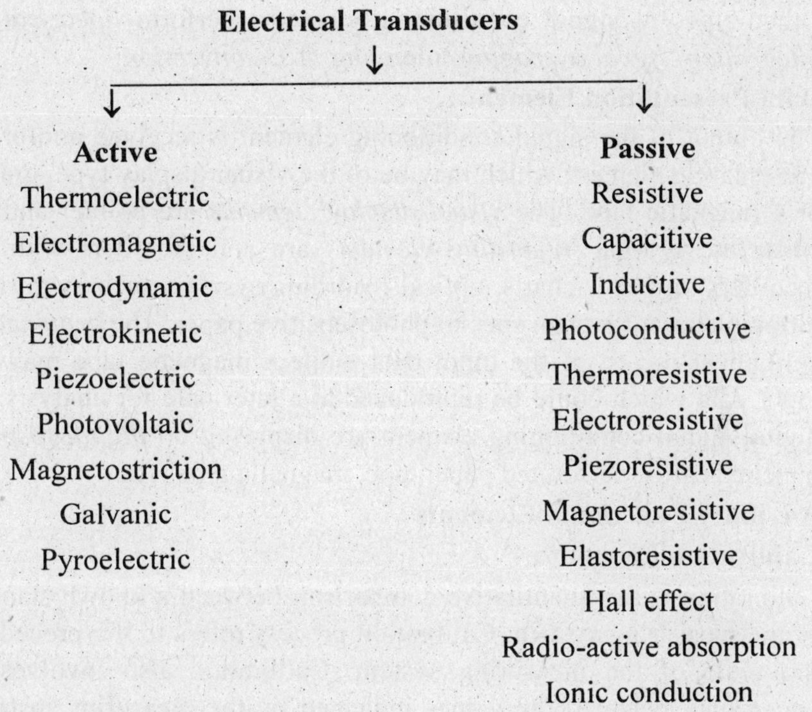

2. **Signal Conditioning Element :**

The signal conditioning elements manipulate or process the output of a transducer in a form suitable for display and control devices. The output of a transducer is fed to the signal conditioning element by mechanical means (through levers, linkages, etc.), electrical cables, fluid transmission through liquids or by pneumatic transmission using air. Remote transmission of signals can be achieved using telemetry systems. The signal conditioners perform one or more of the following operations :

Amplification :

The magnitude of output of transducer may be so small that it could not operate an indicator or recorder elements. Therefore amplifiers are used in conditioner which increase the amplitude of signal. Depending upon the type of signal, types of amplifiers used are : mechanical (levers, gears or their combination), electrical (transistor or integrated circuits), hydraulic/pneumatic (using valves or restrictions such as orifice meter, venturi meter), optical (lenses, mirrors or their combinations, lamp and scale arrangement).

Signal Filtration :

Signal filtering devices remove the unwanted noise signals which interfere the transducer signal corresponding to the measurand. The types of filtration elements used for different types of signals are mechanical, pneumatic or electrical in nature.

Other types of signal conditioning elements perform *linearization, differentiation, integration, signal averaging, sampling, A/D conversion.*

3. **Data Presentation Element :**

The output of the signal conditioning element is received and presented by the data presentation element which may be of the visual display type, graphic recording type or a magnetic tape. The *visual display elements* are pointer and scale meter, CRO, while the *graphic recording elements* are pen recorders with stylus or pen, ink recorders on paper charts, optical recording systems such as mirror galvanometer or ultraviolet recorders on special photosensitive paper. The *graphical displays* maintain permanent record of the input data while a magnetic tape may be used to acquire input data which could be reproduced at a later date for analysis. The outputs of the digital signal conditioning element are displayed on *digital display devices* such as punched cards, perforated paper tape, magnetic type, etc.

(B) Auxiliary Functional Elements :

1. **Calibration Element :**

Calibration is the quantitative comparison between a known standard and the output of the measuring system. Calibration process refers to the procedure for determining the scale of the measuring system. Calibration also involves the estimation of uncertainty between the values indicated by the measuring instrument and the true value of the input. The calibration procedures are classified as primary, secondary, direct, indirect or routine.

2. **External Power Source :**

This element provides power to the elements like transducer, signal conditioning element and data processing element.

3. **Feedback Element :**

These elements control the variation of the physical quantity to be measured. The potentiometric or Wheatstone bridge devices are used as feedback elements.

4. **Microprocessor Element :**

These elements are used for manipulation of data which are used in conjunction with A/D converter.

1.6 INTERMEDIATE ELEMENTS

The intermediate elements are nothing but signal conditioning elements which modify or process the output of transducer into suitable form. These elements include amplifiers, compensators, differentiating and integrating devices, filters, A/D, D/A converters and data transmission elements.

1. Amplifiers :

Amplifiers are used to increase the magnitude of the signal from a transducer so as to operate recording or display devices. The type of amplifying element depends upon the type of signal to be amplified i.e. mechanical, hydraulic, electrical/electronic or optical.

(i) Mechanical Amplifiers :

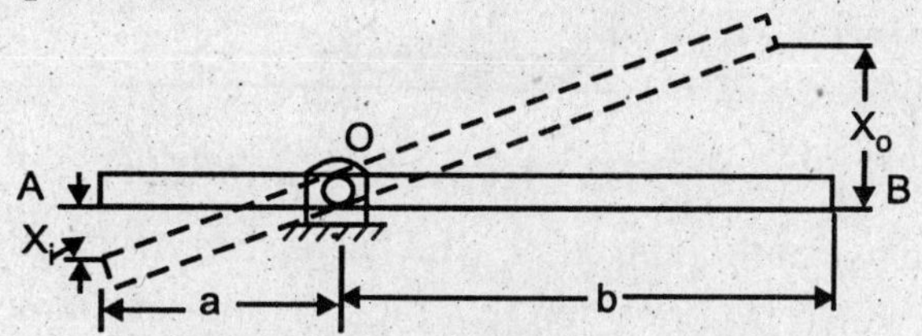

Fig. 1.2 : Mechanical amplifier

Fig. 1.2 shows a lever type mechanical amplifier which consists of a lever AB of length l (=a + b) pivoted at point 'O'. The input signal to be amplified acts downwards at end 'A' of the lever which produce downward deflection X_i corresponding to input signal. Due to this downward force acting at end 'A', the lever rotates about the fulcrum 'O' so that the other end 'B' undergoes vertical displacement X_o. According to lever principle, taking moments about fulcrum O, we get

$$X_i\, a = X_o\, b$$

$$X_o = \left(\frac{b}{a}\right) X_i \qquad \ldots (1.1)$$

Since $b > a$, $X_o > X_i$, i.e. the input signal gets **amplified**.

If $b < a$, $X_o < X_i$, i.e. the input signal gets **attenuated**.

In case of angular motion θ_i applied to a gear having N_i number of teeth, which is meshed with another larger gear having N_o number of teeth, the output signal is given by

$$\theta_i \times N_i = \theta_o \times N_o$$

$$\theta_o = \left(\frac{N_o}{N_i}\right) \theta_i \qquad \ldots (1.2)$$

Since $N_o > N_i$, $\theta_o > \theta_i$, i.e. amplification effect.

The advantages of mechanical amplifiers are simple in construction, rugged and inexpensive.

The disadvantages of mechanical amplifiers are friction and stiction effects, inertial effects due to higher mass and backlash effects. The output of these amplifiers is also affected by surrounding temperature effects.

The examples of mechanical amplifiers are compound lever mechanism used in extensometers, system of gears in dial gauge indicators, combination of levers and gears in Bourdon gauge.

(ii) Hydraulic Amplifiers :

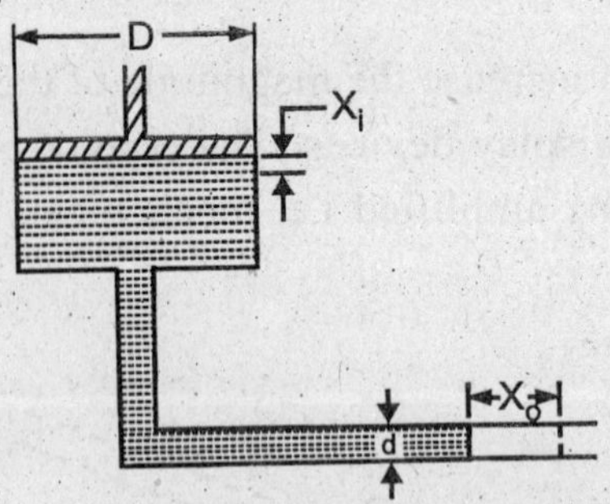

Fig. 1.3 : Hydraulic amplifier

Fig. 1.3 shows hydraulic amplifier which consists of a cylinder fitted with a plunger of diameter D which is connected to a pipe of smaller diameter d. The system is filled with hydraulic medium such as oil. When input signal X_i is applied to the plunger, the pressure force exerted on the oil surface in the cylinder is $\frac{\pi}{4} D^2 X_i$. The same force is transmitted to the pipe fluid, thus generating output signal X_o acting on smaller pipe area $\frac{\pi}{4} d^2$.

Now, input force = output force

$$\therefore \quad \frac{\pi}{4} D^2 X_i = \frac{\pi}{4} d^2 X_o$$

$$\therefore \quad X_o = \left(\frac{D}{d}\right)^2 X_i$$

Since D >> d, $X_o >> X_i$, therefore input signal X_i is amplified into output signal X_o.

The applications of hydraulic amplifiers are in automobile hydraulic brakes and hydraulic steering systems.

The advantage of these amplifiers is compact construction and main *disadvantage* is leakage problem.

(iii) Pneumatic Amplifiers :

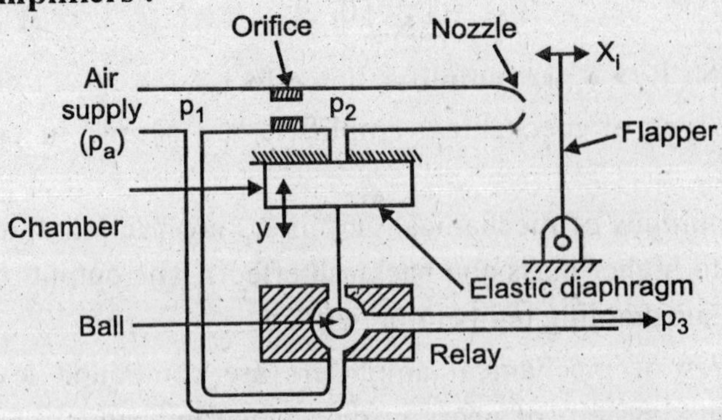

Fig. 1.4 : Flapper-nozzle relay as a amplifier

Fig. 1.4 shows flapper-nozzle type pneumatic amplifier which consists of a flapper which is pivoted at one end and free at the other end. A nozzle is held near the free end of the flapper through which air continuously bleeds out through orifice at pressure p_1. As flapper moves towards the nozzle, flow of air gets obstructed which result in increase in back pressure p_2. On the other hand as flapper moves away from the nozzle, back pressure p_2 decreases. Thus mechanical displacement X_i at free end of the flapper is converted into pneumatic signal p_2. Hence, it is known as *pneumatic transducer*. The output signal p_2 is amplified using a ball type relay system shown in Fig. 1.4. The back pressure p_2 acts on the diaphragm connected to the ball placed in the spherical seat. As p_2 increases, the diaphragm and hence the ball move downwards, so that air flow is completely blocked so that output pressure p_3 nearly equals to atmospheric pressure p_a. On the other hand, as p_2 decreases, the diaphragm and hence the ball get raised in the seat, so that output pressure p_3 equals to the air supply pressure p_1. Thus, in response to small change in input displacement signal X_i, back pressure p_2 and consequently output pressure p_3 change from atmospheric pressure p_a (zero gauge pressure) to supply pressure p_1. Thus, relay can be treated as a pneumatic amplifier.

(iv) Electrical/Electronic Amplifiers :

Earlier vacuum tubes (diodes and triodes) were used as electrical amplifiers, but now they have become obsolete. Now-a-days, electronic transistor circuits or suitable integrated circuits (ICs) are used as amplifiers.

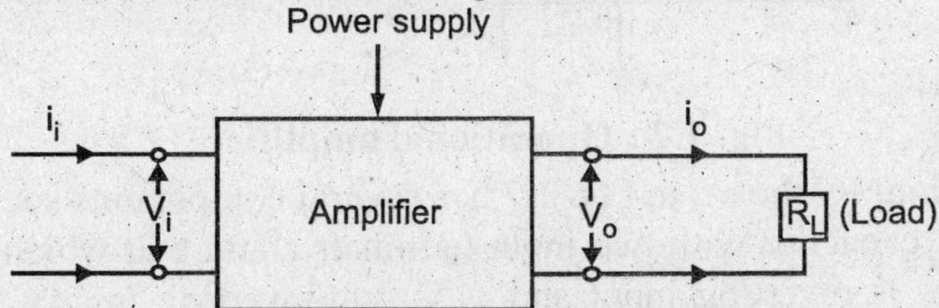

Fig. 1.5 : Electrical amplifiers

Fig. 1.5 shows electrical amplifiers used to amplify input voltage V_i into voltage signal V_o. The voltage gain of the amplifier is defined as :

$$G = \frac{\text{Output voltage}}{\text{Input voltage}} = \frac{V_o}{V_i}$$

In decibel (dB) scale, $$G = 20 \log \left(\frac{V_o}{V_i}\right) \text{dB}$$

$$\text{Current amplification} = \frac{\text{Output current}}{\text{Input curernt}} = \frac{i_o}{i_i}$$

$$\text{Power gain} = \frac{\text{Output power}}{\text{Input power}} = \frac{V_o\, i_o}{V_i\, i_i} = \frac{P_o}{P_i}$$

In dB scale, $$\text{Power gain} = 10 \log \frac{P_o}{P_i}$$

Two-stage transistor amplifiers shown in Fig. 1.6 with or without feedback are used for a.c. and d.c. amplification.

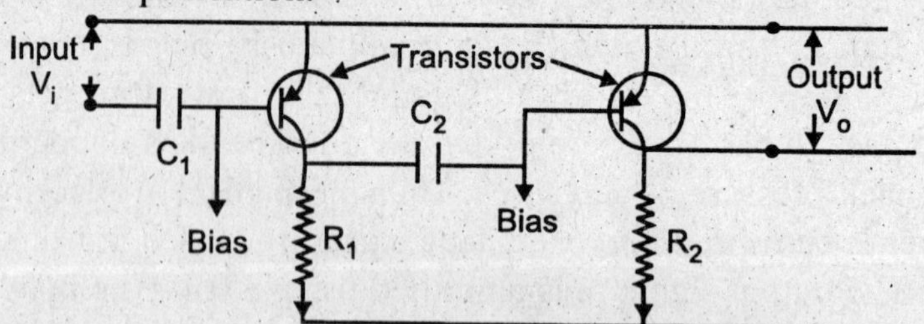

Fig. 1.6 : Two-stage transistor amplifier

The ideal amplifier should possess the following characteristics :

- infinite input impedance
- zero output impedance
- a very large gain (theoretically infinite)
- good frequency response
- ability to filter input noise signal
- should provide zero output for zero input

(v) Operational Amplifiers (Op-amps) :

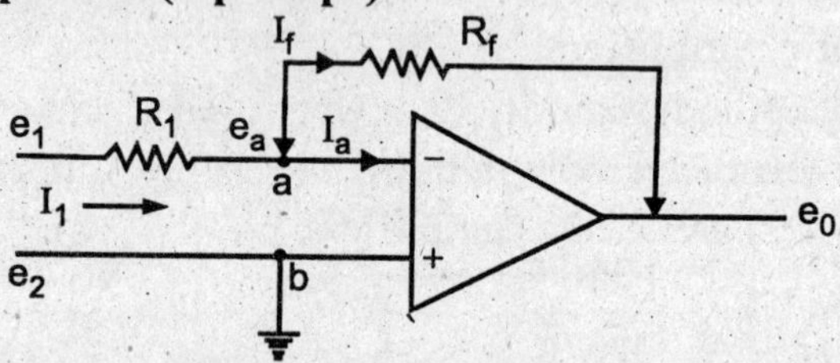

Fig. 1.7 : Operational amplifier

A typical op-amp IC shown in Fig. 1.7 has several components such as 20 transistors, 12 resistors, 1 capacitor with two input terminals a and b at which voltages e_1 and e_2 are applied (e_1 is inverting input and e_2 is non-inverting input). This amplifier has high d.c. gain (upto 10^5) with high input impedance and low output impedance. In the ideal op-amp, no current flows into the input terminals ($I_a = 0$), and the output voltage is not affected by the load connected to the terminal. Since the op-amp has high gain, negative feedback is provided through resistance R_f to make the amplifier stable. The op-amp is used along with outside resistances and capacitances. The maximum differential input of 30 V can be applied to the amplifier. These amplifiers are used as amplifiers, summing and difference amplifiers, integrating amplifiers, differential amplifiers, sensor linearization, etc., as follows. Fig. 1.7 shows **inverting amplifier.** If single ended voltage e_1 is applied to one of the inputs and another input is grounded (i.e. $e_2 = 0$), then summing the currents at point a :

$$I_1 = I_f + I_a \qquad \dots \text{(i)}$$

For ideal op-amp, $I_a = 0$

so that equation (i) becomes :

$$I_1 = I_f$$

Applying Ohm's law across the resistances R_1 and R_f,

$$\frac{e_1 - e_a}{R_1} = \frac{e_a - e_o}{R_f}$$

with $e_a \approx 0$,

$$\frac{e_1}{R_1} = -\frac{e_o}{R_f}$$

$$\frac{e_o}{e_1} = -\frac{R_f}{R_1} \quad \text{... (ii)}$$

Negative sign in above equation indicates that the input and output signals are out of phase i.e. have phase difference of 180°. Therefore, these amplifiers are called **inverting amplifiers.**

If $R_f = 6\ M\Omega$ and $R_1 = 0.6\ M\Omega$, then equation (ii) gives

$$\text{Voltage gain, } G = \frac{e_0}{e_1} = -\frac{6}{0.6} = -10$$

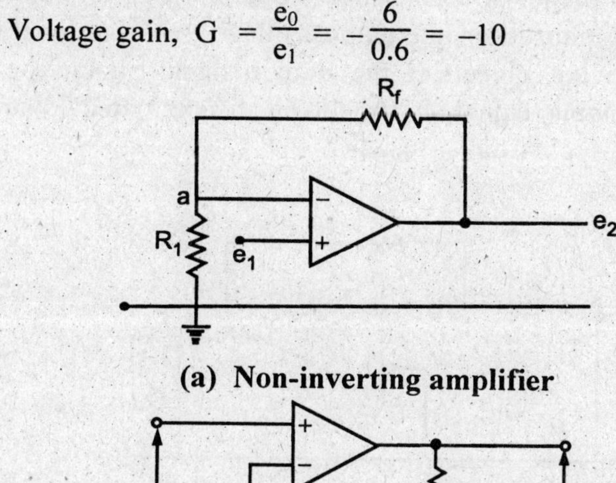

(a) Non-inverting amplifier

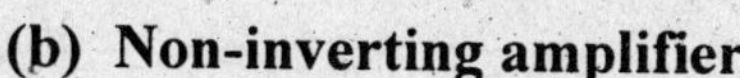

(b) Non-inverting amplifier

Fig. 1.8

Fig. 1.8 (a) shows non-inverting amplifier in which inverting input is grounded while input signal e_1 is applied to the non-inverting input. From the equivalent circuit shown in Fig. 1.8 (b),

$$e_a \approx e_1$$

$$\left(\frac{R_1}{R_1 + R_f}\right) e_o = e_1$$

$$e_o = \left(\frac{R_1 + R_f}{R_1}\right) e_1$$

$$= \left(1 + \frac{R_f}{R_1}\right) e_1 \quad \text{or } e_0 \propto e_1$$

Since e_o and e_1 have same signs (i.e. they are in same phase), this is called as non-**inverting amplifier**.

If $R_f = 0$, i.e. feedback loop is shorted, then $e_o \approx e_1$ or voltage gain $\frac{e_o}{e_1} \approx 1$.

This arrangement is called **voltage follower** which has infinite input impedance. This is used where impedance loading is to be avoided.

2. **Differentiating Elements :**

In some applications output of a transducer needs to be differentiated. For example, in an electrodynamic transducer, the output voltage is proportional to input velocity signal from the moving object. If the output signal should be proportional to acceleration of the input signal, it should be differentiated [since acceleration = $\frac{d}{dt}$ (velocity)].

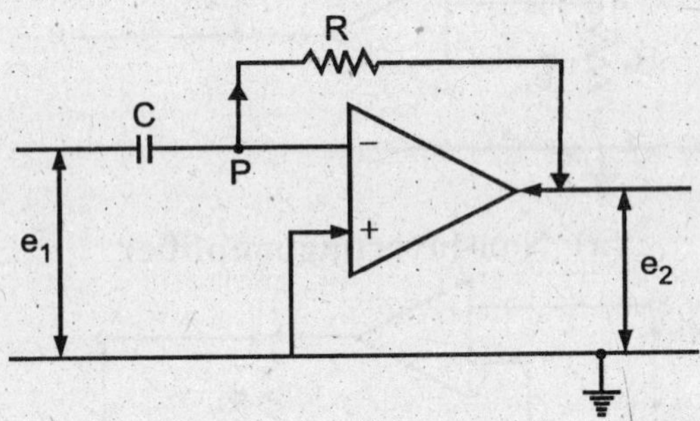

Fig. 1.9 : Differentiating element using op-amp.

Fig. 1.9 shows differentiator circuit using high-gain op-amp with capacitance C at the input and feedback resistance R. The gain G of an op-amp is very high and negative, therefore the potential at point 'a' can be considered to be very small or it can be considered as a virtual earth (i.e. zero potential). Since potential at point 'a' is nearly zero, the current i_3 entering the op-amp is also nearly zero; i.e. the amplifier has an infinite input impedance. Summing up the currents at point 'a',

$$i_1 = i_2 + i_3$$

Since, $$i_2 = 0, \quad i_1 = i_3$$

$$C\frac{de_1}{dt} = -\frac{e_2}{R}$$

$$e_2 = -RC\frac{de_1}{dt}$$

Therefore output $e_2 \propto \frac{de_1}{dt}$, i.e. derivative of input signal e_1.

3. Integrating Element :

In some applications the output of a transducer needs to be integrated. For example, in an electrodynamic transducer, the output voltage is proportional to input velocity signal from the moving object. If the output signal should be proportional to the displacement of moving object, it should be integrated [since displacement $\propto \int_0^t$ (velocity) dt.]

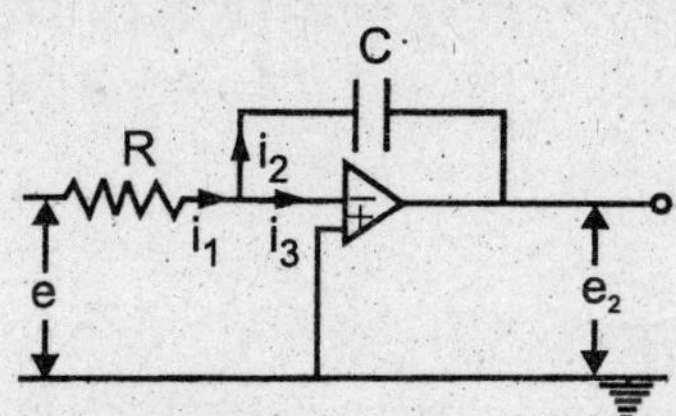

Fig. 1.10 : Integrating amplifier using op-amp.

Fig. 1.10 shows integrator circuit using high gain op-amp with resistance R at the input and capacitor C in the feedback path. If the gain G of an op-amp is high, potential at point 'a' is nearly zero, therefore current $i_3 \approx 0$. Summing up currents at point 'a',

$$i_1 = i_2$$

$$\frac{e_1}{R} = C\frac{de_2}{dt}$$

$$e_2 = \frac{1}{RC}\int_0^t e_1\, dt$$

Therefore, output $e_2 \propto \int_0^t e_1\, dt$ i.e. integration of the input signal.

4. Filters :

Filters remove unwanted signals (i.e. noise) from the desired transducer signal as shown in Fig. 1.11. Filters can be mechanical, electrical, pneumatic or hydraulic depending on the type of signal. Filters may be classified based on the frequencies of signal they pass through as low pass, high pass, band-pass, notch type. **The low pass filters** pass signals of low frequencies, while the **high pass filters** pass signals of high frequencies. The **band-pass filters** pass signals lying between certain frequencies f_1 and f_2, while the **notch-pass filters** block the frequencies in certain range between f_1 and f_2, and allow the remaining frequencies to pass through.

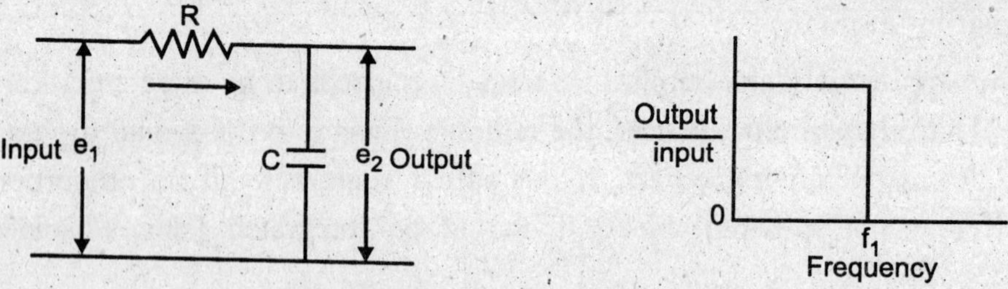

(a) Low-pass electrical filter

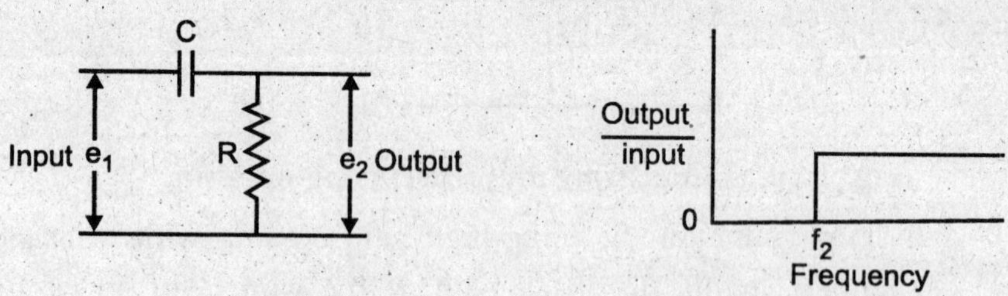

(b) High-pass electrical filter

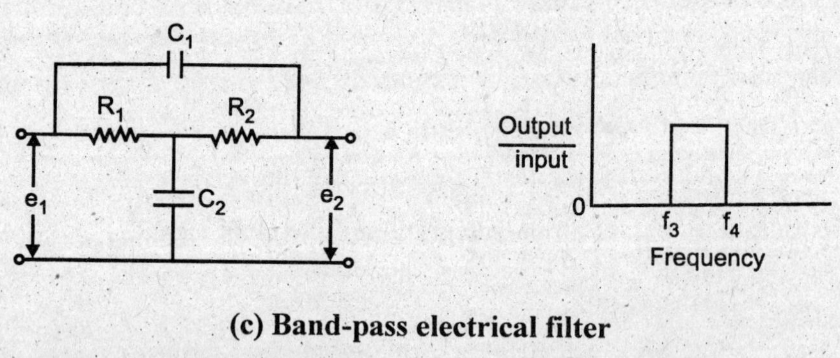

(c) Band-pass electrical filter

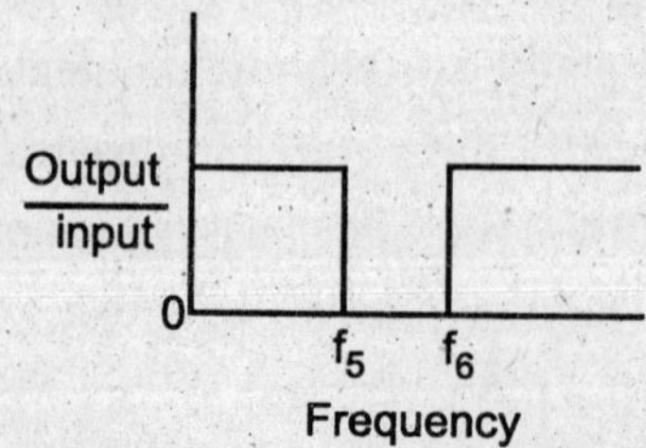

(d) Notch-pass electrical filter

Fig. 1.11 : Types of electrical filters

The RC circuits shown in Fig. 1.11 are used as electrical filters.

5. **A/D and D/A Converters :**

A/D converters convert analog voltage output of transducer into digital form which is further processed by digital computer. Digital numbers are represented in terms of two distinct states, viz., ON and OFF or true and false or 0 and 1 i.e. binary form. A binary symbol is called a **bit** and a group of bits representing a given analog signal is known as **byte**. A selective arrangement of 7 bits provides 128 distinct character combinations or 128 bytes. A/D conversion can be achieved using potentiometric type, successive approximation type, counting type and dual slope integrating type converters.

D/A converters convert digital signals generated by digital devices such as digital computer into an analog, signal which further operates the analog display and control devices. D/A conversion can be achieved using potentiometric type converters.

6. **Data Transmission Elements (Telemetry Units) :**

The data transmission elements are used to transmit data over long distances from the measuring points to a remote location for display or recording purposes. A typical data transmission system transmits data from the **source** to the **destination** (sink) through a suitable medium. The transmission elements are broadly of two types; land line or cable type (i.e. through pipeline or wires) or radio-frequency (RF) type in which the data is transmitted using radio waves. The land-line elements may be electrical, pneumatic or position type in nature.

(i) **Electrical Data Transmission System :**

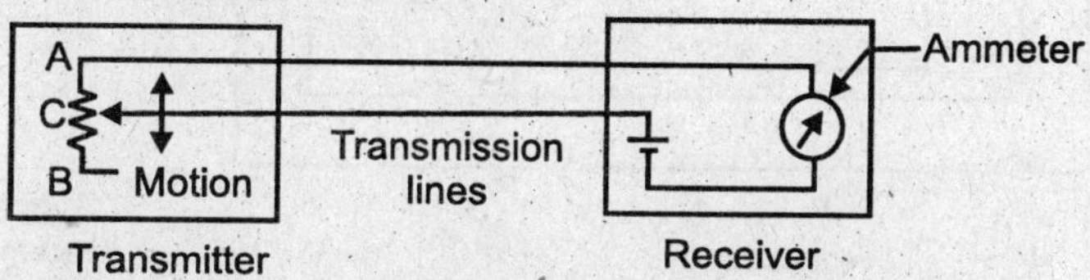

Fig. 1.12 : Electrical data transmission system

Fig. 1.12 shows electrical data transmission system used for transmitting motion signal from the transmitter end to the receiver end in the form of electrical current. The transmitter consists of a variable resistance AB with sliding contactor C through which electric current is passed. The motion signal to be transmitted positions the contactor C on slide wire AB which determines current through the connecting wires. Thus, ammeter connected at the receiver end shows change in current as a measure of the input measurement signal. Instead of ammeter, a potentiometer circuit with galvanometer may be used as a receiver, so that adjustment of potentiometer sliding contact for getting zero or null deflection in the galvanometer indicates the input motion signal given to the contactor C.

(ii) Pneumatic Transmission System :

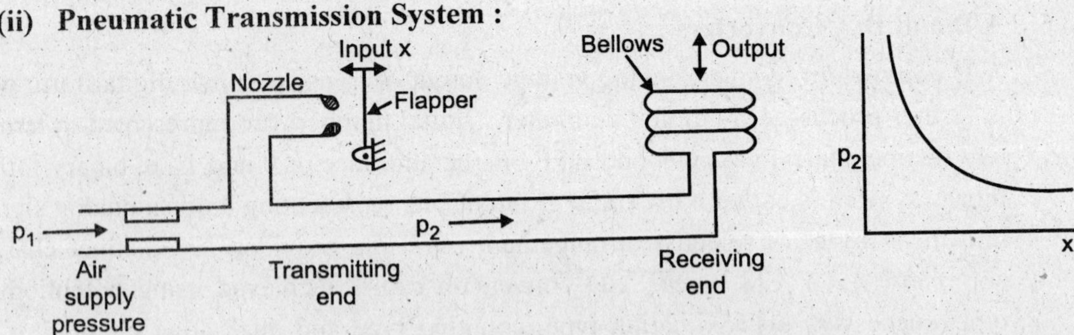

Fig. 1.13 : Pneumatic transmission system

Fig. 1.13 shows a pneumatic transmission system which consists of a flapper-nozzle arrangement which transmits the input motion signal X applied at free end of the flapper as pneumatic pressure signal P_2 or output motion signal Y at the free end of the bellows at the receiving end.

(iii) Motion-type Transmission System :

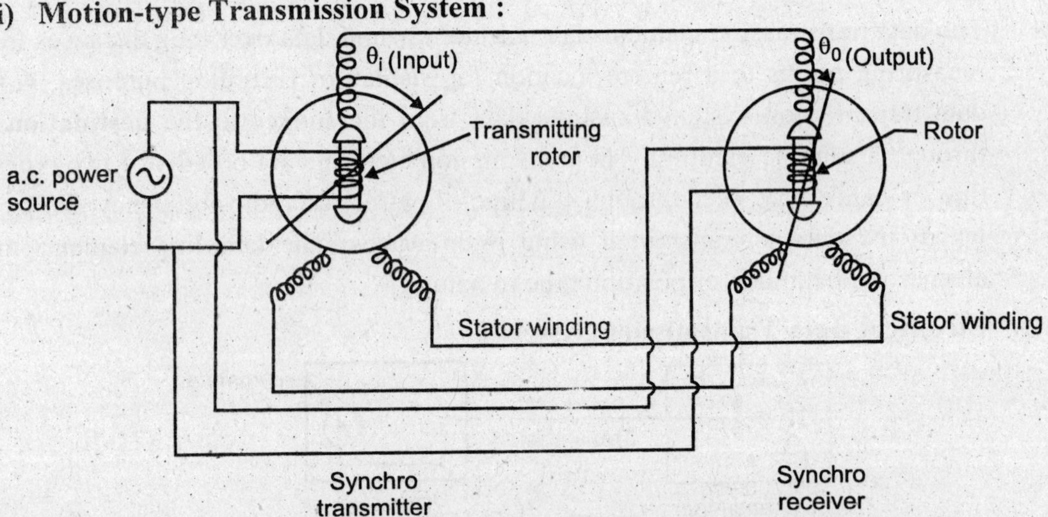

Fig. 1.14 : Motion-type transmission system

Fig. 1.14 shows a motion-type transmission system in which motion at the transmitter end is transmitted as the motion at the receiver end through synchrony systems at either ends. **A synchrony system** consists of a stator with three coils at 120°, inside which a **rotor** can move freely. The transmitting synchrony is energized by a.c. power supply. If the rotors in transmitting and receiving synchrony are in identical position (same angular displacement), the voltages induced in stator coils are equal in magnitude but opposite in sense, hence no current flows in the stator wires. If the input motion signal (such as rotation of pointer) is applied to the rotor of transmitter synchro, it gets rotated through angular displacement θ_i. Since two rotors are not symmetrically positioned with respect to the respective stator coils, differential voltage is induced in the stator coils which forces current in the stator wires. The current in the stator coils of the receiving synchro produce a torque on the rotor of receiving synchro so that it rotates through angle θ_o, thereby the rotors are again aligned (i.e. $\theta_i = \theta_o$). Thus input motion signal θ_i is transmitted as the output motion θ_o.

(iv) Radio-frequency (RF) Transmission System :

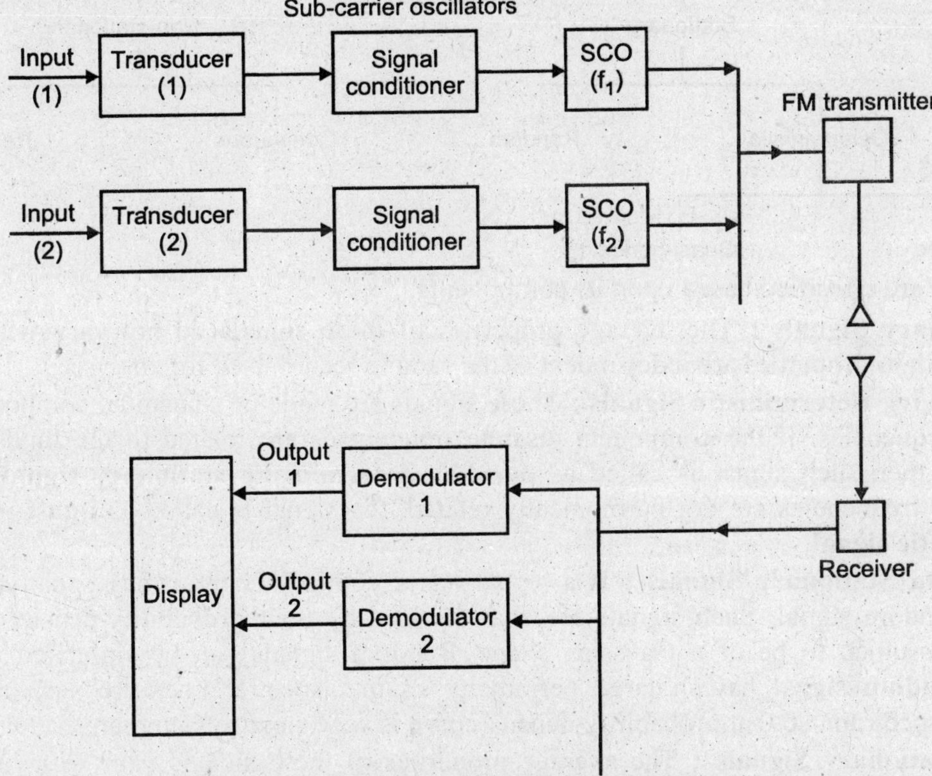

Fig. 1.15 : Radio-frequency transmitter

Fig. 1.15 shows radio-frequency transmission system which is used to transmit number of signals from different transducers using radio-frequency waves. In this system, transducer outputs are scanned at fixed intervals and multiplexed by frequency division method. In this method, the transmission bandwidth is divided between the various transducers, or channels. Each channel is associated with a sub-carrier frequency (SCO) which is modulated by output signal from transducer. For example, channel 1 output modulates the SCO1 frequency i.e. f_1, channel 2 modulates SCO2 frequency f_2 and so on. The outputs of all SCOs are mixed and then transmitted by FM transmitter which is received by a suitable antenna at the receiving end. Then transmitted signal is demodulated and filtered to recover the original signal for display or recording.

1.7 SIGNAL ANALYSIS

A signal is assumed to be composed of sinusoidal components at different frequencies, each having a given amplitude and initial phase. Signals are classified as given in flow chart below.

Classification of signals:

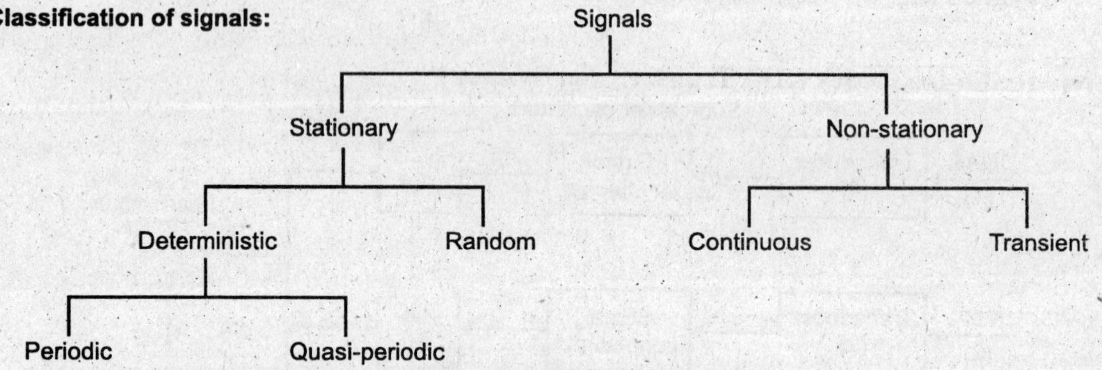

Signals are classified based upon its components.

Stationary Signals : The average properties of these signals do not vary with time. Therefore, their properties are independent of the sample record used for analysis.

Stationary Deterministic Signals : These signals are made of sinusoidal components at discrete frequencies. If the component discrete frequencies are related to the fundamental frequency, then such signal is called as **periodic deterministic stationary signal**. If the component frequencies are not harmonically related, the signal is called as **quasi-periodic deterministic signal**.

Random Stationary Signals : If a signal has a continuous frequency spectrum, it is called a random signal. Such signals are characterized by their probability-density curves, which is assumed to be of a Gaussian shape. Random signals can be simulated using a **pseudo-random** signal having large periodicity so that spectral lines are very close in frequency spectrum, so that probability-density curve is very close to Gaussian shape.

Non-stationary Signals : The average properties of these signals vary with time and hence depend on the sample chosen for analysis. Such signals are analyzed over short time interval during which they are considered quasi-stationary.

Signal analysis means obtaining its frequency spectrum by passing through a number of analog filters with different centre frequencies and outputs of these filters are recorded on a single tunable filter whose centre frequency is changed discretely or swept continuously.

Signal analysis is used for identification of defects in machine components such as shafts, compressor blades, and also for analysis of structural vibrations. This can be done by comparing signal analysis of prototype (standard) component with that of the sample test specimen.

1.8 DATA ACQUISITION AND CONVERSION

Fig. 1.16 shows data acquisition system for collecting data (signals) from various transducers, conditioning them, multiplexed together and then send to analog recording or display devices. For digital output, the multiplexed analog signal is converted into digital signal by A/D converters for the purpose of processing, transmission, display and storage. A standard digital panel meter (DPM) or high-speed high-resolution device are used for acquiring data in digital form.

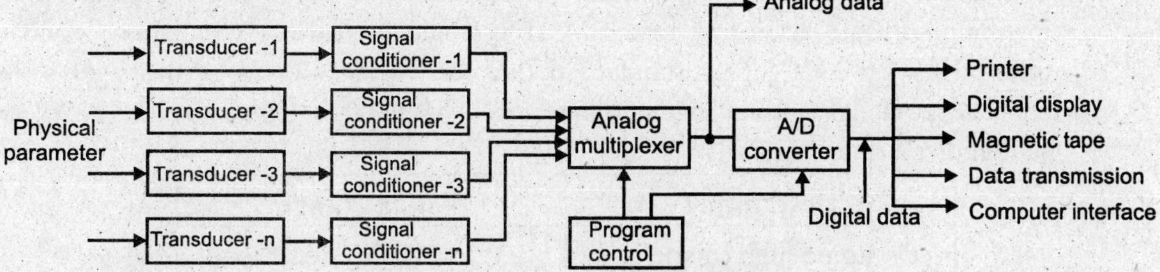

Fig. 1.16 : Data acquisition system

The data acquisition systems for laboratory instruments have high sensitivity. Calibration test equipments are oriented more towards making sensitive measurements rather than protecting the integrity of the analog data. This is because such equipments are operated over narrow temperature ranges with much less electrical noise. The high sensitivity and precision devices are used for getting high accuracy and precision.

The data acquisition systems for hostile environments such as industrial process control systems, aircraft control systems, and measurements in industrial environments are aimed at protecting the integrity of the analog data. The devices used for this purpose are capable of wide temperature range operation and good shielding from outside world signals. The data acquisition systems are either single-channel or multi-channel systems.

The signal conditioners shown in Fig. 1.16 scale the gains of input signals (from transducers) to match with converter's full range. Signal conditions perform ratiometric conversion and logarithmic compression operations on the transducer signal.

1.9 DIGITAL SIGNAL TRANSMISSION AND PROCESSING

Digital signal information is in the form of binary (two-valued) digit, known as a **bit** and group of bits is called a **byte**.

Digital data can be transmitted using one of the following methods.

1. **Modulation Techniques :**

   In modulation technique, a sine wave carrier is employed to convey the data by means of change in its amplitude, frequency, or phase.

2. **Serial Data Communication :**

   In order to reduce the number of connecting wires required to send digital data over long distances, the data is usually sent in the serial form, i.e., various bits forming a data byte are sent one after the another, one bit at a time. The rates at which the bits are sent are expressed as the BAUD rate (Bd), which is the inverse of the time required for passing 1 bit. The commonly used rates are 110, 300, 600, 1200, 4800, 9600, 19200 Bd.

RS-232C :

The data communication equipments (DCE) and data terminal equipments (DTE) intercommunicate according to a EIA (Electronic Industries Association) standard referred as RS-232C. This standard define the voltage levels of the signals, the handshake signal and a 25-pin connector. The voltage levels for RS-232C are standardized as follows :

Description	Voltage range
Logic high (mark)	(–3) to (–15 V) under load
Logic low (space)	+3 and –15V under load

The RS-232C is used for a maximum Baud rate of 20,000 Bd for distances upto 15 m. At lower Baud rates, wires as long as 600-900 m can be used.

The serial data communication between a terminal and personal computer is done through a telephone line, using MODEMS (modulators-demodulators) at both ends.

The IEEE-488 Standard Bus :

This bus can be used to interconnect upto 15 instruments over lengths upto 20 m at the data rates upto 500 kBytes/sec. The instruments connected using this bus are of three types viz. the listener, the talker and the controller. A talker transmits the data to other devices while the **listener** receives the data from other devices (such as printer). The **controller** device manages the communication over the bus by sending addresses and commands. Some devices such as ADC can talk as well as listen the data.

1.10 INDICATING, RECORDING AND DISPLAY ELEMENTS

The display element gives an indication of the input quantity being measured/sensed by transducer. These elements may be of analog or digital type, depending on whether the indication is in continuous or discrete form.

1. **Indicating Elements :**

The indicating elements indicate the present value of the measurement without any record of the past values. These elements are classified as follows :

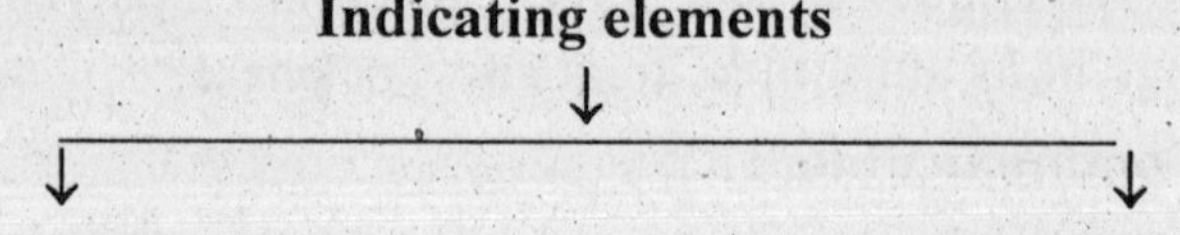

Analog Elements

(1) Voltmeters and ammeters

(2) Vacuum tube voltmeters

Digital Elements

(1) Digital voltmeters (DVM)

(2) Cathode Ray Oscilloscope (CRO)

Analog Indicating Elements :

Conventional voltmeters and ammeters are the examples of analog indicating elements. These elements work on d'Arsonval type galvanometer principle of electromagnetic induction, according to which when a current to be measured is passed through a coil placed in a magnetic field, the coil rotates and the pointer attached to it indicates the magnitude of current. The vacuum tube voltmeters also work on the same principle but they have amplifiers built in them.

Digital Indicating Elements :

Digital Voltmeters (DVM) convert analog signals into digital signals. Therefore, ADCs discussed earlier are the examples of DVM. There are two types of DVM viz. non-integrating type and integrating type. Potentiometric DVM shown in Fig. 1.17 is the example of non-integrating type.

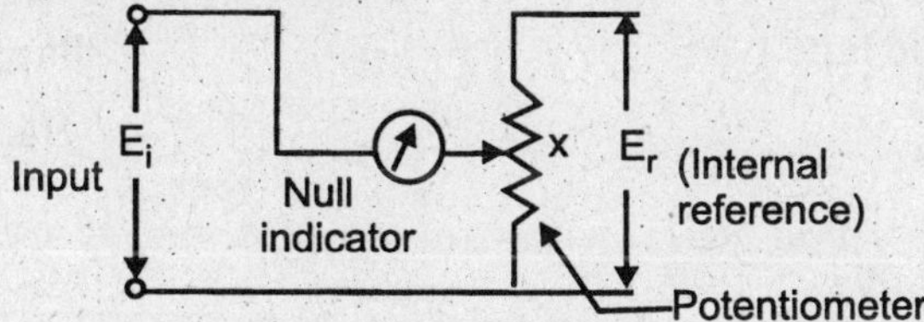

Fig. 1.17 : Potentiometric type DVM

In manual type device shown in Fig. 1.17 the input voltage E_i to be measured is compared with the standard voltage E_r generated inside, which is applied to a potentiometer circuit. When two voltages are equal, galvanometer shows zero indication. When these two voltages are not equal, the contactor (on the slide wire) is so adjusted that galvanometer shows null deflection. Therefore, the position x of the contactor would be an indication of unknown voltage E_i. This operation can be made automatic by comparing the two voltages by feedback action.

Integrating-type DVM is essentially a voltage-to-frequency converter, in which a d.c. signal is converted into a periodic signal of frequency proportional to magnitude of the signal. The pulses obtained are counted by a counter which gives an indication of E_i.

Cathode Ray Oscilloscope (CRO) is used as the digital indicating element, which is essentially a high input impedance voltage measuring device. A CRO consists of cathode ray tube in which electrons are released from a cathode and accelerated towards the screen by positively charged anode. The electron scatter is collimated by application of voltages in horizontal and vertical planes. The impingement of the electron beam on a phosphorescent screen results in emission of light so that the spot becomes visible. A CRO essentially consists of a display device, vertical amplifier, horizontal amplifier, time base, trigger circuit and power supply. The signals given to the horizontal and vertical amplifiers are compared from the Lissajous figures produced on the screen. In a conventional CRO, the indication persists only for few seconds, while storage CROs can capture and store the signal indications. A digital CRO can store, analyze and display a signal. The stored signal can be deleted as in a personal computer.

2. Recording Elements :

The recording elements keep the record of variation in the values of measurement. Various types of recording elements are discussed below.

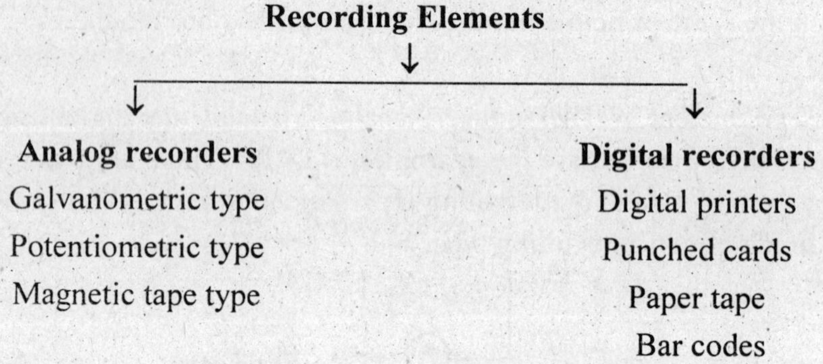

Analog Recorders :

Galvanometric recorders :

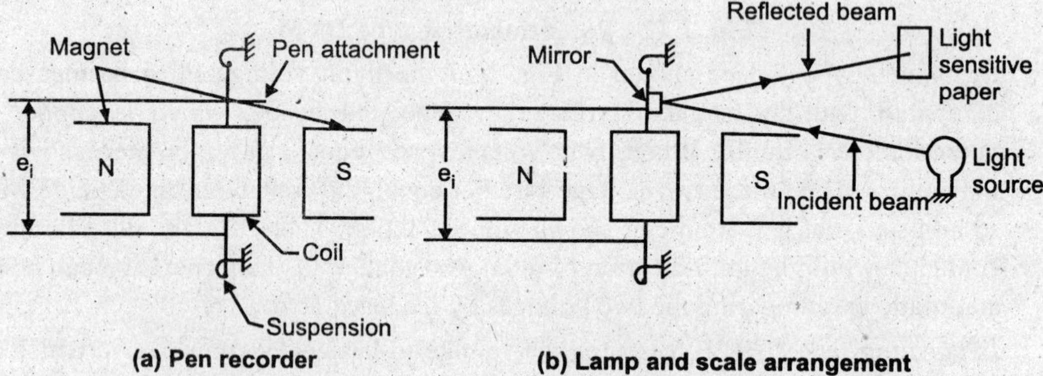

Fig. 1.18 : Galvanometric recorders

The galvanometric recorders work on the principle of moving coil galvanometer, i.e. when current signal to be measured is passed through a coil suspended in the magnetic field, the coil gets rotated through an angle proportional to the current passed through it. An ink pen is connected to the coil which transfer motion of the coil onto a paper wrapped around a rotating drum which is rotated at a known speed [Refer Fig. 1.18 (a)]. The linkages convert the angular rotation of the coil into a straight line motion of the pen. In some designs, a heated stylus (or pen) is used which is moved against a heat-sensitive chart paper. Since large initial torgue is required, sensitivity of this type of recorder is low.

In some arrangements as shown in Fig. 1.18 (b) (lamp and scale arrangement) the pen attachment is replaced by a light beam from a mercury lamp source, which gets reflected from a small mirror attached to the coil and falls on a photosensitive paper moved precisely over a drum with a clock mechanism. As coil rotates in response to current flowing through it, the light beam gets deflected which is traced on a light-

..nsitised paper. The coil system is either hydraulically or magnetically damped. The recording paper width is typically 10 to 25 cm wide. It is possible to arrange about 16 galvanometers recording their trace on the same paper. The overlapped records can be distinguished using trace identification markers. One of the galvanometers can be used as a time marker by feeding pulse signal from a crystal oscillator which serves as the time scale for the plot.

Potentiometric recorders (self-balancing servo type recorders) :

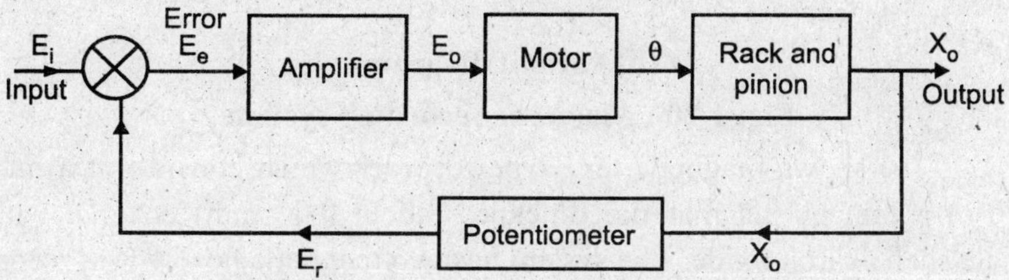

Fig. 1.19 : Potentiometric recorders

In potentiometric type recorders shown in Fig. 1.19, the unknown measurement signal in voltage form (E_i) is compared (or balanced) against a known d.c. potential (E_r) obtained from a slide-wire potentiometer operated from a standard electrical source. The difference between these voltages, i.e. error signal (E_r) is amplified and applied to a drive motor which moves the wiper of the slide-wire potentiometer through rack and pinion arrangement. The wiper is coupled to an ink-operated recording stylus which moves (or writes) on a mechanically-driven chart. These recorders are highly sensitive, linear and rugged. They are suitable for slow-speed measurements such as temperature using thermocouples. These systems are used in process control systems in chemical, metallurgical and textile industries. Two independent servo systems can be used for plotting two variables against each other such as pressure-volume variation of an I.C. engine (i.e. indicator diagram).

Magnetic Tape Type Recorder :

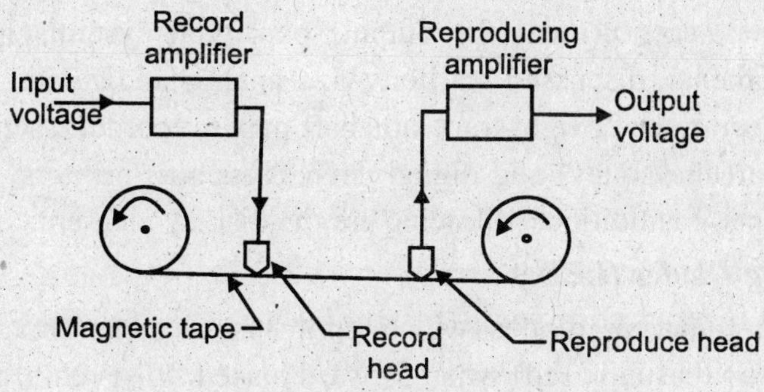

(a) Block diagram

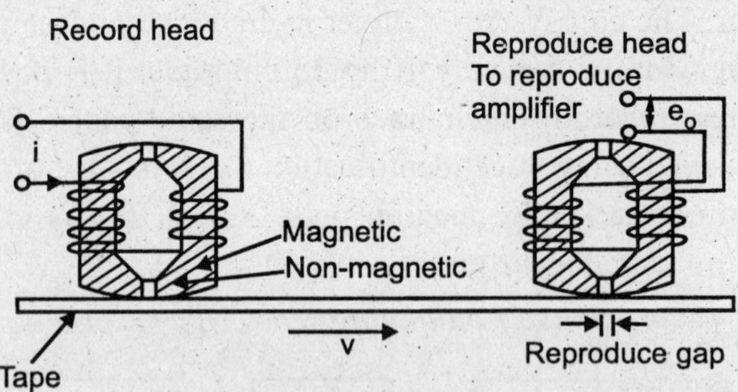

(b) Circuit diagram

Fig. 1.20 : Magnetic recording system

Fig. 1.20 (b) shows magnetic tape type recorder which consists of a magnetic tape made of a thin plastic material (thickness about 0.04 mm) covered with magnetic particle such as iron oxide. The system has two magnetic heads, viz., record head and reproducing head, each having a coil and gap. The input current signal to be measured is passed through the coil of the recording head which produces a magnetic flux at the gap. As magnetic tape passes across this gap, it gets magnetized. The magnetization effect varies with the frequency of input signal. The magnetized tape then passes over a gap in reproducing head thereby generating an output voltage proportional to the magnetic flux in the tape across the gap in the head. With a gap width of 0.002 mm and a tape speed of 300 cm/s, the frequency response upto 1 MHz can be achieved.

Digital Recording Systems :

Digital recorders are the input-output systems (I/O) through which data is fed into the digital computer for processing. The digital I/O devices such as punched cards, paper tape, bar codes, line printer, ink-jet printer, disk files, floppy disk, CRT displays, data plotter are used for digital signal recording. (The detailed construction and working of these devices are beyond the scope of this book.)

3. Display Elements :

The display elements present the outputs of digital systems in visual form. The indicating elements discussed earlier, viz. analog indicators (pointer and scale arrangement, pen trace or light trace on chart paper recorders, screen display in CRO or large TV screen display) and digital devices such as printers, punch cards are the display elements. In addition, following are the display elements used in practice :

Light Emitting Diodes (LEDs) :

LEDs are p-n junction diodes which emit visible electromagnetic radiations of different colours (casually red) when forward biased. In seven-segment numeric LED display (for showing 0 to 9) shown in Fig. 1.21 there is one LED per segment along with a series resistance, (a, b, ... g) all having one terminal (cathode or anode) common. In addition to diodes for seven segments a, b, ... g of the display, there is additional diode and resistance for getting a decimal point in the display. These displays have low power requirement and high reliability. LEDs get illuminated ON or OFF, depending on the output level 1 or 0.

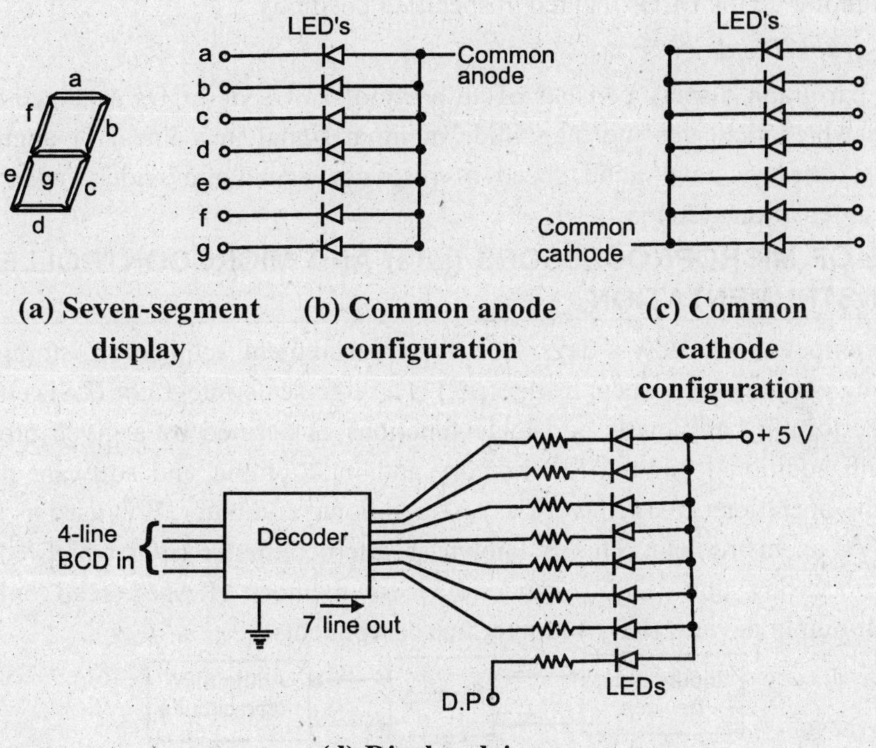

(a) Seven-segment display **(b) Common anode configuration** **(c) Common cathode configuration**

(d) Display driver

Fig. 1.21 : LED Seven-Segment Display

Liquid Crystal Display (LCD) :

The LEDs are active devices that generate light while the LCD is a passive device that modify the light by scattering. LCDs are made from organic molecules which flow like liquids and have crystal-like characteristics. They appear dark or bright depending on voltage range applied across the crystal. This is an electro-optic device in which light from a separate light source is controlled by placing the liquid crystal cell in the light path, and the optical transmission characteristics of the cell are altered using electric field. In the twisted nematic (TN) display, the liquid crystal is sandwiched between two pieces of glass, one of which acts as a polarizer through which the light enters the crystal and the other acts as an analyzer through which the light leaves. When there is no electric field applied there is no transmission of light, so that the background appears dark. The LCD has low power consumption, fast response, but they can operate over short temperature range (0 to 60°C), are less reliable and have short operating life.

Alpha-numeric Displays :

These devices display alphabets as well as numerals in response to electrical input. The arrays of LEDs and CRTs are used for this purpose. The characters are displayed by lighting up the LEDs located in specified positions.

Bar-graph Display :

The bar-graph display consists of an array of LEDs or LCDs arranged in a matrix form which indicates the magnitude of input signal in a linear or angular format. These displays have good speed of response which are widely used in process instrumentation systems.

1.11 USE OF MICROPROCESSORS (μP's) AND MICROCONTROLLERS (μC's) IN INSTRUMENTATION

Digital computers are now-a-days used for measurement acquisition, storage, analysis and processing of data. A microcontroller (μC) is a large-scale integrator (LSI) chip which is capable of performing arithmetic and logic functions as defined by a given program. It is equipped with additional circuits for memory and input/output and software program for controlling the operations so as to work as an operational computer. It is used as a controller in a system or an instrument. This is known as microcomputer (μC) which comprises of μP/central processing unit (CPU), random access memory (RAM), read only memory (ROM), input/output devices (I/O) and interface components.

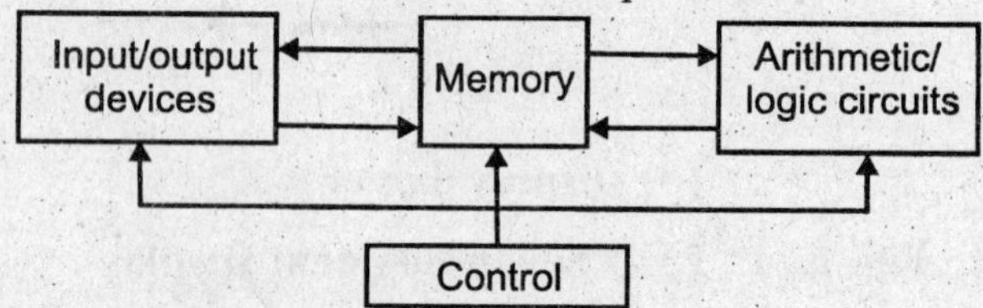

Fig. 1.22 : Block diagram of a microcomputer

The control section operates on the basis of a sequence of instructions (or program) stored in a memory. The data transfer between various units occurs through buses interconnecting them. A standard microcontroller widely used in industrial applications is the 8051 series having 3 variations, viz., 8031, 8051, 8751.

Use of μC for Data Acquisition (Measurement) :

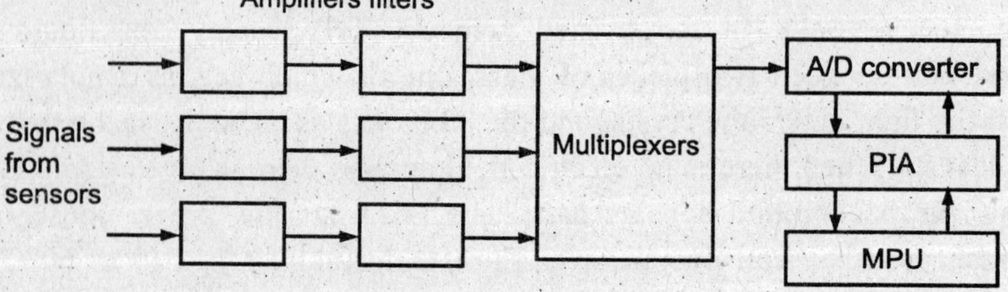

Fig. 1.23 : μP-based measurement system

Fig. 1.23 shows μP-based measurement system. In this system, the measurement signals from a number of sensors are conditioned (i.e. amplified, filtered) and then passed to a DAQ (data acquisition) board plugged in a slot at the back of a computer. The DAQ board includes a multiplexer (which allows only one signal at a time to ADC), A-D converter (for digitizing signals), PIA (Peripheral Interface Adapter) and a μP. The transmitted signal is then stored and analyzed. The advantages of μC-based DAQ systems are : ability and ease of complex mathematical computations (such as linearization), relatively small size and reasonable cost. The example of μC-based DAQ system is a μC-based temperature indicator which can linearize voltage signal from a thermocouple sensor. The indicators can be made intelligent by incorporating validation of the measured data so that incorrect data arising due to noise are rejected. This avoids false alarms due to such disturbances. Such a temperature indicator can be used as temperature controller (P, PI etc.) by using the timer circuit in the μC. The μC allows selection of controller parameters, can adjust the heating rate and cooling rate, thus optimizing the system performance. Such controllers can be made self-tuning or auto-tuning, i.e. the controller initiates a system identification sequence and from the results obtained, optimizes the controller tuning parameters automatically.

1.12 PC (PERSONAL COMPUTER) – BASED INSTRUMENTATION SYSTEMS

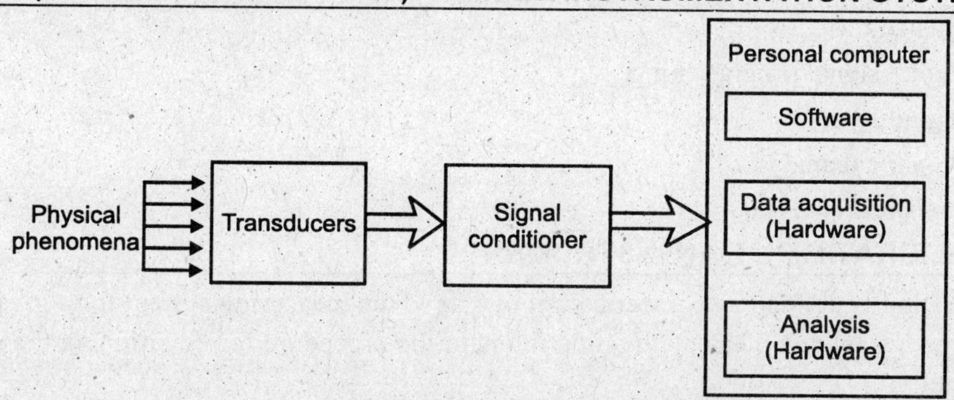

Fig. 1.24 : PC-based instrumentation system

Fig. 1.24 shows PC-based DAQ systems, in which electrical measurement signals from various transducers is communicated to a PC after conditioning by the interface element. The PC ADD-ON cards are used for this purpose which directly interface analog signals to a PC. The PC has, as a part of it, data acquisition hardware and analysis hardware. The softwares include the program to acquire data, perform some computations/manipulations on the same and the result is presented on the VDU. Thus, huge power of PC in communication and analysis of data can be used for measurement of parameters in desired output form. Use of PC in instrumentation system for a big plant enables simultaneous display of various parameters in a plant by suitable colour graphics and attributes along with their trend plots.

1.13 VIRTUAL INSTRUMENTATION (VI)

VI is a layer of software and/or hardware, which is added to a digital computer so as to function as real instrumentation system without any actual use of hardware such as sensors. The VI architecture consists of data acquisition, analysis and presentation on a VDU (Visual Display Unit). In a VI system, the front panel shows emulated (programmed) instruments such as temperature indicator, process controller, chemical instrumentation. For this graphical programming language such as LABVIEW is used in which the functional blocks corresponding to data acquisition and control are selected from a parallel menu. The important features of LABVIEW are given below :

(i) **Front Panel Presentations :**

The front panel shows a GUI which consists of controls and indicators, whose values are automatically logged as data in various forms such as numeric, Boolean, string, strip chart, graph, arrays, cluster or custom.

(ii) **Block Diagram Programming :**

Various icons, controls, structures and graphical elements are used to construct block diagram programs. The functions involved in the programs are arithmatic, comparison, conversion, string, trigonometric, logarithmic etc.

(iii) Data acquisition and control.

(iv) Data analysis.

(v) Digital signal programming.

(vi) Digital filters.

(vii) Numerical analysis.

(viii) Statistical analysis.

1.14 CALIBRATION OF AN INSTRUMENT

Calibration is defined as comparison of output of the measuring system for a given input with a known standard. Thus, calibration refers to the procedure for determining the scale of the system.

Alternatively calibration is the process of checking correctness of the scale of the instrument in terms of the uncertainty between the values indicated by the instrument and the true value of the input. For a linear system it is sufficient to compare a single input value with the standard (i.e. single-point calibration) whereas for non-linear systems, a set of known standard inputs to the measuring systems are used for calibrating corresponding outputs.

Calibration procedures are classified as follows :

Primary calibration : A process of calibrating a system against primary standards is known as primary calibration. The primary standards are laid down by International Bureau of Weights and Measures (at Sevres, France) as the units of measurements of various physical quantities such as mass (kg), length (meters), time (second), luminous intensity (candela). These standards are accurate but not available for day-to-day comparisons.

Secondary calibration : A process of calibrating a system using secondary standards is known as secondary calibration. The secondary standards are basic reference standards employed by industrial measurement laboratories which are periodically compared with primary standards. These standards are freely available to the ordinary users for checking and calibration of instruments.

Direct calibration : Measuring systems can be directly calibrated with a known **input** source. Such systems can be used as secondary calibration devices. For example, a turbine flow meter can be calibrated by measuring the time required for certain quantity (weight) of liquid to flow through turbine (total flow of liquid = time required × number of rotations of the turbine wheel). Such a turbine meter can be used for calibrating other flow meters.

Indirect calibration : In this method, a system is calibrated by comparing its performance with another similar standard instrument; when both are subjected to identical conditions.

Routine calibration : Routine calibration involves periodically checking the accuracy and proper functioning of an instrument with known standards. The steps followed in routine calibration are as follows :

(i) Instruments are calibrated by taking readings both in the ascending and descending order.

(ii) Any physical defects in the system are identified by visual inspection.

(iii) Check zero setting of the instrument.

(iv) Check proper installation and levelling in accordance with the manufacturer's specification.

(v) The standard used for calibration should be more accurate than the instrument to be calibrated.

1.15 PERFORMANCE CHARACTERISTICS OF MEASURING INSTRUMENTS

The basic function of the measuring instrument is to sense or detect a parameter in industrial process (such as temperature, pressure, level, flow, etc.) and changes in it reliably and accurately. The output of instrument is either displayed or used to activate a control device for control purposes. The operating characteristics of measuring instruments are nothing but the functional characteristics which represent their capabilities and limitations for a particular application. The knowledge of the performance characteristics enables us to compare the performance of different instruments used for the same purpose and hence for selection of the suitable instrument for the purpose.

The performance characteristics of a measuring instrument are classified as :

(1) Static characteristics, and

(2) Dynamic characteristics.

When instrument is used for measuring constant or slowly time-varying quantities, the static performance characteristics are considered. On the other hand, when instrument is used for measuring the quantities rapidly varying with time, the dynamic characterics are considered.

1.15.1 Static Characteristics

(1) Accuracy :

Accuracy of a measuring system is defined as closeness of the instrument output to the true value of the measurement quantity. In practice, accuracy is expressed in terms of inaccuracy (deviation) or percentage error in the value of the measurement from the true value. Therefore, the algebraic difference between the actual indicated value and true value of the measurand is termed as the error of the instrument, which is usually expressed in per cent of the full-scale output (% F.S.).

Accuracy can be expressed either in terms of true value of measurand or % F.S. values as follows :

$$\% \text{ Accuracy} = \frac{\text{Measured value} - \text{True value}}{\text{True value}} \times 100$$

or

$$= \frac{\text{Measured value} - \text{True value}}{\text{F.S. value}} \times 100$$

The accuracy specification as a % FS is less accurate than the % true value.

Types of Errors :

Systematic or Cumulative Errors : These errors have the same magnitude and sign for a given set of conditions, hence they get accumulated. They alter the instrument reading by fixed magnitude. These errors are caused due to the following factors :

Instrument errors : These errors are inherent in the system due to improper design of the instrument. Such errors can be avoided by calibrating the instrument against a suitable standard and then applying suitable corrections.

Environmental errors : These errors occur due to variation of conditions around the instrument, such as change in temperature, pressure, humidity etc.

Loading errors : These errors occur due to effect of measurement on the physical system being tested.

Accidental or Random Errors : These errors occur due to random variations in the parameter. Such errors vary in magnitude and sign (+ve or –ve). The sources of such errors are as follows :

Errors associated with measurement of small quantities, errors due to system defects such as large tolerances in mating parts, friction.

These errors are detected and corrected by measuring the quantity first while increasing and then while decreasing the magnitude.

Miscellaneous Errors : These errors are partly systematic and partly random. These errors include personal or human errors, errors due to faulty components and improper application of the instrument.

(2) Precision :

Precision is defined as the ability of the instrument to reproduce a certain set of readings within a given accuracy.

Precision can be expressed as the mean value of the scatter of the individual measurements or as the closeness with which the individual measurements are distributed about their mean value. It also refers to the degree of agreement of a set of measurements among themselves. The instrument is considered to have high precision if it gives the same output information when the reading is repeated large number of times.

Difference between accuracy and precision :

Accuracy represents the degree of closeness of the measured value to the true value, while precision represents degree of repeatability of several independent measurements of the desired input at the same reference conditions. Accuracy is determined by calibration of the instrument while precision is determined by statistical analysis methods. Both the accuracy and precision depend on systematic and random errors in the measurement. A precise measurement may not necessarily be accurate and vice versa.

(3) Repeatability and Reproducibility :

Repeatability is defined as the ability of the instrument to reproduce measurements of the same input under the same operating conditions and in the same direction. Repeatability is the measure of the deviation of the measured values from the mean value.

Reproducibility is defined as the ability of the instrument to reproduce measurements of the same input while approaching the measurement from both sides (i.e. through the measurements below the input value and also above it) under the same operating conditions.

(4) Linearity :

The instrument is said to be linear if its output varies linearly with the value of the measurand. (i.e. according to the straight line equation $y = mx + c$). The closeness of the actual calibration curve (input-output relationship) to a specified straight line is considered as the linearity of the instrument which is expressed as maximum deviation of the output curve from the best-fit straight line. The non-linearity may be introduced due to presence of non-linear elements in the instrument such as electronic amplifier, viscous flows, mechanical hysteresis, etc. The scale of such non-linear instruments is not uniform and calibrated accordingly. Linearity is classified as follows :

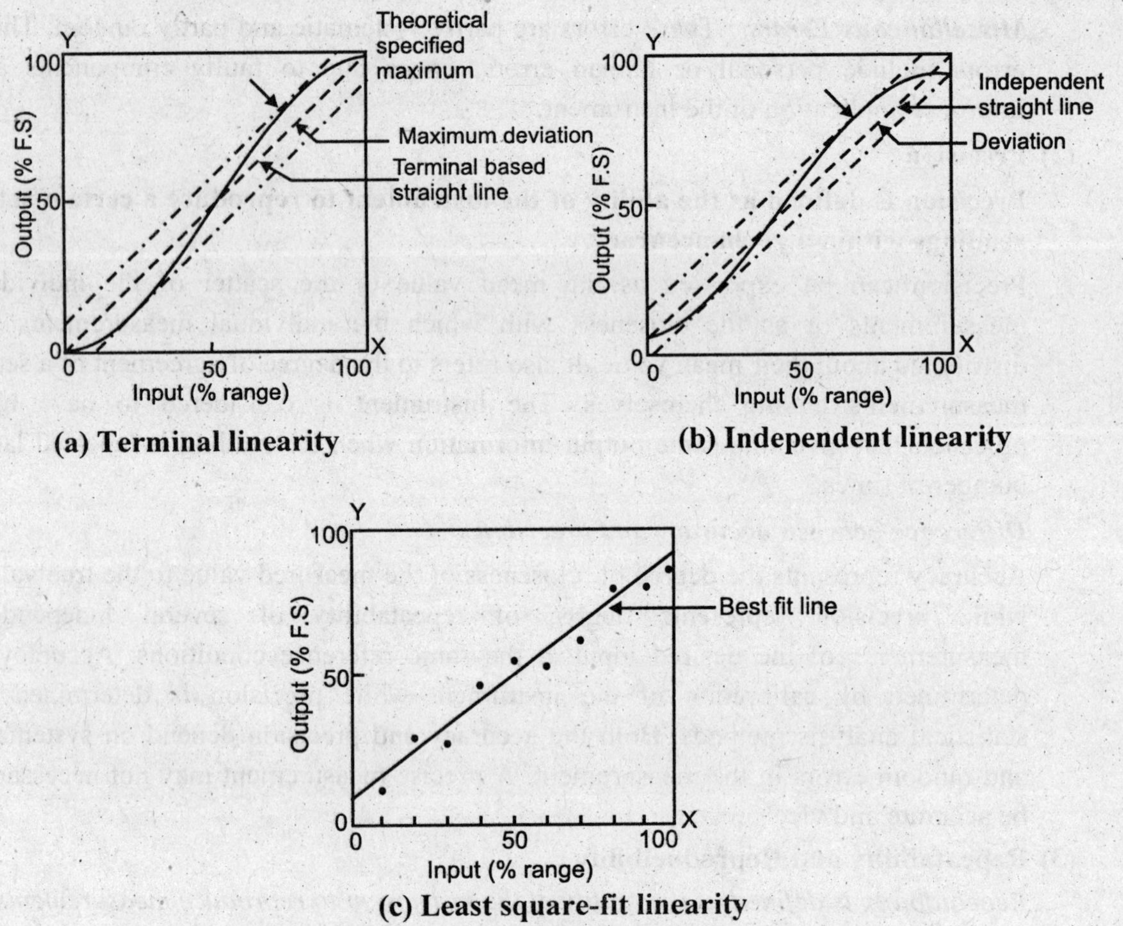

(a) Terminal linearity **(b) Independent linearity**

(c) Least square-fit linearity

Fig. 1.25 : Types of linearity

Theoretical Slope Linearity : This refers to a straight line between the theoretical end points of input and output values (i.e. 0 % and 100 % values). This line is drawn without considering the actual measurement value. Fig. 1.25 (a) shows terminal linearity which is the special case of theoretical slope linearity in which the theoretical end points are exactly 0 % and 100 % of the full-scale (FS) output.

End Point Linearity : This refers to a straight line between the experimental end points, which are obtained during one calibration cycle. (Refer Fig. 1.25 b).

Independent linearity : This refers to the best straight line midway between the closest possible two parallel straight lines enclosing all the output values obtained during one calibration cycle. [Refer Fig. 1.25 (b)]

Least Square Fit Linearity : This refers to the straight line for which the sum of the squares of the residuals (i.e. deviations of the output values from their corresponding points on the best-fit straight line) are minimized.

(5) Resolution (Discrimination) :

Resolution is defined as the smallest increment in the measured value that can be detected by the instrument with certainty. In other words, it is the ability of a measuring system to discriminate between nearly equal values. Resolution also refers to the input increment that produces a perceivable change in the output. Thus, resolution refers to the smallest measurable input change which is nothing but the least count of the instrument.

(6) Threshold : *Threshold is defined as the minimum value of input below which no output change can be detected.* Note that, resolution defines the smallest measurable input change, while threshold refers to the smallest measurable input. Threshold is also expressed as dead band, dead zone, dead space which is defined as the largest change of the measurand to which instrument does not respond. The factors responsible for non-zero threshold and resolution are friction between moving parts, backlash (i.e. play in joints), inertia between moving parts, size of pointer, parallax effect, etc.

(7) Static Sensitivity (Scale Factor or Gain) :

Static sensitivity is defined as the ratio of the change in magnitude of output (response) to the change in input (i.e. the quantity to be measured). Therefore,

$$\textit{Static sensitivity or Gain } K = \frac{\textit{Change in output}}{\textit{Change in input}}$$

Static sensitivity can be determined from the slope of the static calibration curve (input-output curve). For linear instruments, static sensitivity is constant, whereas for non-linear instruments, the sensitivity varies with the input value. The reciprocal of sensitivity is defined as the inverse sensitivity or the deflection factor.

(8) Backlash (Play) :

Backlash is defined as the maximum distance or angle through which any part 'A' of the mechanical system can be moved in one direction without causing motion of the next part 'B' connected with the part 'A'. This refers to mechanical play or tolerance between two mating parts.

(9) Drift :

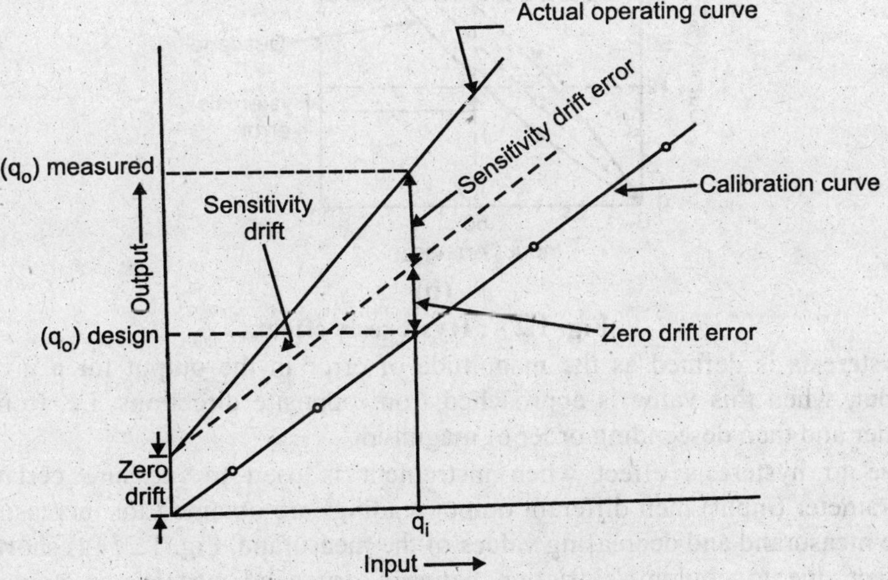

Fig. 1.26 : Zero and sensitivity drift effects

Drift is defined as the variation of output for given input caused due to change in sensitivity of the instrument on account of change in external conditions such as ambient temperature. The output value for zero input is known as zero drift, while change in sensitivity of the instrument due to drift is known as the *sensitivity drift* as shown in Fig. 1.26.

(10) Hysteresis :

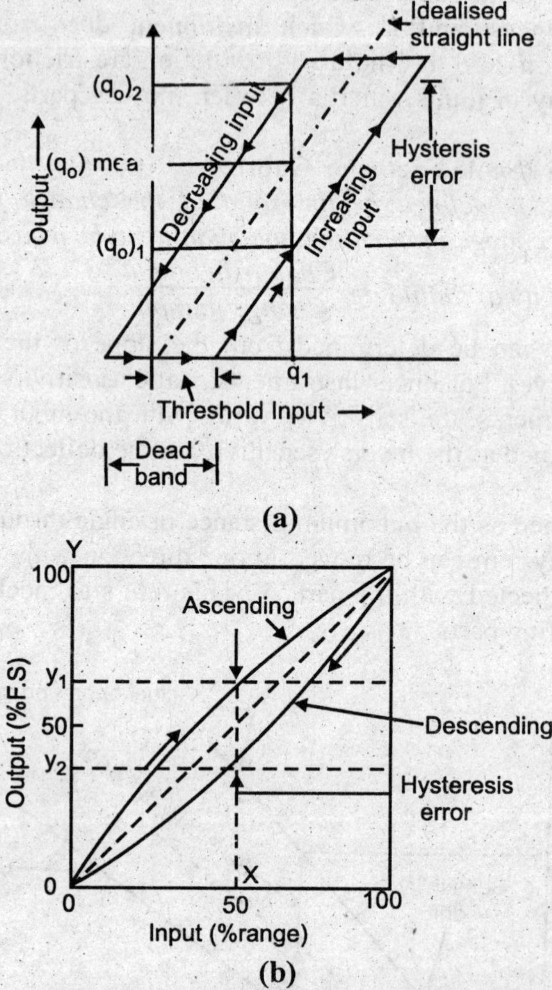

Fig. 1.27 : Hysteresis effect

Hysteresis is defined as the magnitude of error in the output for a given value of input, when this value is approached from opposite directions, i.e. from ascending order and then descending order of magnitude.

Due to hysteresis effect when instrument is used to measure certain value of parameter (input) then different output readings are obtained for increasing values of the measurand and decreasing values of the measurand. Fig. 1.27 (a) shows hysteresis effect due to coulomb's friction between dry solid surfaces in contact, whereas Fig. 1.27 (b) shows hysteresis effect due to viscous friction. Hysteresis is usually expressed as a percentage of the full-scale output measured at 50 % F.S. level as shown in Fig. 1.27 (b). Hysteresis effect depends on the past history of input reversals, lost motion and elasticity of materials. This error is reduced by proper selection and design of mechanical components subjected to heat treatment. Hysteresis effects are eliminated by taking the observations for both ascending and descending values of input and then taking the arithmetic mean of the corresponding readings for a given input. For example, in Fig. 1.27 (b) for a value of input x, the output in ascending order is y_1 and in descending order is y_2 then the mean output reading is

$$y_{mean} = \frac{y_1 + y_2}{2}$$

This mean value approximately corresponds to the straight line calibration curve.

(11) Range and Span :

The range of the instrument is specified as :

Lower limit of measurand – Upper limit of measurand.

The range can be unidirectional (e.g. 0 – 200°C), bidirectional (e.g. –10 to 100°C), expanded type (or zero suppressed type) (e.g. 20 – 100°C). The over-range (or overload capacity) of the instrument is the maximum value of measurand that can be applied to the instrument without any change in its operating characteristics. The amount of time elapsed after the removal of the overload conditions before it operates within the specified range is known as *recovery time*. The algebraic difference between the upper and lower range values is known as *span* of the instrument e.g. a thermometer having range –5 to 100°C, has a span of 100 – (–5) = 105°C.

(12) Reliability and Maintainability :

The reliability of a measurement system is defined as the probability that it will perform its assigned functions for a specified period of time under given operating conditions.

The maintainability of a system is the probability that in the event of the failure of the system, maintenance action under given conditions will restore the system within a specified period of time.

1.15.2 Dynamic Characteristics

Dynamic response of an instrument refers to its output behavior when input signal changes dynamically (i.e. with time). Dynamic characteristics of the instrument are determined when it is used for measurement of dynamic or time-varying quantities.

Standard test signals (Ideal forcing function) :

The dynamic input signal to an instrument may be of the following types :

(i) Transient Input :

The transient input signal varies non-cyclically with time as shown in Fig. 1.28. Such signal is of a definite duration during which its magnitude reaches maximum and then becomes zero after a certain period of time.

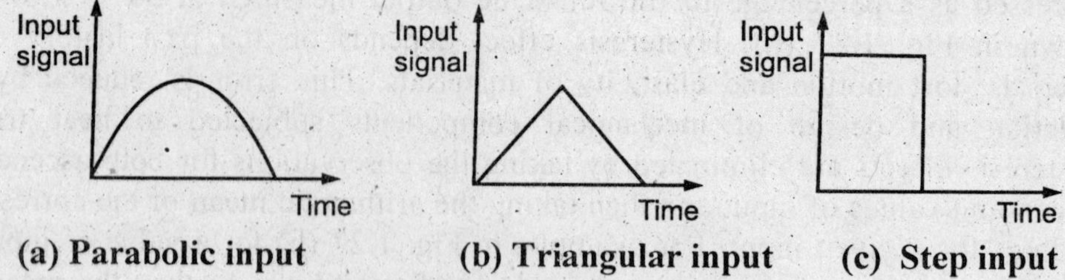

(a) Parabolic input (b) Triangular input (c) Step input

Fig. 1.28 : Transient inputs

In practice, usually the input x_i changes suddenly from initial zero value to a value x_s in certain time t as shown in Fig. 1.28 (c), i.e. known as step change. This can be mathematically represented as :

$$x_i(t) = 0, \quad t < 0$$
$$= x_s, \quad t \geq 0$$

The Laplace transform of such step function gives

$$\bar{x}_i(s) = \frac{x_s}{s} \quad \text{... (1.3)}$$

(ii) Ramp Input :

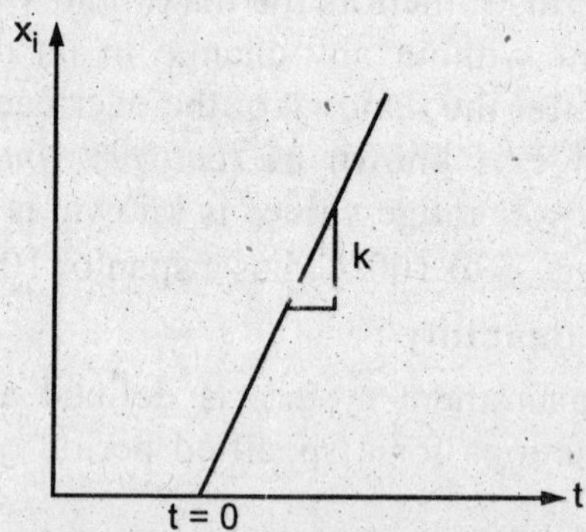

Fig. 1.29 : Ramp input

If input increases (or decreases) linearly with time as shown in Fig. 1.29, it is known as ramp change. In practice, such a change represents gradual, steady change in input at constant rate k. Ramp change can be mathematically represented as :

$$x_i(t) = 0, \quad t < 0$$
$$= kt, \quad t \geq 0$$

The Laplace transform of this function gives :

$$\bar{x}_i(s) = \frac{k}{s^2} \quad \text{... (1.4)}$$

(iii) Impulse Input :

An impulse function is a rectangular pulse of infinitely short duration and infinitely high magnitude as shown in Fig. 1.29. If width of the pulse is A and its height is $\frac{1}{A}$, then area under the pulse is unity ($= A \times \frac{1}{A}$), which is termed as *unit impulse*. In practice an impulse having zero duration and infinite height is a mathematical or theoretical concept, but if magnitude is larger than its duration it is considered as unit impulse.

(iv) Periodic Input :

The periodic input varies cyclically with time as shown in Fig. 1.30 (a) or repeats itself after a constant interval as shown in Fig. 1.30 (b) and (c).

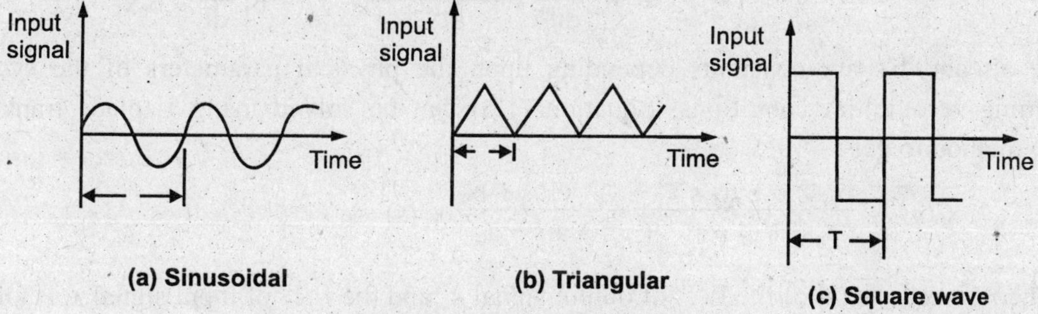

(a) Sinusoidal (b) Triangular (c) Square wave

Fig. 1.30 : Periodic inputs

In practice, the input signals varying gradually between certain bounds (maximum and minimum values) represent cyclic periodic input or sinusoidal input. It is mathematically represented as

$$x_i = A \sin(\omega t)$$

Where, A = amplitude of oscillations

and ω = radian frequency of oscillations.

The Laplace transform of above equation gives

$$\bar{x}_i(s) = \frac{A\omega}{s^2 + \omega^2} \quad \ldots (1.5)$$

(v) Random Input :

Random input varies randomly (but not cyclically) with time with no definite period and amplitude as shown in Fig. 1.31.

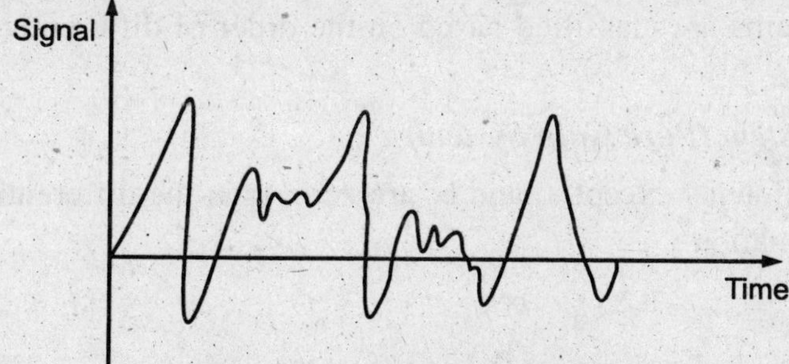

Fig. 1.31 : Random input

In practice, the input signal may be combination of all the above standard or ideal test signals.

Transfer function model of the measurement system : The dynamic response (i.e. output response) of any instrument can be studied by establishing its mathematical model which represents the dynamic relation between input (x_i) and output (x_o) signals. In general, the mathematical model used for dynamic response studies is the ODE (Ordinary Differential Equation) with constant coefficients having the general form :

$$a_0 \frac{dx_0^n}{dt^n} + a_1 \frac{dx_0^{n-1}}{dt^{n-1}} + \ldots + a_1 \frac{dx_0}{dt} + a_0 x_0$$

$$= b_m \frac{dx_i^m}{dt^m} + \frac{b_{m-1}\, d^{m-1}\, x_i}{dt^{m-1}} + \ldots + b_1 \frac{dx_i}{dt} + b_0 x_i \qquad \ldots (1.6)$$

where a's and b's are constants depending upon the physical parameters of the system. Assuming zero initial conditions, Equation (1.6) can be solved using Laplace transform (L.T.) method to get :

$$\overline{x}_0(s) = \frac{b_m s^m + b_{m-1}\, s^{m-1} + \ldots + b_1 s + b_0}{a_n s^n + a_{n-1}\, s^{n-1} + \ldots + a_1 s + a_0}\, \overline{x}_i\,(s)$$

The ratio $\overline{x}_0(s)/\overline{x}_i(s)$ of the L.T. of output signal x_o and the L.T. of input signal x_i is known as the transfer function model of the instrument given by

$$G(s) = \frac{\overline{x}_o(s)}{\overline{x}_i(s)} = \frac{b_m s^m + b_{m-1}\, s^{m-1} + \ldots + b_1 s + b_0}{a_n s^n + a_{n-1}\, s^{n-1} + \ldots + a_1 s + a_0} \qquad \ldots (1.7)$$

The transfer function model can be represented in the form of a block diagram shown in Fig. 1.32 in which the transfer function is written inside the rectangular block with input and output signals as represented by arrow heads in Laplace domain.

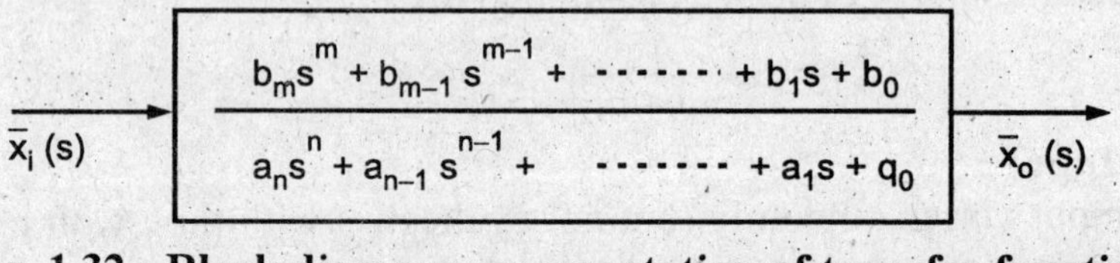

$$\overline{x}_i\,(s) \longrightarrow \boxed{\frac{b_m s^m + b_{m-1} s^{m-1} + \text{------} + b_1 s + b_0}{a_n s^n + a_{n-1} s^{n-1} + \text{------} + a_1 s + q_0}} \longrightarrow \overline{x}_o\,(s)$$

Fig. 1.32 : Block diagram representation of transfer function

The dynamic systems are classified based on the order of differential equation model of the system as follows :

(i) Zero-order system (Pure Gain System) :

If all the coefficients except a_o and b_o are zero, then the differential equation reduces to simply algebraic equation :

$$a_o x_o = b_o x_i$$

Therefore output

$$x_o = \left(\frac{b_o}{a_o}\right) x_i$$

$$= k x_i \qquad \ldots (1.8)$$

where $k = \frac{b_o}{a_o}$; a constant known as *static sensitivity* or *gain* of the system. Equation (1.8) shows that the output x_o varies with (or follows exactly) the input x_i without any deviation or time lag as shown in Fig. 1.32. Such systems are always at steady state, moving instantly from one steady-state to another without any transient behavior in between. Thus, output is identical in form to the input, but differs only in magnitude. For k = 1, output remains unchanged, k < 1 output is attenuated, while for k > 1, output is amplified.

Such systems are called as **pure gain systems**. There are very few physical systems that truly exhibit pure gain characteristics. One of the examples of such systems is a fine bore capillary through which incompressible fluid is flowing at flow rate F. The manometric tubes are installed at the upstream and downstream sides of the capillary. The differential pressure head across the ends of the capillary is measured in terms of difference h in liquid levels in the tubes. It is observed that differential pressure head h varies proportional to flow rate F. Considering 'F' as input (or cause) and 'h' as output (or effect), this system can be modelled by the equation

$$h = (\text{constant})\ F$$

which matches with the standard input-output model of zero-order process (i.e. Eq. (1.8)). Other examples of pure gain systems are mechanical spring and electrical resistor in potentiometer.

Step response :

For step change in input

$$x_i = 0, \qquad t < 0$$
$$= x_s, \qquad t \geq 0$$

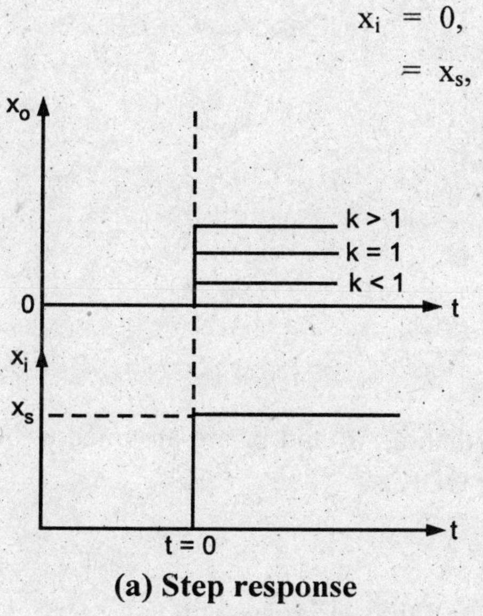

(a) Step response

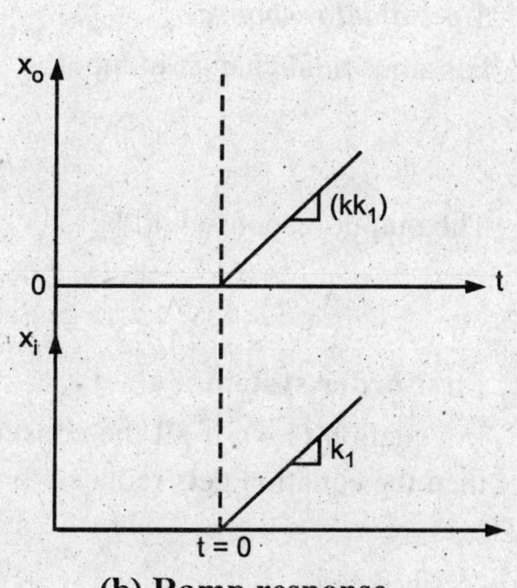

(b) Ramp response

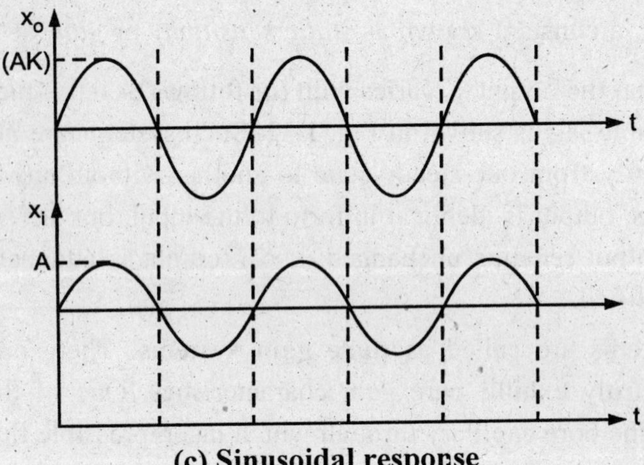

(c) Sinusoidal response

Fig. 1.33

According to equation (1.8),

$$x_o = 0, \quad t < 0$$
$$= kx_s, \quad t \geq 0$$

Ramp response : [Fig. 1.33 (b)]

For ramp change in input

$$x_i = 0, \quad t < 0$$
$$= k_1 t, \quad t \geq 0$$

According to equation (1.8),

$$x_o = 0, \quad t < 0$$
$$= (kk_1)t, \quad t \geq 0$$

Sinusoidal response :

For sinusoidal change in input,

$$x_i = 0, \quad t < 0$$
$$= A \sin \omega t, \quad t \geq 0$$

The output response will be

$$x_o = 0, \quad t < 0$$
$$= (Ak) \sin \omega t, \quad t \geq 0$$

(ii) First-order system :

In equation (1.4), if all the constants other than a_1, a_o and b_o are assumed to be zero, then the equation gets reduced to first order ODE.

$$a_1 \frac{dx_o}{dt} + a_1 x_o = b_o x_i$$

Any system having such a model is known as a first-order system.

Rearranging the above equation

$$\frac{a_1}{a_0}\frac{dx_0}{dt} + x_0 = \frac{b_0}{a_0} x_i$$

Substituting $\frac{a_1}{a_0} = \tau$ = time constant and $\frac{b_0}{a_0} = k$ = gain and taking Laplace transform with zero initial condition,

$$\left.\begin{aligned} \tau_s \bar{x}_o(s) + \bar{x}_o(s) &= k\,\bar{x}_i(s) \\ \bar{x}_0(s) &= \frac{k}{1+\tau_s}\,\bar{x}_i(s) \\ \text{Transfer function } G(s) &= \frac{\bar{x}_o(s)}{\bar{x}_i(s)} = \frac{k}{\tau_s + 1} \end{aligned}\right\} \quad \ldots (1.9)$$

Practical example of first order system is a liquid expansion thermometer shown in Fig. 1.34.

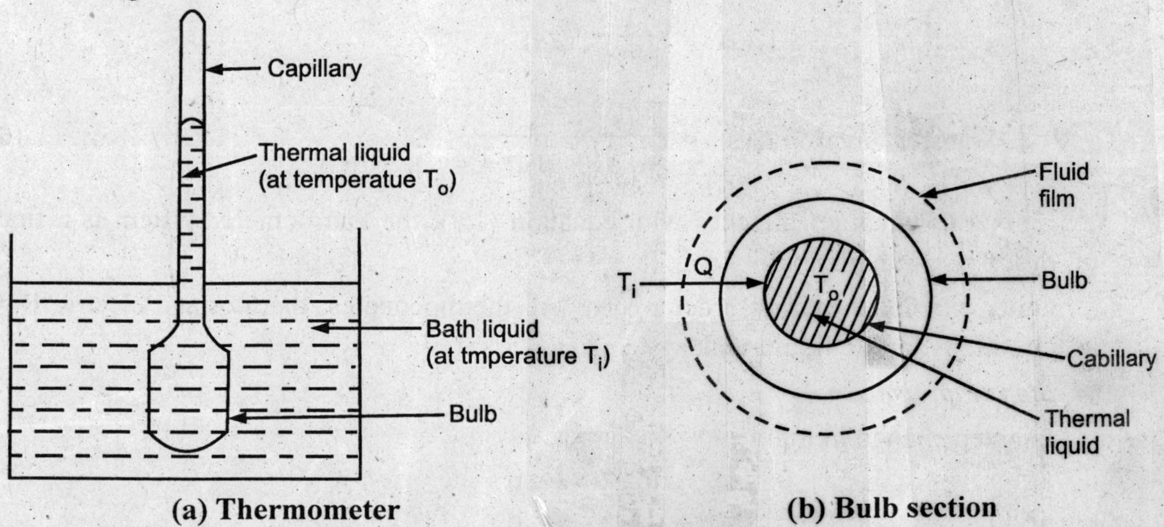

(a) Thermometer **(b) Bulb section**

Fig. 1.34 : Liquid expansion thermometer

A thermometer system consists of a bulb of cylindrical or spherical cross section connected to a fine bore capillary. The system is partially filled with thermal liquid (such as mercury) and capillary is sealed under vacuum. When the bulb is immersed in liquid bath at higher temperature T_i, the thermal liquid gets heated from initial temperature T_m and expands/rises in the capillary tube. Level of thermal liquid inside the capillary indicates the temperature of bath liquid on the calibrated scale. The energy balance equation around the bulb can be written as (assuming no loss of heat).

Rate of heat accumulation = Input heat flow rate – Output heat flow rate

$$mc\frac{dT_0}{dt} = hA\,(T_i - T_o)$$

where m = mass of thermal liquid inside the bulb

c = specific heat of thermal liquid

h = heat transfer coefficient of liquid film around the bulb

A = heat transfer area across the bulb.

Rearranging the above equation,

$$\frac{mc}{hA}\frac{dT_o}{dt} = T_i - T_o$$

Substituting $$\frac{mc}{hA} = \tau$$

$$\tau\frac{dT_o}{dt} + T_o = T_i$$

Taking Laplace transform

$$\tau_s \bar{T}_o(s) + \bar{T}_o(s) = \bar{T}_i(s)$$

$$\bar{T}_o(s) = \frac{1}{1 + \tau_s}\bar{T}_i(s)$$

$$\text{Transfer function } G(s) = \frac{\bar{T}_o(s)}{\bar{T}_i(s)} = \frac{1}{\tau_s + 1} \qquad \text{... (1.10)}$$

Since this equation matches with equation (1.9), the thermometer system is a first-order system having unity gain (k = 1).

Other examples of first-order system are thermocouples, thermostats, electric R–C circuit, hydraulic liquid-tank system.

Step response :

For step change in input,

$$x_i = 0, \quad t < 0$$

$$x_i = x_s, \quad t \geq 0$$

The Laplace transform of input change is

$$\bar{x}_i(s) = \frac{x_s}{s}$$

The output response is given by equation (1.10) as

$$\bar{x}_o(s) = \frac{k}{\tau_s + 1}\frac{x_s}{s} = kx_s\left(\frac{1}{(\tau_s + 1)\,s}\right)$$

Expanding the bracketed term on right hand side using partial fraction expansion and taking inverse Laplace transform

$$x_o(t) = kx_s\,[1 - \exp(-t/\tau)] \qquad \text{... (1.11)}$$

The output response is an exponential curve represented as shown in Fig. 1.33.

Final output response : From equation (1.11)

at $t \to \infty$, $x_o(\infty) = kx_s$

Therefore, $k = \frac{x_o(\infty)}{x_s} = \frac{\text{Steady-state change in output}}{\text{Change in input}}$

$= \text{Steady-state or static gain}$

For k = 1, $x_0(\infty) = x_s = \text{change in input.}$

Significance of time constant : From equation (1.11), at $t = \tau$, $x_o = 0.632 \times kx_s$

Therefore, within one time constant period, the output response reaches $(0.632 \times kx_s)$ or 63.2 % of its final steady-state value (kx_s).

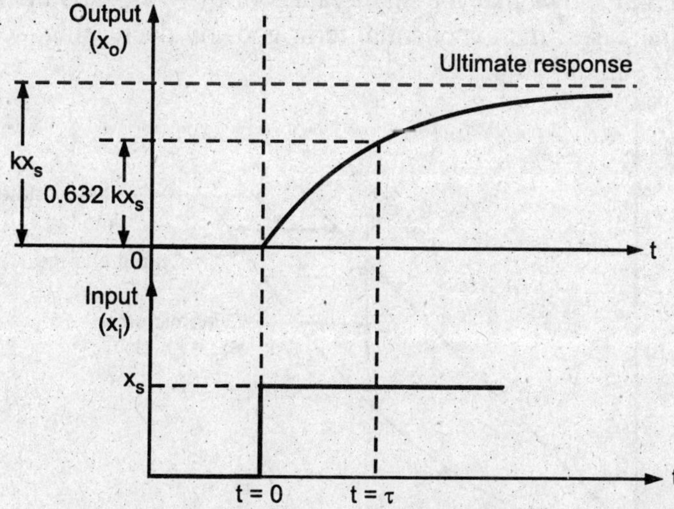

Fig. 1.35 : Step response of first-order system

For $t = 2\tau$, $x_o = 0.865 \times kx_s$ or 86.5 % of steady-state value,

$t = 3\tau$, $x_o = 0.95\ kx_s$ or 95 % of steady-state value,

$t = 4\tau$, $x_o = 0.98\ kx_s$ or 98 % of steady-state value.

Thus, time constant τ is a measure of speed of response, i.e. time necessary for the output to adjust to a change in input. Smaller the value of τ, faster is the output response and vice versa. Note that output changes slower than input, or output lags behind the input. Therefore, first-order system is also called as *first-order lag or transfer lag system.*

Ramp response :

For ramp change in input

$$x_i = 0, \quad t < 0$$
$$= (k, t), \quad t \geq 0$$

The Laplace transform of ramp change in input is

$$\bar{x}_i(s) = \frac{k_1}{s^2}$$

The output response is given by equation (1.11) as

$$\bar{x}_o(s) = \frac{k}{\tau_s + 1} \times \frac{k_1}{s^2} = (kk_1)\left(\frac{1}{(\tau_s + 1)\, s^2}\right)$$

Expanding bracketed terms on right hand side of the above equation,

$$\bar{x}_o(s) = (kk_1)\left(\frac{-\tau}{s} + \frac{1}{s^2} + \frac{\tau}{s + \frac{1}{\tau}}\right)$$

Taking inverse Laplace transform, we get output response equation

$$x_o(t) = kk_1 [-\tau + t + \tau \exp(-t/\tau)]$$

$$= kk_1 [t - \tau \{1 - \exp(-t/\tau)\}] \quad \text{... (1.12)}$$

Equation (1.12) shows that for small values of t ($\rightarrow$ 0), $x_o(t)$ increases exponentially, while as t increases, the exponential term goes on decreasing, so that $x_o(t)$ will vary linearly with t as shown in Fig. 1.36

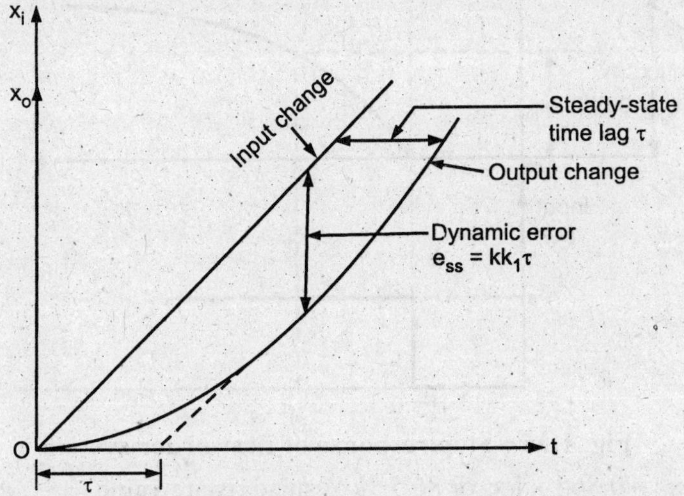

Fig. 1.36 : Ramp response of a first-order system

Dynamic error between input and output :

If output also would have been changed at the same rate k according to ramp function $x_i = kt$, then

$x_o\ (\text{ramp}) = k_1 x_i = kk_1 t$.

But from equation (1.12), actual value of output is

$t \rightarrow \infty$ is $x_o(\infty) = kk_1(t - \tau)$

Therefore output response is asymptotic to a ramp input function with slope kk_1, displaced by τ time units, from the origin at $x_o = 0$. Thus, steady-state time lag between input ramp and output is τ.

Dynamic steady-state error between ramp output and actual output is

$$e_{ss}(\infty) = x_o\,(\text{ramp}) - x_o\,(\infty)$$

$$= kk_1 t - kk_1 (t - \tau)$$

$$= kk_1\tau \quad \text{...(1.13)}$$

With smaller values of τ, the steady-state dynamic error is also small.

Frequency response :

The frequency response of a first-order system for sinusoidal change in input $x_i = A \sin(\omega t)$ is calculated from equation (1.11) as follows :

$$\bar{x}_o(s) = \frac{k}{\tau_s + 1} L(A \sin \omega t) = \frac{k}{\tau_s + 1}\, \frac{A\omega}{s^2 + \omega^2}$$

$$= \frac{kA\omega}{\tau}\left(\frac{1}{s + \frac{1}{\tau}} \times \frac{1}{(s + j\omega)} \times \frac{1}{(s - j\omega)}\right)$$

Expanding bracketed term on right hand side using partial fractions,

$$\bar{x}_o(s) = \frac{kA\omega}{\tau}\left(\frac{c_1}{s + \frac{1}{\tau}} + \frac{c_2}{s + j\omega} + \frac{c_3}{s - j\omega}\right)$$

Evaluating the values of c_1, c_2, c_3 and taking inverse Laplace transform,

$$x_o(t) = \frac{kA\omega\tau}{1 + (\omega\tau)^2} e^{-t/\tau} - \frac{kA\omega\tau}{1 + (\omega\tau)^2} \cos \omega t + \frac{kA}{1 + (\omega\tau)^2} \sin \omega t$$

As $t \to \infty$, $e^{-t/\tau} \to 0$ and the first term in the above equation disappears. Thus, after a long time, the output response for sinusoidal input is also sinusoidal as

$$(x_o)_{ss}(t) = \left[\frac{-kA\omega\tau}{1 + (\omega\tau)^2}\right] \cos \omega t + \left[\frac{kA}{1 + (\omega\tau)^2}\right] \sin \omega t \qquad \text{... (1.14)}$$

Using the trigonometric identity,

$$a \cos \theta + b \sin \theta = c \sin(\theta + \phi)$$

where, $c = \sqrt{a^2 + b^2}$ and $\phi = \tan^{-1}\left(\frac{a}{b}\right)$

Equation (1.22) takes the form

$$(x_o)_{ss}(t) = \frac{kA}{\sqrt{1 + (\omega\tau)^2}} \sin(\omega t + \phi) \qquad \text{... (1.15)}$$

where, $\phi = \tan^{-1}(-\omega\tau)$

Comparing input sinusoidal function

$$x_i(t) = A \sin(\omega t)$$

and output sinusoidal function

$$(x_o)_{ss}(t) = \frac{kA}{\sqrt{1 + (\omega\tau)^2}} \sin(\omega t + \phi) \text{ or } B \sin(\omega t + \phi)$$

We conclude that,

- Th[illegible]ltimate response of a first-order system to a sinusoidal input is also a sinusoidal wi[illegible]e frequency ω, but having different amplitude B and phase angle $(\omega t + \phi)$.

- The ratio of output amplitude B to input amplitude A is known as *amplitude (or magnitude) ratio* which is given by

$$\text{AR (or MR)} = \frac{B}{A} = \frac{1}{\sqrt{1 + (\omega\tau)^2}} \quad \text{... (1.16)}$$

- The output sinusoidal *lags behind* the input wave (phase lag) by an angle ϕ given by

$$\phi = \tan^{-1}(-\omega\tau) \quad \text{... (1.17)}$$

Equations (1.16) and (1.17) show that both the AR and ϕ are functions of frequency ω of input signal. Note that, negative phase angle ϕ indicates that the output lags behind the input.

Therefore, for different frequencies of input signal, the output response has different magnitude and phase angle.

The frequency response is plotted as two separate curves for AR and ϕ versus frequency ω of input signal as shown in Fig. 1.37.

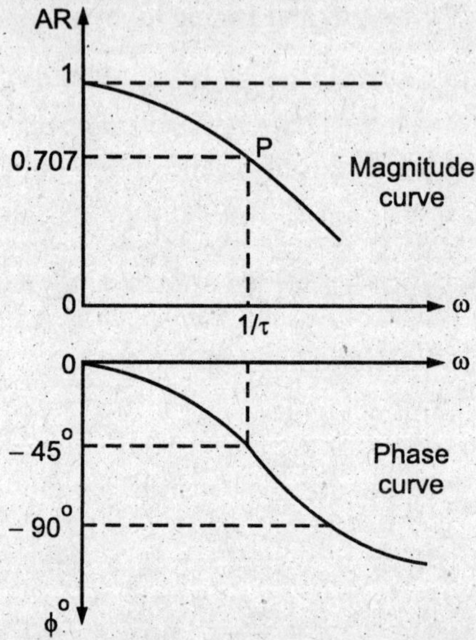

Fig. 1.37 : Frequency response curve of a first-order system

From equation (1.16) at $\omega = 1/\tau$ (known as break-point frequency). AR = 0.707, i.e. the output amplitude is 70.7 % of the input one. Also, ϕ changes from 0° (for $\omega \to 0$) to –90° (for $\omega \to \infty$), with the value of –45° at break-point frequency. Note that for small values of τ, break-point frequency is high, then AR curve is flat.

Impulse response :

The unit impulse response of a first-order system is calculated using equation (1.9) as

$$\bar{x}_o(s) = \frac{k}{\tau s + 1} \times L(u_i(t))$$

$$= \frac{k}{\tau s + 1} \times 1 = \frac{k/\tau}{s + \frac{1}{\tau}}$$

Taking inverse Laplace transform

$$x_o(t) = \frac{k}{\tau} e^{-t/\tau} \qquad \dots (1.18)$$

The output response is as shown in Fig. 1.38.

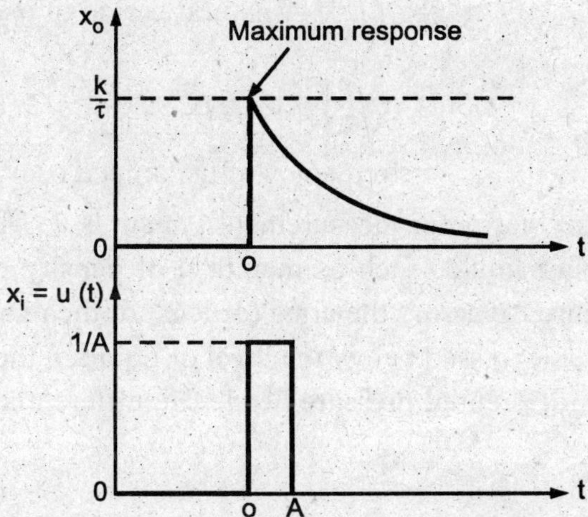

Fig. 1.38 : Unit impulse response of a first-order system

(iii) ***Second-order systems :***

In equation (1.6) if all the constants other than a_2, a_1, a_0, b_0 are zero, then the equation gets reduced to

$$a_2 \frac{d^2x_0}{dt^2} + a_1 \frac{dx_0}{dt} + a_0x_0 = b_0x_i$$

$$\frac{a_2}{a_0} \frac{d^2x_0}{dt^2} + \frac{a_1}{a_0} \frac{dx_0}{dt} + x_0 = \frac{b_0}{a_0} x_i$$

Assuming $\frac{b_0}{a_0} = k, \ \frac{a_2}{a_0} = \tau^2, \ \frac{a_2}{a_0} = 2\zeta\tau$

$$\tau^2 \frac{d^2x_0}{dt^2} + 2\zeta\tau \frac{dx_0}{dt} + x_0 = kx_i \qquad \dots (1.19)$$

Taking Laplace transform with zero initial conditions

$$(\tau^2s^2 + 2\tau\zeta s + 1) \ \bar{x}_o(s) = k \ \bar{x}_i(s)$$

Therefore transfer function is

$$G(s) = \frac{\bar{x}_o(s)}{\bar{x}_i(s)} = \frac{k}{\tau^2s^2 + 2\tau\zeta s + 1} \qquad \dots (1.20 \text{ a})$$

Assuming $\omega_n = \frac{1}{\tau}$, transfer function becomes

$$G(s) = \frac{\bar{x}_o(s)}{\bar{x}_i(s)} = \frac{k\omega_n^2}{s^2 + 2\zeta\omega_n s + \omega_n^2} \qquad \dots (1.20 \text{ b})$$

where, k = static gain or sensitivity

$$\zeta = \frac{a_1}{2\sqrt{a_0 a_2}} = \text{damping ratio}$$

$$\tau = \sqrt{\frac{a_2}{a_0}} = \text{natural period of oscillations}$$

$$\omega_n = \sqrt{\frac{a_0}{a_2}}$$

= frequency of undamped oscillations having $\zeta = 0$.

Practical example of second-order measurement system is a U-tube manometer shown in Fig. 1.39 containing heavier liquid (such as mercury) of density ρ. This system is used to measure differential pressure Δp across the arms (or legs) of the manometer. If $P_1 > P_2$, liquid column in the left arm gets depressed below the level of liquid in the right arm through height 'h' which is termed as the differential pressure head. The differential pressure $\Delta P = P_1 - P_2$ is measured in terms of 'h'.

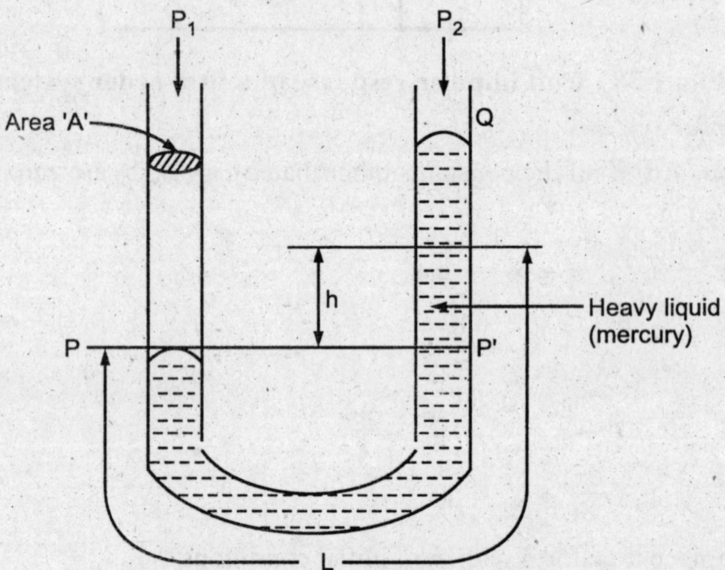

Fig. 1.39 : U-tube manometer

Assume cross-sectional area of the manometer tube as 'A' (having diameter D) and length of heavy liquid as 'L'. Applying Newton's second law on the plane PP',

Net force acting on fluid on plane P

= Mass of fluid × Acceleration of fluid due to differential pressure $(P_1 - P_2)$ – (Force at point Q) – (Force at point 'P')

Density of fluid × volume of fluid × acceleration of fluid =

– (Force due to liquid level of height h) – (Force due to fluid friction)

Force due to fluid friction is calculated as

$$\text{Pressure drop due to friction} \times A = \Delta P \times \frac{\pi D^2}{4}.$$

According to Hagen - Poiseuille equation,

$$\Delta P = \frac{8\mu LQ}{\pi R^4} = \frac{128\mu LQ}{\pi D^4}$$

where, Q = volumetric flow rate of liquid

$$= A \times \frac{dh}{dt} = \frac{\pi D^2}{4}\frac{dh}{dt}$$

and μ = viscosity of liquid

$$\therefore \quad \Delta P = \frac{128\mu L}{\pi D^4} \times \frac{\pi D^2}{4} \times \frac{dh}{dt}$$

$$= \left(\frac{128\mu L}{\pi D^4} \times \frac{\pi D^2}{4}\frac{dh}{dt}\right)\frac{\pi D^2}{4}$$

$$= (8\pi\mu L)\frac{dh}{dt}$$

Equation (1.20) gives

$$P_1A - P_2A - (\rho Ah)\,g - (8\pi\mu L)\frac{dh}{dt} = (\rho AL)\frac{d^2h}{dt^2}$$

Rearranging the equation and putting $P_1 - P_2 = \Delta P$

$$(\rho AL)\frac{d^2h}{dt^2} + (8\pi\mu L)\frac{dh}{dt} + (\rho Ag)\,h = (\Delta P)\,A$$

Dividing throughout by (ρAg),

$$\left(\frac{L}{g}\right)\frac{d^2h}{dt^2} + \left(\frac{8\pi\mu L}{\rho Ag}\right)\frac{dh}{dt} + h = \frac{(\Delta P)\,A}{\rho Ag} \quad \ldots (1.21)$$

Assuming $\frac{L}{g} = \tau^2$, $\quad \frac{8\pi\mu L}{\rho Ag} = 2\tau\zeta \left(\text{or } \zeta = \frac{4\pi\mu}{\rho A}\sqrt{\frac{L}{g}}\right)$

and $\frac{(\Delta P)\,A}{\rho g} = k$

Equation (1.21) has the same form as equation (1.19), therefore, the manometer is taken as the example of a second-order system. Obviously, the transfer function of manometer is given by equation (1.20) as

$$G(s) = \frac{\bar{h}(s)}{\Delta\bar{P}(s)} = \frac{k}{\tau^2 s^2 + 2\tau\zeta s + 1} \quad \ldots (1.22)$$

Step response : For step change in input (i.e. pressure drop) ΔP_s, the output response can be determined from equation (1.22) as

$$\bar{h}(s) = \frac{k}{\tau^2 s^2 + 2\tau\zeta s + 1} \frac{\Delta P_s}{s}$$

$$= \frac{k\,\Delta P_s}{s\,(\tau^2 s^2 + 2\tau\zeta s + 1)} = \frac{k\Delta P_s/\tau^2}{s\left(s^2 + \frac{2\zeta}{\tau} s + \frac{1}{\tau^2}\right)}$$

$$= \frac{\omega_n^2}{s\,(s^2 + 2\zeta\omega_n s + \omega_n^2)} = \frac{(k\Delta P_s)\,\omega_n^2}{s\,(s - s_1)\,(s - s_2)}$$

Partial fraction expansion gives

$$\bar{h}(s) = k\Delta P_s \omega_n^2 \left(\frac{c_1}{s} + \frac{c_2}{s - s_1} + \frac{c_3}{s - s_2}\right)$$

Taking inverse Laplace transform,

$$h(t) = k\Delta P_s \omega_n^2 \,(c_1 + c_2\, e^{s_1 t} + c_3\, e^{s_2 t}) \qquad \dots (1.23)$$

Calculation of c_1, c_2, c_3 gives the output response. In above equation s_1, s_2 are the roots of quadratic expression $s^2 + 2\zeta\omega_n s + \omega_n^2$ calculated as

$$s_1 = \omega_n (\zeta + \sqrt{\zeta^2 - 1}) \text{ and } s_2 = \omega_n (\zeta - \sqrt{\zeta^2 - 1})$$

The nature of the roots s_1, s_2 depends on whether $\zeta > 1$ (s_1 and s_2 are real and distinct), $\zeta = 1$ ($s_1 = s_2$), $\zeta < 1$ (s_1 and s_2 are complex conjugate) which result in three different types of responses as follows :

(i) For $\zeta > 1$ (overdamped response) :

The roots s_1 and s_2 are real and distinct, therefore equation (1.23) gives the output response

$$h(t) = k\,(\Delta P_s)\left[1 - \frac{\zeta + \sqrt{\zeta^2 - 1}}{2\sqrt{\zeta^2 - 1}} \exp\,(-\zeta + \sqrt{\zeta^2 - 1})\,\omega_n t \right.$$

$$\left. + \frac{\zeta - \sqrt{\zeta^2 - 1}}{2\sqrt{\zeta^2 - 1}} \exp\,(-\zeta - \sqrt{\zeta^2 - 1} \times \omega_n t)\right]$$

$$= k\Delta P_s$$

$$\left[1 - \left\{\cosh\,(\omega_n \sqrt{\zeta^2 - 1})\,t + \frac{\zeta}{\sqrt{\zeta^2 - 1}} \sinh\,(\omega_n \sqrt{\zeta^2 - 1}\,t)\right\} \times \exp\,(\zeta\omega_n t)\right] \qquad \dots (1.24)$$

where cosh (......) and sinh (– –) are the hyperbolic functions defined as :

$$\cosh\alpha = \frac{e^{\alpha} + e^{-\alpha}}{2} \text{ and } \sinh\alpha = \frac{e^{\alpha} - e^{-\alpha}}{2}$$

The output response represented by Equation (1.24) is shown in Fig. 1.40, which resembles largely to the step response of a first-order system, except that initial response of second-order process is sluggish than the first-order process. As value of ζ is increased (above 1) the response becomes more and more sluggish and takes longer time to reach steady-state response ($k\Delta P_s$). For a given value of ζ, as ω_n is doubled and t is halved, same output response is achieved. This indicates that ω_n is the measure of speed of response of the system. As ω_n is increased (or τ is decreased), the output response becomes faster.

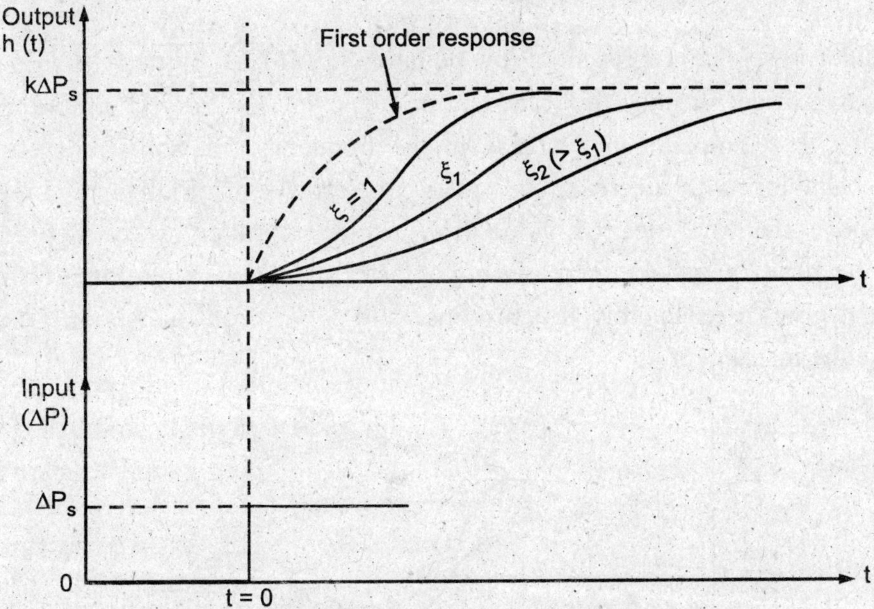

Fig. 1.40 : Step response of overdamped system

(ii) For $\zeta = 1$ (Critically damped response) :

For $\zeta = 1$, the roots s_1 and s_2 are real and repeated ($s_1 = s_2 = \zeta s\omega_n$) therefore equation (1.23) gives the output response as

$$h(t) = k\Delta P_s [1 - (1 + \omega_n t) \exp(-\omega_n t)] \quad \text{... (1.25)}$$

The output response represented by equation (1.25) is shown in Fig. 1.40 which is faster than the response for higher values of ζ (> 1). (Note that critically damped systems approach its ultimate value faster than does an overdamped system.)

(iii) For $\zeta < 1$ (Underdamped response) :

For $\zeta < 1$, the roots s_1 and s_2 are complex conjugates.

$$s_1 = \omega_n\zeta + j\zeta\omega_n \sqrt{1 - \zeta^2}$$

and

$$s_2 = \omega_n\zeta - j\zeta\omega_n \sqrt{1 - \zeta^2}$$

Substituting these values in equation (1.23), we get the output response as

$$h(t) = k\Delta P_s \left[1 - \exp(-\zeta\omega_n t) \left\{ \cos \omega_n \sqrt{1 - \zeta^2}\, t + \frac{\zeta}{\sqrt{1 - \zeta^2}} \sin \omega_n \sqrt{1 - \zeta^2}\, t \right\} \right]$$

This equation may be written in the form

$$h(t) = k\Delta P_s \left[1 - \exp(-\zeta\omega_n t) \sin(\sqrt{1-\zeta^2}\, \omega_n t + \phi)\right]$$

where, $$\phi = \sin^{-1}\sqrt{1-\zeta^2} \text{ or } \tan^{-1}\frac{\sqrt{1-\zeta^2}}{\zeta}. \quad \ldots (1.26)$$

The output response represented by equation (1.26) is plotted in Fig. 1.41 (a) as sinusoidal curve of decreasing amplitude and frequency $\sqrt{1-\zeta^2}\,\omega_n$. Therefore, an increase in the value of ζ (< 1) results in decrease in the frequency of oscillations i.e. decrease in oscillatory behavior with decrease in speed of response. Initially the output response increases above the final desired value $k\Delta P_s$ which is called as *peak overshoot*. As ζ decreases, the peak overshoot increases with faster response. Therefore, value of ζ is so chosen that it gives a reasonably fast response and small peak overshoot. Large overshoot may damage the instrument.

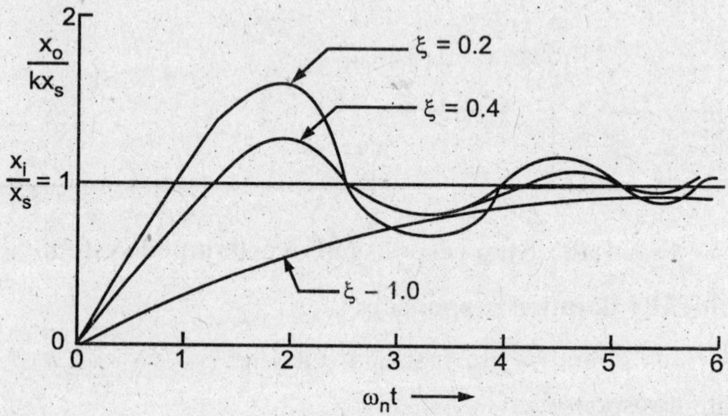

(a) Step response of an underdamped system

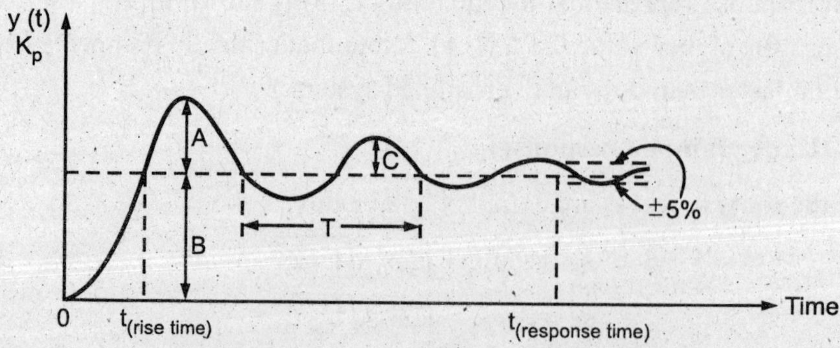

(b) Characteristics of an underdamped system

Fig. 1.41 : Response of an underdamped system

Fig. 1.41 (b) shows characteristics of underdamped response which are defined as follows :

Peak overshoot : The maximum amount A by which output response exceeds its ultimate value B is called as peak overshoot. The ratio A/B is defined as overshoot which is given by

$$\text{overshoot} = \exp\left(-\pi\zeta/\sqrt{1-\zeta^2}\right)$$

Note that as ζ increases, overshoot decreases and as $\zeta \to 1$, overshoot $\to 0$, i.e. critically damped response.

Decay Ratio : The ratio of the amounts above the ultimate value of two successive peaks is called as delay ratio. It is given by the ratio $\frac{C}{A}$ which is given by

$$\frac{C}{A} = \exp\left(-\frac{2\pi\zeta}{\sqrt{1-\zeta^2}}\right) = (\text{overshoot})^2$$

As ζ increases, decay ratio decreases more rapidly towards zero than overshoot.

Period of Oscillations : Equation (1.26) shows the output response is oscillatory having radian frequency

$$\omega = \omega_n\sqrt{1-\zeta^2} \quad \text{(rad/time)} \qquad \dots (1.27)$$

Therefore, period of oscillations i.e. the time elapsed between two successive peaks is given by

$$T = \frac{2\pi}{\omega} = \frac{2\pi}{\omega_n\sqrt{1-\zeta^2}} \dots \text{(time)} \qquad \dots (1.28)$$

Cyclical frequency of oscillations is

$$f = \frac{1}{T} = \frac{\omega_n\sqrt{1-\zeta^2}}{2\pi} \quad \text{(cycles/time or Hertz)} \qquad \dots (1.29)$$

Natural period of oscillations : A second-order system with $\zeta = 0$ is an undamped system which oscillates freely with natural frequency given by equation (1.27) as

$$\omega = \omega_n$$

For $\zeta = 0$, the roots s_1, s_2 are pure imaginary. Therefore, the output response of such undamped system is determined by substituting $\zeta = 0$ in equation (1.26) that gives

$$h(t) = k\Delta P_s \sin(\omega_n t + \phi) \qquad \dots (1.30)$$

Equation (1.30) shows that the output will oscillate continuously with a constant amplitude and a natural frequency ω_n (as shown in Fig. 1.42).

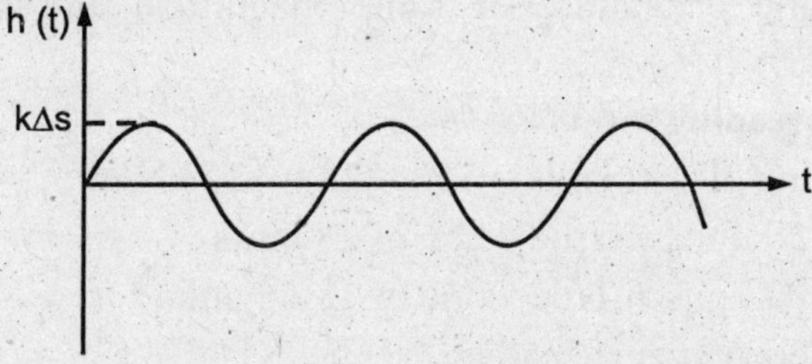

Fig. 1.42 : Natural oscillations of undamped system

Therefore, ω_n in equation (1.20 b) represents natural radian frequency of oscillations. Therefore, natural period of oscillations is given by

$$T_n = \frac{2\pi}{\omega_n} = 2\pi\tau$$

Consequently, since ω_n represents natural frequency of oscillation, its reciprocal $\tau = 1/\omega_n$ represents natural period of oscillation.

Rise Time (t_{rise}) : The time required for the response to reach its final value for the first time is known as rise time which is calculated using the expression

$$t_{rise} = \frac{\pi - \phi}{\omega_n \sqrt{1-\zeta^2}}$$

As ζ (< 1) increases, the rise time increases which indicate slower response with smaller overshoot.

Response Time : As $t \to \infty$, the output response of an underdamped system reaches final value $k\Delta P_s$. The time required for the response to reach within ± 5 % of its final value and stay there is known as the response time.

SOLVED EXAMPLES

Ex. 1.1 : *A millivoltmeter has a range of 0 - 100 mV and its accuracy is ± 0.5 % of f_{sd}. If the meter is used to measure voltage of 40 mV, find the output of the instrument.*

Sol. : Accuracy of the millivoltmeter

$$= \pm (0.005 \times \text{maximum scale value})$$
$$= \pm (0.005 \times 100)$$
$$= \pm 0.5 \text{ mV}$$

$$\text{Output of the instrument} = \text{True value} \pm \text{ \% accuracy}$$
$$= 40 \pm 0.5$$

Therefore output reading of the millivoltmeter lies between 35 mV to 45 mV.

Ex. 1.2 : *A Bourdon type pressure gauge is used to measure pressure inside a pressure vessel. Due to mechanical fault, the pressure readings shown by this gauge are subjected to systematic error. Due to this error, the gauge shows higher readings in a linear fashion. The zero reading on the gauge corresponds to true pressure of 6 kN/m^2 and the reading of 150 units on the scale corresponds to the true value of 28 kN/m^2. Find the true value of pressure for a dial reading of 100.*

Sol. : The systematic errors are of same magnitude and sign, therefore they get accumulated.

Error at zero reading ≡ 6 kN/m^2.

Error at reading of 150 units = 150 – 28 = 122 kN/m^2.

Reading of 150 units ≡ True value of 28 units.

Reading of 100 units ≡ True value of 18.66 units.

Considering error at zero reading,

True value for reading of 100 = 18.66 + 6 = 24.66 kN/mm^2.

Ex. 1.3 : *A thermometer has a first-order response with time constant of 1 sec. It is given a step input of 50 °C from 0 °C. Calculate the temperature indicated 0.6 s after the application of the input. Plot the temperature response characteristics at every 0.2 s interval upto 2s.*

Sol. : $\tau = 1$ sec. $= x_s = 50 - 0 = 50$

The step response of a first-order system is calculated as

$$x_0(t) = kx_s [1 - \exp(-t/\tau)]$$

Assuming k = 1, response after t = 0.6 s will be

$$x_0(0.6) = 50 [1 - \exp(-0.6/1)] = 22.56$$

To draw the response curve (Refer Fig. 1.43) the output response at interval of 0.2 s is calculated as follows :

Time (sec)	0.2	0.4	0.6	0.8	1.0	1.2	1.4	1.6	1.8	2.0
Response (x_o)	9.06	16.48	22.56	27.53	31.6	34.94	37.67	39.9	41.73	43.23

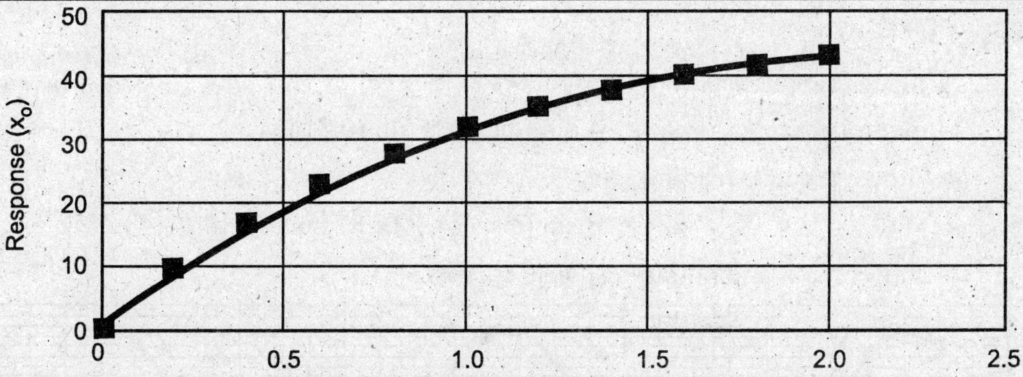

Fig. 1.43

Ex. 1.4 : *A first-order temperature measuring system having time constant of 3 s is used to measure temperature of a heating medium which changes sinusoidally between 250 and 200 °C with a periodic time of 20 s. Find the minimum and maximum values of temperature as indicated by the measuring system and time lag between the output and input signals. Sketch the input and output response curves at interval of 10 s upto 100 s.*

Sol. : The heating medium has mean temperature of

250 – 200 = 225°C and has amplitude of oscillations $= \frac{250 - 200}{2} = 25°C = A$

A system has $\tau = 3$ s and T = 20 s.

Frequency of oscillations, $\omega = \frac{2\pi}{T} = \frac{2\pi}{20} = 0.314$ rad/s

Amplitude of output oscillations

$$B = \frac{A}{\sqrt{1+(\omega\tau)^2}}$$

$$= \frac{25}{\sqrt{1+(0.314 \times 3)}} = 12.87$$

Therefore indicated temperature reading (i.e. output) will oscillate around the mean value 225°C between (225 + 12.87) and (225 – 12.87) i.e. between 237.87°C and 212.13°C.

The phase lag between input and output waves

$$\phi = \tan^{-1}(-\omega\tau) = \tan^{-1}(-0.314 \times 3) = -43.28°$$

Time lag between input and output is calculated as follows :

$$\text{Phase difference} \equiv \text{Time lag (s)}$$

$$360° \equiv 20 \text{ s } (= T)$$

$$43.28° \equiv \frac{43.28 \times 20}{360} = 3.6 \text{ s}$$

Response curves :

Calculate input and output responses at interval of 10 s upto 100s as follows

Input response, $x_i = A \sin(\omega t) = 25 \sin(0.314\, t)$

Output response reading

$$x_o = B \sin(\omega t - \phi) = 12.87 \sin(0.314\, t - 43.28°)$$

Fig. 1.44 shows input and output response curves.

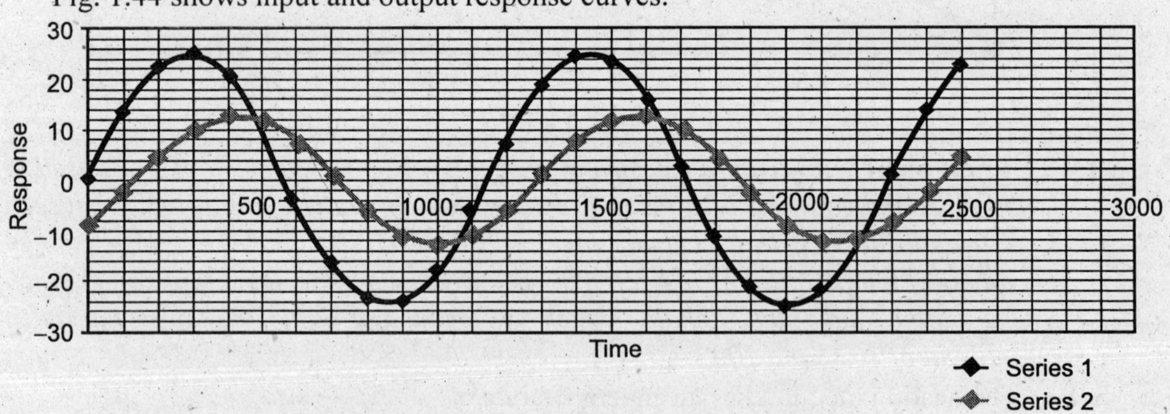

Fig. 1.44

Ex. 1.5 : *A second-order pressure transducer has a natural frequency of 30 rad/s, damping ratio 0.2, static sensitivity of 2 μV/Pa. If a step pressure input of 4 × 10⁵ Pa is applied, determine the expression for output of the transducer.*

Sol. : Given : $\omega_n = 30$ rad/s, $\zeta = 0.2$, $k = 2\ \mu V/Pa$, $x_{ss} = 4 \times 10^5$ Pa

Since $\zeta < 1$, the transducer is an underdamped system. The step response of this system is given by

$$x_0(t) = kx_{ss}\left[1 - \exp(-\zeta\omega_n t)\sin\left(\sqrt{1-\zeta^2}\,\omega_n t + \phi\right)\right]$$

where, $$\phi = \tan^{-1}\frac{\sqrt{1-\zeta^2}}{\zeta} = 78.46°$$

$$\therefore \quad x_0(t) = 2 \times 4 \times 10^5\left[1 - \exp(-6t)\sin(0.97t + 78.46°)\right]$$
$$= (8 \times 10^5)\left[1 - \exp(-6t)\sin(0.97t + 78.46°)\right]$$

Ex. 1.6 : *A measuring element with a time constant of 1 sec and a static sensitivity of 0.05 mV/°C is used to measure the temperature of a medium which changes from 20 to 60°C. (a) If output is zero at 20°C, find the time taken for the output voltage to reach 80 % of the steady-state value, if the temperature change occurs suddenly. (b) Find the output voltage at the end of 5 sec if the temperature changes from 20°C to 60°C at a constant rate in 5 sec.*

Sol. : **Given :** $\tau = 1$ sec, $k = 0.05$ mV/°C

(a) For step change in temperature from 20° to 60°C, $x_s = 60 - 20 = 40$.
Time required for achieving the response of 80 % of steady-state value is calculated as follows.

$$x_0 = 0.8\,kx_s = kx_s\left[1 - \exp(-t/\tau)\right]$$
$$0.8 = 1 - \exp(-t/1)$$
$$\exp(-t/1) = -0.2$$
$$\mathbf{t = 1.6\ s}$$

(b) Now temperature changes at a constant rate from 20°C to 60°C in 5 sec, therefore rate of change is

$$k_1 = \frac{60-20}{5} = \frac{40}{5} = 8°C/s$$

∴ The output response for such ramp (linear) change in input is given by

$$x_0(t) = kk_1\left[t - \tau\{1 - \exp(-t/\tau)\}\right]$$

∴ Output response at the end of 5 sec is calculated as :

$$x_o(5) = 0.05 \times 8\ \left[5 - 1\{1 - \exp(-5/1)\}\right]$$
$$= 1.6\ mV$$

Ex. 1.7 : *A thermometer suddenly put in a water bath kept at 100°C shows the following temperature readings at different time intervals.*

Time t(s)	*Temp T (°C)*
0	*30 = T_i*
1	*50*
3	*64*
6	*80*
8	*89*
11	*95*
15	*98*
18	*99*

(a) *Find time constant of the thermometer.*

(b) *Find the steady-state error if the thermometer is used to measure temperature of a liquid cooling at a constant rate of 1 ℃ for every 6 s.*

Sol. : The initial reading of the thermometer (i.e. at t = 0) is T_i = 30°C.

Therefore output response at the given time instant is calculated as $x_o = T - T_i$, the final desired response being equal to step change in temperature x_s = 100 – 30 = 70°C. (Refer Fig. 1.45).

(a) The time constant of thermometer can be determined by plotting the graph of temperature T (°C) on y-axis versus time t (sec) on x-axis as shown in Fig. 1.45. Time constant τ can be determined as the time required for change in temperature = 0.632 × (70) = 44.24, which corresponds to temperature reading of 30 + 44.24 = 74.24°C.

∴ Time constant, τ = 0.35 sec.

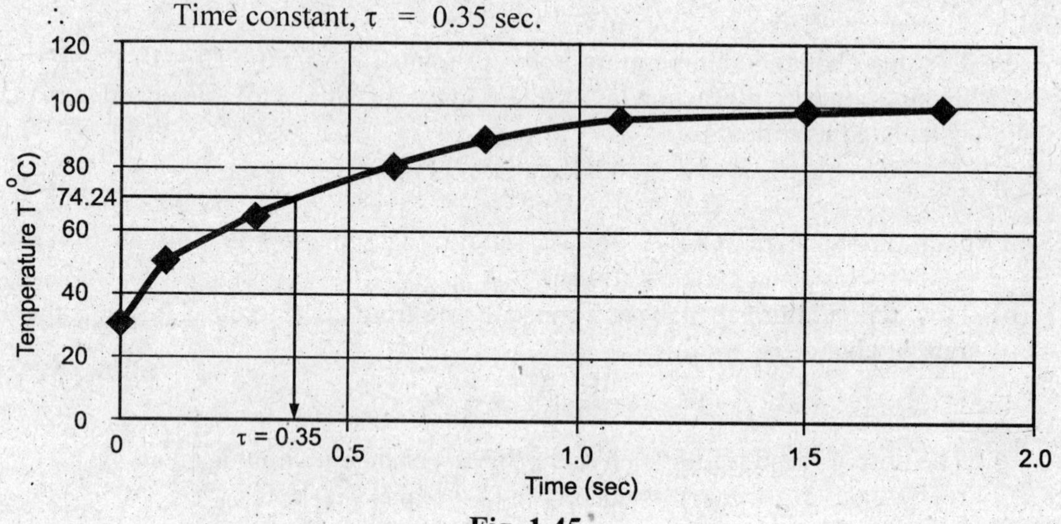

Fig. 1.45

(b) Rate of cooling (k_1) = $\frac{1°C}{6s}$ = 0.17 °C/s

Steady-state error (e_{ss}) = $kk_1\tau$

Assuming sensitivity k = 1, e_{sa} = 0.17 × τ = 0.17 × 0.35 = 0.059

Ex. 1.8 : *A first-order system has time constant of 1.2 s and sensitivity 4. If input of this system is given unit impulse change, find output response at the interval of 0.5 s up to 5 sec. Also sketch the response.*

Sol. : Given τ = 1.28, k = 4

The unit impulse response of a first-order system is given by

$$x_o(t) = \frac{k}{\pi} \exp(-t/\tau)$$

Fig. 1.46 shows the plot of impulse response.

t	0	0.5	1	1.5	2	2.5	3	3.5	4	4.5	5
$x_o(t)$	3.33	2.93	1.44	0.95	0.63	0.42	0.27	0.18	0.12	0.08	0.05

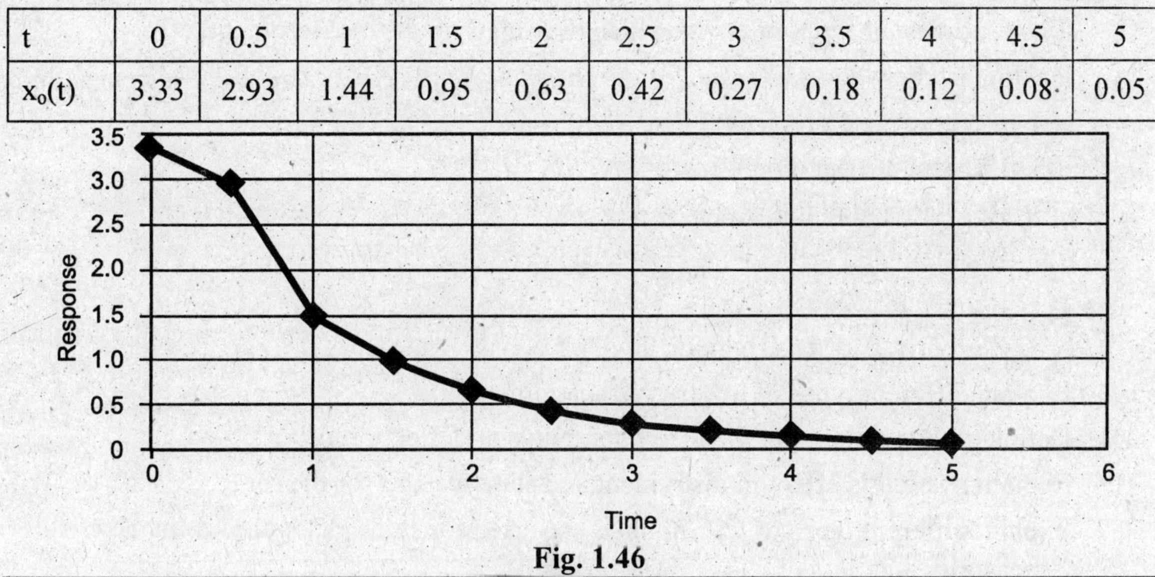

Fig. 1.46

EXERCISES

1. Explain the need and scope of process instrumentation.
2. Explain the basic components of a generalized measurement system.
3. Explain the steps followed in the analysis of measurement problem.
4. Explain the basic and auxiliary functional elements of the measurement system.
5. What is a transducer ? Give classification and desirable properties of transducer.
6. State advantages of electrical transducers over other types of transducers. Give classification of electrical transducers.
7. Explain the operations performed by signal conditioning element.
8. Explain the intermediate elements of measurement system.
9. Explain the basic principles of mechanical, hydraulic, pneumatic and electrical/electronic amplifiers.
10. Explain use of operational amplifiers for amplification, differentiation and integration of input measurement signal.
11. Explain electrical, pneumatic, motion type and RF signal transmission systems.
12. Explain the techniques used for digital signal transmission of processing.
13. Explain various types of indicating, recording and display elements.
14. Explain virtual instrumentation (VI) using Lab View.
15. What is calibration ? Explain the procedures used for calibration of measurement system.
16. Explain the following static characteristics of measuring instruments - accuracy, precision, repeatability, reproducibility, linearity, resolution, sensitivity, backlash, drift, hysteresis, range and span.

17. Explain different types of errors which may incur in the measurement.
18. Distinguish between.
    - (i) Accuracy and precision.
    - (ii) Repeatability and reproducibility.
    - (iii) Resolution and threshold.
    - (iv) Backlash and drift.
    - (v) Range and Span
    - (vi) Zero drift and sensitivity drift.
19. Explain different types of linearity of instrument.
20. Define : Static sensitivity, inverse sensitivity (or deflection factor)
21. Explain hysteresis effect in instrument and state reasons for the same.
22. Explain different types of test input signals used for studying dynamic characteristics of measuring instrument.
23. Classify measurement systems based on their differential equation model.
24. Derive step, impulse, ramp and frequency response characteristics of
    - (i) Zero-order system.
    - (ii) First-Order system.
    - (iii) Second-Order System.
25. Derive transfer functions of first and second-order systems.
26. Derive the differential equation model and transfer function of the mercury expansion thermometer immersed in hot bath liquid. Also derive step response, ramp response, impulse response and frequency response of this system.
27. State transfer function of second-order system. Explain significance of the terms k, ζ, τ and ω_n in the equation.
28. Distinguish between over damped, critically damped and under damped response of second-order system.
29. Derive the differential equation model and transfer function of U-tube manometer.
30. Explain effect of ζ on speed of response and response time for
    - (i) an underdamped system.
    - (ii) an overdamped system.
31. For an underdamped system define the following terms : peak overshoot, decay ratio, natural period of oscillations, rise time, response time. Also state the expression for evaluating these parameters.

❑❑❑

2

CHAPTER

TEMPERATURE MEASURING INSTRUMENTS

Temperature of the substance represents its thermal state i.e. hotness or coldness. According to the Classical Theory, *heat* is a form of energy associated with the random or chaotic thermal motion of the molecules. Temperature is a measure of heat and acts as the driving force or potential for heat transfer.

2.1 INTRODUCTION

Any change in temperature of a body causes change in its physical, chemical and electrical properties. These effects can be employed for temperature measurement purposes. In this chapter, we shall study the operating principle, construction, working and characteristics of temperature sensors.

2.2 TEMPERATURE SCALES

Temperature scales represent the temperature of the body quantitatively.

The International Practical Temperature Scale (IPTS) : IPTS was established by an international commission in 1948 with a text revision in 1960. A revision of the scale was finally adopted in 1968 and is reproduced in Table 2.1. The scale is defined by *fixed points* which are reproducible temperature points established by physical constants of readily available materials. Interpolation between these fixed points is made by several standard measuring instruments.

Table 2.1 : Basic or Primary Fixed Points

Temperature °C	Defining fixed point	Interpolating instrument
– 183.09	Oxygen, liquid-vapour equilibrium	Platinum resistance thermometer
0.00	Water, solid-liquid equilibrium	Platinum resistance thermometer
0.01	Water, triple point	Platinum resistance thermometer
100.00	Water, liquid-vapour equilibrium	Platinum resistance thermometer
419.58	Zinc, solid-liquid equilibrium	Platinum resistance thermometer
444.67	Sulphur, liquid-vapour equilibrium	Platinum resistance thermometer
961.62	Silver, solid-liquid equilibrium	Pt-Pt + 10% Rh thermocouple
1064.4	Gold, solid-liquid equilibrium	Pt-Pt + 10% Rh thermocouple

Absolute Zero Temperature : According to Classical Theory, absolute zero temperature is the state in which molecular motion is at a minimum which is related to Thermodynamics.

There are five different temperature scales used in practice viz. Centigrade or Celcius (°C), Fahrenheit (°F), Kelvin or absolute (K), Rankine or Fahrenheit absolute (°R') and Reaumur (°R).

1. **Centigrade or Celcius Scale (°C) :** It was introduced about 1740 and is commonly used in European Countries. It has *ice-point* at 0°C and *steam-point* at 100°C. This scale depends upon the selection of working substance used.

2. **Fahrenheit Scale (°F) :** It was introduced about 1665 and is used in most English-speaking countries. It has *ice-point* at 32°C and *steam-point* at 212°F. The *zero-point* or starting point temperature is 0°F that represents temperature of certain salt-ice mixture.

°C and °F scale temperatures are related by –

$$°F = (1.8 \times °C) + 32$$

3. **Kelvin or Absolute Scale (°K) :** This is *thermodynamic* temperature scale. It was suggested by Lord Kelvin. This scale is based on mechanical work which may be obtained from a reversible Carnot heat engine working between the two temperature limits. This being thermodynamic property, is independent of the working substance used. The number of such reversible heat engines are arranged to operate on Carnot cycle such that each of them except the first, receives the heat given out by its predecessor, then temperature change through each engine would represent temperature interval on the scale. The engine that discharges no heat is taken as *zero-point* of the scale. This scale has *ice point* at 273.16 °K and *steam point* at 373.16°K. °K and °C scale temperatures are related by

$$°K = °C + 273.16$$

4. **Rankine Scale (°R') :** It is also called Fahrenheit absolute scale and has 491.7°R as *ice-point* and 671.7°R as *steam-point.* °R' and °F scale temperatures are related by

$$°R' = °F + 459.7$$

This is called absolute scale because it has absolute zero as one of the reference points.

5. **Reaumur Scale (°R) :** This scale is often used in alcohol industries. It has 0°R as the *ice-point* and 80°R as the *steam-point.*

Comparison of Temperature Scales :

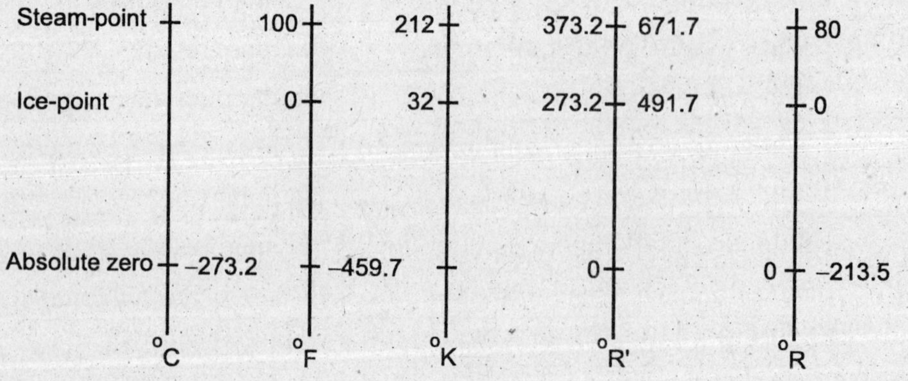

Fig. 2.1

2.3 CLASSIFICATION OF TEMPERATURE SENSORS

Classification of temperature sensors originate from the class of the property of sensor that changes with temperature, followed by the corresponding type of the mechanism used and hence the output signal generated, which is taken as the measure of change in temperature. Hence, thermometers are broadly classified as mechanical (or non-electrical), electrical, optical as given in the classification below.

Classification of temperature sensors :

1. **Mechanical (or non-electrical) sensors :**
   - (a) Solid expansion thermometers (bimetal type).
   - (b) Liquid-in-glass thermometers
     - (i) Thermometers containing non-wetting liquids such as mercury.
     - (ii) Thermometers containing wetting liquids such as pentane, alcohol, toluene.
   - (c) Filled system thermometers :
     - (i) Liquid filled thermometer (mercury-in-steel type).
     - (ii) Constant volume thermometer (gas filled type).
     - (iii) Vapour pressure thermometer.
2. **Electrical sensors :**
   - (a) Thermo-resistive type thermometers :
     (Based on change in electrical resistance)
     - (i) Metallic resistance temperature sensors or detectors (RTD).
     - (ii) Non-metallic or semiconductor resistance temperature sensors (thermistors).
   - (b) Thermo-electric type thermometers :
     (Based on generation of thermo e.m.f.)
     Thermocouples :
   - (c) Solid-state temperature sensors.
   - (d) Quartz thermometers.
3. **Radiation sensors (Pyrometers) :**
   - (a) Total radiation pyrometer.
   - (b) Selective radiation or optical pyrometer.

2.4 MECHANICAL (NON-ELECTRICAL) TEMPERATURE SENSORS

Introduction : Usually matter (solid, liquid or gas) expands or contracts with change in temperature. Hence any change in temperature of matter can be measured in terms of its volumetric expansion.

2.4.1 Solid Expansion Thermometers (Bimetallic Thermometer)

Solid expansion thermometers utilize the changes in thermal expansion of solids with temperature, for measuring temperature around the solid.

I. Principle :

Solids, particularly metals change their volume with temperature and this coefficient of change is not the same for all metals. Hence, any change in temperature around the bimetal strip can be measured in terms of the free end deflection.

II. Construction and Working :

(a) Bimetallic strip :

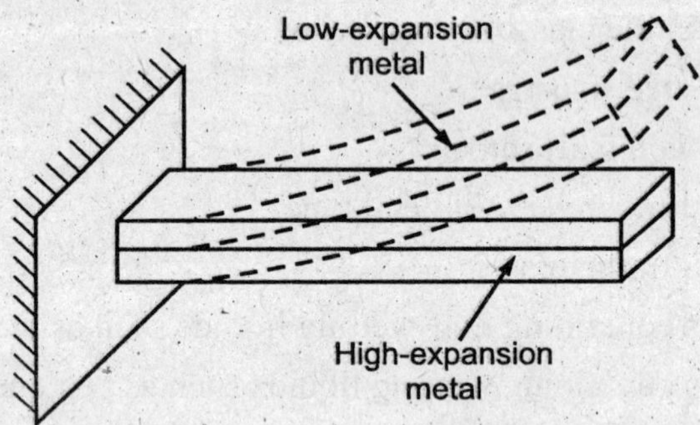

Fig. 2.2 : Bimetallic strip (straight form)

For utilizing thermal expansion of solids for temperature measurement, bimetal strip shown in Fig. 2.2 is used. It consists of two metal strips welded together, each strip made from a metal having different coefficients of thermal expansion. In simple straight form, bimetal strip is fixed at one end in the form of cantilever beam, while its other end is free to move.

Working : Since two metals used in bimetal strip have different *coefficient of thermal expansion* (i.e. expansion per unit length per unit temperature change), the metal having high coefficient expands more in length than the metal having relatively low coefficient of thermal expansion. Since these two metals are bonded in cantilever form, as temperature around the strip increases, the strip bends towards the metal having low thermal expansion coefficient. Thus, free end of the strip gets deflected and this free end deflection is nearly proportional to the change in temperature. This free end deflection is : (i) directly proportional to the square of the length of the strip, and (ii) inversely proportional to the thickness of the metal. This free end deflection is coupled with the pointer that moves on the scale calibrated in temperature.

Working substance : The metals used in bimetallic strip are – low expansion metal – Invar (64% Fe + 36% Ni), high expansion metal – Brass, Nickel, Ni-Mo alloy.

Temperature range : Range is restricted by creeping (stressing) effect at high temperature to – 75 to 540°C.

Free end deflection of the bimetal strip increases with increase in its length. Hence, to get considerably large deflection for small temperature changes, long bimetal strips are arranged in spiral of helix forms described below. Knowing the coefficient of expansion of two metals, their thickness, the desired scale length and range, the total length of spiral is computed.

(b) Spiral bimetal element thermometer : In spiral arrangement, bimetal strip fixed at one end is wound such that turn diameter goes on increasing as shown in Fig. 2.3. One end of the strip is fastened to the case while other end is connected to the pointer.

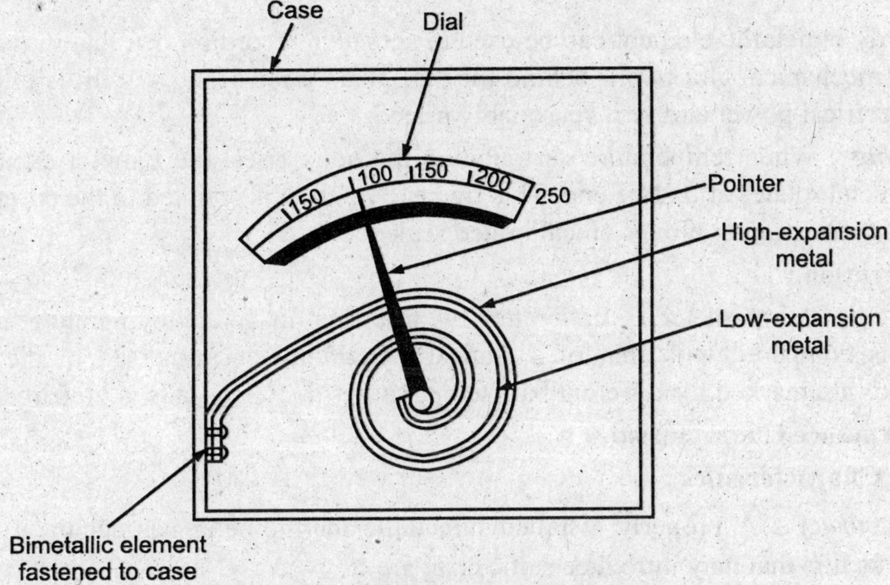

Fig. 2.3 : Spiral bimetal element

Working : As the temperature around the spiral increases, the coil gets tightened or wound. This causes movement of the pointer connected to the free end.

(c) Helix bimetal element thermometer :

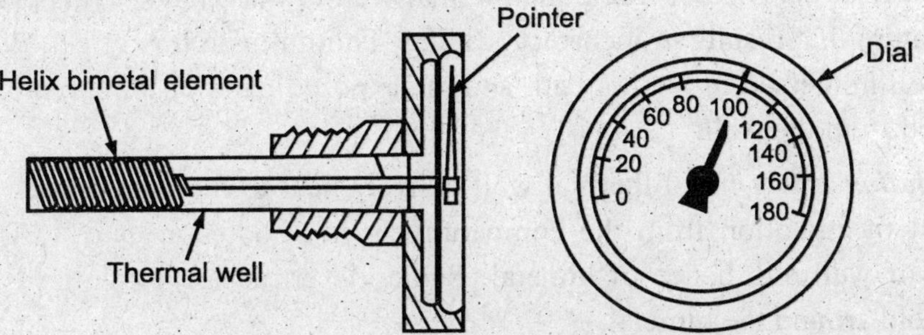

Fig. 2.4 : Helix bimetal element

In helix arrangement shown in Fig. 2.4, bimetal strip is wound coaxially such that all turns are of same diameter. One end of the strip is fastened to the case while its other end is connected to the shaft. The shaft is connected to the pointer that moves on the calibrated scale. A metal thermal well can be used around the helix stem for protection against corrosion and breakage.

In single helix arrangement, the coil moves axially as it winds or unwinds with change in temperature. This requires clearance for vertical movement of the pointer. To overcome this difficulty, a multiple element wound coaxially is used that forms coils within the coils. This construction is more costly, but has an advantage in requiring less immersion depth.

The assembly is sealed using a dry gas in the dial face portion and silicone fluid in the stem around the coils that dampens the vibration and accelerates heat transfer.

Read out dials are available in ranges of 50 to 125 mm in diameter with stem length upto 600 mm.

A sturdy bimetallic element can be used to actuate a recording pen that moves on a chart driven by mechanical clockwork behind the pen. Such a recording system is independent of outside electrical power and very reasonably priced.

Working : When temperature surrounding the helix rises, the bimetal expands and the helical bimetal rotates at its free end. This free end rotation is coupled to the pointer via shaft, due to which the pointer moves on calibrated scale.

III. Calibration :

Bimetallic thermometer is calibrated by inserting in fixed temperature bath and its response is compared with that of a standard thermometer immersed in the same bath. Calibrations are marked for different bath temperatures and then scale is prepared.

IV. Performance Characteristics :

(A) Static Characteristics :

1. Accuracy : A properly installed bimetallic thermometer has accuracy of ± 1% of span. The factors that may introduce static error are :

(a) Ambient temperature effect : The ambient temperature has very little effect on the accuracy, provided bimetallic element is well inserted in the hot bath.

(b) Immersion effect : If the bimetallic element is not well inserted in the hot bath, then conduction of heat takes place along the thermal well to the outside. This causes decrease in well temperature that results in incorrect reading. To minimize this effect, thermometer well should be well immersed in the hot bath and the exposed parts of the thermometer should be well insulated from the well.

(c) Radiation effect : Hot thermal well delivers heat to the cold bodies around it and it receives heat by radiation from the comparatively hot bodies around it. This changes the temperature of well and hence of bimetal. Radiation errors are minimized by constructing radiation shield around the bimetal.

2. Reproducibility : The factors causing calibration drift are :

(a) Mechanical and thermal stresses in bimetal strip.

(b) Fatigue and creep of bimetal strip.

3. Sensitivity : Dead zone depends on the starting friction in moving elements.

(B) Dynamic characteristics :

The speed of response depends upon the installation conditions and characteristics of the fluid surrounding the thermometer. Time constant of response in moving air is normally larger than in a moving liquid.

V. Advantages, Limitations, Applications :

Advantages :

(a) Lowest as compared to thermal and electrical sensors.

(b) Rugged construction, less subjected to breakage.

(c) Reasonably accurate.

(d) Easy installation and little maintenance.

(e) Considerably wide temperature range.

(f) Nearly linear response.

(g) Can be equipped with recorder.

(h) Helical coil can be designed to fit into a stem more easily than the spiral.

Limitations :

(a) High accuracy cannot be obtained.

(b) It is to be mounted at the point of temperature measurement.

(c) Remote indication of temperature cannot be obtained.

(d) Rough handling changes calibration.

Applications : Bimetal thermometer can be used where local temperature indication is required and point of measurement is easily accessible.

2.4.2 Liquid Expansion Thermometers (Liquid-in-Glass Thermometers)

This is the first closed thermal expansion system and has been known since Gabriel Daniel Fahrenheit investigated the expansion of mercury in eighteenth century.

I. Principle :

All liquids expand with rise in temperature. This volumetric expansion of liquid is proportional to the rise in temperature, hence volumetric expansion of liquid can be taken as the measure of its temperature. The relation between volume of a liquid and its temperature is given by

$$V_T = V_o (1 + \alpha T + \beta T^2 + \gamma T^3) \quad \ldots (1)$$

where, V_o = initial volume

V_T = final volume at T°C

T = final temperature in °C

α, β, γ – coefficients of volumetric expansion

II. Construction :

We describe the construction of *mercury-in-glass thermometer*, shown in Fig. 2.5 (a). It consists of a glass stem having a fine, uniform bore *capillary,* with a thin-walled *glass bulb* at lower end. The bulb may be cylindrical or spherical in shape and has volumetric capacity very large as compared to that of the capillary. (If bulb volume is 0.5 cc, then diameter of the capillary is 0.025 mm). Although bulb and capillary could be made from the same type of glass, it is more convenient to make the bulb from a glass with a good stability factor, and the capillary from a glass easier to work. For accurate measurements, the capillary must be properly annealed after it is drawn to the correct bore. Uniformity of bore is desirable, but not absolutely essential if thermometer is calibrated at a sufficient number of points. The front end of the *glass stem* is lens shaped as shown in Fig. 2.5 (b) so as to magnify small diameter mercury column inside the capillary. The rear end of the stem is enameled white, that gives the background for visualising mercury column. *A clinical thermometer* has a restriction purposely placed in the capillary which prevents the mercury from returning towards the bulb when thermometer is removed from the warmer object.

The mercury (or any other working liquid) fills the bulb and the part of the capillary. After filling the capillary open end of the capillary is sealed off under vacuum such that no air is left in the capillary. Occasionally, the space above the mercury inside the capillary may be filled with an inert dry gas such as nitrogen, so as to increase the temperature range.

Industrial thermometers [shown in Fig. 2.5 (c)] have capillary enclosed in a metal case while bulb is inserted into a metal *thermal well*. The thermowell minimizes accidental breakage of the bulb without much effect on accuracy, but it may reduce the speed of response of thermometer. Thermowells are generally made of brass, steel, iron, aluminium etc.

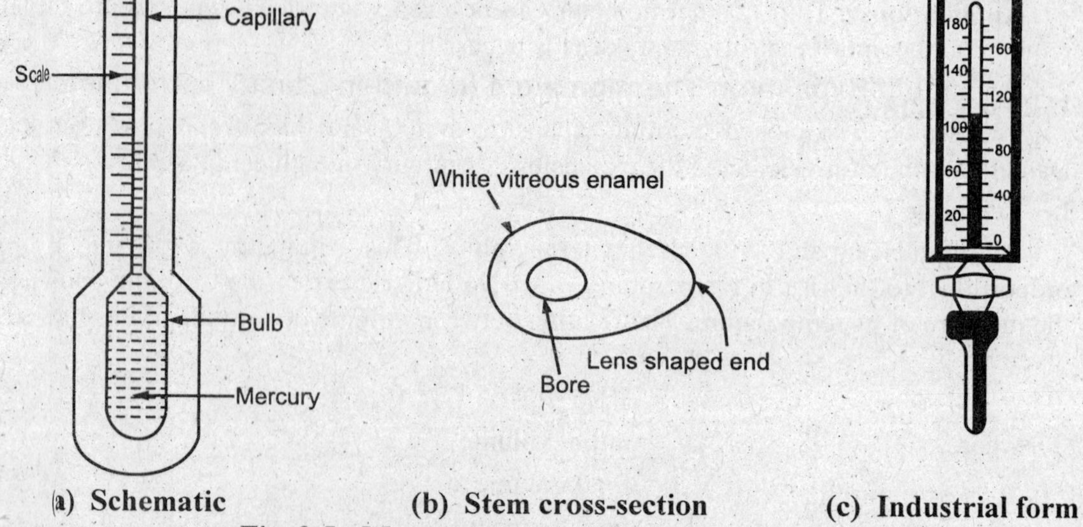

(a) Schematic **(b) Stem cross-section** **(c) Industrial form**

Fig. 2.5 : Mercury-in-glass thermometer

Working substances and their temperature ranges : Usually *mercury* is used as working substance in liquid-in-glass thermometers. The "temperature range" of mercury-in-glass thermometer is restricted by freezing point (–39°C) and boiling point (358°C) of mercury. The upper limit of the range can be increased upto 538°C by elevating the B.P. of mercury, that is achieved by charging pressurized gas (like N_2 at 30 to 300 psi) above mercury in the capillary. For temperatures above 538°C, mercury starts boiling and vapour pressure effects play important role.

Advantages of using mercury in liquid expansion thermometers are :

1. Wide temperature range between its freezing and boiling points.
2. The coefficient of cubical expansion of mercury is nearly eight times that of glass.
3. Non-wetting characteristics towards glass.

The other working substances that can be used in different temperature ranges are :

(a) Alcohol ... (– 80 to 70°C)

(b) Toluene ... (– 80 to 100°C)

(c) Pentane ... (– 200 to 30°C)

(d) Cresole ... (– 5 to 200°C)

III. Working :

For temperature measurement, the bulb of mercury-in-glass thermometer is immersed in the bath to a sufficient depth. Heat energy from the hot bath is transferred to the working substance like mercury through thermal well, stem and bulb mainly by conduction. On receiving heat, mercury expands more than glass because coefficient of cubical expansion of mercury is much greater than that of glass. Since volumetric capacity of capillary is very smaller than that of the bulb, the thermal expansion of mercury causes rise in mercury level inside the capillary. *Thus mercury level inside the capillary changes with temperature of the hot bath.* The top of the mercury column read against the scale gives the bath temperature.

Working of mercury-in-glass thermometer

Change in bath temperature → mercury expands or contracts → mercury level inside the capillary rises or falls to indicate bath temperature

IV. Calibration :

First *ice-point* is marked on the thermometer. For this the thermometer is well inserted in an ice-bath for certain period, then mercury level is marked as 0°C by observing through telescope. Usually mercury-in-glass thermometer is calibrated by comparing its performance with some other standard thermometer, provided both are dipped in the same bath under identical conditions. The type of bath depends upon the temperature range over which thermometer is to be calibrated. When both thermometers reach thermal equilibrium with bath, corresponding temperature reading is marked on the stem. This procedure is repeated for several known bath temperatures within the desired range and then intervals between the corresponding makings are equally divided by a dividing machine.

V. Performance characteristics :

(A) Static characteristics :

*1. **Accuracy :*** ± 1% of span.

To achieve this accuracy, thermometer bulb should be installed such that –

(a) surrounding bath medium would flow around the bulb with sufficient speed so that rapid heat transfer takes place between bath fluid and mercury.

(b) it is dipped into the bath to sufficient depth that reduces immersion error.

(c) the surrounding temperature should be near ordinary room temperature.

Sources of static error are :

(i) Ambient temperature effect

(ii) Immersion effect

(iii) Radiation effect.

2. ***Reproducibility and sensitivity :***

Reproducibility of thermometer depends upon the extent of ambient temperature effects and calibration drift. The contamination of pure working substances at high temperature also cause calibration drift. Since mercury thermometers develop a large force in thermal system, its dead zone is small i.e. within 0.05 to 0.10% of full scale.

(B) Dynamic characteristics :

The dynamic response of mercury thermometer is determined by the following factors :

1. *Thermal characteristics of bulb, well and working substance like*
   (a) thermal capacitance,
   (b) thermal conductivity,
   (c) surface area per unit mass.
2. *The characteristics of bath fluid surrounding the bulb like*
   (a) outside film coefficients of heat transfer,
   (b) mass flow velocity,
   (c) thermal capacitance and conductivity.

For better dynamic response, bulb should have a large area, a small mass, a small specific heat and a high thermal conductivity.

Dip effect : If metal bulb is used, then metal bulb expands suddenly with temperature rise before expansion of liquid in it. This causes temporary net contraction of volume of liquid, that causes the instrument to indicate a reverse direction of temperature change. The lag due to dip effect is 0.01 min.

Effect of bath medium : Time constant of response is larger in moving air than that in moving liquid. At higher temperature, the time constant gets reduced due to radiation effects. Time constant decreases with increasing speed of fluid past the bulb.

Effect of thermal well : Thermal well increases the time lag of the thermometer. This is mainly because due to presence of thermal well, thermometer becomes second-order system. Heat is transferred from well to bulb by conduction, convection and radiation. Since heat transfer by *conduction* depends upon area of contact between bulb and well, the space between them is often filled by metal powder, graphite, oil or mercury. This increases speed of response of the thermometer. When liquid is filled between bulb and well, *convection* heat transfer rate increases. If space between bulb and well is not filled, then at temperature about 540°C, most of the heat is transferred by radiation. For good radiation characteristics the radiating surfaces must be rough and well-oxidised.

VI. Advantages, Limitations, Applications :

Advantages :

(a) Low cost.
(b) Considerably wide temperature range with small bulb volume.
(c) Less space is required.
(d) Easy installation and long life.

Limitations :

(a) The scale of thermometer is not exactly linear because

(i) expansion and contraction of glass envelope cause change in volume of mercury inside the bulb.

(ii) coefficient of cubical expansion of mercury varies with temperature.

(iii) when mercury rises in the capillary, it compresses nitrogen present above it (i.e. used to elevate the B.P. of mercury) that causes elastic expansion of thermometer walls and compression of mercury volume.

(b) Thermometer cannot be used for measuring rapidly fluctuating temperatures.

(c) It is to be mounted near to the point of measurement.

(d) Difficult reading.

(e) Non-adaptability to recording or automatic control.

(f) Liable to breakage.

Applications : Mercury thermometer is used for temperature measurement in –

(a) open tanks containing liquids,

(b) cooking kettles,

(c) molten-metal baths,

(d) steam-lines and

(e) air-ducts.

2.4.3 Filled System or Pressure Spring Thermometers

Filled thermal elements consist of a small bore tubing having bulb connected at one end and a pressure gauge modulated in a readout instrument at the other end. The whole system is gas-tight and filled with an appropriate confined gas or liquid under pressure.

SAMA classification of filled system : The Scientific Apparatus Maker's Association (SAMA) has classified filled system thermometers into four major categories according to filling material and then according to method of ambient temperature compensation. (Table 2.1)

Table 2.1 : SAMA classification of filled system thermometers

SAMA category	Type of compensation	Filling medium
I I-A I-B	None Full Case	Liquid
II-A II-B II-C II-D	Not-required	Vapour
III-A III-B	Full Case	Gas
V-A V-B	Full Case	Mercury

I. Principle :

Liquid-filled thermometers : These thermometers utilize volumetric expansion of liquid with rise in temperature for indicating temperature of liquid.

Gas-filled thermometers : Pressure of certain fixed volume of gas varies with temperature of the gas. Thus, any change in temperature of the gas can be measured in terms of change in its pressure.

Vapour-pressure thermometers : Vapour-pressure of a volatile liquid varies with temperature of liquid. Hence, any change in temperature of a volatile liquid can be measured in terms of change in its vapour pressure.

II. Construction and Working :

In general, a filled system thermometer consists of a *bulb, capillary, thermal well and extension neck.* It is preferred to use the largest possible bulb that decreases ambient temperature errors, permits smaller spans and larger capillaries. Plain bulbs without any covering are used where the measured medium is not under pressure and will not harm the bulb material. *Long, thin bendable bulb* gives high speed of response if used for sensing the average temperature in large areas. A long bulb may be *coiled* for measuring temperature of gas flowing with low velocity. Bulbs are usually made of stainless steel which is relatively inert and withstand high temperature.

The capillary is usually relatively fragile, thin-walled and it is protected by a flexible armored stainless steel or PVC covered bronze tubing.

An extension neck to bulb prevents the tubing from being immersed directly in the measured medium.

2.4.3.1 Construction and Working of Liquid-Filled Thermometers (Class-I Type)

Construction :

System is completely filled with inert hydrocarbon liquids such as xylene, toluene, alcohol etc. (other than mercury) which has coefficient of expansion 6 times that of mercury and makes smaller bulbs possible. The criterion for any liquid used is that :

(i) Pressure inside the system must be greater than the vapour pressure of liquid to prevent bubbles of vapours from flowing in the pressure spring; and

(ii) Liquid should not be allowed to solidify even in cold storage, otherwise calibration may be affected. Fig. 2.6 shows Class-II type filled thermometer having a bulb, a capillary tube and Bourdon tube with pointed mechanism. Note that in glass stem expansion thermometers, system is partially filled with working liquid, while in filled system thermometers the system is completely filled with liquid without any space left.

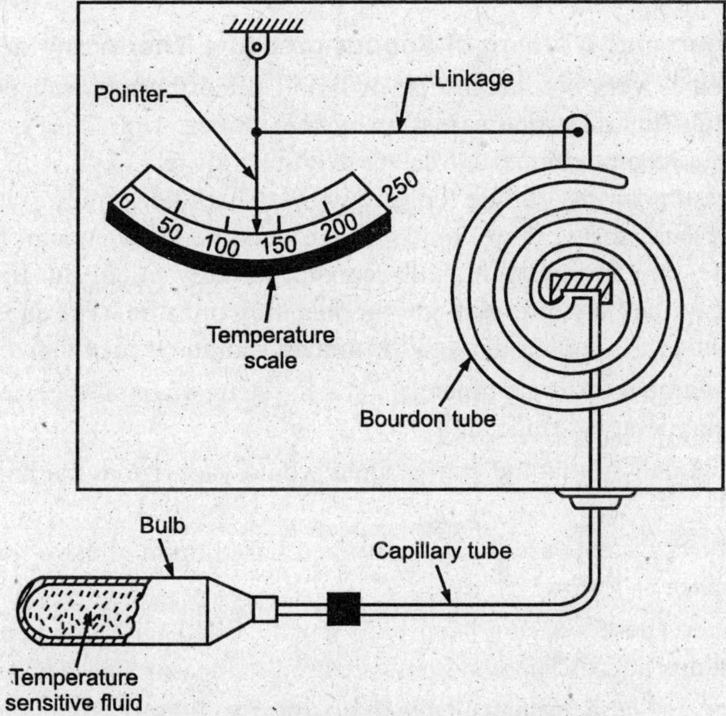

Fig. 2.6 : Liquid-filled thermometer

Class-I type systems are further classified based upon the extent of ambient temperature compensation. Rise in ambient temperature causes thermal expansion and increases pressure that affects reading slightly if compensation is not provided. *The case compensation* is provided only for instrument case i.e. Bourdon spiral.

If compensation is provided for both capillary and case, then it is called as *full compensation*. The further classification of class-I type systems is given below :

Class I-A type : These systems have full compensation against ambient temperature effect.

Class I-B type : These systems have case compensation only, against ambient temperature effect.

(Compensation details are discussed under sources of static error at the end of this article.)

Working : When bulb is sufficiently inserted in the bath whose temperature is to be measured, the bulb liquid receives heat from the bath until its temperature equals bath temperature. With change in temperature, liquid expands or contracts that causes winding or unwinding of the Bourdon tube. This free end deflection of the Bourdon is coupled with the pointer that moves on the calibrated scale or with the pen of recorder. Thus, strictly speaking, liquid-filled thermometer is a volume thermometer rather than pressure thermometer. The volume of liquid required in the bulb is determined by the expansion coefficients of liquid and change in volume required to operate the pointer over the full desired range.

Temperature range : –87°C to 371°C

2.4.3.2 Construction and Working of Vapour-pressure Thermometer (Class II Type)

The construction is very similar to that of liquid-filled thermometer shown in Fig. 2.7 except that a volatile liquid partially fills the system. Since vapour pressure of liquid is a function of its surface temperature, its free surface must always exist at the bulb and not in the capillary or pressure spring. If bulb temperature (i.e. bath temperature) is higher than that of capillary and pressure spring then liquid volume must be large enough to fill completely the capillary and pressure spring while, bulb remains partially filled. But if bulb temperature is less than that of capillary and pressure spring, then bulb must be large enough to contain all the liquid. The volume of liquid required in the system should be such that :

(i) it is not too large so as to completely fill the system when all the vapour condenses at the lowest temperature range, and

(ii) it is not too small so that the entire liquid would vaporize at the highest temperature range.

Class-II type filled systems are further classified based upon relative positions of liquid space and vapour space as follows :

Class II-A type : These systems have bulb mostly filled with gas, while capillary and Bourdon spiral contains liquid. These systems are used to measure temperatures.

Class II-B type : These systems have bulb mostly filled with volatile liquid while capillary and spiral contains gas. These systems are not suitable when ambient temperature is same or close to the measured temperature due to difficulty in having the vapour-liquid interface in the bulb. These systems are used to measure temperature below ambient upto –184°C.

Class II-C type : These systems permit measurement of temperatures on both sides of the ambient temperature. These systems experience cross-ambient effect while crossing the ambient temperature. These systems can be used above and below ambient temperature, but not through it.

Class II-D type : These systems overcome the cross-ambient effect associated with Class II-C type filled systems. Alongwith a volatile working liquid, a non-volatile liquid is filled partly in bulb, capillary and spiral that acts as a hydraulic transmitter for transmitting vapour pressure of volatile liquid to the pressure spring. These systems can be used to measure temperatures above, below and through the ambient temperatures.

Working substance : Temperature ranges of different working substances are :

Methyl chloride	...	(0° to 50°C)
Sulphur dioxide	...	(30° to 120°C)
Ethyl alcohol	...	(90° to 170°C)
Toluene	...	(150° to 250°C)
Ethyl chloride	...	(30° to 100°C)
Water	...	(120° to 220°C)

Working : When bulb of vapour pressure thermometer is well inserted in the bath, then liquid receives heat from the bath and it vapourizes. The liquid continues to boil until pressure in the system equals the vapour pressure of the boiling liquid at that temperature. This vapour pressure is sensed by the Bourdon tube and pointer indicates the bath temperature on the calibrated scale. When temperature surrounding the bulb decreases, the vapour inside the system condenses, which results in decrease in pressure inside the system. This decreased pressure is sensed by the Bourdon tube.

2.4.3.3 Construction and Working of Gas-filled Thermometers (Class III Type)

Construction : The construction is very similar to that of liquid-filled systems. The size of bulb depends upon the type of working gas, temperature span and length of the capillary tubing. A long capillary can be avoided by terminating a short capillary at a small diaphragm chamber, that transmits the pressure with the help of spring. This arrangement is expensive, but permits much smaller bulbs than could otherwise be used.

Working substance : Gas thermometers contain gases like Helium, Hydrogen, Nitrogen, etc. Nitrogen is inert and cheap but it does react somewhat with steel bulb material at temperature above 427°C.

Working : For measuring hot bath temperature, the bulb of gas-filled thermometer is well inserted in the hot bath. Gas inside the bulb receives heat from the bath with corresponding change in pressure (Gay-Lussac's law) which is indicated by moving pointer coupled with the Bourden spiral. Hence, any changes in temperature around the bulb are noticed by pointer deflections on the scale calibrated in terms of bath temperature.

Working of gas-filled thermometer
As bath temperature changes → gas pressure changes → pointer deflects

2.4.3.4 Construction and Working of Mercury filled Thermometer (Class V Type)

Being liquid filled system, the construction and working of mercury filled system is exactly similar to that of Class I type systems. Advantages of using mercury as filling liquid are rapid response, high accuracy, large power for operating control elements. These systems can be used at high working pressure upto 2.8 MPa at high temperature that minimizes any head effect error. Ambient temperature compensation is negligible because of incompressible nature of mercury.

III. Calibration :

All pressure-spring thermometers are calibrated by comparing their response with that of standard thermometer, when both are dipped in same bath under identical conditions.

IV. Performance characteristics :

(A) Static characteristics :

1. *Accuracy :* ± 0.5% of full range

   ± 1% of span for gas systems.

Sources of static error are :

(a) Ambient temperature effect (For liquid-filled thermometers) : Since bulb and receiving element like Bourdon are separated by long capillary tubing, any changes in ambient temperature around the capillary and receiving element causes error in temperature reading.

(i) Ambient temperature compensation : If the ratio of the volume liquid in the bulb to volume of liquid in the capillary and receiving element is large, say 1000 : 1, then ambient temperature effect is negligible.

(ii) Compensation using bimetal strip (case compensation) : Change in ambient temperature at capillary and receiving element causes free end deflection of the Bourdon tube, that causes error in the temperature reading. This deflection is compensated by equal and opposite deflection of bimetal strip (connected as shown in Fig. 2.7) with temperature change. Thus any effect of ambient temperature is compensated or nullified.

Case compensation is adequate when case and capillary are at same temperature (near ambient) and the length of capillary is not too long.

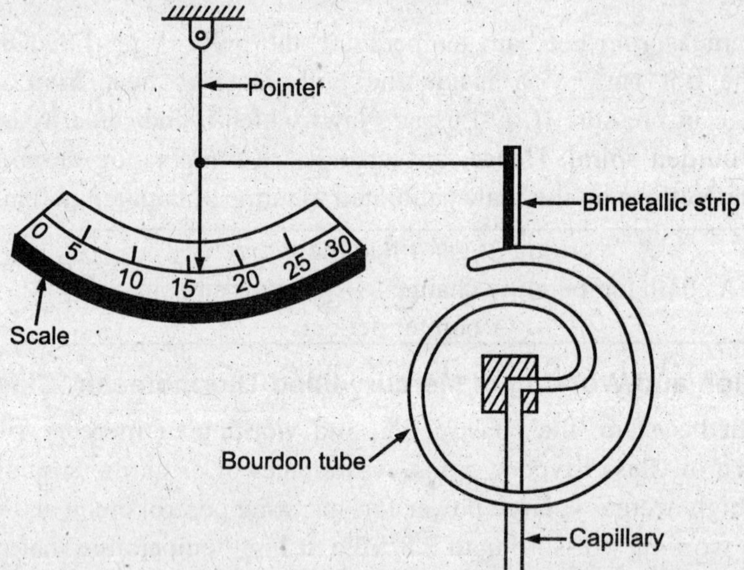

Fig. 2.7 : Ambient temperature compensation using bimetal strip

(iii) Full compensation (capillary and case compensation) : This method provides compensation at the case i.e. Bourdon tube and along the capillary.

In capillary and case compensation shown in Fig. 2.8, second receiving element and capillary filled with liquid or gas is used. The capillary tubings of measuring system and compensating system both run adjacent to each other. Changes in ambient temperature cause equal deflections of the Bourdon tube. But these measuring and compensating Bourdon tubes are connected in opposition, due to which these deflections due to ambient temperature change cancel each other. Full compensation is adequate for narrow range and for small bulb, long capillary systems.

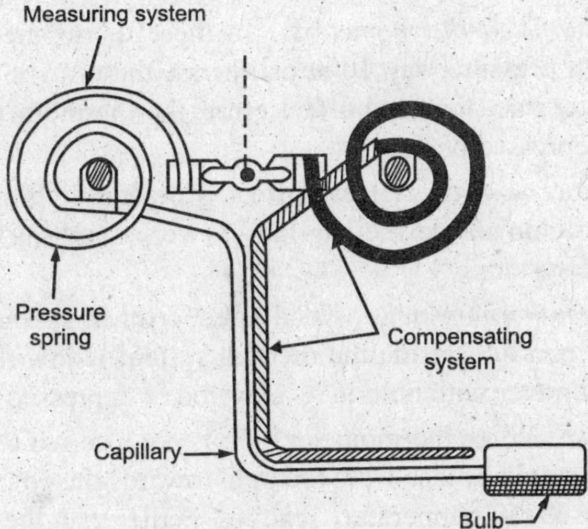

Fig. 2.8 : Capillary and case compensation

Ambient temperature effect in gas-filled thermometers : Gas-thermometers have wide temperature range and hence ambient temperature effect is small as compared to liquid-filled thermometers. Compensation can be achieved by using second-gas-filled capillary and receiving element.

Ambient temperature effect in vapour-filled thermometers : In vapour-actuated thermometers pressure in the thermal system is determined only by the temperature at the free surface of liquid inside the bulb. Hence, these thermometers do not require any ambient temperature compensation. Any changes in volume due to ambient temperature change are compensated by establishing a new vapour-pressure equilibrium at the liquid surface.

(b) Head effect : When thermometer bulb is at a considerably higher or lower elevation than the receiving element like Bourdon tube, then pressure head of liquid inside the capillary affects the pressure spring reading. This is called as *head effect*. Due to head effect, pressure spring shows pressure reading i.e. greater or smaller than the pressure corresponding to bulb temperature.

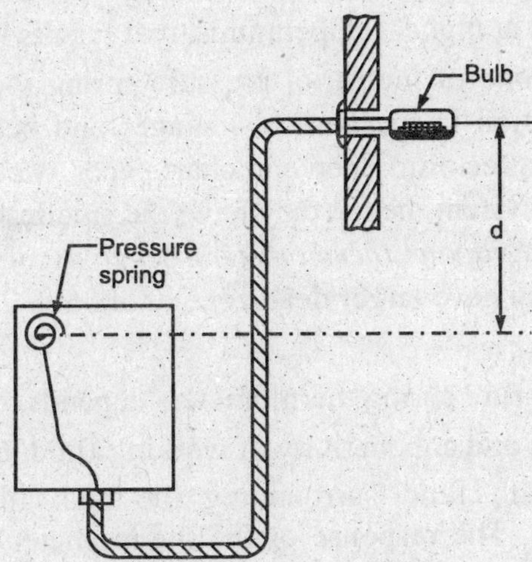

Fig. 2.9 : Head effect

Head effect in liquid-filled thermometers : In these thermometers, working liquid like mercury is filled at high pressure, say 1000 psi, hence the error in the reading due to head effect is negligible. To correct for head effect error, the thermometer is calibrated with the bulb in its elevated or depressed position.

Head effect of gas thermometers : Head effect is negligible in gas thermometer because pressure head of gas column inside the capillary is very small as compared to pressure at which gas is filled in the system.

Head effect in vapour-thermometers : Head effect error in vapour-actuated thermometers is considerable because pressure inside the thermal system is low. Head effect is accounted by calibrating the thermometer with bulb in its elevated or depressed position.

(c) Immersion effect : When thermometer bulb is not inserted to a sufficient depth in the bath, then heat conduction takes place from the bulb towards the cold un-immersed portion of the bulb or well. This results in temperature reading smaller than the actual bath temperature. This is called as *immersion effect.* To minimize this effect in case of liquid and gas-filled thermometers, bulb and well should be well immersed in bath and extension neck of the thermometer should be well insulated from the bulb.

For vapour-actuated thermometer bulbs, it is not very essential to immerse the bulb far inside the bath. But in these thermometers, the whole free surface of volatile liquid in the bulb should be in good thermal contact with bath fluid.

(d) Radiation effect : While measuring temperature of gas or air, the thermometer bulb has tendency to exchange heat with the surrounding hot or cold solid bodies. This results in error in temperature reading. To minimize radiation error, a radiation shield is constructed around the bulb, that reduces radiation heat loss.

2. Reproducibility : The reproducibility depends upon the effectiveness of ambient temperature compensation. The calibration may drift after certain time period. Hence, the calibration should be checked periodically. The working fluids like nitrogen, mercury are used in pure form and they remain stable over long period. But these fluids may get contaminated or decomposed at higher temperatures, that results in calibration drift.

3. Sensitivity : *Dead zone* of industrial pressure spring thermometers depends on the starting friction and lost motion in mechanical linkages and bearings of receiving element like Bourdon tube or between recording pen and chart paper. *Mercury thermometers* develop a larger force in the thermal system, hence they have the smallest dead zone of about 0.05 to 0.10% of full scale. *Gas and vapour thermometers* develop comparatively smaller force in the thermal system, hence they have larger dead zone of about 0.25% of full scale.

(B) Dynamic characteristics :

Dynamic response of pressure spring thermometers depends upon

(i) Thermal capacitances and conductivity of working fluid, bulb and thermal wall.

(ii) Characteristics of bath fluid surrounding the bulb like mass velocity, thermal capacitance and conductivity. The response of the thermometer depends on the size of the bulb, its area and method of installation. For better speed of response, thermometer bulb should have a large area, small mass, small specific heat and high thermal conductivity. The time constant* for a pressure thermometer having its bare bulb placed in a well-agitated liquid is 0.1 min.

Dip effect : When metal bulb containing fluid is used in pressure thermometer, then sudden expansion of the metal bulb takes place before the expansion of fluid. This causes temporary contraction of fluid volume, that results in reverse temperature reading. This is called as *dip effect*. Dip effect causes time lag of 0.01 min in *liquid-filled thermometer,* while the effect is negligible in *gas and vapour-pressure thermometers.*

Effect of fluid surrounding the bulb : For a bare thermometer bulb placed in moving air, time constant is 5 to 10 times larger than that when bulb is placed in a moving liquid. At higher temperature above 200°C, radiation heat transfer becomes predominant, that results in decreased time constant.

Cross-ambient effect in vapour-pressure thermometers :

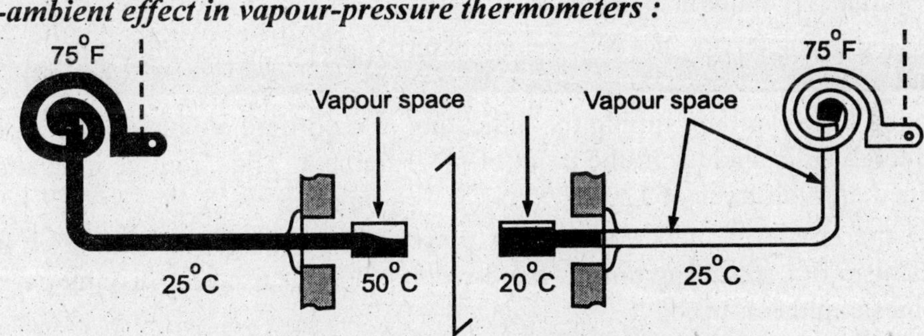

Fig. 2.10 : Cross ambient effect

Consider a vapour-actuated thermometer having capillary and receiving element at room temperature of 25°C. Now if thermometer bulb is at a higher temperature of say 50°C, then capillary and the receiving element are completely filled with liquid and vapour space is present in the bulb as shown in Fig. 2.10 (a). On the other hand, if bulb is at a lower temperature of say 20°C, then vapour space is present in capillary and the receiving element as shown in Fig. 2.10 (b).

Now suppose the temperature range of the instrument is say 0° to 100°C. Then, when temperature at the bulb crosses from below to above the room temperature of 25°C, liquid must migrate from the bulb and fill the capillary and the receiving element. On the other hand, when the bulb temperature drops below the room temperature of 25°C, vapour in capillary and the receiving element condenses into liquid at the bulb. This change of position of liquid and vapour space takes some time and introduces time lag in the measurement. This is called *cross-ambient* effect. Therefore vapour-pressure thermometer should not be used in cross-ambient ranges if high speed of response is desired. Cross-ambient effect can be overcome by using *dual-fill thermal system.* In dual-fill system, receiving element and capillary are completely filled with a non-vapourizing liquid, which just transmits the actual vapour pressure in the bulb to the receiving element, without any condensation or evaporation. Thus, the volatile working liquid is confined only to the bulb, that avoids cross-ambient effect.

* *Time constant : It is the time required for the instrument to respond 63.2% of the final desired response.*

Effect of thermal well : Thermal well around the thermometer bulb increases the response lag. Heat is transferred between the bulb and well by conduction, convection and radiation. Heat transfer rate by *conduction* can be increased by filling the space between the bulb and well with a metal powder, graphite, oil or mercury. This increases the speed of response by 10%. Filling of the space between the bulb and well also prevents any heat transfer by *convection* that otherwise may introduce additional time lag. At temperature above 550°C, most of the heat is transferred by radiation. Radiation being the fastest mode of heat transfer, causes very small time lag in the measurement. For effective radiation heat transfer, surfaces should be rough and well-oxidized rather than smooth and polished.

V. Advantages, Limitations, Applications :

Advantages :

(a) Rugged, self-contained construction without any external power supply required.

(b) Low initial and maintenance cost.

(c) These thermometers do not require any external power source and in this respect they are automatic.

(d) By using long capillary tubing the indicating or recording element can be located at a considerable distance from the point of measurement. Thus, remote indication can be obtained upto distance of 120 m.

(e) These thermometers generate enough power to operate the recording or indicating mechanism or controlling unit. If hand-wound clock is used for driving chart, system becomes explosion-proof.

(f) Accuracy and sensitivity are sufficient to meet most industrial requirements.

(g) Mercury thermometer has greater sensitivity than other filled thermometers.

(h) Vapour-actuated thermometers are most widely used because they are less costly and simpler to maintain. It does not require any compensation and has good speed of response.

(i) Gas thermometer has better accuracy and it can reach considerably low temperature.

(j) Three or more separate systems can be put in a single instrument case.

(k) Filled thermometers are intermediate in cost and performance between the simplest devices like glass stem and bimetallic thermometers and more complex electrical elements.

Limitations :

(a) Accuracy, sensitivity and temperature span are low as compared to electrical temperature sensors. For increasing accuracy, large size bulb be used, that requires larger space at the point of measurement.

(b) All pressure thermometers contain working fluid at certain fixed pressure, hence system cannot be broken without affecting the calibration.

(c) In case of any breakage, the entire system should be replaced.

(d) For separation distance of more than 30 m between sensing element and indicating element, use of transmitters becomes economical.

(e) Vapour-pressure thermometers indicate only temperature at the liquid surface.

Comparison of Pressure Spring Thermometers :

Property	Mercury	Gas	Vapour
1. Scale shape	Linear	Linear	Non-linear
2. Temperature range (°C)	–49 to 649	–268 to 760	–184 to 343
3. Smallest span (°C)	38	70	26
4. Largest span (°C)	537	426	176
5. Ambient effect	Yes	Yes	No
6. Cross-ambient effect	No	No	Yes
7. Head effect	No	No	Yes
8. Barometric effect	No	Yes	Yes
9. Dip effect	Yes	No	No
10. Immersion effect	Yes	Yes	Yes (little)
11. Response speed	Slow	Slow	Fast
12. Sensitivity	Greater	Low	Low

2.5 ELECTRICAL TEMPERATURE SENSORS

The output of electrical temperature sensors is in the form of electrical signals i.e. either voltage or current. In this chapter, we study the following temperature sensors :

1. Thermo-resistive type sensors.
   (Resistance temperature detectors, RTD and Thermistors).
2. Thermo-electric type (Thermocouples).
3. Solid state temperature sensors.
4. Quartz thermometers.

2.5.1 Thermo-Resistive Type Sensors

2.5.1.1 Resistance Temperature Detectors (RTD) (Resistance Thermometers)

History : The application of the property of electrical conductors to increase electrical resistance with rise in temperature, was first described by Sir William Siemens at the Bakerian Lecture of 1871 before the Royal Society in Great Britain. The necessary methods of construction were established by Callendar, Griffiths, Holborn and Wein between 1885 to 1900.

I. Principle :

Electrical resistance of a substance changes with change in its temperature. This substance can be a metal or a nonmetal like semiconductor. Hence, any changes in temperature of a metal can be measured in terms of change in its electrical resistance. The resistance of most metals increases with rise in temperature and the relationship between resistance and temperature for metals is given by

$$R_t = R_o (1 + a_1 t + a_2 t^2 + a_3 t^3 + \ldots) \quad \ldots (2.1)$$

where,
R_t = resistance at temperature t°C
R_o = resistance at 0°C
a_1, a_2, a_3 = constants i.e. coefficients of resistance

For small temperature ranges, only constant a_1 is considered, so that relationship between temperature and resistance becomes linear.

II. Construction :

(A) Sensing element (Resistance bulb) : Industrial resistance thermometer bulb essentially consists of a coil of fine resistance wire wound on or inside the frame of insulating material. Different forms of the resistance bulb are described below :

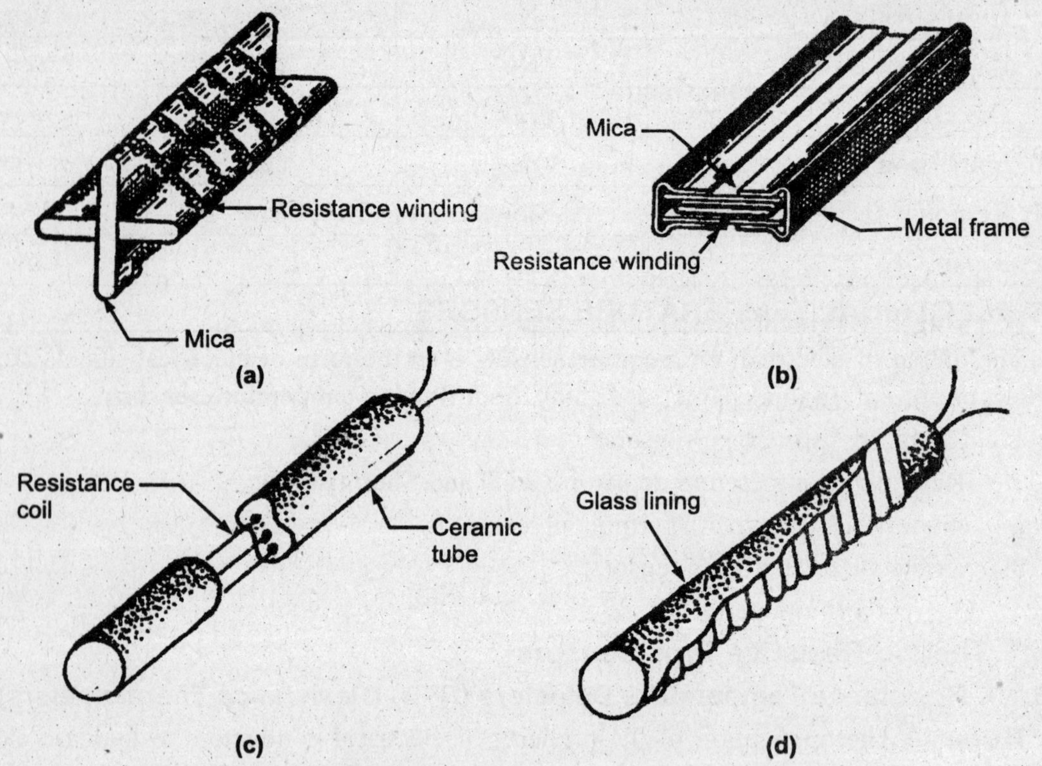

Fig. 2.11 : Resistance bulb

High resistance metal wires (like platinum) are wound on a notched or perforated mica frame as shown in Fig. 2.11 (a). Such a bulb appears as a round coil.

Resistance wire is clamped between two mica plates as shown in Fig. 2.11 (b). This arrangement is more compact than that shown in Fig. 2.11 (a).

For high temperature measurement resistance wires are passed through small holes drilled in ceramic rod as shown in Fig. 2.11 (c).

The robust form of resistance bulb i.e. shown in Fig. 2.11 (d), in which resistance wire is wound on solid ceramic rod and coil is sealed by glass. This form is used in aircrafts. For surface temperature measurement, resistance element is made in the form of woven-wire mesh cloth.

Low resistance wires made of copper, nickel etc. can be wound on glass or plastic insulators, instead of using mica.

Precautions to be taken while winding resistance wire on insulating frame are :

(a) Good thermal conductivity and high rate of heat transfer is obtained.

(b) The windings should be free from any physical strain, because electrical resistance of winding changes with change in mechanical stress or strain in it.

(c) The resistance wire material should have a continuous and stable relationship between resistance and temperature and also it should have a high thermal coefficient of resistance.

(d) Resistance wire should be homogeneous so that entire wire would be at same, uniform temperature. This avoids generation of any localized thermo-e.m.f. due to temperature difference along the wire.

(e) While making connections of the resistance wire, the contact resistance and thermo-electric effects must be avoided. Contact resistance is avoided by soldering, fusing or welding the joints, while thermoelectric effects are avoided by maintaining all such connections at same temperature.

Working Substance (Resistance elements) : Resistance elements used are made of Platinum (Pt) or base metals such as Nickel (Ni) or Copper (Cu) or the alloys such as Balco.

(a) Platinum Resistance Thermometers : Pt elements are available as fine wire or as a deposited film. There are two types of Pt resistance thermometers :

(i) Standard Pt-resistance thermometer (SPRT) : These are used as international standard for temperature measurements between the triple point of Hydrogen (13.81 K) and the freezing point of Antimony (630°.75°C). The temperature standard of SPRT is 25.5 Ω at ice-point to stay within the range of practical Muller bridges while providing a nominal 0.1 ohm/°C sensitivity. SPRT are constructed in a manner to be almost totally strain free, using very lightly supported wires of larger size than typical in an industrial thermometer. Such elements provide high TCR and maximum thermal stability at the expense of fragility and larger size.

(ii) The Industrial Pt-resistance Thermometer (Industrial RTD) : The RTD has fully supported and rugged construction that uses a reference grade wire that gives a TCR over the interval 0 to 100°C between 0.003817 to 0.003915 ohm/°C - ohm with the common value of 0.003902 ohm/ohm °C with winding over pure alumina mandrel. This value slightly differs from that of SPRT element (0.003927 ohm/ohm°C). The international grade Pt-RTD curves (temperature Vs. resistance) are obtained with slightly doped Pt-wire having TCR of 0.00385 ohm/ohm °C. *Wire-wound designs* are most common at ice point resistance of 100 ohm alongwith availability of 200 ohm and 500 ohm at higher cost. The *thick or thin film-type designs* are also available with ice point resistance of 100 ohm and 100 ohm at same cost with slightly lower TCR specified at 100 ohm.

PT 100 sensor has 100 ohm resistance at room temperature with fundamental interval of 38.5 ohms.

Resistance-temperature relationship for Pt-elements is given by Callendar equation

$$T = \left(\frac{R_T - R_0}{R_{100} - R_0}\right) 100 + \delta\left(\frac{T}{100} - 1\right)\frac{T}{100}$$

where R_0, R_T and R_{100} are resistances at 0°C, T°C and 100°C respectively.

δ = Constant lying between 1.49 to 1.5 determined from sulphur point.

(b) Base-metal RTDs :

Nickel RTD : Second in usage to Platinum is a high purity Nickel (Ni) which offers the highest TCR, second highest temperature range and lower assembled cost than wire-wound Pt at high resistance values. Resistances of 120 and 500 ohm are most common with 1000 ohm availability. Nickel has a non-linear TCR that increases with rise in temperature. Ni is highly strain sensitive and requires great care by the manufacturer to obtain interchangeability. The TCR of Ni is highly influenced by both purity and state of anneal. There is no internationally standard temperature-resistance curve for Ni-sensors, although there are national standards and several manufacturers can provide sensors to a common curve characteristic by TCR between 0 to 100°C of 0.00672 ohm/ohm °C.

Copper RTD : Cu-RTDs are available only at 10 or 100 ohm ice point resistance of winding wire. TCR of Cu is almost same as Pt and it is very linear above the ice point. Cu in bifilar winding is used in electrical machine due to very low inductive or capacitive reactance. There is no internationally standard recognised curve for Cu, although some national standards exit.

Balco RTD : Balco is an alloy of Fe and Ni (70% Ni to 30% Fe) having high specific resistance that makes possible high resistance windings without much increase in size. It has ice-point resistance of 2000 or 10,000 ohm and second highest TCR alonwith third highest temperature capability. It does not have recognised standard curve.

Thermal well (Protective sheathing) : Thermal well is used with resistance bulb, when the thermometer is used to measure temperatures in corrosive, oxidising medium. Well is usually made of porcelain, brass or stainless steel and it is in the form of a tube that covers the bulb. Well prevents any contamination of resistance element.

Lead-wires : Lead-wires are used to connect the resistance bulb with the indicating element (Wheatstone bridge) because both are separated by a distance of 100 feet or more. Lead-wires of silver or platinum have larger diameter than resistance wire and they are welded to resistance wire inside the glass seal. Lead wires transmit the information regarding temperature surrounding the bulb to indicating element.

Industrial RTD sensor has 0.025 mm diameter Pt-wire wound into coil and inserted into ceramic tube. The winding is embedded and fused within or on ceramic tube.

(B) Indicating Element (Wheatstone Bridge Circuit) : We have seen that the electrical resistance of the sensing element i.e. of resistance bulb changes with change in temperature surrounding it. Hence, for measuring temperature around the bulb, it is necessary to measure the resistance of the bulb, which then can be correlated with the corresponding temperature value. We study Wheatstone bridge circuit used to measure resistance of the bulb.

Basic Wheatstone Bridge Circuit :

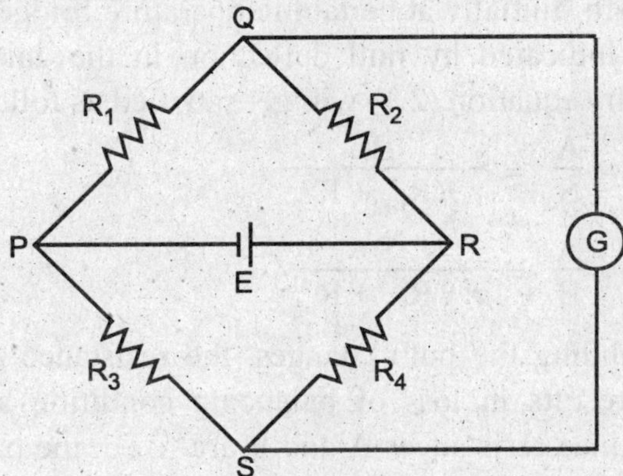

Fig. 2.12 : Wheatstone bridge circuit

Wheatstone bridge circuit consists of *four resistances* R_1, R_2, R_3, R_4 arranged in diamond shaped form as shown in Fig. 2.12. A *battery* of e.m.f. E is connected between terminals P and R, while a *galvanometer* G is connected between points Q and S. This circuit is said to be in *balanced condition* when galvanometer shows *null* or *zero deflection.* It can be proved that in balanced condition the resistances satisfy the relation

$$\frac{R_1}{R_2} = \frac{R_3}{R_4} \quad \text{(Balancing condition)} \qquad \dots (2.2)$$

Whatstone bridge as the indicating element for resistance thermometer :

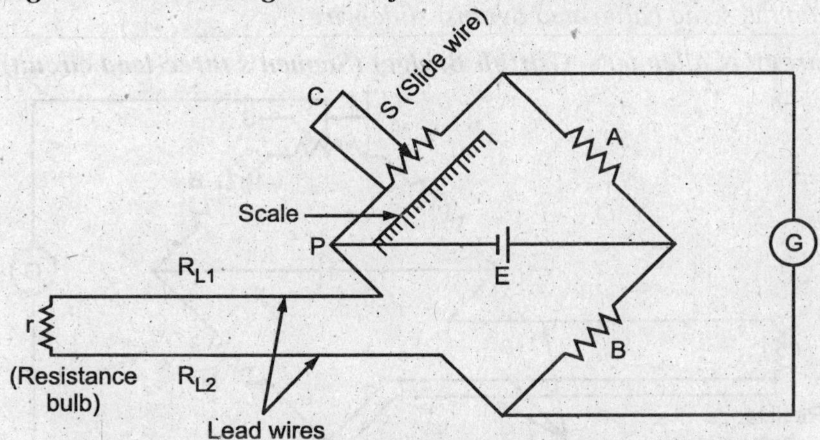

Fig. 2.13 : Indicating element of resistance thermometer

Wheatstone bridge indicating element shown in Fig. 2.13 is the modified form of basic bridge circuit shown in Fig. 2.12. In this circuit, A and B are fixed resistances while S is the variable resistance whose value can be adjusted by changing the contactor (C) position. Resistance bulb 'r' is connected in the bridge circuit with lead wires having resistances R_{L_1} and R_{L_2}. All resistances are made of Manganin so that their value does not change much with temperature.

III. Working of Resistance Thermometer :

The *sensing element* (resistance bulb) is connected to the indicating element (Wheatstone bridge) by lead wires as shown in Fig. 2.13. For temperature measurement using resistance bulb it is inserted in the bath. Initially at certain temperature bridge, circuit is assumed to be in balanced condition as indicated by null deflection in the galvanometer G. Hence the balancing condition given by equation (2.1) will get satisfied as follows :

$$\frac{A}{S} = \frac{B}{r + R_{L_1} + R_{L_2}}$$

i.e.

$$\frac{A}{B} = \frac{S}{r + R_{L_1} + R_{L_2}} \qquad \ldots (2.3)$$

As temperature surrounding the bulb changes, the resistance r of the bulb changes its value to say r' and this results in loss of balancing condition as indicated by non-zero galvanometer deflection. Since resistances A and B are fixed, the balancing condition can be obtained at this new value r' of bulb resistance, only by changing the value of sliding wire adjustable resistance S. Thus for every value of r, there exists certain fixed value of S, for which circuit gets balanced. Value of S can be adjusted by changing the contactor position accordingly. Thus contactor position can be marked on the scale in terms of bulb temperature. This balancing can be achieved automatically using potentiometers.

> ***Working of resistance thermometer :***
>
> *Temperature around resistance bulb changes → resistance 'r' of bulb changes → loss of balancing condition → variable resistance 's' is adjusted by changing contactor position so as to restore the balancing condition → contactor position shows the temperature on the scale calibrated against slide wire.*

Modified circuit (Callender – Griffith Bridge) (Siemen's three-lead circuit) :

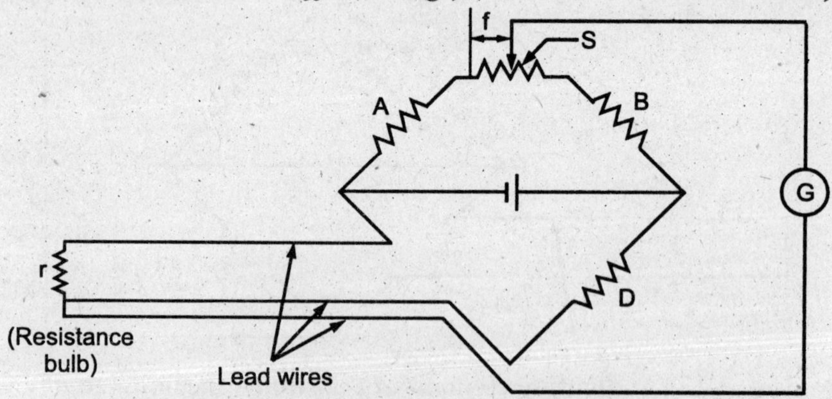

Fig. 2.14 : Callender-Griffith bridge

We have already discussed the working of industrial resistance thermometer in which basically any change in resistance of the bulb due to change in temperature is used to determine temperature around the bulb. Hence care should be taken that the change in electrical resistance of the bulb must be only due to change in temperature around it. But there are some factors which cause change in bulb resistance without any change in temperature. These factors are :

(a) Contact resistance between slide wire 's' and contactor 'c'.

(b) Lead wire resistance that changes with the ambient temperature.

(c) Joule heating effect rises the temperature of the bulb that changes its resistance.

The Wheatstone bridge circuit shown in Fig. 2.13 is modified as shown in Fig. 2.14 in order to compensate for change in resistance due to above factors. This modified circuit has three lead wires and slide-wire s is placed at the top of the bridge where it may lie in both arms of the bridge. If 'f' is the fraction of slide-wire present in left arm of the bridge, then balancing condition for this modified circuit becomes :

$$\frac{r + R_L}{D + R_L} = \frac{\frac{A}{s} + f}{\frac{B}{s} + 1 - f} \quad \text{where } R_L = \text{lead-wire resistance}$$

(a) Compensation of contact resistance : In the modified circuit shown in Fig. 2.14 slide-wire 's' and contactor 'c' are not in the bridge circuit directly, but they are in galvanometer circuit. Hence, any change in contact resistance due to dirt, dust and mechanical wear causes a negligible change in galvanometer reading, while the balancing condition and hence the accuracy remain unaffected.

(b) Compensation of change in lead-wire resistance (Siemen's three lead method) : For achieving this compensation three lead-wires are connected as shown in Fig. 2.14, so that galvanometer is directly connected to the bulb by third lead wire. All lead wires are identical in material, size and they are passed through same cable, so that they are subjected to same ambient temperature change. Note that approximately equal length of lead-wire is present in both the arms of bridge, that achieves compensation. It can be proved that the balance of the bridge-circuit is independent of lead-wire resistance provided :

(i) Contactor C is placed at 50% of the scale.

(ii) Resistances A and B are equal in magnitude.

At this particular temperature setting bulb resistance 'r' equals resistance 'D' and compensation is exact, while at other temperatures the error is negligible.

(c) Compensation of change in bulb resistance due to Joule heating of bulb : Electrical current flowing through the bulb causes Joule heating of the resistance element with heat produced = $(\text{current})^2 \times$ resistance. This heat produced and hence the resistance varies with the current. From circuit diagram [Fig. 2.14] , the current through the bulb would be $\left(\frac{E}{r + D}\right)$.

Therefore, heat produced $H = I^2 r = \left(\frac{E}{r+D}\right)^2 r.$

But for lead-wire compensation $r = D$

$$H = \frac{E^2}{4r}$$

Thus, heat produced would be minimum if battery voltage is small and bulb resistance is large, that leads to negligible change in bulb resistance.

IV. Calibration :

Resistance thermometers are calibrated either by reference to fixed point or by comparing the performance with the standard, reference thermometer when both are installed in identical surrounding. The reference thermometer may be a thermocouple, a liquid-in-glass thermometer or another RTD.

V. Performance characteristics :

(A) Static characteristics :

(a) Accuracy : Accuracy of resistance thermometer is ± 0.25% of span and is better than that of other thermometers. The static error in the reading can be minimized by using the standard resistance bulb.

(b) Reproducibility : Reproducibility is better than thermocouple and expansion thermometers.

(B) Dynamic characteristics :

Speed of response depends upon the nature of flowing medium around the bulb. The response is faster when bulb is installed in fast-flowing liquid than when the same bulb is placed in moving air. Thermal well around the bulb introduces lag in the temperature measurement. This lag is more when thermometer is installed in liquid than that in air. When thermometer is installed in air, heat transfer takes place by radiation and for effective radiation well surface should be dark and rough. It takes 6 seconds for 63.2% change when it is dipped in water heated from 0 to 50°C.

VI. Advantages, Limitations, Applications :

Advantages :

(a) Considerably wide temperature range between –200 to 650°C that can be obtained comparatively in small size.

(b) High accuracy.

(c) No drift over long period.

(d) Fast speed of response.

(e) Good reproducibility.

(f) Does not require any ambient temperature compensation.

(g) Remote indication can be obtained.

Limitations :

(a) The coefficients of resistance in equation (2.1) vary considerably with the purity of resistance winding and its heat treatment. Hence, sensing bulb requires protection against contamination and oxidation.

(b) High cost.

(c) It requires external electrical power supply.

(d) Bulb size is larger than that of thermocouple and filled thermometers.

Applications :

(a) Resistance thermometer having its galvanometer calibrated in temperature (i.e. called deflectional RTD) can be used as ambient-temperature detector.

(b) Deflectional RTD can be used in aircraft thermometers.

(c) RTD can be used as the standard thermometer for calibration of other thermometers.

2.5.1.2 Temperature Measurement using Thermistor

I. Principle :

Thermistor is a semiconductor material whose electrical resistance decreases with rise in temperature around it and vice versa. Thus, any change in temperature around the thermistor can be measured in terms of change in its electrical resistance.

II. Construction :

Sensing element : Thermistors are made from a specific mixture of pure oxides of Ni, Mn, Cu, Co, Fe, Mg, Ti. Thermistor was first introduced in 1940 and its name has been derived from *thermally sensitive resistors*. Thermistors have very large positive or negative TCR (temperature coefficient of resistance). For positive TCR material, its resistance increases with temperature rise; while for negative TCR material, resistance decreases with rise in temperature. The different shapes of thermistor sensors are as shown in Fig. 2.15.

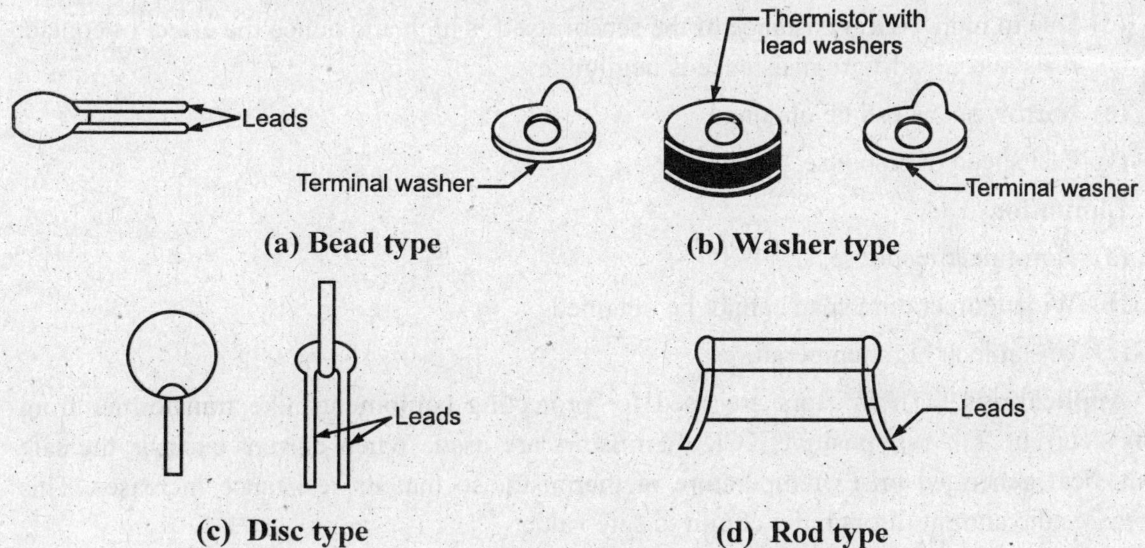

Fig. 2.15 : Thermistor sensors

Thermistors can have bead type, washer type, disc type or rod type configuration shown in Fig. 2.15. It can also be encapsulated in plastic, cemented, soldered in bolts, encased in glass tubes. Thermistor beads are 1 to 2.5 mm in diameter, discs are 5 to 25 mm in diameter and rods are 1 to 6 mm in diameter upto 50 mm length.

Indicating element : For temperature measurement, thermistors are connected in Wheatstone bridge circuit shown in Fig. 2.13 in article 2.5.1.1.

III. Working :

Thermistor sensing element is placed in the bath whose temperature is to be measured. As bath temperature changes, electrical resistance of thermistor changes. This causes the unbalance in Wheatstone bridge circuit. This unbalance signal is indicated by galvanometer deflection. Hence, galvanometer can be calibrated in terms of bath temperature.

IV. Calibration :

Calibration procedure is same as that for resistance thermometer discussed in art. 2.5.1.1.

V. Performance characteristics :

All performance characteristics of thermistors are comparable with those of resistance thermometers, but the response is faster than RTD.

VI. Advantages, Limitations, Applications :

Advantages :

(a) Low cost.

(b) Small size.

(c) For negative TCR thermistor, sensitivity is high.

(d) Due to high TCR, resistance of the sensor itself is high and hence the effect of contact resistance, lead-wire resistance is negligible.

(e) Narrow spans can be obtained.

(f) Fast speed of response.

Limitations :

(a) Non-linear response.

(b) Wide temperature span cannot be obtained.

(c) Unstable at high temperatures.

Applications : Thermistors are used for protecting equipments like transformer from heavy current. For this positive TCR thermistors are used. When current exceeds the safe limit, heat generated raises temperature of thermistor so that its resistance increases. This decreases the current through the circuit to safe value.

2.5.2 Thermoelectric Temperature Measurement

(Temperature measurement using thermocouple) :

The word *thermocouple* is a combination of *thermo* for heat requirement and *couple denoting two junctions.*

Thermocouple consists of wires of two dissimilar metals soldered or welded at the ends to form two junctions. The junction at higher temperature is called *hot or measuring junction,* while the junction at lower temperature is called *cold or reference junction.*

I. Principle :

(a) Seebeck effect : In 1821, Seebeck discovered that when there is temperature difference between two junctions of the thermocouple, electromotive force (e.m.f.) is developed between the junctions. This e.m.f. causes electric current to flow through the thermocouple circuit. This is called as *thermoelectric effect* by which thermal energy is converted into electrical energy. The e.m.f. developed is called as *thermo-e.m.f.*, while the resulting current is called as *thermo-current*. Seebeck effect is the combined effect or Peltier and Thomson effect. This thermo-e.m.f. developed is proportional to temperature difference between junctions.

$$\therefore \qquad \text{e.m.f., } e \propto (T_h - T_c)$$

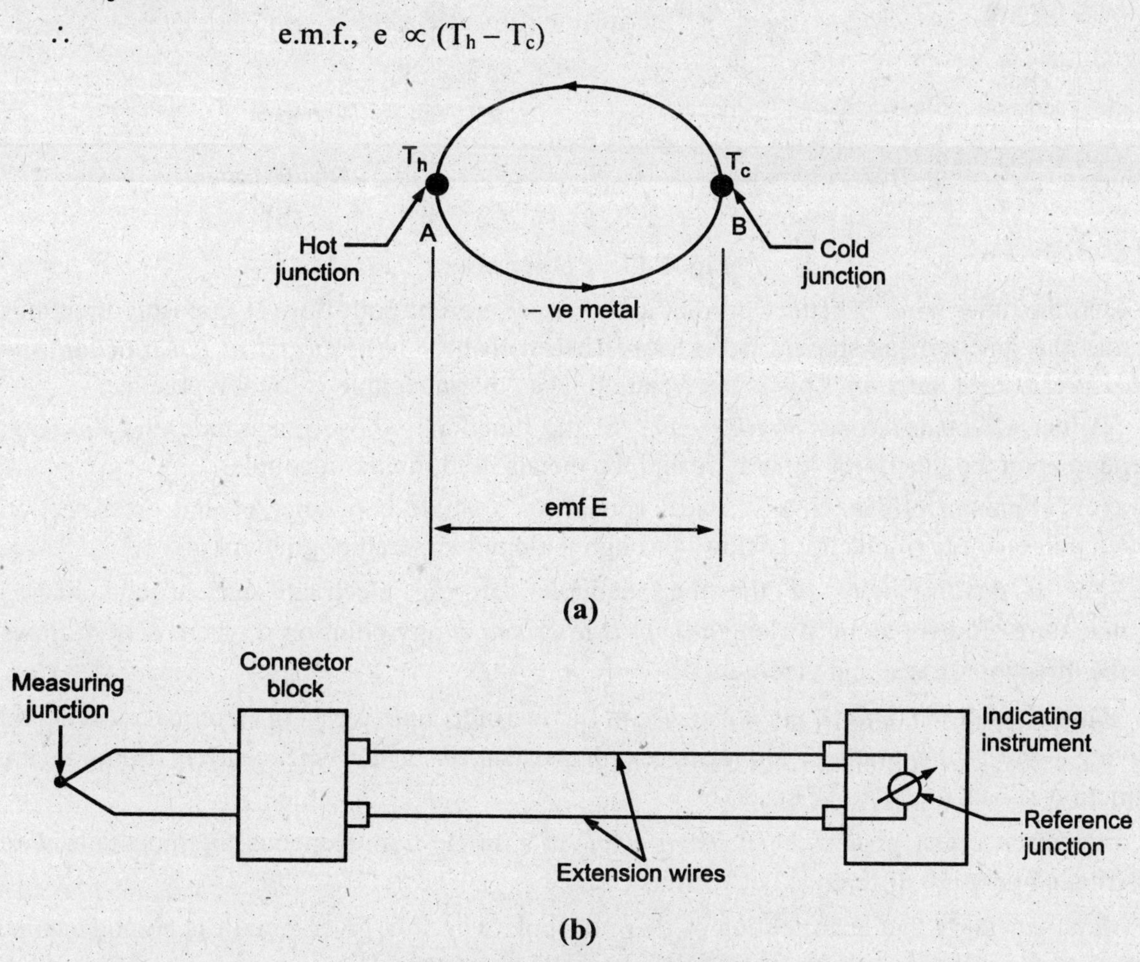

Fig. 2.16 : Thermocouple

If cold junction is maintained at fixed temperature (preferably 0°C) then e.m.f. developed can be taken as a measure of the hot junction temperature.

(b) Peltier effect : Battery is connected in the thermocouple circuit as shown in Fig. 2.17. Battery current and thermocurrent both flow through the circuit across the junctions.

Peltier effect is defined as the change in heat content when 1 coulomb of charge crosses the junction.

If the battery current and thermal current both flow in same direction across the junction [as shown in Fig. 2.17 (a)], then *heat is liberated at hot junction and absorbed at cold junction.*

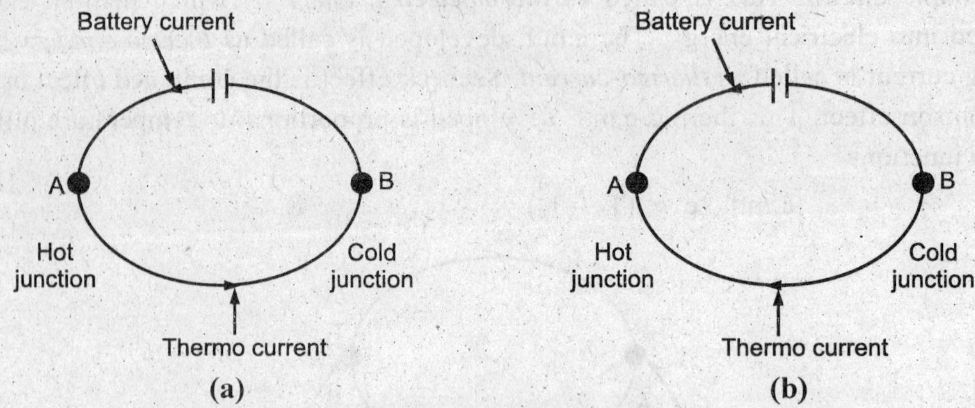

Fig. 2.17 : Peltier effect

On the other hand if battery current and thermal current both flow in opposite directions across the junction [as shown in Fig. 2.17 (b)], then heat is *absorbed at hot junction and liberated at cold junction.* This is the situation when thermocouple is used in practice.

Peltier effect developes *Peltier e.m.f.* at the junctions whose magnitude and direction depend upon the junction temperature and the metals used in thermocouple.

(c) Thomson effect : It gives heat content of a single conductor of unit cross-section when unit quantity of electricity flows through it along temperature gradient of 1 K.

For a positive wire of the thermocouple carrying electrical current and having temperature gradient along its length, *heat is liberated* at any point on it where current flows in the direction of heat and vice-versa.

On the other hand, *for a negative wire* of the thermocouple carrying electrical current and having temperature gradient along its length, heat is *absorbed* when current flows in the direction of heat and vice-versa.

Thomson effect generates *Thomson e.m.f.* in a single homogeneous thermocouple wire having temperature difference between its ends.

It is necessary that each section of thermocouple wire in a given circuit is homogeneous, which has uniform composition and physical properties along its length. With such homogeneous wires, the circuit e.m.f. depends only upon the metals employed and the temperature of their junction, while it is independent of length and diameter of wires.

Thus, thermo e.m.f. predicted in Seebeck effect is the sum of Peltier e.m.f. at junctions and two Thomson e.m.f.s along the wire. Note that Peltier and Thomson effects cannot exist separately for a homogeneous conductor.

Thermoelectric Laws :

(a) Law of homogeneous circuit : An electric current cannot be sustained in a circuit of single homogeneous metal, however varying in its cross-section, by the application of heat alone.

This law is deduced from the experiments which conclude that thermo-e.m.f. developed in the thermocouple depends only upon the hot and reference junction temperatures and it is independent of temperature distribution long the wire and intermediate temperatures along the wire.

(b) Law of intermediate temperatures : The law states that the thermal e.m.f. developed by thermocouple (C) with its junctions at temperatures T_1 and T_2 $(T_1 > T_2)$ equals the algebraic sum of the e.m.f.s generated by two thermocouples, one (A) with its junction at T_1 and some reference temperature T_3 (lying between T_1 and T_2) and the other (B) with its junctions at same reference temperature T_3 and the measuring temperature T_2.

i.e. $$T_1^E T_2 = T_1^E T_3 + T_3^E T_2$$

This law is used for calibration of thermocouple, because calibration can be based on temperatures of hot and cold junctions only without any reference to temperature T_i of intermediate junctions (shown in Fig. 2.18 (b)).

This law is described in Fig. 2.18 (a).

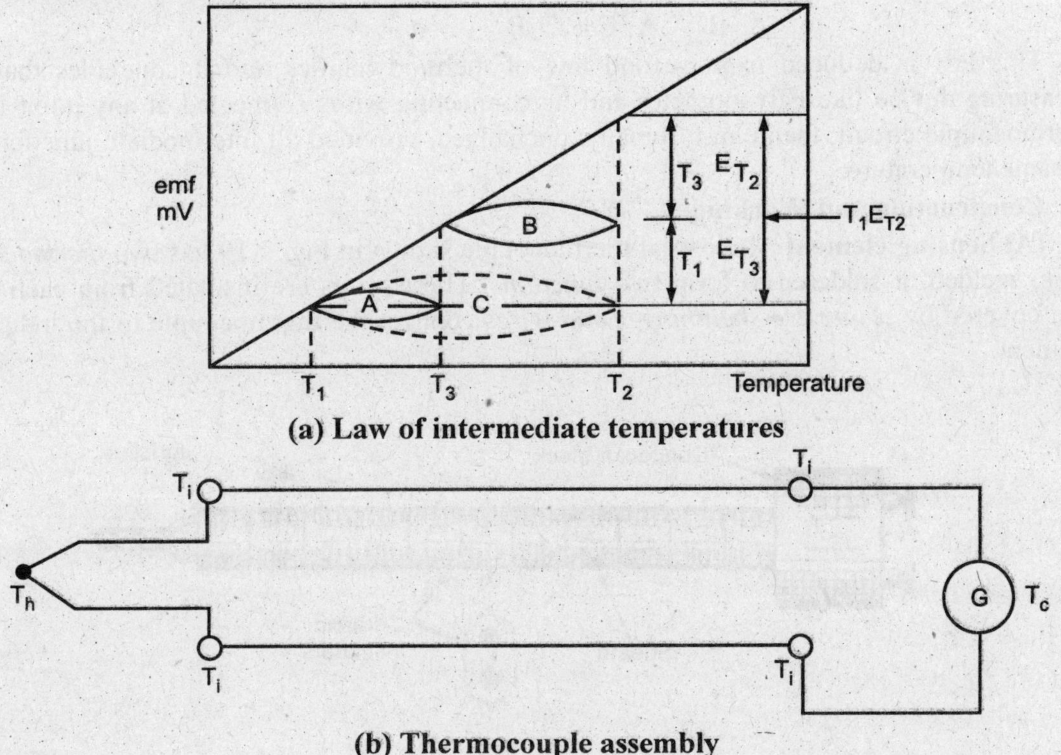

(a) Law of intermediate temperatures

(b) Thermocouple assembly

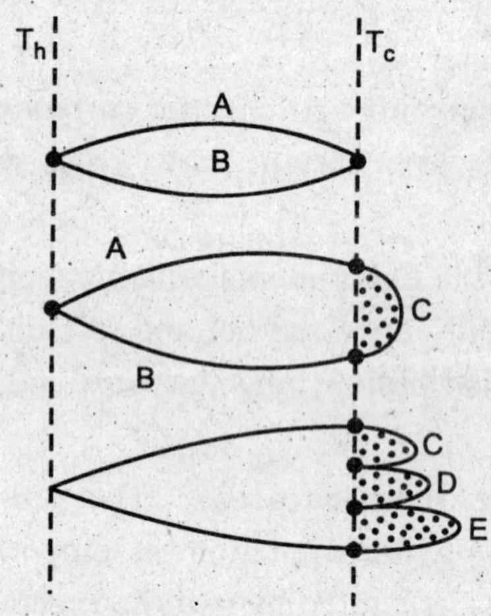

(c) Law of intermediate metals

Fig. 2.18

(c) Law of intermediate metals : The law states that the algebraic sum of the thermo-e.m.f.s in a circuit composed of any number of dissimilar metals is zero, provided all the circuit is at a uniform temperature. Hence, introduction of a third metal into the circuit of two metals will have no effect upon the e.m.f. generated so long as the junctions of the third metal with the other two are at the same temperature. Fig. 2.18 (c) shows different circuits generating same e.m.f., even though the second and third circuit diagrams show materials C, D, E and F inserted between A and B. For second circuit, the law states :

$$A \overset{e}{} B = A \overset{e}{} C + C \overset{e}{} B$$

This law is deduced from second law of thermodynamics and it concludes that if a measuring device like galvanometer and its connecting wires connected at any point in the thermocouple circuit, then e.m.f. remains unchanged, provided all intermediate junctions are at same temperature.

II. Construction and Working :

(A) Sensing element : Industrial thermocouple shown in Fig. 2.19 has two *thermocouple wires* welded or soldered to form two *junctions*. These wires are insulated from each other and covered by *protective sheathing*. *Lead-wires* connect the thermocouple to the indicating element.

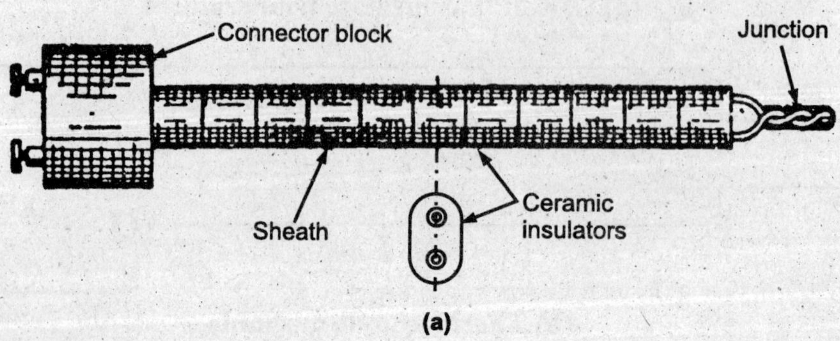

(a)

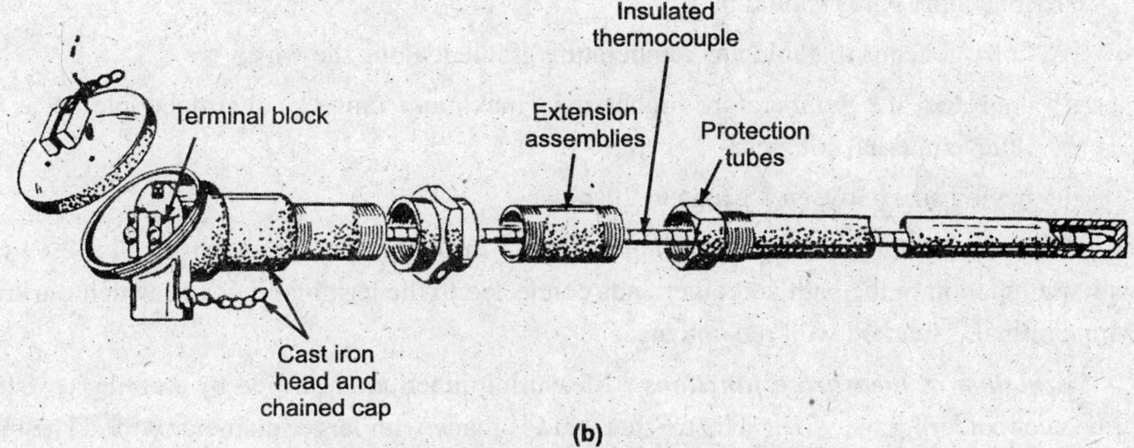

Fig. 2.19 : Thermocouple

Thermocouple wires : The materials used for thermocouple wires predict its type. The properties that determine metal's usefulness in thermocouple wire are melting point, electrical conductance, stability, repeatability, cost, ease of handling, thermoelectric output in combination and reaction to various atmospheres.

Table 2.1 : Thermocouple types

Type	Positive wire	Negative wire	Temperature range (°C)	Linearity
B	Pt-70-Rh-30	Pt-94-Rh-6	0 to 1860	Good at high temperature
E	Chromel	Constantan	(–196) to 999	Good
J	Iron	Constantan	–196 to 760	Nearly linear between 149 to 438°C
K	Chromel	Alumel	–190 to 1371	Most linear
R	Pt-87-Rh-13	Platinum	–18 to 1704	Good at high temperature
S	Pt-90-Rh-10	Platinum	–18 to 1760	Good at high temperature
T	Copper	Constantan	–190 to 399	Same as J
	Tungsten	W 74–Re 26	–18 to 2316	Same as R
	W 94 – Re 6	W 74 – Re 26	–18 to 2316	Same as R
	Copper	Gold-cobalt	–268 to –18	Linear above 60 K
	Ir 40 – Rh 60	Ir	–18 to 2093	Same as R

(Pt – platinum, Rh – rhodium, W – tungsten, Re – rhenium, Ir – irridium)

Thermocouple wires should be :

(i) homogeneous to avoid any temperature gradient along the wire.

(ii) annealed at a temperature higher than maximum range of thermocouple so as to relieve internal stresses.

(iii) having size between 8 gauge to 20 gauge.

The thermocouple wires pass through ceramic insulator spacers shown in Fig. 2.19 (a) with hot junction in the bath and other ends connected to the terminal block in which positive wire terminal is marked with red colour.

Formation of measuring junctions : Measuring junction is formed by welding (twisted or butt) or soldering the wires. The twisted weld is made with larger diameter wires. The butt weld is made by fusing the two wires into a round bead.

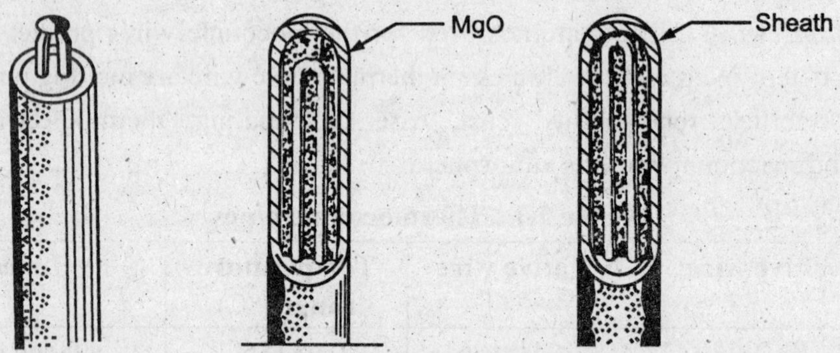

(a) Exposed type (b) Ungrounded type (c) Grounded type

Fig. 2.20 : Types of measuring junctions

(i) Exposed type : In this type the measuring junction extends beyond the protective metallic sheath (covering) as shown in Fig. 2.20 (a). This type gives fast response and can be used for measurement of non-corrosive fluid temperature.

(ii) Ungrounded type : In this type measuring junction is insulated from the thermocouple sheath by soft MgO powder as shown in Fig. 2.20 (b). This junction is isolated from any external electrical noise.

(iii) Grounded type : In this type, the measuring junction is welded to the sheath as shown in Fig. 2.20 (c). This gives faster response than ungrounded type.

Formation of reference or cold junction : The other ends of the thermocouple wires are connected to the fixing screws in the *terminal block* made of insulating material. Lead wires are connected to these screws, whose other ends are connected to thermocouple wires, so as to form reference junction as shown in Fig. 2.21.

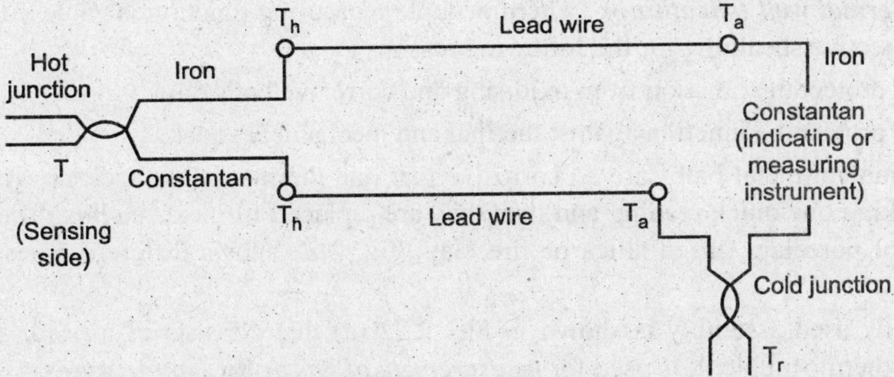

Fig. 2.21 : Location of reference junction

Thermal e.m.f. developed depends upon the difference between measuring junction and reference junction temperatures. Hence, for getting e.m.f. proportional to measuring junction temperature, it is necessary to maintain reference junction at certain fixed temperature. For this purpose, the reference junction is located away from the measuring junction and usually it is located in the measuring instrument where the temperature changes are negligible. When measuring instrument is situated in temperature-controlled or air-conditioned room, this location of reference junction is more effective.

(b) Lead-wires (Compensating cables) : Lead-wires connect the measuring junction of the thermocouple to the indicating instrument, because measuring junction and the indicating instrument are usually far away from each other. Ideally lead wires and thermocouple wires, both should be made of same material, but it becomes costly to use platinum lead-wires for platinum thermocouple. Hence, lead wire material is such that its thermoelectric properties should match with those of thermocouple wires. Also lead wires should have low resistivity.

It can be observed from Fig. 2.21 that two ends of the lead-wire are not at the same temperature. Since thermocouple is far away from the measuring instrument, the temperature difference (Th-Ta) may be very large. Error due to this temperature difference is avoided by selecting lead-wire material as mentioned above. If polarities of thermocouple wires and lead wires are not proper, then large error may result. Lead-wires may be solid or straded for flexibility with insulation of enamel, cotton, asbestos, glass. The lead-wires for different thermocouples are given in Table 2.2.

Table 2.2 : Thermocouple wires and lead wires

Thermocouple wires		Lead wires	
+ve	–ve	+ve	–ve
Copper	Constantan	Copper	Constantan
Iron	Constantan	Iron	Constantan
Chromel	Alumel	Chromel	Alumel
Chromel	Alumel	Iron	Copper-Nickel alloy
Chromel	Alumel	Copper	Constantan (upto 125°C)
Platinum-Rhodium	Platinum	Copper	Copper-Nickel

(c) Thermal well (sheathing) : Thermocouple measuring junction is enclosed in thermal well or protective sheathing for the following reasons :

(i) To protect the junction from oxidising and corrosive bath fluids.

(ii) To protect the junction against thermal and mechanical shocks.

Some molten-metal baths are so corrosive that one thermocouple and one well are used only for taking one quick reading and then they are replaced for next reading. Thermal wells are made of porcelain, fused silica or fire clay. Fig. 2.22 shows different types of thermo wells.

Normally used assembly is shown in Fig. 2.22 (a) that consists of a head, a mounting flange and thermocouple. It is used for *measurement of gas or air temperatures.*

Fig. 2.22 (b) shows the assembly used for *temperature measurement in pressure vessels and pipe lines containing pressurized liquids.*

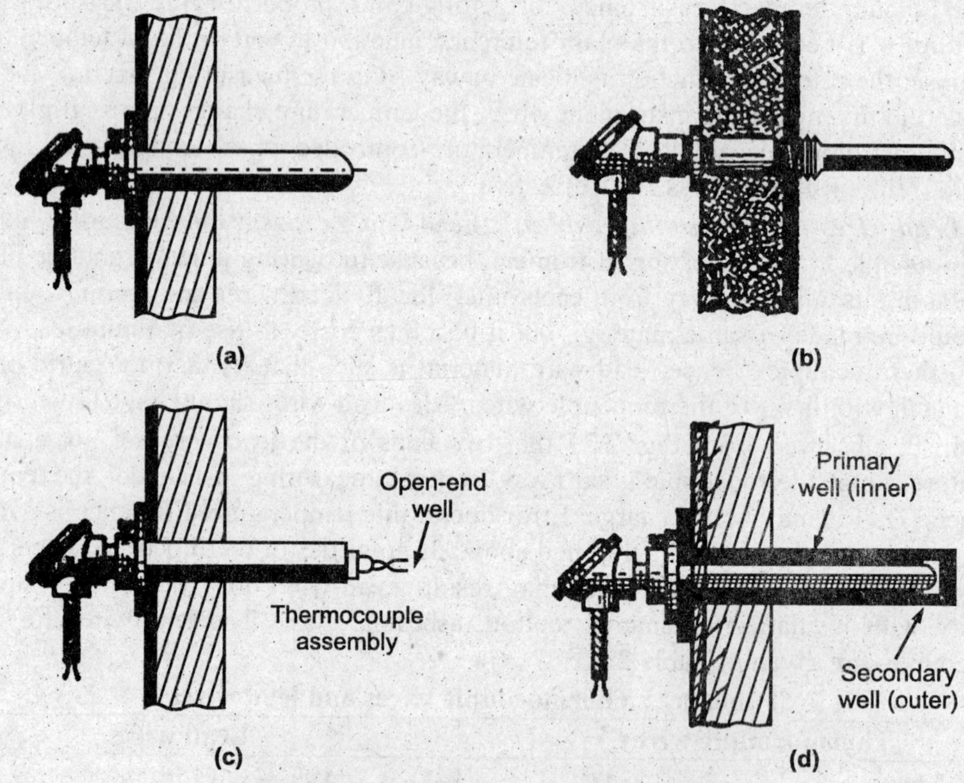

Fig. 2.22 : Thermal wells (sheathing)

Fig. 2.22 (c) shows the assembly used in furnaces at low temperatures where little protection is required. This is called *open-end well assembly* that protects the junction from the erosive effects of fast-moving gases.

Fig. 2.22 (d) shows the assembly used in baths above 1100°C where corrosion may be severe. In this system two wells, primary and secondary are used. Secondary well prevents sagging of the assembly at high temperatures and the surface of primary well is protected. Secondary wells are made of metals like Ni, Cr, Fe for oxidising atmosphere, Cr-Fe for sulphating environments. The mechanical properties to be considered while selecting a thermal well are :

(i) resistance to corrosion and oxidation.

(ii) resistance to thermal and mechanical shock.

(iii) resistance to gas leakge.

(iv) mechanical strength.

(B) Indicating element (Measuring instrument) : Thermocouple generates an e.m.f. proportional to temperature difference between measuring and reference junctions. Hence to measure the measuring junction temperature it is necessary to measure the thermo-e.m.f. correctly. For this purpose, the *Millivoltmeter* or the *potentiometer type instrument* is used.

The millivoltmeters : The millivoltmeter is nothing but a *calibrated dc galvanometer*. It is the simplest and least expensive indicating element for the thermocouple. The millivoltmeter consists of a *rectangular coil* pivoted at the top and bottom and this coil is placed in a steady, permanent *magnetic field* of two poles of *horse-shoe magnet*. Hairsprings are connected at the upper and lower ends of the coil and the springs are connected to the terminals of the millivoltmeter. When electric current passes through coil, the coil rotates and this rotation causes the pointer attached to the coil to deflect. Thus pointer deflection is proportional to the current through the coil and it is calibrated in terms of potential difference across its terminals.

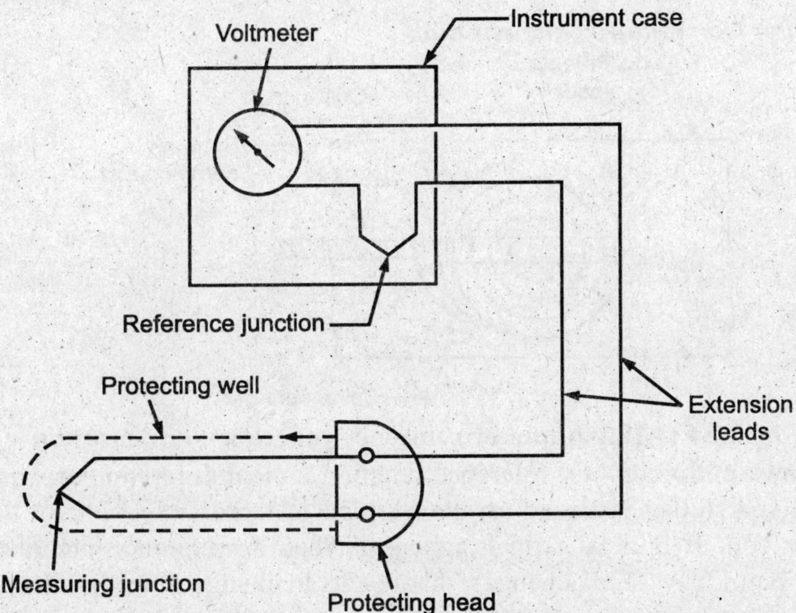

Fig. 2.23 : Thermocouple with millivoltmeter indicator

The millivoltmeter connected with the thermocouple is shown in Fig. 2.23. Figure shows *measuring junction, thermal well, terminal block, lead-wires, reference junction* located inside the millivoltmeter.

Sources of error in millivoltmeter reading :

(i) Due to electrical resistances of thermocouple, lead-wires, millivoltmeter, the millivoltmeter (mV) reading is not exactly equal to the e.m.f. of the thermocouple, but mV reads slightly less than the actual e.m.f. In order to reduce the effect of change in external resistances, the internal resistance of the mV should be as high as possible (about 600 ohms). Then mV is calibrated by taking certain fixed value of external resistance. Now, the error caused by change in external resistance is negligible or it can be compensated.

(ii) Change in ambient temperature may change the internal resistance of the galvanometer, that affects the calibration. This error is avoided by using Manganin resistor which has small TCR.

(iii) Ambient temperature changes cause change in reference junction temperature that results in serious error in the measuring junction temperature. The magnitude of error is proportional to the change in e.m.f. caused by change in reference junction temperature. It is very troublesome to maintain the reference junction at 0°C, hence it is usually maintained at room temperature of 24°C and the millivoltmeter is compensated for any changes in this temperature.

(iv) Since thermocouple e.m.f.s are of low level type, precautions must be taken against stray currents resulting from proximity to electrical wiring. To avoid this, best practice is never to run thermocouple wire in the same conduit with electric power wires.

Reference junction temperature compensation :

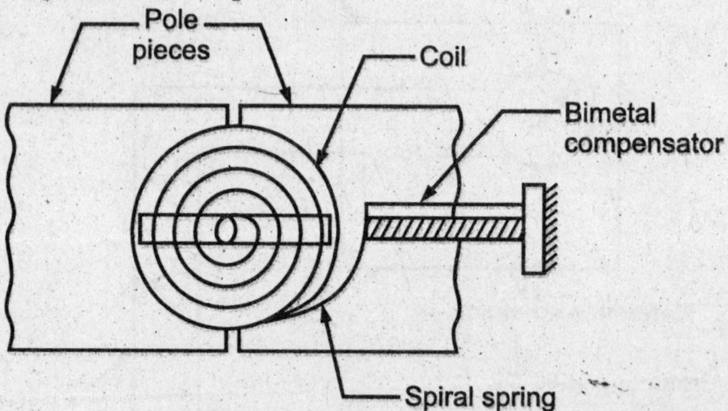

Fig. 2.24 : Millivoltmeter reference junction compensation

Fig. 2.24 shows millivoltmerer reference junction temperature compensation in which a bimetal strip is fixed so that it can adjust the position of fixed end of one of the hairsprings connected to the coil. If bimetal strip is not used, then as reference junction temperature changes, thermo-e.m.f. developed changes, that results in change in millivoltmeter deflection. The bimetallic strip expands or contracts with the change in reference-junction temperature in such a fashion that it cancels the pointer deflection that might occur due to change in reference-junction temperature. Thus pointer deflection is proportional to the difference between measuring junction temperature and the reference-junction temperature at which the millivoltmeter is calibrated.

III. Calibration :

A thermocouple is calibrated by comparing its performance with a standard thermometer when both are dipped in same bath under same conditions. The standard thermometer may be another thermocouple or RTD or mercury thermometer. Above 800°C thermocouple is calibrated by comparing the performance with an optical pyrometer.

IV. Performance characteristics :

(A) Static characteristics :

1. Accuracy : The accuracy of the millivoltmeter and a standard iron-constantan thermocouple is ± 1.5% of full scale.

The sources of error in thermocouple reading :

(a) Depth of immersion : If thermocouple measuring junction and well is not immersed into the bath at sufficient depth, heat conduction takes place along the thermocouple wires or thermal well, that results in decreased temperature reading.

(b) Radiation effect : Radiation errors occur while measuring high air or gas temperatures. At temperatures above 538°C, thermocouples receive most of the heat by radiation from the surrounding. But when thermocouple is used for furnace temperature measurement, then different parts of the furnace like heating element, furnace wall, furnace floor are at different temperatures. Hence, the thermocouple reading depends upon relative amount of radiation received from each of the parts.

While measuring temperature of flowing gases, radiation shield is installed around hot junction. It is essential that the hot gases flow around both the shield and the thermocouple. The velocity of the gases should be as high as possible for which venturi arrangement may be used.

2. Sensitivity : The dead zone of millivoltmeter is quite small, but it depends on the friction in moving coil systems.

(B) Dynamic characteristics :

The dynamic response of the thermocouple depends upon its heat-transfer characteristics, thermal well heat transfer characteristics, size of thermocouple and well.

(a) Effect of heat transfer characteristics of thermocouple and well : When bare thermocouple is installed in a liquid, most of the heat is transferred by conduction. But when bare thermocouple is installed in a gas at temperature less than 200°C, most of the heat is transferred by conduction, some by convection and very little by radiation. For temperatures between 200 to 530°C heat is transferred by all 3 modes, while at temperature above 530°C heat is mostly transferred by radiation, that results in fast speed of response. When a thermal well is used, air space present between the measuring junction and the well introduces time lag in heat transfer. Sometimes there is physical contact between measuring junction and well that improves speed of response. With few exceptions the thermocouple wire material do not affect the speed of response to great extent. Thermal capacitance of well material is important at low temperature because it decides film coefficient of resistance that in turn depends upon velocity of fluid past the thermocouple. The speed of air flow should be at least 0.6 m/s and speed of liquid flow should be at least 0.3 m/s, to get a reasonable speed of response.

(b) Effect of well material and surface : The quality of well surface decides its emissivity and greater emissivity means large amount of heat is absorbed that results in fast speed of response. For this purpose well surface should be rough instead of smooth and polished. Ceramic thermal wells have higher emissivity than smooth oxidized metal wells. Also metallic materials form an oxide scale that reduces conduction of heat through well. Thermal-well materials such as quartz, glass and Vycor transmit the radiations rather than absorbing them. Hence, in such thermocouples speed of response is very fast and well material has very little effect on the speed of response.

(c) Effect of thermocouple and well size : As size of the thermocouple measuring junction increases, its thermal capacity increases that results in slow speed of response, cast materials like Nichrome, Chromel, Iron have thicker walls and slower response than machined wells of Inconel, steel and iron. Heavier thermal wells with thick walls have slow speed of response but they have better resistance to corrosion. *Hence, while selecting thermal well material, there must be good compromise between speed of response and corrosion resistance.* Frequency replacement of corroded light construction wells becomes more economical than using heavier walls.

V. Advantages, Limitations and Applications :

Advantages :

(a) Rugged, inexpensive construction.

(b) Simpler to use and take the readings.

(c) Indicating instrument is compact like millivoltmeter as compared to Wheatstone bridge for RTD.

(d) Wide temperature range from –270° to 2800°C.

(e) The output is in electrical form that is suitable for indicating and controlling devices.

(f) Good accuracy and reproducibility.

(g) Electrical output can be transmitted over long distance, hence sensing and indicating elements can be far away from each other.

(h) No danger of contaminating the process by filling fluid.

Limitations :

(a) Not suitable for spans less than 33°C.

(b) The reference junction must be maintained at constant temperature and compensation arrangements should be made.

(c) Non-linear temperature e.m.f. relationship.

(d) Temperature gradients must be avoided.

(e) Not as simple as direct reading thermometer.

(f) They cannot be used bare in conducting fluid.

Applications : The thermocouple types suitable for various environments are listed below :

Thermocouple type	+ve wire	–ve wire	Suitable atmosphere (advantages)
B	Pt – 70 – Rh 30	Pt – 94 – Rh 6	Inert or slow oxidizing
E	Chromel	Constantan	Oxidizing
J	Iron	Constantan	Reducing
K	Chromel	Alumel	Oxidizing
R	Pt – 87 – Rh 13	Pt	Oxidizing (fast response)
S	Pt – 90 – Rh 10	Pt	Oxidizing
T	Copper	Constantan	Oxidizing or reducing (Good corrosion resistance)
Y	Iron	Constantan	Reducing
–	Tungsten	W – 74 – Re 26	Inert or vacuum (high temperature)

(i) Average Temperature Measurement : Parallel combination :

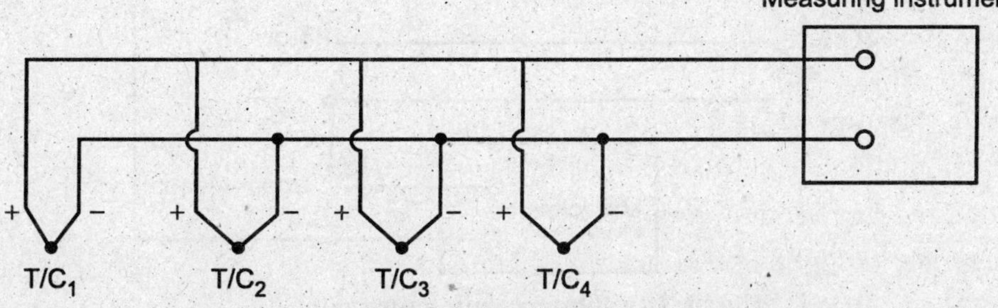

Fig. 2.25 : Average temperature measurement

(ii) Temperature Difference Measurement :

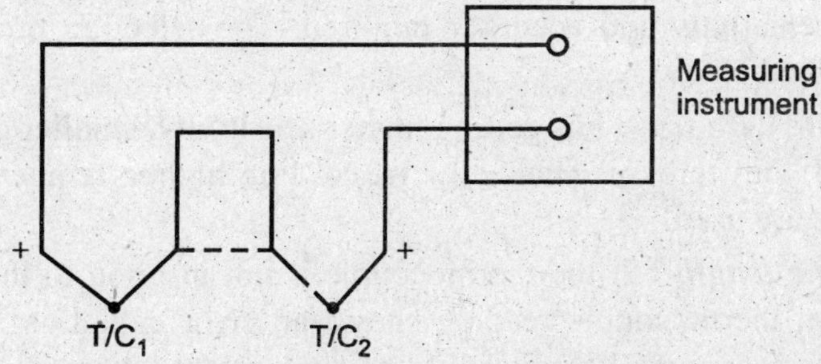

Fig. 2.26 : Temperature difference measurement

(iii) Parallel operation from Common Thermocouple :

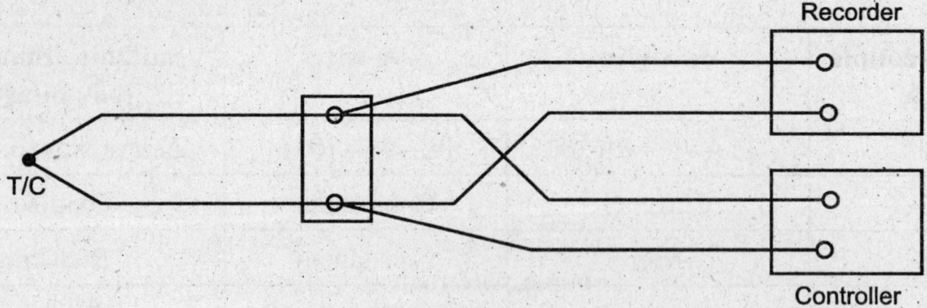

Fig. 2.27 : Parallel operation

(iv) Thermopiles : These are thermocouples connected in series with electrically insulated junction as shown in Fig. 2.28. Thermopiles generate large e.m.f.s thus reducing sensitivity requirements in the indicating millivoltmeter. The principal objections to the use of thermopiles are the necessity for electrical isolation of individual thermocouples and error due to short circuit of one of the thermocouples which might go unnoticed.

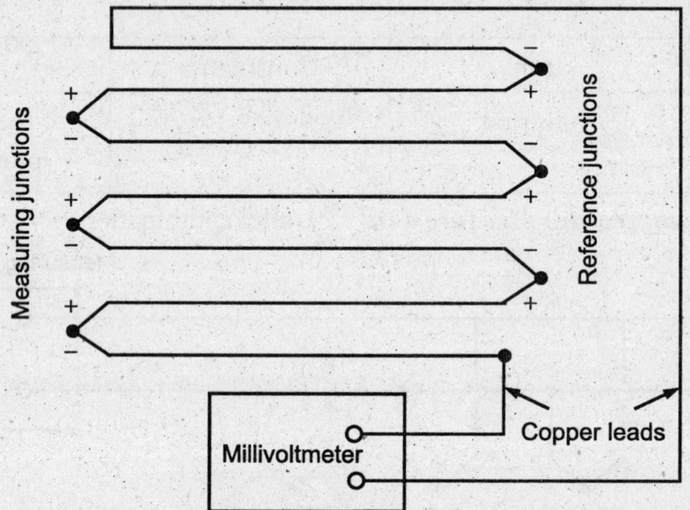

Fig. 2.28 : Thermopile construction

Thermocouple Selection :

While selecting a thermocouple type for temperature measurement, one should consider temperature range, sensitivity and accuracy required. The selection procedure for different components is described below :

1. ***Thermocouple wire size :*** For getting higher sensitivity, smaller diameter wires are to be used, but they are mechanically weak. For higher temperature measurement, heavier wires are used.
2. ***Thermocouple length :*** If the thermocouple is not inserted to the sufficient depth in hot bath, then thermocouple reading shows an error called as immersion error. To avoid this, thermocouple length should be such that the tip of the thermocouple is in most turbulent region, that avoids any formation of film on the well surface. In case

of cylindrical pipes it is better to locate the thermocouple tip at the pipe centre while in case of tanks length should be nearly equal to ten times the diameter of thermowell.

3. ***Well material :*** Following are the well materials alongwith their temperature limits. Carbon steel (540°C), Cast iron (700°C), Stainless steel (980°C), Inconnel (Cr 14% + Ni 80%) (above 980°C), Ceramic tubes (upto 1650°C).
4. ***Lead wire material and size :*** Lead wires are of larger diameter than thermocouple wires so as to reduce their resistivity. Lead wire material should be, as far as possible, same as that of the thermocouple wire material, otherwise both the materials should have matching thermoelectric properties. This reduces error due to change in ambient temperature.
5. ***Single or duplex thermocouple :*** It is not recommended to split the thermocouple connections for two different devices like say recorder and controller. For this purpose duplex element is used that consists of two independent thermocouples housed in same thermal well.

Use of Thermocouple Tables :

All thermocouple tables showing the values of e.m.f. for various measuring junction temperatures are based upon a reference junction temperature of 0°C. Therefore direct conversion of e.m.f. reading into temperature can be made only when ice bath (at 0°C) is used at the reference junction. If it is not possible to maintain the reference junction temperature at 0°C, a correction factor must be applied to the millivolt values given in the thermocouple tables. Note that thermocouple e.m.f. generated is decreased with decrease in temperature difference between the measuring and reference junctions. Hence e.m.f. correction is applied as follows :

(A) Converting e.m.f. (mV) obtained to equivalent temperature (with reference junction at (say) room temperature of 25°C) :

(i) From the thermocouple table for the thermocouple used, obtain the e.m.f. e_{ref} corresponding to the actual temperature of measuring junction (room temperature of 25°C).

(ii) The value obtained in step (i) is added algebraically to the e.m.f. reading obtained on millivoltmeter that gives the corrected e.m.f.

$$e_{corrected} = e_{actual} + e_{ref}$$

(iii) Using the same thermocouple table, the temperature corresponding to corrected e.m.f. is obtained. This might require *interpolation* between two printed values in the tables. This is done by adding algebraically to the smaller value a proportionate part of the difference between two printed values.

T_1 T_2 T_3

e_1 e_2 e_3

$$\frac{T_3 - T_1}{T_2 - T_1} = \frac{e_3 - e_1}{e_2 - e_1}$$

$$e_2 = e_1 + \left(\frac{T_2 - T_1}{T_3 - T_1}\right)(e_3 - e_1)$$

(B) ***Converting measuring junction temperature to equivalent e.m.f. :*** For checking the calibration of instrument, it is necessary to check the e.m.f. obtained for certain hot junction temperature. For this proceed as follows :

(i) From the thermocouple table for the thermocouple used, obtain the e.m.f. e_{ref} corresponding to actual temperature (say room temperature) at the input terminals of the instrument to be checked, which is based upon 0°C reference junction temperature.

(ii) From the same table, obtain the e.m.f. e_T based upon 0°C reference junction for the temperature to be checked.

(iii) Subtract algebraically the value obtained in step (i) above, from the value obtained in step (ii) that gives corrected e.m.f.,

$$e_{corrected} = e_T - e_{ref}$$

2.5.3 Solid-State Temperature Sensors

Principle : Solid-state devices such as semiconductor diodes (p-n junctions) and transistors (p-n-p or n-p-n) can be used as temperature sensing devices.

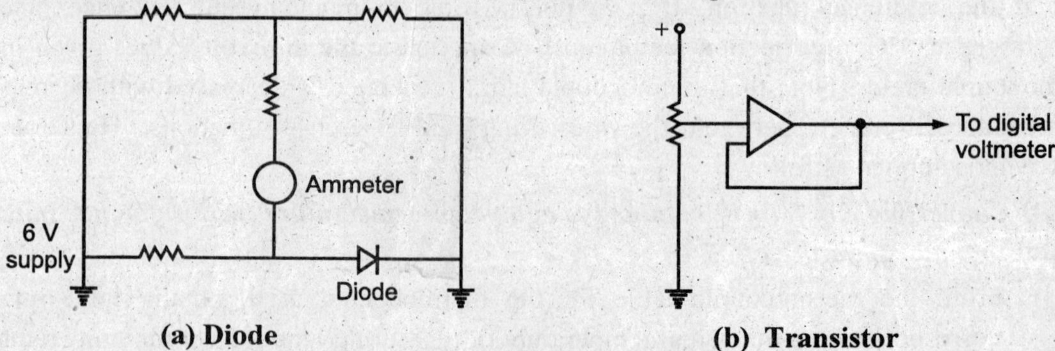

(a) Diode **(b) Transistor**

Fig. 2.29 : Solid state devices

A p-n junction diode connected to d.c. supply as shown in Fig. 2.29 (a) is said to be forward biased. The forward bias voltage across the p-n junction is given by the equation

$$V_{BE} = \frac{KT}{q} \ln\left(\frac{I_c}{I_{es}}\right)$$

where,

V_{BE} = Base-emitter voltage

I_c = Collector current

K = Boltzmann constant (= 1.38×10^{-23} J/K)

T = Absolute temperature (K)

q = Electron charge (= 1.6×10^{-19} coul)

I_{es} = Emitter saturation current.

Therefore, for constant forward current, the emitter-base voltage V_{BE} varies linearly with temperature, i.e. the output of the transducer becomes directly proportional to temperature T (measured input).

In case of a transistor shown in Fig. 2.29 (b),

The emitter-base forward bias voltage V_{BE} is given by

$$V_{BE} = \frac{kT}{q} \ln \left(\frac{I_E + I_{Eo}}{I_{Eo}}\right)$$

where, I_{Eo} = emitter reverse current

I_E = emitter current.

For constant I_E and I_{Eo}, the voltage V_{BE} is a linear function of temperature.

Construction and Working :

Diodes are highly sensitive temperature sensors. If two identical transistors are operated at a constant ratio of collector current densities, then the difference in base-emitter voltages will be directly proportional to absolute temperature. These sensors are available in both voltage and current configurations.

Advantages :

(i) Linear operating characteristics.

(ii) High accuracy of the order of ± 1°C.

(iii) These transducers produce high output level which is capable of direct indication without any signal conditioning.

(iv) The sensitivity of the silicon transistor within its usable range of – 55 to 150°C is of the order of –2 mV/°C.

(v) The output can be used for microprocessor based control applications.

Limitations :

(i) The linear relation between V_{BE} and T exists only above 170 K.

(ii) Limited temperature range 223 to 423 K.

2.5.4 Quartz Thermometers

Principle :

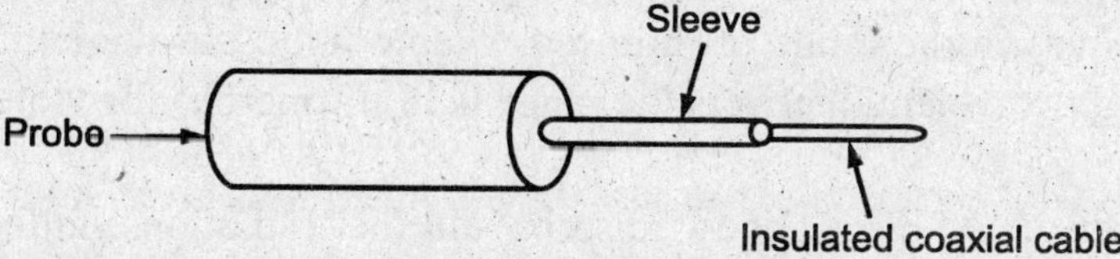

Fig. 2.30 : Quartz thermometer

The quartz crystal is cut in the form of shear type LC cut. As temperature around the crystal changes, the resonant frequency of vibrations of crystal faces varies linearly with temperature according to equation

$$f = f_0 (1 + AT + BT^2 + CT^3)$$

where, f = actual resonant frequency

f_0 = fundamental frequency at a reference temperature

A, B, C are constants.

In the LC cut crystal, the coefficients B and C are negligible in comparison with A, therefore, the resonant frequency f varies linearly with temperature T.

Construction and Working :

The quartz resonator consists of a crystal hermetically sealed in a cylindrical copper case in a helium atmosphere, and the case itself is further enclosed in a stainless steel tubular body. The resonator is thermally isolated from the heat sensitive oscillator circuitry by using a coaxial cable.

Advantages :

(i) The output response is highly linear i.e. of the order of ± 0.5% F.S.

(ii) High sensitivity of the order of 1000 Hz/°C at the operating frequency of 28 MHz.

(iii) The output is in digital form which is insensitive to signal-noise or cable resistance effects.

(iv) High resolution of the order of $\pm 5 \times 10^{-4}$ °C.

(v) Fast speed of response with response time as low as 1 sec.

(vi) Long-term stability and reliability.

Limitations :

(i) Limited measuring range – 40 to 230°C.

(ii) The output reading is pressure-sensitive.

(iii) Expensive.

(iv) Used in laboratory environment.

2.6 RADIATION TEMPERATURE MEASUREMENT (PYROMETRY)

High temperature measurement by means of radiations from a hot body is called as *pyrometry* and the instruments used for this are called as *pyrometers*. In this chapter, we discuss two different types of pyrometers viz. (i) radiation pyrometer and (ii) optical pyrometer.

2.6.1 Basic Concepts of Hot Body Radiation

1. **Radiant energy :** It is the heat energy radiated by a hot body in the form of electromagnetic waves in the range of infra-red, visible light, ultraviolet, X-ray and gamma ray. The visible light wavelength covers the range 0.38 μ (micron) for violet colour to 0.78 μ for red colour.

2. **Black body :** A black body absorbs all the radiations falling on it without transmitting or reflecting any. Also, black body radiates energy at all spectral wavelengths when it is heated and the maximum intensity of radiation depends upon its temperature.

3. **Kirchhoff's law :** Any body in thermal equilibrium with its surrounding emits as much heat radiation as it receives at any given wavelength and temperature.

4. **Stefan-Boltzmann law :** The amount of radiant energy from a black body is given by this law as :

$$\phi_b = \sigma A T^4 \qquad \ldots (2.4)$$

where, ϕ_b = radiant flux = radiant energy per unit time (ergs/sec.)

σ = Stefan-Boltzmann constant

= 5.77×10^{-5} ergs/sec-cm^2 deg^4

A = black body surface area (cm^2)

T = temperature (°K)

5. Planck's radiation law : The emissive power i.e. radiant energy per unit time per unit area at certain wavelength is given by this law as :

$$W_{b\lambda} = \frac{C_1 \lambda^{-5}}{e^{C_2/\lambda T} - 1}$$

where C_1 and C_2 are constants.

λ = wavelength

e = natural logarithm base

T = absolute temperature

6. Wien's displacement law :

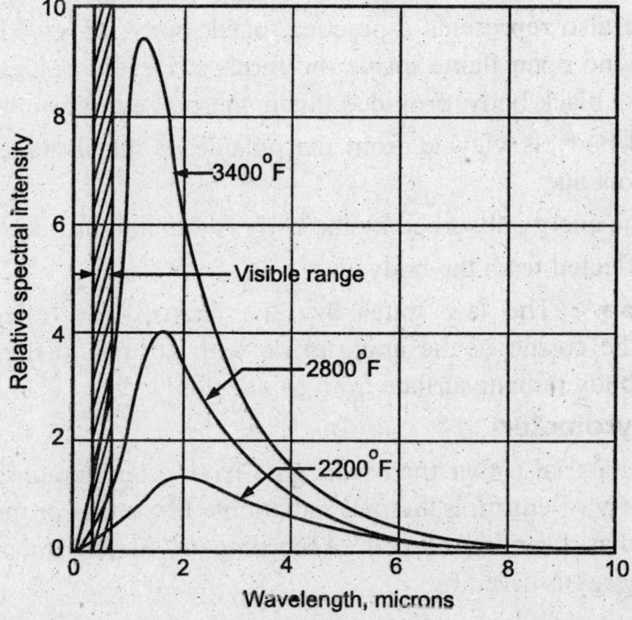

Fig. 2.31 : Spectral distribution of radiant energy

Fig. 2.31 shows the distribution of radiant energy at various wavelengths at different temperatures. Note that intensity of radiation changes with wavelength and intensity becomes maximum at certain wavelength. The Wien's law states that the product of the wavelength at which maximum radiant intensity occurs and the absolute temperature of the hot body remains constant.

Mathematically, $\lambda_m T = 2900$ ... (2.5)

where, λ_m = wavelength at which the radiant intensity is maximum in microns

T = absolute temperature in °K

Above equation predicts that as black body temperature increases, the wavelength of maximum radiant energy goes on decreasing, which can also be verified from the graph. Due to this reason only, when metal is heated, its colour goes on changing from red (a long wavelength) to yellow and white (a short wavelength) with increase in maximum intensity of radiation.

7. Total emissivity (e) : Emissivity of any hot body is defined as the ratio of total radiation energy from that body to total radiation energy from a geometrically similar black body, when both are at same temperature. Obviously emissivity of black body would be equal to 1, while the emissivity of a non-black body would be less than unity. Emissivity of oxidized open, rough surfaces is higher than polished surface.

8. Spectral emissivity (e_λ) : Spectral emissivity of a non-black body is defined as the ratio of the monochromatic radiation energy of wavelength λ from a non-black body to that from a geometrically similar black body at the same temperature.

9. Practical black body : It is impossible to construct a perfectly black body in practice, but bodies having their behaviour matching with black body can be constructed. An industrial furnace also represents a practical black body, provided it has relatively few openings and there is no open flame inside the furnace. Heated bodies inside a furnace can also be considered as a black body, provided it is in thermal equilibrium with furnace.

When the heated body is viewed from the outside of the furnace, the radiated energy consists of two components :

(a) whatever is the energy absorbed by the body is radiated out, and

(b) the energy reflected from the body.

10. Lambert's law : The law states that the intensity of reflected radiation varies approximately with the cosine of the angle made with normal to the surface. This allows viewing of the black body radiant surface from any desired side.

2.6.2 Radiation Pyrometer

Theory : Every material (other than inert gas) having temperature above absolute zero has a universal property of emitting thermal radiations. From this property, the technique of radiation pyrometry has been developed. According to Stefan-Boltzmann law, the total amount of radiated energy is given by

$$\phi_b = \sigma A T^4$$

where A = surface area of target

T = absolute temperature of target

Out of this total radiated energy, only the energy radiations having wavelengths between 0.3 to 20 micron is of sufficient magnitude usable for radiation detectors. This range encompasses the visible spectrum (0.35 to 0.75 microns) and the near infra red (IR) region (wavelengths longer than red i.e. between 0.7 to 20 micron). The intensity and distribution of this energy from a substance may be compared with that of a black body which radiates its energy in a theoretically predictable spectral distribution and intensity. Real targets, however always deviate from an idealized black body to some degree. This deviation can be minimized with high emittance and low reflectance for the target. For materials other than solids, the radiant energy detector will actually see beneath the surface, or if the object is thin, right through it.

I. Principle :

According to Stefan-Boltzmann law, the intensity of radiant energy emitted by hot target varies as the fourth power of its absolute temperature. In radiation pyrometer, the absolute, visible and IR energy is focussed on radiation detector which converts it into proportional electrical signal, that indicates the target temperature.

II. Construction :

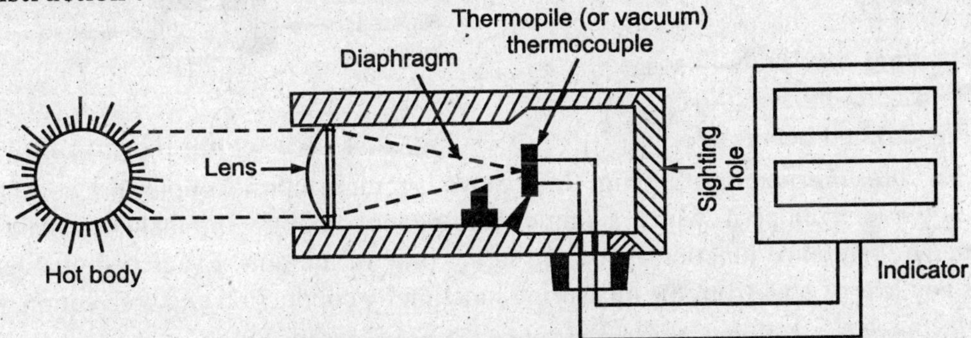

Fig. 2.32 : Radiation pyrometer

Fig. 2.32 shows the construction of radiation pyrometer that consists of a lens, diaphragm, radiation receiving element, sighting hole and recorder or indicator. Diaphragm position can be adjusted for calibration.

The target size is minimum at focal length of objective but it increases with distance from the lens. The target cross-sections can vary from circular to rectangular and even slot-shaped depending on apertures in the housing design. The telescopic eye pieces can magnify the radiant energy such that much smaller targets at greater distance can be viewed. Targets of 1.6 mm diameter are feasible with proper design.

The physical shape of optical system and its mounting control the sighting path; while its material determines optical properties. Glass does not transmit well beyond 2.5 micron and it is suitable only for high temperature where plenty of output is available. Other materials are Quartz (upto 4 micron), CaF_2 (upto 10 micron), lesser used materials (greater than 10 microns).

Windows and filters alter transmission properties. A filter must be purposely placed in front of detector to cut off unwanted wavelengths.

Different types of radiation pyrometer designs used are :

1. broad band total radiation pyrometer,
2. single band-pass pyrometer,
3. the ratio or two-colour pyrometer.

Radiation receiving elements : These elements receive radiant energy from the hot body and generate a signal proportional to the intensity of radiation.

(a) Thermopile : Thermopile consists of a number of thermocouples connected in series with their measuring junctions flattened and blackened as shown in Fig. 2.33. The reference junction of each thermocouple is located at the outer ring where the individual thermocouples are connected.

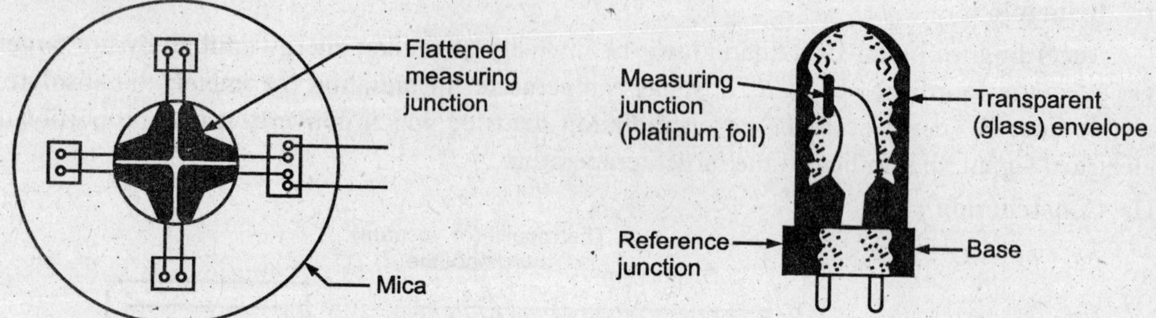

Fig. 2.33 : Thermopile

Fig. 2.34 : A vacuum thermocouple

(b) Vacuum thermocouple : Fig. 2.34 shows vacuum thermocouple that consists of an evacuated glass envelope in which a single thermocouple alongwith blackened platinum foil is placed. The reference junction is located in the base of the unit. Evacuated glass envelope prevents any loss of heat from the measuring junction by conduction and convection.

(c) Bolometer : Bolometer is a resistance thermometer usually in the strip form made of Nickel so as to get about 10 ohm resistance. The strip is coated with gold black or platinum black to increase its absorptivity.

(d) Photomultiplier tubes and Photon detector : If radiant energy falls on semi-crystalline material such as silicon, lead sulphate etc., the electrical charges get released that give electrical output in proportion to intensity of radiant energy. It gives fast speed of response that permits measuring temperature of small objects moving at high speed where relatively energy output is very small. These elements are very sensitive to wavelength, hence they can control the band pass in addition to filters.

III. Working :

Radiations at all possible wavelengths from a hot body (target) are focussed by the lens on the radiation receiving element. When thermopile or vacuum thermocouple is used as radiation receiving element, then radiant energy from the target is focussed on blackened measuring junction. Due to absorption of radiant energy, the measuring junction temperature rises. According to Seebeck effect, e.m.f. is developed between the output leads which is proportional to temperature difference between measuring and reference junction. When this element is connected with millivoltmeter type instrument, the e.m.f. developed can be calibrated in terms of the target temperature. If bolometer element is used, then resistance of the foil changes with change in temperature. Hence the bolometer can be calibrated in terms of target temperature with Wheatstone bridge circuit.

IV. Calibration :

Radiation pyrometer is normally calibrated by comparing its performance with standard optical pyrometer.

V. Performance Characteristics :

(A) Static characteristics :

Accuracy : Under black-body conditions, the accuracy of radiation pyrometer is ± 0.5%.

Sources of static error in the reading :

1. ***Reference junction temperature :*** When radiation receiving element like thermopile is used, temperature of the reference junction of the thermocouples should be kept constant, because e.m.f. developed depends upon temperature difference between measuring and reference junction. Since reference junctions are in close contact with the thermopile housing, temperature rise of housing causes approximately same temperature rise in measuring and reference junctions. Hence, for low temperature measurement, the error is appreciable than that for high temperatures.

But when temperature of the housing rises by more than 65°C, then air or water cooling of the housing is done to maintain the reference junction temperature constant.

2. ***Distance between the hot target and the receiving element :*** The angle of the focussing lens is usually selected so that the target diameter is a given fraction of the distance between the target and receiver. e.g the target–area ratio of 10 : 1 means distance between target and receiver should not be greater than 10 times the maximum useful target diameter, otherwise insufficient radiations are received that results in error.

In lens-type radiation pyrometer shown in Fig. 2.32, lens is so adjusted that the image of the target surface is focussed on the diaphragm opening. Hence, the hot target and the diaphragm opening, both should be located at the conjugate foci of the lens. For this purpose, either lens or diaphragm position is adjusted.

3. ***Absorbing media between target and receiver :*** Substances like smoke, dirt and gases present in the space between the target and receiver may absorb the radiation that results in incorrect, lower temperature reading. If hot gases, flame, high temperature, carbon particles are present, then it results in incorrect, higher temperature reading.

4. ***Reradiation :*** If different parts of the radiation pyrometers are at different temperatures, then energy received may get reradiated between them that may cause a slight error. To minimize this error all parts and the housing are maintained at constant temperature.

5. ***Emissivity of target surface :*** Closed surfaces can be considered as black body, hence temperature measurement does not require any correction for emissivity. But open surfaces like molten metal, hot steel plate have low emissivity and hence their temperature measurement requires emissivity correction. Emissivity of such surfaces is low because of slag and oxides formed over them, which are at lower temperature than the molten metal below it. For such application a target tube is used. For applying the correction, one must know the *total emissivity* of the surface.

Emissivity correction :

Radiant energy from the target that is received by the receiver can be written by Stefan-Boltzmann law by

$$\phi = e\sigma AT^4 \quad \dots (2.6)$$

where, ϕ = radiant energy received by receiver

e = total emissivity of the target

A = target area

T = absolute temperature of the target

If T_a is the *apparent temperature* of the target, that is the temperature indicated by radiation pyrometer, then Stefan-Boltzmann law can be written as

$$\phi = \sigma A T_a^4 \qquad \text{... (2.7)}$$

Solving equations (2.6) and (2.7) simultaneously, we get

$$T = e^{-1/4} T_a \qquad \text{... (2.8)}$$

Above equation (2.8) gives the *actual temperature* of the target in terms of its emissivity and the apparent temperature. It gives the emissivity correction for temperature reading of the radiation pyrometer. The temperature correction given by above equation (2.8) when applied to lens type radiation pyrometer, also has some error and this error is due to the fact that in equation (2.8) *we use total emissivity 'e';* but when lens is used, it passes radiations in certain band of wavelength only. Hence, pyrometer response is restricted to this band only. If the instrument responds to the full wavelength band radiations, then only we can use total emissivity in equation (2.8), otherwise lower value of e should be used in the equation.

When the total emissivity of the surface is below about 0.8, it cannot be determined with certainty and hence temperature measurement cannot be accurate. Under this condition it is preferred to calibrate the radiation unit under the actual operating conditions. This also helps to eliminate any error due to reflection to the target surface from higher temperature surfaces around it.

(B) Dynamic characteristics :

Radiation pyrometer has time constant of about 0.01 to 0.02 mm. Fast speed of response is due to small thermal capacitance of thermopile.

Effect of target tube : For low emissivity targets like molten metal, target tube is used that is made of either a ceramic or a metal such as silicon carbide, inconel, nickel, wrought iron or steel. The tube forms a black body target, and its length and diameter are so proportioned that it absorbs almost all radiations by multiple reflections, thus approaching its emissivity closer to unity. The use of target tube reduces the speed of response.

VI. Advantages, Limitations, Applications :

Advantages : Discussed in Art. 2.6.4.

Limitations :

1. Emissivity of target material affects the temperature measurement.
2. Non-linear scale.
3. Error due to absorbing media.
4. More costlier and fragile than thermocouple and RTD.
5. Requires relatively wide temperature span.

Applications :

1. Radiation pyrometers are used in the corrosive environments where other sensors cannot be used.
2. For temperature measurement of moving objects.
3. For temperature measurement of targets which are not easily accessible.
4. For measurement of average temperature of large surface areas.

Points to be considered while using a radiation pyrometer are :

1. Target temperature (extreme and normal limits).
2. Minimum target size and distance factors.
3. Target material and emittance.
4. Angle of observation.
5. Stationary or moving target. Choose fast responding sensor for moving targets.
6. Ambient temperature.
7. Atmospheric conditions between target and detector.
8. Direct or window sighting of the target.

2.6.3 Optical Pyrometer (Disappearing Filament Type)

I. Principle :

The spectral radiant intensity of the radiated energy from heated body at a given wavelength is proportional to the temperature of the body. Hence, temperature of the body can be measured in terms of spectral radiant intensity at a certain wavelength. Optical pyrometers are narrow band or two-colour radiation pyrometers which operate in the visible spectrum around 0.65 micron point.

II. Construction and Working :

There are two designs of optical pyrometer - Manual and automatic.

1. Manual type :

In manual pyrometer a human eye acts as the detector for comparing a source of known radiant energy generated within the instrument to the incoming unknown source. Fig. 4.5 shows schematic diagram of optical pyrometer which is similar to the telescope having *objective* at one end and the eyepiece at the other end. A red filter is placed between the eye and the two sources of energy, that cuts out the shorter wavelengths and passes radiations having wavelength about 0.65 micron. Thus, filter serves as a dual purpose :

(i) Permits an easier colour match.

(ii) Permits an extension of temperature range beyond the point where eye could no longer tolerate the amount of energy if viewed directly.

The *filament lamp* acts as the standard source which is placed exactly at the focus of objective; so that image of the hot target is focussed on the plane of filament. Due to this target image and filament lamp appears superimposed on one another when viewed through eyepiece. A 2 volt battery alongwith milliammeter anc heostat is connected in series with the lamp. The intensity of filament lamp can be varied by varying current through it with the help of rheostat. A slight modification in this principle maintains the standard source constant and varies the amount of interposing absorbing material in the absorbing path.

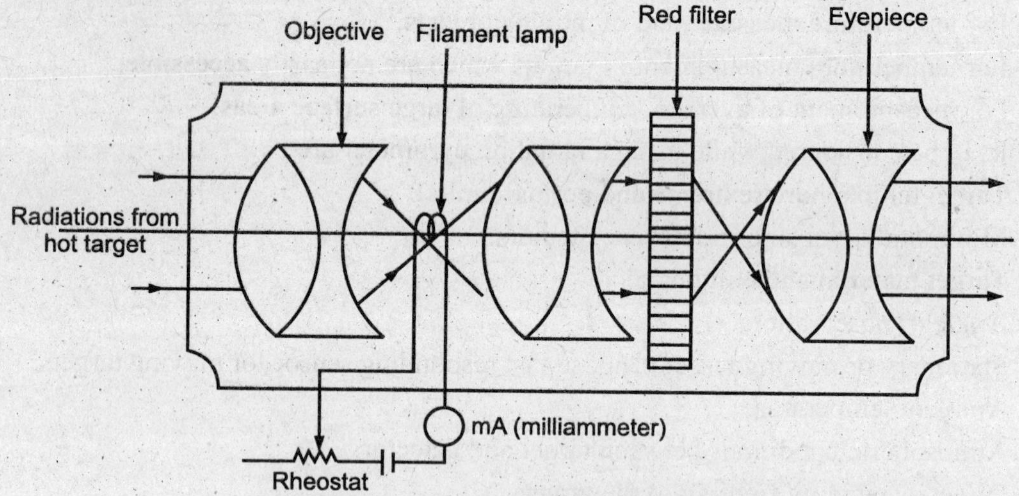

Fig. 2.35 : Optical pyrometer (schematic)

Manual instrument is so shaped to be held in the hand and upto the eye so that it may be sighted on the target. An adjustable focus permits the operator to focus an image of the source or target whose temperature is to be determined.

The temperature range is limited to 760°C on low end because there is insufficient emissions of visible light below 760° C for an accurate comparison.

Advantages of Manual Units :

1. Self-contained unit with its own power supply for operating the current.
2. Can be mounted in place or hand-held by an operator as he takes a sighting.
3. Reasonable accuracy if sighted into near black body furnace.

Limitations of Manual Units :

1. Requires operator to adjust temperature dial manually.
2. Not suitable to alarm and control functions.
3. Use of human eye restricts accuracy somewhat because eye responds to both colour and brightness rather than directly to energy.

III. Working :

In optical pyrometer we are interested in collecting the radiations of particular wavelength from the hot target. The telescope is focussed on the hot target so that image of the target is formed exactly at the filament lamp. When object is viewed through eyepiece, filament is viewed against the background of target image. In optical pyrometer, the brightness or intensity of hot target is matched with the intensity of filament lamp. The matching is done as follows :

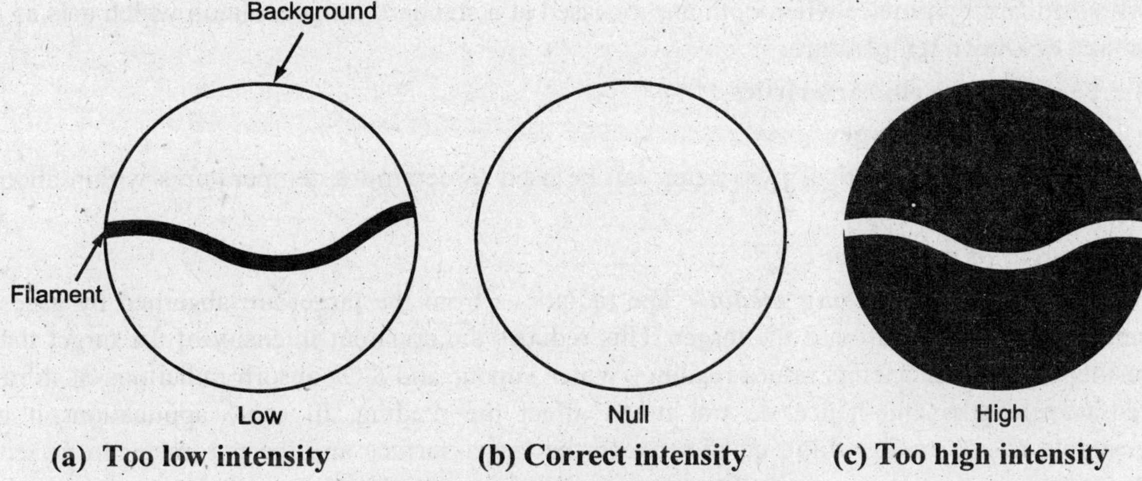

(a) Too low intensity **(b) Correct intensity** **(c) Too high intensity**

Fig. 2.36 : The disappearing filament

If temperature of the target is higher than that of the filament, the filament appears dark against the bright background as shown in Fig. 2.36 (a). On the other hand, when target temperature is lower than that of the filament, then filament appears bright against the dark background as shown in Fig. 2.35 (c). When temperatures of target and filament match, then their intensities become equal and then filament disappears against the target background as shown in Fig. 2.35 (b).

For getting target temperature, the intensity of filament lamp is so adjusted that the filament disappears against the background, hence the name disappearing filament type pyrometer. The filament current required to get this condition can be used for calibrating the instrument. Usually the milliammeter or rheostat is calibrated for target temperature.

Temperature range : 760° to 3500°C.

2. Automatic type :

Automatic units use electrical radiation detector instead of human eye and consequently it is not limited to visible wavelength of spectrum. It can reach far into the IR or near ultraviolet using either a narrow band, or two-colour or a wide band selection in accordance with the optical system and the detector used. It operates essentially by comparing the amount of radiation emitted by target with that emitted by an internally controlled reference source. The system usually consists of two components, the optical head and the electronic amplifier. In some models, optical head contains a temperature-controlled black-body source, a preamplified and an optical chopper. The chopper driven by a synchronous motor alternately exposes the detector to incoming and cavity radiations. The automatic pyrometers are used for measuring temperatures in jet engine rotor blades, furnaces, hot metal filaments, refractory metals, metal processing, textile, plastic, ceramic industries, thin film polymers, etc.

IV. Calibration :

Optical pyrometers are calibrated by focussing them on a standard tungsten strip lamp whose temperature is known. Calibration can also be done by comparing the performance with standard pyrometer when both are focussed at a standard tungsten lamp which acts as a source of known temperature.

V. Performance characteristics :

Static characteristics :

Accuracy : The optical pyrometer can be used to determine temperatures within about ± 5°F.

Sources of static error :

1. ***Effect of absorbing media :*** The radiations from the target are absorbed by gases, smoke, dust present around the target. This reduces the apparent intensity of the target that results in decreased temperature reading. Water vapour and CO_2 absorb radiations of infra-red wavelengths and hence do not much affect the reading. In some applications it is desirable to use an absorbing glass between the target surface and the pyrometer to protect the mechanism used. Knowing the transmission factor of the glass at 0.65 μ wavelength, correction may be applied.

2. ***Effect of spectral emissivity :*** The effect is same as that on radiation pyrometer. But in fact the variations of *spectral emissivity at 0.65 μ* is not large as compared to variation in total emissivity under same conditions. Hence, the emissivity correction for optical pyrometer is smaller than that for radiation pyrometer.

3. Ambient temperature change and distance between target and optical pyrometer have negligible effect on the reading.

VI. Advantages, Limitations, Applications :

Advantages :

1. Light weight and portable construction.
2. Good accuracy.

Limitations :

1. Cannot be used for measuring temperature of clean burning goods because they do not radiate energy in visible range.
2. The working depends upon correct matching of the intensities of target and lamp, hence personnel error is involved in the measurement.

Applications : Optical pyrometers are frequently used for calibration of radiation pyrometers.

2.6.4 Advantages of Pyrometers (Radiation and Optical) over other Temperature Sensors

1. Pyrometers do not require the physical contact with the target whose temperature is to be measured.
2. Pyrometers can be used to measure temperatures of either stationary or moving objects.
3. Theoretically there is no upper limit on the temperature that pyrometers can measure.

4. Since pyrometers do not make any actual physical contact with the target, they can be used to measure the temperatures of targets having contaminating environment.
5. Pyrometers can measure temperature of targets which are difficult to access for other sensors.

2.7 CALIBRATION OF THERMOMETERS

Thermometers are calibrated periodically using one of the following methods.

2.7.1 Comparison Method

In this method, the thermometers are calibrated by comparing their output response with that of a standard device whose accuracy is known; when both are subjected to similar changes in temperature. The accuracy attainable in this method depends on the quality of reference standard used, which should be atleast one order higher in magnitude than that of the sensor to be calibrated.

The standard liquid-in-glass thermometers, RTDs, thermocouples whose errors and accuracies are known can be used as reference devices.

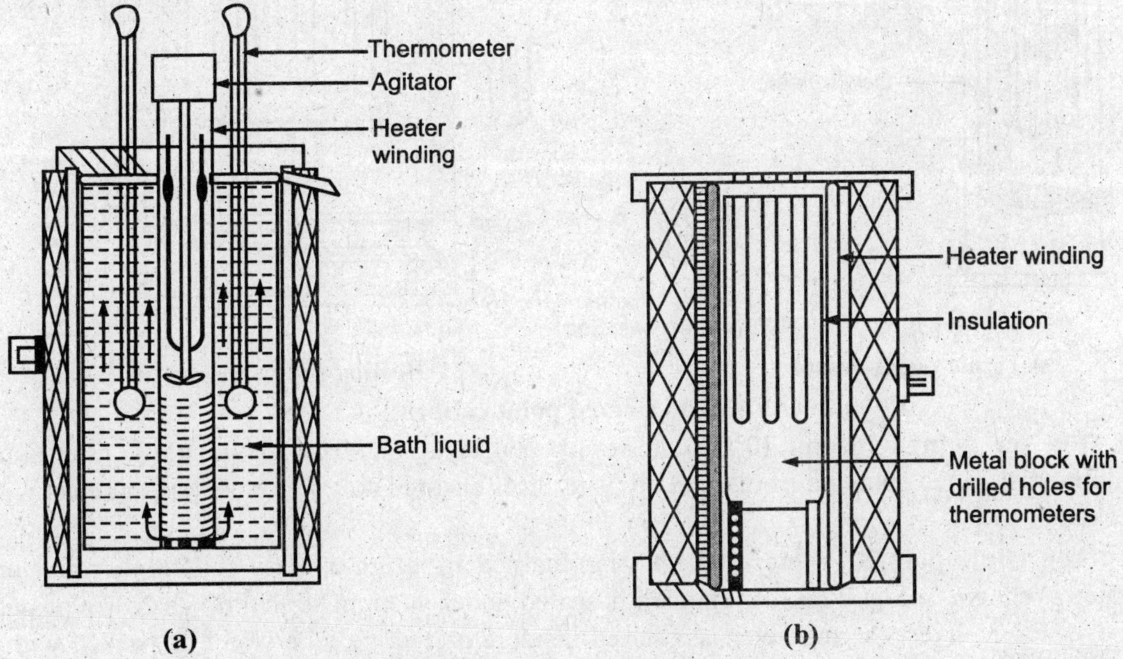

Fig. 2.37 : Comparison calibration

For calibration in the range of –100 to 600°C electrically heated liquid bath [shown in Fig. 2.37 (a)] is used. The bath liquid may be water (between 0 to 99°C), methanol (–100 to 0°C), silicon oil (50 to 250°C), tin (250 to 630°C). For tests below room temperature, the bath liquid can be cooled by a refrigeration system or liquid nitrogen. For higher temperature (upto 800°C), the metal block furnace [shown in Fig. 2.37 (b)] is used.

The metal block is made of aluminium, copper (upto 500°C) or nickel (upto 800°C) is used as a heat reservoir having uniform distribution of heat.

The advantage of comparison calibration method is that the test can be performed at any desired temperature within the desired temperature range.

2.7.2 Calibration using Fixed Point Temperatures

International Temperature Scale ITS-90 defined a reproducible temperature standards (known as fixed points) which are given in Table 2.1.

These temperatures correspond to certain physical state of the specified substance at standard pressure.

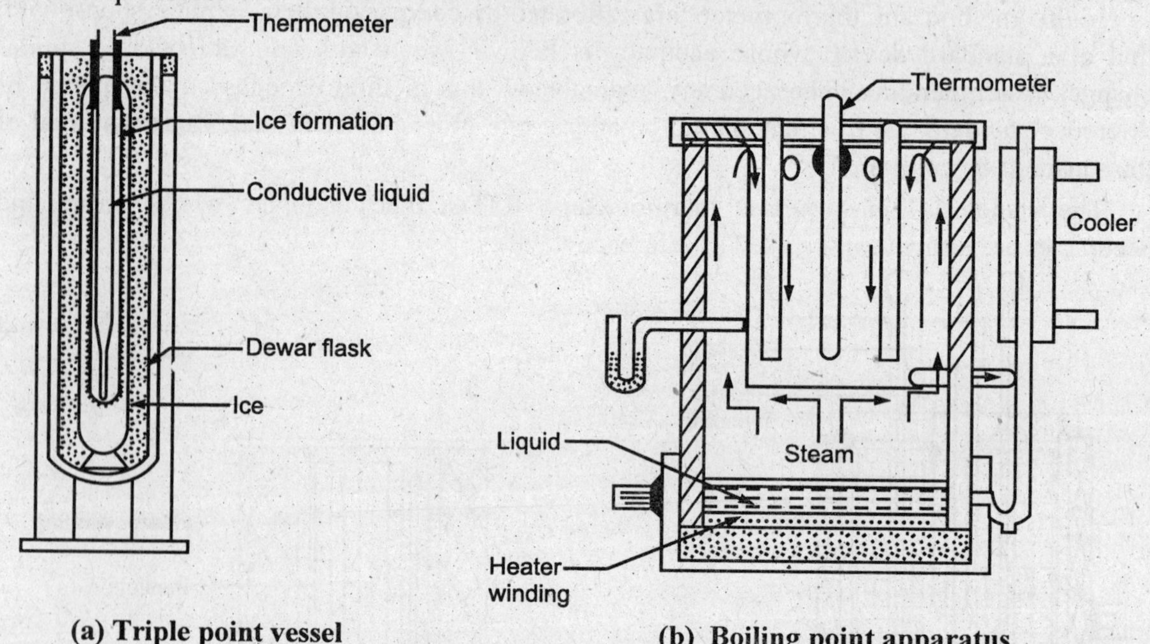

(a) Triple point vessel **(b) Boiling point apparatus**

Fig. 2.38 : Fixed point calibration

The ice point of water (0°C) can be attained using standard Dewar flask filled with finely-crushed ice obtained from distilled water. It is ensured that the sensor is in contact with ice only.

The triple point of water (0.01°C) is obtained by using a glass cell filled with pure water as shown in Fig. 2.38 (a). The cell is sealed under vacuum so that no gases are present above water. A test thermometer is inserted inside a protective tube which is packed with a finely crushed dry ice from outside. At this stage, the ice is taken out and replaced momentarily by water at room temperature, thereby producing a thin layer of water column between the well and the mantle of ice. This layer is at temperature of 0.0075°C at 4.58 mm Hg, which is called as the triple point of water.

The boiling point temperature of any liquid can be obtained with boiler shown in Fig. 2.38 (b) in which the temperature of the condensing vapour at a particular pressure is taken as a reference temperature.

This method of fixed-point calibration allows greatest possible accuracy attainable, but it requires appropriate measurement set-up for achieving each fixed point.

2.8 SELECTION OF TEMPERATURE SENSOR

Temperature sensors are selected to meet the requirement of specific applications. The factors to be considered while selecting the temperature sensor for specific application are temperature level or range, the point or average temperature measurement and the nature of the process environment.

1. Environmental Effects : The temperature experienced by the sensor may be different from the temperature one is attempting to measure because of :

(i) improper size or configuration of sensor.

(ii) improper installation.

(iii) inadequate thermal coupling of sensor with the media of which temperature is measured.

2. Atmospheric Effects : In highly humid or very moist environments, it is essential that the element of RTD or the bead of a thermistor be well insulated electrically, otherwise due to moisture content, the elements may short. Thermocouples in general are less sensitive to moisture than RTD. If null-balance potentiometer or high input impedance readout devices are used, insulation resistance between legs of the couple as low as 10,000 can be tolerated without serious errors in the measurement. If low input impedance current measuring readout devices are used, a high insulation resistance between legs of the couple becomes as important as with RTD and should be in megaohms.

If a sensing device is used in corrosive, reducing or oxidizing environments, it must be protected by some form of envelope or coating. But this increases mass of the sensor, which adversely affects its characteristics.

3. Measuring Temperature of Solids : The correct allowable size and configuration of sensor assures a useful measurement. This requires correct knowledge of the heating or cooling conditions together with an estimate of the magnitude of temperature gradients that are likely to exist in the region in which the measurement is to be made. It is found that the magnitude of Biot modulus $\frac{hL}{K}$ can be used to determine whether significant gradients are likely to exist. (h = surface heat transfer coefficient, L = smallest dimension of the solid, K = thermal conductivity of the solid). If $\frac{hL}{K} < 0.2$, no significant gradient is expected and a measurement anywhere on or within the solid should give identical results regardless of size of configuration of the sensor. On the other hand, if $\frac{hL}{K} < 0.2$, temperature gradients are likely to exist, hence care should be exercised in choosing the size, location and orientation of the sensor within the solid. In such cases, the maximum rate of heat transfer to surface of solid must be known or estimated and the maximum gradient at the point of measurement must be determined. The maximum temperature at the surface of solid is determined from $\frac{\Delta T}{\Delta x} = \frac{q}{k}$. Under certain conditions of heating or cooling if measurement at points other than the surface are important, it may be necessary to evaluate anticipated heat transfer conditions and resulting temperature gradients. On the basis of this gradient, it is possible to establish the limits on the size of the sensing device e.g. the length of any one of the three dimensions of the sensors (excluding lead wires) should not be greater than the distance between two points of the process that are different in temperature by more than the acceptable measurement error. The sensor must have satisfactory thermal coupling with the process material, otherwise the sensor will not indicate the true temperature history experienced by the solid, which is the condition that can produce dynamic errors. The best thermal coupling is achieved by direct bonding of the sensor such as welding a thermocouple to the solid surface, or into a cavity within the solid. The bond line between the sensor and the solid shoud be kept as thin as possible and should not fracture or fail during thermal cycling. Such bondings can be achieved by using various expoxy and ceramic cements with fillers to improve their conductivity.

4. Measuring Temperature of Fluids : The fundamental problem of measuring the temperature of a fluid is one of assuring strong thermal coupling. For fluid temperature measurement, the sensor must come to equilibrium with temperature of the fluid. For rapidly changing temperature, the rate of heat transfer between the sensor and process fluid must be sufficient to overcome the thermal capacitance of the sensor in order that it can follow the fluctuations in fluid temperature. Under such conditions, the temperature T experienced by a sensor which are initially at temperature T_i is given by

$$\frac{T_i - T}{T_i - T_o} = e^{\left(\frac{hA}{WC_p}\right)t}$$

where
h = heat transfer coefficient at surface of sensor
A = surface area of sensor
W = weight of sensor
C_p = specific heat of sensor
t = time after immersing sensor in fluid.

A sensor to respond rapidly to changes in fluid temperature, should have a large surface area to mass ratio. It should also have large heat transfer coefficient which is a direct function of the fluid mass flow rate over the sensor. Hence forced convection or the rapid flow of fluid over the sensor is desirable.

5. Measuring Temperature of Gases : While measuring temperature of gas stream in a heated duct or furnace where temperature difference between sensor and its surrounding exceed 500°C, significant errors can occur due to radiation exchange between sensor and surrounding. Under such conditions, the sensor must be shielded against thermal radiation exchange. This can cause disturbances in the flow of fluid around the sensor and hence affect the directional response characteristics. Another thermal effect in measuring the temperature of gas streams at higher velocities is the recovery factor, which results from an increase in the temperature of the gas at the sensor due to compression heating as the gas is brought to stagnation against the sensor.

EXERCISE

1. List various temperature scales and compare them on the basis of ice point, steam point and absolute zero point.
2. Why Kelvin scale is called as thermodynamic temperature scale ?
3. Describe bimetallic thermometers.
4. Describe liquid expansion thermometers.
5. What is thermal well ? Why it is used ? How thermal well affects the dynamic response of the thermometer ?
6. How will you elevate the upper range of the mercury-in-glass thermometer ?
7. What are the factors affecting dynamic response of mercury thermometer ?
8. Why scale of mercury thermometer is not exactly linear ?
9. Describe gas-expansion thermometers.
10. Why gas-thermometers cannot be used at very high temperatures ?
11. While calibrating gas-expansion thermometers, why corrections are to be applied particularly at low temperatures and high pressures ?
12. How will you differentiate between liquid-expansion thermometer and liquid-filled pressure-spring thermometer ?
13. Give reason : Free liquid surface in vapour-actuated thermometer should be located in the bulb only.
14. Explain various sources of static error in pressure-spring thermometers.
15. Describe various methods of compensating for any error in temperature measurement due to change in ambient temperature.
16. Why the extension neck of the pressure spring thermometer is thermally insulated from the bulb ?
17. Describe cross-ambient effect in case of vapour-actuated thermometers.
18. Why ambient temperature effect is negligible in vapour-pressure thermometers ?
19. Why head effect is negligible in gas thermometers ?
20. Give reason : Vapour-actuated thermometers can measure the temperature of free liquid surface only.
21. State :
    (a) Seebeck effect
    (b) Peltier effect and
    (c) Thomson effect for a thermocouple
22. State three thermoelectric laws and give their significance for thermocouples.
23. Describe the principle, construction and working of thermocouple used for temperature measurement.

24. List various types of thermocouples with the material used for positive and negative wire. Also state the temperature range and suitable atmosphere for each type.
25. Describe different methods by which the measuring junction can be formed.
26. Where is the reference junction of the thermocouple located ? Why it is not located near the measuring junction ?
27. What is the function of lead wires ? How will you select the material of lead wires for a given thermocouple ?
28. What is the function of protective sheathing on the measuring junction ? What are the desirable properties of the thermal well material ?
29. Describe the construction of millivoltmeter and state how it can be used as the indicating element for a thermocouple ?
30. Why the resistance of millivoltmeter should be as high as possible ?
31. Why reference junction temperature compensation is required ? How it is obtained for a millivoltmeter ?
32. What are the sources of error in the thermocouple reading ?
33. Describe the factors affecting dynamic response of the thermocouple.
34. Give reasons :
    (a) Thermocouples have fast speed of response above temperature of 530°C.
    (b) Thermal well surface should be rough.
    (c) Thermocouples having quartz, glass and vycor thermal wells have fast speed of response and these well materials have very little effect on the response.
    (d) While selecting thermal well material, there must be good compromise between speed of response and corrosion resistance.
35. List various thermocouple types which can be used in
    (a) oxidizing
    (b) reducing
    (c) inert or vacuum environments
36. What is the recommended thermocouple length in
    (a) cylindrical pipe,
    (b) tank ?
37. What is the selection criteria for single or duplex element thermocouple ?
38. Describe the principle, construction and working of resistance thermometer.
39. Give reasons :
    (a) Resistance winding of resistance thermometer should be stress free.
    (b) Resistance wire should be homogeneous.
40. What is PT-100 RTD ?

41. What is the function of lead wires ?
42. Describe Callender-Griffith's bridge circuit. How it overcomes the effect of :
    (a) contact resistance
    (b) lead wire resistance
    (c) Joule's heating,

    associated with Wheatstone bridge indicator.
43. Why resistance bulb must be protected from any contamination and oxidation ?
44. What is thermistor ? Draw various configurations of thermistor.
45. Describe the use of thermistors for protecting the electrical devices from damage due to heavy current.
46. What are the advantages of radiation temperature measuring methods over other methods ?
47. Define : (i) Black body, (ii) Total emissivity, (iii) Spectral emissivity.
48. State : (i) Planck's law, (ii) Kirchhoff's law, (iii) Stefan Boltzmann law, (iv) Wien's displacement law.
49. Give reason : When solid is heated, its colour goes on changing from red to yellow and then it becomes white. State the law justifying this statement.
50. Under which conditions a furnace can be considered as a practical black body ?
51. How will you differentiate between the operating principle of radiation and optical pyrometer ?
52. Describe construction and working of : (i) Radiation pyrometer, (ii) Optical pyrometers.
53. Describe the construction and working of radiation receiving elements :

    (i) Thermopile, (ii) Vacuum thermocouple, (iii) Bolometer.
54. Describe the sources of static error in (i) Radiation pyrometer and (ii) Optical pyrometer.
55. State the emissivity correction for temperature measurement with radiation pyrometer.
56. Why red filter is used in optical pyrometer ?
57. Why optical pyrometer is also called as disappearing filament type instrument ?
58. How will you calibrate optical pyrometer ?
59. Emissivity correction for optical pyrometer is much less than for radiation pyrometer. Justify.
60. How will you select the most economic temperature sensor for temperature measurement ?

Practice Problems :

1. A S-type thermocouple having the reference junction at 70°F indicates reading of 8.1 mV. Using the extract of thermocouple table given below, determine the actual temperature around the measuring junction of thermocouple.

Temperature (°F)	70	1615	1620
e.m.f. (mV)	0.120	8.203	8.234

(**Ans.** 1617.75°F)

2. A R-type thermocouple having the reference junction at 75°F indicates reading of 18.7 mV corresponding to measuring junction temperature of 2900°F. Check the calibration of thermocouple with the help of following data for R-type thermocouple and state the error if any :

Temperature (°F)	75	2890	2895	2900
e.m.f. (mV)	0.135	18.560	18.598	18.636

(**Ans.** Error = – 0.071 mV)

3

CHAPTER

PRESSURE AND STRAIN MEASUREMENT

3.1 INTRODUCTION

The measurement of pressure and vacuum is highly essential in continuous processing industries. In many operations it is necessary to measure and control pressure of liquid or gas to avoid any hazards. Hence pressure measurement is one of the most important of all process measurements. In this chapter, we shall study the principle, construction, working and characteristics of pressure sensors.

Pressure is defined as the amount of force applied per unit surface area on which it acts normally.

Units of Pressure : From the definition of pressure, its units can be derived as :

1. newton per square meter (N/m^2).
2. pascal (Pa).
3. atmosphere or bar units (atm, bar)
4. pounds per square inch (psi).
5. micron.
6. torr.
7. Head units – in mm of mercury or water or any other liquid.

Relation between different units :

1. $1 \text{ Pa} = 1 \text{ N/m}^2 = 10^{-5} \text{ kg/cm}^2$
2. $1 \text{ psi} = 6.9 \times 10^{-2} \text{ kg/cm}^2 = 6.9 \text{ kPa}$.
3. $1 \text{ kg/cm}^2 = 14.7 \text{ psi}$.
4. $1 \text{ atm} = 1 \text{ bar} = 1 \text{ kg/cm}^2 = 760 \text{ mm of Hg}$.
5. $1 \text{ micron} = 10^{-6} \text{ m Hg} = 19.34 \times 10^{-3} \text{ psi}$.
6. $1 \text{ torr} = 1 \text{ mm Hg} = 19.34 \times 10^{-3} \text{ psi}$.
7. $1 \text{ mm Hg} = 133 \text{ Pa}$.
8. $1 \text{ inch water} = 24 \text{ Pa}$.

Pressure scales : Unknown pressure can be expressed either in gauge scale, absolute scale or vacuum scale.

Relation between different pressure scales is shown in Fig. 3.1.

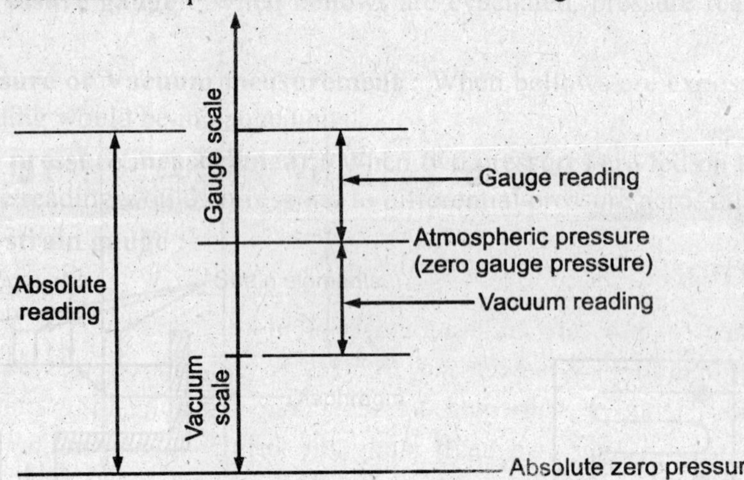

Fig. 3.1 : Relation between pressure scales

1. **Gauge scale :** This scale has atmospheric pressure as the lowest (zero) point. In other words, zero pressure on the gauge scale is nothing but atmospheric pressure of 1 bar or 760 mm of Hg or 1 kg/cm^2 or 14.7 psi.

Head units of pressure measurement :

Pressure head : A liquid column of mass density 'ρ' and weight density ω and height 'h' exerts a hydrostatic pressure 'p' at the bottom of the column given by

$$p = h\rho g = h\omega$$

Hence, pressure 'p' can be expressed in terms of liquid column of height 'h' and mass density ρ as :

$$h = \frac{p}{\rho g} = \frac{p}{\omega}$$

Atmospheric pressure is 76 cm of Hg means the pressure equals the hydrostatic pressure of mercury column of height 76 cm. Usually small pressures are expressed in m or cm or mm of mercury or water column.

A pressure gauge used to measure unknown pressure in gauge units, balances the unknown pressure against atmospheric pressure and it is expressed as 'psig'.

2. **Absolute scale :** This scale has absolute zero pressure as the lowest (zero) point. A pressure gauge used to measure unknown pressure in absolute units, balances the unknown pressure against absolute zero pressure or complete vacuum and the reading is expressed as 'psia'. The unknown pressure in gauge units can be converted into absolute units by using the relation :

$$\text{Absolute pressure} = \text{Gauge pressure} + \text{Atmospheric pressure}$$

3. **Vacuum scale :** Vacuum is nothing but sub-atmospheric (below atmospheric) pressure. Hence, vacuum scale has atmospheric pressure as the reference. Even though gauge scale and vacuum scale both have atmospheric pressure as the reference, the former is higher

than atmospheric while the latter is lower than atmospheric pressure. Thus vacuum can be expressed as negative gauge pressure.

$$\text{Vacuum} = -(\text{Gauge pressure})$$

For measuring unknown pressure in vacuum units, it is balanced against atmospheric pressure.

3.2 CLASSIFICATION OF PRESSURE MEASURING INSTRUMENTS

Different techniques are used for measuring pressures in different ranges, i.e. high (above 1000 atm), low (of the order of 1 mm of Hg and below) and moderate pressure. The static pressures are measured directly, while dynamic pressures are converted into displacement by using an elastic element, which is further converted into electrical signal using any electrochemical transducer. Pressure sensors are broadly classified into gravitational (e.g. manometers) and elastic type. The pressure transducers used in different pressure ranges are given below.

(A) Moderate Pressure Sensors :

(1) Manometers

(2) Elastic element gauges such as Bourdon tube, bellows, diaphragm, capsule.

The output of elastic elements is in the form of displacement which is then converted into electrical signals using transduction elements that give rise to different pressure transducers as follows :

(i) Potentiometric transducer

(ii) Strain gauge transducer

(iii) Variable reluctance transducer

(iv) LVDT sensor

(v) Variable capacitance sensor

(vi) Force-balance transducer

(vii) Solid-state transducer

(viii) Thin-film transducers

(3) Piezo electric pressure transducer

(4) Digital pressure transducer

(5) Measurement of fluctuating pressures

(B) High-pressure sensors :

Resistive transducer (wire type).

(C) Low pressure (vacuum) sensors :

(i) Manometers. (used upto pressure of about 0.1 torr)

(ii) Elastic element gauges. (used upto pressure of about 0.1 torr)

(iii) Mc Leod gauge.

(iv) Thermal conductivity or Pirani gauge.

(v) Ionization gauge.

(vi) Kundsen gauge.

3.3 PRESSURE MEASUREMENT USING MANOMETERS

3.3.1 Barometer

Barometer is used to measure atmospheric pressure. Atmospheric pressure is the pressure exerted by the air surrounding the earth, that goes on decreasing away from the earth surface.

I. Principle :

Barometer liquid balances the atmospheric pressure against vacuum and pressure head reading is obtained in absolute units.

II. Construction and Working :

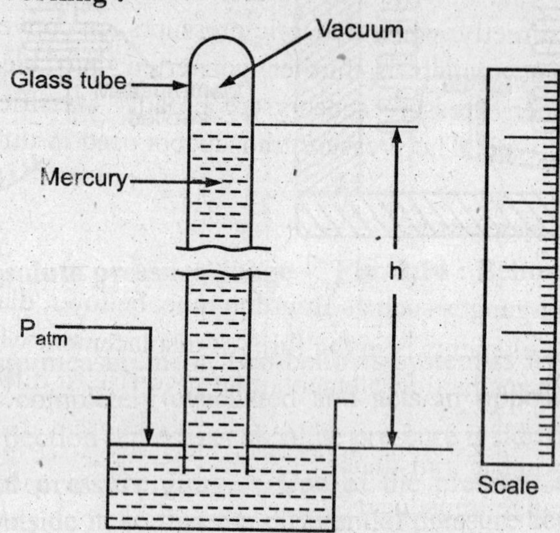

Fig. 3.2 : Liquid barometer

Barometer has a glass tube closed at one end and open at the other. The length of the tube must be greater than 76.2 cm. The tube is first completely filled by mercury and open end is temporarily plugged. Then tube is inverted so that plugged end is immersed in a mercury pan as shown in Fig. 3.2. When the plug is removed, the mercury in the tube drops by a certain amount, creating a vacuum at the top of the tube above the mercury column. The mercury stabilizes at a certain level inside the tube and then reading 'h' is noted. The reading 'h' is proportional to atmospheric pressure acting on mercury in the pan. Note that this atmospheric pressure reading is in absolute units.

We have stated that vacuum is present on the top of the tube above mercury, but actually there is vapour pressure of mercury acting on the mercury. Pressure 'P' is given by

$$P = 6.66 \times 10^{-3} h$$

where h is in cm and P is in kg/cm^2.

3.3.2 Manometers

I. Principle :

All manometers work on the effect of hydrostatic pressure exerted by a liquid column. In manometer unknown pressure is determined by balancing it against some known pressure or vacuum.

II. Construction and Working :

3.3.2.1 U-tube Manometer (Refer to Fig. 3.3)

The U-tube manometer consists of glass U-tube partially filled with a suitable liquid like water, mercury etc. One of the *arms or legs* of the manometer is connected to unknown pressure tap to be measured, while other connected to other pressure tap or it is left open to atmosphere.

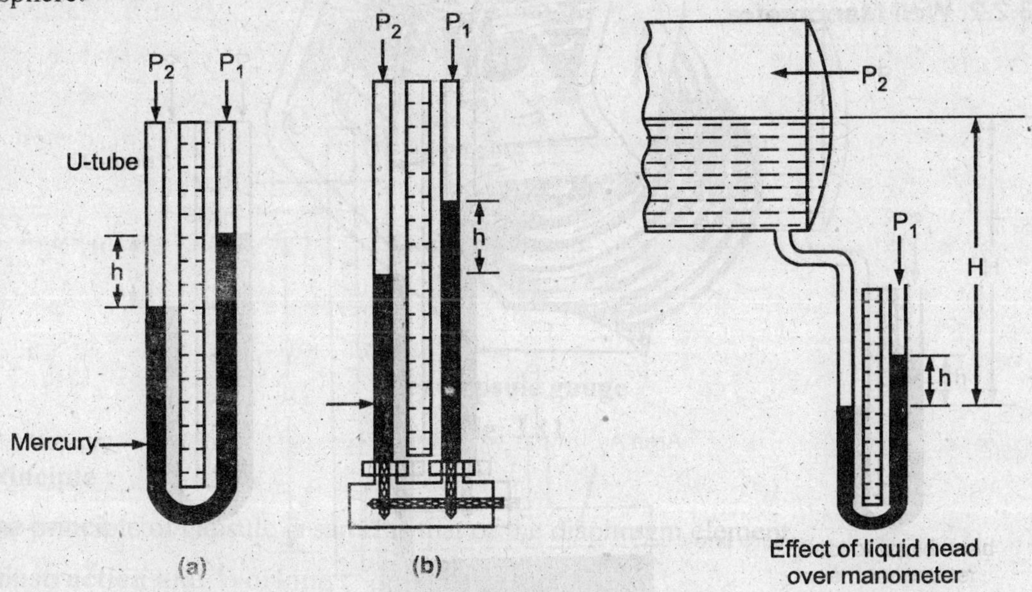

Fig. 3.3 : U-tube manometer

When there is difference of pressure between two arms of the manometer, liquid levels in the two arms do not match. This level difference in the two arms of the manometer represents differential pressure ($P_1 - P_2$). The static balance equation for Fig. 3.3 (a) can be written as :

$$P_2 - P_1 = h\rho g$$

where h = height difference

ρ = mass density of manometric liquid

If the fluid over manometric liquid has appreciable density, then static balance equation can be written as :

$$P_2 - P_1 = h(\rho_m - \rho_{T\cdot L})\, g$$

where h = height difference

ρ_m = mass density of manometric liquid

$\rho_{T\cdot L}$ = mass density of fluid over the manometric liquid.

Measu ment of differential pressure : As shown in Fig. 3.3 the two pressure taps are connected wo arms of the manometer so that height difference 'h' is proportional to difference two pressures.

Measurement of gauge pressure : When the unknown pressure is fed to one of the arms and the other arm is exposed to atmosphere, then 'h' represents the unknown pressure in gauge units.

Measurement of absolute pressure : When the unknown pressure is fed to one of the arms and the other arm is evacuated, then 'h' represents the unknown pressure in absolute units.

3.3.2.2 Well Manometer

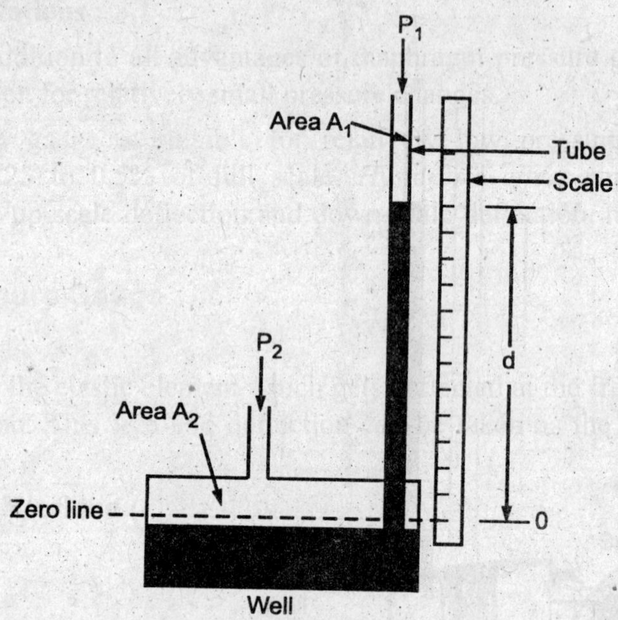

Fig. 3.4 : Well Manometer

This is nothing but a U-tube manometer, modified by replacing one leg by a large diameter well. Usually well area is 300 times greater than the tube area. Due to this, any change in pressure 'P_2' has negligible effect on manometric liquid level inside the well as compared to that on the tube liquid. Hence, manometric liquid level in the well is assumed to be fixed and it is called as zero level.

When pressures P_1 and P_2 are applied as shown in Fig. 3.4, the height 'h'of manometric liquid in the tube is measured from zero line. This height 'h' represents differential pressure $(P_2 - P_1)$. The static balance equation can be written as :

$$P_2 - P_1 = \rho h \left(1 + \frac{A_1}{A_2}\right)$$

where, A_1 = area of the tube

A_2 = area of the well

Limitations :

1. The non-uniformity of tube may produce error in measurement.
2. For getting high accuracy, zero level of the well is set at the zero level of the scale.

3.3.2.3 Enlarged Leg Manometer (Refer to Fig. 3.5)

In this manometer both the legs are enlarged in proportion as shown in Fig. 3.5 and they are connected by a separable tubing. Float is placed in one of the chambers.

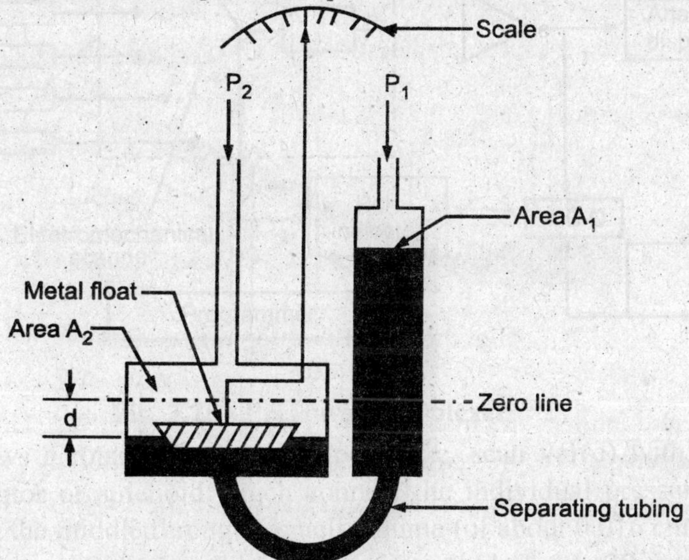

Fig. 3.5 : Enlarged leg manometer

When pressures P_1 and P_2 are applied as shown in Fig. 3.5, the float gets displaced. This float displacement measured from zero line represents the differential pressure $(P_1 - P_2)$. The manometer can be made recording type by connecting pointer mechanism to the float, that makes the pointer to deflect on the calibrated scale. The static balance equation can be written as :

$$P_2 - P_1 = \rho d \left(1 + \frac{A_2}{A_1}\right), \text{ where } A_2 > A_1$$

Advantages :

1. Recording type manometer.
2. The span can be changed by using different size tubes.
3. For recording type manometer mercury level need not be viewed, hence metal arms can be used that permit its use for measurement of high pressures upto 5000 psi.

3.3.2.4 Inclined Leg Manometer

The construction is very similar to enlarged leg manometer except that small diameter tube is inclined to the vertical axis.

When pressures P_1 and P_2 are applied as shown in Fig. 3.6, then liquid rises in the tube. The level of manometric liquid inside the tube is measured from zero level along the inclined tube; which represents the differential pressure $(P_1 - P_2)$. The static balance equation can be written as :

$$P_2 - P_1 = \rho d \sin \alpha \left(1 + \frac{A_1}{A_2}\right)$$

where, α = angle of inclination of the inclined leg

d = height difference measured along the tube

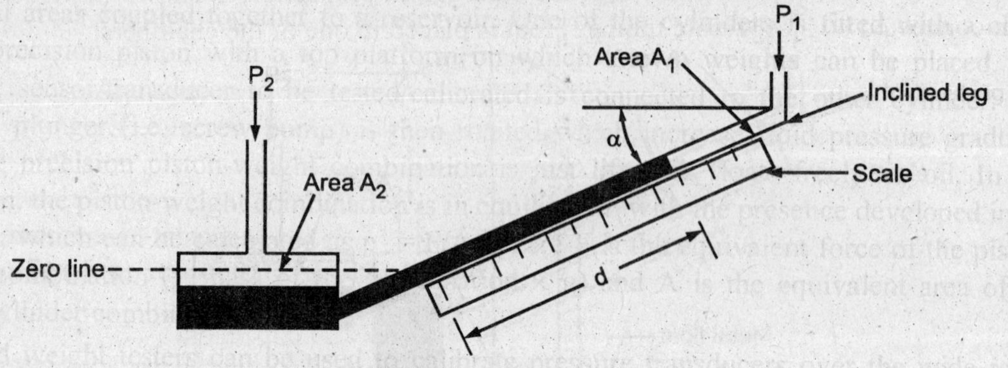

Fig. 3.6 : Inclined leg manometer

Advantages :

1. Due to inclined leg, the manometer reading gets amplified. Hence, it can be used for measurement of low pressures which cannot be measured by other manometers.
2. By reducing angle α, the scale length and hence the sensitivity can be increased.

Manometric Liquids :

Desirable properties of good manometric liquid are low freezing point, high boiling point, non-wetting characteristics, low surface tension, chemically inert, clear visible interface and ability to maintain density at various temperatures. Manometric fluids used in practice are :

1. **Mercury :** Mercury has low F.P. (–38°F) and high B.P. (675°F), but it corrodes many metals and it is poisonous and expensive.
2. **Water with colouring agents :** Colouring agents reduce surface tension of the pure water, that reduces the capillarity effect in manometer.
3. Benzene, kerosene, CCl_4, toluene etc.

III. Calibration :

Manometer is subjected to known differential pressure and corresponding height difference is noted. The calibration curve can be prepared by plotting height difference versus differential pressure. This curve can be used to get the differential pressure for certain height difference.

IV. Sources of Error :

1. **Temperature effect :** Rise in temperature causes decrease in manometric liquid density that affects the calibration which leads to an error.
2. **Capillary rise :** To avoid capillary rise effect, the tube diameter should be over 10 mm, otherwise capillary rise results in error in pressure reading.
3. **Meniscus shape :** For water, the free surface is concave, while for mercury free surface is convex. The level of manometric liquid should be noted at the centre of the meniscus.

V. Advantages, Limitations :

Advantages :

1. Simple, inexpensive construction.
2. High accuracy and sensitivity.
3. Can be used for low pressure measurement.
4. Desired span can be obtained just by using suitable manometric liquid.
5. Pressure range of manometers is 3 to 100 kPa.

Limitations :

1. No overrange protection.
2. Requires large space.
3. Non-portable.
4. Levelling is required.
5. Condensation of test liquid affects the reading.

3.4 PRESSURE MEASUREMENT USING ELASTIC ELEMENTS

Transducer is a device that converts one form of energy into some other form. These pressure gauges have elastic element that converts pressure signal into proportional mechanical displacement. In this article, we study Bourdon gauge, bellows gauge, diaphragm gauge and capsule gauge.

3.4.1 Bourdon Pressure Gauge

I. Principle :

E. Bourdon introduced Bourdon tube in 1852 as a curved or twisted tube having non-circular transverse section. According to Bourdon theory, a tube having internal cross-section that is not a perfect circle if bent or distorted, has the property of changing its shape with internal pressure variation. This causes the free end deflection of the tube which can be taken as the measure of change in pressure inside it.

II. Construction

Bourdon pressure gauges use different types of Bourdon springs as shown in Fig. 3.7. C-shaped Bourdon tube is shown in Fig. 3.7 (a) which is formed by winding the tube to form a segment of a circle having arc-length of about 270°. In spiral type, number of turns are wound in the shape of a spiral about a common axis as shown in Fig. 3.7 (b). In helix type, number of turns are wound in helix form as shown in Fig. 3.7 (c). In these figures, 'P' indicates direction of application of pressure, while 'T' indicates tip travel for rise in pressure.

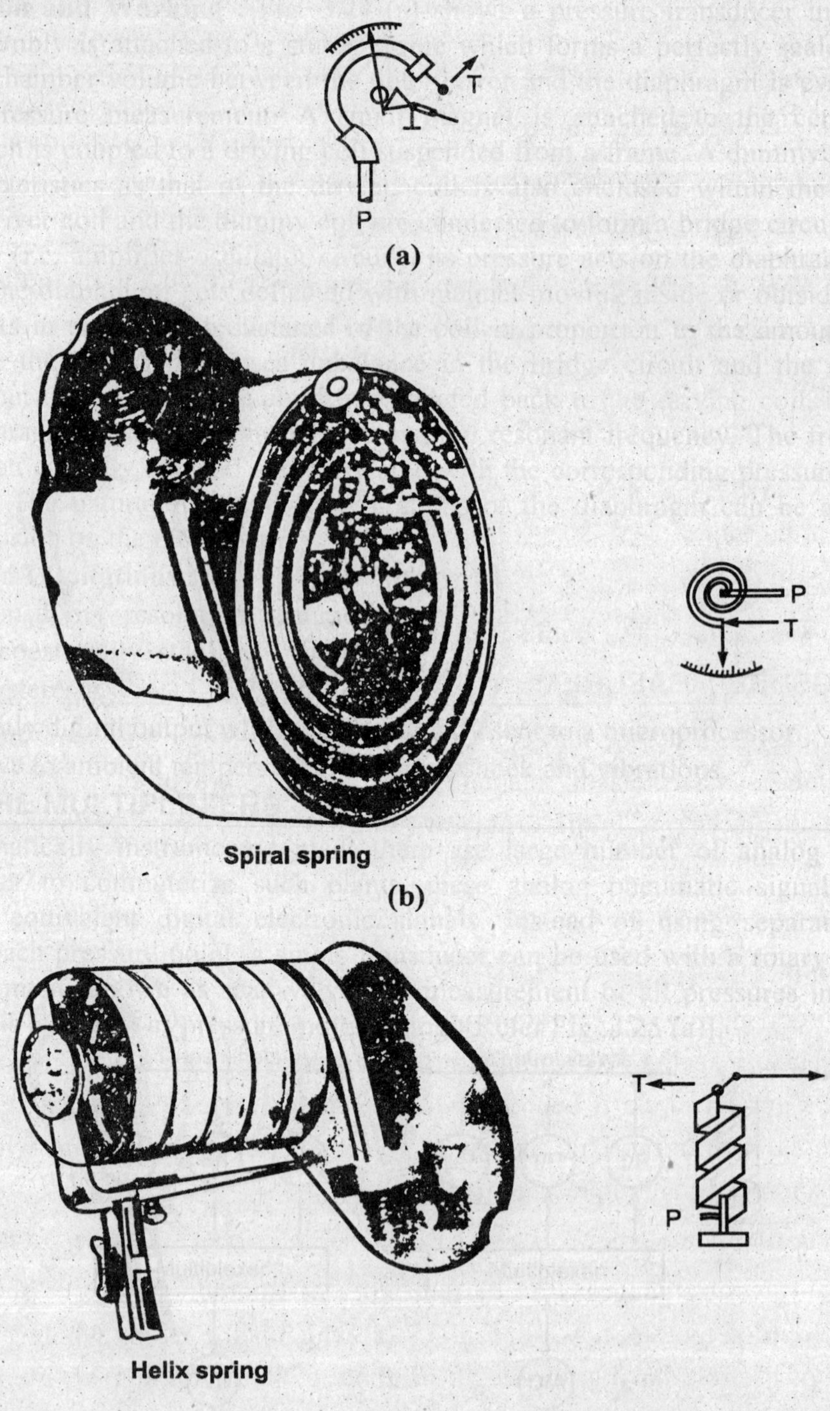

Fig. 3.7 : Bourdon springs

(P → pressure application, T → tip movement for rise in pressure)

We study C-shaped Bourdon tube gauge in detail. (Fig. 3.8). The gauge consists of a C-shaped Bourdon tube, tip, adjustable link, segment lever, sector, pinion, spring and pointer. A C-shaped Bourdon tube is a thin-walled tube having a non-circular or nearly elliptical transverse section as shown in Fig. 3.8. One end of the tube soldered or welded to a socket at the base through which pressure is fed inside the tube, while the other end is sealed by a tip. *Adjustable link, segment lever, sector and pinion* are connected to the tip, that convert linear motion of the tip into proportional rotary motion which is given to the *pointer* that moves on the *scale* calibrated in terms of pressure. A *hairspring* is connected to the spindle on which sector is mounted, that provides the necessary tension for meshing sector and pinion thus liminating any backlash.

Under-range protection is particularly required for gauges having partial ranges (like 20 to 50 psi).

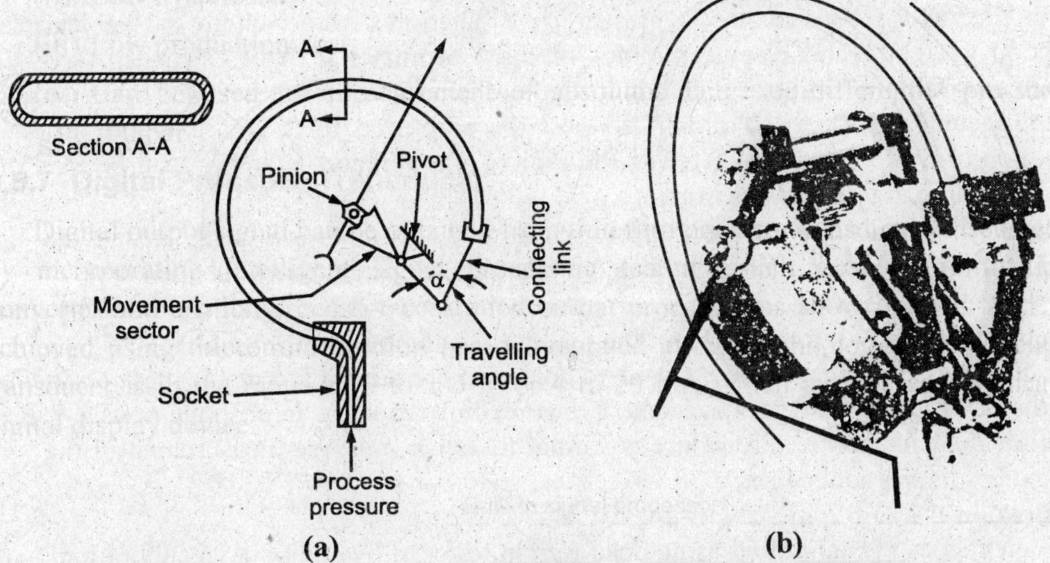

Fig. 3.8 : Bourdon pressure gauge using C-shaped Bourdon tube

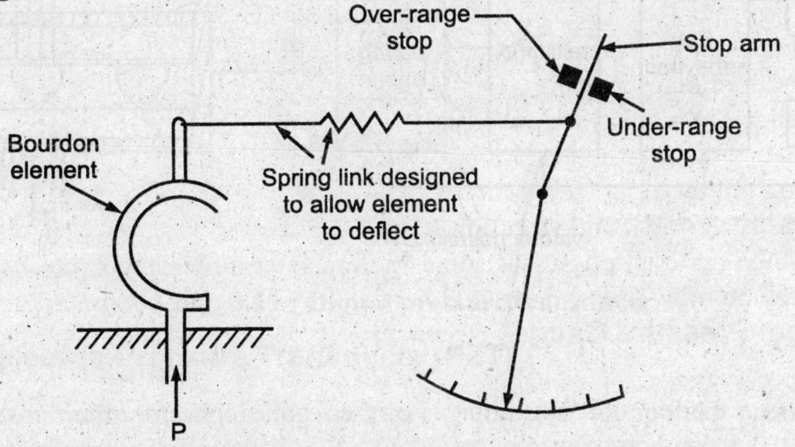

Fig. 3.9 : Over-range and under-range protection

Bourdon tube materials : A Bourdon spring can be made of any metal or alloy that exhibits satisfactory elastic properties. Materials used are – brass, phosphor bronze, monel, beryllium, copper, stainless steel, etc.

Pressure range :

C-shaped tube	:	0 to 1,00,000 psi.
Gauge pressure	:	0 to 12,000 psig (0.83 MPa)
Absolute pressure	:	0 to 100 psia (0.07 MPa)
Vacuum	:	0 to 30" Hg. (vac.)

III. Working :

When fluid under pressure to be measured enters the Bourdon tube, its cross-section tries to become more and more circular that causes straightening of the tube. Since one end of the tube is fixed, straightening causes the free end to deflect, that is called as *tip travel*. The amount of tip travel for given rise in pressure is a function of tube length, wall thickness, cross-section geometry and elastic modulus of the tube material. This linear tip travel is guided and amplified by adjustable link and segment lever and then it is given to sector and pinion arrangement. Sector and pinion convert the amplified tip travel into proportional rotary motion of the pointer connected to the pinion. The pointer deflection can be read on the scale calibrated in terms of pressure.

Helical and spiral type Bourdon tubes have many number of turns, hence the tip movement for given change in pressure is more than that for single turn C-shaped tube.

Gauge pressure measurement : When unknown pressure is fed inside the Bourdon tube and its outside is exposed to atmosphere, the reading would be in gauge units.

Absolute pressure measurement : When unknown pressure is fed inside the tube and its outside (that is instrument case) is evacuated, then reading would be in absolute units.

Vacuum measurement : Procedure is similar to gauge pressure measurement. Bourdon vacuum gauges have poor accuracy.

IV. Calibration :

Bourdon gauges are calibrated using dead weight tester or by comparison calibration.

V. Advantages, Limitations, Applications :

Advantages :

1. Low cost and simple construction.
2. Wide pressure range.
3. High accuracy in relation to low cost.

Limitations :

1. Low spring gradient.
2. Susceptibility to shock and vibration.
3. Bourdon tube material possesses some hysteresis in a pressure cycle. Hysteresis can be kept minimum by proper heat treatment and by using proper materials.

3.4.2 Diaphragm Pressure Gauge

I. Principle :

When pressures are applied on either sides of the tight diaphragm, then it gets deflected. This deflection of the diaphragm is proportional to the differential pressure across it. Thus differential pressure across the diaphragm can be measured in terms of its deflection.

II. Construction and Working :

Diaphragm gauge uses metallic or non-metallic (slack) diaphragms alongwith the pointer mechanism shown in Fig. 3.10.

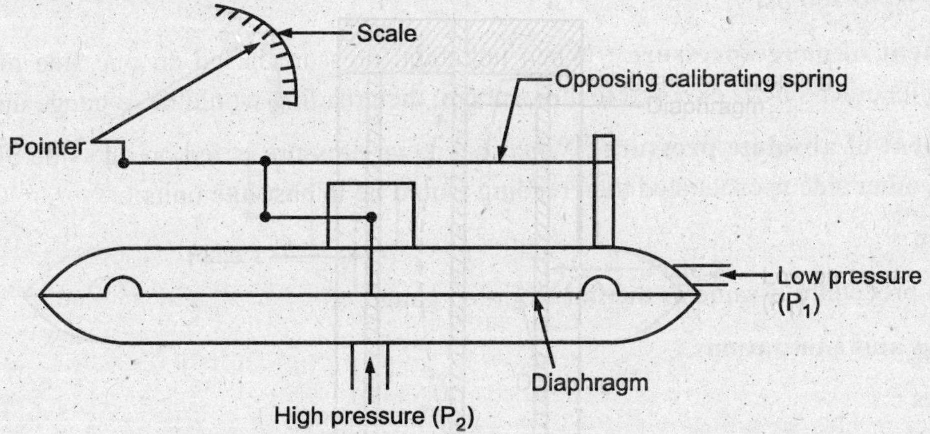

Fig. 3.10 : Diaphragm differential pressure gauge

1. Metallic diaphragms : These elements are flexible circular discs, either flat or corrugated. These elements convert pressure signal to pointer deflection.

The metal is heat-treated before forming a diaphragm to produce maximum elastic limit. After forming, the diaphragms are heat-treated to relieve internal stresses. A diaphragm is usually designed so that the deflection - versus - pressure characteristics are as linear as possible over a specified pressure range and with a minimum of hysteresis and minimum shift in the zero point. *Linearity* and *sensitivity* are determined to a great extent by the depth and number of corrugations and the angle of formation of the diaphragm face. The *sensitivity* can be increased by increasing the number of corrugations and by decreasing the depth of corrugations and with a sacrifice in linearity. The maximum sensitivity can be obtained by using flat, non-corrugated diaphragms. The diaphragm deflection with pressure is dependent on factors like diameter, metal thickness, shape of corrugations, number of corrugations, modulus of elasticity and applied pressure. The deflection varies with fourth power of diameter, hence if diameter is doubled, the deflection increases 16 times for a given pressure change. The diaphragm material should be chosen such that maximum deflection at the centre is one third of its thickness so as to keep material within elastic limit. *Diaphragm seals* are used to prevent the contact of process fluid with diaphragm which is necessary to :

(i) protect the corrosion and clogging of the diaphragm.

(ii) prevent the loss of explosive or hazardous process fluid in case of failure or replacement of the diaphragm.

Metals used are brass, phosphor-bronze, beryllium-copper, stainless steel.

2. Non-metallic or Slack diaphragms : These diaphragms are very flexible and hence they are used in low-pressure and vacuum gauges.

Materials used : Slack diaphragms are made from a variety of materials like synthetic rubber, neoprene, leather, teflon and elastomers reinforced by cotton, nylon or decron. The choice of material depends upon temperature and composition of the process fluid in contact with the diaphragm. The diaphragm deflection is opposed by a light spring.

Pressure range : For non-metallic diaphragm 0 to 10" H_2O :

Minimum – 0" to 2" of H_2O

Maximum – 0 to 400 psi.

Measurement of gauge pressure : When unknown pressure is fed on one side of the diaphragm and its other side is exposed to atmosphere, then reading would be in gauge units.

Measurement of absolute pressure : When unknown pressure is fed on one side of the diaphragm and other side is evacuated then reading would be in absolute units.

II. Calibration :

Calibration procedure is same as that for Bourdon gauge.

V. Advantages and Limitations :

Advantages :

1. Moderate cost and small size.
2. Corrosion resistant materials can be used.
3. Good linearity.
4. Can be used for pressurized slurries.

Limitations :

1. Lack of vibration resistance.
2. Suitable for relatively low pressure.
3. Troublesome repairing.

1.3 Capsule Pressure Gauge

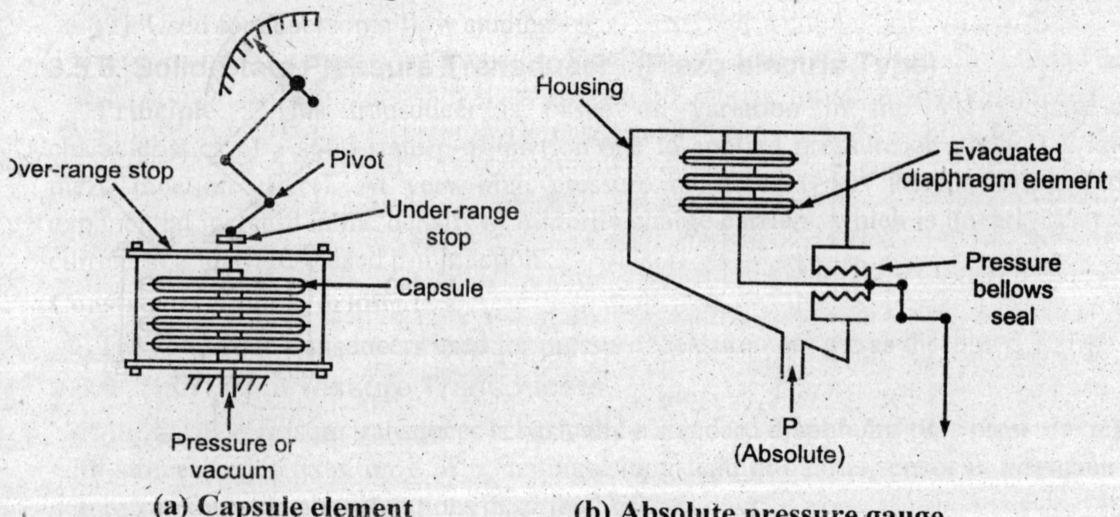

(a) Capsule element (b) Absolute pressure gauge

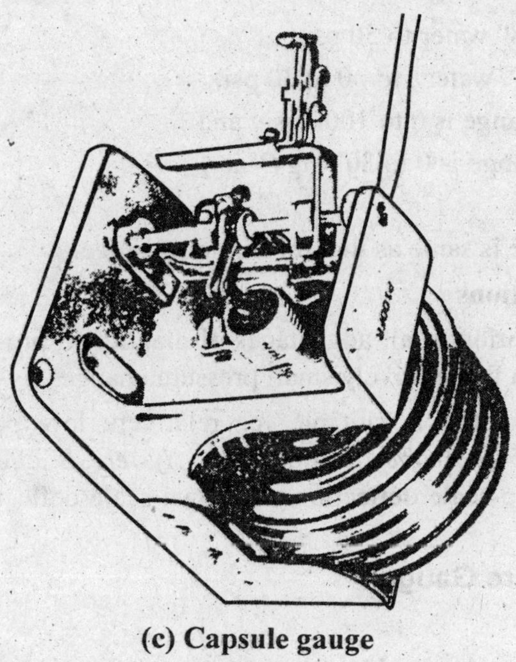

(c) Capsule gauge

Fig. 3.11

I. Principle :

The principle of capsule is same as that of the diaphragm element.

II. Construction and Working :

A capsule is formed by welding or soldering of two diaphragms at their periphery. Number of such capsules are arranged in the stack form as shown in Fig. 3.11. Pointer mechanism is connected to topmost capsule that represents pressure on the calibrated scale.

When pressure inside the first capsule changes, the free end of the last capsule in the stack gets deflected. This deflection depends upon : (i) diameter of the capsule, (ii) thickness of the material, (iii) elasticity of the diaphragm material, (iv) shape and number of corrugations on the diaphragm. The deflection versus pressure relationship is almost linear and any non-linearity can be compensated.

Measurement of gauge pressure or vacuum : Unknown pressure is fed inside the capsule, while its outside is exposed to atmosphere so that reading would be in gauge or vacuum units as shown in Fig. 3.11 (a).

Measurement of absolute pressure : Unknown pressure is fed outside the evacuated capsule so that reading would be in absolute units as shown in Fig. 3.11 (b).

Materia[illegible] used : Phosphor bronze, stainless steel, Ni–SPAN C (Nickel alloy).

Pressur[illegible]ge : The range depends upon number of capsules in the stack.

Phosph[illegible] capsule : 0 to 0.5" water to 0 to 30 psi.

Stainless steel : 0 to 8" water to 50 psi.

Ni – SPAN C : 0 to 4" water : to : 0 to 30 psi.

Maximum pressure range is 0 to 1000 psig and

Maximum vacuum range is 0 to 30" Hg (Vac.)

III. Calibration :

Calibration procedure is same as that for Bourdon gauge.

IV. Advantages, Limitations :

Advantages : In addition to all advantages of diaphragm pressure gauge, capsule gauge provides larger deflection for relatively small pressure changes.

Limitations : The gauge is suitable for relatively low pressures. The capsule has hysteresis effect of 0.25 to 0.5% of full scale. *Hysteresis effect* can be defined as the difference between the up-scale deflection and down-scale deflection, measured at the same applied pressure.

3.4.4 Bellows Pressure Gauge

I. Principle :

Bellows element is the elastic element which gets deflected at the free end when pressure is fed through fixed end. This free end deflection can be taken as the measure of pressure inside it.

II. Construction and Working :

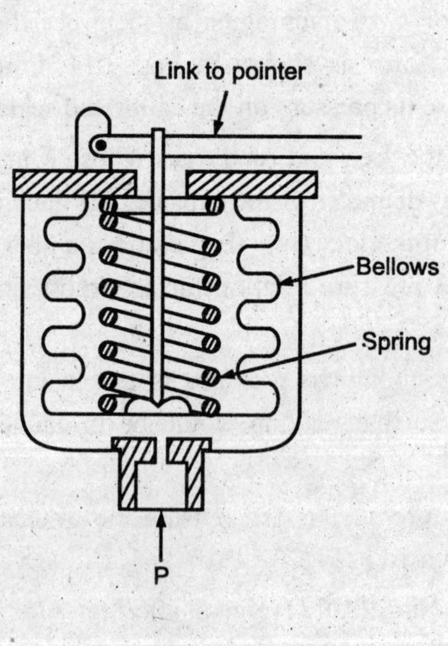

(a)

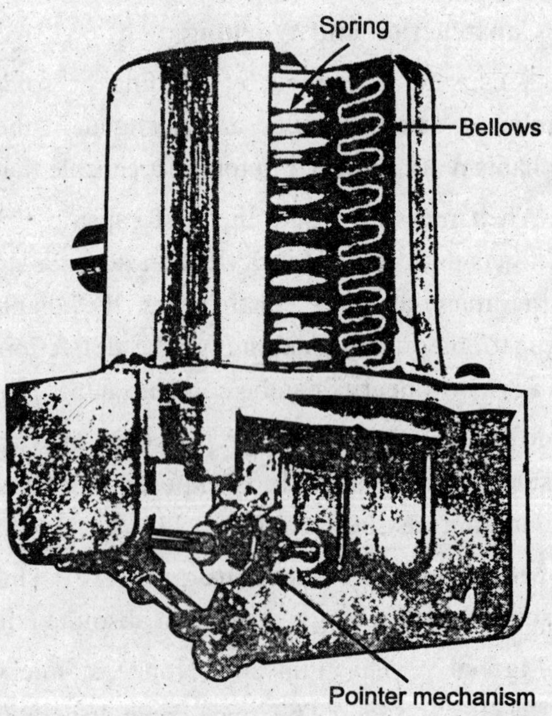

(b)

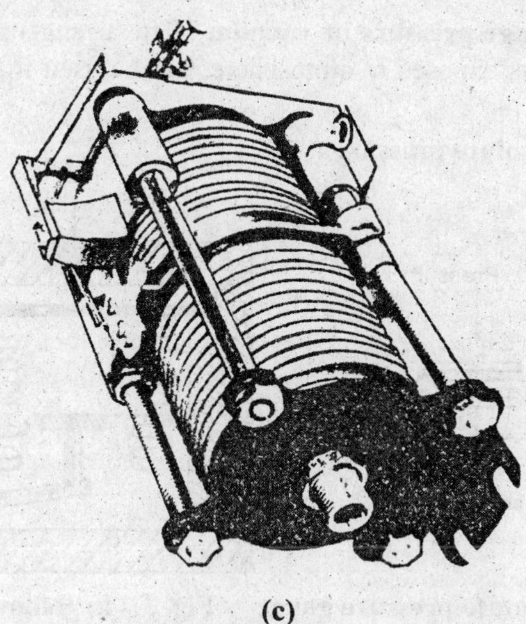

(c)

Fig. 3.12 : Bellows pressure gauge

A *bellows element* is a one-piece collapsible, seamless metallic unit having several convolutions or folds and it is formed from a very thin-walled tubing. Bellows can be considered to be made of capsules connected to each other. Bellows element is manufactured either by turning from a solid stock or by welding stamped annular rings. Bellows may also be manufactured by welding a series of formed plates together at their inner and outer diameters. The bellows element resembles the bulb of household kerosene pump. In *bellows pressure gauge* shown in Fig. 3.12 (a) metallic bellows are enclosed in a shell and bellows movement is opposed by the compression of the spring. A rod rests against the free end of the bellows which is connected to the pointer mechanism.

Materials used : Bellows are made of brass, phosphor bronze, beryllium, copper, monel, stainless steel. The choice of material depends upon pressure range and corrosion resistance.

Working : When pressure is fed inside the gauge, it acts on the outside of the bellows and bellows get compressed. Due to compression, free end of the bellows moves against the opposing force of the spring. This free end movement raises the rod resting against it, that transmits the movement to the pointer. This pointer deflection represents the pressure fed outside the bellows. The bellows movement for given pressure can be increased by increasing bellows diameter, while stroke length can be increased by increasing number of folds. The allowable stroke length should be within 10% of the maximum stroke so as not to exceed the elastic limit of the material. Bellows motion is restricted by the opposing spring. *Maximum pressure rating* for the bellows is the value of pressure that developes maximum allowable stress in given bellows. *Maximum stroke rating* for the bellows is the magnitude of stroke which developes the maximum allowable stress.

Measurement of gauge pressure or vacuum : The arrangement shown in Fig. 3.12 (a) with inside of the bellows exposed to atmosphere, can be used for measurement of pressure in gauge units.

Measurement of absolute pressure :

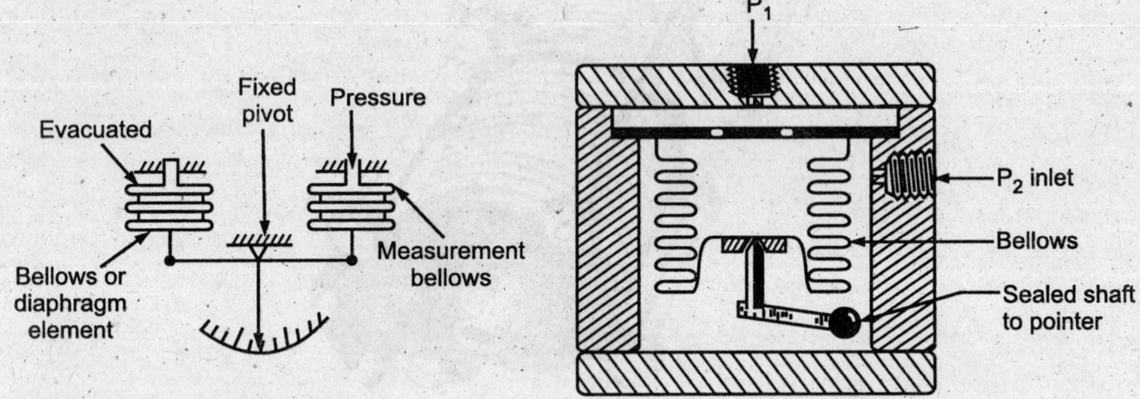

Fig. 3.13 : Bellows absolute pressure guage **Fig. 3.14 : Bellows differential pressure gauge**

For absolute pressure measurement, two-bellows system is used as shown in Fig. 3.13. One of the bellows is completely evacuated and acts in opposition to the measurement bellows. The pointer deflection represents absolute pressure inside the measurement bellows.

Bellows differential pressure gauge : One of the pressure is fed inside the bellows, while the other is fed outside it, so that the differential pressure acts across the bellows. The movement of the free end of the bellows represents the differential pressure. This deflection is communicated to the pointer through sealed shaft as shown in Fig. 3.14.

Pressure Ranges :

Gauge pressure – 0 to 2000 psig

Vacuum – 0 to 30" Hg vacuum.

Differential pressure – 0 to 50 psi at static pressures upto 2000 psig.

III. Calibration :

Calibration procedure is same as that for Bourdon gauge.

IV. Advantages, Limitations :

Advantages :

1. Moderate cost.
2. Adaptability for absolute and differential pressures.
3. Low to moderate pressure range.

Limitations :

1. Not suitable for high pressures.
2. Requires ambient temperature compensation.

3.5 ELECTRICAL PRESSURE TRANSDUCERS

In electricity, *transducer* is a device which converts any form of energy into proportional electrical signal. In pressure measurement with Bourdon, bellows or diaphragm elements, electrical output can be obtained by using transducer that converts mechanical displacement of the elastic element into electrical signal.

3.5.1 Resistance Type Transducer (Strain Gauge)

I. Principle :

Strain gauge consists of an elastic element and strain element attached to it. When pressure acting on elastic element changes, the strain element gets strained so that its length and cross-section area changes. Strain element being in the form of a fine metal wire, its electrical resistance changes with change in strain. This change in electrical resistance of strain element can be used for calibrating the instrument in terms of pressure.

II. Construction and Working :

1. Bellows electrical pressure gauge :

Fig. 3.15 shows bellows electrical pressure gauge using strain gauges. An unbonded strain gauge is connected to the bellows so that bellows displacement causes straining of the strain gauges. The terminals of the strain gauges are connected to one of the arms of the Wheatstone bridge circuit.

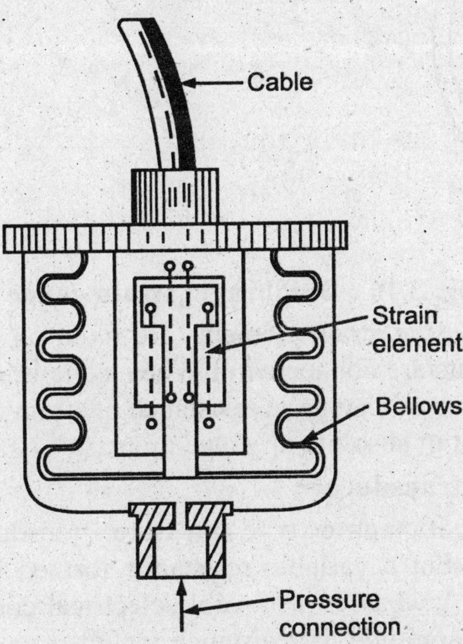

Fig. 3.15 : Bellows strain gauge

Working : As pressure acting against the bellows changes, bellows get compressed or expanded that causes straining of the strain elements. Strain element being a resistance element, its electrical resistance changes with strain produced. This change in resistance can be measured in terms of deflection of the galvanometer in the bridge circuit. Hence, galvanometer can be calibrated in terms of pressure.

Absolute pressure gauge : When bellows are evacuated, pressure reading would be in absolute units.

Gauge pressure or Vacuum measurement : When bellows are exposed to atmosphere, the pressure reading would be in gauge units.

Differential pressure measurement : When two pressures are fed on either sides of the bellows, pressure reading would correspond to differential pressure across the bellows.

2. Diaphragm strain gauge :

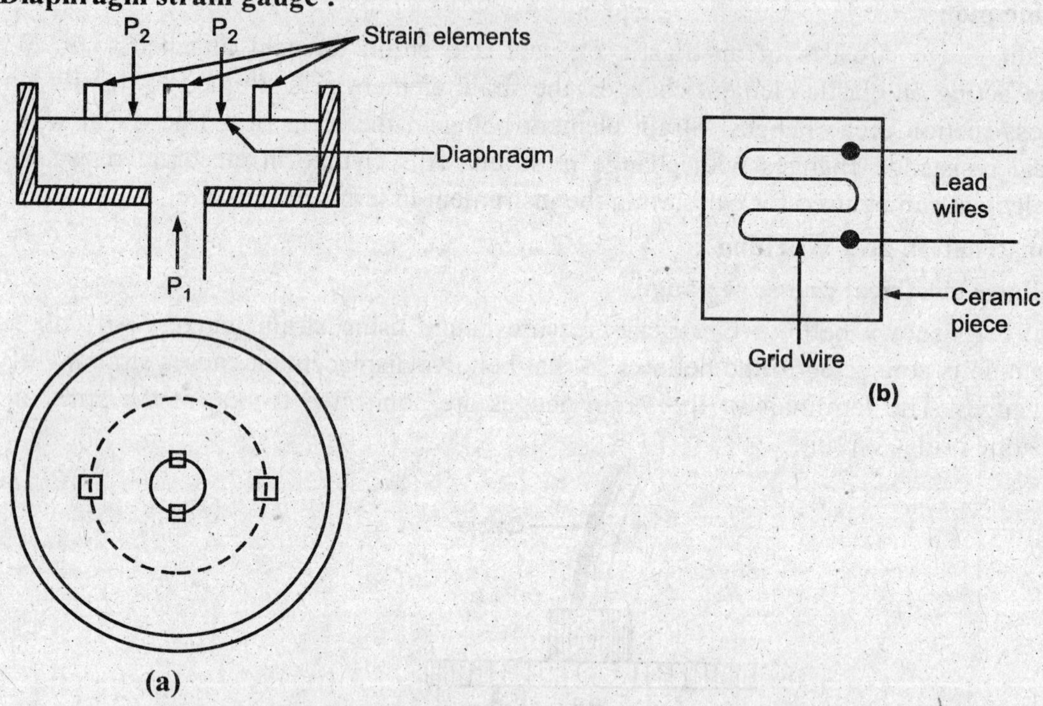

Fig. 3.16 : Diaphragm strain gauge

In diaphragm strain gauge, the strain elements are fixed on the diaphragm as shown in Fig. 3.16. These strain elements are connected in Wheatstone bridge circuit so as to measure the differential pressure in terms of change in resistance of strain elements. This gauge can be used for pressure measurement in absolute or gauge units.

3. Bourdon potentiometric transducer :

Fig. 3.17 shows a potentiometric type pressure transducer which consists of a *potentiometer* that is nothing but a variable resistance formed by winding resistance wire around an insulated cylinder. A *wiper* is a movable electrical contact whose position on the resistance wire decides the magnitude of resistance included in the circuit. Free end of the Bourdon tube is connected to the wiper through mechanical linkages.

Working : As pressure inside the Bourdon tube increases, its free end gets deflected. This free end deflection changes the position of wiper that changes the electrical resistance between terminals A and C shown in the figure. This change in resistance can be calibrated in terms of pressure using Wheatstone bridge circuit. Instead of Bourdon tube, bellows or diaphragm can also be used.

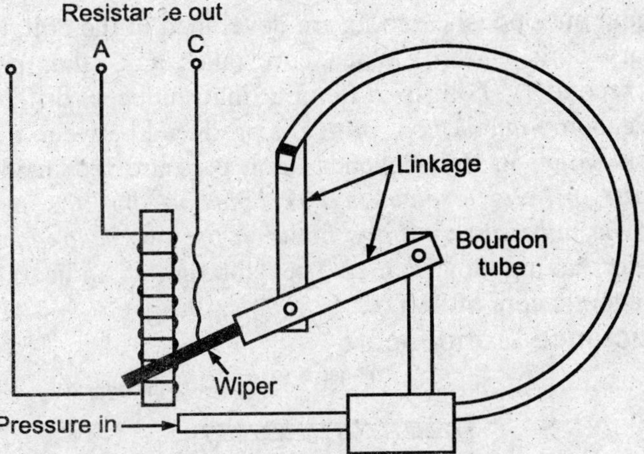

Fig. 3.17 : Bourdon potentiometric pressure transducer

3.5.2 Inductance Type Pressure Transducers

(LVDT – Linear Variable Differential Transformer)

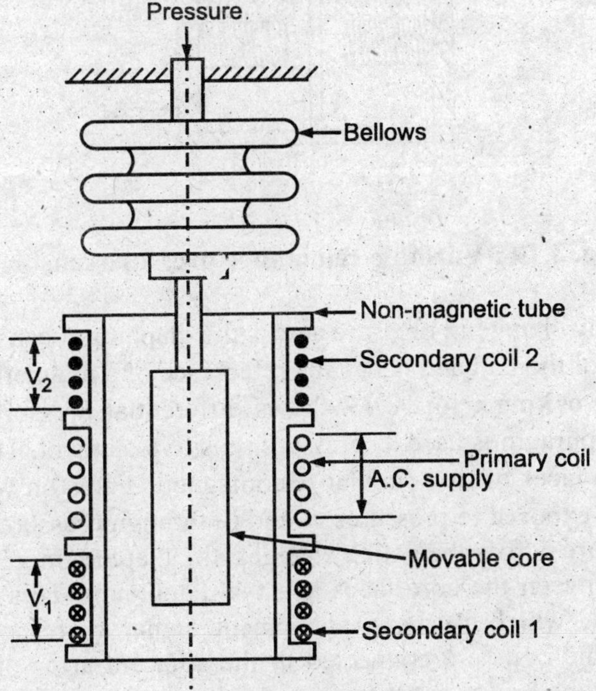

Fig. 3.18 : LVDT

LVDT consists of *three coils* wound on a single *non-magnetic tube*. There is one *primary coil* fed with a.c. supply and *two secondary coils*. A movable *ferromagnetic core* can move inside the coil. The deflection of elastic element like bellows is coupled with this movable core as shown in Fig. 3.18. When pressure inside the bellows changes, its free end gets deflected alongwith the movable core. When core is symmetrically positioned between two secondary coils, then magnetic coupling of the core with both the secondary coils is equal.

In this position the equal but opposite e.m.f.s are developed in the coil, hence the net voltage between two secondary coils is zero. When core takes any other position the magnetic coupling with each secondary coil is different, that induces different voltages in the secondary coils. Hence, some *unbalance voltage* is produced between two coils that depends upon the core position which in turn depends upon pressure fed inside the bellows. Thus *pressure acting against the elastic element like bourdon, bellows or diaphragm can be measured in terms of the unbalance voltage between the two secondaries.* By this method, enlarged leg manometer having float can be used for remote indication by coupling float movement with the magnetic core of LVDT.

3.5.3 Variable Reluctance Transducers

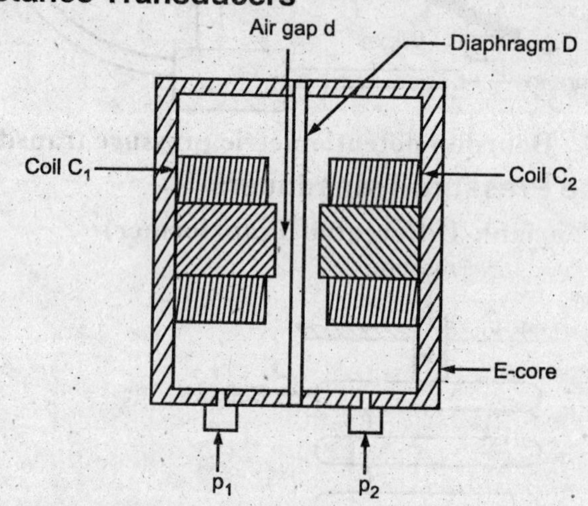

Fig. 3.19 : Variable reluctance pressure sensor

Principle :

In this instrument, any change in pressure across the diaphragm can be measured in terms of change in inductance of the coil and hence the reluctance of a magnetic path.

Construction and working : Fig. 3.19 shows differential pressure gauge in which an elastic ferromagnetic diaphragm is used as pressure sensitive element. This diaphragm acts as an armature between the faces of two circular ferromagnetic cores on which coils C_1 and C_2 are wound. The coils are exposed to pressures p_1 and p_2 through pressure ports.

As differential pressure across the gauge changes, the diaphragm gets deflected resulting in change in air gaps between the core faces and the diaphragm. This leads to a change in inductance of each coil, which is the measurement signal corresponding to change in differential pressure. If the coils are connected in the adjacent arms of an a.c. Wheatstone bridge, then the output of the bridge is proportional to the measurement signal.

Advantages and Limitations :

(1) Fast response due to absence of any mechanical linkages or loading of strain gauges on the diaphragm.

(2) High sensitivity.

(3) Rugged and insensitive to vibrations.

Application :

(1) Used for very low pressure measurements.

3.5.4 Variable Capacitance Type Transducers

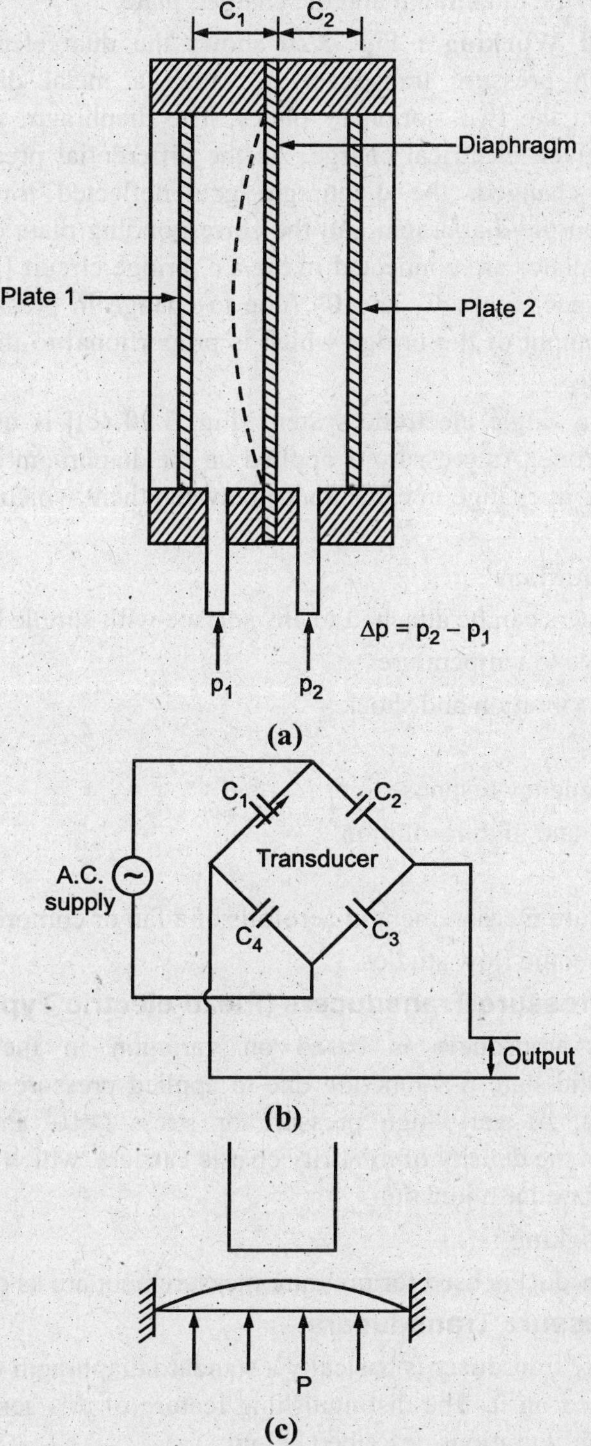

Fig. 3.20 : Variable capacitance type transducers

In this type, any change in pressure across the gauge can be measured in terms of change in capacitance between the diaphragm and the charged plate.

Construction and Working : Fig. 3.20 shows the dual electrode type capacitance arrangement in which pressure transducer in which a metal diaphragm is positioned symmetrically between the two stationary plates. The diaphragm is electrically grounded while the plates are given electrical charge. As the differential pressure ($p_2 - p_1$, $p_2 > p_1$) across the gauge is changed, the diaphragm gets deflected towards plate 1 and the capacitance C_1 between the diaphragm and the corresponding plate changes as compared to capacitance C_2. If the plates are connected in the a.c. bridge circuit [Refer Fig. 3.20 (b)] any unbalance between capacitances C_1 and C_2 (due to change in pressures p_1 and p_2) can be measured across the output of the bridge which is proportional to the change in differential pressure across the gauge.

In some designs, a single electrode system [Fig. 3.20 (c)] is used in which there is a single stationary electrode. As pressure is applied on the diaphragm it moves with respect to the electrode, resulting in change in capacitance between them which is taken as the measure of change in pressure.

Advantages and Limitations :

(1) These transducers can be attached to any surface with simple bondings.

(2) Highly sensitive to temperature.

(3) Susceptible to vibration and shock.

(4) Small size.

(5) Good high frequency response.

(6) Good linearity and high resolution.

Applications :

(1) Used for pressure measurement in aerofoils of a fan or compressor blade.

(2) Used for supersonic flow studies.

3.5.5 Solid-State Pressure Transducers (Piezo-electric Type)

Principle : This transducer is based on variation in the V-I (voltage-current) characteristics of a solid-state p-n junction due to applied pressure or stress (i.e. known as piezo junction effect). At very high pressure or stress ($>10^8$ Pa for silicon), there is exponential increase in the density of minority charge carriers, which is linearly related to the current in a forward-biased p-n junction.

Construction and Working :

The solid state transducers used for pressure measurement are as discussed below :

3.5.6 Thin Film Pressure Transducers

A thin film pressure transducer is basically a standard diaphragm type pressure transducer with strain gauges fixed on it. The distinguishing feature of this sensor is a special type of diaphragm material configurations described below.

(i) A diffused single crystal chemically milled monocrystalline silicon diaphragm with strain gauges laid down by diffusing boron onto the surface.

(ii) A dielectrically isolated thin film diaphragm on which the strain gauges are electro-formed using vapour deposition technique and photoresist techniques.

(iii) The force sensing beams are fabricated from a highly polished stainless steel wafer with an insulating layer of silicon dioxide deposited on its surface. Then a pressure sensitive polysilicone layer is added with gauge pattern etched on its surface.

Advantages and Limitations :

(i) High accuracy and long-term stability.

(ii) Low hysteresis.

(iii) Low production cost.

(iv) Can be used for measurement of absolute, gauge or differential pressures upto 200 bar.

3.5.7 Digital Pressure Transducer

Digital output signal can be obtained from thin film pressure transducers discussed earlier by incorporating intelligent signal processing features such as pre-amplification A/D converter and a microprocessor-controlled output processor as shown in Fig. 3.21. This is achieved using microminimisation based integrated circuit technology. The output of this transducer is in the range of 0 to ± 5 V or 4 to 20 mA which may be communicated to a digital display device.

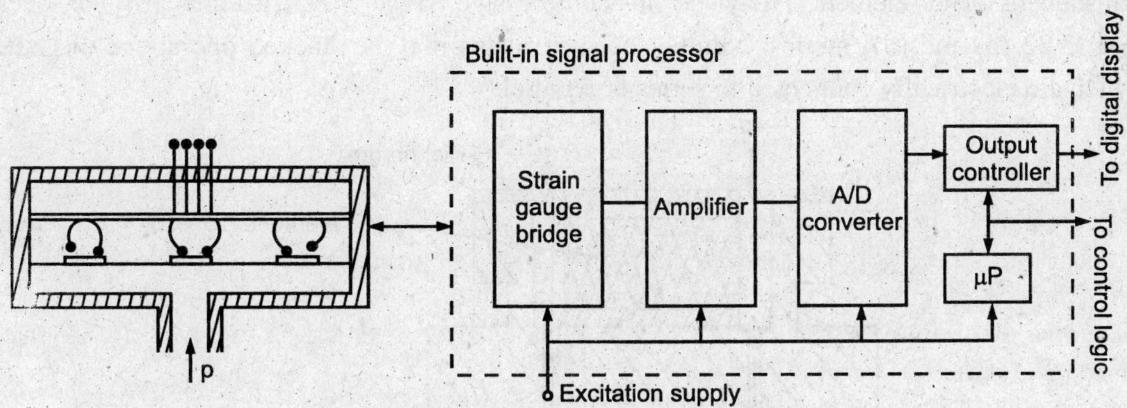

Fig. 3.21 : Digital pressure transducer

3.5.8 Piezoelectric Pressure Transducer (PZT)

When piezoelectric material like quartz is subjected to applied pressure (or stress), electrostatic charge or voltage is generated across the material for few seconds. This is known as piezoelectric effect which can be used for measurement of unknown pressure.

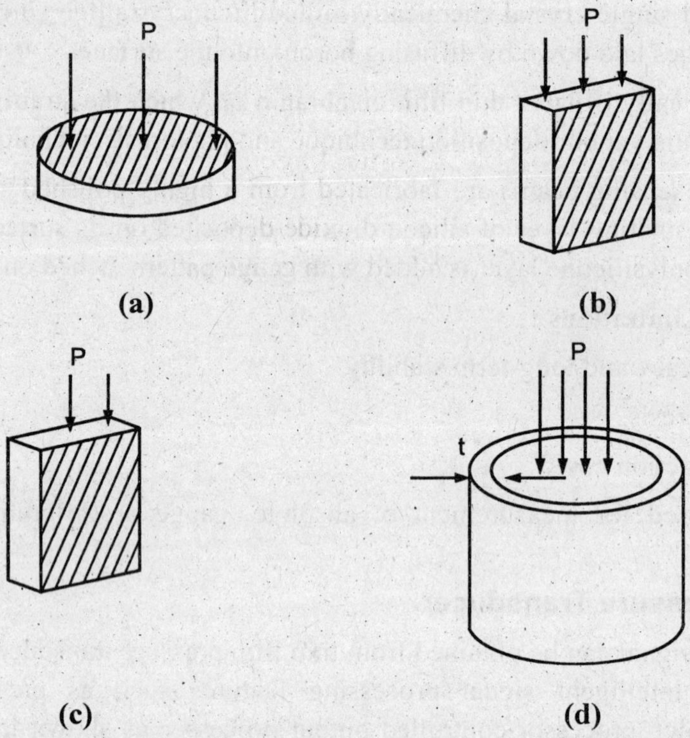

Fig. 3.22 : Piezoelectric elements configurations used in pressure transducers

Fig. 3.22 shows different configurations of piezoelectric elements used in pressure transducers. The elements may be in compressive [Fig. 3.22 (a) and (b)] or shear [Fig. 3.22 (c) and (d)] modes. Number of such plates may be stacked one above the other which are electrically connected in series or parallel.

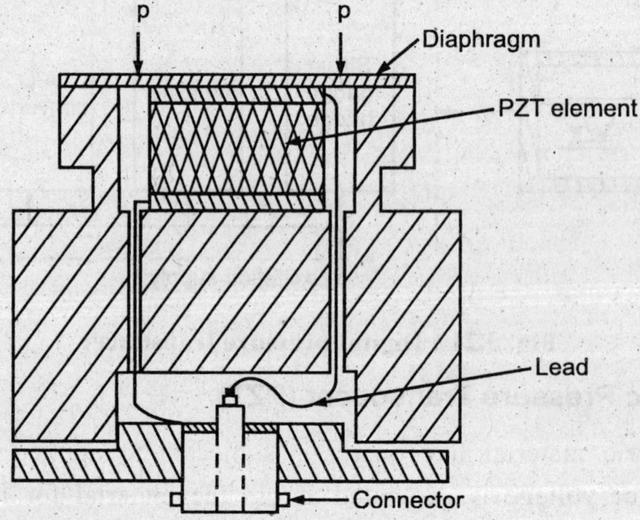

Fig. 3.23 : Piezoelectric pressure transducer (PZT)

Fig. 3.23 shows a PZT using compressive mode transducer element in bending mode bimorph construction. In thin arrangement, a PZT element has similar conducting plates on upper and lower sides, which are connected mechanically and electrically along their common surface. This design gives the largest value of the mode effectiveness which is the product of q_p (charge sensitivity) and f_o (natural frequency of vibration). This is because q_o increase by a factor equal to the number of plates and f_o decreases, thereby maintaining the value of the product ($q_p f_o$) constant.

Advantages and Limitations :

(i) Natural quartz elements are most stable having lower temperature sensitivity and high resistivity, which lead to large time constant.

(ii) The elements having the natural frequency of the order of 50 kHz provide flat frequency response from 1 Hz to 20 kHz. Therefore, these transducers are widely used for measurement of rapidly varying pressures and shock pressures.

(iii) Thcsc clements have small size, rugged construction and fast speed of response.

(iv) Quartz elements can be used over a wide temperature range of – 200°C to + 300°C.

(v) These transducers are used in aeronautics, pumps, turbines and acoustic applications.

(vi) These sensors cannot measure static pressures for more than few seconds, but they can measure dynamic pressures such as shock, vibration, etc.

3.5.9 Pressure Sensors with Vibrating Pressure-Sensitive Elements

Principle : It is observed that the natural resonant frequency of an elastic element like diaphragm changes as a function of the pressure applied on the diaphragm. Thus, applied pressure can be measured in terms of the resonant frequency of vibration of the diaphragm.

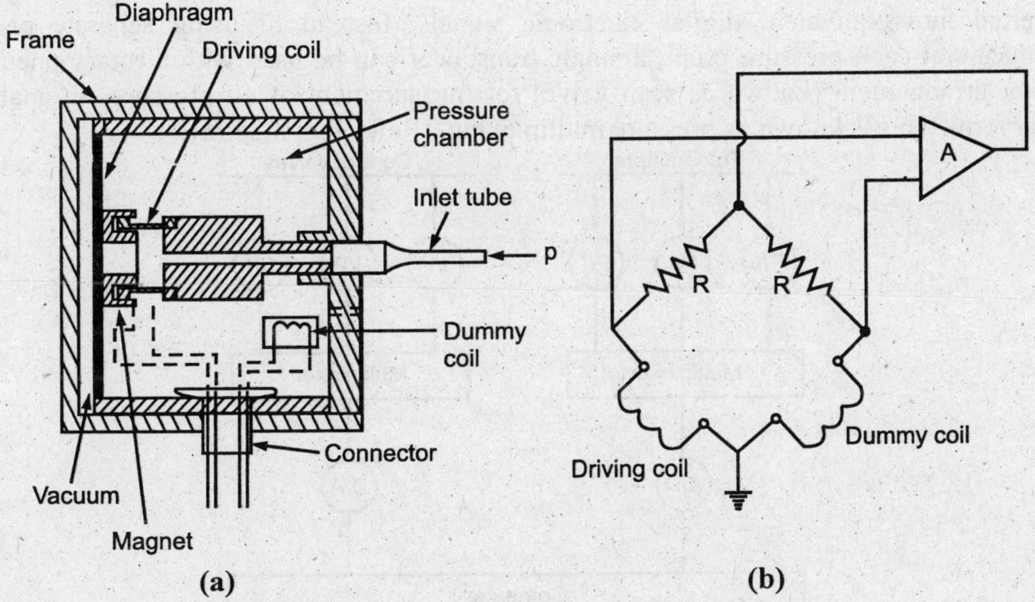

Fig. 3.24 : Vibrating element pressure sensor

Construction and Working : Fig. 3.24 (a) shows a pressure transducer in which the diaphragm assembly is attached to a sturdy frame which forms a perfectly sealed pressure chamber. The chamber volume between the outer cover and the diaphragm is evacuated for the absolute pressure measurement. A small magnet is attached to the centre of the diaphragm which is coupled to a driving coil suspended from a frame. A dummy coil having identical characteristics as that of the driving coil is also enclosed within the transducer housing. The driver coil and the dummy coil are connected to form a bridge circuit as shown in Fig. 3.24 (b) (i.e. amplifier-oscillator circuit), its pressure acts on the diaphragm through pressure tube, the diaphragm gets deflected with magnet moving inside or outside a driving coil. This results in change in inductance of the coil in proportion to the amount of metal (magnet) inside the coil. This causes unbalance in the bridge circuit and the unbalanced signal (i.e. output of the bridge) is amplified and fed back to the driving coil, that further excite the diaphragm so as to vibrate with its natural resonant frequency. The frequency of vibrations is then digitally counted and correlated with the corresponding pressure acting on the diaphragm. The natural frequency of vibrations of the diaphragm can be adjusted by adjusting the tension on the diaphragm.

Advantages and Limitations :

(i) High sensitivity, resolution, accuracy.

(ii) Good repeatability, stability.

(iii) Low hysteresis.

(iv) Inherently digital output which can be directly sent to a microprocessor.

(v) Sensitive to ambient temperature variations, shock and vibrations.

3.6 PRESSURE MULTIPLEXERS

In a pneumatically instrumented plant there are large number of analog pneumatic signals. In order to computerize such plants, these analog pneumatic signals must be converted into equivalent digital electronic signals. Instead of using separate pressure transducers at each pressure point, a single transducer can be used with a rotary pneumatic selector arrangement (known as scan valve) for measurement of all pressures in analog or digital form. This is known as pressure multiplexing. [Refer Fig. 3.25 (a)].

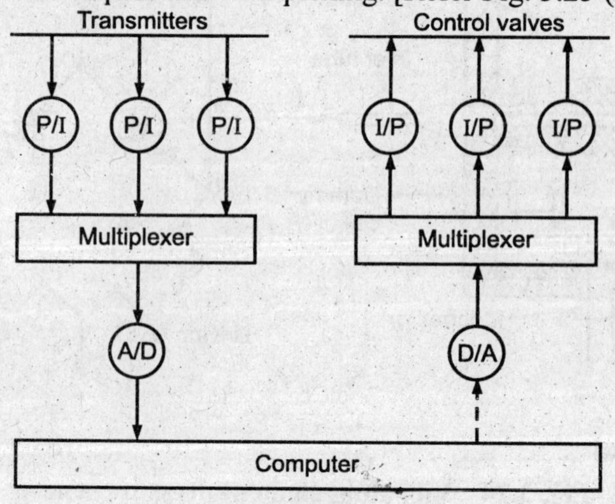

(a)

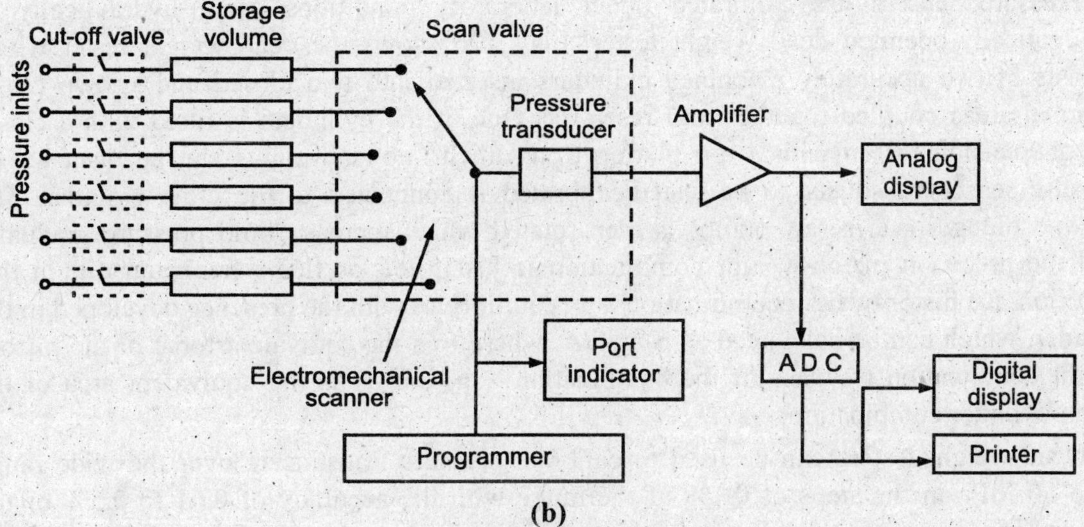

(b)

Fig. 3.25 : Pressure multiplexer

Fig. 3.25 (b) shows a rotary pneumatic selector (i.e. scan valve) with 24 or 48 ports, driven either by a motor or solenoid which connect the individual pressure signals to the common transducer at the middle through a small volume (of about 0.016 cm^3) of the rotating U-tube. This small volume of U-tube allows a scanning speed of upto 20 samples per second, but the scanning speed is limited to 6 samples per second to limit maintenance. The signal from a pressure transducer is processed with a suitable signal conditioner (i.e. P/I conversion followed by A/D conversion) into a digital signal sent to analog or digital display devices. The sampling time of a large number of signals can be increased by decreasing the number of ports per multiplexer.

This system is used for aeronautical measurements.

3.7 CALIBRATION OF PRESSURE SENSORS

1. Calibration using dead weight tester

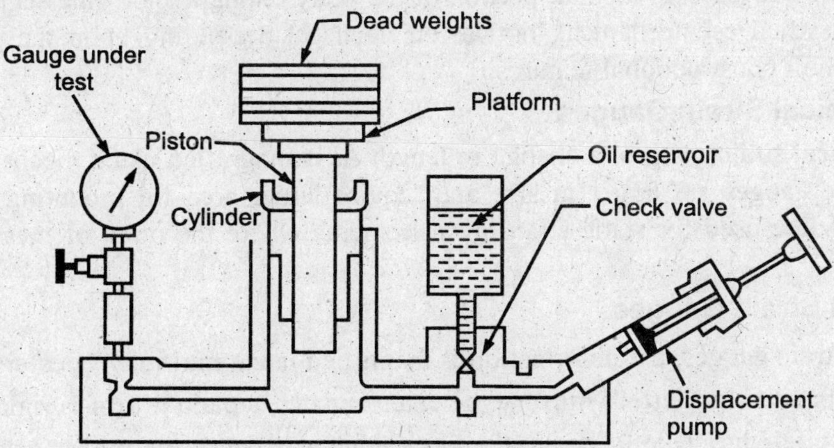

Fig. 3.26 : Dead weight pressure tester

Pressure sensors are calibrated under laboratory conditions using hydraulically or pneumatically-operated dead weight tester. Fig. 3.26 shows the dead weight tester which consists of two accurately machined cylinders inserted into two closed and known cross-sectional areas coupled together to a reservoir. One of the cylinders is fitted with a close-fitting precision piston with a top platform on which known weights can be placed. The pressure sensor/transducer to be tested/calibrated is connected to the other cylinder. The screwed plunger (i.e. screw pump) is then rotated which increase fluid pressure gradually until the precision piston-weight combination is just lifted or floats freely on oil. In this condition, the piston-weight combination is in equilibrium with the presence developed in the cylinder, which can be calculated as $p = F/A$, where F is the equivalent force of the piston-weight combination (= mass of the combination × g) and A is the equivalent area of the piston-cylinder combination.

Dead weight testers can be used to calibrate pressure transducers over the wide range 50 to 50 MPa in the steps of 0.1% of the range with the accuracy of 0.01 to 0.5% of the reading. The air-weight testers can give high accuracy of the order of 0.01%.

(2) Very low pressure transducers can be calibrated using standard mercury or water manometers in the range of few mm of water to 2 atm.

(3) The secondary standards used for calibration are Bourdon gauges and force-balance type pressure transducers which can achieve the accuracy of 0.05% F.S.

(4) The dynamic calibration of sensors may be done by subjecting it to fluctuating pressure (of frequency 100 Hz) created by an electrically driven vibrating piston or diaphragm in a closed chamber. Alternatively, a transducer may be subjected to a step change in pressure input generated with a shock tube having a rise time of 1 ms.

3.8 STRAIN MEASURING INSTRUMENTS (STRAIN GAUGES)

Strength of materials deals with checking the strength of machine components and structures in terms of stress (defined as force applied per unit area) and strain (defined as change in length Δl per unit original length l, i.e. $\Delta l/l$) produced. Strain gauges are used to measure strain produced over a small portion of the body, along a short line segment. Strain gauges are classified as mechanical, optical or electrical depending upon the principle of operation and their constructional features.

3.8.1 Mechanical Strain Gauges

In mechanical strain gauges, a change in length Δl is magnified using mechanical levers or gears. These gauges are larger in size and require larger area for mounting on the test specimen. They are used for static strain measurements where the point of measurement is accessible.

3.8.2 Optical Strain Gauges

In optical strain gauges, the deformation is magnified using multiple reflectors consisting of mirrors and prisms. In Martin's mirror-type extensometer, a plain mirror is rigidly attached to a movable knife edge. Due to stress, the knife edge and hence the mirror gets rotated so that reflected light beam gets rotated through twice the incident angle. These measurements are more accurate and independent of temperature variations.

3.8.3 Electrical Strain Gauges

In electrical strain gauges, their electrical properties such as resistance, capacitance or inductance change proportional to the strain acting on the gauge. Electrical strain gauges basically consists of a metal wire or foil which is bonded to the specimen so that both are subjected to same strain. Due to strain, resistance of the wire increases with tension and decreases with compression. This change in resistance can be accurately measured using Wheatstone bridge circuit and calibrated with the strain acting on the wire. The materials used for wires should have high specific resistance, low temperature coefficient of resistance (TCR), constant gauge factor $\left(\frac{\Delta R}{R} / \frac{\Delta l}{l}\right)$ and constant strain sensitivity over a wide range of strain values. The materials satisfying these properties are pure copper, iron, platinum or alloys such as Constantan Advance (45% Ni + 55% Cu), Nichrome (80% Ni + 20% Cr), Karma (74% Ni + 20% Cr + 3% Al + 3% Fe).

The strain gauges are classified based on the method of fabrication as wire-type and foil-type.

Wire-type strain gauges :

There are two types of wire-type strain gauges namely, bonded and unbonded.

In bonded gauges, the strain gauge is bonded directly to the surface of the specimen to be tested with a thin layer of adhesive cement which transmit the strain from the specimen to the gauge wires and also as an electrical insulator. In these gauges, long, thin metal wires are arranged in flat grid type, wrap around type, single wire type or woven-type as shown in Fig. 3.27.

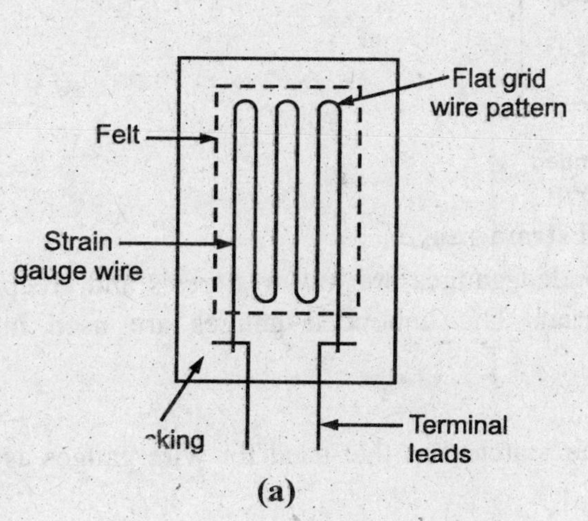

(a)

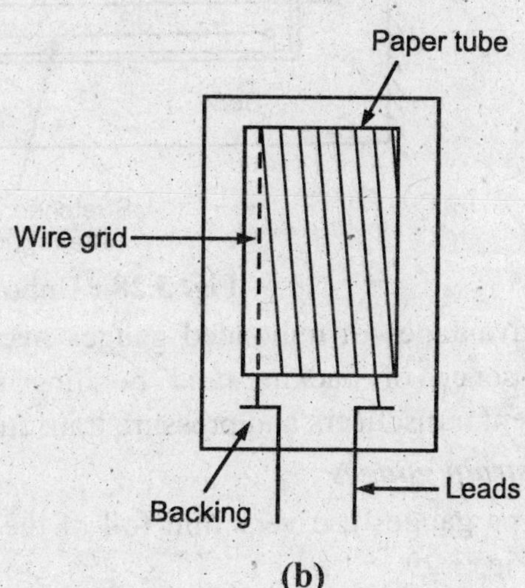

(b)

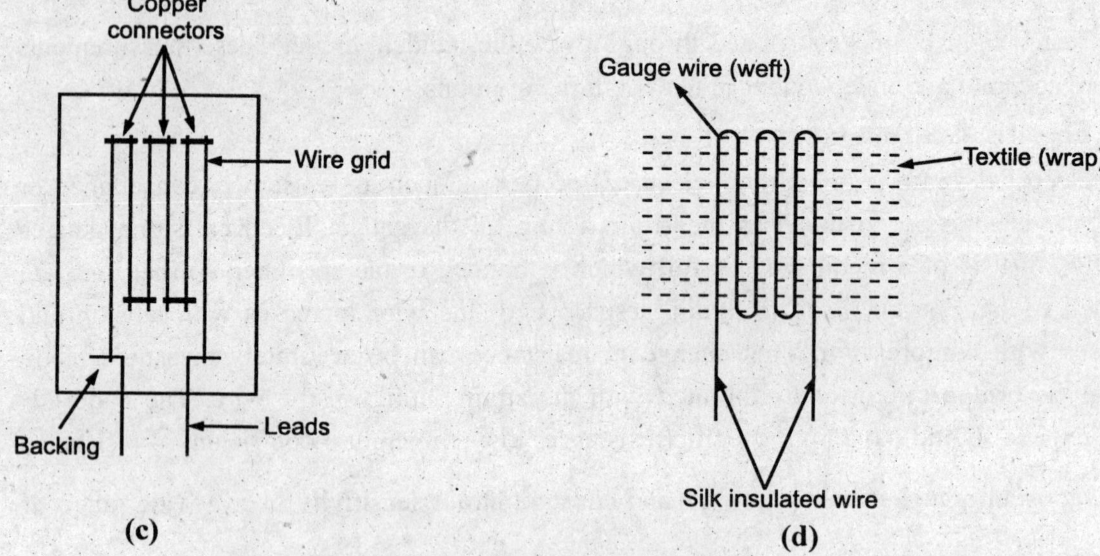

Fig. 3.27 : Bonded strain gauges

The current carrying capacity of the wire-type strain gauges is limited to 10 to 20 mA.

An unbonded strain gauge is basically a free filament-sensing element without any backing so that strain is transferred to the resistance wire directly. These gauges consist of number of loops of resistance wire wound between insulated pins, one of them attached to stationary frame and the other to a movable frame so that the winding gets strained under the applied stress. (Refer Fig. 3.28)

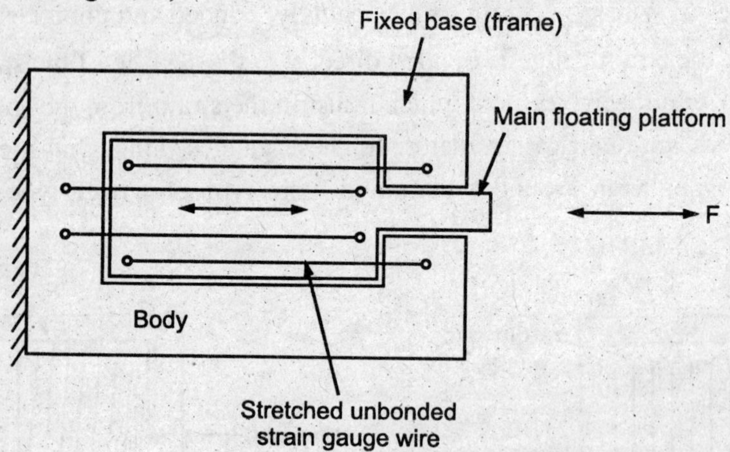

Fig. 3.28 : Unbonded strain gauge

The advantages of unbonded gauges over bonded gauges are low hysteresis and creep due to absence of backing and bonding material. The unbonded gauges are used in displacement transducers and pressure transducers.

Foil-type strain gauges :

Foil-type gauges use very thin foil of the same material as that used for wire gauges as shown in Fig. 3.29.

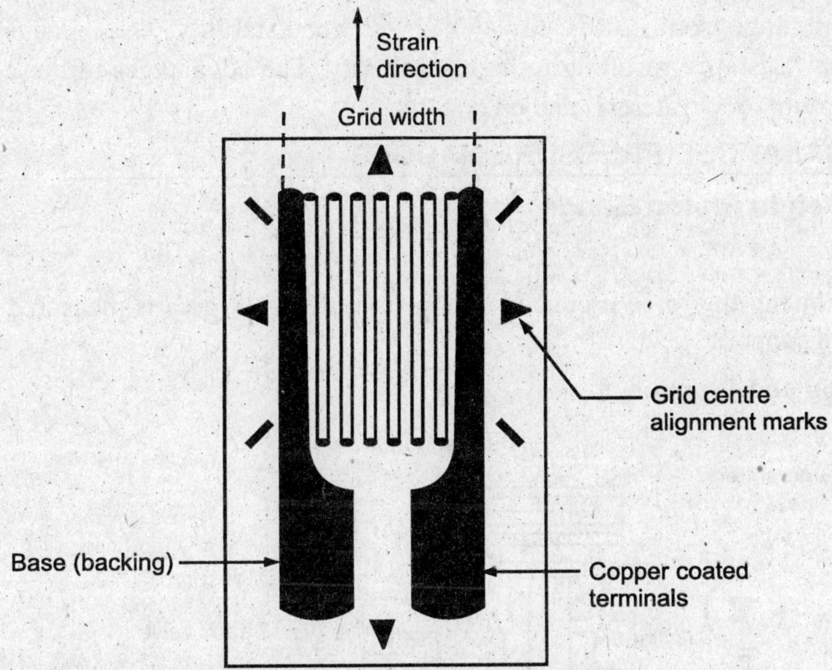

Fig. 3.29 : Foil-type strain gauge

The foil gauge elements have large surface area to area of cross-section ratio and hence higher heat dissipation capability resulting in better thermal stability. In these type of gauges, complex patterns of small sizes can be fabricated using photo-chemical etching process.

Semiconductor Strain Gauges :

Semiconductor strain gauges are fabricated from single crystals of semiconductor materials such as doped silicon and germanium. The strain sensitivity of semiconductor gauges is mainly due to resistivity changes rather than dimensional changes in wire-type strain gauges. This is known as piezo-resistive property which gives high gauge factor of 100 to 140 so that change in resistance due to strain is 40 to 100 times more than that of wire-type gauges. The advantages of these gauges are high gauge factor, chemical inertness, no hysteresis and creep effects, longer fatigue life. The resistivity of semiconductor materials depend on the degree of doping of impurity atoms into pure germanium or silicon. The p-type silicon gives positive gauge factor while n-type silicon gives negative gauge factor elements. Therefore, when p-n junction is used as strain gauge, it forms bridge circuit with two active arms at one location itself. The temperature changes affect the resistance and sensitivity of the gauge. The maximum permissible safe current in these gauges is about 30 mA for 120 ohm gauge on account of heat-dissipation capability to the test specimen.

Thin film-type strain gauges :

Thin films of metals as aluminium, gold, nickel, platinum are formed in desired patterns on a substrate by thermal evaporation technique and then thin substrate is attached to the test specimen by the same technique as that for wire gauges. These gauges can operate over a wide temperature range from –200°C to +400°C with good stability. These gauges have high gauge factor and resistance resulting in high sensitivity. The advantages of these gauges are rugged construction, low hysteresis and creep.

3.9 FORCE BALANCED PRESSURE GAUGES

3.9.1 Dead-Weight Piston Gauge

I. Principle :

In this instrument, the force produced on a piston of known area is measured directly by the weight it will support.

II. Construction and Working :

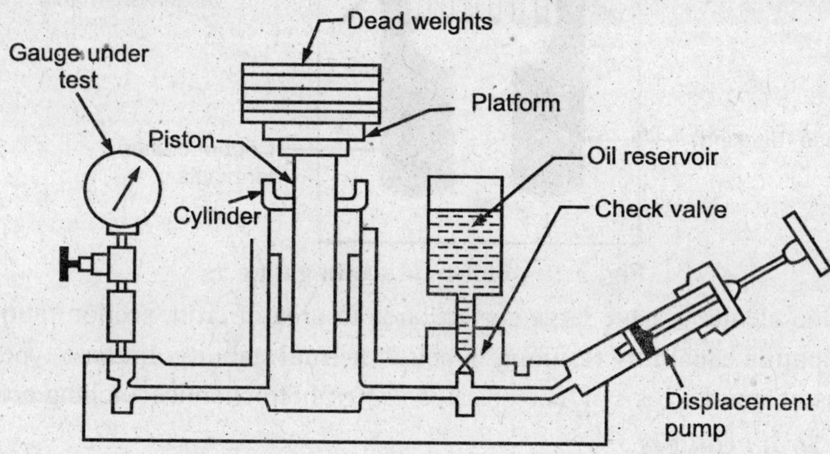

Fig. 3.30 : Dead-weight piston gauge

The gauge consists of well machined and bored *cylinder* having finished *piston* inserted in it. At the top of the piston there is *platform* on which standard, known weights can be placed. *An oil reservoir* with a check valve at its bottom is provided. *Displacement pump* is fitted as shown in Fig. 3.30 that is used to suck the oil from reservoir on upward stroke and pressurize the oil on downward stroke.

Working : Dead-weight gauge is mostly used for calibrating elastic element pressure gauges. The gauge to be calibrated or tested is fitted as shown in Fig. 3.30. A standard known weight is applied on the platform, that pressurizes the oil into pressure gauge. The screw pump is rotated to lift the piston-weight assembly so as to float freely on the oil surface. Now pressure exerted by the weights on the oil can be calculated by force divided by cross-section area of the piston. This pressure is used for calibrating the pressure gauge. Oxygen pressure gauges should not be tested with oil because, if oil enters inside the gauge, then oil vapour may form explosive mixture with oxygen. To avoid this oxygen pressure gauges are tested with water or air in dead weight gauge for pressures upto 300 psig.

3.9.2 Ring Balance Gauge

I. Principle

This gauge measures the differential pressure across the gauge by force balance principle.

II. Construction and Working :

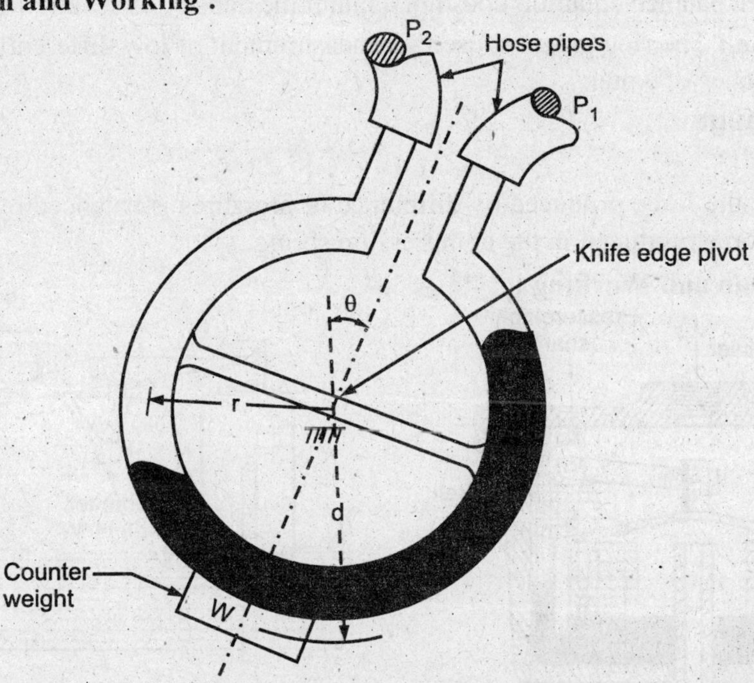

Fig. 3.31 : Ring balance gauge

The ring gauge consists of a hollow ring of circular section supported near its centre by a knife-edge pivot. The ring is divided into two parts by a partition and it is partially filled with suitable manometric liquid. The ring may be made of metal or plastic depending upon the nature of pressure fluid. Counterweight is attached at the bottom of the ring and it is assumed that the centre of gravity of the ring itself without weight is at the pivot.

Working : When pressures p_1 and p_2 are fed through the pressure hoses, the net force due to differential pressure causes rotation of the ring about pivot. The rotation continues until this driving force is balanced by the counterweight so that force due to liquid in both the partitions is same, hence the name *force-balance device*. This rotation of the ring is transferred to an indicating or recording device through linkages, that indicates differential pressure across the ring. The force-balance equation can be written as :

$$p_2 - p_1 = \frac{dW \sin\theta}{rA}$$

where,

d = radial distance of counterweight from pivot

W = counterweight

θ = angle through which counterweight gets deflected

r = average radius of the tube

A = cross-sectional area of the tube

Even though ring gauge resembles manometer, it cannot be considered as manometer in true sense because

1. It does not have two separate arms or legs.
2. Pressure balance equation does not contain the density of sealing liquid.

Application : The ring gauge is used for measurement of low differential pressures of the order of few inches of water.

3.9.3 Bell Gauge

I. Principle :

In this type the force produced by difference of pressures is balanced by the weight of the bell or by the force produced in the compression spring.

II. Construction and Working :

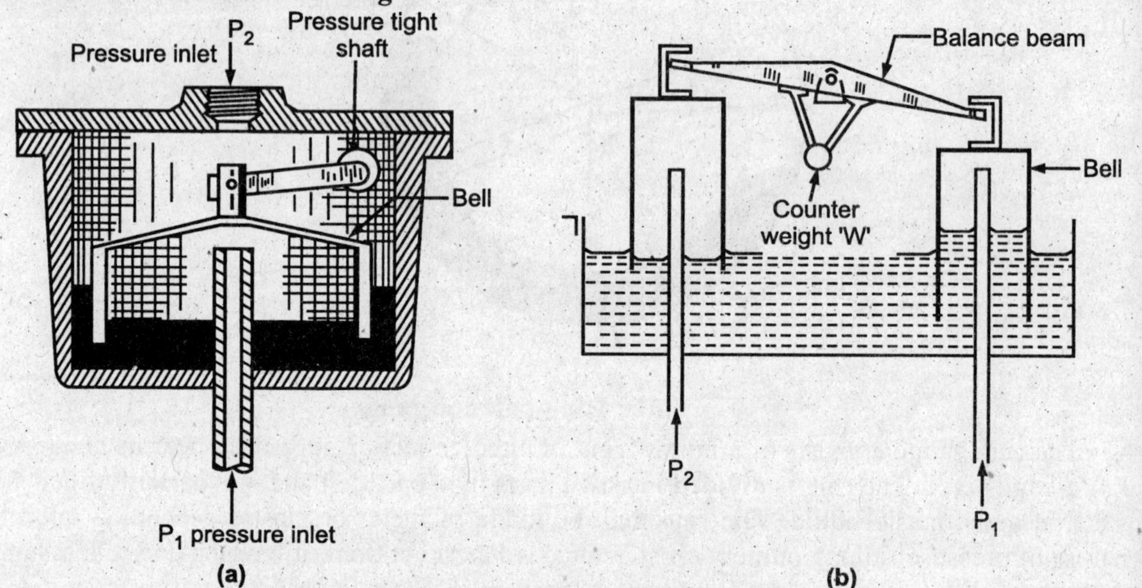

Fig. 3.32 : Bell differential pressure gauge

The gauge consists of a *bell* suspended in a sealed chamber with its open end downwards. The chamber contains liquid such as oil or mercury. The open end of the bell is immersed in the liquid, that forms two separate sealed chambers. The higher pressure P_1 is fed inside and lower pressure P_2 is fed outside the bell as shown in Fig. 3.32 (a). Due to differential pressure $(P_1 - P_2)$, the force acts on the bell due to which bell rises in the liquid. Bell rises until equilibrium is reached between the net upward force and the apparent weight of the bell. Since the pressure inside the bell is higher than pressure outside it, the liquid level outside the bell is higher than that inside the bell. As bell rises in the liquid, its portion immersed in the liquid decreases, that reduces the buoyant upthrust of the liquid on the bell, which ultimately increases the apparent weight of the bell. Thus force due to differential pressure is balanced by increase in apparent weight of the bell. The bell movement is proportional to differential pressure $(P_1 - P_2)$, hence it is communicated to indicator or recording pen by a sealed shaft.

Fig. 3.32 (b) shows alternative arrangement employing two light metal bells supported on a beam pivoted on a knife edge alongwith the counterweight. When pressures are fed inside the bells the beam gets deflected at the pivot and this deflection is used to indicate differential pressure.

Pressure range : Differential pressure of 0.25 to 15 inches water at static pressure of 600 to 800 psig.

3.10 DIFFERENTIAL PRESSURE MEASUREMENT

We have already discussed following differential pressure gauges :

1. Manometers.
2. Bellows gauge.
3. Diaphragm gauge.
4. Capsule gauge.
5. Electrical strain gauge.
6. Ring balance gauge.
7. Bell gauge.

3.11 VACUUM MEASUREMENT

We have discussed following vacuum gauges :

1. Manometer.
2. Bourdon gauge.
3. Bellows gauge.
4. Diaphragm gauge.

3.12 PROTECTION OF PRESSURE GAUGES

(A) High temperature protection : While reading steam pressure, the temperature rise of elastic element should be restricted. This can be obtained by using Siphon arrangement as shown in Fig. 3.33. It consists of brass coil, coiled as shown in Fig. 3.33. Due to this arrangement steam condensate is trapped which helps to reduce the temperature of the pressure gauge.

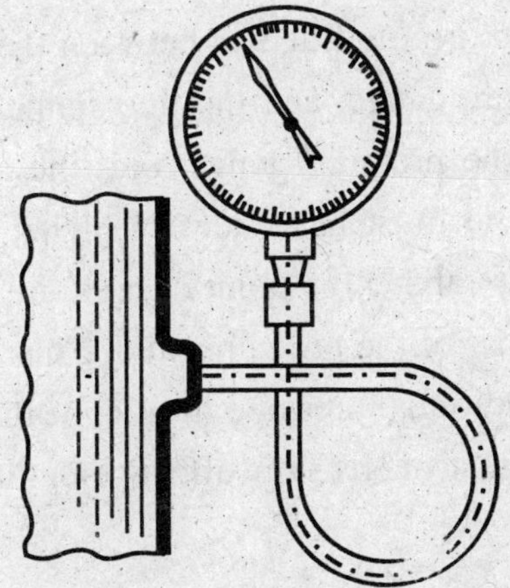

Fig. 3.33 : Siphon arrangement

(B) Protection from hazards due to contact of process fluid and pressure sensitive element (sealing techniques) :

1. Diaphragm seal :

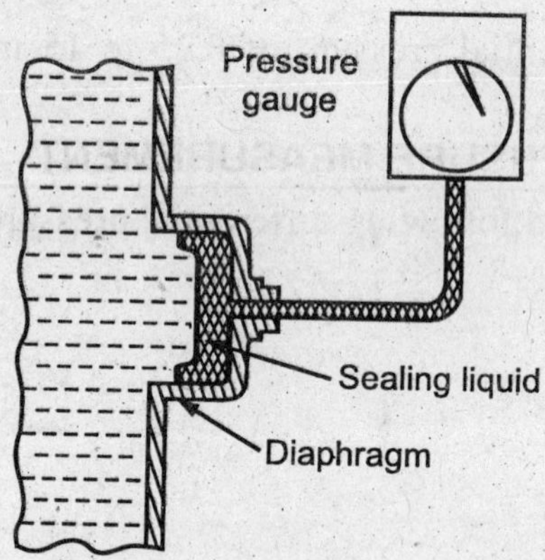

Fig. 3.34 : Diaphragm seal

In this arrangement, a thin *metallic or neoprene diaphragm* having large area is fitted inside the bronze or cast iron unit. The system is filled by a sealing liquid like glycerine or oil. The diaphragm should be quite flexible so that pressures on either sides of the diaphragm would become equal. Sealing liquid just transmits the process fluid pressure to the pressure gauge without actual contact with the elastic element of pressure gauge. This prevents the likely damage of elastic element in the pressure gauge from corrosion, high temperature effect etc. Due to this arrangement, pressure gauge is always filled with clean sealing liquid that prevents clogging of pressure gauges which otherwise may happen due to solids in process fluid. Instead of diaphragm, bellows can also be used.

2. Liquid seal :

A *seal pot* of bronze or cast iron is fitted in between the point of pressure measurement and pressure gauge. The pressure gauge, and the line connecting to seal pot is solidly filled with a suitable liquid. When the pressure gauge and line are below the point of pressure measurement, then sealing liquid must have density higher than that of the pressure fluid. If the pressure gauge and line are above the point of pressure measurement, the sealing liquid must have density lower than that of the pressure fluid. This is necessary for getting constant calibration correction for the additional pressure head of sealing liquid. This method prevents any exposure of pressure gauge to corrosion effect, clogging effect and high-temperature problems.

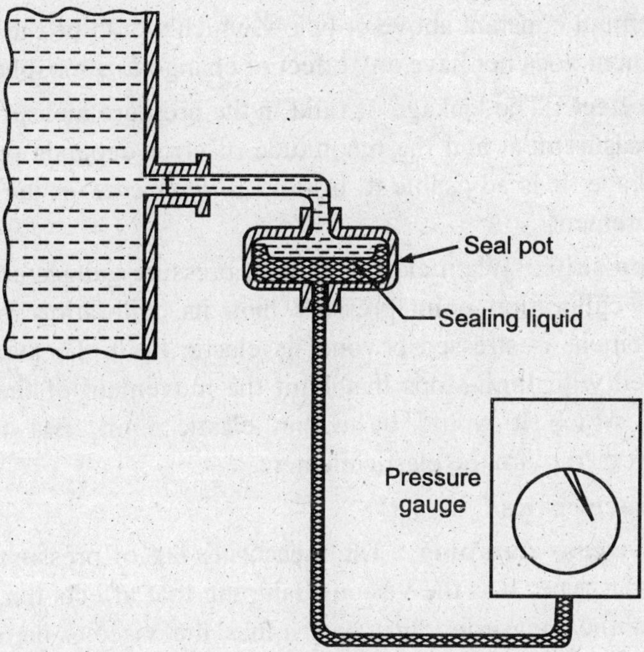

Fig. 3.35 : Liquid seal

3.13 PERFORMANCE CHARACTERISTICS OF PRESSURE GAUGES

(A) Static Characteristics :

Accuracy : The accuracy of the simple dial-indicating pressure gauge when calibrated with a dead weight tester is usually ± 1% of span, while the recording type gauges are generally accurate to ± 0.5% of span.

Source of static error :

1. **Ambient temperature effect :**

(a) Manometers : Ambient temperature rise causes cubical expansion of manometric liquid that affects the calibration. This effect is negligible if ambient temperature changes are less than 30°F

(b) Elastic element pressure gauges : Ambient temperature change may cause linear expansion of the element and change in temperature coefficient, Young's modulus of elasticity of the elastic element. This results in zero shift and span shift of calibration. If the change in elastic modulus with temperature is about 1% per 75°F, then compensation is not required.

2. **Head effect :** The liquid column in the gauge line between point of pressure measurement and the pressure gauge, exerts certain pressure head on the gauge. This head must be considered while calibrating the gauge.

3. **Barometric effect :** The effect of changes in Barometric pressure depends upon the application of pressure measurement. In case of measuring draft pressure, atmospheric

pressure should remain constant above or below which would be the draft pressure. Absolute pressure measurement does not have any effect of change in atmospheric pressure.

4. Leakage effect : The leakage of fluid in the pressure measuring lines introduce error in the pressure measurement and the magnitude of error depends upon the size of the line. To detect any leakage, it is advisable to install a *shutoff cock* in the measuring line close to the point of measurement.

5. Calibration shift : When elastic element pressure gauges are subjected to pressures above the highest calibration point pressure then its calibration may get shifted. This is because elastic element is stressed beyond its elastic limit. To avoid this, pressure gauge element is provided with limit-stops that limit the movement of the elastic element within certain range for which it would be within elastic limit. But too high pressure may permanently distort or rupture the elastic element.

(B) Dynamic characteristics :

1. Effect of viscous damping : The measuring lag of pressure gauges can usually be considered first-order type. It is the viscous damping that affects the speed of response. The length and size of the measuring line determines the viscous damping effect.. Since the viscosity of gases is much lower than that of most liquids, liquid-filled lines should be larger in diameter for a given length than gas-filled lines. When measuring lines are over 50 ft. in length, it increases the lag because of damping and the inertia of liquid.

2. Effect of frequency of pressure variation : The ordinary mechanical pressure gauge is not suitable for measuring rapidly fluctuating pressures such as impact pressures, supersonic air-flow pressures etc. This is because the natural frequency of these gauge elements is very low about 1 per sec. to 0.2 per sec. Electric pressure gauge can be used at frequencies upto 3000 cycles per sec because its mass is small and spring gradient is high.

If pressure frequency matches with the natural frequency of gauge, then *resonance* occurs and gauge starts vibrating with maximum amplitude. To avoid this effect, it is necessary to dampen or slow down the pulsations before they reach the pressure gauge. Shock waves due to water hammer in liquid–filled lines can be absorbed by installing an air trap in the line.

3.14 COMPARISON OF PRESSURE SENSORS

Sr. No.	Element	Local	Remote	Range	Process contact	Relative cost	Accuracy % span
1.	Manometers	✓	✓	0.15 H_2O to 60 psig	✓	low	± 0.1 to 1
2	Bourdon	✓	✓	15 psi to 1,00,000 psi	✓	low	± 0.5 to 15
3.	Diaphragm	✓	✓	0 to 50 psi	✓	medium	± 0.5
4.	Bellows	✓	✓	0 to 3,000 psi	✓	medium	± 0.5 tol
5.	Strain gauge	×	✓	2,00,000 psig	×	high	± 1

SOLVED PROBLEMS

Problem 3.1 : *Express pressure of 1.5 bar into units of : (i) MN/cm^2, (ii) Pa, (iii) psi, (iv) cm of Hg, (v) m of H_2O.*

Solution : (i)

$$1.5 \text{ bar} = 1.5 \text{ kg/cm}^2 = 15 \text{ N/cm}^2 = 15 \times 10^{-6} \text{ MN/cm}^2$$

(ii)

$$1.5 \text{ bar} = 1.5 \text{ kg/cm}^2 = 15 \text{ N/cm}^2 = 15 \times 10^4 \text{ N/m}^2 = 15 \times 10^4 \text{ Pa} = 150 \text{ kPa}$$

(iii)

$$1.5 \text{ bar} = 1.5 \text{ kg/cm}^2 = 150 \text{ kPa}$$

but

$$6.9 \text{ kPa} = 1 \text{ psi}$$

$$\therefore \quad 150 \text{ kPa} = \mathbf{21.73 \text{ psi}}$$

(iv)

$$p = h\rho$$

$$p = 1.5 \text{ bar} = 1.5 \times 10^3 \text{ gm/cm}^2$$

$$\rho = \text{density of Hg} = 13.6 \text{ gm/cm}^3$$

$$h = \frac{p}{\rho} = \frac{1.5 \times 10^3}{13.6} = \mathbf{110.29 \text{ cm}}$$

(v)

$$p = h\rho$$

$$h = \frac{p}{\rho} = \frac{1.5 \times 10^3}{1} = 1.5 \times 10^3 \text{ cm} = 1500 \text{ cm} = \mathbf{1.5 \text{ m } H_2O}$$

Problem 3.2 : *Express pressure of 1000 mm of mercury in kPa.*

Solution :

$$p = h\rho = 100 \times 13.6 = 1360 \text{ gm/cm}^2 = 1.36 \text{ kg/cm}^2 = 1.36 \times 10^4 \text{ kg/m}^2 = 1.36 \times 10^4 \text{ Pa} = \mathbf{13.6 \text{ kPa}}$$

EXERCISE

1. List various units of pressure used in practice.
2. Describe three different pressure scales.
3. State relation between :
   (a) absolute pressure and gauge pressure.
   (b) gauge pressure and vacuum.
4. Describe Barometer.
5. Describe with the help of neat figures :
   (a) U-tube manometer,
   (b) enlarged leg manometer,
   (c) well manometer,
   (d) inclined leg manometer.

   Write static balance equation for each manometer.

6. How will you measure absolute pressure and gauge pressure with the help of liquid manometer ?
7. What are the advantages of inclined leg manometer ?
8. List the desirable properties of manometric liquid.
9. State the sources of error in manometer pressure measurement.
10. Describe Bourdon pressure gauge.
11. How will you measure gauge pressure and absolute pressure with Bourdon gauge ?
12. Describe diaphragm pressure gauge.
13. Give reason : If diameter of the metallic diaphragm is doubled, then for given pressure, its deflection increases 16 times.
14. Describe Bellows pressure gauge.
15. List the factors which decide the deflection of diaphragm with pressure.
16. Describe two bellows system for absolute pressure measurement.
17. Describe various electrical pressure transducers.
18. How will you get electrical output from Bourdon, bellows and diaphragm pressure gauges ?
19. Describe the working of LVDT.
20. Describe force-balance pressure measuring devices.
21. Describe working of bell gauge.
22. List various gauges used for differential pressure measurement and vacuum measurement.
23. How will you protect the pressure gauge from high temperature process fluid ?
24. Describe sealing techniques used with pressure gauges.
25. Describe the factors that introduce static error in the pressure measurement.
26. Describe the factors affecting speed of response of the pressure gauges.
27. Why liquid-filled gauge lines should be larger in diameter than gas-filled lines ?
28. What is resonance effect in pressure gauge ?
29. Compare different pressure gauges.
30. If pressure of 60 psi is applied to one side of mercury manometer and pressure of 65 psi to its other side, calculate the resultant difference in heights of mercury column on the two sides. **(Ans.** 12.55 cm)
31. A mercury manometer attached at the bottom of a water tank with other end open to the atmosphere shows a reading of 36.5 mm. Calculate height of water level inside the tank. **(Ans.** 5.9 cm)
32. A mercury manometer has its one arm open to the atmosphere and the other connected to a chamber. It records a level difference of 55 cm of mercury with higher level in the arm open to atmosphere. Find absolute pressure in the chamber in bar. **(Ans.** 2.74 bar)

4

CHAPTER

LEVEL MEASURING INSTRUMENTS

4.1 INTRODUCTION

In many industrial processes, liquid level measurements are made to infer the quantity of liquid stored in a container or a vessel. Liquid level measurement and/or control is important because it affects both pressure and rate of flow of liquid flowing in and out of the container. In this chapter, we study the direct and indirect methods of measurement of level of liquids and solids.

Applications of Level Measurement

(Importance or Necessity of Level Measurement)

1. It is necessary to measure and frequently control the level of material contained in storage and processing vessels such as tanks, wells, reservoirs, bins, hoppers.
2. In many processes involving liquids contained in vessels such as distillation columns, reboilers, evaporators, crystallizers, the particular liquid level is highly essential for efficient process operation. Too high level in these vessels may upset reaction equilibrium, damage the equipment or cause spillage of valuable process material. Too low level also has bad consequences.
3. Correct level control reduces the storage capacity of continuous processing plant, that reduces the initial cost of the equipment.
4. In steam or vapour generators, such as boiler, the liquid level must be maintained accurately at a predetermined height irrespective of load variations in the process.
5. In evaporators, the tubes must carry heating medium liquid upto optimum depth. Too low level decreases the efficiency of the unit while too high level may require greater heat input.
6. If level measurement and control are used, the size of mixing or reaction vessel may be small.
7. It is necessary to maintain the liquid level in the storage tank from which a centrifugal pump is pumping liquid. If the level becomes too low, flashing or cavitation may occur.
8. In industries like textile manufacturing product quality depends upon correct liquid level. Variation in sizing solution level destroys warp uniformity and may cause breakage of threads on the loom.
9. The data of correct levels of liquid raw materials and finished products is essential for cost accounting of the plant.

4.2 LEVEL MEASUREMENT METHODS (Classification of Level Measuring Methods)

(A) Direct Methods :

1. **Based on direct visual observation :**

(a) gauge stick

(b) hook gauge

(c) gauge glass.

2. **Based on determining the position of detecting member which rides on material surface :**

(a) float gauges.

3. **Buoyancy methods :**

(a) float gauges

(b) displacer gauges.

(B) Indirect or Inferential Methods :

1. **Based on the hydrostatic head developed by liquid :**

(a) pressure gauge method

(b) air-trap method

(c) diaphragm box method.

(d) air or gas purge method.

(e) differential pressure method.

2. Based on attenuation of radioactive radiations.

3. Based on utilization of electrical properties like capacitance, conductance and resistivity that depend upon level.

4. Based on reflection of waves from the liquid surface.

4.3 DIRECT LEVEL MEASUREMENT

In these methods, level of liquid is directly measured on the scale. Direct methods use varying liquid level as the means of level measurement.

4.3.1 Point Contact Methods

In these methods, the liquid surface is contacted by means of certain element and corresponding reading is taken.

1. **Hook gauge :**

Construction : Hook gauge consists of about 1/4 inch diameter wire bent into a U-shape with one arm longer than the other as shown in Fig. 4.1. The shorter arm is pointed with 60° taper, while the longer arm is attached to a slider having a vernier scale which moves over a main scale and indicates the level.

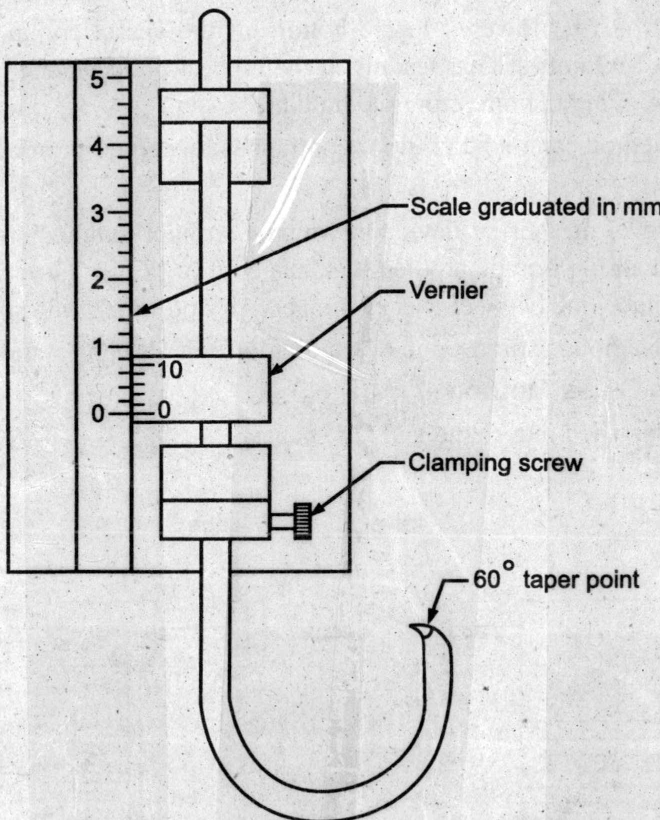

Fig. 4.1 : Hook level gauge

Working : In this method, the hook is pushed below the liquid surface and gradually raised until the taper point is just about to break through the surface. In this position it is clamped and level reading is taken on the scale. This method is useful for measuring liquid level in open tanks.

2. Bob and tape method :

Construction : In this method, a bob or weight is suspended from a tape marked in cm or m.

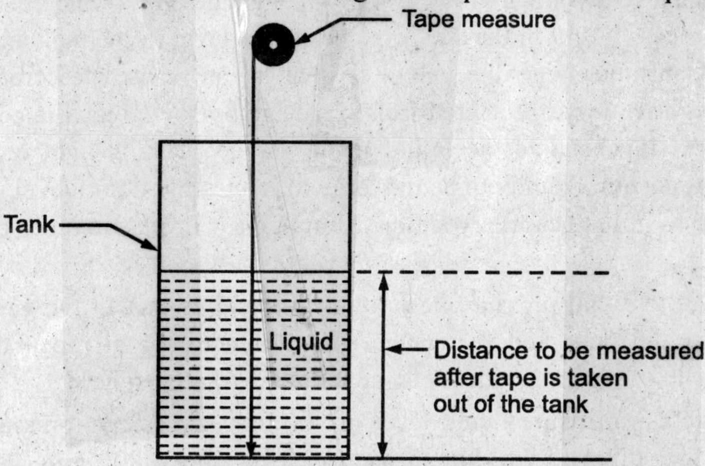

Fig. 4.2 : Bob and tape method

Working : The bob is first lowered to the bottom of the vessel containing liquid and the liquid level is determined by noting tape reading at the highest point reached by the liquid. This reading is noted after removing the tape from the liquid.

Limitation : This method cannot be used for continuous level measurement.

3. **Dip stick :**

This is very crude level measuring device in which a straight notched stick is lowered upto the bottom of vessel containing liquid and then it is taken out of liquid. Then reading on the stick is noted against the interface line between wet portion and dry portion of the stick.

Application : This method is still used in transportation vehicles and stationary engines.

4.3.2 Sight or Gauge Glass Method

Gauge glasses are classified into round and flat shapes.

(A) Tubular gauge glass :

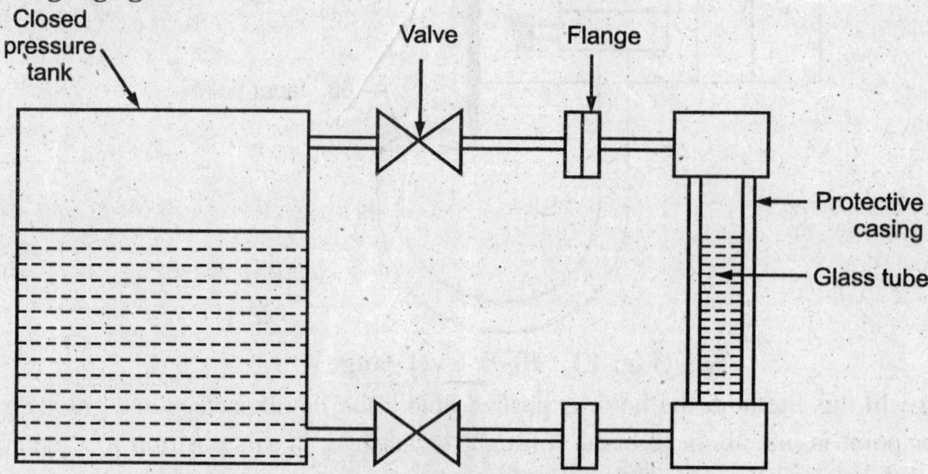

Fig. 4.3 : Tubular gauge glass for closed tanks

Construction and Working : A graduated tubular glass tube is mounted on the side of the vessel by coupling flanges as shown in Fig. 4.3. The gauge glass can be considered as a manometer in which process liquid in the tank assumes same level in the tank and the glass tube. Gauge glass is usually installed with the valves so that it can be isolated from the vessel for repairing purpose. The glass tube is protected from breakage by some metallic covering around it having a slit or window to visualize the liquid level. Gauge glass is light coloured for clear visibility. Gauge glass diameter should not be too large to reduce the liquid level in the tank and it should not be too small to initiate capillary action. Simple glass or plastic tubes can be used upto 450 psi and 400°F.

Working : When differential pressure in the tank is same as that in the gauge glass, liquid occupies same level in the tank and the gauge glass. Hence, for an open tank exposed to atmosphere, the upper end of the gauge glass can be left open to atmosphere.

Range : This gauge can measure liquid level of 900 mm upto steam pressure of 350 psi at 250°C and liquid pressure of 1000 psi. For measuring level above 900 mm, gauge glasses are provided at different levels.

(B) Flat glass gauges :

There are two types of flat glass gauges :

1. Reflex type : In reflex type level gauge, the gauge glass has 90° prismatic grooves running lengthwise on the inside face. When light ray falls normal to the glass plate, it strikes the prism at 45°. If liquid is not in contact with the prism, the incident ray has to cross glass-air interface for which the critical angle is 42°. Since critical angle of 42° for glass-air interface is less than that angle of incidence of 45°, the *total internal reflection takes place*, due to which the portion of gauge glass that does not contain any liquid appears shiny or *silvery white*. On the other hand, when liquid is in contact with the prism, the incident ray has to cross glass-liquid interface for which the critical angle is 62°. Since this critical angle of 62° is greater than angle of incidence of 45°, *total internal reflection does not take place* and light ray passes through the liquid. This enables us to see the inside of the chamber which is usually painted black. Due to this even though liquid inside the gauge is colourless, the liquid portion appears black from which liquid level can be read out.

Limitations :

(a) This gauge does not permit observation of the colour of liquid or an interface between the two liquids.

(b) The method is suitable for clean liquids upto pressure of 260 kg/cm^2 and 400°C.

(c) The method is not suitable for liquid which boils or condenses in the gauge glass.

2. Transparent type : The construction of transparent level gauge is similar to that of the reflex type except that glass has no prisms on it. Transparent gauge can be used for direct observation of interface between the two liquids.

4.3.3 Buoyancy Methods

Principle : These methods use the Archimede's Buoyancy Principle which states that body immersed in a fluid gets buoyed up or it experiences upthrust whose magnitude equals the weight of the fluid displaced. These methods use either floating or partially submerged or fully submerged elements.

(A) Float level gauges :

Construction and Working : Float gauges use the principle of a buoyant member which floats on the liquid surface and it raises or lowers with the liquid level. The float displacement can be taken as the measure of change in liquid level. Fig. 4.4 shows different methods by which *float* displacement can be transferred to an indicating pointer. All these gauges use a spherical float which is us made of metal like nickel plated copper. Float is made with a sloping top so as to avoid any s osition, that otherwise may change its weight.

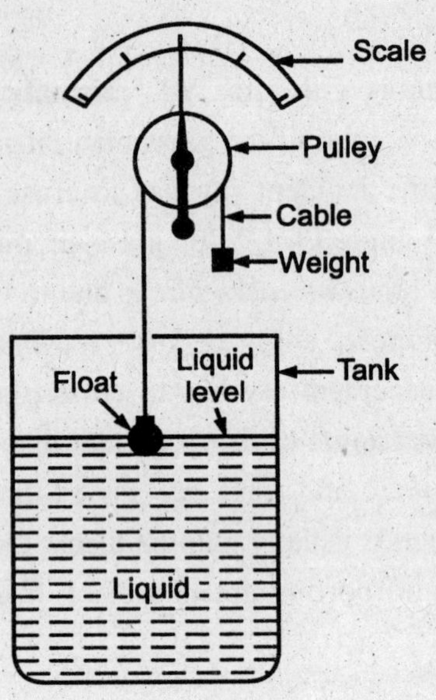

(a) Float and tape gauge

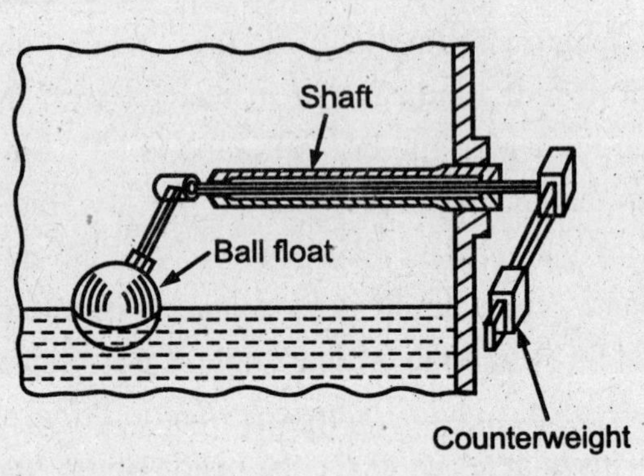

(b) Float and shaft gauge

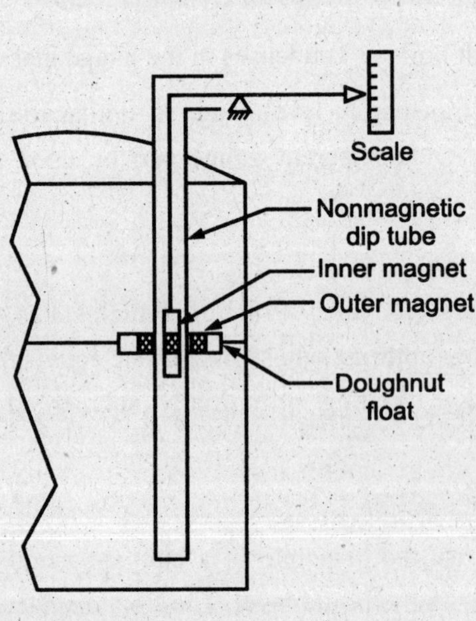

(c) Magnetic float gauge

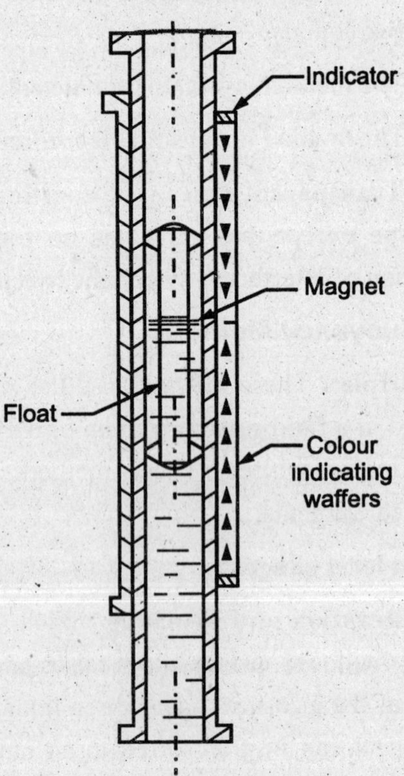

(d) Magnetic level indicator

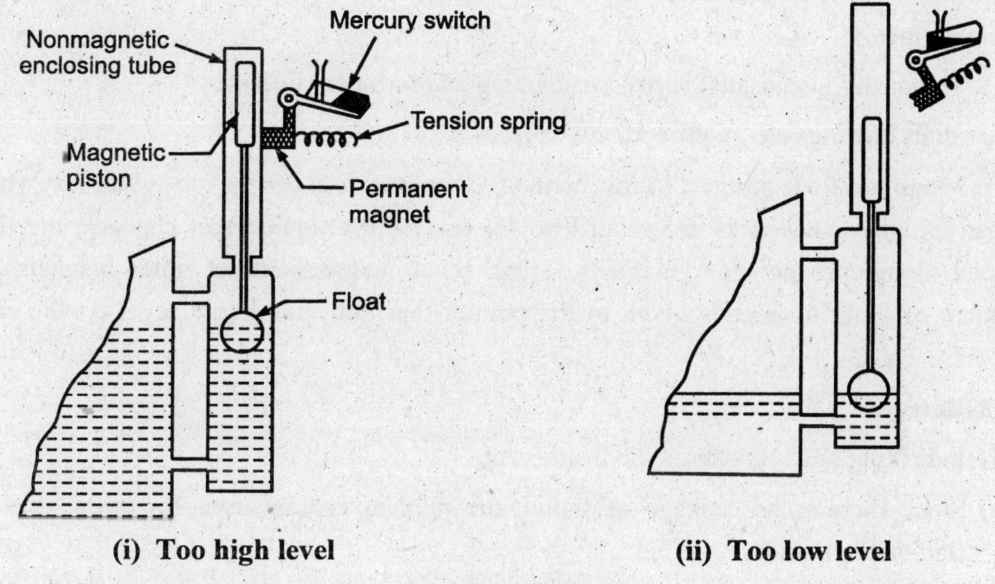

(i) Too high level **(ii) Too low level**

(e) Level switch

Fig. 4.4 : Float gauges

1. Float and tape method : In float and tape method shown in Fig. 4.4 (a), float is attached to a flexible, light-weight *tape* or *chain* which is wound around a drum or *pulley* to which the *pointer* is connected. *Counterweight* is connected to other end of the tape. As liquid level changes, float rises or falls that causes rotation of the drum and pointer. Pointer indicates liquid level on the calibrated scale.

Range : This method is suitable for measuring levels between 4 inches to 60 feet.

Limitation : The method is not suitable for getting remote level indication.

2. Float and shaft method : In this method, float is connected to the shaft and shaft is fitted with a *stuffing box* to provide sealing effect. At the other end of the shaft, adjustable *counterweight* is attached as shown in Fig. 4.4 (b). Counterweight is so adjusted that float remains half-submerged in the liquid. This is necessary because when spherical float is half-submerged, it has sufficient power to overcome bearing friction. As the liquid level changes, float gets displaced that results in rotation of the shaft. Shaft rotations are indicated by the pointer in terms of level of liquid.

Range : Level changes between 10 to 20 inches.

Advantages :

(a) Suitable for level measurement in open or closed pressure vessels upto 1000 psi and 750°F.

(b) Suitable for wide range of liquids and semi-liquids.

(c) Remote indication can be obtained by pneumatic or hydraulic transmission of the shaft rotation.

Limitations :

(a) The method is unsatisfactory for foaming and turbulent liquids.

(b) Shaft bearings etc. require maintenance.

3. Magnetic float gauge : In this method, *doughnut float* carries *outer magnets* while a *dip tube* carries *inner magnet* as shown in Fig. 4.4 (c). As the liquid level changes, the float gets displaced alongwith the outer magnets. These outer magnets attract inner magnets and this movement of inner magnet is given to the pointer that indicates liquid level on the calibrated scale.

Advantages :

(a) Indicating and recording type instrument.

(b) Since there is no leakage of liquid, the method can be used for toxic, explosive or flammable liquids.

Limitations : It must be ensured that float is free-moving, non-stick, and non-freezing.

4. Magnetic level indicator : The indicator consists of float carrying magnet and the front side of the gauge has small bi-coloured steel wafers which are free to rotate through 180°. As the float moves, the wafers against it rotate due to magnetic effect and shows the colour different than that of wafers away from the float. Thus, liquid level is indicated by change in colour of the wafers.

5. Magnetic level switch : Fig. 4.4 (e) shows magnetic level switch consisting of a *magnetic piston*, attached to a *float rod* which raises or lowers inside a non-magnetic *enclosing* tube with liquid level. Outside this tube there is a permanent magnet attached to a pivoted aim with a *mercury switch* mounted on it. When liquid level is too high, the magnetic piston is in the magnetic field and the magnet is drawn on the enclosing tube as shown in Fig 4.4 (e) (i) thereby tilting the mercury switch. This causes opening of the electrical circuit between the wires of the switch which is indicated by the lamp or alarm. When liquid level reduces to a predetermined point, piston moves down and out of the magnetic field as shown in Fig. 4.4 (e) (ii). Due to this magnet flies back to original position due to spring tension. During this fly back of the magnet, the mercury switch gets tilted so that contacts get dipped in mercury, that gives the indication opposite to the previous one. This is a two position self actuating level controller.

The gauge works on Archimede's Buoyancy principle which states that a body which is fully or partially immersed in a fluid gets buoyed up by a force which is equal to the weight of the liquid displaced. Fig. 4.5 shows a *displacer* which is usually cylindrical in shape and it is weighted by lead shots so as to sink in the liquid. The length of the displacer depends upon the level variation expected. Displacer is connected to the *torque-tube* which is a metal tube with a shaft whose inside is connected to the displacer. The outer end of the tube is gasketed and clamped rigidly to the vessel outside. Pointer is attached to the other end of the rod.

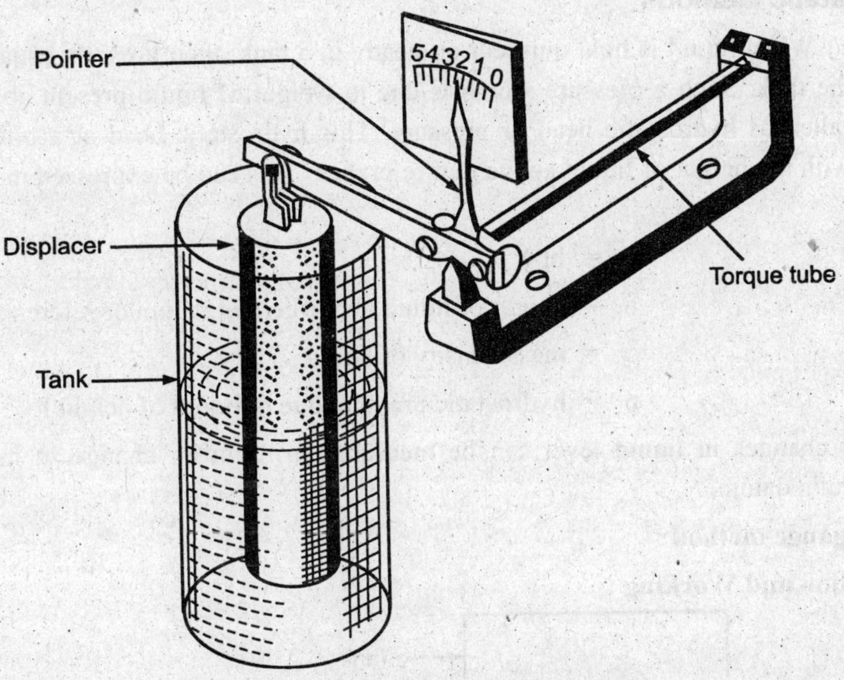

Fig. 4.5 : Displacer level gauge

Working : As liquid level changes, the amount of immersion of the displacer in the liquid changes. Change in displacer immersion causes change in buoyant force acting on it. More the displacer is submerged, larger is the buoyant force and vice-versa. Thus for every particular liquid level, there is certain fixed buoyant force acting on the displacer. This change in buoyant force with liquid level causes rotation of the torque tube and pointer. This rotation can be used for pneumatic transmission.

Advantages :

1. More sensitive to small level changes than float gauges.
2. Torque-tube overcomes the leakage and friction problems of stuffing box.
3. Simple, reliable, accurate and adaptable to wider range of level measurement at very high temperatures.
4. They can be mounted internally and externally and external units can be disconnected for maintenance.

Limitations :

1. These instruments require maintenance.
2. External units require heating to avoid freezing.

4.4 INDIRECT LEVEL MEASUREMENT

In this type, level is measured in terms of the variable which changes with change in level of liquid. Such variables are hydrostatic pressure, attenuation of radioactive energy, electrical properties, etc.

4.4.1 Hydrostatic Methods

Principle : When liquid is held quiscent or steady in a tank, then it exerts equal pressure on the walls of the tank. Such a pressure which is due to weight of liquid present above a certain reference is called as hydrostatic head or pressure. This hydrostatic head at a reference in the liquid varies with the height of liquid above that reference. This can be expressed mathematically as :

$$p = h\rho g$$

where,

h = height of liquid above certain datum or reference

ρ = mass density of liquid

p = hydrostatic pressure due to liquid of height h

Thus, any changes in liquid level can be measured in terms of change in its hydrostatic pressure at certain datum.

1. Pressure gauge method :

Construction and Working :

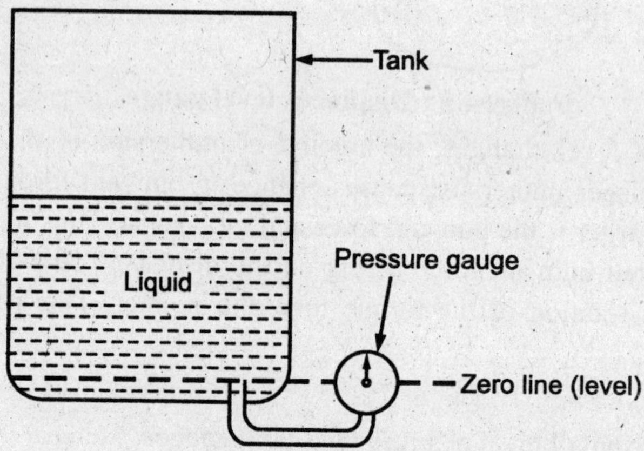

Fig. 4.6 : Pressure gauge method

In this method, a pressure gauge is connected at the lowest or zero level of the tank. Hence, the pressure sensed by the gauge is the hydrostatic pressure of liquid which is proportional to height of liquid above this zero level. Pressure gauge is calibrated in terms of liquid level by considering the density of liquid. A liquid seal can be used between process liquid and the pressure gauge so as to avoid the contact of corrosive process liquid with the pressure gauge elements.

Limitations :

(a) In this method, the pressure gauge must be located at the lowest liquid level, which becomes inconvenient for elevated tanks.

(b) The method cannot be used for measuring interface level between the two liquids.

2. **Diaphragm box method :**

Construction and Working : The method consists of a *diaphragm box* lowered into the liquid as shown in Fig. 4.7 which is usually made of cast iron or bronze.

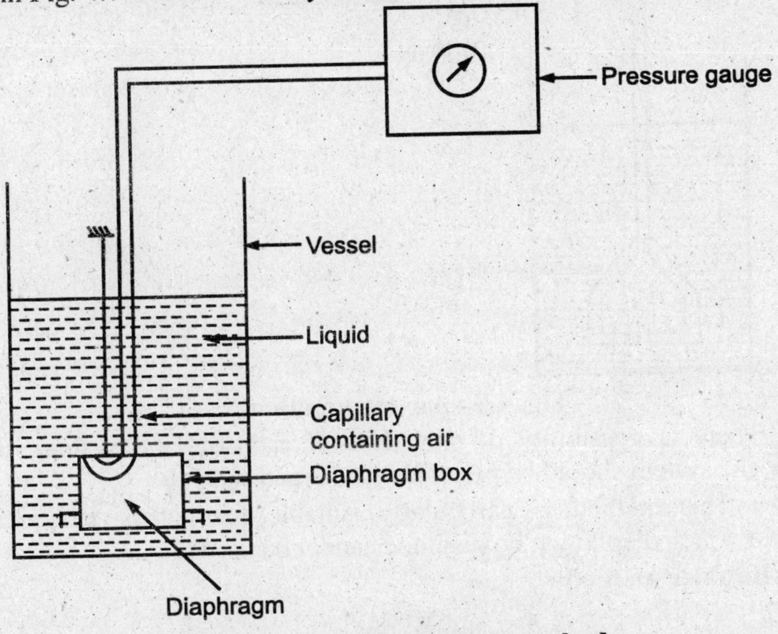

Fig. 4.7 : Diaphragm box method

Diaphragm box has a flexible *diaphragm element* made of rubber or neoprene fixed between the two flanges. The air-filled *capillary* connects the diaphragm box to the pressure gauge. Capillary is bent to prevent the sealing of capillary due to diaphragm deflection. As the liquid level changes, its hydrostatic pressure changes, due to which diaphragm gets deflected. Deflection of the diaphragm changes the air-pressure inside the capillary. Thus pressure gauge reading changes with liquid level which can be calibrated in terms of liquid level. To avoid any damage to the pressure gauge due to liquid, liquid seal may be used. For liquids containing solids, flushing arrangement is used that clears the sediment deposition near the diaphragm box opening.

Range : 20" to 250'.

Limitations :

System must be air-tight, otherwise loss of air would affect the calibration.

Application : This method is suitable where pressure gauge method cannot be used.

3. **Air-trap method :**

Construction and Working :

The arrangement is very similar to that of diaphragm box system except that there is no diaphragm. The system is filled with pressurised air through purging valve and the air-trap is connected to the pressure gauge as shown in Fig. 4.8. As the liquid level changes, the hydrostatic pressure changes and this change in hydrostatic pressure is indicated by the pressure gauge with the help of entrapped air.

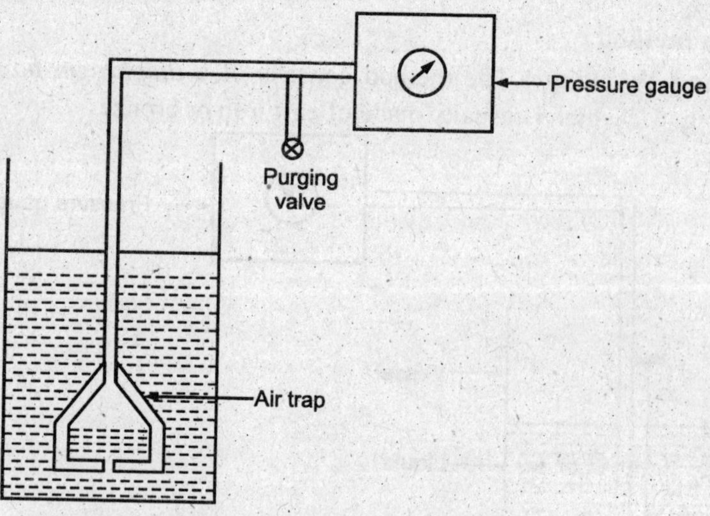

Fig. 4.8 : Air-trap method

Limitation : There is possibility of slow loss of air from the system, that affects the calibration. Hence, the system should be periodically charged with air.

Applications : This method is particularly suitable for corrosive liquids and liquids containing solids for which diaphragm box method cannot be used.

4. Air-purge or Bubbler method :

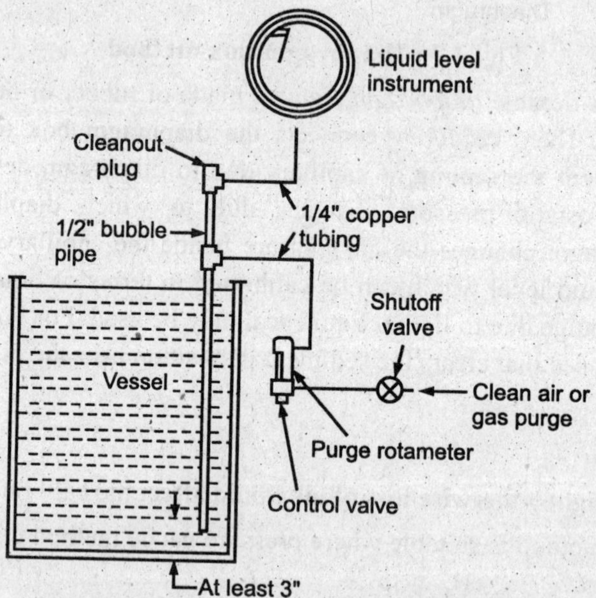

Fig. 4.9 : Air or Gas purge method

Construction : The air-purge system consists of a 1/2" stand pipe or *bubbler pipe*, installed vertically having its open end 3" above the bottom of vessel containing liquid. The bubbler pipe can be of any material and it is notched at the open end to prevent formation of large bubbles. The other end of the bubbler pipe has two connections out of which one is connected to regulated, metered and filtered air or gas supply while the other is connected to the pressure gauge as shown in Fig. 4.9.

Working : Air is passed through a bubbler pipe at a regulated pressure slightly higher than the hydrostatic pressure of liquid, so that it bubbles out into the liquid and usually bubble rate is adjusted as 1 bubble per min. During bubbling, the back pressure in the bubbler pipe exactly equals the hydrostatic pressure which is sensed by the pressure gauge, while the excess air pressure bubbles off into the liquid. Thus, as the liquid level changes, the hydrostatic head changes which is sensed by the pressure gauge calibrated in liquid level. Since air continuously bleeds out through the bubbler pipe, it is called as air-purge method. For periodic level check, a hand-pump may be used for air supply. The air flow can be regulated by using orifice and differential pressure regulator.

Advantages and Applications : The method is suitable mostly for corrosive liquids and liquids containing solids. The pressure gauge can be placed at 1000' from the vessel.

Range : With diaphragm pressure gauge – 4" to 150'

With pressure spring gauge – 150" to 250'.

(For specific gravity of liquid = 1)

Limitations : With semisolids like slurries a bubbler pipe may clog.

5. Differential pressure method :

All the above hydrostatic level measuring techniques can be used only when the vessel containing liquid is exposed to atmosphere. But in case of liquid in a pressure vessel like boiler drum, the bottom pressure corresponds to hydrostatic pressure alongwith the external pressure, hence bottom pressure cannot represent liquid level unless external pressure is balanced. This balancing is achieved by connecting enlarged leg manometer to the pressure vessel as shown in Fig. 4.10. The manometer reading corresponds to the hydrostatic pressure only, hence manometer itself can be calibrated in terms of liquid level.

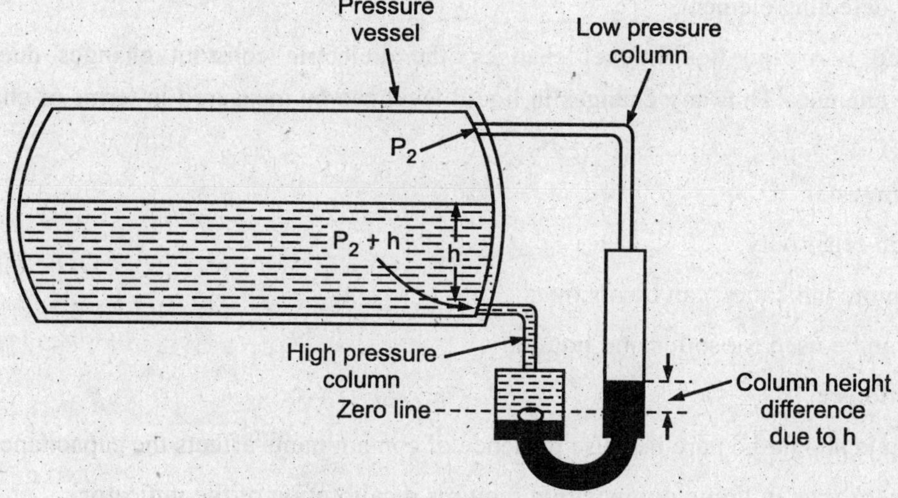

Fig. 4.10 : Differential pressure method

4.4.2 Electrical Capacitance Method

Principle : The electrical capacitance of the sensing probe varies with the level of material and hence level changes can be recorded in terms of changes in electrical capacitance of the sensing probe.

Construction :

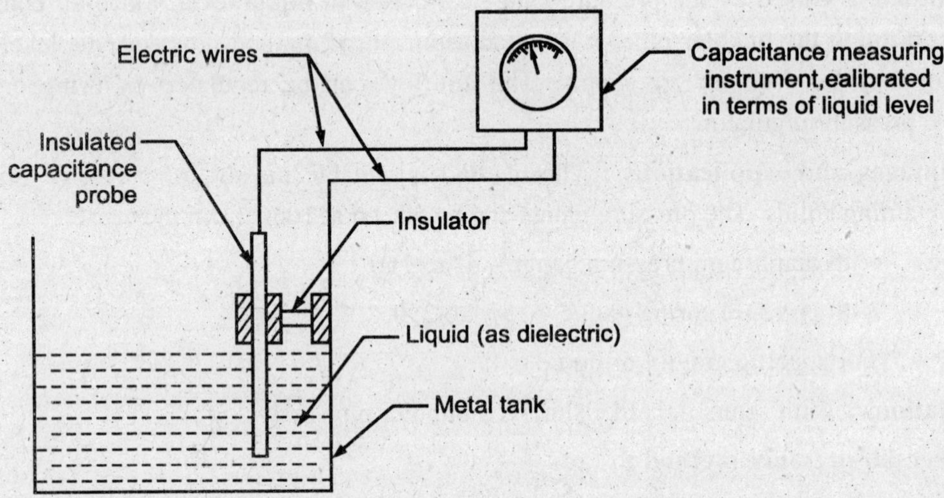

Fig. 4.11 : Capacitance method

The arrangement is very similar to that of parallel-plate condenser in which there are two conductors separated from each other by dielectric material between them. In capacitance level detector shown in Fig. 4.11, there is an insulated capacitance probe fixed near and parallel to tank wall such that the probe and metal tank wall act as the conductors of the condenser with conducting tank liquid as the dielectric medium. These two conductors are connected to capacitance detecting element.

Working : As the liquid level changes, the dielectric constant changes due to which capacitance changes. Thus any changes in liquid level can be measured in terms of change in the capacitance.

Advantages :

(a) High sensitivity.

(b) Remote indication can be obtained.

(c) It can be used for solids and liquids.

Limitations :

(a) Liquid should be pure because presence of contaminants affects the capacitance.

(b) Any change in liquid composition requires recalibration of the indicator.

4.4.3 Radiation Methods

Principle : The extent of absorption of radioactive rays depends upon the level of liquid inside the vessel. Hence any changes in liquid level can be measured in terms of change in intensity of radioactive radiations.

Construction :

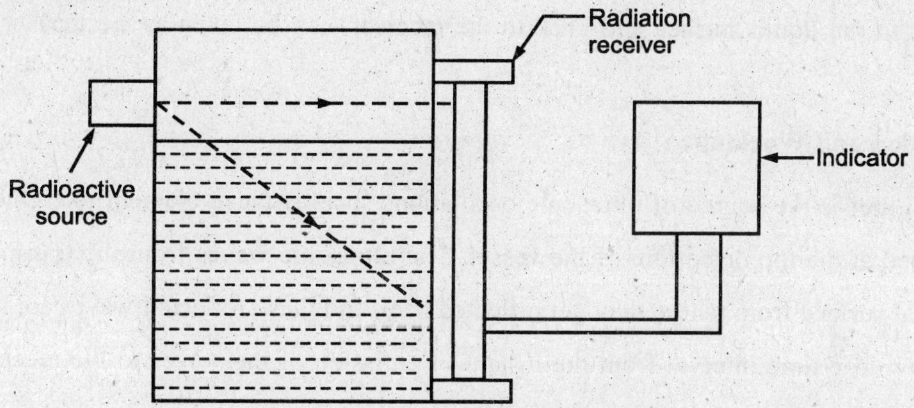

Fig. 4.12 : Radiation method

Radiation level detector consists of radioactive source such as a minute quantity of capsulated radioactive isotope like cobalt-60, cesium-137, radium-226, fixed either inside or outside the vessel. The *radiation receiving element* like Geiger-Muller counter is fixed to the side of the vessel directly across the source location alongwith the indicator.

Working : As liquid or solid level inside the vessel changes, the amount and intensity of radioactive radiations received by the receiver changes. The intensity of radiation varies inversely with the thickness of the vessel walls and the medium inside the vessel. Thus larger is the level of liquid inside the vessel, smaller is the intensity of radiation and vice-versa.

Advantages :

(a) This method is useful particularly when process materials do not allow the use of physical contact type level measuring devices. This method does not require physical contact with the medium.

(b) The method can be employed at very high temperatures and pressures.

(c) Good accuracy.

(d) Continuous level measurement.

Limitations :

(a) Relatively high cost.

(b) The change in density of liquid affects the calibration.

Applications : The method is suitable for corrosive, abrasive, viscous liquids because of non-contact type measurement.

4.4.4 Ultrasonic Level Detector

Principle : This method is based upon utilization of law of reflection of ultrasonic oscillations (having wavelength greater than 20 kHz) from solid or liquid surface or from the interface between two immiscible liquids. The time taken by the wave for its travel from transmitter to the liquid surface and back to the receiver, can be taken as the measure of liquid level.

Construction and Working :

Transmitter is the source of ultrasonic oscillations such as piezo-element like Quartz, which is positioned at the top or bottom of the vessel. The ultrasonic waves from the transmitter reach the material surface from where they get reflected back and these reflected waves are received by the receiver. The time interval from the instant of emission of the waves to the reception of the reflected rays is measured, which varies with the liquid level.

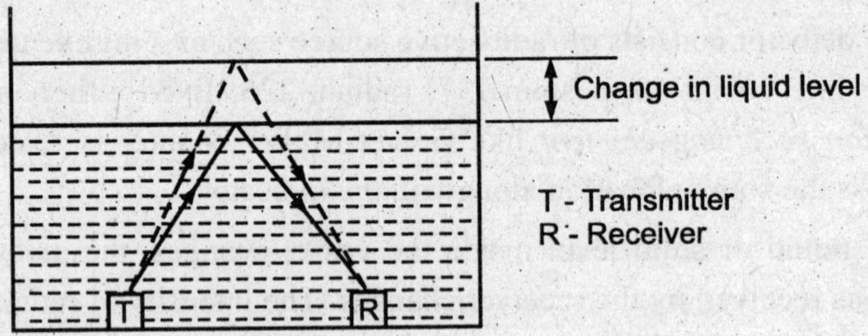

Fig. 4.13 : Ultrasonic method

Advantages :

(a) High accuracy.

(b) Does not require contact with the process material.

(c) It provides continuous level measurement.

(d) Suitable for level measurement in liquid and solid.

4.5 SOLID LEVEL MEASUREMENT

The methods which are commonly used for solid and liquid level measurement are capacitance method, radioactive method and ultrasonic method, which are described in previous articles.

4.6 DENSITY MEASUREMENT

1. Since the hydrostatic pressure of liquid column of certain height is proportional to the density of liquid (as per $p = h\rho g$), the change in density of liquid can be measured in terms of change in its hydrostatic pressure.

2. Density measurement using hydrometer : Hydrometer is a weighted float with small diameter stem so that more or less of the scale is submerged inside the liquid depending upon its density. For density measurement, liquid is maintained at constant level and hydrometer is inserted in it. The immersion of the hydrometer in the liquid represents density on the scale.

3. The density can be calculated by weighing known volume of liquid and the ratio of weight to volume gives density.

EXERCISE

1. How will you differentiate between direct and indirect level measuring methods ? List various direct and indirect methods.
2. State the importance of level measurement and control in various processes.
3. Describe various point contact methods of level measurement.
4. Describe level measuring methods based on Buoyancy effect.
5. How will you differentiate between the operating principles of float level gauge and displacer level gauge ?
6. Describe various sight or gauge glass level indicators.
7. Why reflex type level gauge cannot be used for measuring interface level between the two liquids ?
8. Describe various float level gauges.
9. Describe various hydrostatic level measuring methods.
10. When you will employ differential pressure method for level measurement ? Describe its working.
11. Describe :
    (i) radiation level detector and
    (ii) ultrasonic level detector.

12. List various level measurement methods which are commonly used for solids and liquids.
13. Describe various methods for level measurement of corrosive liquids.
14. Describe a method for electrical measurement of level of conducting liquid contained in a metal vessel.
15. Describe various methods of measurement of specific gravity of liquid.

❑❑❑

5

CHAPTER

FLOW MEASURING INSTRUMENTS

5.1 INTRODUCTION

Flow measurement is the quantitative determination of rates and mass flow of gases and liquids. In this chapter, we study different methods of measurement of flow rates of liquids and gases.

Applications of Flow Measurement

1. Flow measurement is essential for getting information about the proportions and the amount of materials flowing in or out of a process.
2. The flow rates of utilities like air, water, steam are required for cost accounting of the plant.
3. The flow measurement is highly essential for material balancing of the plant process.
4. The quality of product in continuous processing plant mainly depends upon the correct flow rate of raw materials.

5.2 FLOW MEASUREMENT METHODS

There are two types of flow measurement :

1. Rate of flow : It is the amount of fluid that flows past a given point at any given instant.

2. Total flow : It is the amount of fluid that flows past a given point in a definite time period.

(A) Rate of flow measuring instruments (Secondary or inferential type flowmeters) :

1. **Differential-pressure meters :** (Head type flowmeters)
   (a) Orifice meter.
   (b) Venturi meter
   (c) Pitot tube
   (d) Flow nozzle.
2. **Variable-area flowmeters :**
   (a) Rotameter
   (b) Piston type or valve type area meter.
3. **Electromagnetic flowmeter**
4. **Flow integrators**

(B) Total flowmeters (Quantity flowmeters) :

1. Positive displacement meters :

(a) Reciprocating piston type flowmeter
(b) Nutating disc flowmeter
(c) Rotary vane flowmeter.

2. Velocity flowmeters :

(a) Single jet fan type flowmeter
(b) Turbine flowmeter
(c) Propeller type flowmeter.
(d) Anemometers.
(e) Ultrasonic flowmeters.
(f) Vortex flowmeters.
(g) Thermal flowmeters.

(C) Mass flowmeters.

(D) Flow integrators.

RATE OF FLOW MEASURING INSTRUMENTS

5.3 DIFFERENTIAL-PRESSURE TYPE OR HEAD FLOWMETERS

Principle :

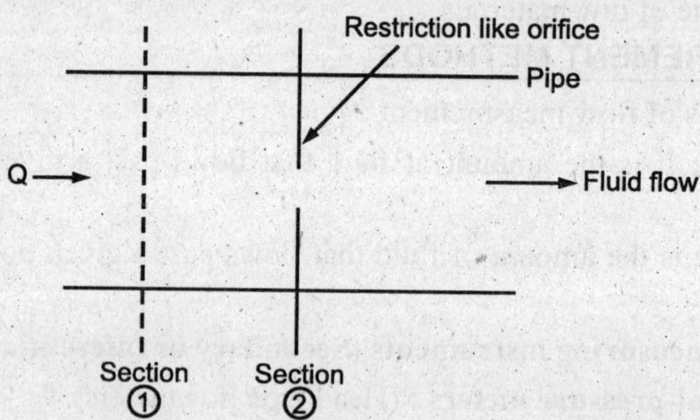

Fig. 5.1 : Principle of head flowmeters

Before stating the principle of head flowmeter, we understand two basic theorems of fluid mechanics. For this consider a flow of incompressible fluid through a pipeline having flow restriction such as orifice as shown in Fig. 5.1.

Continuity equation : If 'Q' is the volumetric fluid flow rate at the restriction, then continuity equation at sections (1) and (2) is stated as :

$$Q = A_1V_1 = A_2V_2 = \text{Constant}$$

where A and V represent the flow area and flow velocity at the respective sections respectively. Thus according to continuity equation, the product of flow area and flow velocity equals the flow rate of fluid at that section. Since flow area 'A_2' at the restriction is smaller than pipe flow, area 'A_1', at a steady fluid flow the flow velocity 'V_2' at the restriction must be greater than the velocity 'V_1' at the section sufficiently away from the restriction. *Thus, according to continuity equation, as flow area decreases, flow velocity increases and vice versa.*

Bernoulli's equation : This is nothing but energy conservation principle which states that in steady flow of fluid the sum of potential energy, kinetic energy and pressure energy remains constant at any section. For Fig. 5.1, Bernoulli's equation between sections (1) and (2) can be written as :

$$\frac{p_1}{\rho} + \frac{V_1^2}{2g} + z_1 = \frac{p_2}{\rho} + \frac{V_2^2}{2g} + z_2 = \text{constant}$$

where p_1, p_2 and z_1, z_2 are static pressures and elevations of sections above some datum and ρ is the density of fluid. We have seen that at the restriction section (2) velocity V_2 increases, hence kinetic energy at this section (2) is greater than that at section (1). According to Bernoulli's equation, this increase in velocity energy would be at the cost of decrease in pressure energy, assuming elevation of the sections same. Thus pressure at the restriction is smaller than that at the point sufficiently away from the restriction. Thus at the flow restriction, flow velocity increases with subsequent decrease in static pressure, that developes differential pressure across the restriction. This differential pressure across the restriction varies with flow rate of fluid passing through it. Thus *any change in fluid flow rate through the restriction can be measured in terms of differential pressure across it. This is the principle of variable head flowmeters.*

5.3.1 Flow Measurement using Orifice Plate

I. Construction :

Orifice flowmeter consists of two separate devices, primary and secondary, that combinely measure the flow rate.

(A) Primary element – (Orifice plate) : Orifice plate is nothing but a circular plate having hole in it. This plate is inserted into a pipeline by means of flanges, so that it acts as the restriction to fluid flow. Orifice plates are made from steel, stainless steel, monel, phosphor bronze, or of any metal which can resist corrosive and erosive action of fluid.

Classification of orifice plates :

(a) Based on shape :

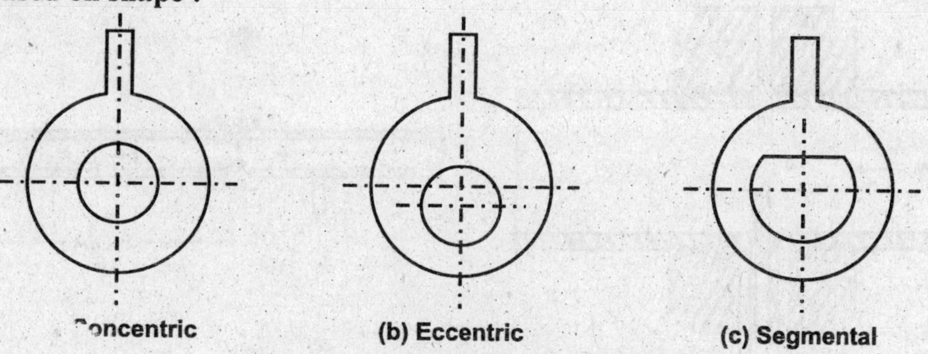

Fig. 5.2 : Shapes of orifice plates

Depending upon the position of the hole in the orifice plates, they are classified as concentric, eccentric and segmental.

The *concentric plate* has a hole concentric with its centre as shown in Fig. 5.2 (a).

The *eccentric plate* has tangential hole having centre above or below the centre of the plate. Usually hole is placed at the bottom of the pipe for gases and at the top for liquids so that entrained water or gases flow through the plate rather than building up in front of it. Also it prevents any accumulation of solid particle that makes it suitable for fluids containing solids, oils containing water and wet steam.

The *segmental plate* has a hole which is segment of a circle, having curved portion coinciding with the lower surface of the pipe.

(b) Based on edge thickness : The orifice plates are classified as thin sharp square, quadrant-edged or conical based on their edge thickness.

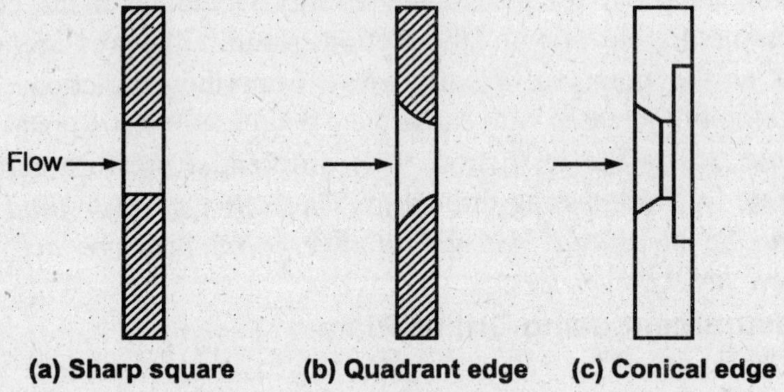

Fig. 5.3 : Orifice edge

Sharp square edged hole is usually bored concentrically in a flat, thin orifice plate.

Quadrant or conical edge hole is rounded to form a quarter circle. This type is more suitable for viscous fluids such as heavy crudes, syrups and slurries.

(c) Based on pressure taps : Orifice plates are classified based upon position of pressure taps used to sense the differential pressure. Different arrangements of taps are flange taps, pipe taps, vena-contracta taps.

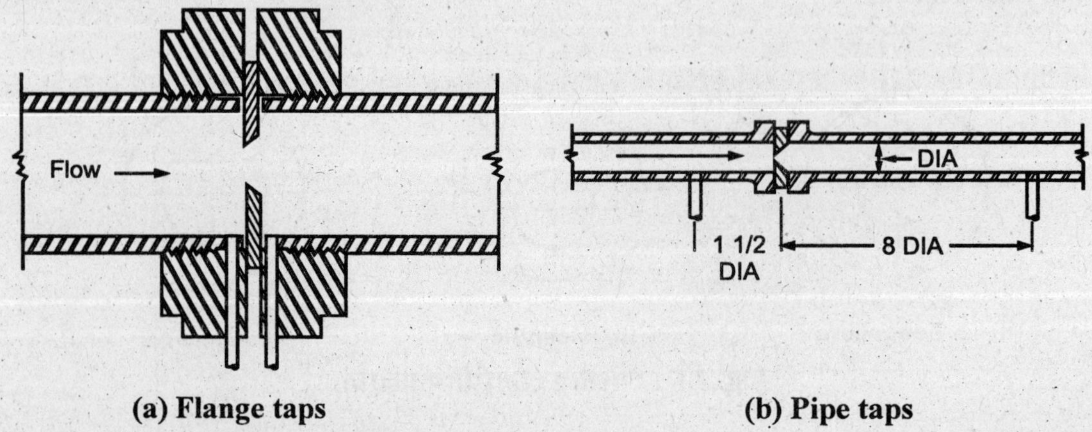

(a) Flange taps **(b) Pipe taps**

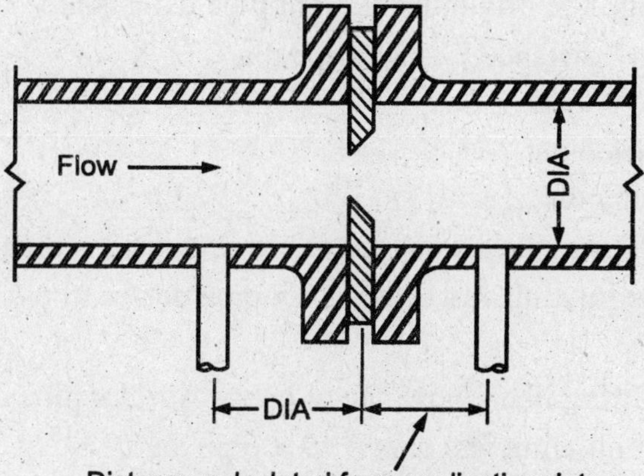

(c) Vena-contracta taps

Fig. 5.4 : Pressure taps

Flange taps are located in the flanges that hold the orifice plate and they are of 25 ± 1 mm from the orifice on either sides.

The flange taps orifice has advantage that the orifice assembly is easily replaceable without any alterations in pipe line.

Pipe taps are located at 2.5 D on the upstream side and 8 D on the downstream side of the orifice as shown in Fig. 5.4 (b) where D is pipe id. These taps are commonly used in measuring flow of gases.

Vena-contracta taps are at a distance equal to pipe id on the upstream side, while downstream tap is located at vena contracta that is at the point of minimum pressure which is determined from calculation. Vena contracta distance varies with β ratio.

(B) Secondary Element : The liquid column manometer acts as the secondary element which is connected to the primary element by lead lines at the pressure taps. The manometer measures differential pressure across the orifice plate, which can be calibrated in terms of flow rate of fluid through it. Differential pressure meters like bellows, ring gauge can be used as secondary element.

Installation of orifice plate in the flow path : There should be minimum recommended straight length of pipe on upstream and downstream side of the orifice plate.

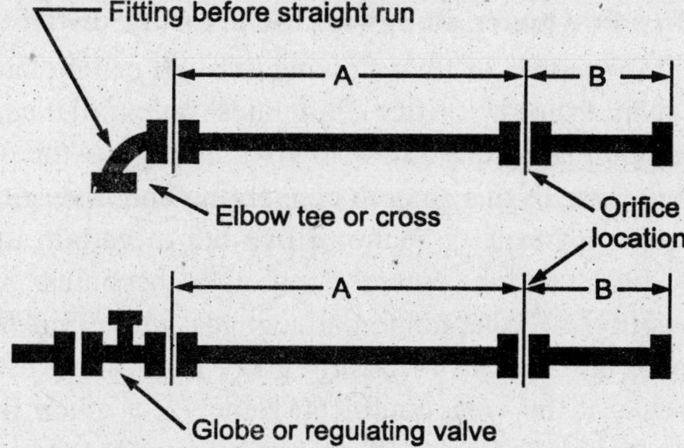

Fig. 5.5 : Orifice plate installation

With reference to Fig. 5.5, minimum straight pipe lengths are :

On downstream side - distance B = 5 × pipe dia.

On upstream side -

For $\beta = 0.6 : \left(= \frac{\text{orifice dia.}}{\text{pipe dia.}}\right)$

1. Distance from fitting like elbow, tee or cross, A = 13 × pipe dia.
2. Distance from regulating valve, A = 31 × pipe dia.

For $\beta = 0.4$:

1. Distance from fitting like elbow, tee or cross, A = 9 × pipe dia.
2. Distance from regulating valve, A = 19 × pipe dia.

II. Working of Orifice-Flowmeter :

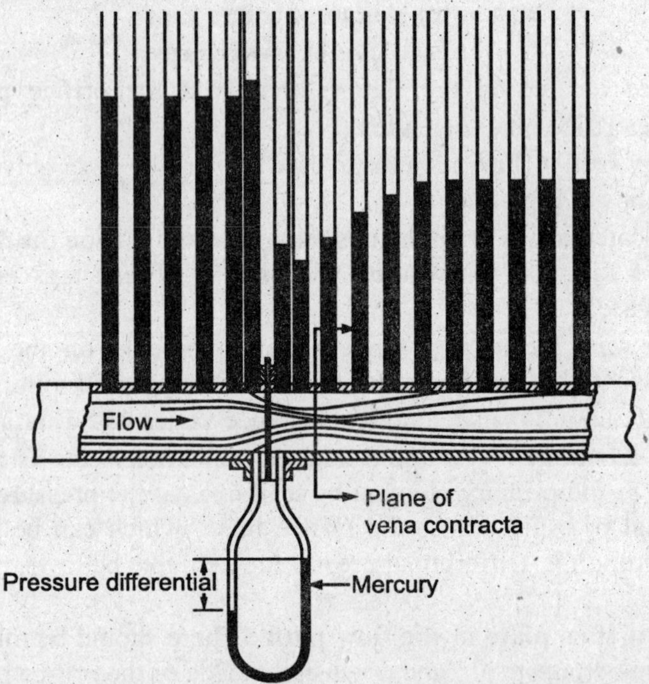

Fig. 5.6 : Orifice flowmeter alongwith the pressure distribution diagram

Fig. 5.6 shows the flow pattern of fluid flowing through orifice installed in a pipe line. At a distance sufficiently away from the orifice, flow lines run parallel and widely spaced, but as fluid approaches the orifice plate, flow lines slowly converge at the orifice and then diverge out to pipe area smoothly. Due to this smooth converging and diverging of the flow lines, the minimum flow area exists not exactly at the orifice but at certain distance on downstream side of the orifice. This location where flow area becomes minimum is called as vena-contracta. The position of vena-contracta changes with fluid flow rate. As discussed earlier, the static pressure at a point sufficiently away from the orifice an its upstream side would be greater than that at the vena-contracta. Hence at a given flow rate, the maximum differential pressure can only be obtained if upstream pressure tap is sufficiently away from the orifice and downstream tap is at the vena-contracta. But it is not possible to correctly locate the vena-contracta, hence pressure taps are located as discussed above. It is to be noted from Fig. 5.6 that on downstream side, pressure does not recover completely, but there is some loss of pressure across the plate which varies inversely with $\beta \left(=\frac{d}{D}\right)$ ratio.

Flow equation of orificemeter :

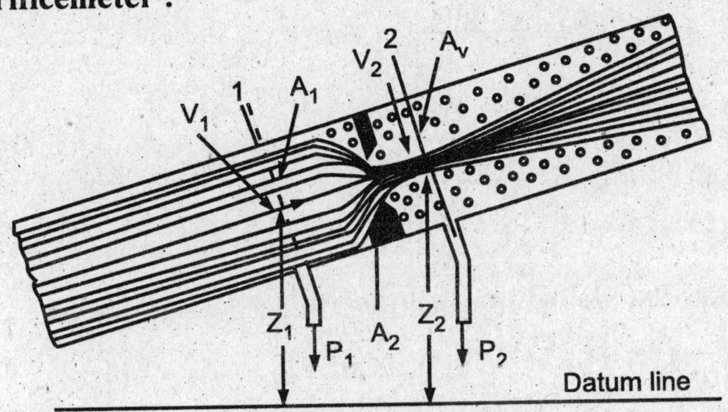

Fig. 5.7 : Orificemeter

Fig. 5.7 shows orifice plate installed in flow line. The symbols A, v, p, Z represent flow area, flow velocity, static pressure, and elevation above some datum respectively at the respective sections (1) and (2). Applying Bernoulli's equation, for the flow of incompressible fluid past the sections (1) and (2), we get

$$\frac{p_1}{\rho} + \frac{v_1^2}{2g} + z_1 = \frac{p_2}{\rho} + \frac{v_2^2}{2g} + z_2 \qquad \text{... (5.1)}$$

where ρ = density of fluid

For fluid flow measurement the difference in elevations $(z_1 - z_2)$ is very small because length of orifice itself is very small. Hence, we neglect this difference so that equation (5.1) becomes

$$\frac{1}{\rho}(p_1 - p_2) = \frac{1}{2g}(v_2^2 - v_1^2)$$

i.e.
$$v_2^2 - v_1^2 = \frac{2g}{\rho}(p_1 - p_2) = 2gh$$

where
$$h = \frac{p_1 - p_2}{\rho} = \text{differential pressure head}$$

i.e.
$$v_2^2 = v_1^2 + 2gh$$

i.e.
$$v_2 = (v_1^2 + 2gh)^{1/2} \qquad \text{... (5.2)}$$

If 'Q' is the flow rate of fluid through pipe line, then according to continuity equation :

$$Q = A_1 v_1 = A_2 v_2$$

i.e.
$$v_1 = \left(\frac{A_2}{A_1}\right) v_2 \qquad \text{... (5.3)}$$

Using this value of V_1, equation (5.2) becomes,

$$v_2 = \left[v_2^2\left(\frac{A_2^2}{A_1^2}\right) + 2gh\right]^{1/2}$$

$$\therefore \quad v_2^2\left[1 - \left(\frac{A_2^2}{A_1^2}\right)\right] = 2gh$$

$$\therefore \quad v_2^2 = \frac{2gh}{\left[1 - \frac{A_2^2}{A_1^2}\right]}$$

$$v_2 = \frac{\sqrt{2gh}}{\left[1 - \frac{A_2^2}{A_1^2}\right]^{1/2}} \qquad \ldots (5.4)$$

Using this value of v_2 in continuity equation, fluid flow rate can be expressed as :

$$Q = A_2\, v_2$$

$$\therefore \quad Q = A_2 \frac{\sqrt{2gh}}{\sqrt{1 - \left(\frac{A_2^2}{A_1^2}\right)}} \qquad \ldots (5.5)$$

Here we assume that flow area A_2 at vena-contracta equals the orifice area.

$$\therefore \quad \frac{A_2^2}{A_1^2} = \frac{(\text{Orifice area})^2}{(\text{Pipe inside area})^2}$$

$$= \frac{\left(\frac{\pi}{4}d^2\right)^2}{\left(\frac{\pi}{4}D^2\right)^2} = \frac{d^4}{D^4}$$

$$= \left(\frac{d}{D}\right)^4 = \beta^4$$

where $\beta = \frac{d}{D} = \frac{\text{Orifice dia.}}{\text{Pipe id.}}$

$\therefore$ Equation (5.5) can be written as :

$$Q = \frac{A_2}{\sqrt{1-\beta^4}}\sqrt{2gh} \qquad \ldots (5.6)$$

Equation (5.6) gives the *theoretical fluid flow rate* through the restriction which differs from the actual flow rate because :

1. Some of the fluid energy is tossed in overcoming pipe friction.
2. Vena-contracta does not occur exactly at the orifice, but its location depends upon the actual flow rate.

The actual flow rate can be expressed in terms of the theoretical flow rate by defining a *discharge coefficient (C)* as the ratio of actual flow rate to the theoretical flow rate.

$\therefore$ Actual flow rate, Q_a = C × theoretical flow rate

$$= \frac{C\,A_2\sqrt{2gh}}{\sqrt{1-\beta^4}}$$

$$= K\,A_2\sqrt{2gh} \qquad \ldots (5.7)$$

where, $K = \frac{C}{\sqrt{1-\beta^4}}$ = flow coefficient

Equation (5.7) gives the actual flow rate. Discharge coefficient can be evaluated by calculating the theoretical flow rate from equation (5.6) and by actually measuring the flow rate by collecting the liquid over certain time interval.

In flow equation (5.7), differential pressure head is given by

$$h = \frac{p_1 - p_2}{\rho_f} \qquad \ldots (5.8)$$

where, ρ_f = density of test fluid flowing through the pipe

If manometer is used to measure differential pressure $(p_1 - p_2)$ then :

$$(p_1 - p_2) = (\rho_m - \rho_f)\,H \qquad \ldots (5.9)$$

where, ρ_m = density of manometric liquid

and H = manometer reading in terms of height difference

Using this value of $(p_1 - p_2)$ in equation (5.8), differential pressure head 'h' can be written as :

$$h = \frac{(\rho_m - \rho_f)\,H}{\rho_f} = \left(\frac{\rho_m}{\rho_f} - 1\right)H$$

Using this value of 'h', flow equation for orificemeter given by equation (5.7) becomes :

$$\boxed{Q = KA_2\sqrt{2g\left(\frac{\rho_m}{\rho_f} - 1\right)H}} \qquad \ldots (5.10)$$

where, $K = \frac{C}{\sqrt{1-\beta^4}}$ = flow coefficient

$$= C \times \frac{1}{\sqrt{1-\beta^4}}$$

= discharge coefficient × velocity of approach factor

A_2 = orifice area $= \frac{\pi}{4}d^2$

ρ_m = density of manometric liquid

ρ_f = density of test fluid

H = manometer reading

$\beta = \frac{d}{D} = \frac{\text{Orifice diameter}}{\text{Pipe id.}}$

Effect of Reynold's number on discharge coefficient :

Reynold's number is a dimensionless number which relates inertia force and viscous force acting on fluid. Reynold's number is defined by :

$$R_e = \frac{\rho v D}{\mu}$$

where,
ρ = density of fluid
v = velocity of fluid
D = pipe id
μ = viscosity of fluid

- If $R_e < 2000$, fluid flow is laminar.
- If R_e lies between 2000 to 4000, fluid flow is said to be in transition state.
- If $R_e > 4000$, fluid flow is turbulent.

The flow coefficient of the orifice depends upon the nature of flow viz. laminar or turbulent. Reynold's number for fluid flow through orifice can be defined as :

$$R_e = \frac{\rho v_2 d}{\mu}$$

where, d = orifice diameter

If Q is the fluid flow rate through orifice, then continuity equation gives

$$Q = A_2 v_2$$

$$\therefore \quad v_2 = \frac{Q}{A_2} = \frac{Q}{\frac{\pi}{4} d^2}$$

Using this value of v_2, expression for R_e can be written as :

$$R_e = \frac{\rho Q d}{\mu \times \frac{\pi}{4} d^2}$$

$$\therefore \quad R_e = \frac{4\rho Q}{\pi \mu d} = \frac{4\rho Q}{\pi \mu \beta D} \qquad \dots (5.11)$$

This gives relation between R_e, β and flow rate for fluid flow through the orifice.

Flow calculation :

1. For a given pipeline having id 'D', orifice diameter 'd' is given alongwith the type of pressure taps. For better accuracy $\beta \left(= \frac{d}{D}\right)$ ratio between 0.2 to 0.6 is used.
2. From flow equation, relation between flow rate 'Q' and flow coefficient 'K' is obtained.
3. Certain value of 'R_e' is assumed and for that value of R_e, value of 'K' is obtained from the standard tables for the desired β-ratio and pressure taps.

4. Using this value of 'K', flow rate is calculated and from this calculated flow rate, 'R_e' is determined from equation (5.11). If this calculated value of 'R_e' does not match closely with its assumed value, recalculation is done until these two values closely match. Finally for this value of R_e, flow coefficient is determined from which correct flow rate is calculated.

III. Performance Characteristics :

1. Linearity : Flow equation for orifice meter is given by :

$$Q = KA_2\sqrt{2gh}$$

Equation shows that :

$$\text{Flow rate, } Q \propto \sqrt{h}$$

$$\propto \sqrt{\frac{p_1 - p_2}{\rho}}$$

Thus there exists a *non-linear square-root relationship* between flow rate 'Q' and differential pressure $(p_1 - p_2)$ across the orifice plate. This relationship also depends upon tap locations, orifice design, etc. and their effects are considered in discharge coefficient.

2. Pressure recovery : On the downstream of the orifice, the decreased pressure head at vena-contracta is recovered. This pressure recovery is not 100%, but there is some permanent loss of pressure head at the orifice. Due to sudden change in flow area, orifice has more pressure loss and hence low pressure recovery than other head flow-meters. Pressure loss at the restriction decides the cost of energy required for pumping fluid.

3. Accuracy : Accuracy of orificemeter ranges from ± 0.8% to 5% of full scale, that depends on fluid, upstream piping configuration, the secondary measuring element and correct value of Reynold's number.

IV. Advantages and Limitations :

Advantages :

1. Simple construction.
2. Easy installation and replacement.
3. Can be used with all types of differential pressure transmitters so as to obtain remote indication.

Limitations :

1. It has relatively high permanent pressure loss as compared to other head flowmeters.
2. It has non-linear, square-root characteristic.
3. The flow characteristics get affected by corrosion, erosion and scaling of the orifice plate.
4. For accurate reading, it requires certain straight pipe run without any pipe fittings and valves on upstream and downstream sides.
5. It cannot be used for slurries that may clog the orifice opening.
6. Low β ratios result in high pressure loss.

5.3.2 Flow Measurement using Venturi Tube

I. Construction :

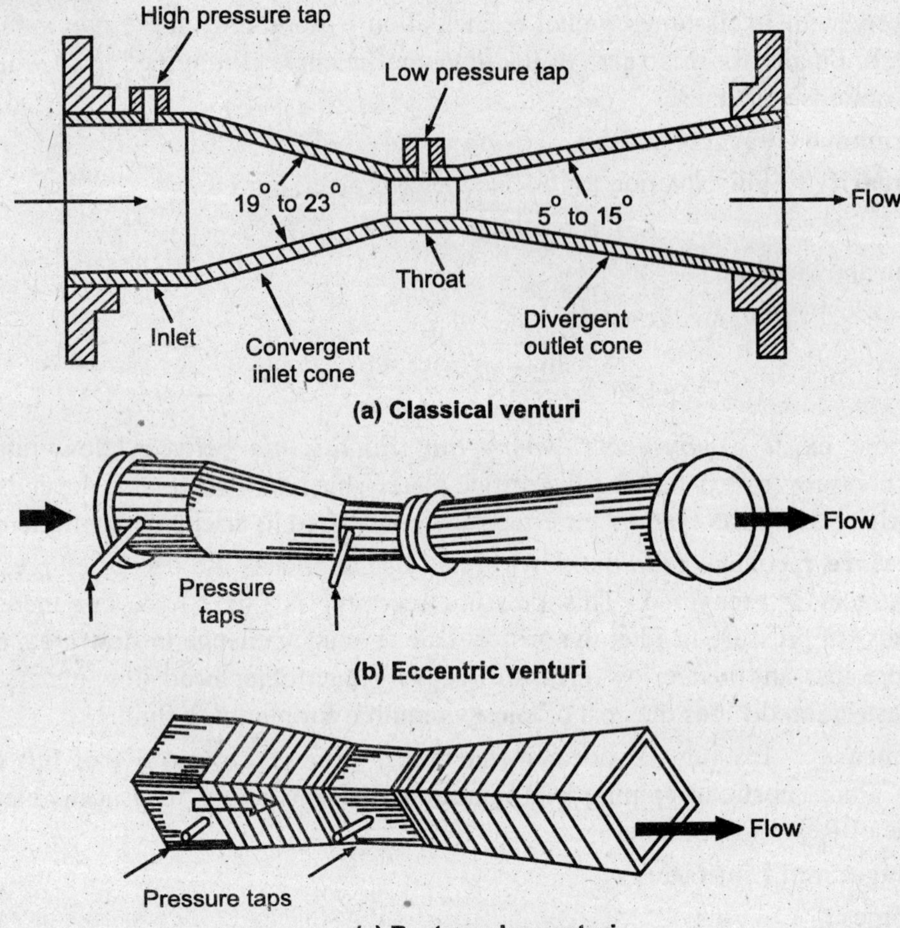

(a) Classical venturi

(b) Eccentric venturi

(c) Rectangular venturi

Fig. 5.8 : Venturi tubes

(a) Classical venturi : Venturi tube is a specially shaped length of pipe resembling two funnels joined at their smaller ends. Classical venturi tube consists of *convergent inlet cone, uniform diameter throat and divergent outlet cone.* The inlet cone has included angle between 19° to 23°, while the outlet cone has included angle between 5° to 15° as shown in Fig. 5.8 (a).

The high pressure tap is located on the convergent section, while low pressure tap is located at the middle of the throat. The venturi tube is usually made of cast iron or steel, but in some cases throat is made of a separate bronze assembly which can be replaced. Very large venturi is made from smooth, poured concrete.

(b) Eccentric venturi tube : In this configuration, throat bottom is in the same horizontal plane as bottom of the connecting pipe. This design prevents any build-up of heavy materials and provides facility to completely drain out the pipe-line.

Venturi tubes have flow coefficient in the range of 0.7 to 1 with usual value 0.98 for β ratios between 0.3 and 0.75.

II. Working :

As fluid enters the inlet convergent cone, it smoothly converges with corresponding increase in flow velocity and decrease in static pressure. In uniform throat section, there is no change in fluid velocity and hence in static pressure, so that throat provides the point for minimum pressure measurement. In divergent section, flow smoothly diverges with increase in pressure head at the cost of decrease in velocity head. The venturi tube has no sudden change in geometrical contour and there are no sharp corners or projections in the flow path. Hence, venturi tube is most preferred for flow measurement of slurries and liquids containing solids, provided pressure taps are protected from plugging. Since the flow area smoothly changes, the pressure recovery of venturi is better than orifice.

Flow equation of venturi tube : Flow equation of venturi tube can be derived by the procedure followed for orifice. The equation gives fluid flow rate by :

$$Q = KA_2\sqrt{2gh}$$

$$= KA_2\sqrt{\frac{2g\,(\rho_m - \rho_{T.L.})}{\rho_{T.L.}} \times H}$$

where,

$$K = \frac{Cd\ A_1}{\sqrt{A_1^2 - A_2^2}} = \frac{Cd}{\sqrt{1-\beta^4}} = \text{Flow coefficient}$$

C_d = discharge coefficient

A_1 = pipe inside area

A_2 = throat area

h = differential pressure head

H = manometer height difference

ρ_m and $\rho_{T.L.}$ = densities of manometric liquid and test fluid respectively

$$\beta = \frac{\text{throat dia.}}{\text{pipe id.}}$$

The flow calculation is done by following the procedure described for orifice-meter.

Performance Characteristics :

1. **Linearity :** Flow rate has non-linear square root relationship with the differential pressure.

2. **Pressure recovery :** Due to smooth geometrical shape, the pressure loss across the venturi is small that results in high pressure recovery. 75% of the total pressure recovery occurs in first half of the length of the divergent cone. The pressure recovery decreases with increase in the included angle of the divergent section. Pressure recovery also depends upon β-ratio.

3. **Accuracy :** The overall accuracy of venturi tube lies between ± 0.25% to ± 3%.

IV. Advantages and Limitations (over orifice) :

Advantages :

1. Low permanent pressure loss and hence high pressure recovery.
2. Can be used for high flow rate measurement.
3. High accuracy over wide flow ranges.
4. Can be used effectively at high and low β ratios.
5. High reproducibility.

Limitations :

1. Venturi tubes are costlier than orifice, but high pressure recovery compensates for the high cost.
2. Venturi tubes are difficult to inspect at site due to its typical geometrical shape.
3. Venturi tubes are not suitable for flow measurement of highly viscous slurries.

5.3.3 Flow Measurement using Flow Nozzle

I. Construction :

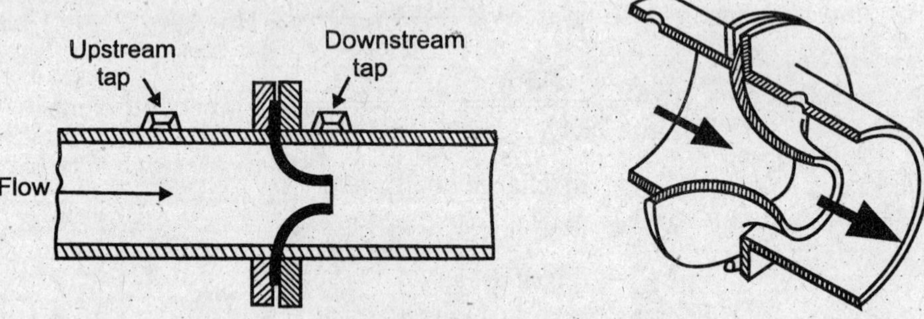

Fig. 5.9 : Flow nozzle

Flow nozzle is a modified venturi tube with the outlet divergent section so that it resembles an orifice with a well-rounded upstream edge as shown in Fig. 5.9. *The inlet section* of flow nozzle can be a quarter-ellipse or a circle. Flow nozzles are made of stainless-steel or any other corrosion resistant material. The upstream or *high pressure tap* is located at about one pipe-dia. from the entrance to the nozzle while *low-pressure tap* is located in the pipe directly opposite to the straight portion of the nozzle as shown in Fig. 5.9 (a).

II. Working :

Working of flow nozzle is similar to that of venturi tube.

III. Advantages and Limitations :

Advantages :

1. Low permanent pressure loss as compared to orifice.
2. It can be used for fluids having Reynold's number as low as 6000 and as high as 50,000.
3. It has high coefficient of discharge with usual value of 0.99, with wide range of β ratio between 0.2 to 0.8.

4. Due to rigid construction, it can be used for metering fluids at high temperatures and flows.
5. Its cost is lower than venturi.

Limitations :

1. Cost is higher than orifice.
2. Low accuracy as compared to venturi.
3. Low pressure recovery.
4. It is not as wear resistant as venturi.
5. Its use is limited to moderate pipe sizes.

5.3.4 Flow Measurement using Pitot Tube

I. Construction :

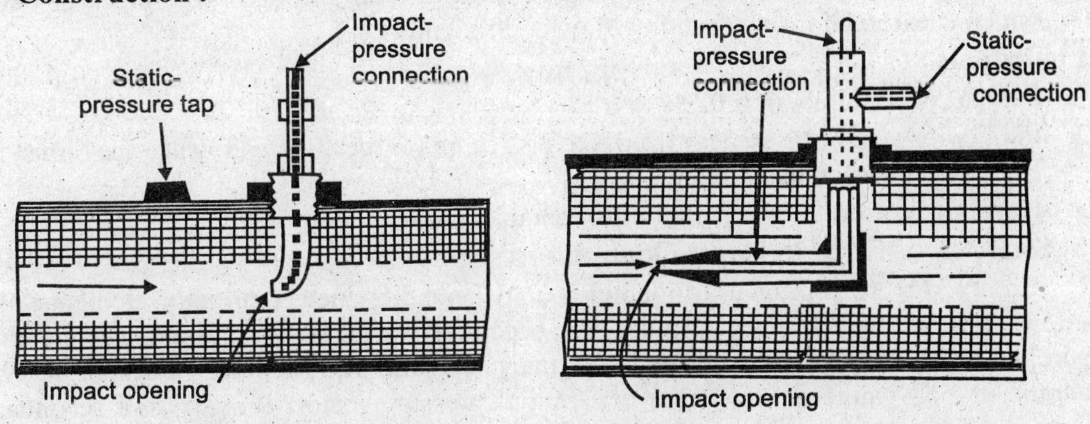

(a) Single opening type **(b) Combined pressure opening type**

Fig. 5.10 : Pitot tube

In simple form, pitot tube consists of a tube supported in the pipe with the impact opening of about $\frac{1}{8}$ to $\frac{1}{4}''$ dia. that points towards the incoming fluid. This opening is connected to impact pressure connection as shown in Fig. 5.10 (a) alongwith static pressure tap directly located on the pipe. In some arrangements, pitot tube consists of two tubes such that the *impact or stagnation pressure* is measured through the inner tube, while outer tube senses the *static pressure* as shown in Fig. 5.10 (b). But in this arrangement, due to eddies formed around the pitot tube, the static pressure is measured with some error.

II. Working :

As fluid approaches the impact opening, it nearly comes to rest so that velocity head gets converted into pressure head. This maximum pressure at the impact opening is called as *stagnation pressure* and the point where fluid comes to rest is called as *stagnation point. The difference between stagnation pressure and the* static pressure is measured that varies with fluid velocity. Thus pitot tube basically measures flow velocity in terms of the differential pressure and flow velocity can be correlated with fluid flow rate by the equation

$$Q = KAV$$

where,
Q = fluid flow rate
A = flow area = pipe inside area
V = flow velocity
K = flow coefficient of pitot tube (normally about 0.8)

III. Advantages and Limitations :

Advantages :

1. Easy installation and removal.
2. Low permanent pressure loss.
3. It can be used where flowing fluid is not enclosed in a pipe or duct such as river water flow rate or air flow measurement in aeroplane.
4. It can be used for velocity traversing of fluid flowing through large pipes or ducts which is essential for determining flow coefficient.

Limitations :

1. Low accuracy of about ± 0.5% to ± 5%.
2. Pitot tubes cannot be standardized like orifice or venturi tube and hence they must be calibrated for each installation.
3. It cannot be used for metering fluids containing solids.

5.3.5 Sources of Error in Head Flowmeters

1. Errors due to piping arrangements : In head flowmeters primary elements like orifice, venturi etc. are connected with the secondary differential pressure meters that measure the differential pressure across the primary element. The secondary element may be a manometer, bell gauge or any other differential pressure meter. Primary and secondary elements should be connected by proper piping. The piping arrangement should not develope any pressure head that otherwise may result in false reading. The precautions to be taken while doing piping are :

(i) There should be no leakage in piping.

(ii) Connecting lines must be clean and free from obstructions and their diameter ranges between 0.25" to 1".

(iii) The connecting lines must be sloped with 2 in. per ft. to prevent gas pockets.

(iv) The connecting lines should not be more than 50 ft. length.

(v) The connecting lines must be maintained at a temperature between 0° to 40°C.

(vi) The secondary element must be connected below the level of primary element if possible.

2. Density of flowing fluid : Flow equation of the head flowmeters contain density of flowing fluid, hence any variation in density causes error in the flow measurement. To avoid these errors, temperature of fluid must be maintained constant.

3. Pressure compensation : The flow equation of head flowmeters used for gas flow measurement contains the static absolute pressure and absolute temperature of the gas. Hence to avoid any errors in flow measurement, the absolute temperature and pressure of gas should be maintained.

4. Fluid viscosity : Viscosity variations cause slight error in the flow measurement. In order to maintain viscosity, temperature must be controlled at certain value. Thus maintaining temperature of fluid constant increases the accuracy of head flowmeter.

5. Flow pulsations : Pulsations or cyclic variations of flow rate are often observed in flow lines connected to reciprocating machines like pumps. In such cases, head meters measure the average flow value because of its sluggish response that causes an unavoidable lag in the measurement. The pulsation can be reduced by providing sufficient fluid capacitance or resistance ahead of the primary element. Also, reducing the pipe size and operating the meter at high differential pressure reduces the pulsations.

6. Non-linearity : We have seen that there exists non-linear square-root relationship between fluid flow rate and differential pressure head across the primary element. Hence, square-root compensation is employed with head flowmeter so that the scale becomes linear. If square-root compensation is not produced, then the recording chart shows that spacing between flow lines increases with flow rate. Square-root compensation can be achieved with bell type differential pressure meter as shown in Fig. 5.11.

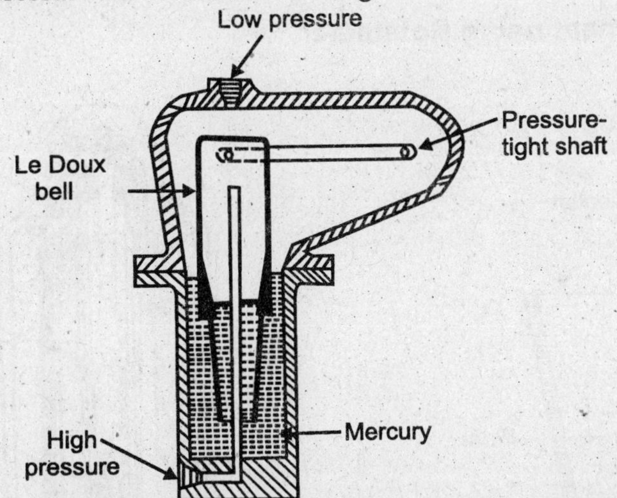

Fig. 5.11 : Bell-differential meter with square-root compensation

In this arrangement bell has parabolic shape that makes the meter response linear so that compensation is achieved by controlling the amount of mercury displaced from the inside of the bell.

The other differential pressure meters like ring gauge have cam arrangement that simply magnifies the lower portion of the scale to linear magnitude. Note that square-root compensation does not improve the accuracy of the flowmeter because first 1% of differential pressure causes the first 10% of flow.

5.3.6 Advantages of Head Flowmeter

1. They can be used for metering almost all fluids except few exceptions.
2. They do not have moving parts in contact with the metering fluid, hence there is little mechanical wearing.

3. They can be indicating or recording type with flow integrating facility.
4. They can be fitted into any configuration of pipe-line like horizontal, vertical or inclined.
5. They can be fabricated to suit any pipe size.

5.4 VARIABLE AREA FLOWMETERS

Principle : The variable area flowmeter operates on the same basic principle as the head flowmeters laid by the continuity equation and the Bernoulli's equation. In the variable area flowmeters, the size of the restriction is varied so as to maintain differential pressure across it constant. This change in restriction size with subsequent change in flow area is proportional to change in fluid flow rate through the restriction. Thus any change in fluid flow rate can be measured in terms of some quantification of change in restriction size or flow area.

Difference between head flowmeter and variable area flowmeter is that in head meters restriction size is fixed and pressure differential across it changes with flow rate, whereas in variable area flowmeters the restriction size changes with flow rate so as to maintain differential pressure across it constant.

5.4.1 Flow Measurement using Rotameter

I. Construction :

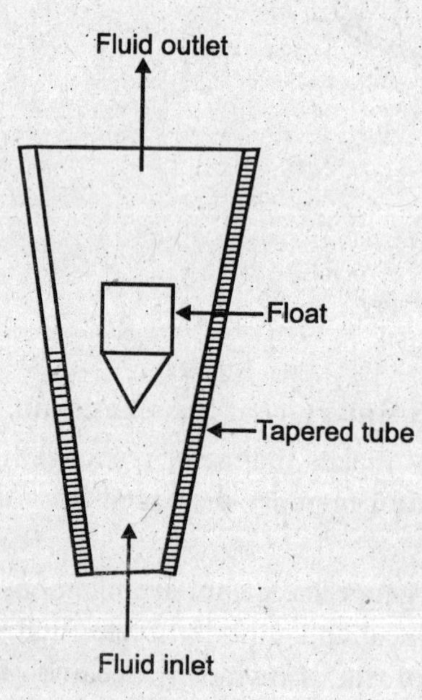

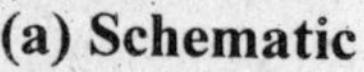

(a) Schematic

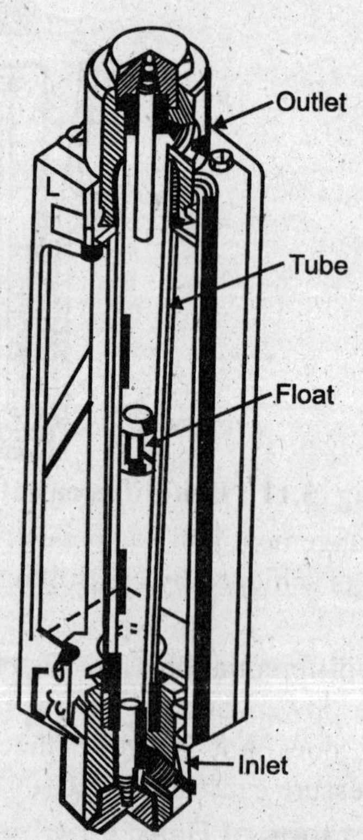

(b) Glass tube rotameter with tube enclosures and metal end fittings

Fig. 5.12 : Rotameter

Rotameter essentially consists of a tapered metering tube and float alongwith scale.

1. Metering tube : Metering tube is tapered glass or metal tube set vertically in piping system with its larger end at the top and the smaller end at the bottom. The tube is placed in a metal housing with front side made of glass for observing the scale. Often the metering tube has protruding vertical ridges at the inside diameter for guiding float movement. Tubes are formed on a mandrel and annealed to prevent internal stresses. For getting exactly linear output conical tube is modified by using internal ribs or beads as shown in Fig. 5.13.

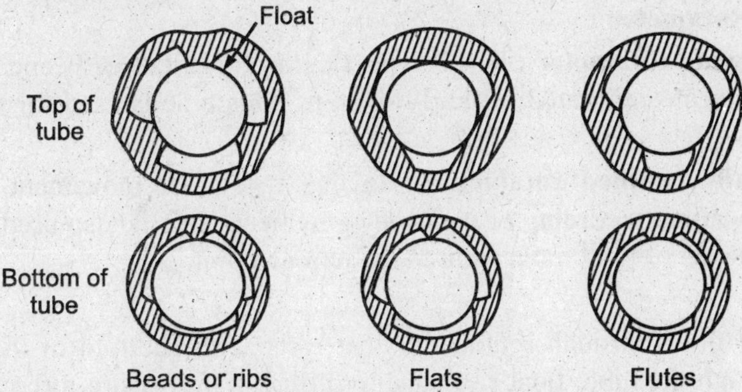

Fig. 5.13 : Bead guided metering tubes

A *float stop* is provided at the upper end of the tube to prevent driving out of the float with fluid stream. The metering tube is made of glass for low temperature and pressure fluids. But for high temperature and pressure service, metal tubes are used. In metal tube rotameters float movement is converted into proportional electrical signal or into rotary motion of the pointer that moves on the calibrated scale.

2. Float : Rotameter floats are usually made of metals which have density higher than liquid, but they can be made of any corrosion resistant materials like aluminium, brass, bronze, monel, nickel, stainless steel. Usually series of slanting notches are cut in the underside of the float rim that gives rotation to float so as to reduce friction. Ball floats are used for measuring low flow rates, while floats having sharp edges are relatively insensitive to viscosity changes over a considerable viscosity range. Fig. 5.14 shows some typical float shapes used in practice.

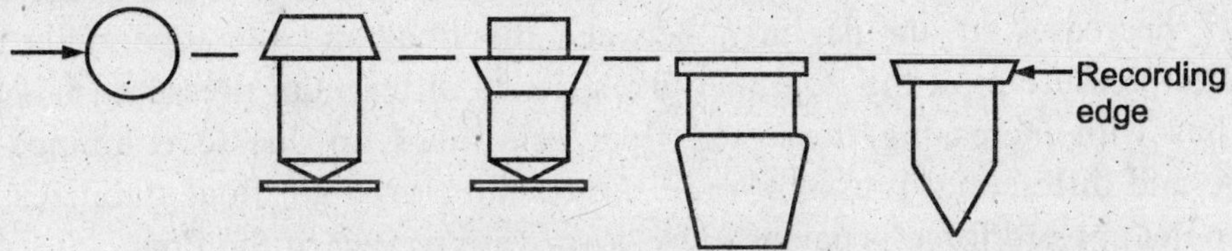

Fig. 5.14 : Float shapes

Flow-range of the rotameter can be changed by changing float material.

Float is stalled in the tube after the meter is mounted in the flow line. Float is inserted from the in ting and not from the outlet fitting so as to avoid float damage due to its free fall in the tı

3. Rotameter scales : Scale is marked on the glass tube or it is mounted close to the metering tube. Scale can be *direct reading type* or *percentage scale* is used which shows the percent value of actual flow relative to maximum flow.

4. Rotameter installation : Rotameter is installed in the pipe line by means of flanges or threads alongwith inlet and outlet piping supported in brackets. The meter must be installed vertically within about 2 geometrical degrees so as to centre the float in the fluid stream.

5. Types of Rotameter :

(a) Direct viewing rotameter : In this type, float is viewed directly and its displacement is measured on the scale calibrated in fluid flow rate. This type is used for free flowing and clear liquids.

(b) Magnetically coupled rotameter : In this type float movement is magnetically coupled to the indicating, recording or controlling element. This is also used for electrical or pneumatic transmission of float movement to the remote point.

II. Working :

When no fluid flows through rotameter, float rests at the bottom of the tube. As fluid starts flowing through the tube, float rises due to differential pressure force and allows fluid to flow through annular space between float edge and the metering tube. Thus as flow rate increases, float moves up in the tube so as to increase the annular orifice area keeping differential pressure across it constant. On the other hand, as flow rate decreases, float falls in the tube so as to reduce the annular orifice area keeping differential pressure across it constant. This is how the operating principle of variable area meter dictates the tapered shape of the metering tube having larger end at the top and smaller at the bottom. At certain fluid flow rate, the float stabilizes at certain position due to balancing of upward differential pressure force and downward weight of the float. *Thus float position varies with flow rate and hence flow rate can be measured in terms of float position.* Usually float has slots on its edge that makes the float to rotate and centre in the tube, due to which the meter is called as rotameter.

Flow equation of rotameter : Fig. 5.15 shows the schematic of rotameter. As flow rate through the meter increases, the buoyancy effect tries to lift the float. Also at the float, flow area suddenly decreases to annular area between the float and the tube. This developes minimum static pressure p_2 at the float that gives rise to differential pressure $(p_1 - p_2)$ across the force. Thus with increasing flow rate, float gets lifted up due to combined effect of buoyant force and differential pressure force. At certain flow rate, float stabilizes at certain position when net upward force is balanced by downward weight of the float.

Let,

D_f = float diameter at the rim

D_t = tube diameter at float position

ρ_f = density of float material

ρ = density of fluid

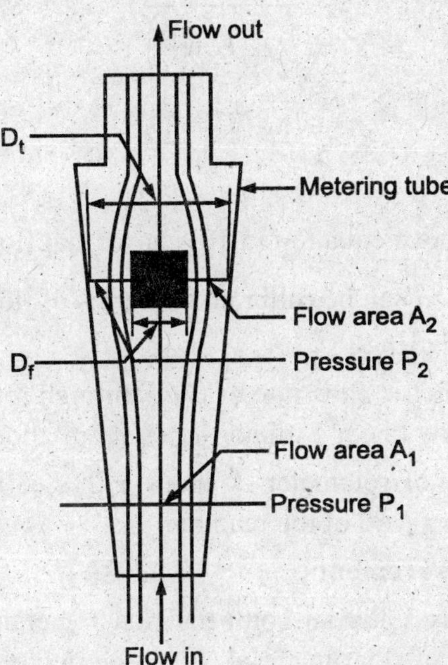

Fig. 5.15 : Schematic of rotameter

p and A represent static pressure and flow area at the respective sections shown in Fig. 5.15. For dynamic equilibrium of float, force balance equation can be written as :

Net upward force = Net downward force on float

i.e. Buoyant force + Differential pressure force = Weight of the float

i.e. $$\rho V_f + (p_1 - p_2)\frac{\pi D_f^2}{4} = \rho_f V_f$$

i.e. $$(p_1 - p_2)\frac{\pi D_f^2}{4} = V_f(\rho_f - \rho)$$

i.e. $$(p_1 - p_2) = \frac{4\,V_f(\rho_f - \rho)}{\pi\,D_f^2} \qquad \ldots (5.12)$$

Now annular flow area between float rim and metering tube can be considered as an orifice having diameter $(D_t - D_f)$ and differential pressure $(p_1 - p_2)$ across it. Hence the flow equation for orifice meter given by equation (5.7) can be written as :

Flow rate : $$Q = K\frac{\pi}{4}(D_t^2 - D_f^2)\sqrt{\frac{2g\,(p_1 - p_2)}{\rho}}$$

i.e. $$Q = \frac{\pi\,K\,(D_t^2 - D_f^2)}{4}\sqrt{\frac{2g}{\rho}\left[\frac{4V_f(\rho_f - \rho)}{\pi\,D_f^2}\right]}$$

(… from equation 5.12)

i.e. $$Q = K\sqrt{\frac{\pi g}{2}}\left(\frac{D_t^2 - D_f^2}{D_f}\right)\sqrt{V_f\left(\frac{\rho_f - \rho}{\rho}\right)}$$

i.e. $$Q = K'\sqrt{V_f\left(\frac{\rho_f - \rho}{\rho}\right)}$$

where $$K' = K\sqrt{\frac{\pi g}{2}\left(\frac{D_t^2 - D_f^2}{D_f}\right)} \quad \text{... (5.13)}$$

The factor $\left(\frac{D_t^2 - D_f^2}{D_f}\right)$ in above equation (5.13) shows that flow rate is the function of float position and hence float position can be calibrated in terms of flow rate.

III. Performance Characteristics :

1. Linearity : The volumetric flow rate of fluid through rotameter is proportional to the area and hence its scale is nearly linear with non-linearity of about 5%.

2. Accuracy : Accuracy of rotameter is about ± 2% of full-scale reading but longer scales increase the accuracy to ± ¼% of the reading.

Sources of error in flow measurement :

(i) Effect of fluid density : Partial compensation for changes in fluid density can be provided by a suitable choice of float material. It can be deduced mathematically that if the density of float material is made twice the density of liquid, then density compensation is almost exact at all flows.

(ii) Effect of fluid viscosity : Viscosity compensation can be provided by suitably shaping the float. The change in fluid viscosity changes the viscous drag acting on the float that disturbs the static equilibrium position of the float at given flow rate. Hence for getting viscosity compensation floats are shaped so that they experience constant viscous drag at all flow rates.

IV. Advantages and Limitations :

Advantags :

1. Rotameter has relatively low and constant pressure drop.
2. Rotameters can handle almost any corrosive fluid.
3. Rotameters can be compensated for changes in fluid density and viscosity.
4. Rotameter has good accuracy particularly at low flow rates.
5. Rotameters are relatively cheaper.
6. Rotameters can be recording, indicating or transmitting type and they can be equipped with alarm switches.

Limitations :

1. Rotameter must be vertically mounted in the pipe line.
2. Glass tube rotameters are not so rugged due to presence of glass tube.
3. Rotameter use is limited to relatively low temperature fluids.

5.4.2 Flow Measurement using Cylinder and Piston Type or Valve Type Areameter

I. Construction :

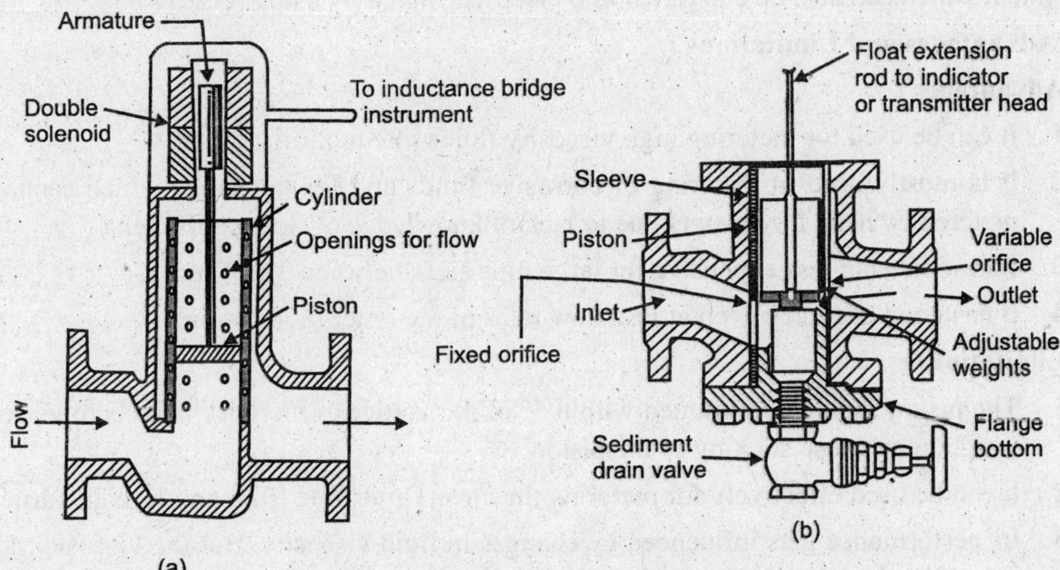

Fig. 5.16 : Piston type areameter

Fig. 5.16 (a) shows cylinder and piston type areameter. It has *cylinder* having holes reamed in its wall fitted with piston. These holes are spaced helically around the cylinder in rows that makes the calibration almost linear. Fig. 5.16 (b) shows the alternative arrangement that consists of a sleeve or cylinder rigidly held in a cast body that is well fitted with piston or metering plug. Orifices, usually rectangular in shape, are cut into sleeve such that bottom of the *variable orifice* at the outlet is above the top of the *fixed orifice* at the inlet. Due to this, when piston is in lowest position, no fluid flows through the meter. The piston may be loaded by weight, placed inside the body. The meter can be made recording or transmitting type by extending piston rod that acts as magnetic rod in the LVDT.

The *meter body* may be of cast iron or any other metal depending upon the corrosion resistance and strength required. The *sleeve* or *cylinder* is usually of heavy construction made of stainless steel. The *piston* is also usually made of stainless steel.

II. Working :

In arrangement shown in Fig. 5.16 (a) as fluid enters below the piston, piston rises and remains steady in certain position. As fluid flow rate increases, piston rises due to differential pressure force. During this upward stroke more and more holes in the walls get uncovered so that flow area increases till differential pressure across the piston is balanced by weight of the piston. Thus at certain flow rate piston occupies certain fixed position. *Hence flow rate can be measured in terms of piston movement and this piston movement can be converted into proportional electrical signal by using LVDT.*

In the arrangement shown in Fig. 5.16 (b), the fluid enters on the underside of the piston through fixed orifice that lifts the piston and uncovers variable orifice through which fluid gets discharged. Thus as flow rate changes, the piston position changes so as to vary the flow area by covering or uncovering of the variable orifice. The piston moves until the differential pressure across it is balanced by its weight. Thus flow rate can be measured in terms of piston movement which can also be converted into electrical signal by using LVDT.

III. Advantages and Limitations :

Advantages :

1. It can be used for metering high viscosity fluids like fuel-oils, tar etc.
2. It is mostly used in metering of corrosive fluids and for the fluids which cannot be metered by head flowmeters due to lack of knowledge of flow coefficient.
3. It is somewhat less expensive for large pipe sizes between 3 to 4 inches.
4. It has good accuracy even at low flow rates of the order 0.08 cc/min.

Limitations :

1. The piston should be mounted within 5° of the vertical, otherwise axial component of weight may cause sticking of the piston.
2. It can be used effectively for metering the clean fluids free from any foreign particles.
3. Its performance gets influenced by changes in fluid viscosity. But the viscosity effect is smaller than that for rotameter.
4. Throttling valves cannot be placed with 10 pipe diameters on the upstream side.

5.5 ELECTROMAGNETIC FLOWMETERS

I. Principle :

Electromagnetic flowmeter works on the principle of Faraday's law of electromagnetic induction which states that, when a current carrying conductor moves through stationary transverse magnetic field, then e.m.f. is induced between the ends of the conductor and this e.m.f. is proportional to relative velocity between the conductor and the magnetic field. This e.m.f. induced is given by

$$E = BLV$$

where, E = emf

B = magnetic induction

L = length of the conductor

V = velocity of the conductor

Thus, $E \propto V$

In electromagnetic flowmeter, flowing conductive fluid acts as the conductor so that e.m.f. developed between the electrodes (located transverse to fluid flow direction and magnetic induction) is proportional to fluid velocity which then can be related with the fluid flow rate by continuity equation

$$Q = AV$$

II. Construction :

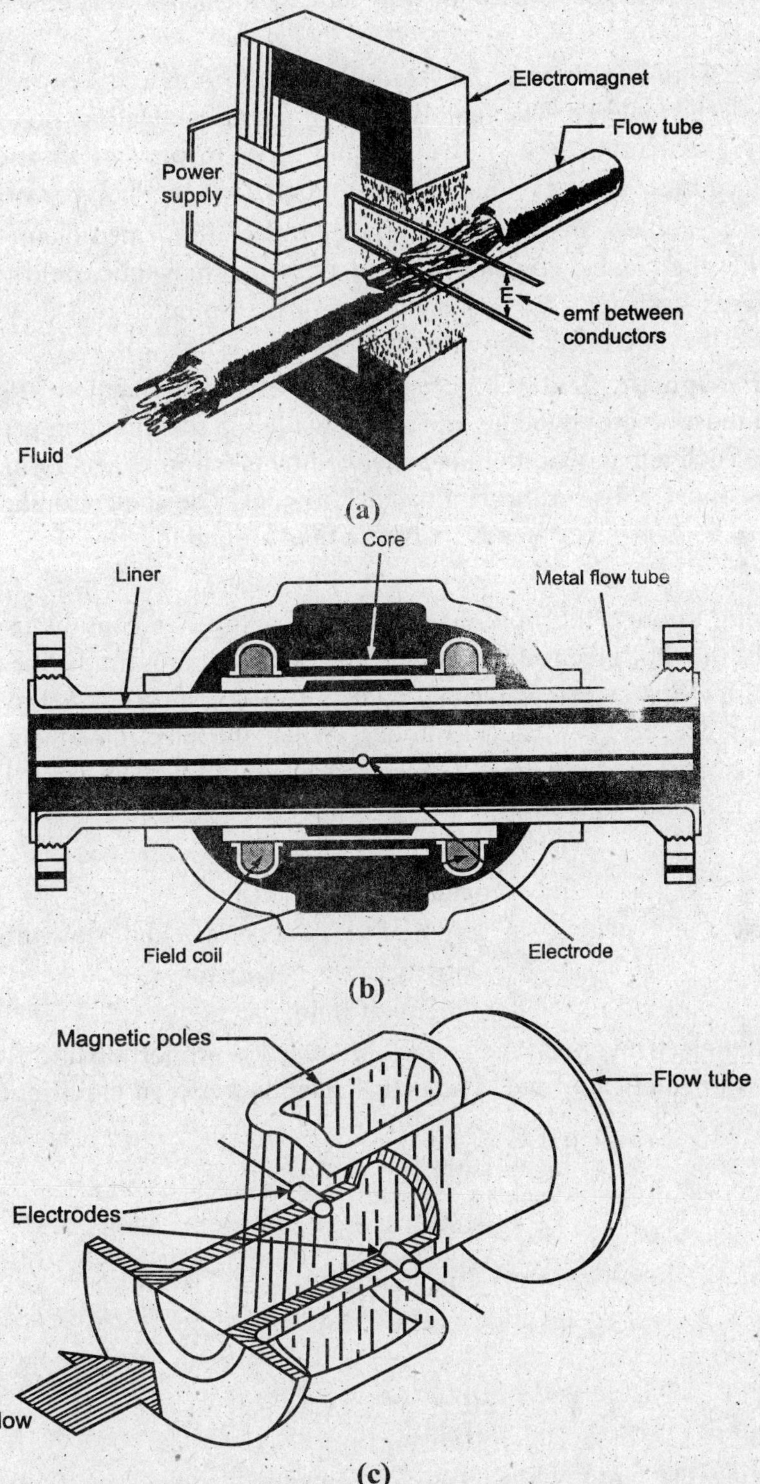

Fig. 5.17 : Electromagnetic flowmeter

The magnetic flowmeter consists of flow tube with electrodes and the source of magnetic field.

Flow tube : This is a separate unit with flanged ends that can be bolted into main pipe carrying liquid to be metered. The tube is made of a non-conducting, non-magnetic alloy and is insulated by glass lining from flowing liquid so as to prevent short-circuiting of e.m.f. between the electrodes. The tube lining can be of polyurethane, polytetra-fluoroethylene.

Electrodes : Stainless steel or platinum electrodes are located diametrically opposite to each other with their axes perpendicular to both the magnetic field and the tube axis. Electrode surfaces flush with the inside surface of the lining so that they do not disturb the flow pattern, but they are in contact with the fluid.

Source of magnetic field : For functioning of electromagnetic flowmeter, a steady magnetic field must be generated around the flow tube in the direction perpendicular to fluid flow direction. Such a magnetic field is generated by electromagnets formed by winding two saddle-shaped copper coils on the laminated iron core. These electromagnets are energized by a.c. supply so as to produce steady magnetic field around the pipe.

III. Working :

Fluid flowing through the flow-tube can be visualised as continuous movement of flat liquid discs past the tube electrodes. Hence, flow of conducting fluids like electrolytes can be considered as a moving current carrying conductor having length equal to inside diameter of the tube or distance between the electrodes. When the electromagnets produce a steady magnetic field around the pipe, then by electromagnetic induction e.m.f. is induced between the electrodes. This emf is given by

$$E = BLV$$

where
B = magnetic induction
L = length of the conductor = id of flow tube
V = velocity of the conductor
= velocity of fluid

Thus for stationary magnetic field e.m.f. produced is proportional to fluid velocity which in turn varies with fluid flow rate. The actual relation between e.m.f. and flow rate can be derived as follows :

We have

$$E = BLV$$

$$= BL\frac{Q}{A} \qquad (\because Q = AV)$$

$$= \frac{BLQ}{\frac{\pi}{4} \times d^2} = \frac{4BQ}{\pi d}$$

$$Q = \frac{\pi d E}{4B}$$

Thus knowing the e.m.f. induced and the magnetic induction, fluid flow rate can be calculated. The meter can be made indicating or recording type.

IV. Advantages and Limitations :

Advantages :

1. Since there are no obstructions in the flow path, very little or no pressure drop occurs.
2. It can be used for metering slurries and greasy materials.
3. It can handle small as well as large flow rates.
4. The flow measurement is not affected by viscosity, density and temperature of the fluid.
5. It has fast speed of response.
6. It can be used to measure flow rates in either directions just by reversing the electrode connections.

Limitations :

1. It can be used for metering conductive liquids only.
2. It cannot be used for metering gases, steam, petroleum products because they have low electrical conductivity.
3. It is relatively expensive.
4. For proper functioning, the flow tube should continuously run full with the liquid.
5. It must be well protected when used in electrical areas to prevent explosion hazards.

5.6 FLOW INTEGRATORS

We have studied various flowmeters that measure the *rate of flow* of fluid. For getting *total flow* over certain time period, the rate of flow must be integrated over that period as :

$$Q = \int_{t=t_1}^{t=t_2} q(t)\, dt$$

where, Q = total flow in time interval $(t_2 - t_1)$

$q(t)$ = flow rate as a function of time.

This integration can be achieved automatically by using flow integrators. Fig. 5.18 shows schematic of flow integrator connected with the differential pressure meter like orifice.

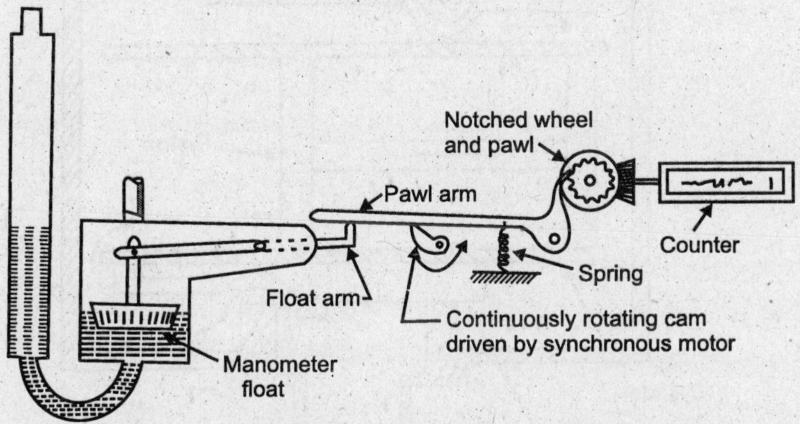

Fig. 5.18 : Wheel and cam type flow integrator

An integrator combines multiplication and addition of flow. The changing flow rate is multiplied continuously by the time elapsed and the product is added continuously to previous trials on counter.

Construction and Working :

Fig. 5.18 shows enlarged leg manometer with float and float arm connected to a counter via gearing. This float arm is made to rest on a rotating cam at high flow, while at low flow it remains away from the cam.

At high flow rates, float arm comes closer to continuously rotating cam, that rotates the arm. Arm rotation drives the counter via mechanical gearing.

As flow rate changes, float position changes that decides the position of float arm above the cam, that causes change in counter reading. Such mechanical integrators operate on 15 sec. cycle. Electrical or pneumatic integrators are also available.

TOTAL FLOWMETERS

5.7 POSITIVE DISPLACEMENT FLOWMETERS (Mechanical Flowmeters or Quantity Meters)

Principle : These meters have two chambers of known volumetric capacity and they are arranged so that when one chamber is being filled, the other is being emptied. Hence for measuring total flow over certain period, the fluid is continuously filled and emptied from the chamber and then the number of times the chamber is filled and emptied in that period is counted which when multiplied by the volumetric capacity of the chamber gives the total flow.

5.7.1 Reciprocating Piston Type Flowmeter

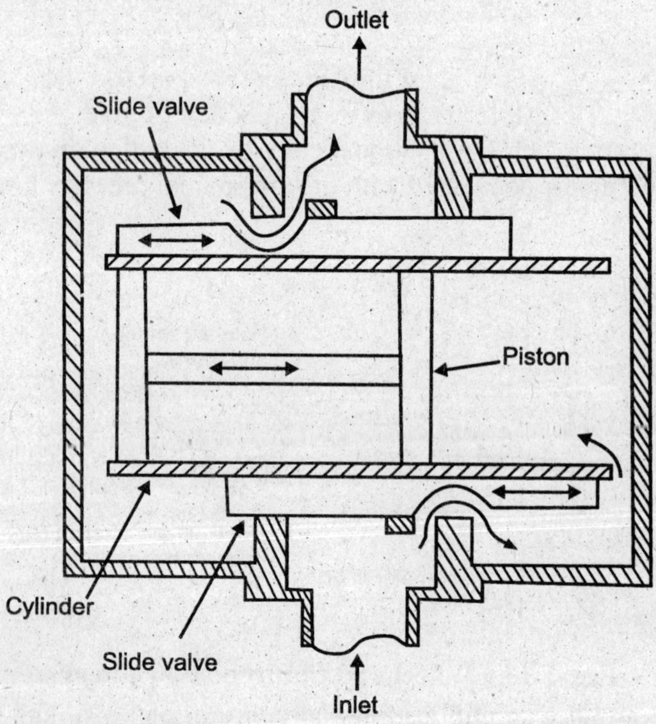

Fig. 5.19 : Reciprocating piston type flowmeter

I. Construction :

The construction is very similar to reciprocating piston pump except that in a pump piston is driven by external power source, while in this flowmeter piston is driven by incoming fluid. It consists of a cast iron cylinder fitted with a piston. Two slide valves are attached at the inlet and outlet ports as shown in Fig. 5.19.

Actually such meters have two to four pistons, all operating on a centre crank arm. The crank arm also operates the valve mechanism which opens and closes the inlet and outlet valves at proper piston positions.

II. Working :

The fluid to be metered enters through the inlet in right portion that forces the piston to the left until the right portion fills the fluid and piston reaches its extreme left position. During this left stroke the fluid already present in the left portion gets discharged through outlet. Now slide valves move in such a fashion that liquid enters in the left portion that forces the piston towards right so as to discharge fluid in right portion. Again sliding valve moves to left and the cycle continues. Thus fluid pressure causes the piston to reciprocate so as to discharge the fluid alternatively from either ends of the cylinder.

Number of piston strokes in a given period represents the number of times cylinder is filled and emptied, which when multiplied by volumetric capacity of the cylinder gives the total flow over that period. This total flow is displayed on the counter driven by the external arm of the slide valve or by the crank arm.

Reciprocating pump flowmeters are available in many forms such as multi-piston meters, double acting piston meters, etc.

III. Advantages and Limitations :

Advantages :

1. It has robust construction.
2. The accuracy of the meter is $\pm$ 0.2 to $\pm$ 0.3%.
3. Its accuracy is not affected by hydraulic conditions around the meter and density, viscosity of fluid.
4. Well designed meters have volumetric efficiency near to 100 %.

Limitations :

1. High cost.
2. Accuracy depends upon leakage of fluid through the meter. Since the amount of leakage depends upon the viscosity of metering liquid, the meters are calibrated on site with the actual liquid before commissioning.
3. It can be used only for non-corrosive and low viscosity liquids.
4. It produces pulsating flow.

5.7.2 Nutating-Disc Flowmeter (Wobbling Flowmeter)

I. Construction :

The meter consists of a *circular disc* pivoted at its geometric centre inside a circular chamber having conical roof and conical floor. A *vertical shaft* is connected to the disc which transmits the disc movement to the *pointer* or indicator via gearing. The inlet and outlet chambers are separated by a partition which fits into a slot in the disc.

II. Working :

The liquid enters through the inlet port and fills the spaces above and below the disc which fits closely and precisely in the measuring chamber. The liquid causes the disc to nutate or wobble about the pivot that causes filling of one chamber and emptying of the other. This disc movement resembles the motion of slowly spinning top.

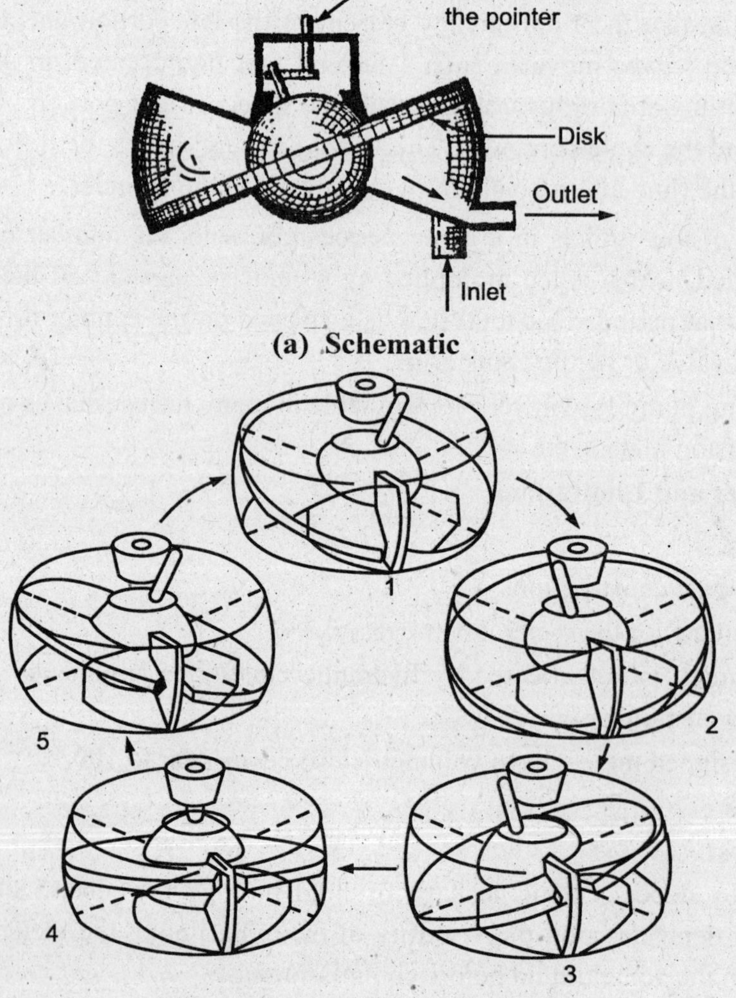

(a) Schematic

(b) One cycle of disc wobbling

Fig. 5.20 : Nutating disc flowmeters

Fig. 5.20 (b) shows one complete cycle of wobbling of the disc that causes the shaft movement to generate a cone with apex downwards. The motion of the disc is controlled by a cam which keeps its lower face in contact with the bottom of the measuring chamber on one side, while the upper face of the disc is in contact with the top of the chamber on opposite side. Thus the measuring chamber is sealed off into separate compartments which are successively filled and emptied and they have a definite volume. The measuring liquid forms a seal between the disc and the chamber wall, that minimizes the leakage and slippage. The motion of the disc is transmitted to indicator via gear train. Zero reset facility is provided with the meter.

III. Advantages and Limitations :

Advantages :

1. Simple and compact construction.
2. Relatively low cost.
3. High accuracy between ± 1 to ± 2%.
4. They can handle a wide range of chemicals with the proper materials of construction.
5. Used in residential water meters.

Limitations :

1. Accuracy depends upon liquid density and viscosity.
2. Can be used only for clear liquids.

5.7.3 Rotating Vane Flowmeter

I. Construction :

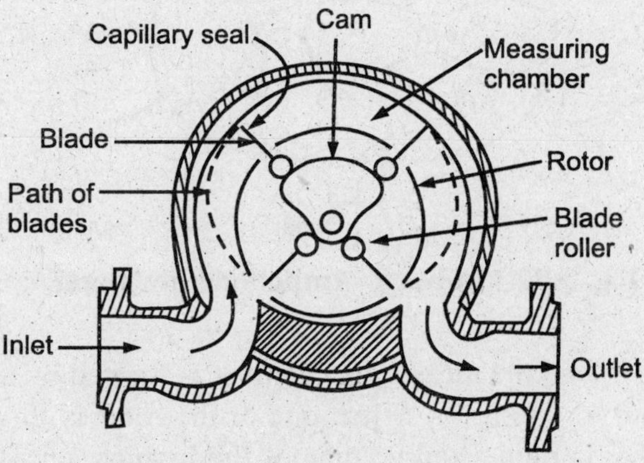

Fig. 5.21 : Rotating vane flowmeter

The sliding vane type flowmeter shown in Fig. 5.21 has a cylindrical rotor that revolves on ball bearing around a central shaft and stationary cam.

II. Working :

As liquid flows against an extended vane or blade, the rotor rotates alongwith the blades. Due to stationary cam position, the blades follow the path shown in Fig. 5.21. Due to this path followed by the blades, measuring chambers are formed and these chambers are sealed by capillary action of the metering fluid. Thus measuring chamber is sealed off into separate compartments which are succesively filled and emptied. The rotations of the rotor are transmitted to a register that indicates total flow in given time period.

III. Advantages and Limitations :

Advantages :

1. They can be used to meter liquids upto temperature of 240°C and pressure of 900 psi.
2. The meter can handle highly viscous slurries because effect of density and viscosity is negligible.
3. It has low pressure loss.
4. Accuracy lies between ± 0.2 to ± 0.3%.

Limitations :

1. Suitable only for clean liquids.
2. Relatively high cost.

5.7.4 Lobbed Impeller Flowmeter

I. Construction :

The meter consists of two rotors, each having two lobes arranged to mesh like gears with fixed relative positions.

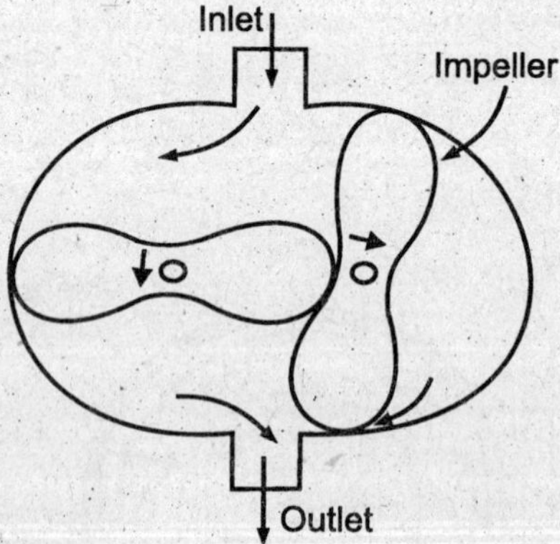

Fig. 5.22 : Lobbed - Impeller Flowmeter

II. Working :

In this meter as rotors rotate, the measuring chamber is formed by the wall of the cylinder and the surface of one-half of one rotor. When one of the rotor is in a vertical position, the measuring compartment has certain fixed volume of fluid which gets discharged through the bottom of the meter with rotation of the rotor. This action takes place four times for a complete revolution. The impeller speed drives the counter that registers total flow over certain time period.

III. Advantages and Limitations :

Advantages :

1. They have wide capacity range of 3.8 to 66.500 LPM.
2. Accuracy is ± 0.2%.
3. They can be used at very high temperatures of 2000C and pressures of 1200 psi.
4. Low pressure loss.
5. Availability of various materials of construction.
6. Applicable to gases and highly viscous fluids like asphalts.

Limitations :

1. Larger and bulky size.
2. Relatively high cost.
3. Sensitivity decreases at low flow rates due to slip effect.
4. Entrained vapours may damage the meter.

5.8 VELOCITY FLOWMETERS

I. Principle :

These flowmeters actually measure the flow velocity which, in turn is a measure of rate of flow in a filled, closed pipe. Thus fluid flow rate is measured in terms of its flow velocity.

5.8.1 Turbine Type Flowmeter

Turbine flowmeter consists of a multiblade rotor mounted at right angles to the axis of the flowing fluid. The rotor is supported on ball bearings either at one end only or at both the ends. This shaft supporting section also acts as straightening vane that directs the flow to turbine.

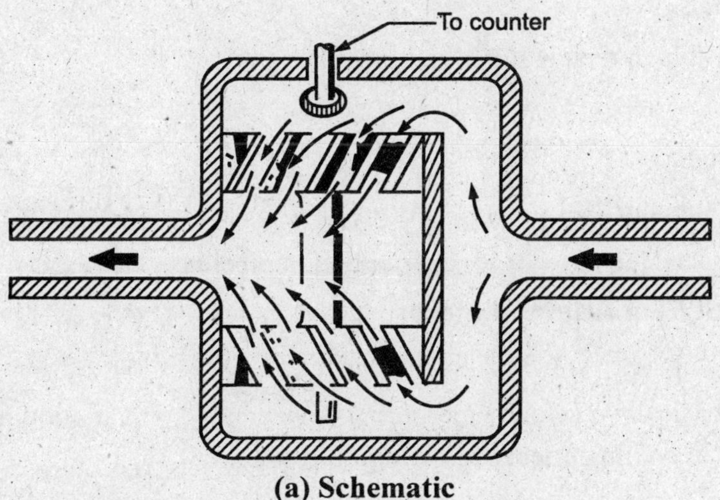

(a) Schematic

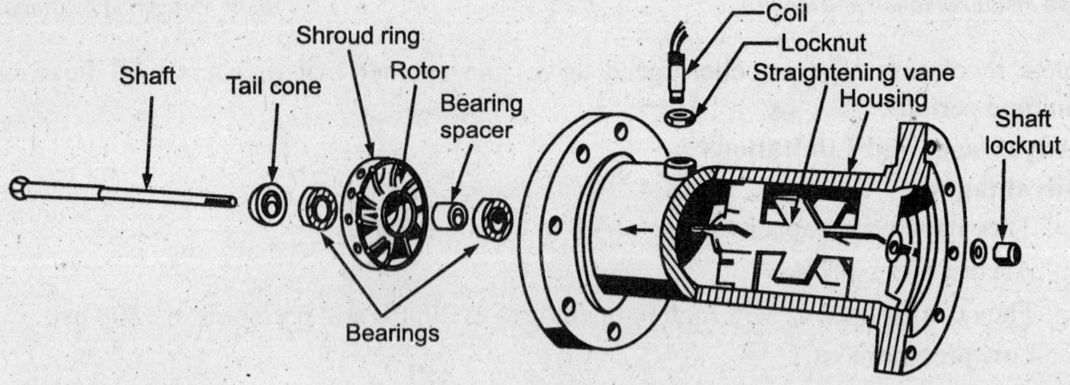

(b) Cutaway and exploded view

Fig. 5.23 : Turbine flowmeter

II. Working :

The flowing fluid impinges on the turbine blades, that imparts force on the blade so as to cause the rotor to rotate. When rotor speed reaches steady value, the speed is proportional to fluid velocity. Turbine wheel operates the counter that indicates rate of flow or total flow. Rotor speed may be transmitted through the meter housing by a mechanical shaft with a magnetic coupling to an external shaft through a suitable gland in the housing.

III. Advantages and Limitations :

Advantages :

1. High accuracy between ± 0.25 to ± 0.5%.
2. Excellent repeatability.
3. Low pressure drop.
4. Particularly suitable in aerospace and air borne applications or energy fuel flow measurements.
5. Can be used at high temperatures and pressures.

Limitations :

1. Relatively high cost.
2. Limited use for slurries.
3. Accuracy depends upon velocity distribution in pipeline.

5.8.2 Hot Wire/Hot Film Anemometers

Principle :

Anemometer is basically a velocity measuring device based on variation in resistance of a thin heated wire due to cooling effect of flowing fluid stream.

Construction and Working :

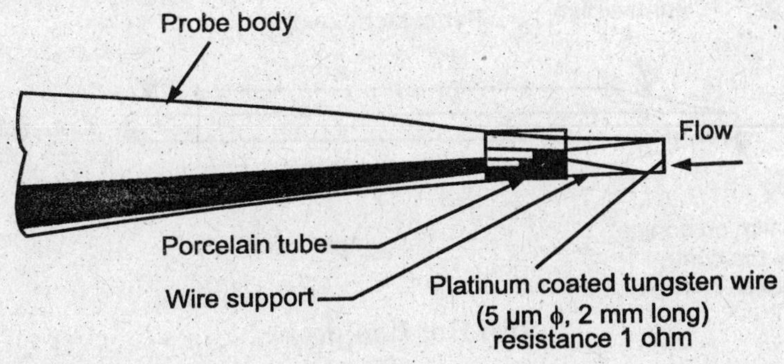

(a)

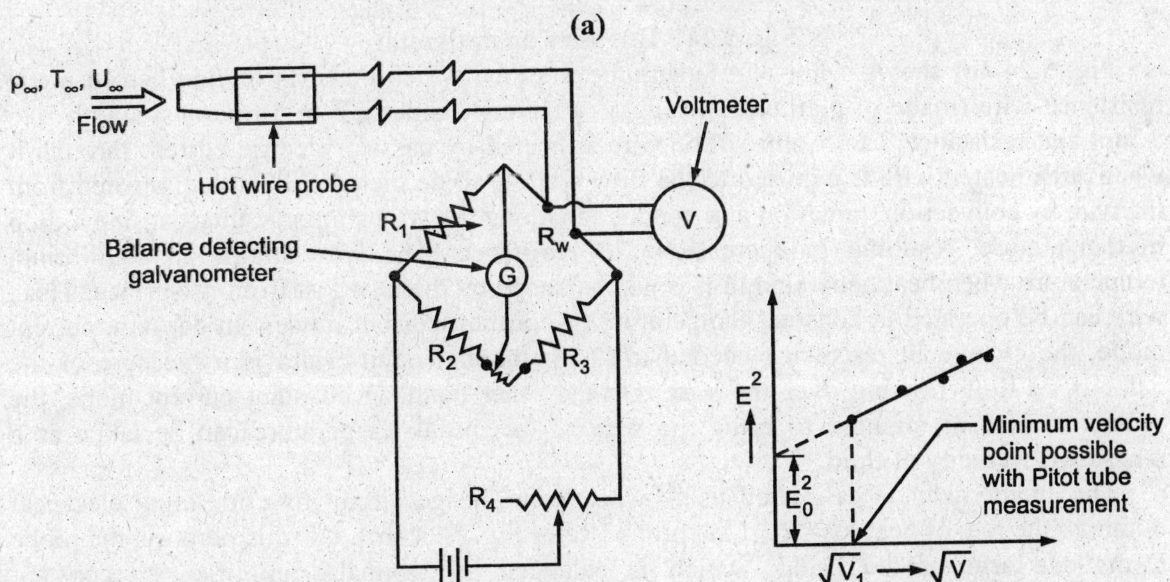

(i) Hot wire bridge circuit

(ii) A typical calibration curve of hot wire anemometer

(b)

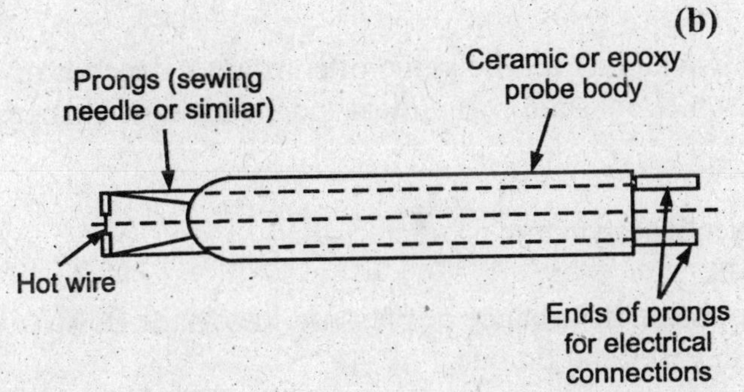

(i) A typical hot wire probe

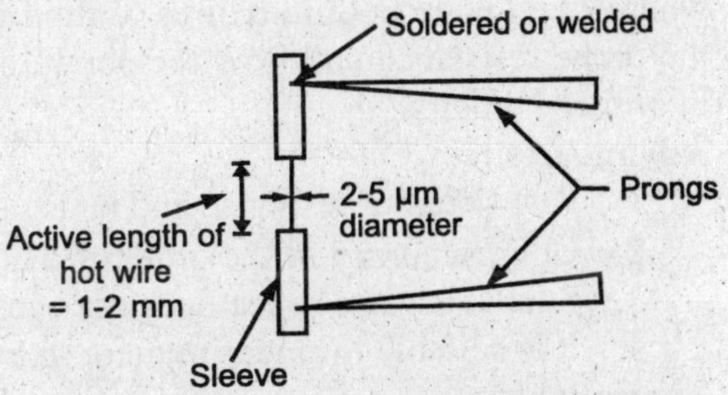

(ii) Constructional details of the wire of the probe

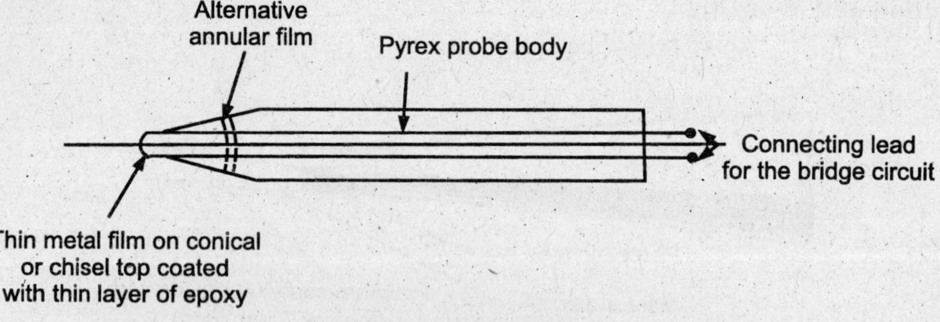

(iii) Hot film probe

(c)

Fig. 5.24 : Hot wire anemometer

Fig. 5.24 (b) shows a hot-wire anemometer probe which consists of fine heated metal resistance wire (made of platinum or tungsten) having diameter 2 to 5 microns, length 2 to 5 mm and resistance 2 to 5 ohms. The wire is heated by passing electric current through it when such heated wire is exposed to the flow of fluid to be metered, heat is dissipated from the wire by convection, radiation and conduction along the wire supports, thus causing a drop in temperature, resulting in decrease in its resistance. The wire attains an equilibrium temperature when heat generated in it is just balanced by the heat lost from its surface. Thus, wire can be operated at constant temperature or constant current modes. In constant current mode, the change in resistance needed to attain thermal equilibrium is a measure of the velocity of fluid flowing over the wire. On the other hand, in constant current mode, the change in current required to bring the wire to the initial temperature can be taken as a measure of velocity of fluid.

The anemometer is calibrated using wheatstone bridge circuit by correlating electrical output to the rate of heat loss from the probe [Refer Fig. 5.24 (b)]. For this purpose, the probe forms one arm of the bridge which is balanced by feedback amplifier. In constant temperature mode, if E is the input voltage to the bridge circuit and E_o is the input voltage corresponding to zero flow of fluid, then heat lost due to force convection can be expressed based on the King's empirical law as

$$E^2 - E_o^2 = ku^2$$

where k and n are both functions of fluid flow velocity u. The value of constant k depends on the probe resistance and flow temperature, while constant n is almost independent of change in probe geometry.

Advantages :

1. Fast speed of response and hence excellent dynamic characteristics.
2. Good accuracy of the order of ± 0.1%.
3. Small size and hence does not cause much disturbance or pressure loss to the flow.
4. It is suitable for measurement in both gases and liquids.

Limitations :

1. Since output depends on cooling of the wire, it is independent of the direction of flow.
2. Sensitivity depends on accumulation of dirt/dust on the hot wire, therefore it needs frequent calibrations.

3. Dust particles in fluid can break the wire, therefore, it is used for clean fluids.
4. Since output voltage is proportional to square of fluid velocity, it has nonlinear operating characteristics.
5. It is expensive and require skilled operations.

5.8.3 Ultrasonic Flow Meter

Principle :

Ultrasonic flow meters work on the principle of apparent change in the velocity of propagation of sound pressure pulses in a fluid with a change in velocity of fluid flow. In practice, short burst of sinusoidal pressure pulse having frequency above audio range (> 20 kHz) is used, with typical value of 10 MHz.

Construction and Working :

There are two types of ultrasonic flow meters viz. Doppler frequency shift and transit time.

In the Doppler method, an ultrasonic transducer (i.e. a piezoelectric crystal) is bonded to a pipe wall which transmit an ultrasonic signal into the fluid flow. The particles suspended in a fluid cause change in frequency of incident radiation which is proportional to velocity of the particle. This frequency shift is measured using electronic counter.

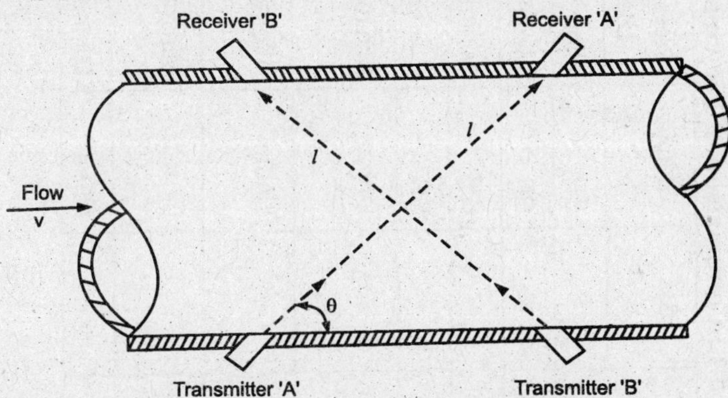

Fig. 5.25 : Ultrasonic flow meter

In the transit flow meter, an ultrasonic transducer is mounted at an angle to the pipe wall as receivers and transmitter as shown in Fig. 5.25. The velocity of the ultrasonic waves emitted by transmitter changes with velocity of fluid flowing through the pipeline.

Advantages :

1. This flowmeter offers negligible resistance to flow of fluid, therefore, there is no much pressure loss.
2. The output is insensitive to temperature, pressure and viscosity.
3. It has good accuracy and fast speed of response.
4. It has linear relation between fluid velocity and output.
5. It is suitable for both liquids and gases flowing through any pipe size.
6. It is used for measurement of ocean currents, vessel and flows of various industrial fluids.

Disadvantages :

The only disadvantages of this flow meter is its relatively high cost which limited its industrial applications.

5.9 COMPARISON OF FLOWMETERS

Table 5.1 : Comparison of Flowmeters

Sr. No	Type	Viscous Liquid	Slurry	Gas	Output	Pressure Loss	Accuracy % full scale	Full range
1.	Orifice	Limited	×	✓	SR	High	± 0.5 to ± 2%	10^{-3} to 5.5×10^3 m³/hr
2.	Venturi	Limited	Limited	✓	SR	Minimal	± 0.5 to ± 3%	1 to 5.5×10^3 m³/hr
3.	Flow nozzle	Limited	Limited	✓	SR	Minimal	± 0.5 to ± 3%	1 to 5.5×10^3 m³/hr
4.	Pitot tube	×	×	✓	SR	×	± 5 to ± 10%	10 to 10^4 m³/hr
5.	Electromagnetic	✓	✓	✓	Linear	Minimal	± 2 to ± 5%	5.5×10^{-4} to 4.95×10^3 m³/hr
6.	Variable areameters	Limited	Limited	✓	Linear	Average	± 0.5%	10^{-7} to 5.5×10^3 m³/hr
7.	Positive displacement	✓	✓	✓	Linear	Minimal	± 0.5 to 1%	10^{-5} to 5×10^2 m³/hr.
8.	Turbine	Limited	×	×	Linear	Minimal	± 2% to ± 5%	0.5 to 4.95×10^2 m³/hr

Note : SR - square root characteristic.

5.10 VORTEX FLOW METER

Principle :

In vortex flowmeter, the fluid entering the meter is swirled or rotated that results in change in velocity of fluid, which is sensed by means of a thermistor in terms of changes in cooling cycles with the velocity variations.

Construction and Working :

In vortex precession type meters, the fluid enters a fixed swirling element and gets swirled or rotated with the center of rotation of the fluid coinciding with that of the meter body. The swirled fluid then enters an enlarged area inside the meter where it leaves the axial path and takes the helical path about the center line. This is known as precession of vortex whose frequency is proportional to volumetric flow rate which is reflected through changes in velocity of fluid i.e. sensed by a thermistor. The de-swirl components of the fluid straighten the flow and leave the meter.

In vortex-shedding type flowmeters triangular-shaped vortex generating objects are used. As the fluid approaches these objects, the flow gets separated from the flow element and the eddies or vortices are formed which grow and then becomes detached or shed from the object on either sides of the triangular object thereby forming a von Karman vortex sheet as shown in Fig. 5.26.

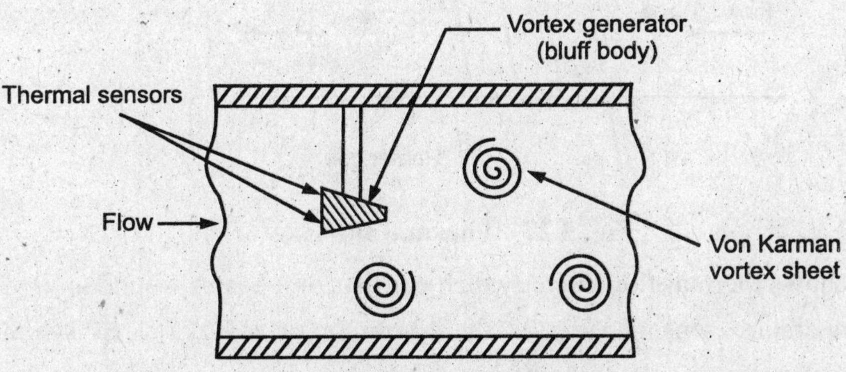

Fig. 5.26 : Vortex shedding

This vortex shedding result in fluctuation in fluid velocity which is sensed by thermistor sensor located on the side of the body.

Advantages :

1. The output signal is independent of gravity, viscosity and temperature of fluid.
2. The calibration depends on dimensions of the flow element, therefore it has same calibration factor for all liquids and gases.

3. Since there are no moving parts, the meters has very low pressure loss and no upper limit on the flow that can be measured except that imposed by the electronics associated with the sensor.
4. These meters can be used for corrosive liquids and gases, slurries and cryogenic liquids.
5. Good repeatability, linearity and fast speed of response.

5.10.1 Thermal Flow Meters

Principle :

As fluid flows through heating coil around the pipeline, temperature of fluid increases in the direction of flow, therefore flow rate of fluid can be measured in terms of temperature difference across the heating coil.

Construction and Working :

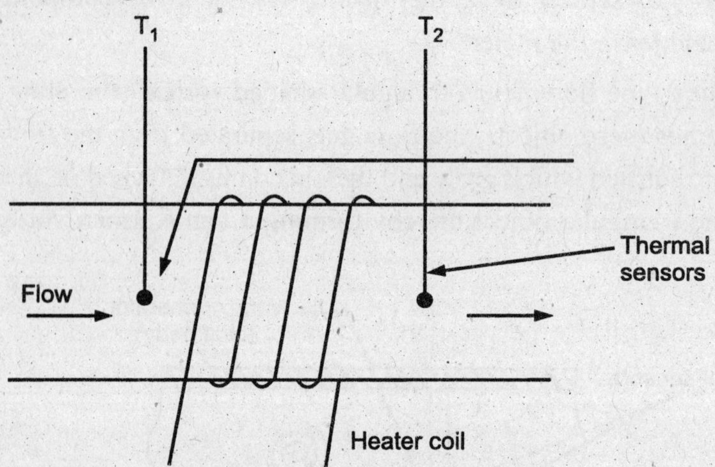

Fig. 5.27 : Thermal flow meter

Fig. 5.27 shows thermal flow meter which consists of a heater wound around the channel with two temperature sensors such as thermocouple or RTD located symmetrically on upstream and downstream side of the heater. When there is no liquid flowing through heater, temperatures T_1 and T_2 measured by the sensors will be the same so that the differential temperature reading $T_2 - T_1$ will be 0. As fluid flow increases, temperature T_1 will fall and T_2 will rise until a steady state is reached. Heat transferred to the liquid by the heater is given by

$$Q = WC_p (T_2 - T_1)$$

where, W = mass flow rate of fluid

and C_p = specific heat of fluid

Thus, at constant heater input power, the temperature difference $T_2 - T_1$ is inversely proportional to the mass flow rate W of fluid.

The limitation of this flow meter is poor speed of response because it depends on flow condition.

5.11 LASER ANEMOMETER

Principle :

This flowmeter works on the principle of Doppler phenomena according to which the particles in fluid scatter the laser light and the frequency of this scattered light differs from that of the incident beam by an amount proportional to velocity of the fluid.

Construction and Working :

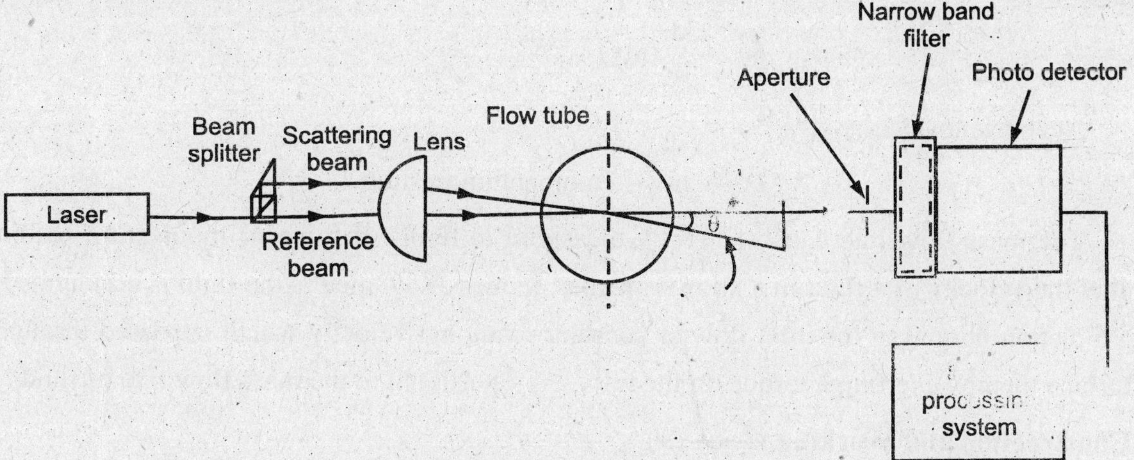

Fig. 5.28 : Laser anemometer

Fig. 5.28 shows the schematic of laser anemometer which consist of laser source of He-Ne or argon ion which emit laser light that pass through splitter and lens so as to focus and collimate on fluid flow. The beam after colliding with fluid particles undergo Doppler effect with frequency shift and then through photo detector and signal processor which convert frequency shift into corresponding voltage fluctuations.

Advantages :

1. Good precision of high resolution.
2. Since there is no flow disturbance, there is no pressure loss.
3. Used for measurement of wind velocity in tunnels.

Disadvantages :

1. Low sensitivity and poor resolution in distinguishing velocity fluctuations.

5.12 MASS FLOWMETERS

In the aircraft fuel requirement is measured in mass unit because the calorific value of fuel is proportional to the mass and not the volume. In many chemical processes, mass flow rate is significant quantity.

Principle :

The volumetric flow rate of fluid measured by flow meters discussed earlier is multipled by density of fluid to get the mass flow rate.

According to Newton's second law of motion, force F acting on fluid in certain direction is given by

$$F = \frac{d}{dt}(mv).$$

At constant velocity v,

$$F = mv = \text{momentum of fluid}$$

The mass flow rate can be directly measured in terms of force or momentum required alter the velocity of a fluid in a known manner. In mass flow meters the fluid is accelerated in a direction normal to the inlet flow at constant rotational velocity which is passed through a turbine thereby exerting a torque on the turbine proportional to the mass flow rate of fluid.

Construction and Working :

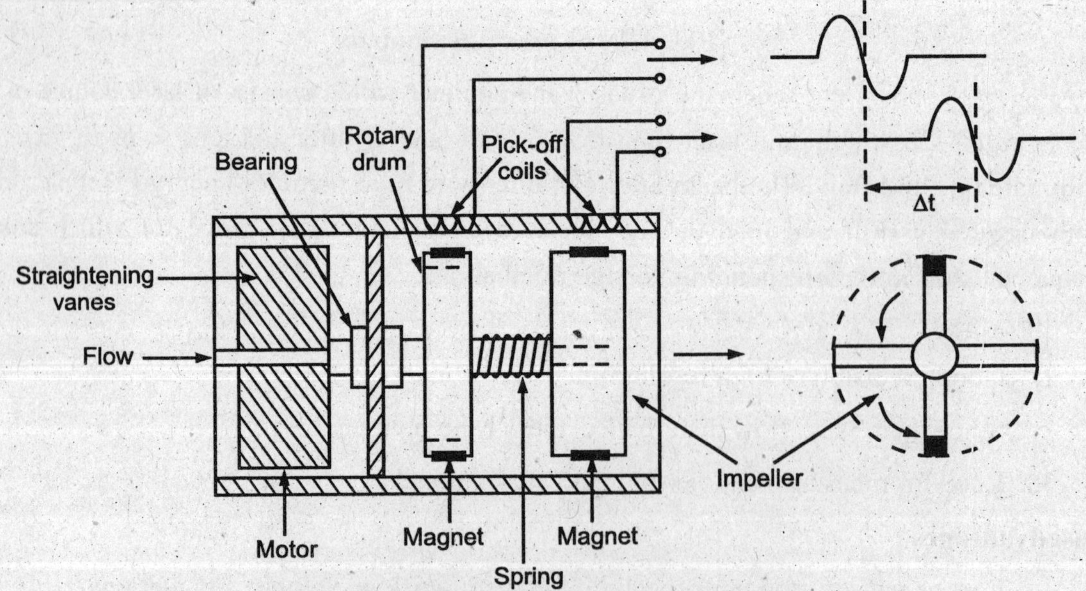

Fig. 5.29 : Rotor torque mass flow meter

Fig. 5.29 shows rotor torque mass flow meter in which fluid flow is smoothened by passing through straightening vanes fitted into an annular space. The axially flowing fluid flows over a rotary drum driven at a constant speed (about 100 r.p.m.). The angular torque is imparted to the impeller by the shaft connected to drum using a torsion spring. This torque is proportional to the mass flow rate of fluid. The voltage pulses are induced in magnets fixed on the periphery of the rotating drum and the time interval between the pulses is measured which is proportional to the spring deflection and hence the mass flow rate.

Advantages :

1. High accuracy of about 6.5%.

EXERCISE

1. State the applications and importance of flow measurement.
2. Differentiate between rate of flow and total flow of fluid.
3. Describe the following flowmeters:

   (i) Orifice, (ii) Venturi, (iii) Pitot tube, (iv) Flow nozzle.
4. Compare the performance of orifice and venturi flowmeters.
5. What is vena-contracta ?
6. Derive the flow equation for :

   (i) Orificemeter, (ii) Venturimeter, (iii) Rotameter.
7. Fora given pipeline, how orifice meter can be used to measure flow rate ?
8. What is the basic difference between a head flowmeter and a variable-area flowmeter ?
9. Describe the following flowmeters : (i) Rotameter, (ii) Valve type flowmeter.
10. How will you measure the flow rate of fluids not enclosed in a pipe, such as river flow ?
11. What are the sources of error in head flowmeters ?
12. What are the advantages of head flowmeters over other flowmeters ?
13. What is the historical background of the word rotameter ?
14. Explain how the operating principle of variable area flowmeter dictates the tapered shape of the rotameter glass tube.
15. Explain the resemblance of variable area meter with head flowmeter when flow stabilizes at certain value.

16. Describe the principle, construction and working of Electromagnetic flowmeter. What are its advantages and limitations ?
17. Explain the function of flow integrators.
18. Describe the following flowmeters :

    (i) Reciprocating piston type, (ii) Rotary vane type

    (iii) Nutating disc type, (iv) Lobbed impeller type.
19. Why square - root compensation is essential in head flowmeters ?
20. Describe turbine type flowmeters.

❑❑❑

6

CHAPTER

INSTRUMENTAL METHODS OF CHEMICAL ANALYSIS

6.1 APPLICATIONS AND IMPORTANCE OF COMPOSITION ANALYSIS

Continuous production processes involve the conversion of raw materials into a single final product. For obtaining uniform, satisfactory finished product quality, it is necessary to measure and control the physical and chemical properties of the constituent materials. This is called as *Composition Analysis* of the product.

Applications of chemical composition measurements :

1. **For Raw Materials :**

(a) To check purchase specifications.

(b) Detection of impurities.

(c) To check the percentage of active-ingredient on which price of the material depends.

2. **For Product Quality :**

(a) To determine product composition.

(b) To determine melting or boiling point, refractive index etc.

(c) To assist in adjustment of product quality to meet the desired specifications.

3. **For Yield Improvement :**

(a) Continuous analysis of process streams helps to measure the effects of variables affecting the product yield.

(b) Analysis of overflow or purge streams, recirculated material is done to determine product losses and build-up of undesirable by-products that affect the yield.

4. **For Process Control :** Continuous process analysis helps to control the continuous process.

5. **For Safety :**

(a) To detect equipment leaks.

(b) To detect any escape of toxic materials from leaks or spills which cannot be detected by human senses.

(c) To detect flammable or explosive mixtures in the atmospheres.

6. **For Waste Disposal :**

(a) To monitor plant stacks for any accidental discharge of toxic gases, vapours, smoke, etc.

(b) To analyse the waste streams for toxic or other objectionable materials.

(c) To control waste recovery facilities.

7. **For Research and Development :**

(a) To get the structural and compositional information which cannot be obtained otherwise.

6.2 BASIC COMPONENTS OF ANALYTICAL INSTRUMENTS

Analytical instruments are used to provide information about the components of sample of matt to obtain qualitative information about presence or absence of one or more components of sample or quantitative data from them.

Elements of an analytical instrument :

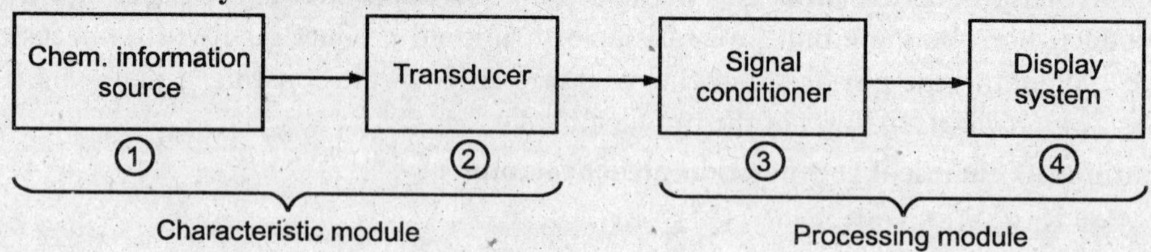

Fig. 6.1

(1) Generates a set of signals containing necessary information generated by sample itself. e.g. yellow radiation by heated sodium to flame photometer.

(2) Converts signal to one of the different nature. e.g. photocell and photomultiplier tube convert radiant energy into electrical signals.

(3) Converts the output of transducer into an electrical quantity suitable for operation of the display system.

(4) Provides a visible representation of the quantity as a displacement on a scale/chart/screen.

Each one of the components of the characteristic module contributes to performance specifications of an instrument. The detector determines the limit of detection of measurement and produces a signal amplitude which is processed in a processing module.

After amplification decision is taken about whether to carry out processing with signal in analog form or to convert to digital form by A/D conversion.

6.3 CLASSIFICATION OF COMPOSITION ANALYSIS METHODS

(A) Methods based on Atomic or Molecular or Crystalline Characteristics of Matter :

1. Absorption Spectroscopy.
2. Emission Spectroscopy.
3. Mass Spectroscopy.
4. X-Ray Diffraction Method.

(B) Methods based on Measurement of following Physical Characteristics of Matter :

1. Thermal Conductivity.
2. Electrolytic Conductivity.
3. Combustibility.
4. Magnetic Susceptibility (O_2 Analyzer).
5. Physical Absorption Characteristics (Chromatography).
6. Refractive Index.
7. Density or Specific Gravity.
8. Viscosity.
9. Acidity or Alkalinity (pH).

6.4 SPECTROSCOPIC METHODS OF COMPOSITION ANALYSIS

Principle : The classification of composition analysis methods given in the section 6.3 is based on the *interactions between energy and matter*. The matter consists of large number of atoms and each atom has positively charged *nucleus* and negatively charged *electrons* orbiting or revolving around it in different *shells.*

The *nucleus* contains *positively charged protons* and *neutral neutrons*. The atomic number of the element is given by the total number of electrons that also equal to total number of protons that make the atom electrically neutral. Electronic configuration of the atom gives the distribution of electrons in different energy levels or shells. When the electrons occupy lowest possible energy levels, atom is said to be in a *ground state*. When atom is *excited* by external energy source like thermal, optical or electrical, then electrons absorb additional energy and jump to higher energy states, thus modifying the electronic configuration. When excitation is removed, these jumped electrons return to their ground energy state and during this jump from higher energy state to lower energy state, the additional energy possessed by the electron is given out in the form of electromagnetic radiations. The wavelength at which energy is absorbed or emitted is the characteristic of the substance used. Hence by studying the absorption or emission spectrum of the substance, its composition can be analysed in terms of presence of certain constituent whose standard spectrum or *fingerprint* is available. When there is *discrete change in energy* during absorption or emission, the line spectrum is produced in which each line corresponds to certain fixed frequency with the characteristic colour. When there is *continuous change in energy* during absorption or emission, then *continuous spectrum* is produced in the form of a patch or band of light. *Absorption line spectrum* shows dark lines on light background, while *emission line spectrum* shows bright lines on dark background on a photographic negative.

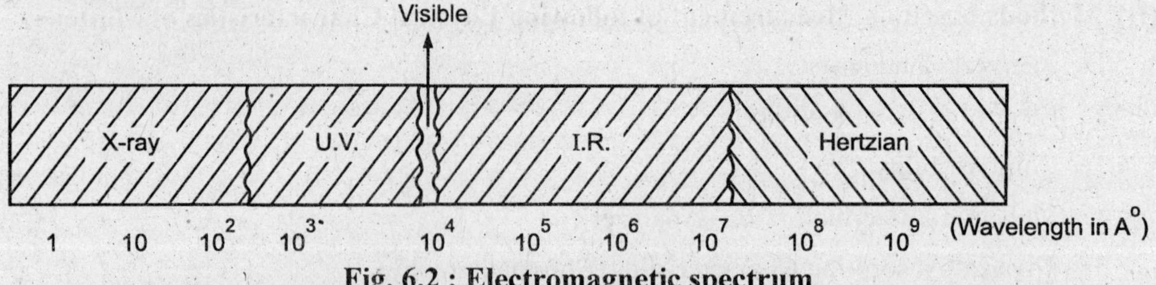

Fig. 6.2 : Electromagnetic spectrum

The electromagnetic spectrum consists of X-ray, ultraviolet (UV), infrared (IR) and hertzian regions with the wavelengths as shown in Fig. 6.2.

6.5 ABSORPTION SPECTROSCOPY

6.5.1 X-Ray Absorption Spectrometers

X-rays occupy the portion of the electromagnetic spectrum between about 0.01 A° to 100 A° (1 A° = 10^{-8} cm = 10^{-10} m). When fast moving electrons are suddenly decelerated by the electric field of nucleus of the target atom, then energy is given out in the form of X-rays. The absorption of X-rays follow Lambert's law given by

$$I = I_0 e^{\mu x \rho} \qquad \dots (6.1)$$

where,
I = intensity of radiation passing through the material
I_0 = intensity of incident radiation
x = thickness of absorbing material
μ = mass absorption coefficient
ρ = density of the absorbing material

The X-ray spectrometer consists of a source of X-rays like X-rays tube providing wavelength range between 0.4 to 1.5 A°. Two beams are taken from the source, one of which passes through a sample cell to a *fluorescent screen*, while the other beam passes through a variable thickness *aluminium attenuator* and then through a second sample cell to the same fluorescent screen. An amplifier is used to measure the difference in the intensity of two beams. The thickness of aluminium attenuator is so adjusted that both the beams have same intensity. Thus the difference between X-ray absorption of two samples can be expressed in terms of thickness of aluminium attenuator. *By trial calibration this aluminium thickness can be related to the content of critical compound.*

Applications :

1. This method can be used for analysis of solids, liquids and gases.
2. The method can be used for measuring -
   (i) sulphur content of oil,
   (ii) lead content of gasoline,
   (iii) metal content of glass,
   (iv) halogen content of plastics,
   (v) ash content of coal.

6.5.2 Ultraviolet (UV) Absorption Spectroscopy

These spectrometers operate in the range from 2000 A° to 8000 A° which actually includes the visible range also. The basic UV absorption analyzer consists of a *radiation source, optical filter, a sample cell, a detector and an output meter*. The absorbance of a substance is given by Beer's law written as

$$A = abc \quad \dots (6.2)$$

where a = molar absorptivity

b = path length

c = concentration

UV source : The source provides the desired UV wavelength and may be either a line source such as mercury arc or a continuous source such as Hydrogen.

Optical filter : It is a spectral dispersing system used for screening out radiations of unwanted wavelengths emitted by the source.

Sample cell : The cell is equipped with windows that are transparent at the chosen wavelengths.

Detectors : Vacuum phototubes, photomultipliers and solid-state cells are used as UT detectors and their output is read with a sensitive meter.

The different types of UV-absorption analyzers are :

(a) Single-beam analyzer : In this method, a single UV beam is passed through the cell, but its output is affected by fluctuations of the light source, dirts or bubbles in the sample cell.

(b) Split-beam analysis : In this method radiations from the source are partially absorbed while passing through the sample and the radiations leaving the sample are divided into two beams by a *semitransparent mirror*. Each beam passes through an optical filter to a phototube. Radiations of the analytical wavelength are absorbed strongly by the component whose concentration is to be measured, while the other radiations of the reference wavelength are absorbed weakly or not at all by the component. Each phototube developes a current which is converted to d.c. potential and *hence the difference between the potentials of two tubes is proportional to the sample concentration.* These analyzers are used to monitor process liquid and gas streams in pipeline and for monitoring the thickness of film or film coatings. This method compensates for any effect of dirt and bubbles in the cell.

Applications of UV-absorption analyzers :

1. For analyzing vitamin components.
2. For analyzing benzene and toluene in petroleum distillates.
3. For analyzing ethylene and carbonyl compounds.
4. For analyzing elemental halogens like Cl_2, F_2.

6.5.3 Infra-Red (I.R.) Absorption Spectroscopy

The I.R. portion of the electromagnetic spectrum extends from 7500 A° to 10^7 A°. The manner in which electromagnetic radiation interacts with matter is a function of the wavelength of the radiation. I.R. radiations in the wavelength range of 30,000 to 10^5 A° have sufficient energy to excite molecular vibration and hence they can be used for detecting the presence of molecular species. The frequency of vibration is a function of the weights of the atomic elements bound in the molecule and the strength of the molecular bond. *This characteristic vibration frequency results in an IR absorption band which indicates the presence of a particular molecular bond.* For example, C–H bond is excited at 34,000 A°, while C-O bond is excited at 47,000 A°.

Non-dispersive I.R. Analyzer (NDIR) : The NDIR analyzer consists of a source of IR radiation, a means of restricting the wavelength range of source radiation, IR-detector, a sample chamber, a means of modulating the source radiation and the signal processing unit.

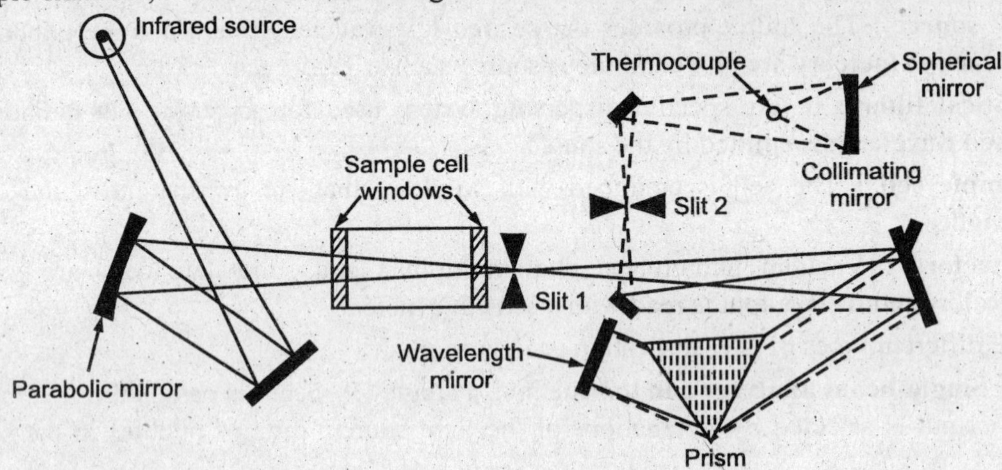

Fig. 6.3 : IR Spectrometer

Fig. 6.3 shows the optical system of IR spectrometer. The IR radiations are produced by an electrically heated resistor and the IR-beam passes to a plane mirror, then to parabolic mirror, which then falls on the slit through the sample to be analyzed. The beam then passes to the collimating mirror, where it is made parallel. This parallel beam passes through the prism, where it is refracted. The wavelength mirror reflects the beam back through the prism where it is once again refracted. The beam is then reflected by the collimating mirror to a plane mirror and then to slit. Finally the beam is reflected to the thermocouple where the beam intensity is measured. The wavelength of IR radiation received by the thermocouple is determined by the angle of setting of the wavelength mirror. Thus by rotating the prism, the intensity of each wavelength can be measured. Finally the graph of IR-wavelength versus the intensity is plotted which is called as IR-spectrogram. Every component has got characteristic spectrogram. The concentration of various components of the sample substance can be determined from the amount of absorption at any wavelength which is based on the Beer's law given by

$$C = \frac{1}{\alpha x} \log_{10} \frac{I_o}{I_x} \quad \dots (6.3)$$

where, C = concentration of substance

α = absorption factor of substance

x = sample thickness along the optical path

I_o = intensity of the beam before passing through the sample

I_x = intensity of the beam after passing through the sample.

These constants are found by a trial calibration of the spectrometer, using a known sample of substance with known concentration. Thus concentration may be determined at any one wavelength in the spectrogram.

Applications :

1. To monitor CO_2 in the manufacture of ethylene oxide and ammonia.
2. Acetylene monitoring in the manufacture of acetylene and vinyl chloride.
3. CO_2 monitoring in steel converting and in the heat-treatment process.
4. CO_2 monitoring in greenhouses, in storage facilities and during formation.
5. Monitoring of explosive and toxic hazards.
6. Monitoring of stack gases for pollution control and flue gas monitoring for combustion efficiency.

6.6 EMISSION SPECTROSCOPY

Emission spectroscopy is accomplished by placing the sample to be analyzed in a flame or in an arc, which causes emission of radiation which is the characteristic of each substance. Emitted radiations are collected and they are separated by refraction or diffraction so as to measure their intensity.

6.6.1 Electric Arc Method

In this method, the electric spark is used for producing emission and a diffraction grating is used for separating the different wavelengths in the emission spectrum. The intensity of radiation at various wavelengths in UV region of about 800 to 2500 A° is measured by a multiplier phototube.

Applications :

Arc type analyzers are used for analysis of Mg, Al, steel.

6.6.2 The Flame Method

In this method an aqueous sample solution is atomized and sprayed into illuminating gas and oxygen flame. The emitted radiations are concentrated by a lens on a phototube. An amplifier operates an indicating instrument that indicates concentration of the sample. Filter may be used to utilize wavelengths between 2800 A° to 8500 A° in the visible range. After atomizing and spraying the sample on the flame, the image of the flame is focussed on the entrance slit of the spectrometer and the spectral line intensity is measured by the phototube, amplifier a[illegible] the recording instrument. For measuring concentration of a single component, the intensit[illegible] particular spectral line can be measured, otherwise the complete spectrum is analyzed fo[illegible] analysis of the sample.

6.6.3 Fluorescence Method

This method is used in applications where the sample allows photochemical deterioration. In this method the substance or sample is irradiated with light of desired wavelength. The absorbed energy causes the sample to emit or fluoresce radiations at wavelengths which are characteristic of certain component in the sample. By measuring the intensity of this radiation the concentrations of different components in the sample can be determined. These units can be operated by X-ray source so that the fluorescence is also in the form of X-rays of various wavelengths. These fluorescent rays pass through a collimating system to a crystal where individual rays of different wavelengths are diffracted at specific angles. The cone of such refracted ray is measured by a Geiger counter.

Applications :

The emission spectroscopy can be used for analyzing metals like Na, K, B, Ca, Co, Cu, Fe, Li, Mg, Mn, Ni.

6.7 MASS SPECTROSCOPY

In this method a sample substance, usually a vapour or gas, is bombarded by an electron beam in an evacuated chamber. This causes "*Knocking off*" of the electrons from each of the different types of atoms present in the substance. Such atoms, from which electrons are knocked off, are called as ions. These ions are then accelerated into a circular path by magnetic field. The radius of circular path varies with the mass of the ions. Thus ions are sorted into beams. The strength of each beam is measured from which different kinds of atoms can be counted and identified, that enables to determine the composition of the substance. The knocked off electrons are collected at the plate in the ionization chamber. The spectrum of ions is compared to the spectrum of a pure substance and mole fractions of the components are obtained by direct proportion. The mass spectrometer can separate masses differing by one part in 300 to one part in 1200. Hence mass spectrometer can be used for analyzing isotopes.

Applications :

This method is most useful in analyzing

1. Aliphatic and cyclic hydrocarbon compounds.
2. Light gases, olefins, paraffins, wet gas, propylene in petroleum refining.
3. Organic and inorganic gases and vapours in chemical manufacturing.

6.8 COMPOSITION ANALYSIS OF SOLIDS BY X-RAY DIFFRACTIONS

Many crystalline and amorphous solids have their atoms arranged in regular fashion that form space lattice. When monochromatic X-ray radiations are directed into a small solid sample, then some rays get reflected in some direction from atoms in certain rows, while some rays get reflected in another direction by atoms in other rows or planes. Hence a photograph of the diffracted beam indicates certain arrangement and spacing of the atoms of the substance. The X-ray diffraction beams are in the form of concentric circle as shown ir Fig. 6.4.

Fig. 6.4 : An X-ray diffraction pattern

Since arrangement and spacing of the atoms in the molecule and of the molecules in the crystals is unique for given solid, the X-ray diffraction pattern is also unique. These diffracted X-ray radiations are counted by Geiger counter, which is connected with the amplifier and potentiometer-type instrument which produces beam intensity versus dimensional spacing of atoms. The actual X-ray diffraction pattern is compared with that of pure substances and then concentrations of components are calculated by simple proportion. Note that this technique cannot be used for liquids and gases because they do not have regular lattice arrangement of atoms and molecules at ordinary temperatures and pressures.

Applications :

1. For control of dyes and fillers in rubber manufacturing.
2. For selection of manganese ore in battery manufacture.
3. For selection of particle size of clay used in ceramics.

6.9 COMPOSITION ANALYSIS METHODS BASED ON MEASUREMENT OF PHYSICAL CHARACTERISTICS OF THE COMPONENT

6.9.1 Composition Analysis of Gases by Thermal Conductivity Measurement

I. Principle :

The ability of gas to conduct heat is called as its *thermal conductivity*. Various gases differ in their thermal conductivity. The thermal conductivity of gas mixture depends on the nature and concentration of its constituent gases. Hence thermal conductivity measurement of the gas mixture can be used for composition analysis of the mixture. The thermal conductivity of air at 0°C is considered as unity. The thermal conductivities of other gases are listed below.

CO_2 (0.585) N_2(1.015)

CO (0.958) O_2 (1.007)

He (6.08) H_2 (7.35)

II. Construction and Working :

The system mainly consists of measuring cell and Wheatstone bridge circuit.

1. Measuring cell : Fig. 6.5 shows *direct flow type* measuring cell made from glass which consists of a platinum filament held under constant tension by a spring. The filament and spring are glass-coated and they are mounted coaxially within a cylindrical chamber containing the gas.

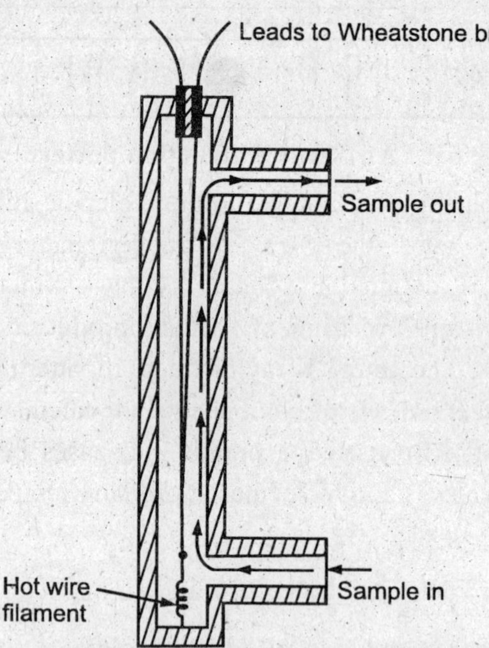

Fig. 6.5 : Direct flow type cell

The filament is maintained at an elevated temperature with respect to the cell walls by passing an electric current through it so that gas flow occurs at a constant rate by natural convection through the cell. The measuring cell may receive the sample gas by diffusion, convection or a combination of these or in gas-chromatography cell, the cell cavity itself is a part of the gas channel through which all the sample gas flows. The rise in filament temperature due to heating current depends on the rate at which heat is conducted away by the sample gas from the filament, which in turn depends on the thermal conductivity of sample gas. Finally an equilibrium temperature is attained by the element when its electrical power input equalizes the thermal losses from the filament mainly by conduction. The filament can serve a dual function of heat source and a sensor for equilibrium temperature in terms of resistance.

2. Wheatstone bridge circuit : Fig. 6.6 shows Wheatstone bridge circuit alongwith measuring cell and reference cell connected for single-pass gas analysis in which sample gas affects the resistance of only one arm of the bridge circuit. The bridge uses a regulated power supply delivering current of 100 to 300 mA which also heats the measuring filaments.

The sample gas to be analyzed flows over the heated filament in the sample cell at a rate of 50 to 200 cc/min, while the reference gas of known and constant composition passes over the filament in the reference cell at a rate of 40 to 100 cc/min, (Sometimes reference cell is scaled by reference gas.) The reference gas has known, fixed thermal conductivity, depending on which it conducts heat from the heated filament which decides the filament surface temperature. The reference filament has certain fixed resistance that depends on its temperature, which in turn depends on the composition of the reference gas. Similarly sample gas concentration decides the resistance of filament in the sampling cell. When the compositions of the sample gas and the reference gas are same, the bridge is in balanced condition as indicated by zero detector reading. But when the compositions of sample and reference gas differ, the resistances of the measuring and reference filament are different that causes the unbalance in the bridge circuit. This unbalance signal represents the difference in compositions of sample gas and reference gas.

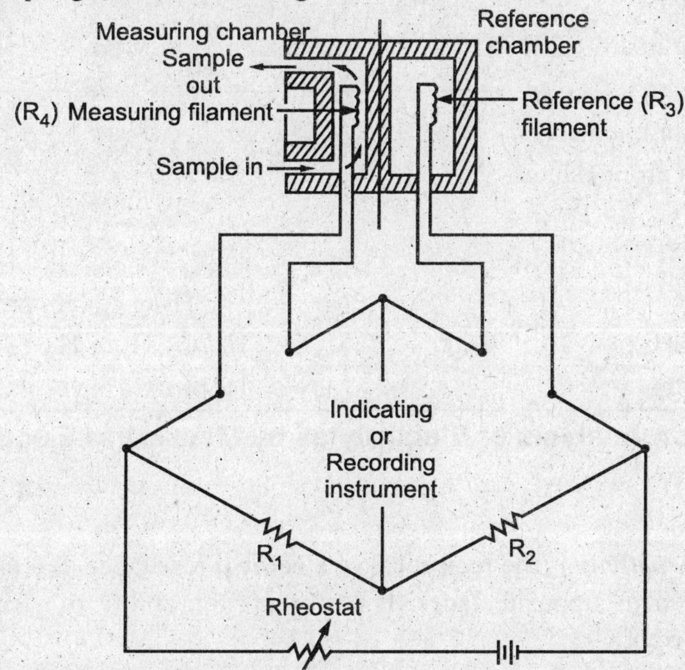

Fig. 6.6 : Wheatstone bridge circuit for single-pass analysis

For differential measurement of one component in a multicomponent mixture, the gas coming out of the measuring cell is passed through a reactor or absorber to remove one component and then it is passed through reference cell. To increase the accuracy, two measuring and two reference cells are connected in the opposite arms of the bridge.

Conditioning of gas sample : Water vapour is the most common component of the industrial gases to be analyzed. Unless the purpose is to analyze for water vapour concentration, it is necessary either to remove the water vapour from gas stream or its thermal conductivity effect is made negligible. It is most convenient to fix the concentration of water vapour. This can be done by saturating the sample gas at a constant temperature.

Gas sampling and cleaning : The sampling line should have a minimum number of elbows with smooth inner surface and it should be made of material that can withstand the thermal and corrosive action of sample gas. The sampling gas should be free from suspended solids, smoke and other particulates.

III. Applications :

The following mixtures can be analyzed by thermal conductivity analyzers with the reference gas mentioned below. Usually reference gas is taken as air which is assumed to have fixed composition.

Table 6.1

Gas mixture	Reference gas
H_2 in air	H_2 or air
Ne in air	air
Cl_2 in air	air
acetone in air	air
NH_3 in air	air
O_2 in enriched air	air
CO_2 in air or flue gas	air
H_2 in O_2	O_2, air or H_2
H_2 in Cl_2	H_2 or Cl_2
H_2 in N_2	H_2 or N_2 or air
H_2 in CH_4	H_2 or CH_4 or $H_2 + CH_4$
H_2 in CO_2	H_2 or CO_2 or $H_2 + CO_2$

6.9.2 Composition Analysis of Electrolytes by Measuring Electrolytic Conductivity

I. Principle :

Electrolytic conductivity is the reciprocal of electrical resistance of a unit cube of solution as measured between its opposite faces. It represents the ability of electrolyte solution to carry the electric current.

Very pure water has practically zero electrical conductivity. Hence the conductivity of water in which electrolyte is dissolved is almost exclusively due to electrolyte ions rather than due to water ions. The conductivity of solutions of strong electrolytes uniformly and linearly varies with its concentration. Hence the electrolyte concentration in its water solution can be determined by measuring its electrical conductivity.

II. Construction and Working :

The conducting solutions are in general electrolytic conductors which carry electricity by positive and negative ions, during which current enters and leaves the system through the metallic electrodes on the surface of which chemical reactions occur while carrying electricity. Positive ions or cations move towards the cathode where reduction takes place, while negative ions or anions move towards the anode, where oxidation takes place. The conductivity of solution depends on the concentration and mobility of the ions which in turn depends on the size and charge on the ions, dielectric constant of the solvent, temperature and viscosity of the solution. Electrolytic conductivity is most often measured by placing electrodes in contact with the electrolyte solution and electrical conductance (reciprocal of resistance) is measured by the measuring Wheatstone bridge circuit.

1. Conductivity cell : Conductivity cell consists of two metal plates or electrod spaced within an enclosure made of electrically insulating material such as glass or pla

This arrangement holds and isolates the portion of the solution that makes the conductivity measurement independent of sample volume and proximity to conductive or non-conductive surfaces.

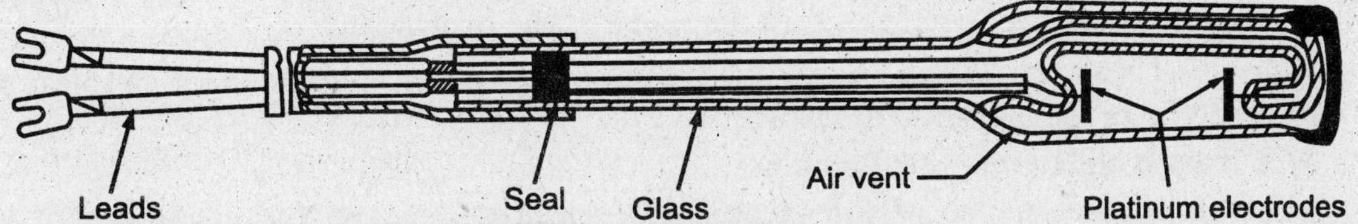

Fig. 6.7 : Conductivity cell

In laboratory cells, platinum electrodes are mounted in glass enclosure. For all practical work, electrodes are of stainless steel, nickel, platinum, gold, etc., while insulating envelope is of glass, rubber, epoxy, polystyrene and teflon. While inserting the cell in liquid, care must be taken to ensure that uppermost air vent is well immersed below the liquid surface. The cell is usually mounted in a pipeline or through a tank wall and the following requirements govern the cell location :

(a) Good liquid circulation.

(b) Linear velocity at the cell location should not be great enough to cause cavitation or damage to the cell.

(c) The temperature variations at the location should be small.

(d) The cell can be mounted at suitable angle, provided it does not become air-bound or gradually fills with sediments.

2. Measuring circuit :

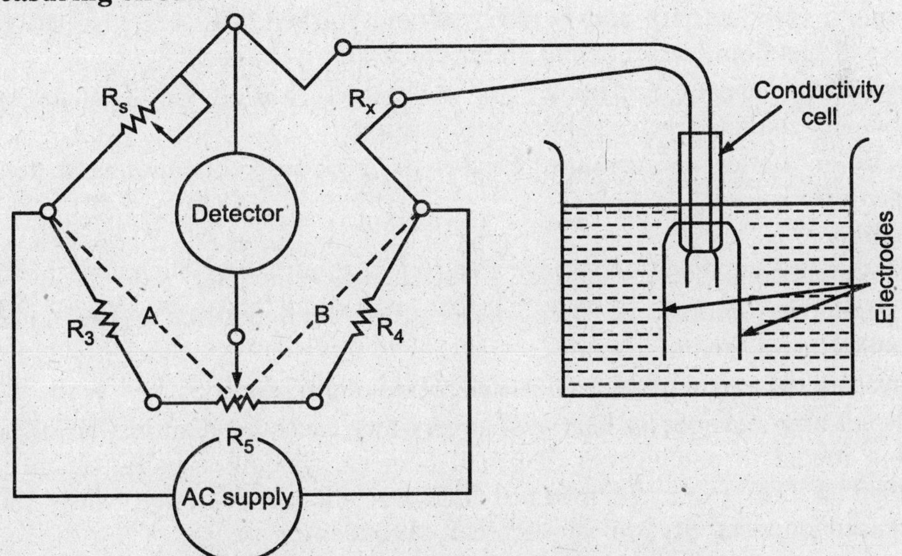

Fig. 6.8 : A.C. Wheatstone bridge circuit for electrolytic conductivity measurement

Fig. 6.8 shows A.C. Wheatstone bridge connected with the conductivity cell. The A.C. supply for the bridge can be obtained from a low voltage tap of a transformer or a battery.

The frequency of A.C. supply used is kept low for low-conductivity or high-resistance solutions, while high frequency supply is used for high-conductivity or low-resistance solutions. The various resistances used in the bridge circuit are :

R_S – Variable resistance, used to adjust the range of the instrument.

R_3 and R_4 – These resistances decide the limits of the bridge calibration. When they are short circuited, the range is from 0 to infinity.

R_5 – Calibrated slidewire potentiometer.

R_X – This is the resistance of the electrolyte measured between the electrodes of the conductivity cell immersed in the test liquid.

For certain concentration of electrolyte in the test solution, the resistance R_X has certain fixed value. For this value of R_X, the balancing condition of the bridge ($AB = R_s/R_X$) is obtained by adjusting slide-wire resistance R_s until detector shows zero reading. Thus resistance R_s can be calibrated in terms of concentration of electrolyte in the solution. In various conductivity monitors, controllers and recorders, the Wheatstone bridge is mechanically rebalanced by a servomechanism operated by the detector.

Sources of Error in Conductivity Measurement :

1. **Insufficient liquid circulation** : Detected by sluggish or slow response to concentration change.

   Remedy : Relocation of the cell or more agitation of solution.

2. **Electrical leakage in the cell** : Detected by change in reading with change in position or angle of immersion of conductivity cell.

   Remedy : Tightening of electrode seals to prevent any leakage of solution.

3. **Leaching of electrolyte :** Detected by higher conductivity reading.

   Remedy : Conductivity cell is removed and washed with hot distilled water and density of platinum black coating on the electrodes is reduced.

4. **Temperature errors** : Detected by instrument reading that changes with time without any changes in electrolyte concentration.

   Remedy : Better temperature control is produced or automatic temperature compensator is used.

III. Applications :

1. To determine concentrations of NaCl, NaOH, H_2SO_4 in water.
2. To gauge the quality of pure distilled or demineralized water in terms of concentration of salts in it.
3. To measure the extent of neutralization, precipitation reactions.
4. To detect any leakages in heat exchangers that causes contamination of heating or cooling media in equipments like acid coolers, condenser coils, steam coils, etc. Leakage in heat exchange medium increases the conductivity, while increase in condensate conductivity indicates a break in condenser tubes.
5. To analyze water in terms of dissolved solids and salinity.
6. To detect the interface between a conductive and a non-conductive liquid like oil-water interface, which also helps to distinguish non-conductive water-in-oil emulsions from the conductive oil emulsions from the conductive oil-in-water.

6.9.3 Composition Analysis of Fuels by Combustibility (Combustibility Component Analysis)

I. Principle :

When a fuel is burned, the amount of heat evolved depends upon the completeness of combustion. (The products of complete combustion are heat, CO_2 and H_2O). If combustion is not complete, instead of CO_2, CO is liberated. *Hence the combustion efficiency of fuel or the extent of completeness of combustion can be measured in terms of concentration of CO in fuel gases.* Since every process material has its own characteristic value of heat of combustion, its concentration in fuel can be determined by measuring heat of combustion of fuel gas in terms of temperature and hence the resistance of filament in thermal conductivity analyzer.

II. Construction and Working :

Measurement of Combustibility of Fuel (Flue gas analysis) : The flue gas produced by burning of fuels is passed through one thermal conductivity chamber and then it is passed through an apparatus which converts CO to CO_2 as shown in Fig. 6.9. This CO_2 is then passed through other thermal conductivity chamber. Due to difference in thermal conductivities of CO and CO_2, the resistances of the filaments in two chambers differ that causes the bridge to unbalance. This degree of unbalance is due to concentration of CO in flue gas. Hence, the bridge indicator represents composition of the gas which indicates the combustibility of fuel burned. The moisture is removed from the flue gas before supplying it to the cell.

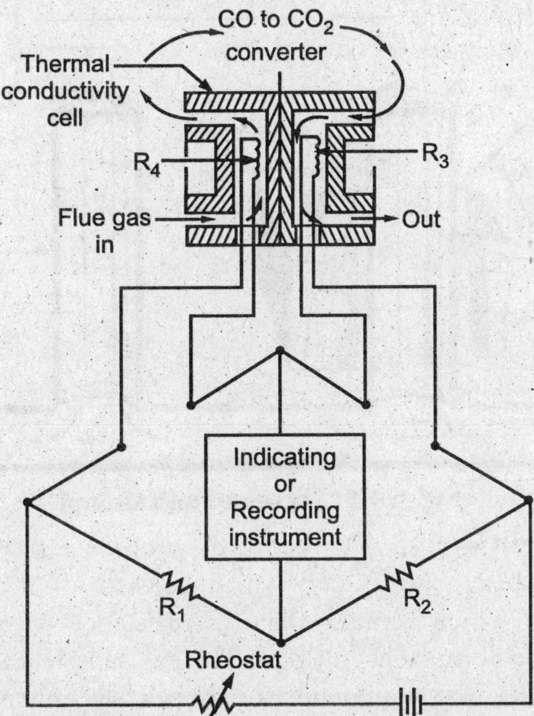

Fig. 6.9 : Thermal conductivity bridge for flue gas analysis

III. Applications :

1. **Total combustibles analyzer :** These instruments are used for detecting the presence of a wide range of combustible gases and vapours in usually inert atmospheres so as to prevent the explosions. By this method the combustible gas concentrations are controlled within safe limits below the *lower explosive limit* (LEL). Hence the instruments are commonly calibrated in terms of the LEL like 0 to 1 % , 0 to 2%, 0 to 5%, 0 to 10%, 0 to 20%, 0 to 25%, 0 to 100% LEL.
2. **Total hydrocarbons analyzer :** It is necessary to determine the concentration of total hydrocarbons in analyzing internal combustion engine exhausts, in detecting breakthroughs in carbon adsorption beds, in detecting leakages in refrigerant systems.

6.9.4 Oxygen Analysers

1. Magnetic Susceptibility Method :

I. Principle :

When matter gets attracted to the strongest part of the non-uniform magnetic field, then it is classed as *paramagnetic or ferromagnetic*. When matter tends to go to the weakest part of the field, then it is classed as *diamagnetic*. The ratio of the intensity of magnetism induced in a unit volume to the magnetic intensity of the field acting on it is called the *susceptibility per unit volume*. Oxygen and nitric acid both have very high volume susceptibility and this property of oxygen is used in measurement of oxygen concentration in gas mixture.

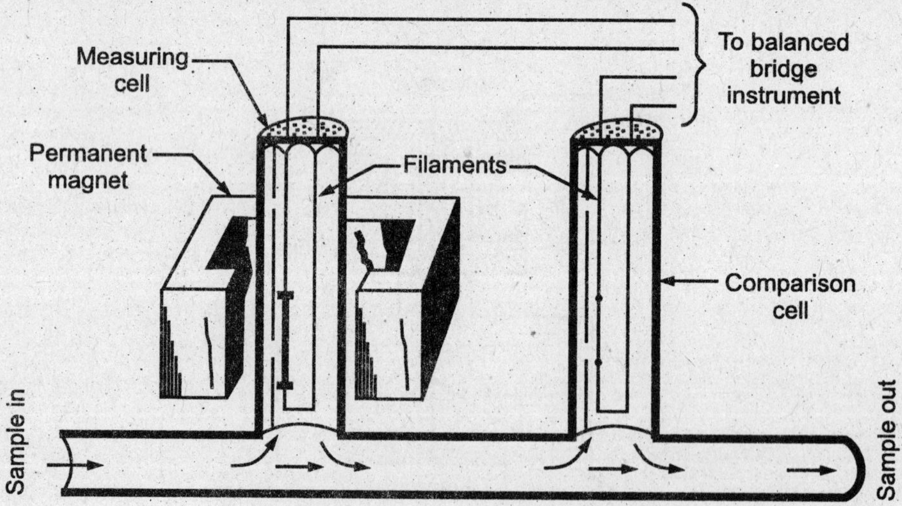

Fig. 6.10 : Oxygen analysis cell

II. Construction and Working :

Fig. 6.10 shows oxygen analysis cell which consists of the measuring cell and the comparison cell, both of which contain identical resistance wires. The measuring cell is situated in the field of the permanent magnet. The gas sample passes across the bottom of both the cells. The gas is drawn into measuring cell by either an aspirator pump or a centrifugal blower. The oxygen content of the gas gets attracted towards the magnetic field and comes closer to the heated filament. As oxygen gets heated by the filament, its magnetic susceptibility decreases so that it is pushed down into the cell by incoming cool oxygen. Thus oxygen circulation, which is called as *magnetic wind*, is established that cools the filament to certain temperature that decides the resistance of the filament. The same gas then passes over the filament in comparison cell whose resistance depends on the thermal conductivity of gas. The difference in resistances of the measuring and the comparison filaments cause unbalance in the bridge circuit and this unbalance is indicated by the indicator or recorder calibrated in terms of oxygen concentration in the gas.

2. Polarizing Cell Method :

This is an electrochemical O_2 detector that involves the ionization of oxygen in both a sample and a known reference stream.

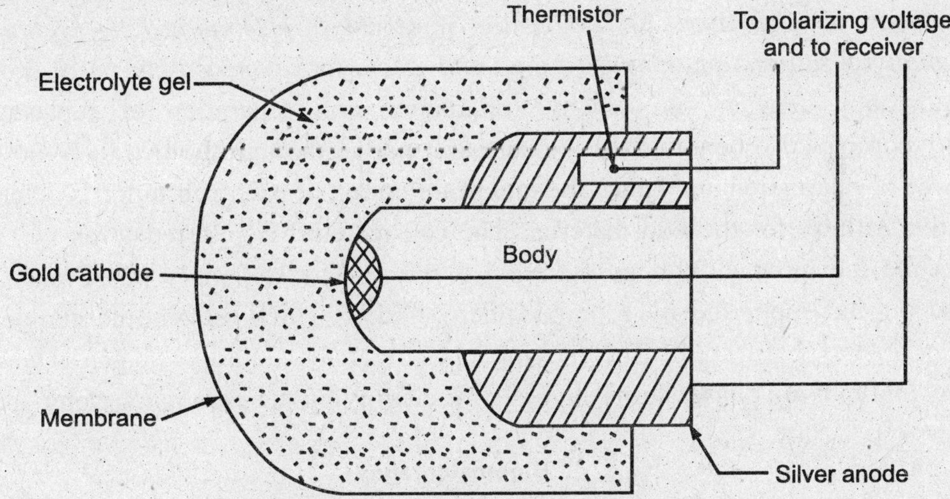

Fig. 6.11 : Polarizing cell O_2 detector

Fig. 6.11 shows basic polarographic cell which has two noble-metal electrodes across which a constant polarizing voltage (usually 0.8 V) is applied. When this detector is immersed in the sample liquid, the dissolved oxygen in the sample diffuses through the membrane into the electrolyte which usually is an aqueous KCl solution at the cathode with the production of negatively charged OH^- ions. These ions move towards positively charged anode, thus establishing flow of electric current which is directly proportional to the oxygen content of the electrolyte. The oxidation-reduction reactions in the case of gold-silver cell with KCl electroyte, are as follows.

At the gold cathode, $O_2 + 2H_2O + 4 \text{ electrons} \rightarrow 4 (OH^-)$

At the silver anode, $4 Ag + 4Cl^- \rightarrow 4 AgCl + 4 \text{ electrons}$.

The silver chloride (AgCl) formed at the anode can be converted back to silver by reversing the polarizing voltage. The working of this cell is temperature sensitive, hence either controlled sample temperature or temperature compensation is required to attain high precision measurement. For accurate results, the minimum sample flow velocity must be ensured, otherwise low flow velocity form stagnant layers of sample over the membrane that interfere with the continuous transfer of oxygen into the cell.

6.9.5 Composition Analysis by Chromatography

I. Principle :

Chromatography is an instrumental procedure based on physical absorption principles for separating various components from the mixture. This procedure is useful for analyzing mixtures of compounds whose chemical characteristics and physical properties are so nearly identical that other separation techniques become impractical. This technique was first used to separate plant pigments. For this the pigment sample was washed through a vertical adsorbent bed, that results in a series of coloured bands along the column. This being graphic representation of colours, the chromatography was called as *colour-writing*, but now-a-days the technique is also used for colourless materials. *Chromatography technique is a combination of separation, identification, and quantitative measurement of components.* Chromatography depends on selective retardation and separation of substances by a stationary porous, adsorbent bed, as they are transported through the bed by a moving fluid. The degree of retardation and hence the rate of migration of each substance is determined by the relative affinity for the bed material. The bed material is referred to as the *stationary phase*, while the moving fluid as the *moving phase*. The stationary phase may be liquid dispersed on and supported by a porous inert solid in which the sample components are soluble or it may be a solid. The moving phase may be liquid or a gas. The nature of stationary and moving phases form the basis for classifying the chromatography operation as follows.

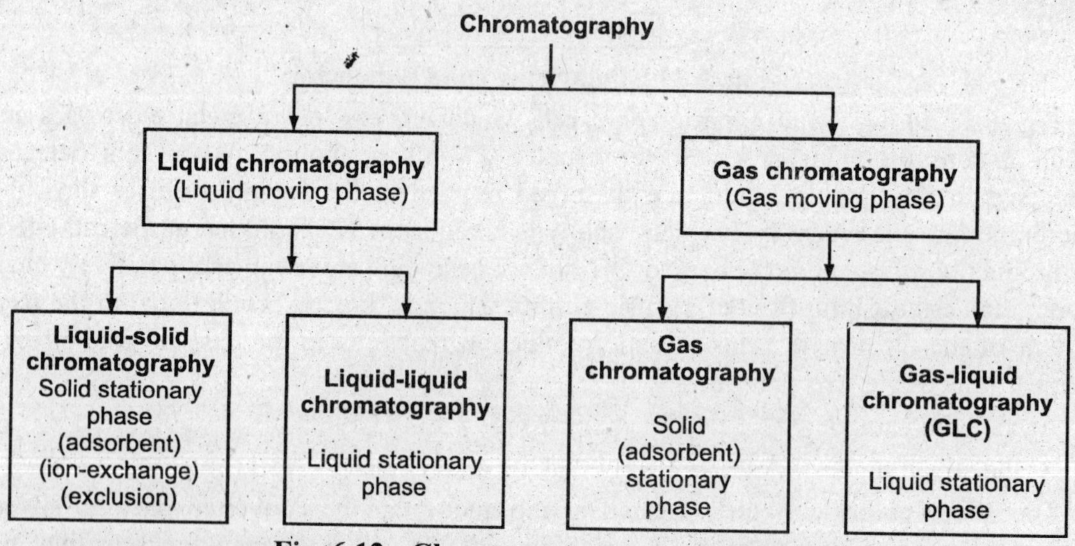

Fig. 6.12 : Chromatography Techniques

II. Construction and Working :

Fig. 6.13 shows the set up for gas chromatography analyzer which consists of carrier gas bottle, chromatography column, reference and measuring thermal conductivity cells connected in bridge circuit and fraction collection, measurement facility.

Carrier gas : It just forces the sample gas through the column, hence it may be any gas that does not react with sample or adversely affect the detector. Usually He, N_2, H_2 or air are used as carrier gas. The carrier gas is supplied at constant pressure by pressure regulator.

Sample injection : The sample gas to be analyzed is injected in the analyzer at a point shown in Fig. 6.13 that flows to the column alongwith carrier gas. A flash heater is provided at this point to vaporize the sample.

Separation column : For gas-liquid chromatography usually partition type columns are used, which consist of an inert solid material of small mesh coated with high boiling liquid. This liquid coating absorbs the sample gas constituents at different rates. Thus each constituent of sample gas travels through the column at different rates because each of them is retained for different time by the column adsorbent like silica gel, activated carbon, etc.

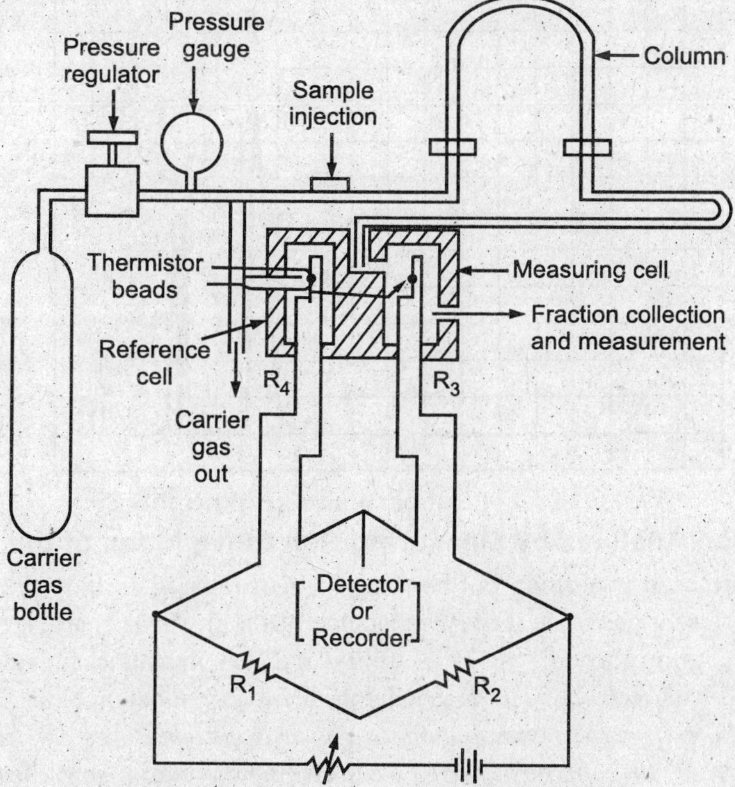

Fig. 6.13 : Gas chromatography analyzer

Measuring and reference chambers :

These chambers have thermistor as sensing deceive. The carrier gas alone passes through reference chamber whose thermal conductivity decides the temperature and hence the resistance of thermistor bead. The carrier gas alongwith the component separated from the mixture passes over thermistor bead in the measuring chamber whose resistance depends upon the thermal conductivity of carrier gas component mixture. Hence the difference in resistance of measuring and reference beads is only due to the separated component of the mixture. Hence the detector reading can be calibrated in terms of concentration of the separated component.

Indicator or recorder : The output of the bridge circuit is amplified and it is fed to the strip chart recording instrument. The record produced is in the form of series of peaks and valleys as shown in Fig. 6.14. By comparing the height of each peak with that produced by passing a calibrated sample (of known composition) over the measuring filament, the percentage by volume of each constituent of sample gas can be determined.

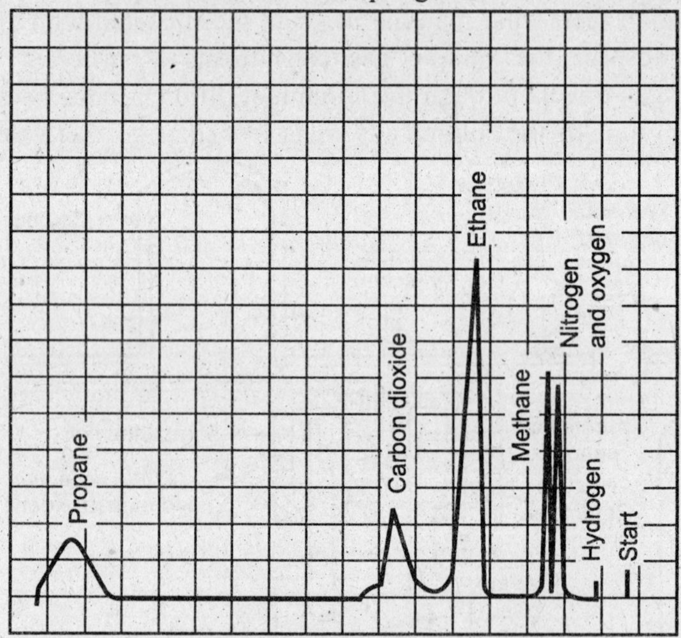

Fig. 6.14 : Typical chromatographic chart

6.9.6 Composition Analysis by Measuring Refractive Index of the Sample

Principle : *Refraction* is nothing but bending of light rays when they cross the boundary of media having different densities. Every substance has a physical characteristic that causes refraction of light coming through air. The ability of every substance to refract the light is expressed in terms of its *Refractive Index* (R.I.). Since every substance has its characteristic R.I., *the concentrations of known components in gas or liquid mixtures can be determined by measuring the R.I. of the mixture*. There exists linear relationship between R.I. and concentrations of two components in the mixture.

Refractometer : When light ray crosses the boundary from denser medium to rarer medium, its angle of refraction increases with angle of incidence. This continues until at certain angle of incidence called the *critical angle*, the refracted ray emerges along the boundary between the two media. If angle of incidence is increased beyond the critical angle, the refraction does not take place, but the ray gets *total internally reflected* with maximum intensity. The R.I. of the sample solution with respect to glass is measured in terms of the critical angle for this glass-liquid boundary that varies with the composition of liquid. Refractometers measure the R.I. of sample liquid in terms of its critical angle from which the composition of liquid can be determined. When telescope is directed along the critical angle towards the interface, then reading is taken by focussing on sharp division between dark and light portions in the field of view.

6.9.7 Composition Anlaysis by Measuring Density or Specific Gravity of the Sample

Principle : The *density* of a material is defined as its weight per unit volume. The *specific gravity* of the liquid is the ratio of its density with the density of water at 4°C while the specific gravity of gas is defined as the ratio of its density with density of air at 0°C at 14.7 psi absolute pressure. By definition, the specific gravity of water is unity and hence that of oils and spirits lies below unity while all the aqueous solutions have specific gravity above unity. *Every substance has got characteristic value of density or specific gravity, hence its measurement can be used for analyzing the sample fluid.*

1. Density measurement using hydrometer : A hydrometer is weighted float with small diameter stem so that more or less scale is submerged inside the liquid depending upon the density of liquid. Since hydrometer weight is constant, the hydrometer displaces a volume of liquid equal to its own weight. Specific gravity measurement using hydrometer is nothing but measuring the volume of liquid equivalent to weight. Smaller the density of liquid, greater is the volume of liquid displaced, that lowers the position of the hydrometer in the liquid.

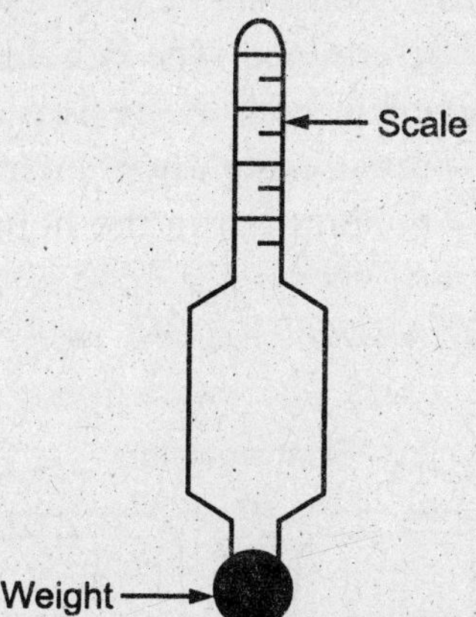

Fig. 6.15 : Hydrometer

The density or specific gravity scale is marked on the upper portion of the hydrometer. The reading is taken on the scale at the point to which liquid rises. Since density varies with temperature, the density reading should be corrected if liquid temperature changes.

For getting remote indication of density, a long metal rod is connected to the hydrometer as the weight. This rod raises or lowers with the hydrometer between the coils of LVDT that gives proportional electrical output corresponding to density of liquid. For continuous density measurement, the hydrometer is kept floating in a constant volume chamber in which constant liquid level is maintained by overflow arrangement.

2. Displacer density meters : Fig. 6.16 shows displacer density meter in which liquid flows continuously through the displacer chamber at a constant rate. Since motion of displacer is quite restricted, the buoyant force acting on the displacer varies with the density of liquid.

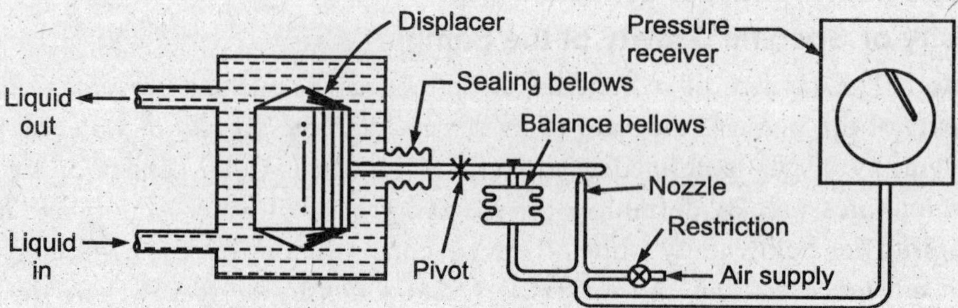

Fig. 6.16 : Displacer density meter

This force on the displacer acts on the balance beam whose other end gets deflected about the pivot. This deflection of the beam moves the flapper of the flapper-nozzle system. As density of liquid increases, the upthrust on the displacer increases that causes pressing of the flapper against the nozzle. This increases the air backpressure to the indicator or recorder. Thus indicator signal changes with density of liquid.

3. Differential pressure method : Fig 6.17 shows two similar vessels, one containing a reference liquid like water of known, constant density and the other vessel contains the process fluid whose density is to be determined. The bubbler tubes are immersed in both the vessels to same depth. The liquid levels in both the vessels are held constant. Bubbler pipes are fed with regulated air supply at pressure slightly greater than the hydrostatic pressure of liquid in the tanks so that air slowly bubbles out in the liquid. *Since liquid level in both the tanks is same, the differential pressure across the bubbler pipe varies only with change in density of process liquid. Thus differential pressure meter can be calibrated in terms of density of process liquid.*

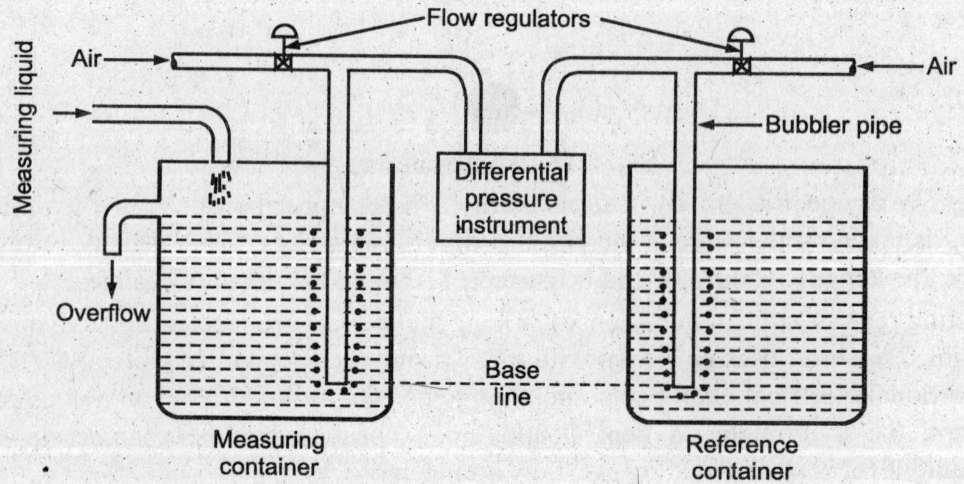

Fig. 6.17 : Air bubbler method for density measurement

6.9.8 Composition Analysis by Viscosity Measurement

The viscosity of a fluid represents its resistance to flow. The fluids whose viscosity considerably changes with temperature or on shaking are called as *non-Newtonian fluids*, while the fluids whose viscosity does not change with temperature are called as *Newtonian fluids*. The viscosity measuring methods are different for Newtonian and non-Newtonian fluids. In this article we describe the viscosity measurement of Newtonian fluids only for analyzing the sample.

Units of viscosity :

Absolute viscosity : It is the ratio of applied shear stress to the rate of shear. The SI unit of absolute viscosity is pascal-second (Pa.s) or $\frac{\text{N-sec}}{\text{m}^2}$, while the CGS unit is poise (P) or $\frac{\text{dyne-sec}}{\text{cm}^2}$, 1 P = 0.1 Pa.s.

Kinematic viscosity : It is the ratio of absolute viscosity to density of fluid. Hence the SI unit of kinematic viscosity is m^2/s, while its CGS unit is stoke (ST) or cm^2/s.

Viscosity Measurement :

1. **Falling ball or piston :** In this method, the time required for a ball or piston to fall through liquid through certain distance is measured that varies with the viscosity of liquid.

2. **Continuous viscosity meter :** In this method, a metering pump draws some of the liquid from the main stream and pumps it through the rotameter at a fixed rate.

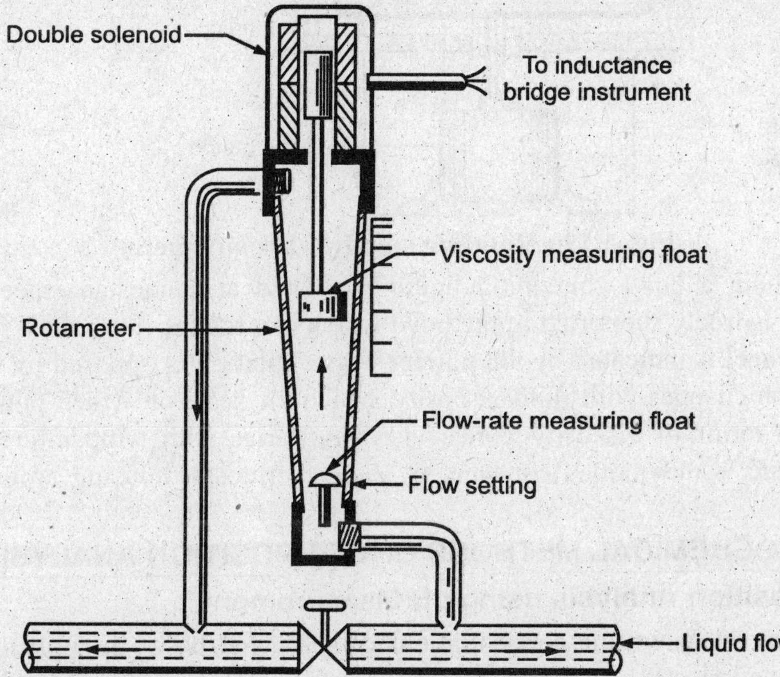

Fig. 6.18 : Continuous viscosity measurement using rotameter

The rotameter has two floats, the lower one is shaped to sense the fluid flow rate independent of the fluid viscosity. The upper float is made sensitive to fluid viscosity changes. The flow rate through the tube is controlled at constant value by adjusting the lower float at flow-setting mark. Now the upper float changes its position only if liquid viscosity changes. Hence the upper float displacement can be calibrated in terms of liquid viscosity. The electrical output can be obtained by transmitting the position of the upper float to the recorder using LVDT.

3. Drag torque method :

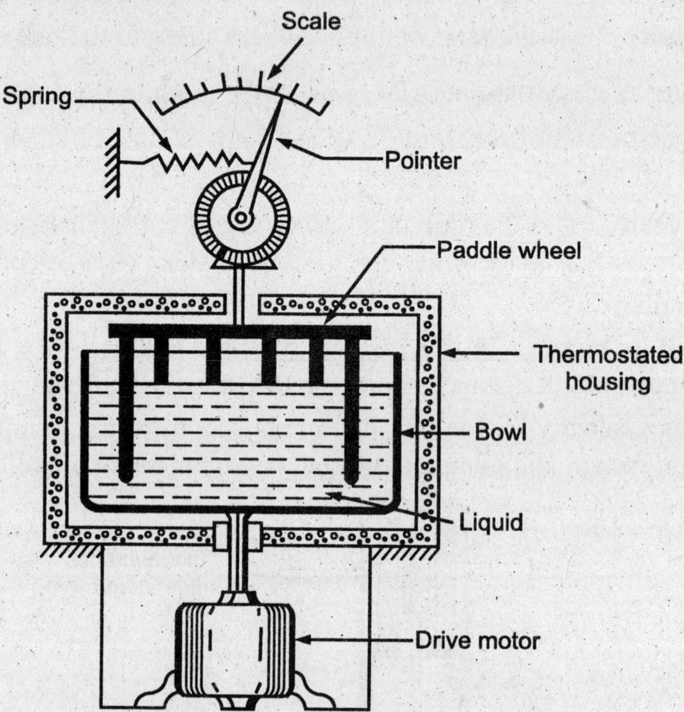

Fig. 6.19 : Rotating spindle viscosity meter

In this method, a bowl containing liquid is rotated at a constant speed by a motor. A paddle wheel is freely supported in the bowl which can rotate with liquid. The drag torque on the paddle wheel is indicated by the pointer whose rotation is opposed by the spring. The pointer deflection changes with fluid viscosity, hence the scale on which pointer moves can be calibrated in terms of viscosity. Since viscosity varies with temperature of liquid, the liquid temperature is maintained constant by using thermostat housing around the rotating bowl.

6.10 ELECTROCHEMICAL METHODS OF COMPOSITION ANALYSIS

6.10.1 Composition Analysis using pH Measurement

It is necessary to determine concentrations of acids and bases in applications like food industry, medicine industry and other chemical industries. This can be done by measuring pH of the sample solutions.

Definition : pH of an aqueous solution is defined as negative logarithm of its hydrogen ion concentration. i.e. pH = – log [H^+].

pH Scale :

Neutral pH : When pure water dissociates into positive hydrogen (H^+) ions and negative hydroxyl (OH^-) ions in equimolar proportions, then neutrality is said to exist and water is said to be neutral. It is found that in pure water at 22°C, the concentrations of H^+ and OH^- ions equal 10^{-7}, hence pH value equals to – log (10^{-7}) = 7. Hence, pure water is neither acidic nor basic. The acidity of solution increases as pH value falls below 7 with ultimate value of 0, while the alkalinity of solution increases as pH value rises above 7 with ultimate value of 14. Thus pH scale ranges from 0 to 14. *pH of 0 means an acid solution of unit strength and pH of 14 means base solution of unit strength.* Note that pH measures only the concentration of H^+ ions actually dissociated in a solution and not the total acidity or alkalinity. Due to this reason, the pH value changes with temperature of liquid. As the water temperature increases, the dissociation into H^+ and OH^- ions increases that results in decrease in pH value.

pH Measurement :

Electronic pH measurement system consists of a measuring electrode, a reference electrode and a potential measuring system.

Measuring electrode : We describe the *glass electrode* as the pH measuring electrode.

The glass electrode is made of a thin glass membrane of special composition that could develope potential proportional to difference in H^+ ion concentration of liquid on either sides of the membrane. The glass envelope has pH sensitive glass membrane at the bottom that contains constant pH buffer solution. This electrode is dipped in the measuring solution so that potential is developed at the platinum electrode which is proportional to the pH of the measuring solution. This potential is measured by completing the circuit with the reference electrode.

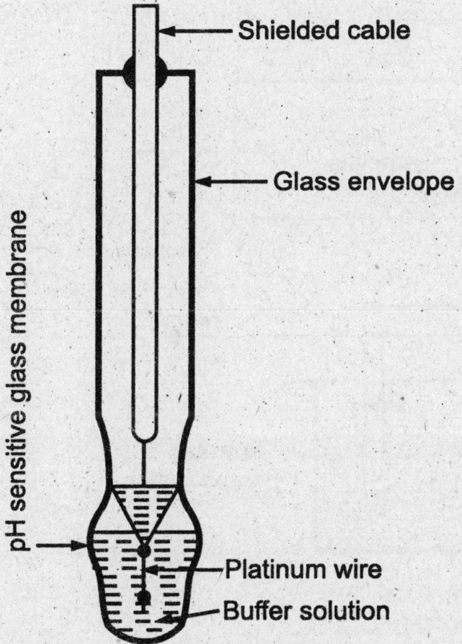

Fig. 6.20 : pH measuring glass electrode

Reference electrode : We describe *calomel electrode* as the reference electrode for pH measurement.

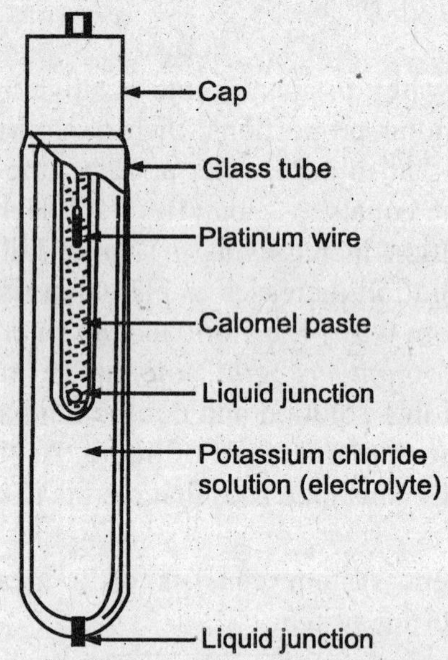

Fig. 6.21 : Calomel electrode

Calomel electrode has glass envelope that contains glass tube which contains calomel (mercury and mercurous chloride) solution alongwith platinum wire dipped in it. This tube is surrounded by KCl solution that slowly diffuses or leaks into process liquid through liquid junction provided by asbestos fibre. Due to this the reference electrode developes constant potential.

Potential measuring system : The measuring and the reference electrode together form an electrolytic cell whose output equals the sum of the voltage produced by the two electrodes.

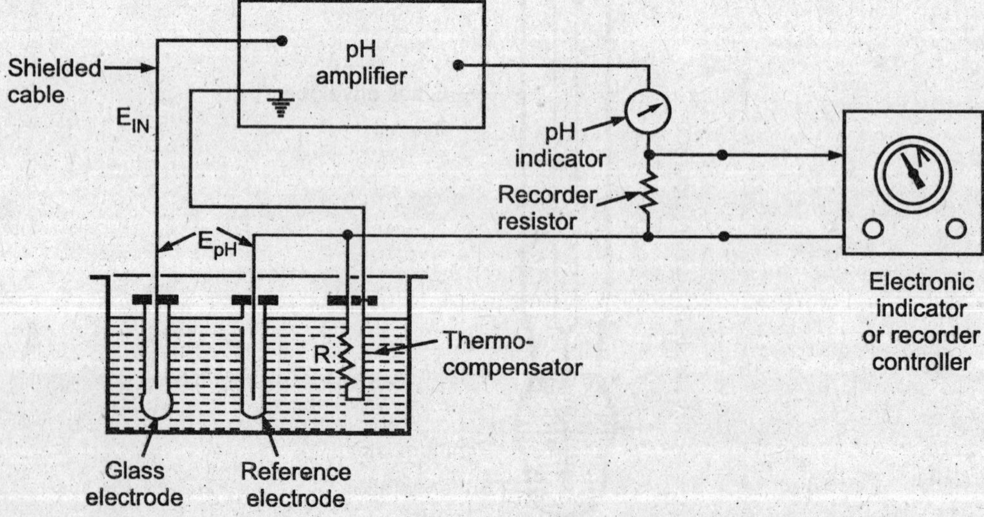

Fig. 6.22 : Circuit for electronic pH measurement

This net voltage is applied to a null-balance millivolt potentiometer in which the slide-wire can be calibrated in terms of the pH of the measuring liquid. Since the electrode operation depends upon the electrical resistivity of glass, change in temperature may cause error in pH reading. To compensate for changes in temperature of the measuring solution, temperature compensating resistance is included in the circuit which is immersed in the solution. The resistance of this resistor changes with temerature. Fig. 6.22 shows the electronic circuit for pH measurement alongwith temperature compensating resistor.

6.10.2 Colorimetric Analysis

Colorimetric method uses only the human eye as a measuring instrument. It involves comparison by visual means of the colour of an unknown solution with the colour produced by single standard or series of standards. The comparison is made by obtaining a match between the colour of the unknown and that of the particular standard by comparison with a series of standards prepared in a similar manner to thc unknown.

The visual methods used earlier are now being replaced by more precise photoelectric methods for quantitative colorimetric measurements. Hence, it is referred as photometric method also. This involves measurement of colour in visual region of the electromagnetic spectrum (400 – 700 mμ).

Construction and Working : Sample compartment of a colorimeter is provided with a holder to contain the cuvette, in which the liquid is examined. This holder is mounted on a slide with positions for at least 2 cuvettes, so that sample and reference cuvette are measured first and a shutter is moved into or out of the light beam until the microammeter gives a full-scale deflection. The sample is moved into the beam and the light passing through it is measured as a percentage to the reference value.

$$\text{Sample concentration} = \begin{pmatrix} \text{Standard} \\ \text{concentration} \end{pmatrix} \times \frac{\text{Sample reading}}{\text{Reference reading}}$$

Colorimeters are used were high accuracy is not desired.

Disadvantage :

A range of filters is required to cover different wavelength regions.

Single beam filter photometers :

Construction and Working : As shown in figure the source of light is a tungsten filament lamp, which is held in a reflector and throws light on the sample holder through filter. The sample holder is a cuvette with parallel walls or a test tube. The light passing through the sample holder, then falls on the surface of the photocell.

The output of the cell is measured either on the light spot galvanometer or microammeter. The lamps must be energized from a highly stabilized dc source or by output of constant voltage transformer.

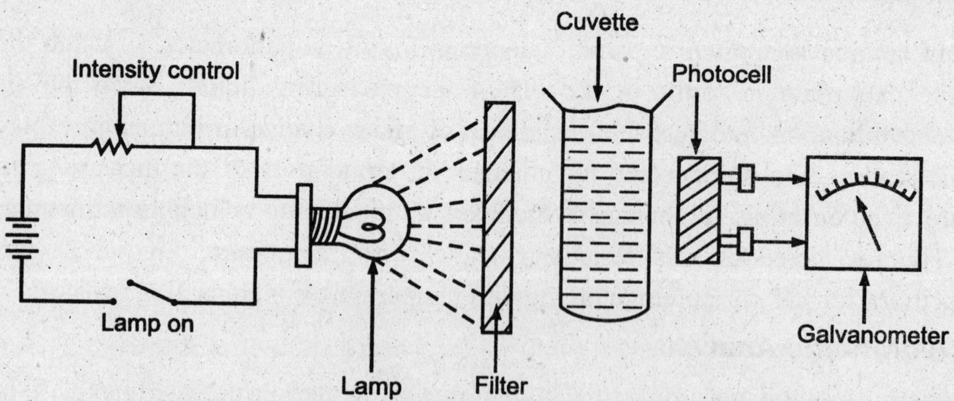

Fig. 6.23 : Basic components of a filter photometer

6.10.3 Conductometers

Principle : The conductivity of an electrolyte is a measure of the ability of the solution of carry electric current. Thus, the conductance of a solution of electrolyte is related to the concentration of electrolyte.

The reciprocal of the resistance R of electrolytic solution (1/R) is called the conductance.

The resistance of a solution depends upon length l, area a and its intrinsic properties.

$$R = \frac{\rho l}{a}$$

where ρ is specific resistance.

$$\therefore \quad \frac{1}{R} = \frac{1}{\rho}\left(\frac{a}{l}\right) = K\left(\frac{a}{l}\right)$$

where K is specific conductance expressed in $ohm^{-1}\ cm^{-1}$.

K is a function of concentration. As the solution is diluted specific conductance will decrease due to less number of ions present to carry electric current in each cm^3 of solution volume.

The ability of individual ions to conduct is called equivalent conductance function (^). Equivalent conductance is the conductance of a hypothetical solution containing one gram equivalent of an electrolyte per cm^3 of solution.

$$\wedge = 1000\ K/C$$

Methods of measurement of conductance :

(1) Null method :

Conductivity is determined by measuring the resistance of a column of solution using Wheatstone bridge, where the conductivity cell forms one of the arm of the bridge. As the conductivity cell contains electrodes separated by a dielectric, an appreciable cell capacitance is invariably present. The commonly employed frequency is 1000 Hz.

Due to less sensitivity of null detector, use of magic eye or cathode ray oscilloscope is more popular.

(2) Direct reading method :

In this the necessity of converting resistance readings into conductance readings is eliminated. The unbalanced bridge current is amplified in an electronic amplifier and displayed on a calibrated panel meter.

(3) High frequency method :

Conductivity cells : A conductivity cell comprises of two electrodes, of two parallel sheets of platinum fixed in position by sealing the connecting tubes into the sides of the measuring cell. Electrode effective area is increased by coating with platinum black. These cells are available in different types, sizes, shapes.

Dip type cells : These are immersed in liquid to be tested as an open container with volumes in the range of 5 ml.

Pipette cells : These are employed for small volumes of solution as small as 0.01 ml.

Epoxy cells are used for high temperature analysis.

Two terminal conductivity cells are used commonly when dirty solutions, fatty acids or other sticky deposits, fouling has to be analysed.

Temperature compensation in conductivity measurements is essential as solutions conductivity varies with temperatures. This is done by introducing into the bridge circuit a resistive element which will change with temperature at the same rate as the solution under test.

Construction and Working : The container with sample is placed between the plates of a capacitor, forming a part of the high frequency generator circuit. Any change in composition of the solution results in changes in plate and grid currents and voltages due to change in conductance and capacitance of the cell. The frequency of a parallel resonant circuit is given by

$$f = \frac{1}{2\pi}\sqrt{LC}$$

The advantage of placing the electrodes outside the solution container and out of direct contact with it is offered in this method. This eliminates the possibility and danger of electrolysis or electrode polarization.

EXERCISE

1. State applications of composition analysis in manufacturing industries.
2. State the principle based on which emission and absorption spectroscopic methods are used for composition analysis.

3. Describe the following techniques of composition analysis :

   (a) X-ray absorption spectroscopy, (b) UV absorption spectroscopy,

   (c) IR absorption spectroscopy, (d) Emission spectroscopy,

   (e) Mass spectroscopy, (f) Fluorescence method, (g) X-ray diffraction method.

4. Distinguish between single-beam and split-beam method used in UV-absorption analysis method.
5. State the applications of UV and IR spectroscopic analysis methods.
6. Why mass spectrometer is preferred for analyzing isotopes ?
7. Describe the use of following measurements for composition analysis : (a) Thermal conductivity of gases, (b) Electrical conductivity of electrolytes, (c) Heat of combustion of fuel, (d) Refractive index of liquid, (e) Density of liquid, (f) Viscosity, (g) pH.
8. Describe the magnetic susceptibility method for oxygen analysis.
9. Describe chromatography method for analyzing multicomponent systems.
10. How will you differentiate between electrolytic conductivity and pH of the liquid ?
11. How will you locate the electrolytic cell pipeline containing liquid ?
12. List different sources of error in electrolytic conductivity measurement. State the means of minimizing these errors.
13. State the applications of electrolytic conductivity measurement for composition analysis.
14. What do you understand by "Combustibility Component Analysis" ?
15. How will you determine combustion efficiency of fuel ?
16. How chromatography is superior separation technique over other techniques like, melting, boiling, evaporation, drying etc. ?
17. Classify the chromatography methods.
18. Draw typical chromatographic recorder chart and describe its use for determining concentrations of components of the mixture.
19. What is refraction ? Why the separation between dark and bright portions is observed in view of refractometer ?
20. Describe various fluid density measurement methods.
21. Describe various viscosity measurement methods.
22. Why temperature correction is necessary for pH meter reading ? How is it generated ?

PART – II

PROCESS DYNAMICS AND CONTROL

7

CHAPTER

FUNDAMENTALS OF PROCESS DYNAMICS

7.1 INTRODUCTION

In process control the natural response of the process is modified to some desired form. But for this one must first understand the inherent, dynamic behaviour of the process itself without any interference of the controller. Therefore, study of the process dynamics is a precursor to the study of process control. Process dynamics refers to analyzing the dynamic or time-varying behaviour of a process in response to different types of inputs. This will enable us to characterize a wide variety of actual processes into a relatively small number of well-defined categories.

In this chapter, we study the tools used for studying the process dynamics and control. Then processes are characterized based on their mathematical models which are further analyzed for dynamic behaviour with different types of inputs. Lastly process identification using step response data is discussed.

7.2 TOOLS OF DYNAMIC ANALYSIS

Dynamic behaviour of processes can be studied experimentally by changing the inputs and recording corresponding output responses. But this method requires the actual physical process to exist, which is not so during the control system design for a new proposed process.

In addition, the experimental investigation carried on single, specific process may not provide critical theoretical information useful for characterizing the behaviour of the entire class of processes.

To overcome this limitation, the mathematical approach is used in which a process is given some form of mathematical representation (i.e. a process model) and then output response is calculated for a given change in input variable.

This approach provides knowledge about *idealized process* behaviour, but it is very much useful in understanding and characterizing the real behaviour of the process. This method involves solving the mathematical equations using the mathematical tools such as Laplace transform (for analog systems), Z-transform (for discrete-time systems), and matrices (for multivariable systems).

7.2.1 The Laplace Transform (LT)

The process models represent unsteady-state behaviour of the process, therefore, the models are usually in the form of differential equations in input and output variables, which may be linear, non-linear, ordinary (ODE) or partial (PDE) in form.

The Laplace transform converts linear, ordinary differential equation (ODE) into simpler algebraic equations in Laplace variable 's', which can be comparatively easily solved to calculate output response for changes in input variable. This process involves the transfer function models form which is widely used in process dynamics and control studies.

Definition of the Laplace transform :

Let f (t) be a real function of real variable 't' (say time) defined for t > 0, then the Laplace transform of f (t) is defined as -

$$L[f(t)] = F(s) = \int_{0^+}^{\infty} f(t)\, e^{-st}\, dt$$

where 's' is a complex variable defined as $s = \sigma + j\omega$, having σ and ω as real variables and $j = \sqrt{-1}$.

Note that in this definition, the lower limit in the integral has been taken as 0^+, which means that all information contained in f(t) for t < 0 is ignored or considered to be zero. This assumption does not place any serious limitation on application of Laplace transform for analyzing linear systems because : (i) in the usual time-domain studies the time reference is chosen at t = 0 i.e. f (t) = 0, for t < 0; and (ii) for a practical system, when input change or excitation is applied at t = 0, the system response never precedes the excitation i.e. the response does not start before or earlier than t = 0.

Definition of the Inverse Laplace Transform :

Let F (s) be the Laplace transform of function f (t), for t > 0, then the inverse Laplace transform of F (s) is defined as :

$$L^{-1}[F(s)] = f(t) = \frac{1}{2\pi j} \int_{c-j\infty}^{c+j\infty} F(s)\, e^{st}\, ds$$

where 'c' is a real constant greater than all the singularities of F (s).

Properties of Laplace Transform :

(1) If $L[f(t)] = F(s)$, then $L[kf(t)] = KF(s)$ where K = constant.

(2) If $L[f_1(t)] = F_1(s)$ and $L[f_2(t)] = F_2(s)$ then, $L[f_1(t) \pm f_2(t)] = F_1(s) \pm F_2(s)$

(3) If $L[f(t)] = F(s)$

then, $$L\left[\frac{d^n}{dt^n} f(t)\right] = S^n F(s) - \lim_{t \to 0^+} \left[s^{n-1} f(t) + s^{n-2} \frac{d}{dt} f(t) + s^{n-3} \frac{d^2}{dt^2} f(t) + \ldots\ldots + \frac{d^{n-1}}{dt^{n-1}} f(t) \right]$$

Corollary (i) : $$L\left[\frac{d}{dt} f(t)\right] = SF(s) - \lim_{t \to 0^+} f(t) = SF(s) - f(0^+)$$

Corollary (ii) : $$L\left[\frac{d^2}{dt^2} f(t)\right] = S^2 F(s) - Sf(0^+) - f'(0^+)$$

Note that the Laplace transform changes the operation of differentiation of function f (t) with respect to 't' to that of multiplication of the Laplace transform F (s) of f (t) by 'S' alongwith some polynomial terms involving the initial values of f (t) and its derivatives.

(4) If $L[f(t)] = F(s)$

then, $$L\left[\int_0^t f(t)\,dt\right] = \frac{F(s)}{S}$$

(5) Initial value theorem : If $L[f(t)] = F(s)$, then initial value of f (t) at $t = 0$ is given by

$$f(0^+) = \lim_{t \to 0^+} f(t) = \lim_{s \to \infty} SF(s) \quad (\text{for } t > 0)$$

(6) Final value theorem : If $L[f(t)] = F(s)$ and if SF (s) is analytic on the imaginary axis and in the right half of the plane, then final value of f (t) as $t \to \infty$ is given by

$$f(\infty) = \lim_{t \to \infty} f(t) = \lim_{s \to 0} SF(s)$$

(7) Time scaling : If $L[f(t)] = F(s)$, then for any constant 'a'

$$L[f(t/a)] = aF(as)$$

(8) Time delay : If $L[f(t)] = F(s)$, then

$$L[f(t-T)] = e^{-st} F(s)$$

(9) Complex translation : If $L[f(t)] = F(s)$, then

$$L[e^{-at} f(t)] = F(s+a)$$

(10) Frequency scaling : If $L^{-1}[F(s)] = f(t)$, then

$$L^{-1}[F(s/a)] = af(at), \text{ where } a = \text{constant}$$

Laplace Transforms of Standard Test Inputs :

1. The step function : It represents sudden change of value of the input e.g. suddenly opening or closing a valve. The step function of magnitude 'A' is mathematically described by the equation

$$r(t) = 0, \text{ for } t < 0$$
$$= A, \text{ for } t > 0$$

The unit step function corresponds to $A = 1$.

The Laplace transform of step function is given by

$$L[r(t)] = R(s) = \frac{A}{S}$$
$$= \frac{1}{S}, \text{ for unit step function}$$

2. The ramp or linear function : It starts with the value of zero at $t = 0$ and increases linearly with time. It is mathematically described by equation

$$r(t) = 0, \text{ for } t \le 0$$
$$= t, \text{ for } t > 0$$
$$= 1, \text{ for } t > 0 \text{ (unit ramp)}$$

The Laplace transform of unit ramp function is given by

$$L[r(t)] = R(s) = \frac{1}{s^2}$$

3. **The impulse function :** It is mathematically described by equation

$$r(t) = 0, \; t < 0$$
$$= \frac{1}{h}, \; 0 < t < h$$
$$= 0, \; t > h$$

Graphically, this represents a rectangular pulse having height $= \frac{1}{\text{width}}$.

The Laplace transform of impulse function is given by

$$L[r(t)] = \frac{1 - e^{-hs}}{hs}$$

Table 7.1 : Laplace Transforms and Inverse Laplace Transforms of some Standard Functions :

Sr. No.	f (t)	L [f (t)] = F (s)	Sr. No.	F (s)	L^{-1} [F (s)] = f (t)
1.	1	$\frac{1}{s}$	1.	$\frac{1}{s}$	1
2.	t^n	$\frac{n!}{s^{n+1}}$	2.	$\frac{1}{s^{n+1}}$	$\frac{t^n}{n!}$
3.	e^{at}	$\frac{1}{s-a}$	3.	$\frac{1}{s-a}$	e^{at}
4.	sin at	$\frac{a}{s^2+a^2}$	4.	$\frac{1}{s^2+a^2}$	$\frac{(\sin at)}{a}$
5.	cos at	$\frac{s}{s^2+a^2}$	5.	$\frac{s}{s^2+a^2}$	cos at
6.	sinh at	$\frac{a}{s^2-a^2}$	6.	$\frac{1}{s^2-a^2}$	$\frac{(\sinh at)}{a}$
7.	cosh at	$\frac{s}{s^2-a^2}$	7.	$\frac{s}{s^2-a^2}$	cosh at
8.	$e^{at} t^n$	$\frac{n!}{(s-a)^{n+1}}$	8.	$\frac{1}{(s-a)^{n+1}}$	$t^n \frac{e^{at}}{n!}$
9.	e^{at} sin bt	$\frac{b}{(s-a^2)+b^2}$	9.	$\frac{1}{(s-a^2)+b^2}$	$e^{at} \frac{\sin bt}{b}$
10.	e^{at} cos bt	$\frac{s-a}{(s-a^2)+b^2}$	10.	$\frac{s-a}{(s-a^2)+b^2}$	e^{at} cos bt
11.	t sin at	$\frac{2as}{(s^2+a^2)^2}$	11.	$\frac{s}{(s^2+a^2)^2}$	$\frac{t \sin at}{2a}$
12.	t cos at	$\frac{s^2-a^2}{(s^2+a^2)^2}$	12.	$\frac{s^2-a^2}{(s^2+a^2)^2}$	t cos at

Process control application of Laplace transform :

As mentioned earlier, Laplace transform is used in process control to solve linear differential equation model of the process to be studied. The unsteady-state behaviour of the process is described in terms of the output of the process as linear, ordinary differential equation with time t as a independent variable.

On taking Laplace transform of this equation it is transformed in terms of the Laplace variable 's', which is then solved in s-domain to get the output response for change in input variable. This s-domain solution, on taking inverse Laplace transform, gets transformed back into time domain solution. This process is represented in Fig. 7.1.

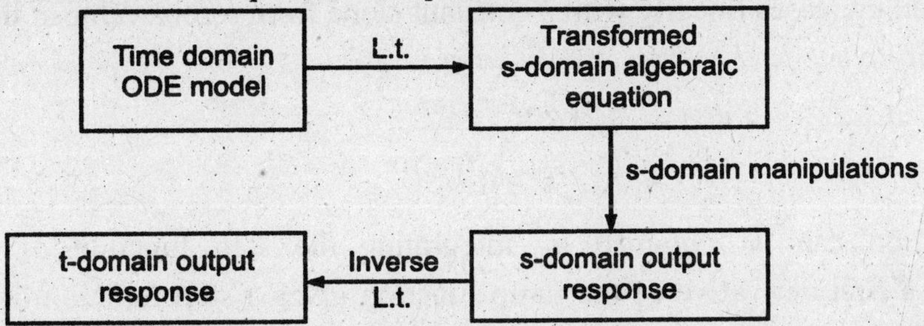

Fig. 7.1 : Application of Laplace transform in process control

7.2.2 Standard Input Functions (Ideal Forcing Functions)

The standard input functions resemble the likely modes of input variations in practice.

The ideal step function :

The ideal step function represents sudden instantaneous change in input. The value of ideal step function remains at zero until it takes the value A instantaneously at the starting time set arbitrarily to t = 0 and remains constant. This is mathematically represented as :

$$f(t) = 0, \quad t < 0$$
$$= AH(t), \quad t \geq 0$$

where $H(t)$ = Unit step function, known as Heaviside function, defined as

$$H(t) = 0, \quad t < 0$$
$$= 1, \quad t \geq 0$$

This function is represented graphically as shown in Fig. 7.2.

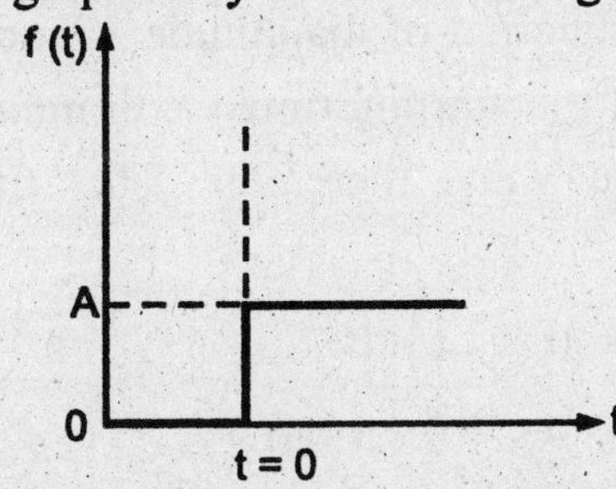

Fig. 7.2 : The ideal step function

The ideal step function may be realized in practice **e.g.** flow rate of liquid flowing through pipeline can be suddenly increased by changing the opening of valve in the line suddenly. But step change cannot be realized exactly in practice. The Laplace transform of step function is

$$L[f(t)] = f(s) = \frac{A}{s}$$

The ideal ramp function :

The ideal ramp function represents gradual change in input at a constant rate. The value of such function increases linearly with a constant slope from a zero value at the starting time by the equation

$$f(t) = 0, \quad t < 0$$

$$= At, \quad t \geq 0$$

This function can be obtained by integrating the step function of magnitude A. Alternatively, a first derivative of the ramp function gives a step function of magnitude A. This function is graphically represented as shown in Fig. 7.3.

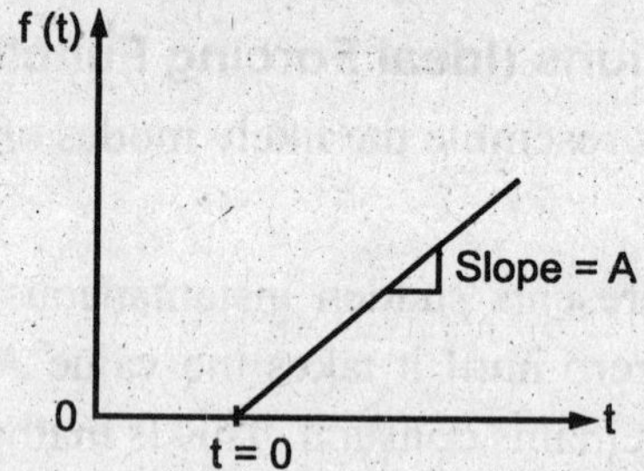

Fig. 7.3 : The ideal ramp function

The Laplace transform of ideal ramp function is

$$L[f(t)] = \bar{f}(s) = \frac{A}{s^2}$$

The ideal rectangular pulse function :

The ideal rectangular pulse function of magnitude A and duration b time units takes on the value of A instantaneously at the starting time t = 0, maintains this new value for b time units and returns to initial zero value thereafter. This function can be mathematically represented as :

$$f(t) = 0, \quad t < 0$$

$$= A, \quad 0 < t < b$$

$$= 0, \quad t > b$$

The ideal rectangular pulse function is graphically represented as shown in Fig. 7.4.

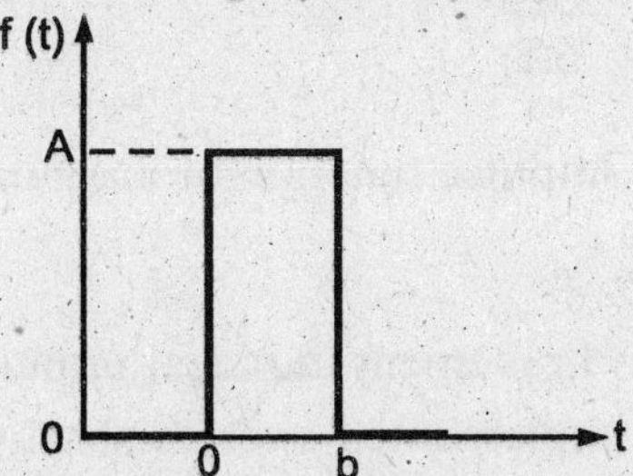

Fig. 7.4 : The ideal rectangular pulse function

The Laplace transform of rectangular pulse function is

$$\bar{f}(s) = \frac{A}{s}[1 - \exp(-bs)]$$

The ideal impulse function :

The ideal impulse function of magnitude A is mathematically represented as :

$$f(t) = A\,\delta(t)$$

where δ(t) is known as the Dirac delta function.

The Dirac delta function has a zero value elsewhere and infinite at the point t = 0, with total area under the curve equal to unity. It is mathematically expressed as :

$$\delta(t) = \infty, \quad t = 0$$
$$= 0, \quad \text{elsewhere}$$

Area under Dirac delta function is :

$$\int_{-\infty}^{\infty} \delta(t) = 1$$

The impulse function of magnitude A can be obtained from the rectangular pulse function of magnitude A = 1/b so that area under the pulse is $A \times b = \frac{1}{b} \times 1 = 1$.

Thus in the limit as pulse width $b \to 0$, so that $A = \frac{1}{b} \to \infty$, while maintaining the constant area of unity gives the Dirac delta function of zero width and unit area.

The ideal Dirac delta function is shown in Fig. 7.5.

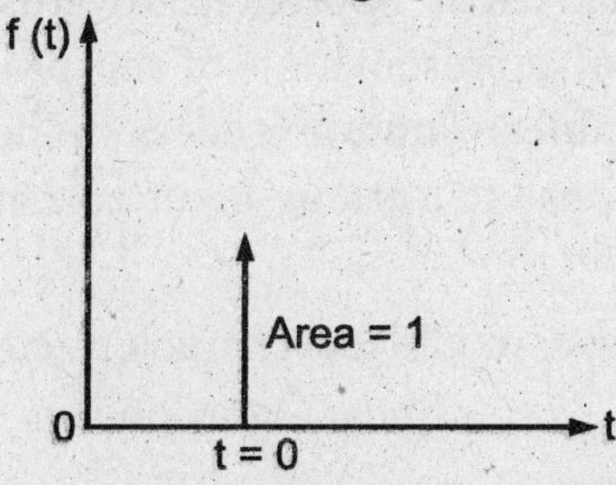

Fig. 7.5 : The ideal Dirac delta function

It may be noted that if H(t) is a unit step function, then

$$\frac{d}{dt}[H(t)] = \delta(t)$$

The Laplace transform of the impulse function of magnitude A is

$$\bar{f}(s) = A$$

In practice, it is impossible to implement the ideal impulse function exactly, however for slow processes a pulse function implemented over as short time interval as possible gives a good approximate impulse change.

The ideal sinusoidal function (frequency function) :

The sinusoidal function represents oscillatory behaviour of input. The sinusoidal function of magnitude A and frequency ω is represented as

$$f(t) = 0, \quad t < 0$$
$$= A \sin \omega t, \; t \geq 0$$

The Laplace transform of sinusoidal function is

$$\bar{f}(s) = \frac{A\omega}{s^2 + \omega^2}$$

The sinusoidal function is represented graphically as shown in Fig. 7.6.

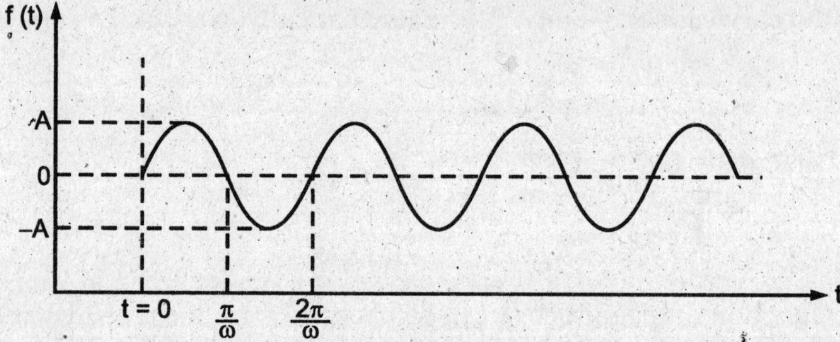

Fig. 7.6 : Sinusoidal function

It is quite difficult to implement a perfect sinusoidal input function in practice, but theoretical response of a process to sinusoidal change in input gives valuable information for designing controllers.

7.2.3 The Process Model

As discussed earlier the theoretical approach towards process dynamics requires a process model, i.e. a mathematical representation of the process in terms of a collection of relationship between process variables. Thus, a process model can be used as a surrogate for the physical system to study response to various input conditions, rather than experimenting on a real, actual physical process.

Enumerous number of processes could be characterized into a few types based on the nature of mathematical models, i.e., linear, non-linear, lumped parameter, distributed parameter and discrete-time systems.

Classification of process variables :

The process variables represent the performance or progress of the process. For example, temperature, pressure, level, flow are the process variables of a chemical process. The process variables are classified based on whether they represent or influence process conditions as follows :

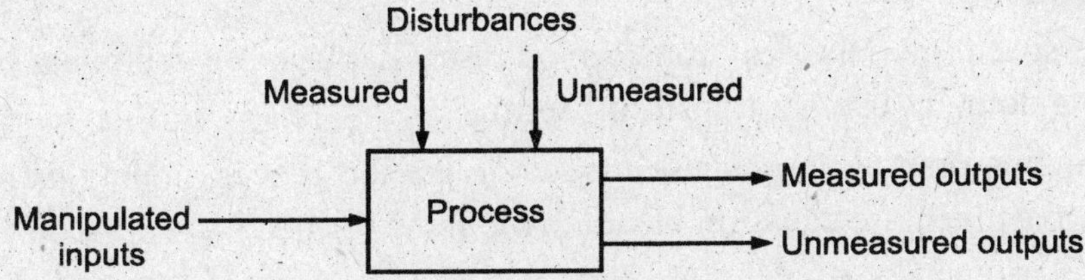

Fig. 7.7 : The process variables

Input variables : The input variables independently stimulate the system and thereby induce change in the internal conditions of the process.

Output variables [y(t)] : The output variables are those which give information about the internal state of the process.

State variables : The minimum set of variables that completely represent the internal state (or condition) of the process. The state of the process is represented by measurement of the output variable.

Manipulated variables [control variables u(t)] : The input variables which can be manipulated freely at out disposal are called as *manipulated variables* while the other variables on which we have no control are called as *disturbance variables [d(t)]*.

Some input and output variables are measurable while others are not measurable.

Forms of process models :

The process models are formulated from first principles such as the conservation principles, transport rate equations, chemical kinetic rate equations and thermodynamic relations.

State-space models :

The process models derived from first principles mentioned above are usually in state space form in which the state variables occur explicitly alongwith the input and output variables. These models are in the form of differential equation (for continuous-time systems) or difference equation (for discrete-time systems) which usually occur in the time domain.

State-space model forms are most useful for obtaining real-time behaviour of linear and non-linear systems.

A state space model of a linear, lumped parameter, first-order system having one input variable u(t), one output variable y(t) and state variable x(t) is in the form :

$$\frac{dx}{dt} = x(t) = Ax(t) + Bu(t) + \gamma d(t)$$

$$y(t) = Cx(t)$$

Input-output model :

Excluding the state variables from state-space model, we get input-output model which strictly relate only the input and output variables. Input-output models can be obtained in different domains as follows :

Transform domain models :

The state-space models are transformed into Laplace or s-domain (using Laplace transform) or z-domain (using z-transform) form.

For continuous time systems these models relate the process inputs u(t) and d(t) to the output y(t) by the algebraic equation in s-domain in the form :

$$\bar{y}(s) = G(s)\,\bar{u}(s) + G_d(s)\,\bar{d}(s) \qquad \text{... (7.1)}$$

where $G(s)$ = process transfer function

and $G_d(s)$ = disturbance transfer function

For discrete-time systems, the z-transform relates sampled input signal to sampled output signal by z-domain equation in the form :

$$\hat{y}(z) = \hat{G}(z)\,\hat{u}(z) + \hat{G}_d(z)\,\hat{d}(z) \qquad \text{... (7.2)}$$

where $\hat{G}(z)$ and $\hat{G}_d(z)$ are z-domain transfer functions.

The transform-domain transfer functions models are used for dynamic analysis and design of control systems.

Frequency response models :

For continuous-time systems, substituting $s = j\omega$ in Laplace transform domain model (Equation 7.1), we get frequency response model in the form :

$$y(j\omega) = G(j\omega)\,u(j\omega) + G_d(j\omega)\,d(j\omega)$$

where $G(j\omega)$ and $G_d(j\omega)$ are frequency response transfer functions, which are functions of frequency ω of input variable.

For discrete-time systems, frequency response models are obtained by substituting $z = \exp(j\omega\Delta t)$ in equation (7.2).

The frequency response models are used as non-parametric models for analysis and design of control systems. The frequency-domain transfer functions can be obtained from experimental data obtained from pulse or sinusoidal inputs in the form :

$$G(j\omega) = R_e(\omega) + j\,I_m(\omega)$$

where $R_e(\omega)$ and $I_m(\omega)$ are obtained experimentally over a range of frequencies.

Impulse-response models :

If input of the process is in the form of unit impulse function, the corresponding output response is known as impulse response G(t).

If the impulse response G(t) of a process is known, then output response of this process to any arbitrary input u(t) and disturbance d(t) is given by the impulse response model in the form :

$$y(t) = \int_0^t g(t-\sigma)\, u(\sigma)\, d\sigma + \int_0^t g(t-\sigma)\, d(\sigma)\, d\sigma$$

where σ is a dummy time argument and integral terms in the equation are known as *convolution integrals*. Therefore, this model is also called as *convolution model*.

For discrete-time process, the impulse response model relates sampled input $\hat{u}(k)$ to output $\hat{y}(k)$ by the equation :

$$y(k) = \sum_{i=1}^{k} G(i)\, u(k-i) + \sum_{i=1}^{k} G_d(i)\, d(k-i) \qquad \ldots (7.3)$$

The impulse-response models are used for dynamic analysis problems involving arbitrary function u(t). For this the discrete-time form of the model [given in Equation (7.3)] is particularly useful because it requires only the input values u(k – i) at different instants i = 1, 2, …, k, irrespective of the functional form of Equation (7.3).

For building such models we require experimental data sampled at an interval Δt that gives data record G(k).

As mentioned earlier, the step response function β(t) is related to impulse response function G(t) by the equation :

$$\frac{d}{dt}[\beta(t)] = G(t)$$

or $$\beta(t) = \int_0^t G(\sigma)\, d\sigma \quad \text{(for continuous time process)}$$

or $$\beta(k) = \sum_{i=1}^{k} G(i) \quad \text{(for discrete-time process)}$$

and $$G(k) = \beta(k) - \beta(k-1) \qquad \ldots (7.4)$$

Therefore discrete-time version of step-response model is :

$$y(k) = \sum_{i=1}^{k} \beta(i)\, \Delta u(k-i) \qquad \ldots (7.5)$$

where $$\Delta u\,(k-i) = u(k) - u(k-i)$$

Since step function is easier to implement on a physical system than an impulse, sampled step response data β(i) can be used to determine sampled impulse response data G(k) from which output can be determined from Equation (7.3).

We study the transfer function model form in more detail.

7.2.4 The Transfer Function

The transfer function of a process allows a quick analysis of process dynamics.

Consider a single-input-single output (SISO), process having one input variable (or forcing function) f(t) and one output variable (forced function) y(t) as shown in Fig. 7.8 (a).

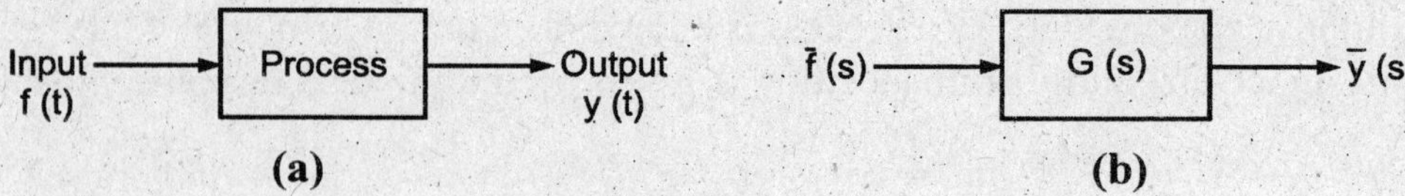

Fig. 7.8 : Transfer function of a SISO process

The dynamic behaviour of such a process is represented by n^{th}-order linear ordinary differential equation :

$$a_n \frac{d^n y}{dt^n} + a_{n-1} \frac{d^{n-1} y}{dt^{n-1}} + \ldots + a_1 \frac{dy}{dt} + a_0 y = bf(t)$$

where $a_0, a_1, \ldots, a_n$, b are constants.

This equation can be expressed in terms of deviation (or perturbation) variables

$$Y(t) = y(t) - y(0) \quad \text{and} \quad F(t) = f(t) - f(0) \text{ as}$$

$$a_n \frac{d^n Y}{dt^n} + a_{n-1} \frac{d^{n-1} Y}{dt^{n-1}} + \ldots + a_1 \frac{dY}{dt} + a_0 Y = bF(t) \qquad \ldots (7.6)$$

Assuming that system is initially at steady-state, so that all derivatives of Y at initial condition t = 0 are zero, i.e.

$$Y(0) = \left.\frac{dY}{dt}\right|_{t=0} = \left.\frac{d^2Y}{dt^2}\right|_{t=0} = \ldots \left.\frac{d^{n-1}Y}{dt}\right|_{t=0} = 0 \qquad \ldots (7.7)$$

Taking Laplace transform of Equation (7.6) and substituting zero initial conditions given by Equation (7.7), we get

$$(a_n s^n + a_{n-1} s^{n-1} + \ldots + a_1 s + a_0)\, \bar{Y}(s) = b\bar{F}(s)$$

$$\frac{\bar{Y}(s)}{\bar{F}(s)} = \frac{b}{a_n s^n + a_{n-1} s^{n-1} + \ldots + a_1 s + a_0} \qquad \ldots (7.8)$$

The ratio $\frac{\bar{Y}(s)}{\bar{F}(s)}$ of Laplace transform of output Y(t) to the Laplace transform of input F(t), both in deviation form is known as transfer.

Function G(s) which relates output to input in Laplace domain.

The transfer function model of a process is represented as shown in Fig. 7.8 (b) in which transfer function G(s) is written inside a rectangular block with input and output signals in Laplace domain with arrow heads.

Note that the transfer function G(s) operates on the input F(t) to produce an output Y(t).

As discussed earlier the process has two types of inputs a manipulated variable u(t) and a disturbance variable d(t).

Therefore, a complete input-output process model is represented in terms of two transfer functions : process transfer function G(s) (which relates the manipulated input to the output variable) and disturbance transfer function $G_d(s)$ (which relates disturbance variable with output variable) as shown in Fig. 7.9. (Assuming that all variables u(t), d(t), y(t) are expressed in deviation form).

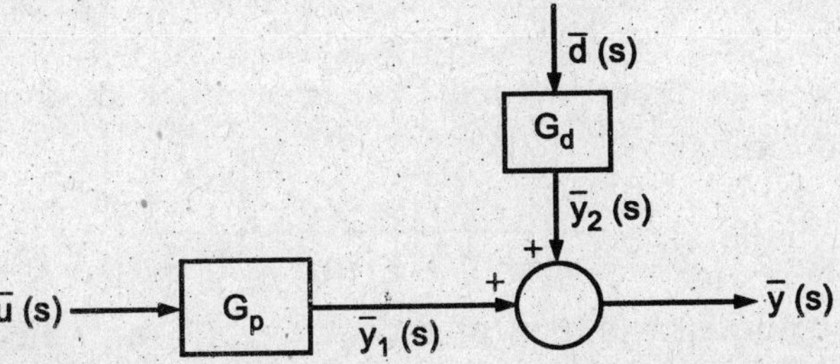

Fig. 7.9 : The input-output form of a process model

The circle shown in Fig. 7.9 represents a summing junction which adds the signals $\bar{y}_1(s)$ and $\bar{y}_2(s)$ which are the output signals of the blocks $G_p(s)$ and $G_d(s)$ respectively.

$$\therefore \qquad G_p(s) = \frac{\bar{y}_1(s)}{\bar{u}(s)} \qquad \text{or} \qquad \bar{y}_1(s) = G_p(s)\,\bar{u}(s)$$

$$\text{Also} \qquad G_d(s) = \frac{\bar{y}_2(s)}{\bar{d}(s)} \qquad \text{or} \qquad \bar{y}_2(s) = G_d(s)\,\bar{d}(s)$$

The output
$$\bar{y}(s) = \bar{y}_1(s) + \bar{y}_2(s)$$
$$= G_p(s)\,\bar{u}(s) + G_d\,\bar{d}(s) \qquad \dots (7.9)$$

This represents linearity property of transfer function which allows superposition of two transfer functions.

Properties of transfer function :

Consider the transfer function $G(s) = \dfrac{\bar{Y}(s)}{\bar{F}(s)}$.

$$\therefore \qquad \bar{Y}(s) = G(s)\,\bar{F}(s)$$

Thus, transfer function describes completely the dynamic behaviour of the output $\bar{Y}(s)$ for a particular change in input F(t) (having Laplace transform $\bar{F}(s)$).

The inverse Laplace transform of $\bar{Y}(s)$ gives output response Y(t) in the time domain.

2. ***Poles and zeros of a transfer function :***

Consider a transfer function defined as :

$$G(s) = \frac{\bar{y}(s)}{\bar{f}(s)} \qquad \dots (7.10)$$

Since the Laplace transforms $\overline{f}(s)$ and $\overline{y}(s)$ are s-domain functions, the transfer function G(s) will be the ratio of two polynomials in 's' as :

$$G(s) = \frac{N(s)}{D(s)}$$

If polynomial N(s) is of order 'm' and D(s) is of order 'n', then N(s) and D(s) can be expressed in factorized form as :

$$G(s) = \frac{k_1 (s - z_1)(s - z_2) \dots (s - z_m)}{k_2 (s - p_1)(s - p_2) \dots (s - p_n)} \quad \dots (7.11)$$

The numerator polynomial N(s) has 'm' roots $z_1, z_2, \dots, z_m$ which are called as *the zeros* of the transfer function.

The denominator polynomial D(s) has 'n' roots $p_1, p_2, \dots, p_n$ which are called as *the poles* of the transfer function. The transfer function G(s) becomes infinite at these values of s.

The poles and zeros of G(s) play important role in the dynamic analysis of systems and design of controllers.

3. Finding the output response y(t) :

Knowing the transfer function G(s), the output response $\overline{y}(s)$ to a given change in input f(t) having Laplace transform $\overline{f}(s)$ is given by

$$\overline{y}(s) = G(s)\,\overline{f}(s)$$

The product $G(s)\,\overline{f}(s)$ will also be a ratio of polynomials in the form

$$\overline{y}(s) = \frac{A(s)}{B(s)}$$

If $r_1, r_2, \dots, r_n$ are the roots of the denominator polynomial B(s), then

$$\overline{y}(s) = \frac{A(s)}{(s - r_1)(s - r_2) \dots (s - r_n)}$$

Resolving the right hand side into partial fraction expression :

$$\overline{y}(s) = \frac{c_1}{s - r_1} + \frac{c_2}{s - r_2} + \dots + \frac{c_n}{s - r_n}$$

Taking inverse Laplace transform :

$$y(t) = c_1 e^{r_1 t} + c_2 e^{r_2 t} + \dots + c_n e^{r_n t}$$

Thus the actual values of $r_1, r_2, \dots, r_n$ (i.e. real or complex) will decide the dynamic behaviour of output y(t) to a given change in input f(t).

Alternatively, in graphical sense, if values of the poles are plotted in complex plane, then location of the poles may predict the dynamic behaviour of the process qualitatively as follows :

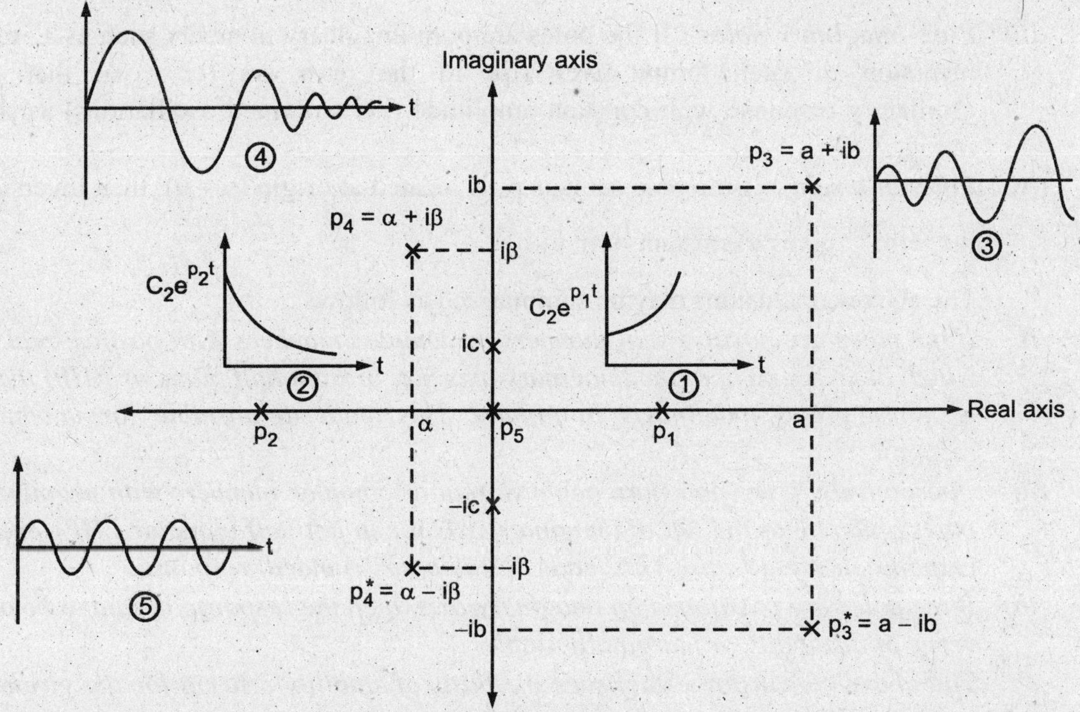

Fig. 7.10 : Qualitative analysis of dynamic behaviour based on location of poles

(i) ***Real, distinct poles :*** If the poles are real and distinct such as p_1 (> 0), p_2 (< 0) as shown in Fig. 7.10 then inversion of terms $\frac{c_1}{s - p_1}$ and $\frac{c_2}{s - p_2}$ give rise to exponential terms $c_1e^{p_1t}$ and $c_2e^{p_2t}$ respectively.

For positive real pole such as p_1, the term $c_1^{p_1t}$ causes the response to increase exponentially to infinity as shown in Fig. 7.10.

For negative real pole such as p_2, the term $c_2e^{p_2t}$ causes the response to decay exponentially to zero as shown in Fig. 7.10. (The above conclusions are also applicable for multiple poles such as $\frac{1}{(s-p)^2}, \frac{1}{(s-p)^3}, \ldots$).

(ii) ***Complex conjugate poles :*** The complex poles always occur in pair of complex conjugates such as $p_3 = a + ib$, $p_3^* = a - ib$. Inversion of such terms gives rise to terms such as $e^{at} \sin (bt + \phi)$ [or $e^{\alpha t} \sin (\beta t + \phi)$] that gives oscillatory response with amplitude e^{at} (or $e^{\alpha t}$).

The amplitude of oscillations increases or decreases with time depending on whether real part of complex pole is positive or negative respectively.

For $p_3, p_3^* = a \pm ib$, if the real part 'a' is positive, then the response grows to infinity in an oscillatory manner as shown in Fig. 7.10. For $p_4, p_4^* = \alpha \pm i\beta$, if the real part '$\alpha$' is negative, then the response decays to zero in an oscillating manner as shown in Fig. 7.10.

(iii) ***Pure imaginary poles :*** If the poles are pure imaginary numbers such as ± ic, then inversion of such terms gives rise to the term sin (ct + ϕ) that gives oscillatory response with constant amplitude (i.e. sustained oscillations) as shown in Fig. 7.10.

(iv) ***Poles at origin :*** If the pole such as p_5 is located at origin (s = 0), then inversion of the term $\frac{c_5}{s}$ gives a constant term c_5.

The above conclusions may be summarized as follows :

(i) *If the poles are positive real numbers or complex numbers with positive real part, which lie to the right of the imaginary axis (i.e. in right half plane or RHP) then the response grows indefinitely to infinity. This leads to unstable (or unbounded) response.*

(ii) *Alternatively, if the poles are negative real or complex numbers with negative real part, which lie to the left of imaginary axis (or in left half plane or LHP), then the response decays to zero. This leads to stable (or bounded) response.*

(iii) *If the poles are positioned on imaginary axis, then the response is said to be on the verge of instability or marginally stable.*

The above conclusion establishes the basis of stability criteria for the given open and closed-loop systems.

7.3 CLASSIFICATION OF PROCESSES BASED ON THEIR DYNAMIC BEHAVIOUR

Enumerous number of processes are characterized into a few types based on the nature of their input-output model, which further predict the dynamic behaviour of the process. The processes are classified based on the order of differential equation models as follows :

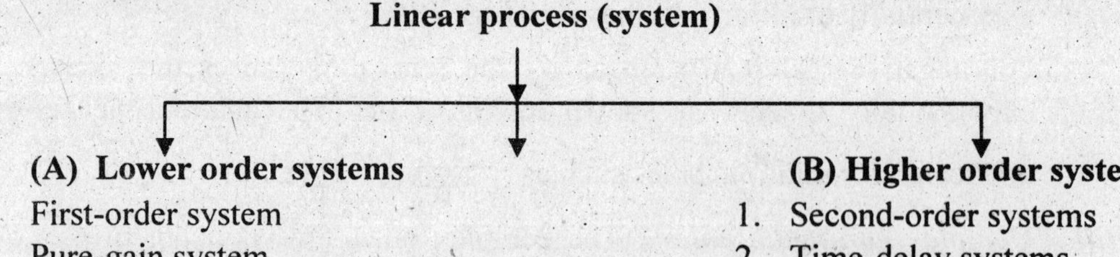

7.4 DYNAMIC BEHAVIOUR OF LINEAR FIRST-ORDER SYSTEM (FIRST-ORDER LAG OR LINEAR LAG SYSTEM)

The model : The output y(t) of a linear first-order system is modelled by a first-order, linear differential equation in the form

$$a_1 \frac{dy}{dt} + a_0 y = bf(t) \qquad \dots (7.12)$$

where f(t) is the input or forcing function.

The transfer function :

Assuming $a_0 \neq 0$, divide equation (7.12) by a_0 to get

$$\frac{a_1}{a_0}\frac{dy}{dt} + y = \frac{b}{a_0} f(t)$$

Substituting $\frac{a_1}{a_0} = \tau_p$ = time constant

and $\frac{b}{a_0} = k_p$ = steady-state gain

$$\tau_p \frac{dy}{dt} + y = k_p f(t) \quad \ldots (7.13)$$

Assume that initially, at t = 0 the system is at steady state with steady values of input and output variables f(0) and y(0) respectively.

Initially at t = 0, equation (7.13) takes the form

$$\tau_p \frac{dy(0)}{dt} + y(0) = k_p f(0) \quad \ldots (7.14)$$

Subtracting equation (7.14) from equation (7.13), we get

$$\tau_p \frac{d}{dt}[y(t) - y(0)] + [y(t) - y(0)] = k_p [f(t) - f(0)]$$

Introducing the deviation variables

$$F(t) = f(t) - f(0) \text{ and } Y(t) = y(t) - y(0)$$

in the above equation :

$$\tau_p \frac{dY}{dt} + Y = k_p F(t)$$

Taking Laplace transform :

$$\tau_p [s\bar{Y}(s) - Y(0)] + \bar{Y}(s) = k_p \bar{F}(s)$$

Substituting Y(0) = y(0) – y(0) = 0 and rearranging the equation, we get the transfer function of a first-order system in the form :

$$G(s) = \frac{\bar{Y}(s)}{\bar{F}(s)} = \frac{k_p}{\tau_p s + 1} \quad \ldots (7.15)$$

Poles and zeros :

Equation (7.15) shows that the transfer function of a first-order system has no zero, but it has a single negative real pole at $s = -\frac{1}{\tau_p}$. Also the denominator polynomial in G(s) is a first degree polynomial in 's'.

Characteristic model parameters :

The characteristic parameters of a first-order system are steady-state or static gain k_p and time constant τ_p, which are defined in the discussion to follow.

Response to various ideal forcing functions (inputs) :

1. Step response :

If value of input variable f(t) is suddenly changed from initial steady-state value f(0) to a new steady-state value f(new), i.e. a step change of magnitude A (= f(new) – f(0) = Δf) is applied as an input then the Laplace transform of the input variable is given by

$$\bar{F}(s) = \frac{A}{s} = \frac{\Delta f}{s}$$

Substituting this value in equation (7.15), the output response is given as :

$$\bar{Y}(s) = \frac{k_p}{\tau_p s + 1} \frac{A}{s}$$

Resolving the right-hand side of above equation into partial fractions :

$$\bar{Y}(s) = (Ak_p) \left(\frac{1}{s} - \frac{\tau_p}{\tau_p s + 1}\right)$$

Taking inverse Laplace transform,

$$Y(t) = Ak_p [1 - \exp(-t/\tau_p)] \quad \text{... (7.16)}$$

In dimensionless form,

$$\frac{Y(t)}{Ak_p} = 1 - \exp(-t/\tau_p) \quad \text{... (7.17)}$$

Step response characteristics :

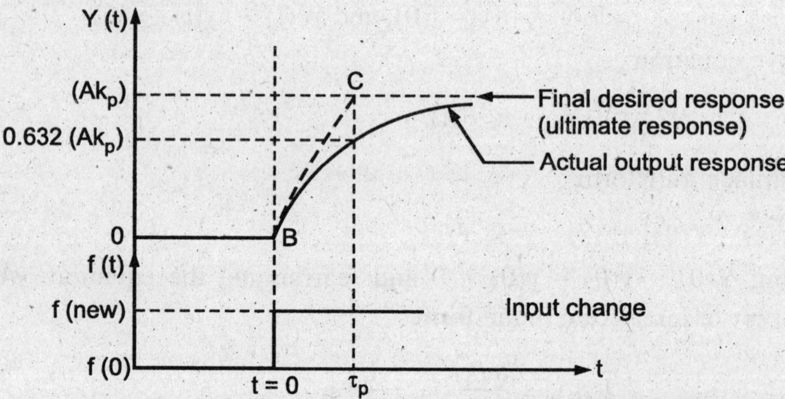

Fig. 7.11 : Step response of a first-order system

The output response of a first-order system for step change in input is represented graphically (shown in Fig. 7.11) as the plot of output Y(t) on y-axis against time t on x-axis. The output response exhibits following characteristics :

(i) Equation 7.16 shows that output response curve is an exponential curve, hence first-order systems are also called as exponential lag systems.

(ii) The output response starts changing at starting time t = 0 without any time lag.

(iii) As $t \rightarrow \infty$, output response $Y(t) \rightarrow Ak_p$. Therefore, for step change of magnitude A in input, the output response Y(t) increases from 0 to a final steady-state value $Y(\infty) = Ak_P$. This implies the significance of response parameter k_p as follows :

Definition of k_p :

Since $Y(\infty) = Ak_p$,

$$k_p = \frac{Y(\infty)}{A} = \frac{Y(\infty)}{\Delta f} = \frac{y(\infty) - y(0)}{f(new) - f(0)} = \frac{\Delta\,(output)}{\Delta\,(input)}$$

Thus, k_p represents change in output per unit change in input, hence it is known as ady-state or static gain or simply gain. If the process gain k_p is known, change in output for step change in input is calculated as :

$$\Delta\,(output) = k_p\,(input)$$

$$y(\infty) - y(0) = k_p\,[f(new) - f(0)]$$

Final steady-state output

$$y(\infty) = y(0) + k_pA \qquad \text{... (7.18)}$$

Thus, k_p is the measure of magnitude of change in output for given change in input.

(iv) From equation (7.16),

At $t = \tau_p$,

$$Y(t) = 0.632\,(Ak_p)$$

$$= 0.632\text{ (ultimate response)}$$

$$= 63.2\%\text{ of ultimate response}$$

Definition of time constant τ_p :

Time constant τ_p of a first-order process is the time elapsed for the output response to reach 63.2% of its final value (i.e. desired response).

The actual output response for time elapsed in terms of multiples of τ_p can be determined from equation (7.16) as given in the following table :

Table 7.1

Time elapsed	% output response
τ_p	63.2
$2\tau_p$	86.5
$3\tau_p$	95
$4\tau_p$	98
$6\tau_p$	99

Thus output response approaches the final desired response after nearly $4\tau_p$ period. The time constant τ_p of the process is the measure of its speed of response. Larger the value of τ_p, slower is the output response, while smaller values of τ_p indicate faster response to change in input.

Since step response of a first-order process approaches new steady-state value, systems are known as self-regulated systems.

(v) The slope of the response curve at origin is :

$$\left.\frac{dY(t)}{dt}\right|_{t=0} = \frac{Ak_p}{\tau_p} = \text{slope of tangent to the response curve at origin}$$

$$= \text{initial rate of change of response}$$

This implies that if the initial rate of change of output were to be maintained, the response would reach its final (ultimate) value in one time constant (τ_p). This is represented by point C on tangent BC in Fig. 7.10.

The smaller the value of τ_p, the steeper the initial response of the system, i.e. faster response.

2. ***The rectangular pulse response :***

If the input variable is changed according to pulse function as :

$$\begin{aligned} f(t) &= 0, \quad t < 0 \\ &= A, \quad 0 < t < b \\ &= 0, \quad t > b \end{aligned}$$

Laplace transform of input variable is :

$$\bar{f}(s) = \frac{A}{s}(1 - e^{-bs})$$

The output response for such rectangular pulse function is given by equation (7.15) as :

$$\begin{aligned} \bar{Y}(s) &= \frac{k_p}{\tau_p s + 1} \frac{A}{s}(1 - e^{-bs}) \\ &= \frac{Ak_p}{s(\tau_s + 1)}(1 - e^{-bs}) \\ &= \frac{Ak_p}{s(\tau_s + 1)} - \frac{Ak_p e^{-bs}}{\tau_s + 1} \end{aligned}$$

The two terms on right-hand side of above equation indicate a translation in time (Refer properties of Laplace transform in article 7.2.1).

Therefore inverse Laplace transform of the above equation gives different values in different time intervals as :

$$\begin{aligned} Y(t) &= Ak(1 - e^{-t/\tau}), \; t < b \\ &= Ak[(1 - e^{-t/\tau}) - (1 - e^{-(t-b)/\tau})], \; t > b \qquad \ldots (7.19) \end{aligned}$$

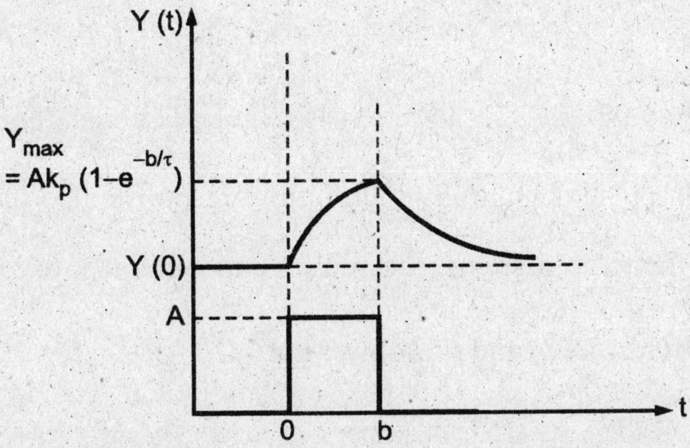

Fig. 7.12 : Rectangular pulse response of a first-order system

Fig. 7.12 shows output response represented by equation (7.19).

Response characteristics :

(i) During pulse width ($0 < t < b$) the response increases exponentially to ultimate value at $t = b$ which is given by

$$Y_{max} = Y(t = b) = Ak_p \left(1 - e^{-b/\tau_p}\right)$$

(ii) After reaching the ultimate value, output decreases exponentially to initial value $Y(0) = 0$.

3. *Impulse response :*

If the input variable is changed according to impulse function having unit area :

$$f(t) = A\,\delta(t)$$

then
$$\bar{f}(s) = A$$

The output response for such impulse change in input is given by equation (7.15) as :

$$\bar{Y}(s) = \frac{k_p}{\tau_p s + 1} A$$

Taking inverse Laplace transform,

$$Y(t) = \frac{Ak_p}{\tau_p} \exp(-t/\tau_p) \qquad \text{... (7.20)}$$

The output response is represented graphically as shown in Fig. 7.13.

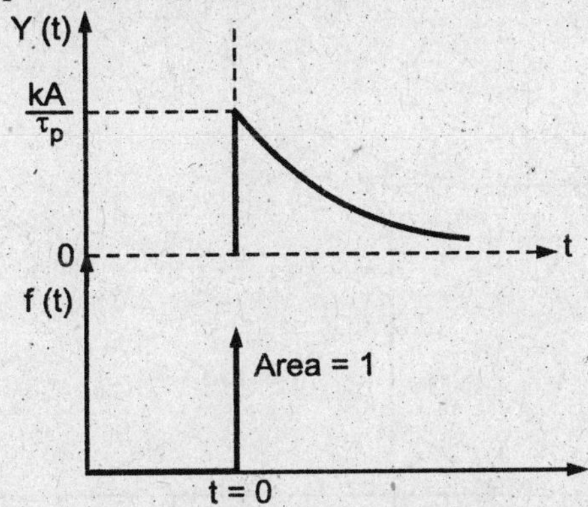

Fig. 7.13 : Impulse response of a first-order system

Response characteristics :

(i) At t = 0, $Y(t) = \frac{Ak_p}{\tau_p}$

Therefore, for ideal impulse change in input, output response also jumps to a value $\frac{Ak_p}{\tau_p}$ instantaneously and then the response decreases exponentially to zero. ($\because$ as $t \to \infty$, $Y(t) \to 0$)

(ii) Comparing equations (7.17) and (7.20), we get

$$\frac{d}{dt}(Y_{step}) = Y_{impulse}$$

4. ***Ramp response :***

If input variable f(t) changes according to ramp function :

$$f(t) = 0, \quad t < 0$$
$$= At, \quad t > 0$$

then, $\bar{f}(s) = A/s^2$

The output response for ramp change in input is given by equation (7.15) as :

$$\bar{Y}(s) = \frac{k_p}{\tau_p s + 1} \frac{A}{s^2}$$

Resolving right-hand side into partial fraction expansion :

$$\bar{Y}(s) = (Ak_p)\left(-\frac{\tau_p}{s} + \frac{1}{s^2} + \frac{\tau_p}{s + \frac{1}{\tau_p}}\right)$$

Taking inverse Laplace transform :

$$Y(t) = (Ak_p)\left[-\tau_p + t + \tau_p \exp(-t/\tau_p)\right]$$
$$= (Ak_p\tau_p)\left[\exp(-t/\tau_p) + \frac{t}{\tau_p} - 1\right] \quad \dots (7.21)$$

The output response is represented graphically as shown in Fig. 7.14.

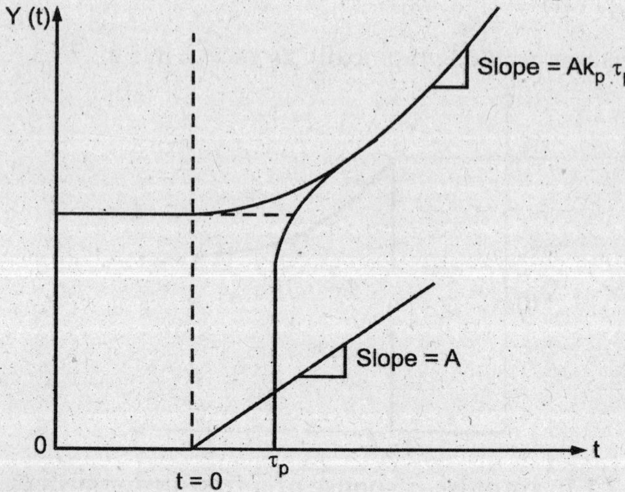

Fig. 7.14 : Ramp response of a first-order system

Response characteristics :

(i) At $t = 0$, $Y(t) = 0$.

As time increases, output response increases from zero exponentially. After sufficiently large time (as $t \to \infty$), the exponential term diminishes and output response is given by

$$Y(t) = (Ak_p)(t - \tau_p)$$

This represents linear output response with slope (Ak_p), but displaced by τ_p units from the origin at $Y(t) = 0$. Thus output response is asymptotic to a ramp function.

(ii) Comparing equations (7.17) and (7.20),

$$\frac{d}{dt}(Y_{ramp}) = Y_{step}$$

5. *Frequency response (sinusoidal response) :*

If input is changed according to sinusoidal function of magnitude A and frequency ω given by :

$$f(t) = A \sin(\omega t), \quad \text{then } \bar{f}(s) = \frac{A\omega}{s^2 + \omega^2}$$

[Comparing this equation with equation (7.9)

$$G_p = G_{load} = \frac{1}{A_c}$$

Input variables : q_i (disturbance d)

q_o (control variable or manipulated variable u)

Output variable : h (output or measured variable)

Above equation becomes :

$$\frac{dy}{dt} = \frac{1}{A_c} d - \frac{1}{A_c} u]$$

The output response for sinusoidal change in input is given by equation (7.15) as :

$$\bar{Y}(s) = \frac{k_p}{\tau_p s + 1} \frac{A\omega}{s^2 + \omega^2}$$

Resolving right-hand side into partial fraction expansion

$$\bar{Y}(s) = Ak_p\omega\tau_p \left[\frac{c_1}{s + 1/\tau_p} + \frac{c_2}{s + j\omega} + \frac{c_3}{s - j\omega}\right]$$

Evaluating the values of c_1, c_2, c_3 and taking inverse Laplace transform, we get the output response :

$$Y(t) = \frac{Ak_p\,\omega\tau_p}{1 + (\omega\tau_p)^2} e^{-t/\tau_p} - \frac{Ak_p\omega\tau_p}{(\omega\tau_p)^2 + 1} \cos \omega t + \frac{Ak_p}{(\omega\tau_p)^2 + 1} \sin \omega t$$

$$= (Ak_p)\left[\frac{\omega\tau_p}{1 + (\omega\tau_p)^2} e^{-t/\tau_p} + \frac{1}{1 + (\omega\tau_p)^2} \sin(\omega t_p) - \frac{\omega\tau_p}{1 + (\omega\tau_p)^2} \cos(\omega\tau_p)\right]$$

Using the trigonometric identity for last two terms inside the bracket,

$a \cos \theta + b \sin \theta = r \sin (\theta + \phi)$ (where $r = \sqrt{a^2 + b^2}$, $\theta = \tan^{-1}$ (b/a)), above equation becomes

$$Y(t) = (Ak_p)\left[\frac{\omega\tau_p}{1 + (\omega\tau_p)^2} e^{-t/\tau_p} + \frac{\sin(\omega t + \phi)}{\sqrt{1 + (\omega\tau_p)^2}}\right] \quad \ldots (7.22)$$

$$\phi = \tan^{-1}(-\omega\tau_p)$$

The output response is represented graphically as shown in Fig. 7.15.

The output response can also be determined by substituting $s = j\omega$ in the transfer function G(s) so that $AR = |G(j\omega)|$ and $\phi = \angle G(j\omega)$.

(If $G(j\omega) = a + jb$, $|G(j\omega)| = \sqrt{a^2 + b^2}$ and $\angle G(j\omega) = \tan^{-1}\left(\frac{b}{a}\right)$)

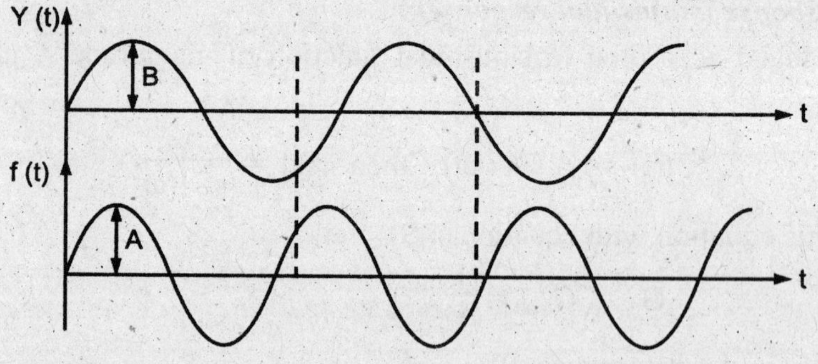

Fig. 7.15 : Sinusoidal response of a first-order system

Response characteristics :

(i) Initially at small values of t, the first term inside the bracket is predominant over the second term. But as time increases to about $4\tau_p$, the first term decays with time, but the second term persists.

(ii) As $t \to \infty$, the ultimate response will be a pure sine wave given by

$$Y(t)|_{t \to \infty} = \frac{Ak_p}{\sqrt{1 + (\omega\tau_p)^2}} \sin(\omega t + \phi) \quad \ldots (7.23)$$

$$= B \sin(\omega t + \phi)$$

This is known as ultimate periodic response (UPR).

(iii) Comparing this ultimate output response with sinusoidal change in input $f(t) = A \sin(\omega t)$, it can be concluded that magnitude of output response is

$$B = \frac{Ak_p}{\sqrt{1 + (\omega\tau_p)^2}}$$

Therefore, ratio of amplitude of output and input sinusoidals is :

$$AR = \frac{B}{A} = \frac{Ak_p/\sqrt{1 + (\omega\tau_p)^2}}{A} = \frac{k_p}{\sqrt{1 + (\omega\tau_p)^2}}.$$

Also the output sinusoidal lags behind the input sinusoidal by angle ϕ given by

$$\phi = \tan^{-1}(-\omega\tau_p)$$

The UPR is characterized by the parameters AR and ϕ which are functions of frequency ω of sinusoidals. Variation in AR and ϕ with ω is called *frequency response* of the process which is represented by Bode diagram consisting of two separate plots : log (AR) Vs. (log ω) and ϕ Vs. (log ω).

Physical examples of first-order systems :

1. Liquid level system :

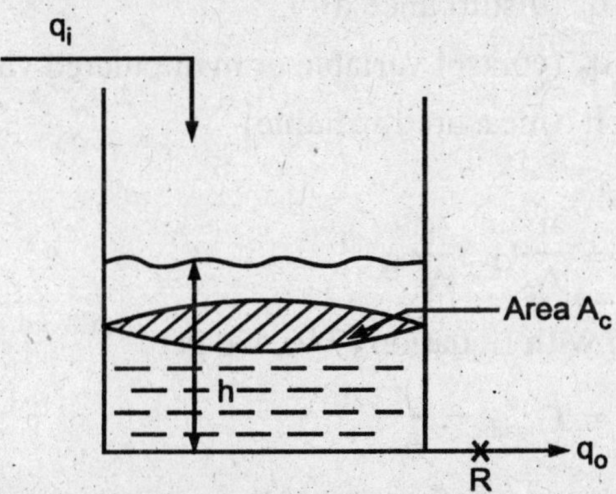

Fig. 7.16 : Liquid level system

Fig. 7.16 shows liquid level system consisting of a cylindrical tank having cross-section area A_c. A liquid of constant density ρ enters the tank at a volumetric flow rate of q_i (volume/time) and it leaves the tank via exit line at a volumetric flow rate q_o through resistance R. The resistance R is associated with pumps, valves, weirs and inlet or exit pipe lengths.

The process model

The unsteady-state (transient) mass balance equation at any instant around the tank is :

Rate of accumulation of liquid mass in the tank

= Inlet mass flow rate – Outlet mass flow rate

$$\frac{d}{dt}(\rho V) = \rho q_i - \rho q_o$$

where V = Volume of liquid inside the tank at moment t

$= A_c h$

Assuming constant density of liquid,

$$A_c \frac{dh}{dt} = q_i - q_o \quad \text{... (7.24)}$$

Assuming that output flow rate q_o is related linearly to the hydrostatic pressure of the liquid level h, through the resistance R by the relation

$$q_o = \frac{h}{R} = \frac{\text{Driving force for flow}}{\text{Resistance to flow}}$$

(This equation is analogous to Ohm's law in current electricity.)

Substituting this value of q_o in equation (7.24),

$$A_c \frac{dh}{dt} = q_i - \frac{h}{R}$$

$$\frac{dh}{dt} = \frac{1}{A_c} q_i - \frac{1}{A_c} q_o$$

$$(A_c R) \frac{dh}{dt} + h = q_i R$$

If process variables are defined as input variables –

q_i (disturbance d)

q_o (control variable or manipulated variable u)

Output variable – h (measured variable)

Above equation becomes :

$$\frac{dy}{dt} = \frac{1}{A_c} d - \frac{1}{A_c} u \qquad \text{... (7.25)}$$

Comparing this equation with Equation (7.9), we get

$$G_p = G_{load} = \frac{1}{A_c}$$

This equation is in the form of first-order linear differential equation (equation 7.13) with :

Input variable : q_i

Output variable : q_o

Time constant, τ_p = $A_c R$

and Steady-stage gain,

$$k_p = R$$

Therefore, first-order systems are characterized by a time constant τ_p which is the product of storage capacitance (A_c) and resistance to flow (R).

Initially at t = 0, the tank system is at steady state with $q_i = q_i(0)$ and corresponding liquid level h(0). Equation (7.24) can be written for initial condition as :

$$(A_c R) \frac{dh(0)}{dt} + h(0) = R q_i(0) \qquad \text{... (7.26)}$$

Subtracting equation (7.25) from equation (7.24)

$$(A_c R) \frac{d}{dt} [h - h(0)] + [h - h(0)] = R [q_i - q_i(0)]$$

Introducing deviation variables

$$H(t) = h(t) - h(0) \text{ and } Q_i(t) = q_i(t) - q_i(0)$$

$$(A_c R) \frac{dH}{dt} + H = RQ_i \qquad \text{... (7.27)}$$

The transfer function :

Taking Laplace transform of equation (7.26) with zero initial condition, the transfer function of liquid tank is :

$$G(s) = \frac{\bar{H}(s)}{\bar{Q}_i(s)} = \frac{k_p}{\tau_p s + 1} = \frac{R}{(A_c R)\, s + 1} \qquad \text{... (7.28)}$$

The output response of this system for step, ramp, impulse or sinusoidal change in input Q_i can be determined as discussed earlier.

2. The continuous stirred-tank heater (CSTH) :

The Process :

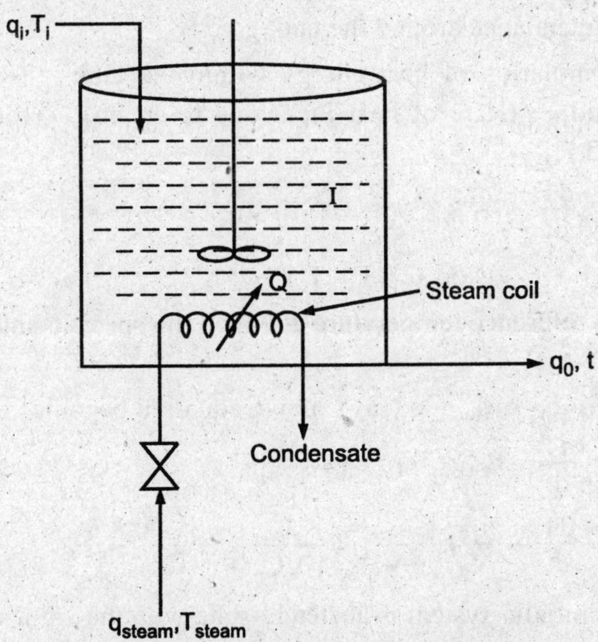

Fig. 7.17 : The stirred tank heater

Fig. 7.17 shows a stirred-tank heater in which liquid enters at volumetric flow rate q_i at temperature T_i. The liquid inside the tank is heated to temperature T by steam circulated through steam coil immersed in the liquid. Due to continuous stirring temperature (T) of liquid inside the tank is uniform.

Liquid leaves the tank at same volumetric flow rate q_i and temperature T.

The Process Model :

Let V = Volume of liquid inside the tank

ρ = Density of liquid

C_p = Specific heat of liquid

λ = Latent heat of vaporization of steam

q_{st} = Flow rate of steam

(i) Overall mass balance equation around the tank gives :

$$\frac{d}{dt}(\rho V) = \rho q_i - \rho q_o$$

$$= 0 \qquad (\because q_i = q_o)$$

Assuming constant density ρ,

$$\frac{dV}{dt} = 0$$

or $$V = \text{constant}$$

This indicates that the tank is a constant volume process which is obvious due to assumption that $q_i = q_o$.

(ii) Overall energy balance around the tank gives

Rate of accumulation of heat energy within the tank = (Rate of heat input with entering liquid) + (Rate of heat input due to steam) – (Rate of heat output with leaving liquid.)

$$\rho V C_p \frac{dT}{dt} = \rho\, q_i\, C_p\, (T_i - T^*) + \lambda q_s$$

$$- \rho q_o C_p\, (T - T^*)$$

where T^* is a reference temperature at which the specific enthalpy of liquid is taken to be zero.

Since $q_i = q_o = q$ (say), above equation becomes :

$$\rho V C_p \frac{dT}{dt} = \rho q C_p\, (T_i - T) + \lambda q_s$$

$$\frac{dT}{dt} = \frac{q}{V} T_i - \frac{q}{V} T + \frac{\lambda}{\rho V C_p} q_s \qquad \ldots (7.29)$$

Assume that initially system is at steady-state with the values of process variables :

$$T = T(0),\ T_i = T_i(0),\ q_s = q_s(0)$$

Therefore equation (7.28) becomes

$$\frac{dT(0)}{dt} = \frac{q}{V} T_i(0) - \frac{q}{V} T(0) + \frac{\lambda}{\rho V C_p} q_s(0) \qquad \ldots (7.30)$$

Subtracting equation (7.29) from equation (7.30), we get

$$\frac{d}{dt}[T - T(0)] = \frac{q}{V}[T_i - T_i(0)] - \frac{q}{V}[T - T(0)] + \frac{\lambda}{\rho V C_p}[q_s - q_s(0)]$$

Now we define the process variables as :

Input variables :

Control or manipulated variable $u = q_s - q_s(0)$.

Disturbance variable $d = T_i - T_i(0)$.

State or output variable : y = T – T(0).

Therefore above equation becomes

$$\frac{dy}{dt} = -\frac{1}{\theta}y + \frac{1}{\theta}d + \beta u$$

where $\theta = \frac{V}{q}$ and $\beta = \lambda/\rho VC_p$ = residence time of the tank.

The transfer function :

Taking Laplace transform of above equation :

$$s\bar{y}(s) = -\frac{1}{\theta}\bar{y}(s) + \frac{1}{\theta}\bar{d}(s) + \beta\,\bar{u}(s)$$

$$(\theta s + 1)\,\bar{y}(s) = \beta\theta\,\bar{y}(s) + \bar{d}(s)$$

$$\bar{y}(s) = \left(\frac{\beta\theta}{\theta s + 1}\right)\bar{u}(s) + \left(\frac{1}{\theta s + 1}\right)\bar{d}(s) \qquad \text{... (7.31)}$$

This equation is in the form of equation (7.9) with transfer functions :

$$G_p(s) = \frac{\beta\theta}{\theta s + 1} \quad \text{and} \quad G_d(s) = \frac{1}{\theta s + 1}$$

7.5 DYNAMIC BEHAVIOUR OF PURE GAIN SYSTEMS

The Model :

Recall the mathematical model of a first-order system in the form :

$$\tau_p \frac{dy}{dt} + y = k_p\, f(t)$$

If $\tau_p = 0$, this equation takes the form :

$$y(t) = k_p\, f(t) \qquad \text{... (7.32)}$$

Taking Laplace transform,

$$\bar{y}(s) = k_p\, \bar{f}(s)$$

The transfer function : $G(s) = \frac{\bar{y}(s)}{\bar{f}(s)} = k_p$ ... (7.33)

Poles and zeros : This transfer function neither have a pole nor a zero.

Model parameters :

Since transfer function of such a system has only a single parameter k_p without any poles and zeros, therefore, it is known as pure gain system.

Response to ideal forcing functions :

Equation (7.32) shows that the output of a pure gain process is directly proportional to the input with the process gain k_p as the constant of proportionality. Therefore the input and output responses are identical in form, but differing only in magnitude depending on the value of k_p as follows :

$k_p > 1$: y(t) is amplified as compared to f(t)

$k_p < 1$: y(t) is attenuated as compared to f(t).

$k_p = 1$: y(t) has magnitude same as f(t).

Since $\tau_p = 0$, such systems theoretically respond instantaneously and infinitely fast to change in input.

Step response :

Input : $f(t) = 0, \quad t < 0$

$= A, \quad t > 0$

Output : $y(t) = 0, \quad t < 0$

$= Ak_p, \quad t > 0$

Rectangular pulse response :

Input : $f(t) = 0, \quad t < 0$

$= A, \quad 0 < t < b$

$= 0, \quad t > b$

Output : $y(t) = 0, \quad t < 0$

$= Ak, \quad 0 < t < b$

$= 0, \quad t > b$

Impulse response :

Input : $f(t) = 0, \quad t < 0$

$= A\,\delta(t), \quad t > 0$

Output : $y(t) = 0, \quad t < 0$

Ramp response :

Input : $f(t) = 0, \quad t < 0$

$= At, \quad t > 0$

Output : $y(t) = 0, \quad t < 0$

$= Ak_p, \quad t > 0$

Sinusoidal response :

Input : $f(t) = 0, \quad t < 0$

$= A \sin \omega t, \quad t > 0$

Output : $y(t) = 0, \quad t < 0$

$= (Ak) \sin \omega t, \quad t > 0$

Therefore, the output response is a sine wave having amplitude (Ak) with zero phase angle ($\phi = 0$) i.e. in phase with input.

Physical examples of pure gain system :

First-order or higher-order systems which are fast responding (i.e. having smaller time constants) may be conveniently approximated as pure gain processes. The examples are :

(i) A pneumatic control valve with very rapid response may be approximated as a pure gain process.

(ii) The proportional controller is a pure gain system whose output is proportional to the input, i.e. error signal.

7.6 DYNAMIC BEHAVIOUR OF A PURE CAPACITIVE SYSTEM (PURE INTEGRATOR)

The Model :

In the mathematical model of a first-order system if $a_0 = 0$, then it takes the form :

$$\frac{dy}{dt} = \frac{b}{a_1} f(t) = k_p' f(t) \qquad \ldots (7.34)$$

The transfer function :

Assuming that f and y are input and output variables in deviation form respectively, the Laplace transform of above equation gives :

$$s\bar{y}(s) = k_p' \bar{f}(s)$$

$$\therefore \quad \text{Transfer function } G(s) = \frac{\bar{y}(s)}{\bar{f}(s)} = \frac{k_p'}{s} \qquad \ldots (7.35)$$

Response characteristics :

Assuming zero initial condition, the output response of such systems can be determined by integrating equation (7.34) regardless of specific nature of the input change as :

$$y(t) = k_p' \int_0^t f(t)\, dt$$

Since this equation involves integration of input function, such systems are known as pure integrator systems.

Equation (7.35) shows that such systems are characterized by the presence of 1/s term in the transfer function, which corresponds to Laplace transform of integral term $\int f(t)\, dt$.

Also from equation (7.13), for $a_0 = 0$,

$$\tau_p = \frac{a_1}{a_0} \to \infty \text{ and } k_p = \frac{b}{a_0} \to \infty$$

$$\text{While} \qquad k_p' = \frac{b}{a_1} = \frac{b/a_0}{a_1/a_0} = \frac{k_p}{\tau_p} = \text{constant}$$

Therefore, even though k_p and τ_p both approach infinity, their ratio remains constant at the value k_p'. Thus, a pure capacitive system may be imagined to be a first-order system whose gain k_p and time constant τ_p are extremely large, but for which their ratio $\frac{k_p}{\tau_p}$ is a fixed, finite constant.

Step response :

Input : $f(t) = 0, \quad t < 0$

$= A, \quad t > 0$

$$\bar{f}(s) = \frac{A}{s}$$

Output response : $\bar{y}(s) = \frac{k_p'}{s} \times \frac{1}{s} = \frac{k_p'}{s^2}$

Taking inverse Laplace transform :

$$y(t) = Ak_p't \qquad \text{... (7.36)}$$

Therefore for step change in input, output response continuously increases with time at a constant rate k_p' as shown in Fig. 7.18. Therefore such systems are called as *non-self regulated systems.*

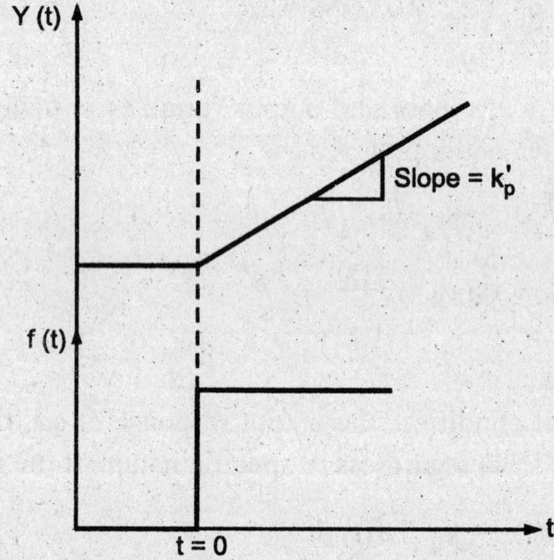

Fig. 7.18 : Step response of pure capacitive process

Rectangular pulse response :

Input : $f(t) = 0, \quad t < 0$

$= A, \quad 0 < t < b$

$= 0, \quad t > b$

Output : $\bar{y}(s) = \frac{k_p'}{s} \times \frac{A}{s}(1 - e^{-bs})$

$$= \frac{k_p'A}{s^2} - \frac{k_p'A}{s^2} e^{-bs}$$

Taking inverse Laplace transform :

$y(t) = 0, \quad t < 0$

$= (Ak_p't), \quad 0 < t < b$

$= (Ak_p'b), \quad t > b$

Therefore, output response starts out as a linear or ramp function at a rate (Ak_p') (for $0 < t < b$) and then at $t = b$, response settles down to a new steady-state value ($Ak_p'b$) as shown in Fig. 7.19.

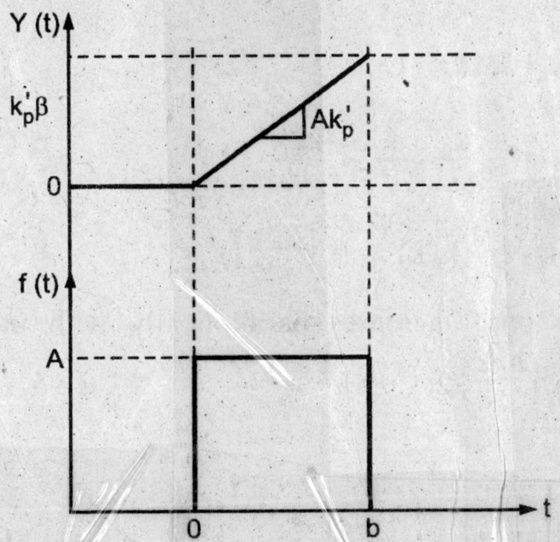

Fig. 7.19 : Rectangular pulse response of a pure capacitive process

Impulse response :

Input : $f(t) = 0, \quad t < 0$

$= A\,\delta t, \; t > 0$

$\bar{f}(s) = A$

Output response : $\bar{Y}(s) = \dfrac{k_p'}{s} \times A$

Inverting : $Y(t) = k_p'A$

Therefore output response steps out from initial steady-state value [$Y(0) = 0$] to a new steady-state value (Ak_p') as shown in Fig. 7.20.

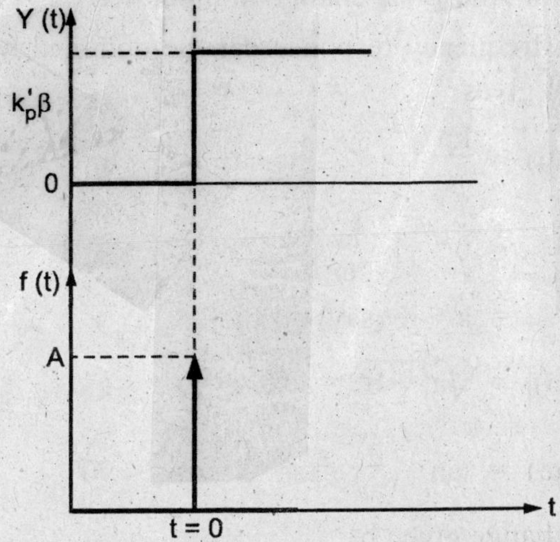

Fig. 7.20 : Impulse response of a pure capacitive process

Ramp response :

Input : $f(t) = 0, \quad t < 0$

$= kt, \quad t > 0$

$$\bar{f}(s) = \frac{k}{s^2}$$

Output response, $\bar{Y}(s) = \frac{k_p'}{s} \times \frac{k}{s^2} = \frac{k_p'k}{s^3}$

Inverting, $Y(t) = (k_p'k)\frac{t^2}{2} = \left(\frac{k_p'k}{2}\right)t^2$

Therefore, ramp response increases parabolically with increasing rate as shown in Fig. 7.21 $\left(\text{since } \frac{dY(t)}{dt} = \left(\frac{k_p'k}{2}\right)2t\right)$.

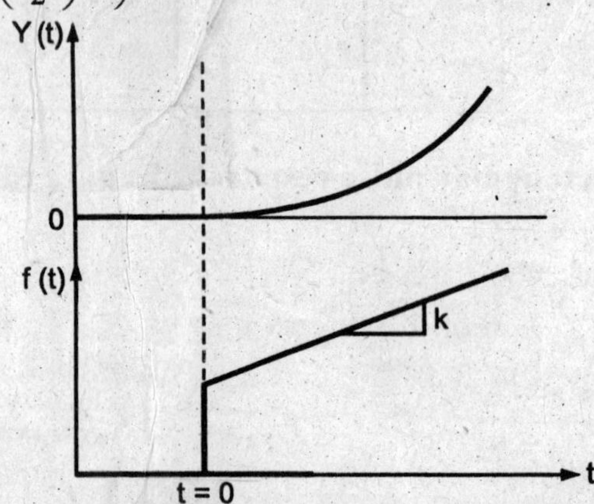

Fig. 7.21 : Ramp response of a pure capacitive process

Sinusoidal response :

(i.e. output response for sinusoidal change in input $f(t) = A \sin \omega t$)

As described earlier, frequency response can be obtained by substituting $s = j\omega$ in the transfer function G(s) that gives :

$$G(j\omega) = \frac{kp'}{j\omega}$$

$$= 0 + j\left(-\frac{k_p'}{\omega}\right)$$

$$= a + jb \text{ (say)}$$

$$\therefore \quad AR = |G(j\omega)| = \sqrt{a^2 + b^2} = \frac{k_p'}{\omega} = \frac{B}{A}$$

$$\phi = G(j\omega) = \tan^{-1}\left(\frac{b}{a}\right) = \tan^{-1}(-\infty) = -90°$$

Therefore, for input change given by

$$f(t) = A \sin \omega t$$

the output response is given by

$$Y(t) = B \sin(\omega t - \phi)$$

$$= \frac{Ak_p'}{\omega} \sin(\omega t + 90°)$$

$$= \frac{Ak_p'}{\omega} \cos(\omega t)$$

Thus, input and output responses are sinusoidal but output lags behind the input signal by –90° as shown in Fig. 7.22.

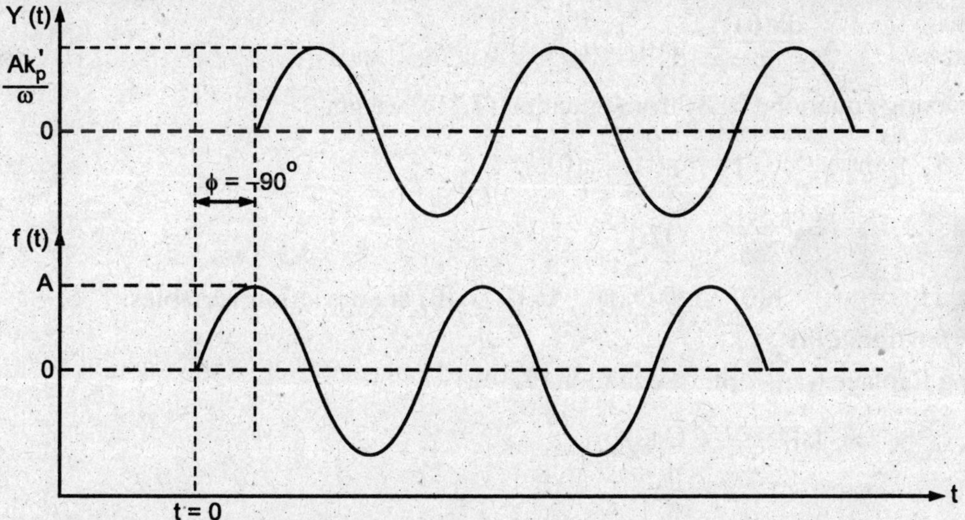

Fig. 7.22 : Sinusoidal response of a pure capacitive process

Physical examples of a pure capacitive process :

Liquid storage tank (or surge tank) with an outlet pump :

Fig. 7.23 shows a typical storage tank with an outlet pump, which is typically used as a process tank for intermediate storage between the two processes.

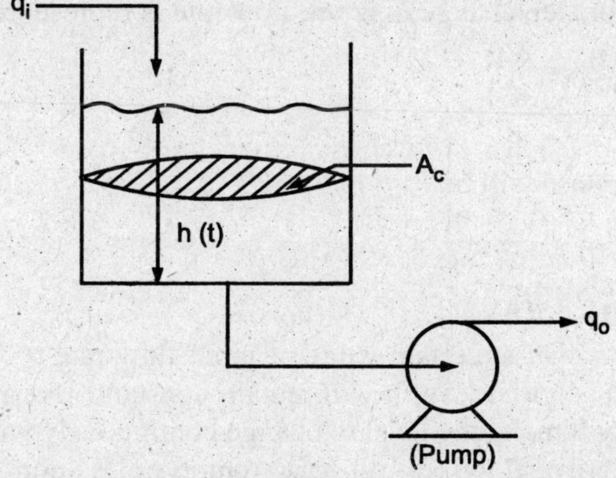

Fig. 7.23 : The storage tank with an outlet pump

The model :

Liquid of constant density ρ enters the tank at volumetric flow rate q_i. A constant displacement pump at the outlet discharges the liquid at a constant rate q_o. If h is level of liquid inside the tank (having cross-section area A_c) at any moment of time t, then mass balance equation around the tank yields :

$$A_c \frac{dh}{dt} = q_i - q_o \quad \text{... (7.37)}$$

At steady-state condition represented by $h = h(0)$, $q_i = q_i(0)$, equation (7.37) becomes

$$A_c \frac{dh(0)}{dt} = q_i(0) - q_o \quad \text{... (7.38)}$$

Subtracting equation (7.38) from equation (7.37), we get

$$A_c \frac{d}{dt}[h(t) - h(0)] = q_i(t) - q_i(0)$$

$$A_c \frac{dH}{dt} = Q_i(t) \quad \text{... (7.39)}$$

where $H(t) = h(t) - h(0)$ and $Q_i(t) = q_i(t) - q_i(0)$ are deviation variables.

The transfer functions :

Taking Laplace transform of equation (7.39),

$$A_c [s\bar{H}(s)] = \bar{Q}_i(s)$$

$$\bar{H}(s) = \frac{\frac{1}{A_c}}{s} \bar{Q}_i(s)$$

$$\text{Transfer function } G(s) = \frac{\bar{H}(s)}{\bar{Q}_i(s)} = \frac{\frac{1}{A_c}}{s} = \frac{k_p'}{s}$$

Therefore, this system behaves as a pure capacitive process.

As discussed earlier for step change in input, flow rate is represented as :

$$Q_i(t) = A$$

$$\bar{Q}_i(s) = \frac{A}{s}$$

Therefore, output response will be :

$$\bar{H}(s) = \frac{k_p'}{s} \times \frac{A}{s} = (Ak_p') \frac{1}{s^2}$$

Inverting $\quad H(t) = (Ak_p')\, t$

This equation indicates that at certain value of input flow rate q_i, the speed of pump can be so adjusted that $q_o = q_i$, so that level h will remain constant. But any small change in the flow rate of inlet stream will make the level to change continuously with time (at a rate Ak_p'), so that tank may flood (overflow) or run dry (empty), i.e. non-self-regulated process. Therefore such pure capacitive process may cause serious control problems.

7.7 DYNAMIC BEHAVIOUR OF A LINEAR SECOND-ORDER SYSTEM

The model :

The output response of a linear second-order system is modelled by a second-order linear differential equation in the form :

$$a_2 \frac{d^2y}{dt} + a_1 \frac{dy}{dt} + a_0 y = bf(t)$$

where f(t) is input or forcing function.

If $a_0 \neq 0$, above equation becomes :

$$\frac{a_2}{a_0}\frac{d^2y}{dt^2} + \frac{a_1}{a_0}\frac{dy}{dt} + y = \frac{b}{a_0} f(t)$$

$$\tau^2 \frac{d^2y}{dt^2} + 2\zeta\tau \frac{dy}{dt} + y = k_p\, f(t) \qquad \ldots (7.40)$$

where $\tau^2 = \frac{a_2}{a_0}$, $2\zeta\tau = \frac{a_1}{a_0}$ and $k_p = \frac{b}{a_o}$

The transfer function :

Equation (7.40) may be expressed in deviation variables Y(t) = y(t) – y(0) and F(t) = f(t) – f(0) as :

$$\tau^2 \frac{d^2Y}{dt^2} + 2\zeta\tau \frac{dY}{dt} + Y(t) = k_p\, F(t)$$

With zero initial conditions, the Laplace transform of above equation gives :

$$\tau^2 [s^2 \bar{Y}(s)] + 2\zeta\tau [s\bar{Y}(s)] + \bar{Y}(s) = k_p \bar{F}(s)$$

$$(\tau^2 s^2 + 2\zeta s + 1)\, \bar{Y}(s) = k_p \bar{F}(s)$$

Transfer function,

$$G(s) = \frac{\bar{Y}(s)}{\bar{F}(s)} = \frac{k_p}{\tau^2 s^2 + 2\tau\zeta\, s + 1} \qquad \ldots (7.41)$$

The denominator of second-order transfer function is a second-order polynomial.

The characteristic parameters of second-order system are :

k_p = Steady-state or static gain or simply gain

τ_p = Natural period of oscillations

ζ = Damping factor

$\omega_n = \frac{1}{\tau}$ = Natural frequency of oscillations.

Substituting $\tau = \frac{1}{\omega_n}$ in equation (7.41),

$$G(s) = \frac{k_p \omega_n^2}{s^2 + 2\zeta\, \omega_n s + \omega_n^2} \qquad \ldots (7.42)$$

Poles and zeros :

The transfer function of second-order system has no zero, but has 2 poles located at $s = p_1$ and $s = p_2$, where p_1 and p_2 are roots of denominator polynomial given by

$$p_1, p_2 = -\frac{\zeta}{\tau} \pm \frac{\sqrt{\zeta^2 - 1}}{\tau}$$

so that,
$$G(s) = \frac{k_p}{(s - p_1)(s - p_2)}$$

For $\zeta > 1$: The poles p_1 and p_2 are real and distinct.

For $\zeta < 1$: The poles p_1 and p_2 are complex conjugates given by

$$p_1, p_2 = -\frac{\zeta}{\tau} \pm i \frac{\sqrt{1 - \zeta^2}}{\tau} \qquad \text{... (7.43)}$$

For $\zeta = 1$: The poles p_1 and p_2 are real and equal given by

$$p_1 = p_2 = -\frac{1}{\tau} = p \text{ (say)}$$

The dynamic behaviour of second-order process depends on the nature of the poles p_1, p_2 that are dependent on the values of the parameter ζ.

7.7.1 Response to Various Ideal Forcing Functions

1. Step response of second-order system :

Let input variable f(t) be changed according to step function of magnitude A by the equation :

$$f(t) = 0, \qquad t < 0$$
$$= Au(t), \qquad t \geq 0$$

$$\therefore \qquad \bar{f}(s) = \frac{A}{s}$$

The output response of a second-order system for step change in input is determined from equation (7.41) as :

$$\bar{Y}(s) = \frac{k_p}{\tau^2 s^2 + 2\tau\zeta s + 1} \frac{A}{s}$$

$$= \frac{Ak_p}{\tau^2} \frac{1}{s\left(s^2 + \frac{2\zeta}{\tau} s + \frac{1}{\tau^2}\right)}$$

$$= \frac{Ak_p}{\tau^2} \left[\frac{1}{s(s - p_1)(s - p_2)}\right]$$

Resolving right-hand side into partial fraction expansion

$$Y(t) = \frac{Ak_p}{\tau^2} \left(\frac{c_1}{s} + \frac{c_2}{s - p_1} + \frac{c_3}{s - p_2}\right)$$

Taking inverse Laplace transform :

$$Y(t) = \frac{Ak_p}{\tau^2} (c_1 + c_2 e^{p_1 t} + c_3 e^{p_2 t}) \qquad \text{... (7.44)}$$

Case 1 : $0 < \zeta < 1$ (underdamped response) :

For $\zeta < 1$, the roots p_1 and p_2 are complex conjugates given by equation (7.43). Substituting values of p_1, p_2 in equation (7.44),

$$Y(t) = \frac{Ak_p}{\tau^2}[c_1 + c_2 e^{(\alpha + i\beta)t} + c_3 e^{(\alpha - i\beta)t}]$$

$$= \frac{Ak_p}{\tau^2}[c_1 + e^{\alpha t}(c_2 e^{i\beta t} + c_3 e^{-i\beta t})]$$

$$= \frac{Ak_p}{\tau_2}[c_1 + e^{\alpha t}\{c_2(\cos\beta t + i\sin\beta t) + c_3(\cos\beta t - i\sin\beta t)\}]$$

$$= \frac{Ak_p}{\tau^2}[c_1 - e^{\alpha t}\{(-c_2 - c_3)\cos\beta t + i(c_3 - c_2)\sin\beta t\}]$$

$$= \frac{Ak_p}{\tau^2}[c_1 - e^{\alpha t}(p\cos\beta t + q\sin\beta t)]$$

$$= \frac{Ak_p}{\tau^2}[c_1 - e^{\alpha t}\cdot R\sin(\beta t + \phi)] \quad \dots (7.45)$$

where, $R = \sqrt{p^2 + q^2}$ and $\phi = \tan^{-1}\left(\frac{p}{q}\right)$

Evaluating constants c_1, c_2, c_3 in equation (7.44), the constants p, q and hence R, ϕ can be calculated, which gives the step response as :

$$Y(t) = Ak_p\left[1 - e^{\alpha t}\frac{1}{\sqrt{1-\zeta^2}}\sin(\beta t + \phi)\right]$$

or

$$Y(t) = Ak_p\left[1 - \frac{e^{-\zeta t/\tau}}{\sqrt{1-\zeta^2}}\sin\left(\frac{\sqrt{1-\zeta^2}}{\tau}t + \phi\right)\right]$$

In the normalized, dimensionless form :

$$\frac{Y(t)}{Ak_p} = 1 - \frac{e^{-\zeta t/\tau}}{\sqrt{1-\zeta^2}}\sin\left(\frac{\sqrt{1-\zeta^2}}{\tau}t + \phi\right) \quad \dots (7.46)$$

where, $\phi = \tan^{-1}\left(\frac{\sqrt{1-\zeta^2}}{\zeta}\right) = \sin^{-1}(\sqrt{1-\zeta^2}) = \cos^{-1}(\zeta)$

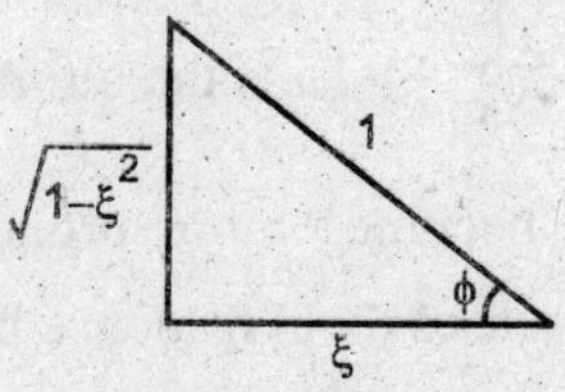

$\sqrt{1-\xi^2}$ 1 ϕ ξ

Fig. 7.24 : Triangle of phase angle ϕ

Response characteristics :

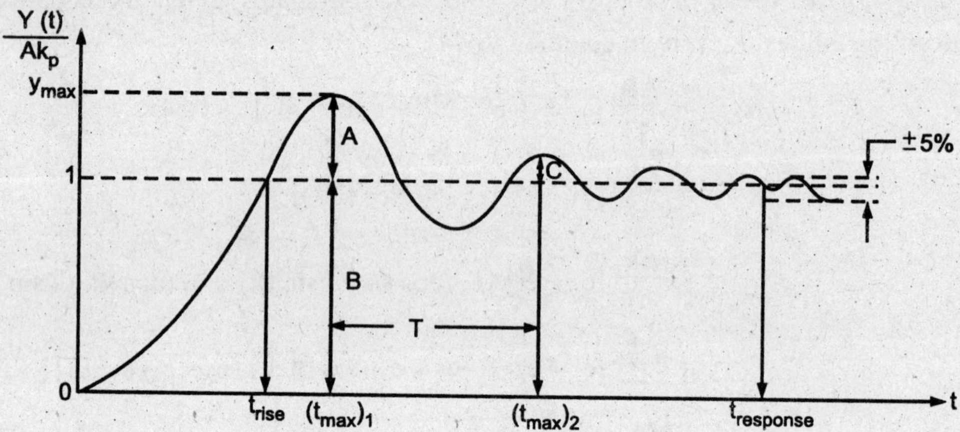

Fig. 7.25 : Step response characteristics of second-order system ($0 < \zeta < 1$)

Fig. 7.25 shows step response of a second-order system ($0 < \zeta < 1$); which is known as *underdamped response*. The response shows the following characteristics :

(i) The initial rate of output response is calculated as :

$$\left.\frac{dY(t)}{dt}\right|_{t=0} = 0$$

Therefore, initially response is slow which increases faster beyond the ultimate value $\frac{Y(t)}{Ak_p} = 1$ to certain value Y_{max} (i.e. overshoot). Then response becomes oscillatory with frequency $\frac{\sqrt{1-\zeta^2}}{\tau}$ [due to sin (...) term in equation (7.46)] with progressively decreasing amplitude [due to exponential term $e^{-\zeta t/\tau}$ in equation (7.46)]. Thus output response is in the form of a damped sinusoidal with frequency $\frac{\sqrt{1-\zeta^2}}{\tau}$ and of decreasing amplitude $\frac{e^{-\zeta t/\tau}}{\sqrt{1-\zeta^2}}$ which ultimately reaches to zero as $t \to \infty$. As $t \to \infty$, $\frac{Y(t)}{Ak_p} \to 1$ i.e. the ultimate response.

(ii) The oscillatory response becomes more pronounced with smaller values of ζ. Alternately, as ζ value increases (< 1) response becomes more and more sluggish as shown in Fig. 7.26.

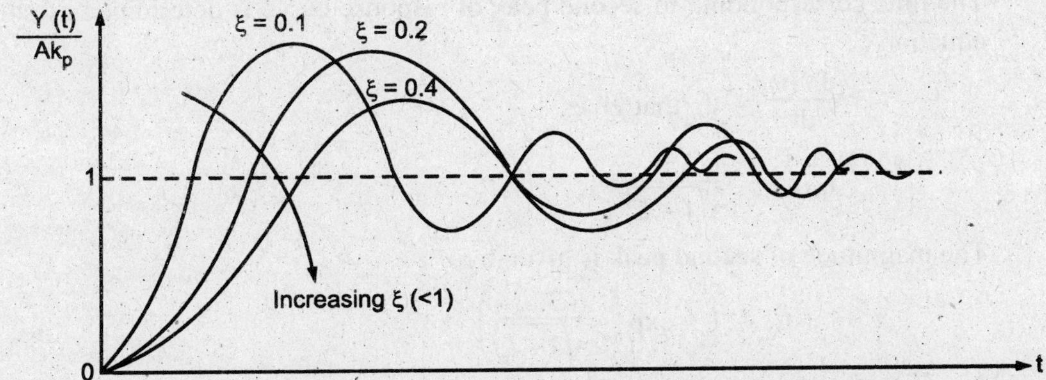

Fig. 7.26 : Step response of second-order underdamped system for different values of ζ

(iii) **Overshoot (OS) :** If A represents magnitude of ultimate response and B represents magnitude by which response exceeds above the ultimate value, then the ratio A/B is called as overshoot. It is the measure of how much the response exceeds the ultimate value. The time at which the response reaches maximum value is determined by solving the equation :

$$\frac{dY(t)}{dt} = 0$$

which gives $(t_{max})_1 = \frac{\pi\tau}{\sqrt{1-\zeta^2}}$ or $\frac{\pi}{\omega_n\sqrt{1-\zeta^2}}$

Maximum response is :

$$\frac{Y_{max}}{Ak_p} = \left.\frac{dY(t)}{dt}\right|_{t = t_{max}} = 1 + \exp\left(-\frac{\pi\zeta}{\sqrt{1-\zeta^2}}\right)$$

$$= A + B = 1 + B$$

Therefore, $$OS = \exp\left(-\frac{\pi\zeta}{\sqrt{1-\zeta^2}}\right)$$

(iv) **Rise time (t_{rise}) :** The time taken by the output response to first reach ultimate value is called as rise time which is determined by solving the equation :

$$\frac{Y(t)}{Ak_p} = 1 - \frac{e^{-\zeta t/\tau}}{\sqrt{1-\zeta^2}} \sin\left(\frac{\sqrt{1-\zeta^2}}{\tau} t + \phi\right) = 1$$

This gives $$t_{rise} = (\pi - \phi)\frac{\tau}{\sqrt{1-\zeta^2}} \text{ or } (\pi - \phi)\frac{1}{\omega_n\sqrt{1-\zeta^2}}$$

Rise time is the measure of speed of response of second-order system. Higher rise time results slow speed of response.

(v) **Decay ratio (DR) :** The ratio C/A of sizes of successive peaks above the ultimate value is known as decay ratio.

The time corresponding to second peak of response curve is determined by solving equation :

$$\frac{dY(t)}{dt} = 0, \text{ that gives}$$

$$t_{(max)_2} = \frac{3\pi\tau}{\sqrt{1-\zeta^2}}$$

The magnitude of second peak is given by

$$1 + C = 1 + \exp\left(-\frac{3\pi\zeta}{\sqrt{1-\zeta^2}}\right)$$

$$\therefore \quad C = \exp\left(-\frac{3\pi\zeta}{\sqrt{1-\zeta^2}}\right)$$

$$\therefore \quad DR = \frac{C}{A} = \exp\left(-\frac{2\pi\zeta}{\sqrt{1-\zeta^2}}\right) = \left[\exp\left(-\frac{\pi\zeta}{\sqrt{1-\zeta^2}}\right)\right]^2$$

$$= (OS)^2$$

Therefore, DR decreases rapidly than OS with increasing values of ζ (< 1) as shown in Fig. 7.27.

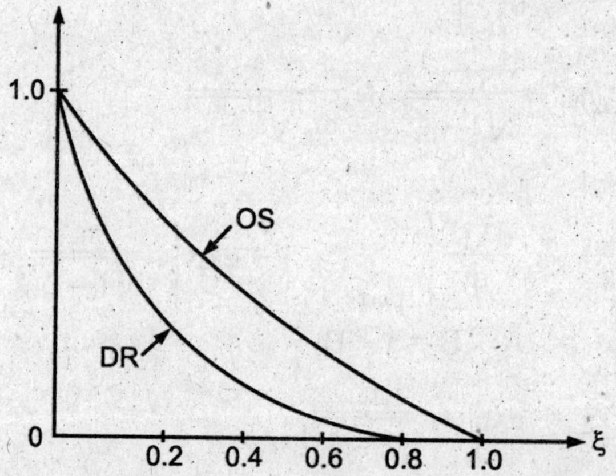

Fig. 7.27 : Effect of damping factor on OS and DR

(vi) **Period of oscillations :** The response equation (7.46) indicates that the radian frequency of oscillations is :

$$\omega = \frac{\sqrt{1-\zeta^2}}{\tau} = \omega_n\sqrt{1-\zeta^2} = \omega_{damped}$$

The time elapsed between two successive peaks is called as periodic time which is given by

$$T = (t_{max})_2 - (t_{max})_1$$

$$= \frac{2\pi\tau}{\sqrt{1-\zeta^2}} \text{ or } \frac{2\pi}{\omega_n\sqrt{1-\zeta^2}} = \frac{2\pi}{\omega_d}$$

This is in accordance with the standard expression

$$T = \frac{2\pi}{\omega}$$

(vii) **Natural period of oscillations :** A second-order system with $\zeta = 0$ is a system free of any damping, which exhibit *natural or free response*. Frequency of such natural oscillations is $\omega_n = \omega|_{\zeta=0} = \frac{1}{\tau}$.

Therefore, τ is called as *natural period of oscillations of the system.*

The corresponding cyclical period is given by

$$T_n = \frac{2\pi}{\omega_n} = 2\pi\tau$$

For $\zeta = 0$, the poles of transfer function are given by

$$\tau^2 s^2 + 2\tau\zeta s + 1 = \tau^2 s^2 + 1 = 0$$

$$\therefore \quad s = \pm i/\tau$$

The unit step response of such undamped system is given by equation (7.46) as

$$\frac{Y(t)}{Ak_p} = 1 - \sin\left(\frac{t}{\tau} + \frac{\pi}{2}\right) \text{ or } Y(t) = Ak_p\left[1 - \sin\left(\frac{\pi}{2} + \frac{t}{\tau}\right)\right]$$

Therefore output will oscillate continuously with a constant amplitude and natural frequency ω_n.

(viii) **Response time :** As $t \to \infty$, the response of an underdamped system will reach its ultimate value in an oscillatory manner. For practical purposes it is assumed that the response reaches its final value when it comes within ± 5% of its final value and stays there. The time needed for the response to reach within this region around the final value is known as response time.

Case 2 : $\zeta > 1$ (overdamped response) :

For $\zeta > 1$ the roots p_1, p_2 given by equation (7.43) are real and distinct given by :

$$p_1, p_2 = -\frac{\zeta}{\tau} \pm \frac{\sqrt{\zeta^2 - 1}}{\tau} = \alpha \pm \beta \text{ (say)}$$

Substituting these values of p_1, p_2 in equation (7.44),

$$Y(t) = \frac{Ak_p}{\tau^2}[c_1 + c_2 e^{(\alpha+\beta)t} + c_3 e^{(\alpha-\beta)t}]$$

$$= \frac{Ak_p}{\tau_2}[c_1 + c_2 e^{\alpha t} \cdot e^{\beta t} + c_3 e^{\alpha t} \cdot e^{-\beta t}]$$

$$= \frac{Ak_p}{\tau^2}[c_1 + e^{\alpha t}(c_2 e^{\beta t} + c_3 e^{-\beta t})]$$

Substituting $e^{\beta t} = \cosh \beta t + \sinh \beta t$ and $e^{-\beta t} = \cosh \beta t - \sinh \beta t$

(where $\cosh \beta t$ and $\sinh \beta t$ are hyperbolic trigonometric functions)

$$= \frac{Ak_p}{\tau^2} [c_1 + e^{\alpha t} \{c_2 (\cosh \beta t + \sinh \beta t) + c_3 (\cosh \beta t - \sinh \beta t)\}]$$

$$= \frac{Ak_p}{\tau^2} [c_1 + e^{\alpha t} \{(c_2 + c_3) \cosh \beta t + (c_2 - c_3) \sinh \beta t\}]$$

Evaluating constants c_1, c_2, c_3, above equation takes the form

$$Y(t) = \frac{Ak_p}{\tau^2}\left[\tau^2 + e^{\alpha t}\left(-\tau^2 \cosh \beta t - \frac{\tau^2 \zeta}{\sqrt{\zeta^2 - 1}} \sinh \beta t\right)\right]$$

$$= Ak_p\left[1 - e^{\alpha t}\left(\cosh \frac{\sqrt{\zeta^2 - 1}\, t}{\tau} + \frac{\zeta}{\sqrt{\zeta^2 - 1}} \sinh \frac{\sqrt{\zeta^2 - 1}\, t}{\tau}\right)\right]$$

In normalized, dimensionless form,

$$\frac{Y(t)}{Ak_p} = 1 - e^{-\zeta t/\tau}\left(\cosh \frac{\sqrt{\zeta^2 - 1}\, t}{\tau} + \frac{\zeta}{\sqrt{\zeta^2 - 1}} \sinh \frac{\sqrt{\zeta^2 - 1}\, t}{\tau}\right) \quad \text{... (7.47)}$$

Response characteristics :

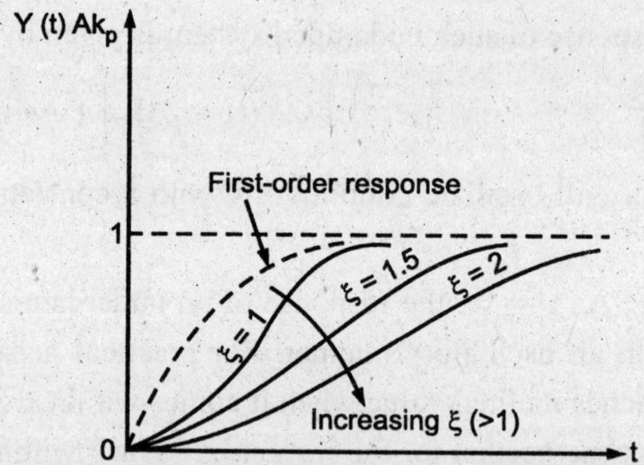

Fig. 7.28 : Step response of an overdamped system

Fig. 7.28 shows step response curve of an overdamped system for various values of ζ (> 1).The response characteristics resemble a little to the response of a first-order system. But initial response is rather sluggish than that of a first-order system. The response curve has a sigmoidal (or S-shape) curve whose slope (i.e. speed of response) increases from zero at start, becomes maximum for intermediate value of t and finally it again approaches zero as $t \to \infty$. This indicates that as time goes on the response approaches its ultimate value of unity asymptotically.

(Since as $t \to \infty$, $Y(t)/Ak_p \to 1$ or $Y(t) \to Ak_p$).

For increasing values of ζ (> 1), the response becomes more and more sluggish as shown in Fig. 7.28. Note that underdamped response is oscillatory but overdamped response is non-oscillatory.

Case 3 : $\zeta = 1$ (Critically damped response) :

For $\zeta = 1$ the roots p_1, p_2 given by equation (7.43) are real and equal given by :

$$p_1 = p_2 = -\frac{1}{\tau} = p \text{ (say)}$$

$$\therefore \quad s^2 + \frac{2\zeta}{\tau}s + \frac{1}{\tau^2} = s^2 + \frac{2}{\tau}s + \frac{1}{\tau^2} = \left(s + \frac{1}{\tau}\right)^2$$

Therefore step response is given by :

$$\bar{Y}(s) = \frac{Ak_p}{\tau^2}\frac{1}{s(s-p)^2}$$

Resolving right-hand side into partial fraction expansion :

$$\bar{Y}(s) = \frac{Ak_p}{\tau^2}\left[\frac{c_1}{s} + \frac{c_2}{s-p} + \frac{c_3}{(s-p)^2}\right]$$

Taking inverse Laplace transform :

$$Y(t) = \frac{Ak_p}{\tau_2}[c_1 + c_2 e^{pt} + c_3 e^{pt} t]$$

$$= \frac{Ak_p}{\tau^2}[c_1 + e^{pt}(c_2 + c_3 t)]$$

Evaluating constants c_1, c_2, c_3 above equation becomes :

$$Y(t) = \frac{Ak_p}{\tau_2}\left[\tau^2 + e^{-t/\tau}\left(-\tau^2 - \frac{1}{\tau}t\right)\right]$$

$$= Ak_p\left[1 - e^{-t/\tau}\left(1 + \frac{t}{\tau}\right)\right]$$

$$\frac{Y(t)}{Ak_p} = 1 - e^{-t/\tau}\left(1 + \frac{t}{\tau}\right) \qquad \text{... (7.48)}$$

Response characteristics :

The step response represented by equation (7.48) is plotted as shown in Fig. 7.28 which is similar to the response of an overdamped system, except that the former approaches the ultimate value faster than the later. Therefore, the system having $\zeta = 1$ is called as critically damped system.

Comparison of step response of underdamped ($\zeta < 1$), overdamped ($\zeta > 1$) and critically damped systems :

Fig. 7.29 shows step response of underdamped, overdamped and critically damped second-order systems. Note that :

(i) The response of an underdamped system is oscillatory which initially overshoots above the ultimate value and then approaches the ultimate value oscillatorily with decreasing amplitude.

(ii) The response of critically damped and overdamped systems approach the ultimate value without any oscillations. But the critically damped response is faster than overdamped response.

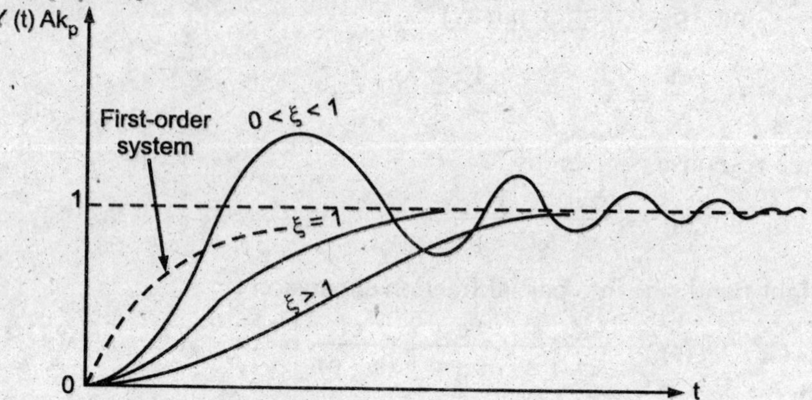

Fig. 7.29 : Comparison of step response of systems having $\zeta > 1, = 1, < 1$

2. Impulse response of second-order system :

Let input variable be changed according to the impulse function of magnitude A by the equation :

$$f(t) = 0, \quad t < 0$$
$$= A\,\delta(t), \quad t > 0$$

$$\therefore \quad \bar{f}(s) = A$$

The output response of a second-order system for impulse change in input is determined from equation (7.41) as :

$$\bar{Y}(s) = \frac{k_p}{\tau^2 s^2 + 2\tau\zeta s + 1} A$$
$$= \frac{Ak_p/\tau^2}{s^2 + 2\zeta/\tau s + \frac{1}{\tau^2}}$$

Resolving right-hand side into partial fraction expansion,

$$\bar{Y}(s) = \frac{Ak_p}{\tau^2}\left[\frac{c_1}{s - p_1} + \frac{c_2}{s - p_2}\right]$$

Taking Laplace transform :

$$Y(t) = \frac{Ak_p}{\tau^2}(c_1 e^{p_1 t} + c_2 e^{p_2 t}) \qquad \dots (7.49)$$

where, $$p_1, p_2 = -\frac{\zeta}{\tau} \pm \frac{\sqrt{\zeta^2 - 1}}{\tau}$$

Case 1 : $\zeta < 1$ (underdamped response) :

For $\zeta < 1$, the roots are :

$$p_1, p_2 = -\frac{\zeta}{\tau} \pm \frac{\sqrt{1 - \zeta^2}}{\tau} = \alpha \pm i\beta \text{ (say)}$$

Output response is given by equation (7.49)

$$Y(t) = \frac{Ak_p}{\tau^2}[c_1 e^{(\alpha + i\beta)t} + c_2 e^{(\alpha - i\beta)t}]$$

$$= \frac{Ak_p}{\tau^2}[c_1 e^{\alpha t} \cdot e^{i\beta t} + c_2 e^{\alpha t} \cdot e^{-i\beta t}]$$

$$= \frac{Ak_p}{\tau^2}[c_1 e^{\alpha t}(\cos \beta t + i \sin \beta t) + c_2 e^{\alpha t}(\cos \beta t - i \sin \beta t)]$$

$$= \frac{Ak_p}{\tau^2}[e^{\alpha t}\{(c_1 + c_2) \cos \beta t + i (c_1 - c_2) \sin \beta t)\}]$$

Evaluating constants c_1 and c_2, above equation gives :

$$Y(t) = \frac{Ak_p}{\tau^2} e^{\alpha t} \frac{\sin \beta t}{\beta} \qquad \text{... (7.50)}$$

Response characteristics :

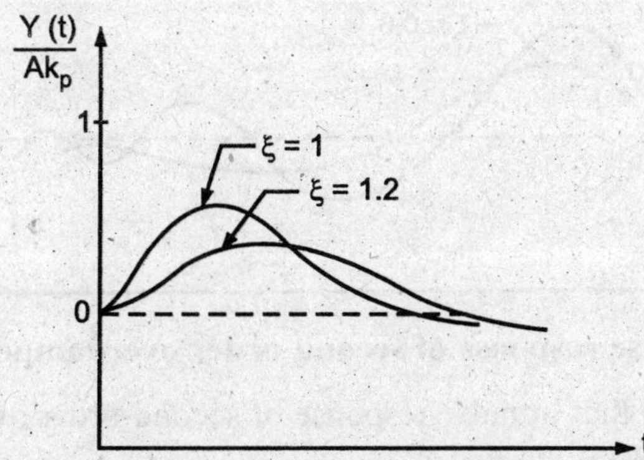

Fig. 7.30 : Impulse response of an underdamped second-order process

Equation (7.50) shows that impulse response of a second-order underdamped response is oscillatory with diminishing amplitude as shown in Fig. 7.30.

As $t \to \infty$, $\quad \frac{Y(t)}{Ak_p} \to 0$

Therefore, response approaches the ultimate zero value.

Case 2 : $\zeta > 1$ (overdamped system) :

For $\zeta > 1$, the roots are real and distinct given by

$$p_1, p_2 = -\frac{\zeta}{\tau} \pm \frac{\sqrt{\zeta^2 - 1}}{\tau} = \alpha \pm \beta$$

Therefore, output response is given by equation (7.49) as :

$$Y(t) = \frac{Ak_p}{\tau^2}[c_1 e^{(\alpha + \beta)t} + c_2 e^{(\alpha - \beta)t}]$$

$$= \frac{Ak_p}{\tau^2}[c_1 e^{\alpha t} \cdot e^{\beta t} + c_2 e^{\alpha t} \cdot e^{-\beta t}]$$

$$= \frac{Ak_p}{\tau^2}[c_1 e^{\alpha t}(\cosh \beta t + \sinh \beta t) + c_2 e^{\alpha t}(\cosh \beta t - \sinh \beta t)]$$

$$= \frac{Ak_p}{\tau^2}[e^{\alpha t}\{(c_1 + c_2)\cosh \beta t + (c_1 - c_2)\sinh \beta t\}]$$

Evaluating constants c_1 and c_2,

$$Y(t) = \frac{Ak_p}{\tau^2}\left[e^{\alpha t} \cdot \frac{1}{\beta}\sinh \beta t\right]$$

$$= \frac{Ak_p}{\tau\sqrt{\zeta^2 - 1}} e^{-\zeta t/\tau} \sinh\left(\frac{\sqrt{\zeta^2 - 1}\, t}{\tau}\right) \quad \text{... (7.51)}$$

Response characteristics :

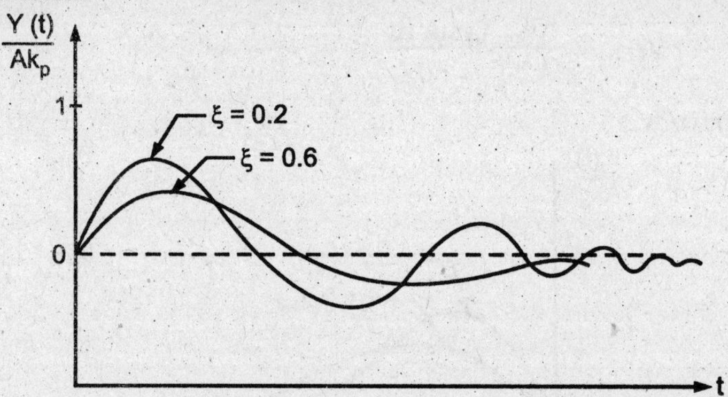

Fig. 7.31 : Impulse response of second-order overdamped ($\zeta > 1$) system

Equation (7.51) shows that impulse response of second-order overdamped system ($\zeta > 1$) is non-oscillatory which initially increases to maximum value and then approaches ultimate zero value exponentially as shown in Fig. 7.31.

Case 3 : $\zeta = 1$ (Critical damped system) :

For $\zeta = 1$, the roots are real and equal given by :

$$p_1 = p_2 = -\frac{1}{\tau} = p \text{ (say)}$$

Therefore, output response is given by equation

$$\bar{Y}(s) = \frac{Ak_p}{\tau^2}\left(\frac{1}{(s - p)^2}\right)$$

Taking inverse Laplace transform :

$$Y(t) = \frac{Ak_p}{\tau^2} e^{pt} \cdot t$$

$$= \frac{Ak_p}{\tau^2} t\, e^{-t/\tau} \quad \text{... (7.52)}$$

Response characteristics :

- Equation (7.52) shows that impulse response of a second-order critically damped system initially reaches maximum value and then approaches ultimate zero value as shown in Fig. 7.31.

  Note that critically damped response is faster than overdamped response.

7.7.2 Physical Examples of Second-Order Systems

1. Two first-order systems in series (Multicapacity process) :

We have studied that when material or energy flows through a single capacity system then the system is characterized as a first-order system. On similar grounds it may be expected that when material or energy flows through two capacities, the behaviour of the system will be described by second-order dynamics. In other words, if two first-order systems are connected in series, the resulting system behaves as second-order system. If two liquid holding tanks are connected in series, the resulting combined system is a physical example of second-order system.

These two tanks can be connected in two different configurations that give rise to non-interacting and interacting systems described below.

(A) Two non-interacting systems in series :

The process :

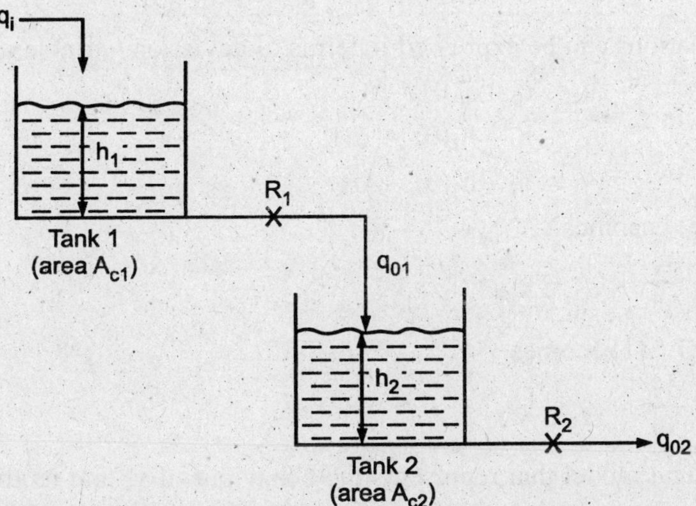

Fig. 7.32 : Two non-interacting systems in series

Fig. 7.32 shows two liquid tanks 1 and 2 (having areas A_{c1}, A_{c2}) connected in non-interacting configuration. In this arrangement, liquid of density ρ enters the tank 1 at volumetric flow rate q_i and leaves at the flow rate of q_{o1} through resistance R_1, freely in the atmosphere and then enters into tank 2, which then leaves at a flow rate of q_{o2} through resistance R_2. In this arrangement, flow rate q_{o1} from tank 1 solely depends upon level of liquid h_1 in tank 1, hence the name non-interacting system. Note that the conditions in tank 1 influence conditions in tank 2, but conditions in tank 2 no way influence tank 1. The mathematical models for tanks 1 and 2 are obtained by carrying out material balances for each tank as follows (assuming linear resistances).

For tank 1 : $(A_{c1}R_1)\dfrac{dh_1}{dt} + h_1 = R_1 q_i,$

$$\tau_1 \frac{dh_1}{dt} + h_1 = k_1 q_i \qquad \text{... (7.53)}$$

where, $\tau_1 = A_{c1} R_1$ and $k_1 = R_1$

For tank 2 :

$$A_{c2}\frac{dh_2}{dt} = q_{o1} - q_{o2}$$

$$= \frac{h_1}{R_1} - \frac{h_2}{R_2}$$

$$(A_{c2}R_2)\frac{dh_2}{dt} + h_2 = h_1 \frac{R_2}{R_1}$$

$$\tau_2 \frac{dh_2}{dt} + h_2 = k_2 h_1$$

where, $\tau_2 = A_{c2}R_2$ and $k_2 = \dfrac{R_2}{R_1}$

The above equations can be expressed in terms of deviation variables :

$$u = q_i - q_i(0) = \Delta Q_i$$

$$y_1 = h_1 - h_1(0) = \Delta H_1$$

$$y_2 = h_2 - h_2(0) = \Delta H_2$$

Equation (7.53) becomes :

$$\tau_1 \frac{dy_1}{dt} + y_1 = k_1 u \qquad \text{... (7.54)}$$

and Equation (7.54) becomes

$$\tau_2 \frac{dy_2}{dt} + y_2 = k_2 y_1 \qquad \text{... (7.55)}$$

The mathematical model that represents the behaviour of y_2 and its direct dependence on u is obtained by eliminating y_1 from equations (7.54) and (7.55) as follows :

Differentiating equation (7.55) with respect to time t,

$$\tau_2 \frac{d^2y_2}{dt^2} + \frac{dy_2}{dt} = k_2 \frac{dy_1}{dt}$$

Substituting value of $\dfrac{dy_1}{dt}$ from equation (7.54)

$$\tau_2 \frac{d^2y_2}{dt^2} + \frac{dy_2}{dt} = \frac{k_2}{\tau_1}(k_1 u - y_1)$$

Substituting value of y_1 from equation (7.55)

$$\tau_2 \frac{d^2y_2}{dt^2} + \frac{dy_2}{dt} = \frac{k_2}{\tau_1 k_2}\left(k_1 u - \tau_2 \frac{dy_2}{dt} - y_2\right)$$

$$(\tau_1 \tau_2)\frac{d^2y_2}{dt^2} + (\tau_1 + \tau_2)\frac{dy_2}{dt} + y_2 = k_1 k_2 u \qquad \text{... (7.56)}$$

This equation is in the form of second-order differential equation model in the form

$$\tau^2 \frac{d^2y}{dt^2} + 2\zeta\tau \frac{dy}{dt} + y = k_p u$$

where,

$$\tau^2 = \tau_1 \tau_2 = (A_{c1}R_1)(A_{c2}R_2)$$

$$2\zeta\tau = \tau_1 + \tau_2 = (A_{c1}R_1) + (A_{c2}R_2)$$

$$\zeta = \frac{\tau_1 + \tau_2}{2t}$$

and

$$k_p = k_1 k_2 = \frac{R_1 R_2}{R_1} = R_2$$

Equation (7.56) represents the combined system of two hold-up tanks as a second-order system with output variable y_2 (= $h_2 - h_2(0) = \Delta H$), input or forcing function u (= $q_i - q_i(0) = \Delta Q_i$) and the parameters k_p, τ, ζ as mentioned above.

Transfer function model :

The transfer functions of individual tanks 1and 2 in terms of deviation variables are :

For tank 1 :

$$G_1(s) = \frac{\bar{y}_1(s)}{\bar{u}(s)} = \frac{\Delta \bar{H}_1(s)}{\Delta \bar{Q}_i(s)} = \frac{k_1}{\tau_1 s + 1} \qquad \text{... (7.57)}$$

For tank 2 :

$$G_2(s) = \frac{\bar{y}_2(s)}{\bar{y}_1(s)} = \frac{\Delta \bar{H}_2(s)}{\Delta \bar{H}_1(s)} = \frac{k_2}{\tau_2 s + 1} \qquad \text{... (7.58)}$$

Multiplying the transfer functions $G_1(s)$ and $G_2(s)$, we get the transfer function of the combined non-interacting system as :

$$G(s) = G_1(s)\, G_2(s) = \frac{\bar{y}_1(s)}{\bar{u}(s)} \frac{\bar{y}_2(s)}{\bar{y}_1(s)}$$

$$= \frac{\bar{y}_2(s)}{\bar{u}(s)} = \frac{\Delta \bar{H}_2(s)}{\Delta \bar{Q}_i(s)} = \frac{k_1 k_2}{(\tau_1 s + 1)(\tau_2 s + 1)}$$

$$= \frac{k_1 k_2/\tau_1 \tau_2}{\left(s + \frac{1}{\tau_1}\right)\left(s + \frac{1}{\tau_2}\right)} = \frac{k_1 k_2/\tau_1 \tau_2}{(s - p_1)(s - p_2)} \qquad \text{... (7.59)}$$

where $k_1 k_2 = k$ = the combined steady-state gain and $\tau_1 = A_{c1}R_1$ and $\tau_2 = A_{c2}R_2$ are the time constants of the individual tanks.

The above transfer function may also be derived by taking Laplace transform of second-order differential equation model (equation 7.56) with zero initial conditions.

Poles and Zeros :

Equation (7.59) shows that the combined system does not have a zero, but it has two poles at $p_1 = -\frac{1}{\tau_1}$ and $p_2 = -\frac{1}{\tau_2}$. Therefore this combined system behaves as undamped system.

Block diagram :

Since the combined transfer function is simply the product of transfer functions of individual tanks, the block diagram for the combined system can be represented as shown in Fig. 7.33.

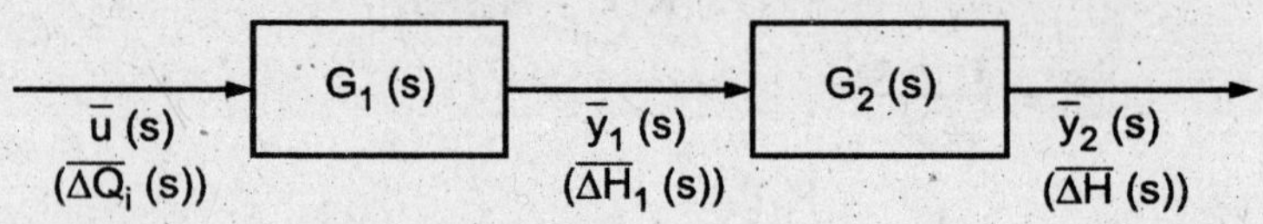

$$\xrightarrow[\left(\overline{\Delta Q_i}(s)\right)]{\bar{u}(s)} \boxed{G_1(s)} \xrightarrow[\left(\overline{\Delta H_1}(s)\right)]{\bar{y}_1(s)} \boxed{G_2(s)} \xrightarrow[\left(\overline{\Delta H}(s)\right)]{\bar{y}_2(s)}$$

Fig. 7.33 : Block diagram of two first-order systems in non-interacting configuration

Step response :

When input u(t) [i.e. $q_i(t)$] is changed according to step function of magnitude A as

$$\begin{aligned} Q_i(t) = u(t) &= 0, \qquad t < 0 \\ &= AH(t), \quad t > 0 \end{aligned}$$

then
$$\bar{u}(s) = \frac{A}{s} = \bar{Q}_i(s)$$

Substituting this value of $\bar{u}(s)$ in equation (7.59), the output response is :

$$\begin{aligned} \bar{H}_2(s) = \bar{y}_2(s) &= G(s)\frac{A}{s} = \frac{k}{(\tau_1 s + 1)(\tau_2 s + 1)} \cdot \frac{A}{s} \\ &= \left(\frac{Ak}{\tau_1 \tau_2}\right)\left(\frac{1}{s\left(s + \frac{1}{\tau_1}\right)\left(s + \frac{1}{\tau_2}\right)}\right) \\ &= \left(\frac{Ak}{\tau_1 \tau_2}\right)\left(\frac{c_1}{s} + \frac{c_2}{s + \frac{1}{\tau_1}} + \frac{c_3}{s + \frac{1}{\tau_2}}\right) \end{aligned}$$

Taking inverse Laplace transform :

$$H_2(t) \text{ or } y_2(t) = \frac{Ak}{\tau_1 \tau_2}\left(c_1 + c_2 e^{-t/\tau_1} + c_3 e^{-t/\tau_2}\right)$$

Evaluating constants c_1, c_2, c_3 :

$$\begin{aligned} H_2(t) \text{ or } y_2(t) &= Ak\left[1 - \left(\frac{\tau_1}{\tau_1 - \tau_2}\right)e^{-t/\tau_1} - \left(\frac{\tau_2}{\tau_2 - \tau_1}\right)e^{-t/\tau_2}\right] \\ &= Ak\left[1 + \frac{1}{\tau_2 - \tau_1}\left(\tau_1 e^{-t/\tau_1} - \tau_2 e^{-t/\tau_2}\right)\right] \qquad \text{... (7.60)} \end{aligned}$$

Special case : If $\tau_1 = \tau_2 = \tau$ (say), equation (7.60) gives

$$\bar{y}_2(s) = \frac{k}{(\tau s + 1)^2} \frac{A}{s}$$

$$= \frac{Ak}{\tau^2}\left(\frac{1}{s\left(s + \frac{1}{\tau}\right)^2}\right)$$

$$= Ak\left(\frac{c_1}{s} + \frac{c_2}{s + \frac{1}{\tau}} + \frac{c_3}{\left(s + \frac{1}{\tau}\right)^2}\right)$$

Taking inverse Laplace transform :

$$y_2(t) \text{ or } H_2(t) = Ak\left[1 - e^{-t/\tau} - \frac{t}{\tau} e^{-t/\tau}\right] \quad \ldots (7.61)$$

Response characteristics :

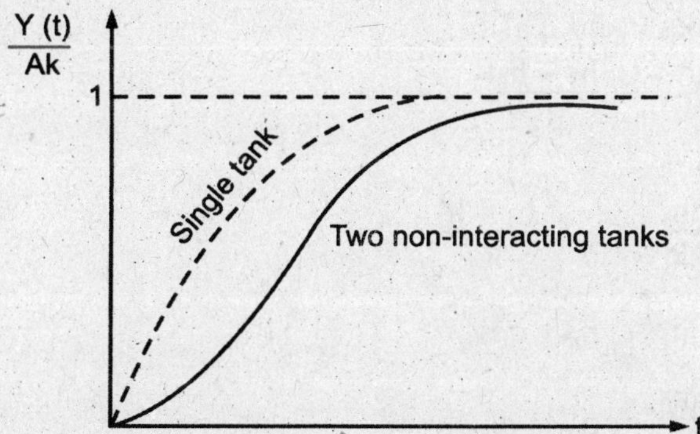

Fig. 7.34 : Step response of liquid level in two-tank non-interacting systems

Equation (7.59) shows that the transfer function of the combined system has real, distinct poles at $p_1 = -\frac{1}{\tau_1}$ and $p_2 = -\frac{1}{\tau_2}$, the system will exhibit overdamped response as shown in Fig. 7.34. As compared to step response of a single-tank first-order system, the step response of two non-interacting tanks is characterized by initial sluggish response (at $t = 0$) followed by speeding up, while finally approaches the ultimate response (as $t \to \infty$). This sluggishness is also known as transfer lag which is the characteristic of multicapacity process.

(B) Two interacting systems :

The Process :

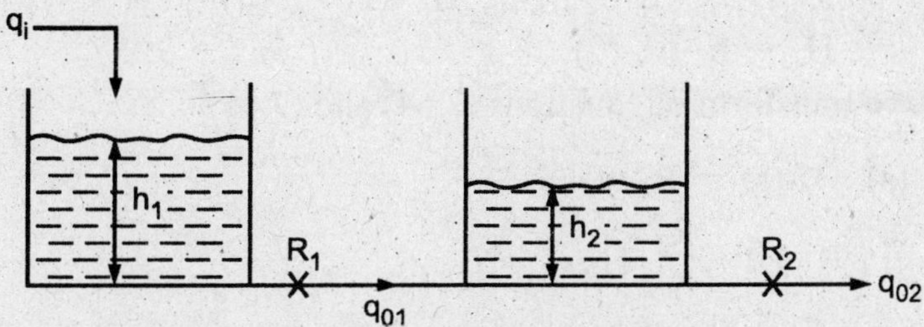

Fig. 7.35 : Two interacting systems in series

Fig. 7.35 shows the liquid tanks 1 and 2 connected in interacting configuration. In this arrangement, liquid enters the tank 1 at volumetric flow rate q_i and exits from the tank at volumetric flow rate q_{o1} through resistance R_1. The water flowing through outlet of tank 1 enters at the bottom of tank 2 and leaves tank 2 at the flow rate of q_{o2}. In this arrangement, flow out of tank 1 now depends on the difference between the levels in two tanks. Therefore, variations in the conditions in tank 2 will influence the conditions in tank 1 or tank 2 interact with tank 1, hence the system is called as interacting system.

The Model :

The mathematical models for tanks 1 and 2 are obtained by carrying out material balances around each tank as follows :

For tank 1 : $$A_{c1}\frac{dh_1}{dt} = q_i - q_{o1} \qquad \text{... (7.62)}$$

Assuming linear resistance R_1, the outflow from tank 1 is proportional to difference between levels in tanks 1 and 2 as :

$$q_{o1} = \frac{h_1 - h_2}{R_1} \qquad \text{... (7.63)}$$

Equation (7.62) becomes

$$A_{c1}\frac{dh_1}{dt} = q_i - \frac{h_1 - h_2}{R_1}$$

$$(A_{c1}R_1)\frac{dh_1}{dt} + h_1 = h_2 + q_iR_1 \qquad \text{... (7.64)}$$

For tank 2 : $$A_{c2}\frac{dh_2}{dt} = q_{o1} - q_{o2}$$

Assuming linear resistance R_2,

$$q_{o2} = \frac{h_2}{R_2}$$

Substituting this value of q_{o2} and value of q_{o1} from equation (7.63) in equation (7.64).

$$A_{c2}\frac{dh_2}{dt} = \frac{h_1 - h_2}{R_1} - \frac{h_2}{R_2}$$

$$(A_{c2}\,R_2)\frac{dh_2}{dt} + \left(1 + \frac{R_2}{R_1}\right)h_2 = \frac{R_2}{R_1}h_1 \qquad \text{... (7.65)}$$

Introducing deviation variables :

$$Q_i = q_i - q_i(0) = \Delta q_i,\ \ H_1 = h_1 - h_1(0)$$
$$H_2 = h_2 - h_2(0)$$

and taking Laplace transform of equations (7.64) and (7.65).

$$(\tau_1 s + 1)\,\bar{H}_1(s) - \bar{H}_2(s) = R_1\,\bar{Q}_i(s) \qquad \text{... (7.66)}$$

and $$-\frac{R_2}{R_1}\bar{H}_1(s) + \left(\tau_2 R_1 + 1 + \frac{R_2}{R_1}\right)\bar{H}_2(s) = 0 \qquad \text{... (7.67)}$$

$$(\tau_1 = A_{c1}\,R_1 \text{ and } \tau_2 = A_{c2}\,R_2)$$

Solving equations (7.66) and (7.67) simultaneously for $\bar{H}_1(s)$ and $\bar{H}_2(s)$:

$$\bar{H}_1(s) = \frac{(\tau_2 R_1)\, s + (R_1 + R_2)}{(\tau_1\tau_2)\, s^2 + (\tau_1 + \tau_2 + A_1R_2)\, s + 1}\,\bar{Q}_i(s) \quad \text{... (7.68)}$$

$$= G_1(s)\, Q_i(s)$$

and

$$\bar{H}_2(s) = \frac{R_2}{(\tau_1\tau_2)\, s^2 + (\tau_1 + \tau_2 + A_1R_2)\, s + 1}\,\bar{Q}_i(s) \quad \text{... (7.69)}$$

$$\bar{H}_2(s) = G_2(s)\,\bar{Q}_i(s)$$

Equations (7.68 and 7.69) indicate that the transfer functions of both the tanks are of second-order type, therefore tanks follow second-order dynamics.

Poles and Zeros :

(i) The transfer functions G_1 and G_2 have common poles given by :

$$p_1, p_2 = \frac{-(\tau_1 + \tau_2 + A_1R_2) \pm \sqrt{(\tau_1 + \tau_2 + A_1R_2)^2 - 4\tau_1\tau_2}}{2\tau_1\tau_2} \quad \text{... (7.70)}$$

Since $(\tau_1 + \tau_2 + A_1R_2)^2 > \tau_1\tau_2$, the poles p_1 and p_2 are distinct and real. Therefore, the response of interacting tank system is always *overdamped.*

(ii) The transfer functions of non-interacting and interacting systems [i.e. equations (7.59) and (7.68)], differ only in the coefficient of s in the denominator by the term A_1R_2. This term is considered as the *interaction factor* which indicates the degree of interaction between the two tanks.

(iii) Equation (7.69) can be expressed in terms of poles p_1 and p_2 as :

$$G_1(s) = \frac{\bar{H}_2(s)}{\bar{Q}_i(s)} = \frac{R_2}{\tau_1\tau_2\left(s^2 + \dfrac{\tau_1 + \tau_2 + A_1R_2}{\tau_1\tau_2} + \dfrac{1}{\tau_1\tau_2}\right)}$$

$$= \frac{R_2/\tau_1\tau_2}{(s - p_1')\,(s - p_2')}$$

$$= \frac{R_2/\tau_1\tau_2}{(-p_1')\left(-\dfrac{1}{p_1'}\, s + 1\right)(-p_2')\left(-\dfrac{1}{p_2'}\, s + 1\right)}$$

$$= \frac{(R_2/\tau_1\tau_2)\,\tau_1'\,\tau_2'}{(\tau_1's + 1)\,(\tau_2's + 1)}$$

$$= \frac{(R_2/\tau_1\tau_2)\,\tau_1'\tau_2'}{(\tau_1's + 1)\,(\tau_2's + 1)} \quad \text{... (7.71)}$$

where $\tau_1' = -\dfrac{1}{p_1'}$ and $\tau_2' = -\dfrac{1}{p_2'}$

Comp[illegible] transfer function of interacting system given by equation (7.71) with the transfer fu[illegible]f non-interacting system given by equation (7.59) it can be concluded that interacting tank system can be viewed as non-interacting tank system with modified effective time constants τ_1' and τ_2'. Therefore when two tanks having time constants τ_1 and τ_2 are connected in interacting configuration, their time constants are modified to τ_1' and τ_2'.

Special case :

If two tanks have same time constants i.e. $\tau_1 = \tau_2 = \tau$ (say), then poles p_1 and p_2 of non-interacting system are equal $\left(\because \frac{p_1}{p_2} = \frac{-1/\tau_1}{-1/\tau_2} = \frac{\tau_2}{\tau_1} = 1\right)$

On the other hand, poles of interacting transfer function are :

$$p_1', p_2' = \frac{-(2\tau + A_1R_2) \pm \sqrt{4\tau^2 + (A_1R_2)^2 + 4\tau_1 A_1 R_2 - 4\tau^2}}{2\tau^2}$$

$$= \frac{-(2\tau + A_1R_2) \pm \sqrt{(A_1R_2)^2 + 4\tau A_1R_2}}{2\tau^2}$$

$$\therefore \quad \frac{p_1'}{p_2'} = \frac{-1/\tau_1'}{-1/\tau_2'} = \frac{\tau_2'}{\tau_1'}$$

$$= \frac{-(2\tau + A_1R_2) + \sqrt{(A_1R_2)^2 + 4\tau A_1R_2}}{-(2\pi + A_1R_2) - \sqrt{(A_1R_2)^2 + 4\tau A_1R_2}}$$

$$\neq 1$$

Thus effect of interaction of two tanks is to change the ratio of the effective time constants of the two tanks. Since $\tau_1' \neq \tau_2'$, dynamic response of one tank is faster than the other tank. In interacting tanks, the overall response of $h_2(t)$ is affected by both tanks, the slower tank becomes controlling and the overall response becomes more sluggish due to the interaction. Therefore, dynamic response of interacting system is sluggish than non-interacting system as shown in Fig. 7.36.

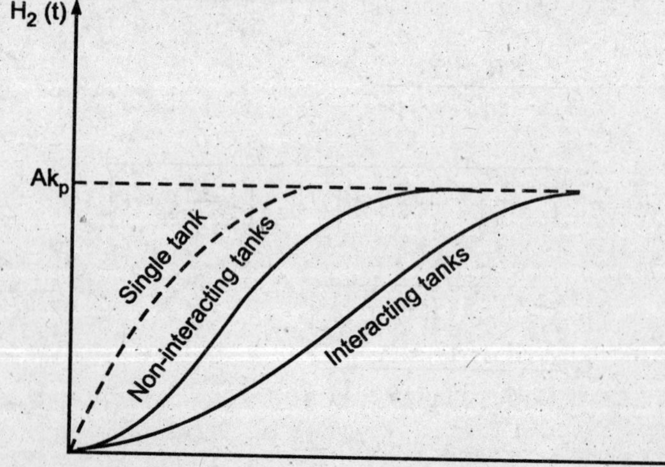

Fig. 7.36 : Comparison of dynamic response of interacting and non-interacting systems

The other examples of second-order system are : U-tube manometer (refer article in chapter 1) and spring-sock absorber (or damped vibrator).

7.8 DYNAMIC BEHAVIOUR OF TIME-DELAY OR DEAD TIME SYSTEMS

In case of first and second-order systems discussed earlier, it was assumed that when input is changed, output starts changing without any time delay. But in practice there is some time delay between the instant the input change is implemented and when the output starts responding. Such systems are called as time-delay systems. Systems involving transportation of material and/or energy from one part of a plant to the other is usually accompanied by dead time or transportation lag which is also known as distance-velocity lag. The examples of such processes are recycle loops and flow through connecting pipes.

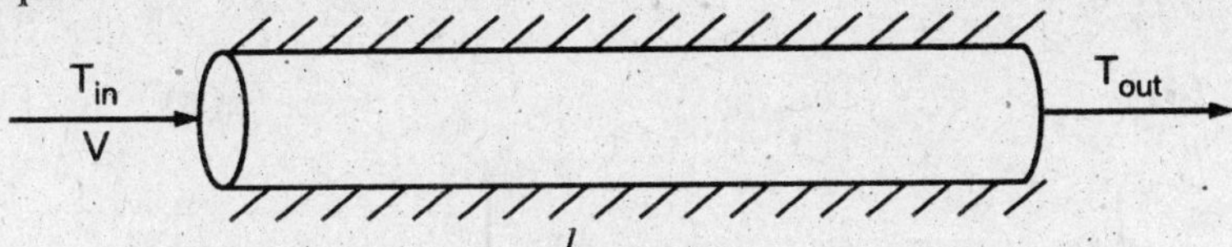

Fig. 7.37 : Flow through an insulated pipe

Consider an insulated pipe of length *l* shown in Fig. 7.37 through which fluid flows at constant velocity v. The fluid element at the inlet require time $t = l/v$ to traverse the length of pipe and reach the outlet. Therefore any change in temperature of fluid at inlet (i.e. input) will be reflected at the outlet (i.e. output) only after the time $t = l/v$ which is known as dead time or time lag. In such case the process output has exactly the same form as the input, but only delay by l/v time units.

The transfer function :

Temperature at exit of the pipe is related to temperature at entrance by the relation :

$$T_{out}(t) = T_{in}(t - t_d) \quad \text{... (7.72)}$$

In above illustration, the input and output variables are related by the equation

$$T_{out}(t) = T_{in}(t - t_d)$$

Taking Laplace transform :

$$\overline{T}_{out}(s) = e^{-t_d s}\, \overline{T}_{in}(s)$$

In general

$$y(t) = f(t - t_d)$$

$$\overline{y}(s) = e^{-t_d s}\, \overline{f}(s) \quad \text{... (7.73)}$$

Transfer function :

$$G(s) = \frac{\overline{y}(s)}{\overline{f}(s)} = {}^{-t_d s} \quad \text{... (7.74)}$$

(Refer properties of Laplace transform in article 7.2.1 of this chapter.)

Response to ideal forcing functions (inputs) :

Equation (7.73) shows that output response of pure dead-time process to any given arbitrary input has same form as the input but delayed by dead time t_d as shown in Fig. 7.38.

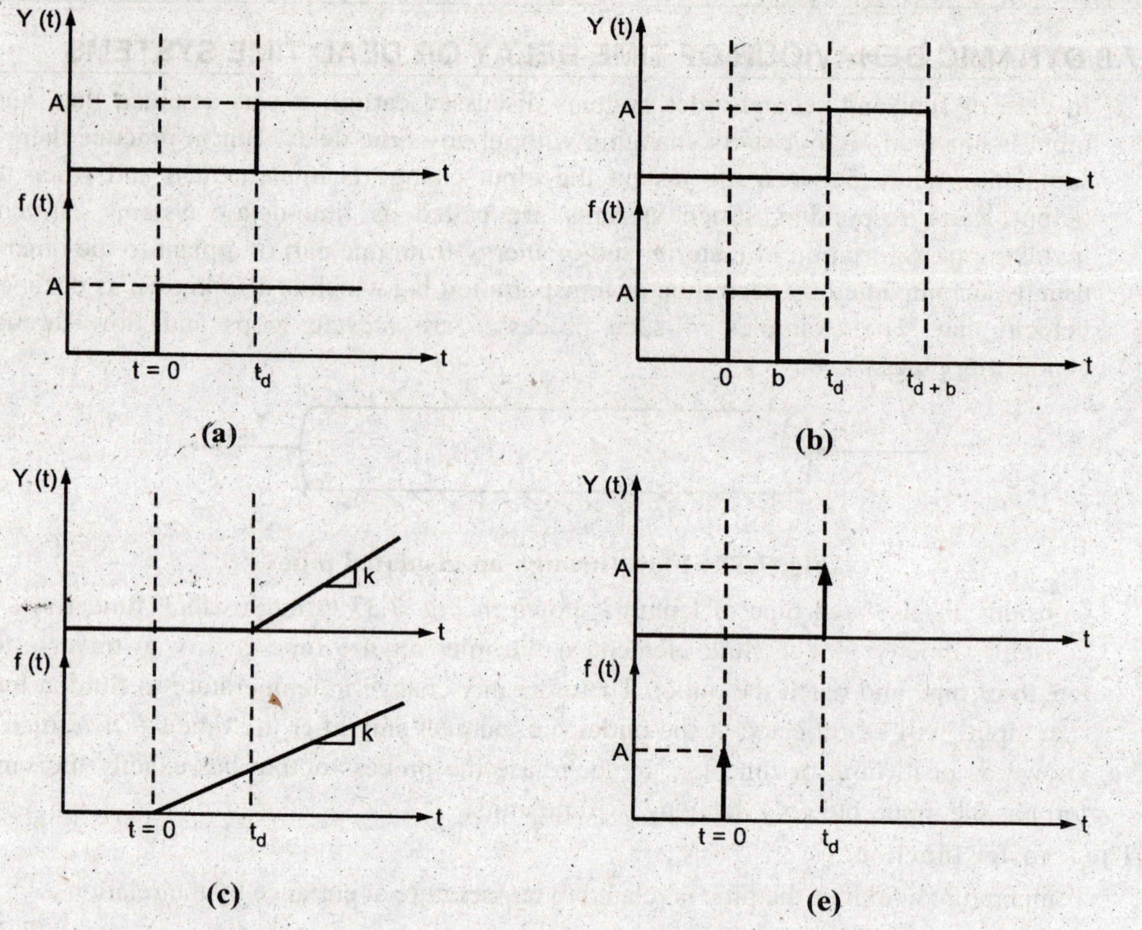

(a)

(b)

(c)

(e)

Fig. 7.38

7.8.1 Systems with Dead Time

As stated earlier, virtually all physical processes involve some time delay between the input and output. The first or second-order systems having long length of pipe at the exit, introduces time lag in the output of the process.

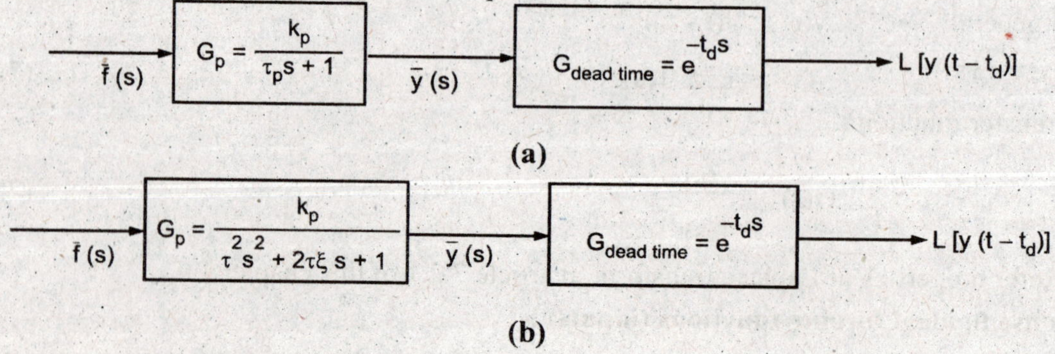

Fig. 7.39 : Systems with dead time

Fig. 7.39 (a) shows a first-order process with dead-time t_d. The transfer function of this combined system is :

$$G(s) = \frac{L\,[y(t-t_d)]}{L\,[f(t)]} = G_p\, G_{dead\ time} = \frac{L\,[y\,(t-t_d)]}{L\,[y(t)]} \times \frac{L\,[y(t)]}{L\,[f(t)]}$$

$$= \frac{k_p\, e^{-t_d s}}{\tau_p s + 1} \quad \ldots (7.75)$$

Fig. 7.39 (b) shows a second-order system with dead-time, which has the overall transfer function as :

$$G(s) = G_p\, G_{dead\ time}$$

$$= \frac{k_p\, e^{-t_d s}}{\tau^2 s^2 + 2\tau\zeta s + 1} \quad \ldots (7.76)$$

7.8.2 Pade Approximations of Dead Time

The exponential term in the transfer function of dead time can be approximated by a rational function. For this $e^{-t_d s}$ is represented by the ratio of lower order polynomials in s as :

$$e^{-t_d s} \approx \frac{1 - \frac{t_d}{2} s}{1 + \frac{t_d}{2} s} \quad \ldots \text{(first-order approximation)}$$

$$\approx \frac{(t_d)^2\, s^2 - 6 t_d s + 12}{(t_d)^2\, s^2 + 6 t_d s + 12} \quad \ldots \text{(second-order approximation)}$$

7.9 PROCESS IDENTIFICATION (EMPIRICAL PROCESS MODELING)

In previous articles, we have discussed theoretical modeling of processes in terms of fundamental material, energy balance equations alongwith constitutive equations. But this approach requires a priori knowledge about internal working (or mechanisms) of the process. Instead, in empirical modeling approach the system is treated like a black box and the characteristics of the system are determined (or identified) entirely from its response to known input functions. For this the unknown process is subjected to a forcing function u(t) and the output response y(t) is measured. The model of this system is developed directly by correlating the input and output data. Therefore, process identification involves constructing a process model directly from experimentally obtained input/output data without any concern to the fundamental nature and properties of the system.

The typical input functions used for process identification are step, impulse, pulse, sine wave (frequency), white noise or pseudo random binary sequences (PRBS).

In this article we study process identification using step-response data.

Step-response identification :

In step-response identification, theoretical step response function is fitted to experimental step-response data.

For this, step test is carried out on the process in which a step input is given to the process and output response is gathered.

The steps followed in process identification are :

1. **Model formulation :**

   Typical candidate process model used for fitting the experimental step-response data is a *first-order-pulse-time delay (FOPDT)* having transfer function

$$G(s) = \frac{ke^{-t_d s}}{\tau s + 1}$$

   The parameters of this model are k, t_d, τ.

2. **Parameter estimation :**

   This step involves estimating the unknown parameters k, t_d and τ of a postulated FOPDT model. The experimental data is fitted to this model form as follows :

   The theoretical step response of a FOPDT system is given by :

$$\begin{aligned} y(t) &= (Ak)\,[1 - \exp\,(+\,t - t_d)/\tau)] \\ &= y(\infty)\,[1 - \exp\,(t - t_d)/\tau] \end{aligned} \qquad \dots (7.77)$$

where,
- A = Magnitude of step change
- k = Process gain
- τ = Time constant
- t_d = Dead time
- $y(\infty)$ = Ultimate response = Ak

Steady-state gain (k) :

For input step change of magnitude A, the ultimate output response (in deviation form) is given by

$$y(\infty) = Ak$$

Therefore, an estimate of steady-state gain is given by

$$\hat{k} = \frac{y(\infty)}{A} = \frac{\text{Ultimate response}}{\text{Step change in input}}$$

Time-constant τ and time delay τ :

Equation (7.77) can be expressed as :

$$\frac{y(t)}{y(\infty)} = 1 - \exp\,[-\,(t - t_d)/\tau]$$

$$\frac{y(t)}{y(\infty)} - 1 = -\exp\,[-\,(t - t_d)/\tau]$$

$$\frac{y(\infty) - y(t)}{y(\infty)} = \exp\,[-\,(t - t_d)/\tau]$$

Taking natural log on both the sides :

$$\ln\left(\frac{y(\infty) - y(t)}{y(\infty)}\right) = -\frac{t}{\tau} + \frac{t_d}{\tau} \qquad \dots (7.78)$$

This equation shows that a plot of the term $\ln\left(\frac{y(\infty) - y(t)}{y(\infty)}\right)$ on LHS of above equation against time t should give a straight line with a slope of $-1/\tau$ and an intercept on the y-axis of τ_d/τ. This line will intersect time-axis at point $t = t_d$ as shown in Fig. 7.40.

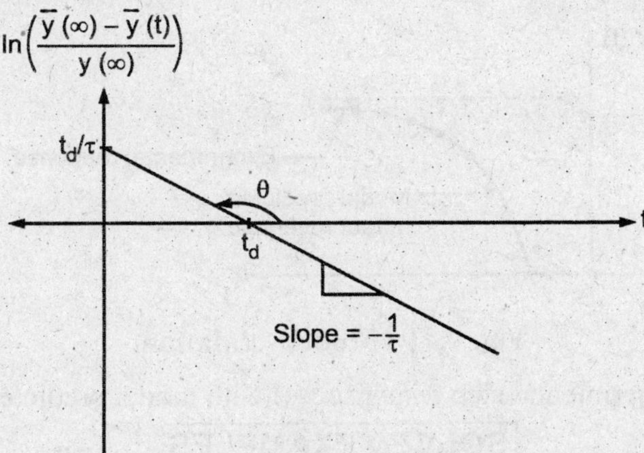

Fig. 7.40 : Estimation of τ and t_d of a FOPDT model form step-response of τ and t_d

To determine the values of τ and t_d graphically from the experimental step response data, calculate $\ln\left(\frac{y(\infty) - y(t)}{y(\infty)}\right)$ and plot it on y-axis against corresponding time (t) values on x-axis to get a straight line plot. Then

Dead time, t_d = Time co-ordinate corresponding to the point of intersection of straight line with t-axis

$$\text{Time constant, } \tau = \frac{1}{\text{Slope of straight line}} = \frac{1}{\tan\theta}$$

(where θ = angle made by straight line with t-axis)

The parameters k, τ and t_d can also be estimated by non-linear regression of equation (7.77) or by linear regression of equation (7.78) using computer programs.

3. Model validation :

Model validation involves checking how the empirical model formulated with the calculated parameters k, τ and t_d fits the actual experimental data it is supposed to represent. This is usually done by comparing model predicted values of output $\hat{y}(t)$ with additional process data y(t) and evaluating the fit (i.e. deviation between the actual and predicted response curves) as shown in Fig. 7.41. In this plot, the addition step response data y(t) is plotted against time t to get the experimental step response curve and the output values $\hat{y}(t)$ predicted from the formulated model are also plotted on the same graph. The closeness of these model-predicted values $\hat{y}(t)$ with the actual experimental response curve given the extent of fit the experimental data y(t) with the model-predicted data $\hat{y}(t)$.

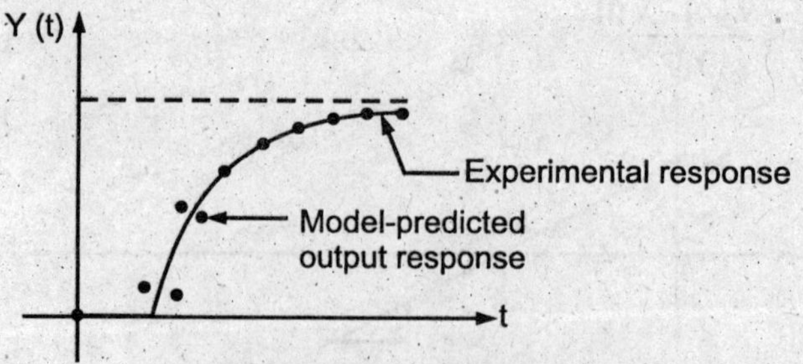

Fig. 7.41 : Model validation

(Comparison of experimental step response y(t) with model predicted response $\hat{y}(t)$.)

SOLVED EXAMPLES

Example 7.1 : *Find the output response of a first-order lag system with τ_p = 0.5 and k_p = 1 to*

(a) a step change of magnitude 2 units

(b) a unit impulse input change

(c) a unit pulse change of duration 5

(d) a sinusoidal input change sin (0.5 t)

(e) a unit ramp change.

Sketch the response and determine the behaviour of the output after long time (t → ∞) for each case above.

Solution : The transfer function of given system is :

$$G(s) = \frac{\bar{y}(s)}{\bar{f}(s)} = \frac{k_p}{\tau_p s + 1} = \frac{1}{0.5s + 1}$$

(a) Response to step change of magnitude 2 : Output response is given by

$$y(t) = Ak_p [1 - \exp(-t/\tau_p)] = 2 [1 - \exp(-t/0.5)] = 2 [1 - \exp(-2t)]$$

Find the output response at the interval of 0.2 sec.

t	0	0.2	0.4	0.6	0.8	1.0	1.2	1.4	1.6	1.8	2.0	2.2	2.4
y(t)	0	0.66	1.1	1.4	1.6	1.72	1.82	1.88	1.92	1.95	1.96	1.97	1.98

Fig. 7.42 : Step response

(b) Unit impulse response (A = 1) : Unit impulse response is given by :

$$y(t) = \frac{Ak_p}{\tau_p} \exp(-t/\tau_p)$$

$$= 2 \exp(-2t)$$

t	0	0.2	0.4	0.6	0.8	1.0	1.2	1.4	1.6	1.8	2.0	2.2
y(t)	2	1.34	0.9	0.6	0.4	0.3	0.18	0.12	0.08	0.05	0.04	0.02

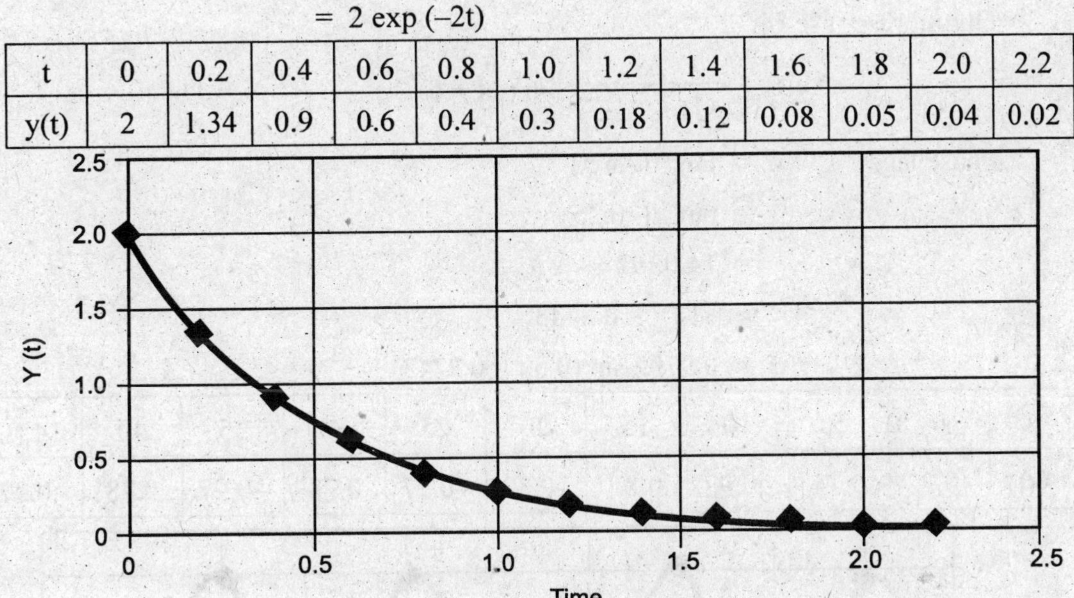

Fig. 7.43 : Unit impulse response

(c) Unit pulse response : A = 1, b = 5.

$$y(t) = Ak_p [(1 - e^{-t/\tau}) - (1 - e^{-(t-b)/\tau})]$$

$$= (1 - e^{-2t}) - (1 - e^{-(t-5)/2})$$

t	0	0.2	0.4	0.6	0.8	1.0	1.2	1.4	1.6	1.8	2.0	2.2
y(t)	11.18	10.35	9.52	8.72	7.96	7.25	6.59	5.99	5.43	4.93	4.46	4.04

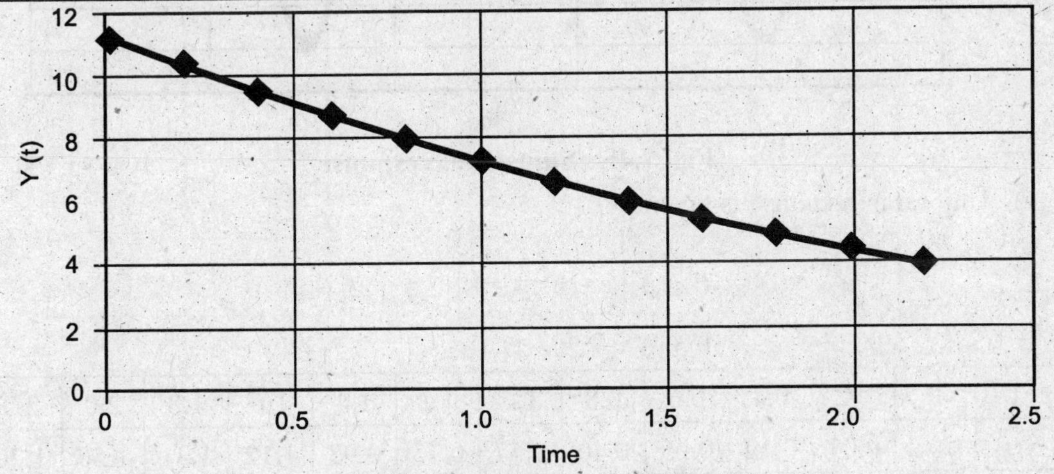

Fig. 7.44 : Unit pulse response

(d) Sinusoidal response :

$$f(t) = \sin(0.5\,t)$$

$$A = 1,\ \omega = 0.5$$

Output response is :

$$y(t) = \frac{Ak_p}{\sqrt{1+(\omega\tau_p)^2}}\sin(\omega t + \phi)$$

Phase lag,

$$\phi = \tan^{-1}(-\omega\tau_p)$$

$$= \tan^{-1}(-0.25)$$

$$= 14.0362$$

$$\approx -14° = 0.2443°$$

$$\therefore \quad y(t) = 0.9702 \sin(0.5\,t - 0.2243)$$

t	0	5	10	15	20	25	30	35	40	45
y(t)	−0.22	0.74	−0.97	0.81	−0.33	−0.27	0.78	−0.97	0.78	−0.27

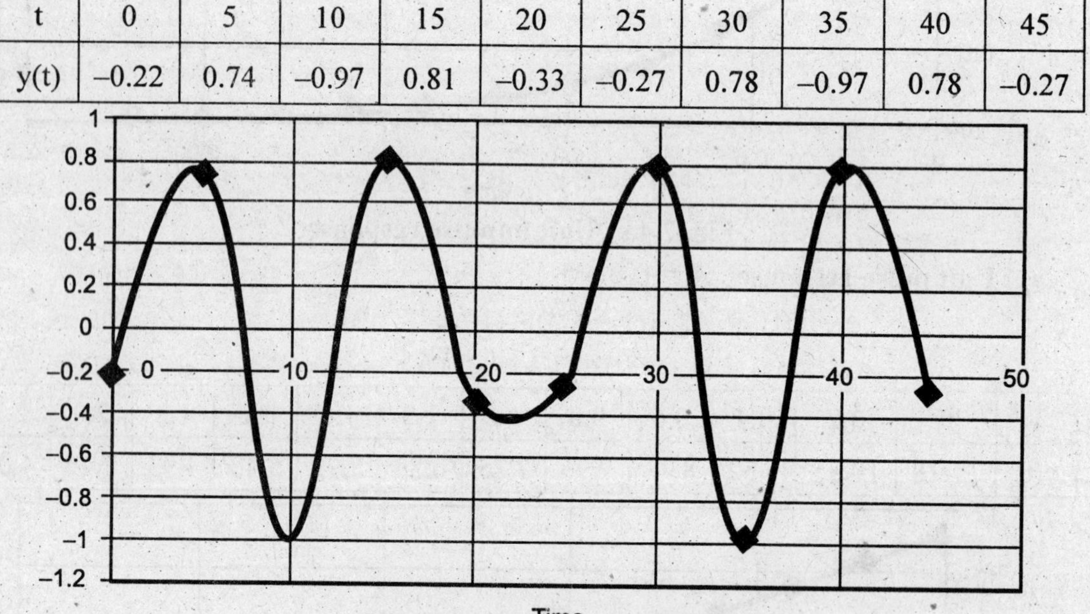

Fig. 7.45 : Sinusoidal response

(e) Unit ramp response is given by :

$$y(t) = (k_p\tau_p)\left[e^{\frac{-t}{\tau_p}} + \frac{t}{\tau_p} - 1\right]$$

$$= 0.5\,[e^{-2t} + 2t - 1]$$

t	0	0.2	0.4	0.6	0.8	1.0	1.2	1.4	1.6	1.8	2.0	2.2
y(t)	0	0.03	0.12	0.25	0.40	0.57	0.75	0.93	1.12	1.31	1.50	1.70

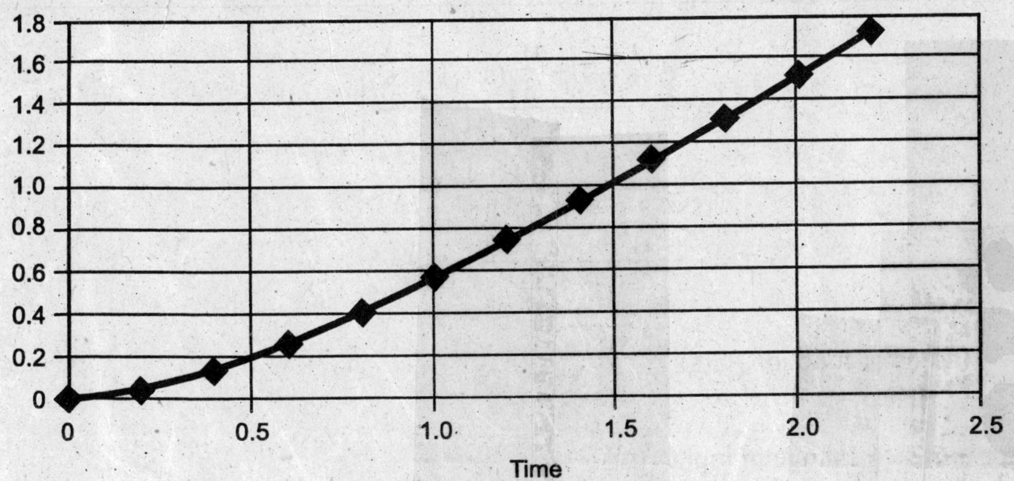

Fig. 7.46 : Ramp response

Example 7.2 : *Find the time response, initial value and final values of the following transfer functions using Laplace transform.*

$$\bar{y}(s) = \frac{s\,(s+8)}{(s+2)\,(s+4)\,(s+5)}$$

Solution : Resolving right-hand side into partial fraction expansion :

$$\bar{y}(s) = \frac{c_1}{s+2} + \frac{c_2}{s+4} + \frac{c_3}{s+5}$$

$$c_1 = \frac{-12}{6} = -2,\ c_2 = \frac{-16}{-2} = 8,\ c_3 = \frac{-15}{3} = -5$$

$$\bar{y}(s) = -\frac{2}{s+2} + \frac{8}{s+4} - \frac{5}{s+5}$$

Taking inverse Laplace transform :

$$y(t) = -2e^{-2t} + 8e^{-4t} - 5e^{-5t}$$

$$\text{Initial value} = \lim_{t \to 0} y(t) = 1$$

$$\text{Final value} = \lim_{s \to 0} s\,\bar{y}(s)$$

$$= \lim_{s \to 0} \frac{s^2\,(s+8)}{(s+2)\,(s+4)\,(s+5)}$$

$$= 0$$

Example 7.3 : *The unit step response of a system is given by*

$$y(t) = \frac{3}{2} + 5t - \frac{3}{2}e^{-t}$$

Solution : Taking Laplace transform of given equation :

$$\bar{y}(s) = \frac{3}{2s} + \frac{5}{s^2} - \frac{3}{2\,(s+1)}$$

$$= \frac{3}{2}\left[\frac{1}{s} + \frac{10/3}{s^2} - \frac{1}{s+1}\right]$$

$$= \frac{3}{2}\left[\frac{s+1+\frac{10}{3}(s+1)-s^2}{s^2(s+1)}\right]$$

$$= \frac{3}{2}\left[\frac{-3s^2+13s+13}{s^2(s+1)}\right]$$

$$= \frac{-9s^2+39s+39}{2s^2(s+1)}$$

$\therefore$ Transfer function, $G(s) = \frac{\bar{y}(s)}{\bar{f}(s)}$

For unit step change in input $\bar{f}(s) = \frac{1}{s}$.

$$\therefore \quad G(s) = \frac{-9s^2+39s+39}{2s^2(s+1)} \times s$$

$$= \frac{-9s^2+39s+39}{2s(s+1)}$$

Example 7.4 : *Find poles of the following systems and comment on their dynamic response qualitatively (i.e. stable, unstable or marginally stable.)*

(a) $G(s) = \frac{1}{s+2}$

(b) $G(s) = \frac{s}{s-3}$

(c) $G(s) = \frac{s+1}{(s+2)(s+3)}$

(d) $G(s) = \frac{1}{2s^2+3s+2}$

(e) $G(s) = \frac{1}{s^2-4s+1}$

(f) $G(s) = \frac{1}{s^2+4}$

Solution : (a) $p = -2 < 0$, stable response

(b) $p = 3 > 0$, unstable response

(c) $p = -2, -3 < 0$, stable response (overdamped)

(d) $p = \frac{-3 \pm \sqrt{9-16}}{4}$

$$= -\frac{3}{4} \pm i\frac{\sqrt{7}}{4}$$

Since real part is negative, response is oscillatory with decreasing amplitude (underdamped resonse).

(e) $$p = \frac{+4 \pm \sqrt{16+4}}{2} = \frac{+4 \pm \sqrt{20}}{2} = +2 \pm i\sqrt{5}$$

Since real part is positive, response is oscillatory with increasing amplitude (overdamped response).

(f) $$G(s) = \frac{1}{s^2+4} = \frac{1}{s^2+2^2}$$

$$p = \pm 2i$$

Response is oscillatory with constant amplitude, i.e. sustained oscillations (natural or undamped response).

Example 7.5 : *A rectangular cross-section tank 150 mm × 150 mm is initially at steady-state with inlet liquid flow rate 200 LPH and liquid level 5 cm. The tank has linear resistance the outlet pipeline. If input flow rate is suddenly changed to 300 LPH.*

(a) Find the transfer function of the tank.

(b) Find new steady-state level of liquid in the tank at flow rate of 300 LPH.

(c) Find the time required for 90% response.

(d) Find the time taken by the level to reach 60 mm.

Solution : At initial steady-state,

$$q_i = 200 \text{ LPH} = \frac{200 \times 10^3}{3600} \text{ cc/s} = 55.55 \text{ cc/s} = q_o$$

$$h_i = 50 \text{ mm} = 5 \text{ cm}$$

Cross-section area of tank,

$$A_c = 15 \times 15 = 225 \text{ cm}^2$$

Time constant, $$\tau = A_c \times R = 225 \times 0.09$$

$$= 20.25 \text{ sec}$$

Setady-state or static gain $k = R = 0.09 \text{ cm}^{-2}\text{s}$.

(a) Transfer function is :

$$G(s) = \frac{\bar{H}(s)}{\bar{Q}_i(s)} = \frac{k}{\tau_s + 1} = \frac{0.09}{20.25s + 1}$$

(b) Magnitude of step change in input flow rate

$$A = \Delta q_i = q_f - q_i = 300 - 200$$

$$= 100 \text{ LPH} = 27.78 \text{ cc/s}$$

Steady-state gain, $$k = \frac{\Delta H}{\Delta Q_i} = R = 0.09 \text{ cm}^{-2}\text{ s}$$

$$\Delta H = 0.09 \times 27.78 = 2.5 \text{ cm}$$

$$= h_f - h_i$$

∴ New steady-state level,

$$h_f = \Delta H + h_i$$
$$= 2.5 + 5$$
$$= 7.5 \text{ cm}$$
$$= 75 \text{ mm}$$

(c) The step response of height is given by :

$$H(t) = Ak_p (1 - e^{-t/\tau})$$

$$\frac{H(t)}{Ak_p} = 0.91 - e^{-t/\tau_p}$$

$$0.1 = e^{-t/\tau_p}$$

$$t = -20.25 \ln (0.1) = 46.62 \text{ sec}$$

(d) For level reading h(t) = 60 mm or 6 cm, level response is

$$H(t) = h(t) - h_i = 6 - 5 = 1 \text{ cm}$$

$$\frac{H(t)}{Ak_p} = (1 - e^{-t/\tau})$$

$$\frac{1}{27.78 \times 0.09} = 1 - e^{-t/20.25}$$

$$0.4 = 1 - e^{-t/20.25}$$

$$0.6 = e^{-t/20.25}$$

$$t = -20.25 \ln (0.6) = 10.34 \text{ sec}$$

Example 7.6 : *In the liquid tank system described in example 7.5, if inlet flow rate is changed gradually from 200 LPH to 300 LPH in 10 sec, find level response actual level after 30 sec from start of change in input flow rate.*

Solution : $\Delta q_i = 300 - 200 = 100 \text{ LPH} = 27.78 \text{ cc/s}$

Rate of change of input flow rate

$$A = \frac{\Delta q_i}{t} = \frac{27.78}{10} = 2.77$$

Output response is given by :

$$H(t) = (Ak_p \tau_p)\left[e^{-t/\tau_p} + \frac{t}{\tau_p} - 1\right]$$

At t = 30 sec.

$$H(t = 30) = (2.77 \times 0.09 \times 20.25)\left(e^{-30/20.25} + \frac{30}{20.25} - 1\right)$$

$$= 3.57 = h(t) - h_i$$

Actual level after 30 sec.

$$h(t) = H(t) + h_i$$

$$= 3.57 + 5 = 8.57 \text{ cm}$$

Example 7.7 : *If in the liquid tank system described in example 7.5 the input flow rate is suddenly changed from 200 LPH to 300 LPH, maintained at this value for 15 sec and then again suddenly returned to initial value of 200 LPH.*

(a) Find level response.

(b) Find maximum response and maximum actual level reached alongwith time required to reach this level.

(c) Find level response and actual level after 20 sec from start.

Solution : $q_i = 200$ LPH, $q_f = 300$ LPH

The input flow rate is given by rectangular pulse input of width b = 15 sec and height A = 100 LPH = 27.78 cc/s.

(a) The pulse response of level is given by

$$H(t) = Ak\left[(1 - e^{-t/\tau}) - (1 - e^{-(t-b)/\tau})\right]$$
$$= (27.78 \times 0.09)\,[(1 - e^{-t/20.25}) - (1 - e^{-(t-15)/20.25})]$$

(b) Maximum response is reached at t = b = 15 sec from start.

∴ Maximum response,

$$H_{max} = Ak_p\,(1 - e^{-b/\tau_p})$$
$$= (27.78 \times 0.09)\,(1 - e^{-15/20.25})$$
$$= 1.3$$
$$= h_{max} - h_i$$

Actual maximum level,

$$h_{max} = H_{max} + h_i$$
$$= 6.3 \text{ cm}$$

(c) Level response,

$$H\,(t = 20) = (27.78 \times 0.09)\,[(1 - e^{-20/20.25}) - (1 - e^{(20-15)/20.25})]$$
$$= 2.5\,[(1 - e^{-0.99}) - (1 - e^{-0.25})]$$
$$= 1 \text{ cm}$$

Actual level, $h(t = 20) = H(t) + h_i = 1 + 5 = 6$ cm

Example 7.8 : *If in the tank system described in example 7.5, if the input flow rate is given ideal impulse change of magnitude 100 LPH.*

(a) Find the level response.

(b) Find maximum level response and actual maximum level reached.

(c) Find level response after 20 sec from start.

Solution : (a) The impulse response of height is given by :

$$H(t) = \frac{Ak_p}{\tau_p}\,e^{-t/\tau_p}$$
$$= \frac{27.78 \times 0.09}{30.25}\,e^{-t/20.25} = 0.082\,e^{-(t/20.25)}$$

(b) Maximum level response $= H(\infty) = \dfrac{Ak_p}{\tau_p} = 0.082$ cm

Actual maximum level $= h(\infty) = H(\infty) + h_i = 0.082 + 1 = 1.082$ cm

(c) Level response after 20 sec $= H(t = 20) = 0.082\ e^{-(20/20.25)} = 0.03$

Actual level $h(t = 20) = H(t = 20) + h_i = 0.03 + 1 = 1.03$ cm

---

Example 7.9 : *A storage tank shown in Fig. 7.47 contains a liquid which is pumped by a centrifugal pump at a steady-rate. Liquid enters the tank at a volumetric flow rate 200 LPH and liquid level reaches steady-state value of 40 cm. If input flow rate is suddenly increased to 300 LPH, find level response and height of liquid after 1 min.*

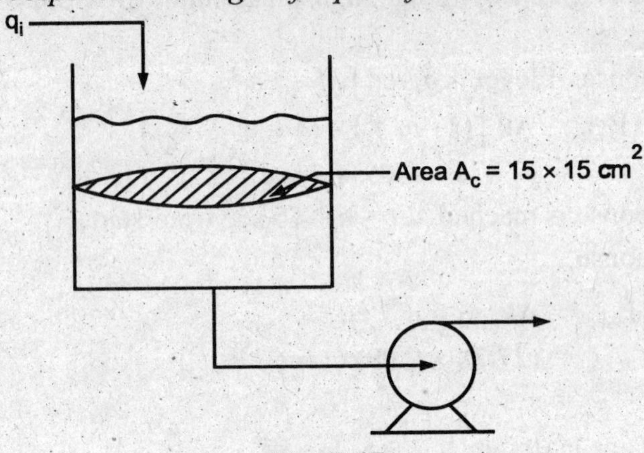

Fig. 7.47

Solution : $A_c = 15 \times 15 = 225\ \text{cm}^2,\ h(0) = 40$ cm

Step change in input flow rate A = 300 – 200 = 100 LPH = 27.78 cc/s

Transfer function of the tank system is

$$G(s) = \frac{\bar{H}(s)}{\bar{Q}_i(s)} = \frac{1}{A_c s}$$

Step response of height is :

$$H(t) = \left(\frac{A}{A_c}\right) t = \left(\frac{27.78}{225}\right) t = (0.1234\ t)\ \text{cm}$$

At t = 1 min, $H(t) = 0.1234 \times 60 = 7.408$ cm

∴ Actual liquid level after 1 min,

$$h(t = 1\ \text{min}) = H(t) + h(0)$$

$$= 40 + 7.408 = 47.408\ \text{cm}$$

Example 7.10 : *A system has transfer function $G(s) = \dfrac{k}{s\,(s + 10) + k}$. Find the value of gain k so that the system will have a damping ratio of 0.5. For this value of k determine % overshoot, decay ratio, settling time and time to peak overshoot for a unit step input.*

Solution : $G(s) = \dfrac{k}{s^2 + 10s + k}$

Comparing this transfer function with standard form of second-order system,

$$G(s) = \frac{\omega_n^2}{s^2 + 2\zeta\omega_n s + \omega_n^2}$$

$$2\zeta\omega_n = 10,$$

$$\omega_n = \frac{10}{2\zeta} = \frac{10}{2 \times 0.5} = 10 \text{ rad/s}$$

and $k = \omega_n^2 = 100$

$$\% \text{ overshoot} = \exp\left(-\frac{\pi\zeta}{\sqrt{1-\zeta^2}}\right) = 16.3\%$$

$$\text{Decay ratio} = (\text{overshoot})^2 = (0.163)^2 = 0.026$$

$$\text{Settling time } t_s = \frac{4}{\zeta\omega_n} = 0.8 \text{ sec.}$$

$$\text{Time to peak overshoot } t_{max} = \frac{\pi}{\omega_n\sqrt{1-\zeta^2}} = 0.362 \text{ sec.}$$

Example 7.11 : *The transfer function of a control system is given by*

$$G(s) = \frac{1}{(1+5s)^2} = \frac{\bar{y}(s)}{\bar{f}(s)}$$

Find the value of ζ and predict the output response for unit step change in input. Find the output response after 30 seconds.

Solution : $G(s) = \dfrac{1}{25s^2 + 10s + 1}$

Comparing this transfer function with standard form :

$$G(s) = \frac{1}{\tau^2 s^2 + 2\tau\zeta s + 1}$$

$$k_p = 1$$

$$\tau^2 = 25, \quad \tau = 5$$

$$2\zeta\tau = 10, \quad \zeta = \frac{10}{2\tau} = 1$$

∴ The output response will exhibit critically damped second-order response characteristics.

(Alternately, the transfer function is :

$$G(s) = \frac{1/25}{\left(s + \frac{1}{5}\right)^2}$$

G(s) has repeated, real negative pole at s = –1/5 = 0.2, therefore, output response will exhibit second-order critically damped response.)

If input is changed by a unit step function, output response is given by

$$y(t) = k_p\left[1 - e^{-t/\tau}\left(1 + \frac{t}{\tau}\right)\right]$$

∴ Output response after 30 seconds.

$$y(t = 30) = 1 - e^{-30/5}\left(1 + \frac{30}{5}\right) = 0.9826$$

Example 7.12 : *The transfer function of a second-order system is given by :*

$$G(s) = \frac{\bar{y}(s)}{\bar{f}(s)} = \frac{1}{ps^2 + qs + r}$$

The input variable F(t) is given step change of 8 units, which cause the output y(t) to approach steady-state ultimate response of 0.5 units as shown in Fig. 7.48.

Find the values of p, q and r.

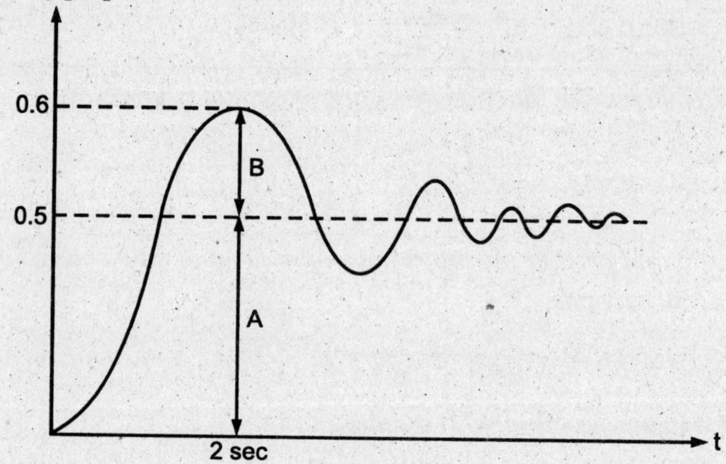

Fig. 7.48

Solution : For step change in F(t),

$$\bar{F}(t) = \frac{8}{s}$$

Therefore, output response is

$$\bar{y}(s) = \frac{8}{s\,(ps^2 + qs + r)}$$

$$\text{Ultimate response } y(\infty) = \lim_{s \to 0} s\bar{y}(s) = \frac{8}{r} = 0.5 \text{ (given)}$$

$$\therefore \qquad \mathbf{r = 16}$$

Fig. 7.48 shows that time for maximum response

$$t_{max} = 2 \text{ sec} = \frac{\pi}{\omega_d}$$

$\therefore$ Damped frequency, $\omega_d = \frac{\pi}{2} = 1.571$ rad/s

$$\text{Overshoot} = \frac{B}{A} = \frac{0.1}{0.5} = 0.2 = e^{-(\pi\zeta/\sqrt{1-\zeta^2})}$$

$$\therefore \quad \ln(0.2) = \frac{\pi\zeta}{\sqrt{1-\zeta^2}}$$

$$1.609\sqrt{1-\zeta^2} = \pi\zeta$$

$$1.609(1-\zeta^2) = \pi^2\zeta^2$$

$$1.609 = \zeta^2(\pi^2 + 1.609)$$

$$\therefore \quad \zeta = 0.14$$

Now,

$$\omega_d = \omega_n\sqrt{1-\zeta^2}$$

$$\omega_n = \frac{\omega_d}{\sqrt{1-\zeta^2}} = \frac{1.571}{\sqrt{1-(0.14)^2}} = 11.22 \text{ rad/s}$$

$$\tau = \frac{1}{\omega_n} = 0.089 \text{ sec}$$

The transfer function may be expressed as :

$$G(s) = \frac{1}{ps^2 + qs + 16} = \frac{1}{16\left(\frac{p}{16}s^2 + \frac{q}{16}s + 1\right)} = \frac{1/16}{\frac{p}{16}s^2 + \frac{q}{16}s + 1}$$

Comparing this with $G(s) = \frac{k}{\tau^2 s^2 + 2\tau\zeta s + 1}$

$$\tau^2 = \frac{p}{16} = (0.089)^2, \quad \mathbf{p = 0.356}$$

$$\frac{q}{16} = 2\tau\zeta$$

$$\mathbf{q = 32\tau\zeta = 32 \times 0.089 \times 0.14 = 0.3987}$$

Example 7.13 : *Consider two tanks having*

$$A_1 = A_2 = A \quad \text{and} \quad R_1 = R_2/2$$

Find the transfer function and hence response of liquid level in tank 2 for unit step change in inlet flow rate if tanks are connected in

(i) non-interacting configuration

(ii) interacting arrangement.

Explain the effect of interaction on effective time constants of tanks.

Solution : The time constants of the tanks are :

$$\tau_1 = A_1R_1 = AR_1 = \frac{AR_2}{2} = \frac{\tau_2}{2} = \tau \text{ (say)}$$

(i) For non-interacting arrangement,

$$\frac{\bar{H}_2(s)}{\bar{Q}_i(s)} = \frac{R_2}{(\tau_1 s + 1)(\tau_2 s + 1)} = \frac{R_2}{(\tau s + 1)(2\tau s + 1)} \quad \text{... (1)}$$

For unit step change in Q_i, $\bar{Q}_i(s) = \frac{1}{s}$.

$$\bar{H}_2(s) = \frac{R_2}{s(\pi s + 1)(2\tau s + 1)} = R_2\left(\frac{c_1}{s} + \frac{c_2}{\tau s + 1} + \frac{c_3}{2\tau s + 1}\right)$$

Finding the constants c_1, c_2, c_3 and taking inverse Laplace transform

$$H_2(t) = R_2(1 + e^{-t/\tau} - 2e^{-t/2\tau}) \quad \text{... (2)}$$

(ii) For interacting arrangement :

$$\frac{\bar{H}_2(s)}{\bar{Q}_i(s)} = \frac{R_2}{(\tau_1\tau_2)s^2 + (\tau_1 + \tau_2 + A_1R_2)s + 1}$$

$$= \frac{R_2}{(2\tau^2)s^2 + (3\tau + A \cdot 2R_1)s + 1}$$

$$= \frac{R_2}{(2\tau^2)s^2 + (5\tau)s + 1}$$

$$= \frac{R_2}{(0.44\tau s + 1)(4.56\tau s + 1)} \quad \text{... (3)}$$

For step change in input flow rate $\bar{Q}_i(s) = \frac{1}{s}$.

$$\bar{H}_2(s) = \frac{R_2}{s(0.44\tau s + 1)(4.56\tau s + 1)}$$

Resolving into partial fractions and taking inverse Laplace transform :

$$H_2(t) = R_2[1 - 1.11\, e^{-t/4.56\tau} + 0.11\, e^{-t/0.44\tau}] \quad \text{... (4)}$$

Comparing equations (1) and (3), it can be observed that due to interaction between the tanks, the effective time constants get changed from τ to 0.44τ and 2τ to 4.56τ. Therefore, time constant of one tank decreases, while that of the other tank increases. The ratio of time constants change from $\frac{\tau}{2\tau} = 0.5$ to $\frac{0.44\tau}{4.56\tau} = 0.1$.

Thus due to interaction, dynamic response of interacting tanks is sluggish than non-interacting configuration.

Example 7.14 : *A 250 litre tank has uniform cross-sectional area 0.25 m^2 and outlet flow resistance 10 m^{-2} min. The system is initially at steady-state with inlet flow rate of 200 LPH.*

(i) Find the initial level in the tank and transfer function model for the tank.

(ii) If the inlet flow rate is suddenly changed to 500 LPH, obtain an expression for how the liquid level in the tank will vary with time.

(iii) Find the time required to reach the level of 0.8 m.

(iv) Find the final steady value of liquid level.

Solution :

$$V = 250 \text{ lit}, \ A_c = 2.5 \text{ m}^2, \ A = 10 \text{ min/m}^2$$

$$q_i = 2000 \text{ LPH} = \frac{2000 \times 10^{-3}}{60} = 0.033 \text{ m}^3\text{/min}$$

$$q_f = 5000 \text{ LPH} = \frac{5000 \times 10^{-3}}{60} = 0.083 \text{ m}^3\text{/min}$$

(i) **Initial level :** Outflow rate is related to height by the relation,

$$q_o = \frac{h}{R}$$

Initially, at steady-state,

$$q_o = q_i = 0.033 \text{ m}^3\text{/min}$$

(ii) Initial steady-state height,

$$h_i = \frac{q_i}{T} R = 0.033 \times 10 = 0.33 \text{ m}$$

Time constant of the tank,

$$\tau = A_c R$$

$$= 0.25 \times 10 = 2.5 \text{ min}$$

Steady-state gain of the tank k = R = 10 min m^{-2}.

∴ Transfer function of the tank in terms of deviation variables H(t) and $Q_i(t)$ is,

$$G(s) = \frac{\bar{H}(s)}{\bar{Q}_i(s)} = \frac{k}{\tau s + 1} = \frac{10}{2.5s + 1}$$

(iii) Step change in input flow rate,

$$A = q_f - q_i = 5000 - 2000$$

$$= 3000 \text{ LPH} = \frac{3000 \times 10^{-3}}{60} = 0.05 \text{ m}^3\text{/min}$$

Change in level for step change in input flow rate is given by

$$H(t) = Ak\,(1 - e^{-t/\tau})$$

$$= (0.05 \times 10)\,(1 - e^{-t/2.5})$$

$$= 0.5\,(1 - e^{-0.4t}) \qquad \dots (1)$$

For actual level of h = 0.8 m, level response is given by

$$H = h - h_i = 0.8 - 0.33 = 0.47 \text{ m}$$

Time required to reach this level is calculated using equation (1) as

$$0.47 = 0.5\,(1 - e^{-0.4t})$$

$$t = 7.03 \text{ min}$$

(iv) Final steady-state response

$$H(\infty) = k = AR$$

$$= 0.5$$

Final steady-state level,

$$h_f = H(\infty) + h_i = 0.5 + 0.33 = 0.83 \text{ m}$$

EXERCISE

1. Explain mathematical tools used for dynamic analysis.
2. Explain process control applications of
   (i) Laplace transform,
   (ii) Complex variable,
   (iii) Z-transform.
3. Explain the standard ideal input functions used for dynamic analysis of systems.
4. Give classification of process variables with respect to process control.
5. What is process model ? State the following model form used in process control :
   (i) State-space model,
   (ii) Transform-domain models (L.t., Z.t.).
   (iii) Frequency-response models.
   (v) Impulse response models.
6. Derive transfer function model of a system having a general n^{th}-order ODE model.
7. What are poles and zeros of a transfer function model of system ? Explain how the nature of poles affect the dynamic behaviour of system. Starting from a standard first-order linear ODE model derive the transfer function of first-order system.
8. Explain dynamic behaviour of a first-order process for step change in input. Sketch the response curve and explain significance of the model parameters k_p and τ_p.

9. Explain the response characteristics of a first-order process to
   (i) Impulse change in input.
   (ii) Rectangular pulse change in input.
   (iii) Ramp change in input.
   (iv) Sinusoidal change in input.
10. Explain effect of variation in (i) k_p and (ii) τ_p on dynamic behaviour of a first-order process.
11. Justify the first-order behaviour of a simple liquid tank process in which liquid enters the tank at a flow rate q_i and leaves at q_o assuming linear resistance R. Derive the transfer function and hence response of liquid level for step change in q_i.
12. Justify the first-order behaviour of a continuous stirred tank heater. Derive the transfer function and hence step response characteristics of the system.
13. What is a pure gain process ? Derive its step, impulse, ramp, sinusoidal response. Give physical example of such process.
14. What is a pure capacitive process ? Derive its step, pulse, impulse, ramp and sinusoidal response. Give physical example of such process.
15. Starting from a second-order linear ODE model, derive the transfer function of a linear second-order process. Explain the effect of ζ on nature of poles and hence dynamic response characteristics of this system.
16. Explain classification of second-order systems based on values of damping ratio ζ. Compare the step response characteristics of underdamped, overdamped and critically damped systems.
17. Starting from transfer function model, derive step response of an underdamped system. Sketch the response curve and represent the following response characteristics :
   (i) Overshoot.
   (ii) Decay ratio.
   (iii) Rise time.
   (iv) Settling time.
   (v) Period and frequency of damped response.
   (vi) Period and frequency of undamped (or natural) response.
18. Derive step response characteristics of an overdamped second-order system.

19. Derive impulse response characteristics of overdamped system.
20. What are interacting and non-interacting capacity processes ?
21. Derive transfer function and hence step response characteristics of
    (i) interacting tank system
    (ii) non-interacting tank system.
22. Compare dynamic behaviour of interacting and non-inverting systems.
23. What are time-delay systems ? How does time delay affect the dynamic behaviour of a process ?
24. What is process identification ? Explain steps involved in step response identification of process.

❑❑❑

8

CHAPTER

FEEDBACK CONTROL SYSTEMS

8.1 INTRODUCTION

This chapter covers the fundamentals of feedback control system. The essential hardware components of control system are discussed in detail. The characteristics of basic control actions are explained. At the end of the chapter, industrial process control systems are discussed.

8.2 CONCEPT OF FEEDBACK CONTROL

In chapter 7 we studied the natural response of first and second order systems. ***The objective of process control is to modify the natural response of dynamic process to some desired form by the influence of controller connected to it.***

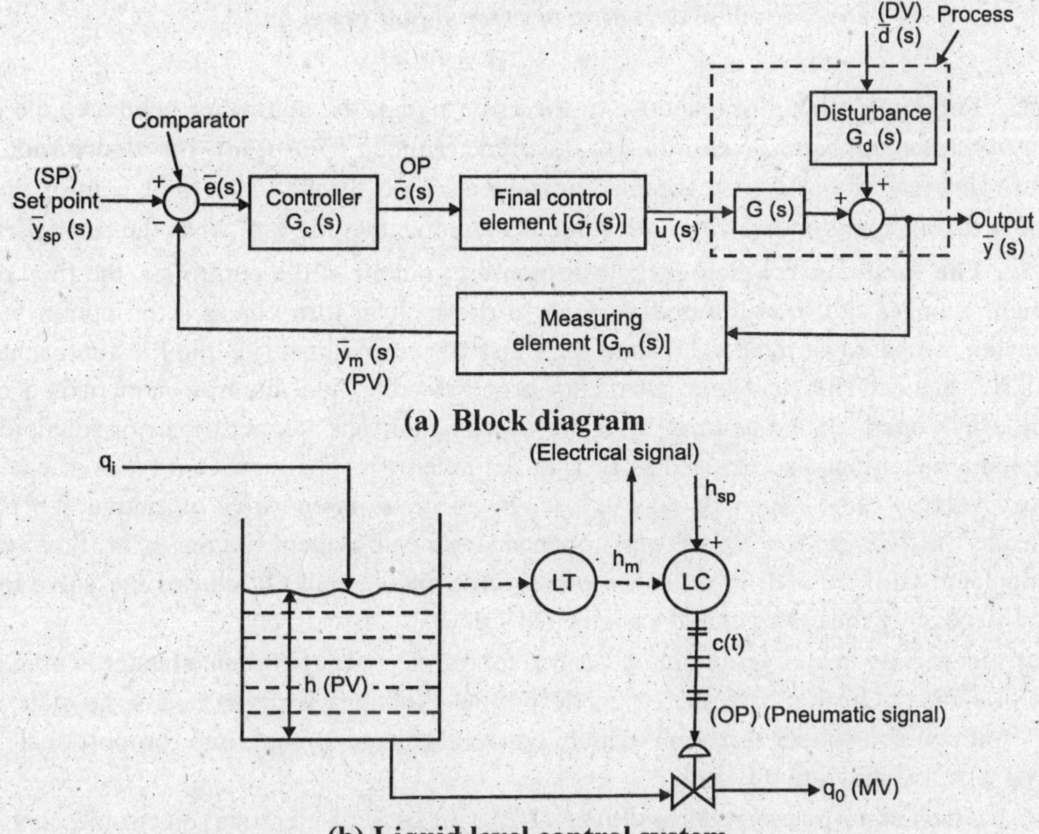

(a) Block diagram

(b) Liquid level control system based on manipulation of output flow rate (q_o)

Fig. 8.1 : Feedback control system

Block diagram :

Fig. 8.1 (a) shows the block diagram of a feedback control system. The system has the following hardware elements :

1. **The process :** As discussed earlier the process has input : manipulated variable $\bar{u}(s)$, disturbance variable $\bar{d}(s)$ and output variable $\bar{y}(s)$. The purpose of control system is to maintain the value of output variable y(t) at the desired value, known as ***set point $y_{sp}(t)$***. The effect of manipulated variable $\bar{u}(s)$ on $\bar{y}(s)$ is represented by the transfer function $G_p(s)$ while the effect of disturbance $\bar{d}(s)$ on $\bar{y}(s)$ is represented by the transfer function $G_d(s)$.

2. **The measuring element (feedback element) :** This element is a suitable sensor which measures the present value of output y(t) as the measurement signal $y_m(t)$ which is also known as ***process variable (PV) or control variable (CV)***. For example, a thermocouple measures temperature [y(t)] in terms of e.m.f. [$y_m(t)$] as the PV.

3. **The comparator :** The comparator compares the measurement signal (PV) with set-point signal (SP) and obtain the ***deviation or error signal given by***

$$e(t) = y_{sp}(t) - y_m(t) = SP - PV$$

4. **The controller :** In response to the error signal, the controller generates the output (OP) ***(or command signal)*** according to the predetermined ***control law (or algorithm)***, which in turn changes the value of the manipulated variable through the final control element. Usually the comparator and the controlling element together are known as the *controller*.

5. **The final control element :** In response to output of the controller, the final control element changes the ***manipulated variable u(t)*** which in turn changes the output y(t) and hence the measured variable $y_m(t)$ so as to reduce the error signal (i.e. the PV approaches SP). Usually for most chemical and petroleum processes, the final control element is a control valve which operates on pneumatic (air pressure) signal. The stepper motor or solenoid valve or potentiometer can also be used as final control element. There are two types of pneumatic control valves : air-to-open or air-to-close. In an ***air-to-open*** *valve* as output (OP) of the controller increases, the valve gets opened with subsequent increase in flow rate of manipulated variable u(t). In an ***air-to-close valve***, increase in OP causes the valve to close thereby reducing the manipulated variable (MV).

In electrically heated temperature control loops, electrical resistance heater is used a final control element. In this case the controller output (voltage) is given to a solid state device SCR (silicon-controlled rectifier) which convert voltage signal into proportional power output which is given to the heater.

6. **Current-to-pressure transducer (I/P) :** In case of electrical/electronic controllers, the output of controller (OP) is in the form of electrical current signal (I), which is converted into pneumatic (or pressure) signal by I/P transducer, that further actuate the control valve so as to vary the manipulated variable.

7. Transmission lines : The electric cables and pneumatic tubings connecting various components of the control system are the transmission elements which transmit current or pressure signals. The standard range of current signal is 4-20 mA, voltage signal is 0-5 V DC, pressure signal is 3-15 psig.

The variables (or signals) involved in feedback control are : the process variable (PV), the set-point (SP), the error signal, the output of controller (OP), the disturbance variable (DV), the manipulated variable (MV).

Thus feedback control strategy is implemented in the following steps :

(1) ***Measuring*** the value of the output variable (PV).

(2) ***Comparing*** the measured value of the output variable (PV) with the desired value (set-point SP) to calculate the error signal (e) as e(t) = SP – PV.

(3) ***Generating the correction signal (OP)*** (or command signal) which actuates the final control element, which in turn changes the manipulated variable (MV) so as to reduce the error signal (i.e. PV approaches SP).

(4) If OP is unable to reduce error to zero (i.e. PV = SP), then above steps are repeated until zero or steady error is obtained. Therefore, feedback control is also called as ***closed-loop control***. The significance of the term ***feedback control*** is that feedback of effect of OP on PV is used to decide the controller output signal in the next cycle. Note that in feedback control strategy, changes in set-point (servo operation) or disturbance (regulator operation) affect the output of the process and then the controller changes the OP so as to return the output (PV) to initial desired value.

The level control system :

Fig. 8.1 (b) shows a feedback control system used to maintain level of liquid at the desired set-point (h_{sp}).

The process variables of this system are :

The measured variable (PV) – Liquid level (h).

The manipulated variable (MV) – Exit liquid flow rate (q_o).

The disturbance variable (DV) – Inlet liquid flow rate (q_i).

Liquid level h(t) is measured or sensed by a ***level transducer*** (such as capacitance type). A ***level transmitter*** (LT) converts the measurement signal from the sensor into a control variable h_m (CV or PV). The ***level controller*** (LC) compares the control variable (h_m) with the desired level i.e. set-point (h_{sp}), that generate the error signal (e = PV – SP) in response to which the controller output (OP) is generated according to the predetermined control law. If electronic controller is used, the command signal is in the form of electric current, which is converted into proportional pneumatic signal by I/P converter. This pneumatic command signal (OP) operates (or actuates) control valve placed in the exit pipeline (i.e. final control element) which adjust the exit liquid flow rate q_o (i.e. manipulated variable MV) so as to reduce the error i.e. the measured level (h_m) approaches the set-point (h_{sp}). If h_m does not match with h_{sp}, the sequence of control action (i.e. measurement – comparison – correction) is repeated number of times until $h_m = h_{sp}$ (or atleast the measured level reach steady-state value). This is why feedback control is known as closed-loop control. In this method, the command signals is calculated based on the effect of previous correction on error (i.e. feedback). Since measurement signal is compared (or subtracted from) with the set-point signal, this is known as negative feedback system.

Also note that in Fig. 8.1 (b) electrical signals are shown by dotted line while pneumatic signal is represented by (—//—//—//—) representation.

8.3 FEATURES OF CONTROLLERS

1. Reverse or Direct action :

Fig. 8.2 : The controller element

Fig. 8.2 shows the controlling element which takes in the error signal [e(t)] and generates command signal or output (OP).

Direct-acting controller (increase - increase and decrease - decrease type) : In case of direct-acting controller, as the PV and hence the error signal increase, the output (OP) also increases (alternately as error decreases, the output also decreases).

Therefore as PV increases above SP, the error and hence the output OP will also increase and vice versa. The working of direct-acting controller is summarized in Fig. 8.3.

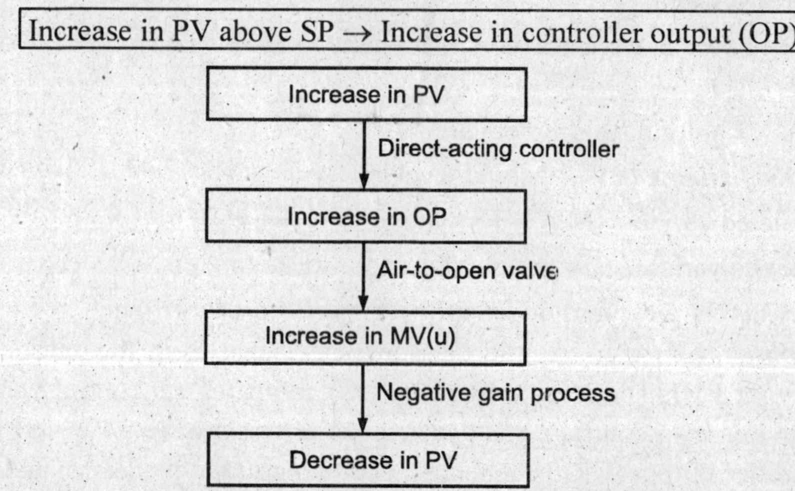

Fig. 8.3 : Direct-acting controller

Reverse-acting controller (increase-decrease and decrease-increase type) : In case of reverse-acting controller, as PV and hence the error signal increase, the output (OP) of the controller decreases.

Alternately, as PV and hence error decrease which will decrease the output (OP).

The working of reverse-acting controller is summarized in Fig. 8.4.

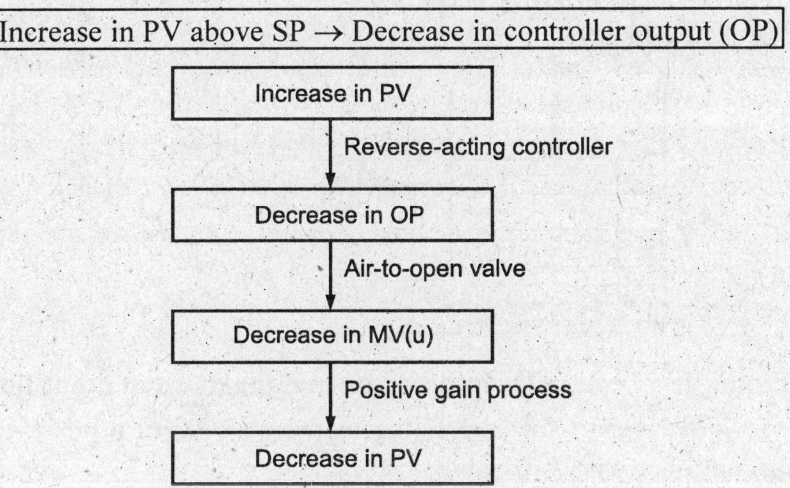

Fig. 8.4 : Reverse-acting controller

Selection of direct or reverse action :

For a given process, choice of direct or reverse-acting controller depends on whether the steady-state gain (K) of the process is positive or negative.

Process gain is defined as :

$$\text{Process gain K} = \frac{\text{Change in output of process } [y(t) \text{ or } y_m(t)]}{\text{Change in input of process } [u(t) \text{ or } d(t)]}$$

If increase in process input (u(t)) results in increase in process output [y(t) or $y_m(t)$] (or vice-versa), then process gain is positive. On the other hand, if increase in process input [u(t)] results in decrease in process output [y(t)] [or decrease in u(t) results in increase in y(t)] then process gain is negative.

In case of a ***positive gain*** process, if PV starts increasing above SP, then in order to decrease PV towards SP a ***direct-acting controller*** should be used with an ***air-to-close (A/C) type control valve.*** (If air-to-open (A/O) valve is used, then reverse-acting controller should be used.)

In case of liquid level control loop shown in Fig. 8.5 (a), if liquid level (PV) starts increasing above SP, then this rise can be counteracted by decreasing the inlet flow rate q_i (MV). Therefore, there is positive gain between h_m (PV) and q_i (MV). For such a positive gain process, if air-to-close (A/C) type control valve is used, then a direct-acting controller should be used, so that any rise in level h_m (PV) can be compensated by decreasing q_i (MV), through an A/C type control valve, which can only be achieved by using direct-acting controller (whose output OP increases with increasing PV, that results in decrease in q_i (MV), followed by arresting decrease in level h_m (PV) towards SP.)

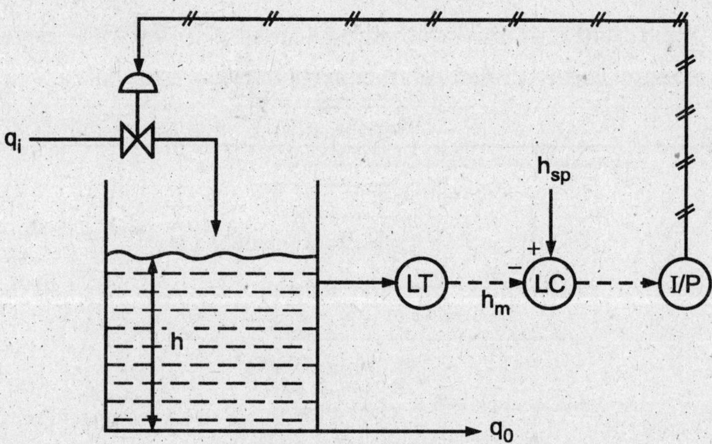

Fig. 8.5 (a) : Liquid-level control loop based on manipulation of input flow rate (q_i)

Fig. 8.5 (b) shows flow-chart for controlling increase in PV of a positive gain process using direct-acting controller with A/C valve.

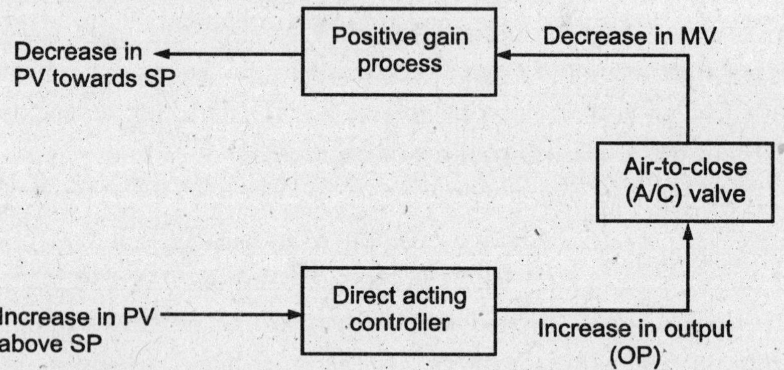

Fig. 8.5 (b) : Flow-chart for controlling output of a positive-gain process using direct-acting controller with air-to-close control valve

In case of a ***negative gain process*** if PV starts increasing above SP, then in order to decrease PV towards SP, a ***reverse-acting controller*** should be used with an ***air-to-close (A/C) type control valve***. (If air-to-open (A/O) type valve is used, a direct-acting controller should be used.)

In case of liquid-level control loop shown in Fig. 8.1 (b), if liquid level (PV) starts increasing above SP, then this rise can be counteracted by increasing outlet flow rate q_o (MV). Therefore, there is negative gain between h_m (PV) and q_o (MV). For such a negative gain process, if air-to-close (A/C) type control valve is used, then a reverse-acting controller should be used, so that any rise in h_m (PV) can be compensated by increasing q_o (MV) through an A/C type control valve, which can only be achieved by using a reverse-acting controller (whose output OP decreases with increasing PV, that result in increase in q_o (MV), followed by decrease in level h_m (PV) towards SP.

Fig. 8.6 shows the flow chart for controlling increase in PV of a negative gain process using reverse-acting controller with A/C type control valve.

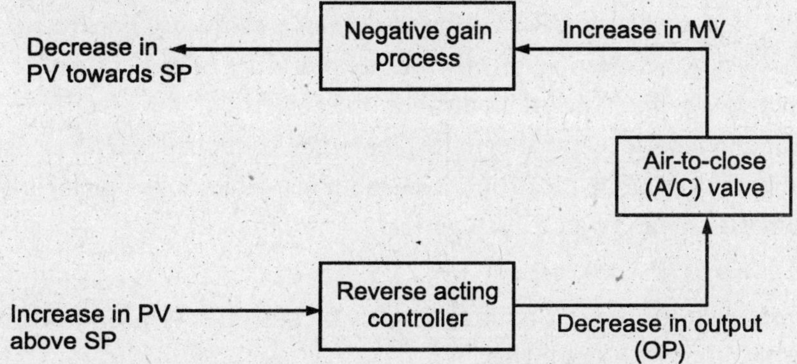

Fig. 8.6 : Flow-chart for controlling output of a negative-gain process using reverse acting controller with air-to-close control valve

The above conclusions can be summarized into the following guidelines for selection of direct or reverse-acting controller :

Process gain	Type of control valve	Control action
Positive	Air-to-close (A/C) (or fail open)	Direct
	Air-to-open (A/O) (or fail close)	Reverse
Negative	Air-to-close (A/C) (or fail open)	Reverse
	Air-to-open (A/O) (or fail close)	Direct

2. Automatic / Manual control mode :

In manual mode, the controller output (OP) is adjusted by the operator so that final control element (say control valve) gets actuated, which in turn bring the desired change (increase or decrease) in measured variable (PV). This is useful during plant start-up, shutdown or emergency situation, in which sudden large change in PV is demanded.

In automatic mode, the controller output OP is decided by the controller itself depending upon the control algorithm (equation or law). This mode is used during routine process operation to maintain PV nearby the SP. A manual/automatic switch, or its software equivalent, is used to transfer the controller from the automatic mode to the manual mode, and vice versa. But during these transfers, it is ensured that the controller output does not change abruptly and bump the process. The controllers have ***bumpless transfer*** characteristics.

8.4 CLASSICAL FEEDBACK CONTROLLERS (CONTROL MODES OR ACTIONS)

As seen from Fig. 8.1 (a) an error signal (e = SP – PV) is input the controller, while its output is command signal [c(t) or OP]. Different control actions are generated depending on the mathematical relation between error e(t) and output (OP) of the controller. The form of output signal depends on the type of controller (i.e. electrical for electronic controller or compressed air for pneumatic controller). If a pneumatic control valve is used as a final control element, then output of an electronic controller (i.e. electrical signal) is converted into proportional pneumatic signal by an I/P converter.

1. Proportional control (P-control) :

The control law (algorithm) : The output of a P-controller is proportional to the error e(t). Therefore, control law of P-controller is :

$$OP(t) = k_c\, e(t) + (OP)_{ss} \qquad \dots (8.1)$$

where, k_c = proportional gain or sensitivity of a controller

and $(OP)_{ss}$ = manual reset or bias signal

Controller Parameters :

Manual reset or bias $(OP)_{ss}$: From equation (8.1), at controller output OP = $(OP)_{ss}$, error e approaches zero (i.e. PV = SP or exact control is achieved). ***Therefore, controller bias is defined as the output of the controller when error is zero.*** At OP = $(OP)_{ss}$, the control valve is set at fixed opening, so that the manipulated variable (MV) is at steady-state value that approach the error to zero.

For non-zero error, (i.e. PV ≠ SP), the difference between the actual controller output OP(t) [or y(t)] and the steady-state bias signal OP_{ss} is known as the control command signal c(t) which is given by equation (8.1) as

$$c(t) = OP(t) - (OP)_{ss} = k_c\, e(t) \qquad \dots (8.2)$$

(Note that c(t) is controller output in deviation form).

Proportional gain (k_c) :

From equation (8.2),

$$k_c = \frac{c(t)}{e(t)} \quad \text{or} \quad \frac{OP(t) - (OP)_{ss}}{e(t)} \qquad \dots (8.3)$$

Therefore, proportional gain k_c represents the ratio of the controller command signal (or change in OP signal) to an error signal.

If OP and e(t) signals are in same units, k_c is dimensionless. The value of k_c can be adjusted in both magnitude and sign to get the desired response. ***Large value of k_c*** makes the controller ***aggressive*** (i.e. produce large change in OP) in response to the error signal, that result in fast control action. On the other hand, for ***small values of k_c***, the controller is ***less aggressive*** in response to the error signal, that result in slow control action. The sign of k_c determines whether the OP signal will inerease (for a positive k_c) or decrease (for a negative

k_c) as a error signal increases. This requirement depends on the nature of the process to be controlled.

In digital controllers, c(t) and e(t) are expressed in % form, i.e. as a number between 0 and 100%.

Thus magnitude of k_c determines the magnitude of OP, while the sign of k_c determines the direction of OP (i.e. increasing or decreasing).

Proportional Band (PB) : The P-controller parameter can also be expressed as a proportional band which is defined as the reciprocal of a non-dimensional proportional gain k_c, expressed in % form :

$$\% \text{PB} = \frac{100}{k_c} = \frac{e(t)}{c(t)} \times 100 \qquad \ldots (8.4)$$

Therefore the PB characterizes the % range over which the error signal must change in order to drive the command signal over its full range (i.e. 100%).

A ***small (or narrow) PB*** corresponds to a large gain k_c, which requires comparatively little change in error to change the OP signal by 100% which in turn will operate the control valve through complete span from 0% (closed) to 100% (full open) or vice versa. Therefore, a narrow PB makes P-controller ***more sensitive*** towards change in input error signal that will result in change in OP by 100%.

Usually, the range of PB is

$$1 \leq \text{PB} \leq 500$$

The transfer function of a P-controller :

In equation (8.2), both the command signal c(t) and input error signal e(t) are in deviation form, therefore taking Laplace transform of this equation, we get the transfer function of a P-controller as :

$$G_c(s) = \frac{\overline{c}(s)}{\overline{e}(s)} = k_c \qquad \ldots (8.5)$$

Thus, transfer function of a P-controller is a pure number, ***without any poles or zeros.***

Step response of a P-controller :

For step change of magnitude A in error, represented as :

$$e(t) = 0, \quad t < 0$$
$$= A, \quad t \geq 0$$

The output response is given by equation (8.2) as

$$c(t) = 0 \ [\text{or OP}(t) = \text{OP(ss)}], \ t < 0$$
$$= Ak_c \ [\text{or OP}(t) = \text{OP(ss)} + Ak_c], \ t \geq 0$$

Thus for change of A in error, the output of P-controller also shows step change of (Ak_c), as sho . 8.7.

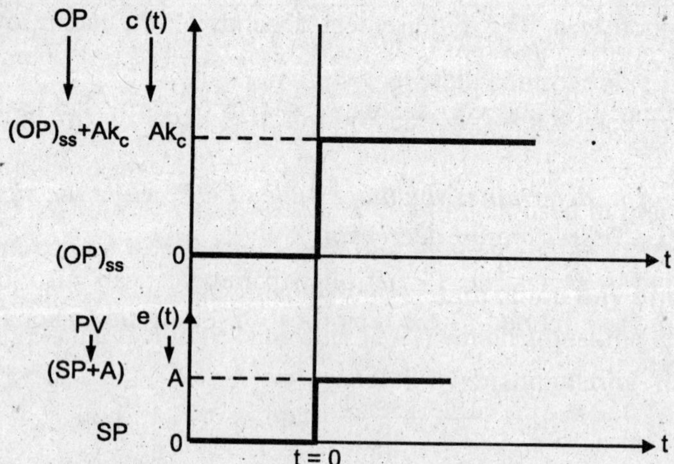

Fig. 8.7 : Step response of a P-controller

Response characteristics :

(i) The output of P-controller is proportional to error which actuates the final control element so as to change the manipulated variable in such a manner that error is reduced to zero. For the error signal sensed by the controller, the magnitude and direction of controller output OP depend upon the value of gain k_c (or PB) chosen.

(ii) As seen from Fig. 8.1 (a) the output of a process [or PV or y(t)] depends on the disturbance variable d(t) and manipulated variable u(t). For certain constant set-point SP, the P-controller can maintain the output PV of process at the desired value SP [so that error e(t) = 0] by generating the output signal $(OP)_{ss}$. Therefore, at certain SP the controller output $(OP)_{ss}$ can achieve exact control of PV at SP [e(t) = SP – PV = 0]. Now if the set-point or disturbance (or load) signal are changed, then the controller output $(OP)_{ss}$ could not achieve zero error, but it results in non-zero steady error in PV known as offset (or droop), defined as :

$$\begin{aligned} \text{Offset} &= \text{SP} - \text{steady-state value of PV} \\ &= \text{SP} - (\text{PV})_{ss} \end{aligned}$$

Therefore, a P-controller has an inherent disadvantage that a steady-state error (or offset) occurs after a set-point change or a sustained disturbance. In principle, offset can be eliminated by manually resetting the SP to new steady-state value $(PV)_{ss}$ or bias $(OP)_{ss}$, which should be done continuously. In practice, the integral control action is added to P-only control, which eliminates offset by automatically resetting the SP.

In level control example explained in Fig. 8.1 (b), assume that, initially the inlet liquid flow rate is 200 LPH (i.e. disturbance q_i) so that controller output of 50% (= bias or $(OP)_{ss}$) maintains liquid level (PV) at the desired value SP (say at 50%).

Therefore, initially at q_i = 200 LPH, OP = $(OP)_{ss}$ = 50% maintains zero error [PV = SP = 50% $(PV)_{ss}$]. Now if the disturbance, i.e. inlet water flow rate is suddenly increased to 60%, the level (PV) will start increasing above SP. This increased input flow rate will require higher value of OP (say 60%) that will open the control valve (air-to-open type) more so as to increase exit flow rate q_o, thereby maintaining the level at the desired value (SP = 50%). Therefore, if controller generate 50% output, liquid level will increase to a new steady-state value PV(∞) (say 55%). Therefore, the output of process (PV) shows a steady-state error of $e_1 = (PV)_{ss} - PV(\infty) = 50 - 55\% = -5\%$, which is known as an offset. This offset can be removed by either changing the SP to 55% or by changing the bias to 55%. Fig. 8.8 shows the offset of a P-controller.

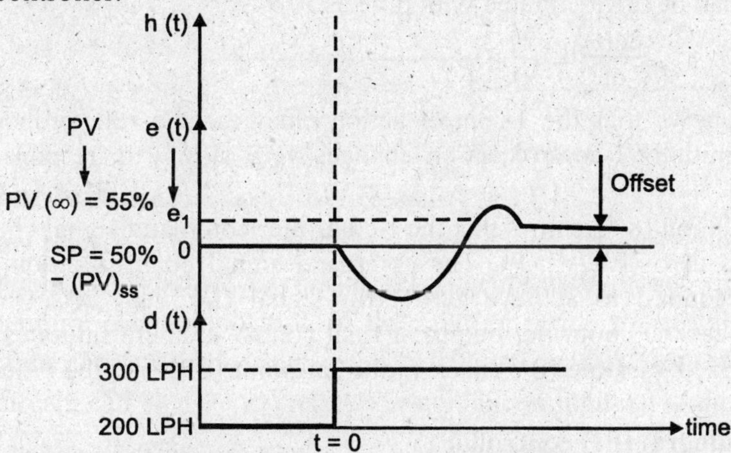

Fig. 8.8 : Offset of a P-controller

2. **Integral (or I) control (Reset action) :**

The control law : The output of I-controller is proportional to the integral of error signal over time by relation,

$$OP = \frac{1}{\tau_I} \int_0^t e \, dt + (OP)_{ss} \qquad \dots (8.6)$$

where τ_I is an adjustable parameter, called as ***integral time or reset time***, while $\frac{1}{\tau_I}$ is called as reset rate (T_R).

The transfer function : Equation (8.6) gives the control command signal :

$$c(t) = OP - OP(ss) = \frac{1}{\tau_I} \int_0^t e \, dt \qquad \dots (8.7)$$

Taking Laplace transform,

$$\bar{c}(s) = \frac{1}{\tau_I} \frac{\bar{e}(s)}{s}$$

Therefore, transfer function is :

$$G(s) = \frac{\bar{c}(s)}{\bar{e}(s)} = \frac{k_c}{\tau_I s} \qquad \dots (8.8)$$

This transfer function has a ***pole at origin (s = 0)***.

Response characteristics :

(i) Equation (8.6) shows that the output of I-controller is proportional to the integral of error (i.e. accumulation of error) with time. Therefore, I-controller will produce little control action unless error persists for some time. This is in contrast to comparatively large initial control action produced by a P-controller as soon as an error is detected. Therefore, I-control action is seldom used by itself, but it is used in conjunction with P-control that gives a PI-controller.

Equation (8.8) can be differentiated with time as :

$$\frac{dc(t)}{dt} = \frac{1}{\tau_I} e(t) \qquad \ldots (8.9)$$

This equation shows that the I-control action changes at a rate proportional to error signal. Therefore, initially I-control action changes very slowly in response to increasing error signal.

(ii) Offset : Equation (8.9) shows that the I-controller command signal changes with time until error becomes zero (PV = SP). The command signal changes automatically until it attains the value required to achieve zero error signal (i.e. zero offset). This desirable situation occurs unless the controller output or final control element saturates and thus could not bring the controlled variable (PV) back to the set-point (SP) (i.e. the value is completely open or closed).

3. Proportional-integral (PI) controller :

The control law : The output of a PI-controller is related to the error signal by the equation

$$OP = (OP)_{ss} + k_c\, e(t) + \frac{k_c}{\tau_I} \int_0^t e\, dt \qquad \ldots (8.10)$$

(P-term) (I-term)

The transfer function :

The command signal is given by

$$c(t) = OP(t) - (OP)_{ss} = k_c\, e(t) + \frac{k_c}{\tau_I} \int_0^t e\, dt \qquad \ldots (8.11)$$

Taking Laplace transform,

$$\bar{c}(s) = k_c \left(\bar{e}(s) + \frac{k_c}{\tau_I s} \bar{e}(s) \right)$$

$$= k_c\, \bar{e}(s) \left(1 + \frac{1}{\tau_I s} \right)$$

Transfer function is $G(s) = \dfrac{\bar{c}(s)}{\bar{e}(s)} = k_c \left(1 + \dfrac{1}{\tau_I s} \right)$

$$= k_c \left(\frac{\tau_I s + 1}{\tau_I s} \right) \qquad \ldots (8.12)$$

The transfer function has a ***zero at*** $s = -\dfrac{1}{\tau_I}$ ***and a pole at origin.***

Response characteristics :

(i) If error signal changes by a unit step function

$$e(t) = 0, \quad t < 0$$
$$= 1, \quad t \geq 0$$

then output of PI-controller is given by equation (8.11) as

$$c(t) = 0, \quad t < 0$$
$$= k_c, \quad t = 0$$
$$= k_c + \left(\frac{k_c}{\tau_I}\right) t, \quad t > 0$$

or

$$k_c \left(1 + \frac{t}{\tau_I}\right)$$

At time t = 0, the controller output signal changes instantaneously due to P-action, and then I-action causes the linear (or ramp) increase at a rate k_c/τ_I as shown in Fig. 8.9.

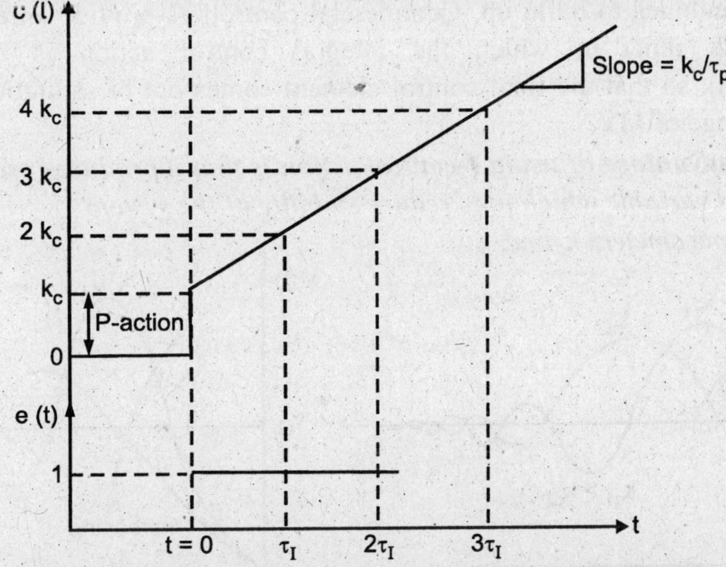

Fig. 8.9 : Response of PI-controller to unit step change in e(t)

Definition of integral time (τ_I) :

Equation (8.11) shows that for unit step change in error, initially only P-term will produce output k_c. But after a period of τ_I minutes, the integral term contributes the correction of

$$\frac{k_c}{\tau_I}\int_0^{\tau_I} 1 \, dt = \frac{k_c}{\tau_I}\tau_I = k_c$$

Therefore, after a period of τ_I minute, the total command signal will be

$$c(t) = k_c + k_c = 2k_c$$

Thus, within integral time τ_I, integral action repeats the proportional action once. This repetition occurs at every τ_I minutes, hence τ_I is called as reset time. ***Therefore, integral time τ_I is defined as the time needed by the PI-controller to repeat the initial P-action once. Hence, τ_I is expressed in the units of minutes or minutes/repeat. Some PI-controllers are calibrated in terms of reset rate $T_R = 1/\tau_I$, expressed as repeats/minute.***

(ii) Reset windup : As explained earlier the output of the PI-controller changes continuously until it attains the value required to make the steady-state error (offset) to zero (or SP = PV). This desirable action occurs until the controller output changes to extreme value (0% or 100%) so that final control element such as control valve gets completely open or closed. This condition is known as ***saturation or integral (reset) windup***. If error still persists even after the controller gets saturated, it is unable to bring the controlled variable (PV) back to the set-point. This condition occurs when the disturbance or set-point change is so large that it is beyond the range of the MV, i.e. during start-up, shut-down or change-over operations.

Reset windup occurs when a PI controller encounters a sustained error, so that the integral term continues to build up. Commercial controllers provide ***antireset windup*** (also called as batch unit) in which the integral control action is temporarily halted (or disconnected), so that the final control element comes out of saturation state and within the operating range of MV.

(iii) The disadvantage of using I-control action is that it produces oscillatory behaviour of the controlled variable which may reduce stability of the system.

Effect of tuning parameters k_c and τ_I :

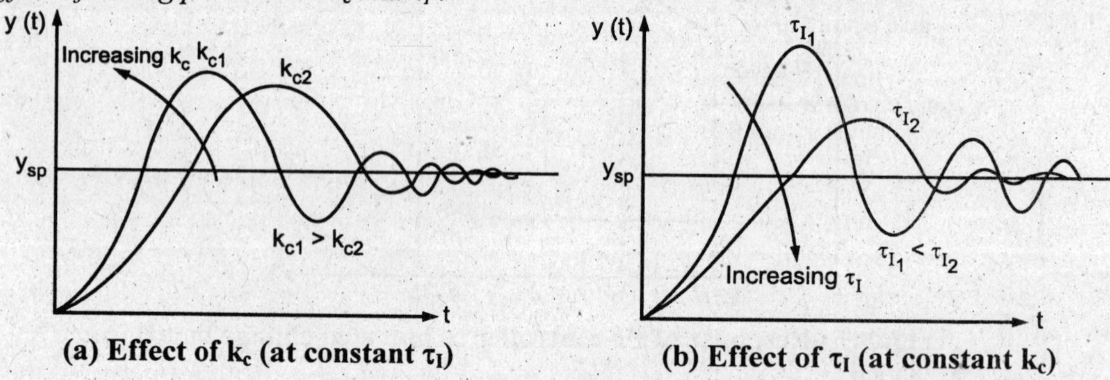

(a) Effect of k_c (at constant τ_I) **(b) Effect of τ_I (at constant k_c)**

Fig. 8.10 : Effect of tuning parameters on a PI-controller

Effect of k_c :

Fig. 8.10 (a) shows the effect of k_c on output response (at constant τ_I). As k_c is increased, the output response becomes faster but more oscillatory with increasing overshoot and decay ratio.

Effect of τ_I :

Fig. 8.10 (b) shows the effect of τ_I on output response. As τ_I is decreased, reset or integral action increases, which results in increased faster, but more oscillatory response with increased overshoot and decay ratio.

Therefore, in PI-controller, the control action can be increased by increasing k_c and decreasing τ_I, which make the output response more sensitive (faster but more oscillatory).

4. Derivative (D) control action (Rate action, preact control, anticipatory control) :

The control law : The output of a D-controller is proportional to the rate of change of the error signal by the equation

$$OP(t) = (OP)_{ss} + \tau_D \frac{de}{dt} \quad \text{... (8.13)}$$

where τ_D is called as the derivative or rate time.

The transfer function :

Equation (8.13) gives the D-controller command signal

$$c(t) = OP(t) - (OP)_{ss} = k_c \tau_d \frac{de}{dt}$$

Taking Laplace transform

$$c(s) = k_c \tau_d e(s)$$

Therefore, transfer function is

$$G(s) = \frac{\bar{c}(s)}{\bar{e}(s)} = (k_c \tau_d) s \quad \text{... (8.14)}$$

This transfer function has ***no pole, but has a zero at origin***.

Response characteristics :

(i) For sudden, instantaneous change in error (however small in magnitude and short in duration), its time rate is very high. Therefore, D-controller will produce comparatively larger instantaneous change in output. Thus, D-control action shall not wait for error signal to change by significant magnitude and then generate proportional output (OP) signal, as in case of a P-controller. For sudden change in error, D-control action occurs too early as compared to P only control action. This can also be expressed as ***anticipatory feature*** of a D-controller, because D-controller anticipates what the error will be in immediate future and applies to a comparatively large correction proportional to current rate of change error. With reference to this D-control action is described as ***preact control or anticipatory control***.

(ii) For fast changes in error the output of D-controller changes by large magnitude, that drastically reduce the error and produce stabilizing effect on the process variable. But if error remains steady ($de/dt = 0$), then D-controller output remains steady at nominal value $(OP)_{SS}$. Therefore, D-action is never used alone, but it is used in conjunction with a P or PI-controller.

(iii) For a noisy error signal fluctuating around a very small value, due to large value of de/dt, D-controller output changes by large mount, which leads to unstable behaviour of PV.

5. Ideal proportional-derivative (PD) controller :

The control law : The output of a PD-controller is given by

$$OP(t) = (OP)_{ss} + k_c e + k_c \tau_D \frac{de}{dt} \quad \text{... (8.15)}$$

(P-term) (D-term)

The transfer function :

The command signal is given as :

$$c(t) = OP(t) - (OP)_{ss} = k_c e + k_c \tau_D \frac{de}{dt} \quad \text{... (8.16)}$$

Taking Laplace transform,

$$\bar{c}(s) = k_c (1 + \tau_D s)\, \bar{e}(s)$$

Transfer function,
$$G(s) = \frac{\bar{c}(s)}{\bar{e}(s)} = k_c (1 + \tau_D s) \quad \text{... (8.17)}$$

The transfer has a zero at $s = -1/\tau_D$, but no pole.

Response characteristics :

(i) For a small step change in error, the value of the derivative de/dt is infinite, which will change the output of PD-controller through 100%, so that control valve will get completely open or closed. This could not give stable control, therefore, ***D-control action is not used for step change in error.***

(ii) Definition of τ_D : For gradual or unit ramp change in error represented as

$$e(t) = 0, \quad t < 0$$
$$= t, \quad t > 0$$

The output of PD-controller is :

$$OP(t) = (OP)_{ss} + k_c t + k_c \tau_D$$
$$c(t) = OP(t) - (OP)_{ss} = k_c (t + \tau_D) \quad \text{... (8.18)}$$

Equation (8.18) shows that ***derivative time τ_D represents the time period by which the output of the PD-controller differs from the output of a P-only controller (i.e. $k_c t$), therefore, it is expressed in the units of time (minutes).***

Fig. 8.11 compares the output response of a P-only and PD-controllers for unit ramp change in error. The output of a P-only controller varies linearly from initial steady-state value $(OP)_{ss}$ at the same rate as the error. But the output of PD-controller changes suddenly by $k_c\tau_D$ at $t = 0$ (D-action) and then increases linearly at the same rate as error (P-action). Therefore, within time period t_1, the output of PD-controller is higher than that of a P-only controller by an amount $k_c\tau_D$. On the other hand, the controller output of magnitude $(k_c t_1)$ is produced by PD-controller τ_D seconds earlier than P-only controller. This explains the terminologies of preact control and anticipatory control for derivative control action.

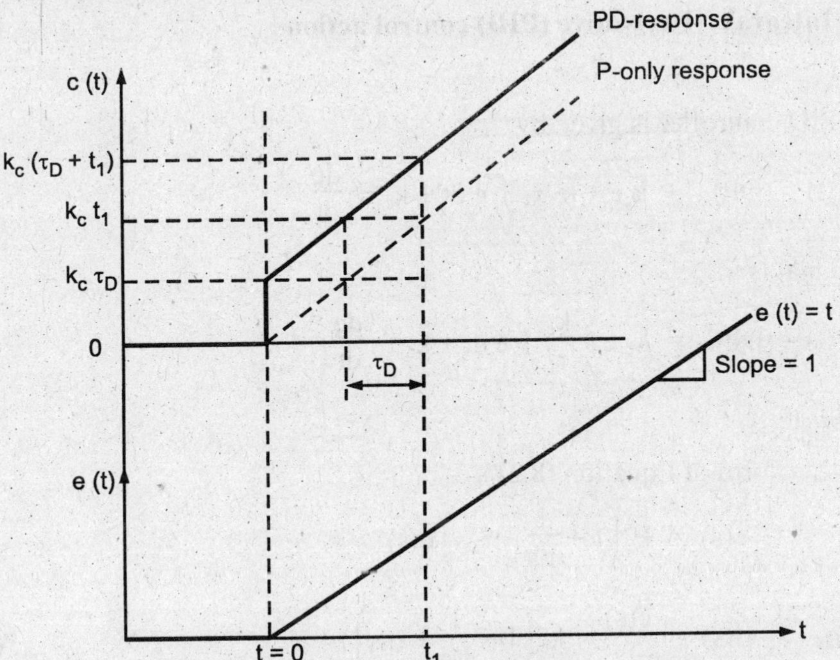

Fig. 8.11 : Response of a PD-controller for unit ramp change in error

(iii) Due to anticipatory action, the D-mode tends to stabilize the controlled process. Therefore, if it is used alongwith PI-controller, the ***D-control action counteracts the destabilizing tendency of the I-control action***.

(iv) Derivative control action tends to improve the dynamic response of the controlled variable (PV) by decreasing the process settling time. But if the process measurement is noisy, i.e. if it contains high-frequency random fluctuations, then the derivative de/dt will change wildly and derivative action will amplify the noise leading to unstable behaviour. Due to this reason, ***D-control action is not used for flow control because flow measurements tend to be noisy***.

(v) Due to noisy measurement signal, the ideal PD-control algorithm in equation (8.15) is physically unrealizable, because it cannot be implemented exactly using either analog or digital components. For analog controllers, the ideal transfer function of PD-controller given by equation (8.17) is modified as

$$\frac{\bar{c}(s)}{\bar{e}(s)} = k_c \left(1 + \frac{\tau_D s}{\alpha \tau_D s + 1}\right) \quad \ldots (8.19)$$

where α is a constant whose value lies between 0.05 and 0.2, with 0.1 being a typical value, that reduce the sensitivity of control calculations to high frequency noise in the measurement.

6. Proportional – Integral – Derivative (PID) control action :

The control law :

The output of a PID controller is given by

$$OP(t) = (OP)_{ss} + k_c e + k_c \tau_I \int_0^t e\,dt + k_c \tau_D \frac{de}{dt} \qquad \dots (8.20)$$

The command signal is

$$c(t) = OP(t) - (OP)_{ss} = k_c e + \frac{k_c}{\tau_I} \int_0^t e\,dt + k_c \tau_D \frac{de}{dt} \qquad \dots (8.21)$$

The transfer function :

Taking Laplace transform of Equation (8.21),

$$\bar{c}(s) = k_c \left(1 + \frac{1}{\tau_I s} + \tau_D s\right) \bar{e}(s)$$

Transfer function,

$$G(s) = \frac{\bar{c}(s)}{\bar{e}(s)} = k_c \left(1 + \frac{1}{\tau_I s} + \tau_D s\right) \qquad \dots (8.22)$$

Response characteristics :

We have seen that in case of PI-controller, due to effect of increasing k_c and decreasing τ_I, the output response becomes faster but more oscillatory, which may lead to instability. If D-mode is added to PI-controller, it brings a stabilizing effect to the system. ***Thus, PID-controller gives reasonably fast speed of response with moderate overshoots and decay ratios.***

Fig. 8.12 shows comparison of output response characteristics with P, PI and PID controllers.

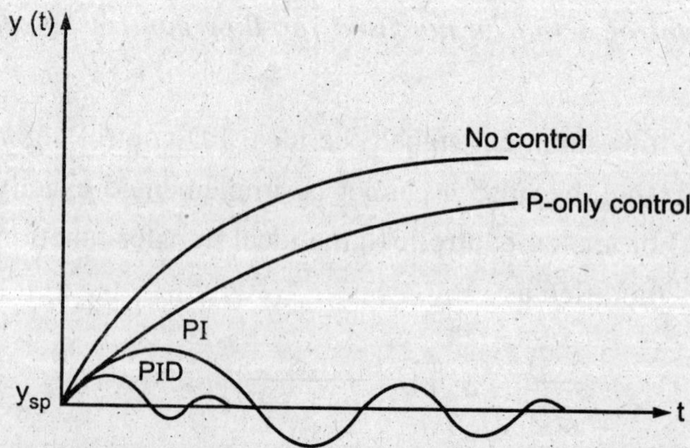

Fig. 8.12 : Comparison of process response with P, PI, PID controllers

7. On-off controller (Two position or bang-bang controllers) :

The control law :

The output of an ideal on-off controller has only two possible extreme values (without any intermediate values) depending on whether error is positive (SP > PV) or negative (SP < PV) as :

$$\begin{aligned} OP(t) &= (OP)_{max}, \quad \text{if } e \geq 0 \ldots \text{on condition} \\ &= (OP)_{min}, \quad \text{if } e < 0 \ldots \text{off condition} \end{aligned}$$

For a typical digital electronic controller,

$$\begin{aligned} (OP)_{max} &= 100\% \ (= 20 \text{ mA}) \\ (OP)_{min} &= 0\% \ (= 4 \text{ mA}) \end{aligned}$$

For a pneumatic controller,

$$\begin{aligned} (OP)_{max} &= 100\% \ (15 \text{ psi}) \\ (OP)_{min} &= 0\% \ (3 \text{ psi}) \end{aligned}$$

Response characteristics :

As the controlled variable (PV) cross the set-point (SP), from above (PV > SP or e > 0) or from below (PV < SP or e < 0) or error changes its sign (from positive to negative or vice versa), the output of controller suddenly changes from one extreme value (100%) to another 0% (or vice versa), which further drive the control valve (i.e. final control element) from fully closed to fully open condition (assuming that control valve is air-to-close type). Note that output of an on-off controller is independent of magnitude of error, but it depends only on sign of error. Note that on-off control can be considered as a special case of P-control with a very high controller gain.

Since on-off controller has only extreme output values, it provides faster correction to the process, but the process output continuously oscillates or fluctuates around the set-point as shown in Fig. 8.13. This produces excess wear on the control valve.

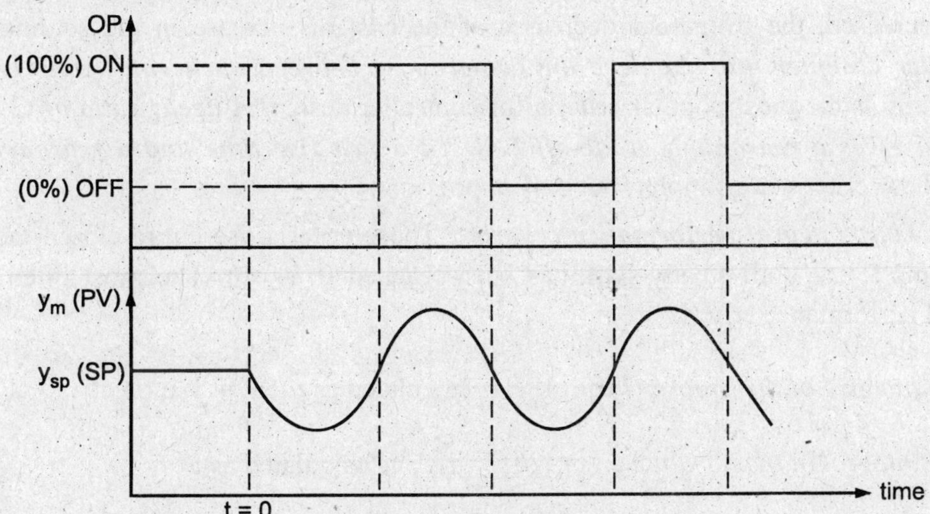

Fig. 8.13 : On-off controller characteristics

To avoid this, solenoid valve or solenoid switch is normally used as final control element with on-off controller (solenoid valve opens and closes with change in electric supply from the controller).

On-off controllers are comparatively inexpensive controllers, which are commonly used as thermostats in home heating systems and refrigerators. They are also used in non-critical industrial applications such as level control loops, where exact level control is not desired, but level is maintained in certain range (band) around the set-point.

8.5 SIMPLE CONTROLLER PERFORMANCE MEASURES

The performance of controller is expressed in terms of the following criteria :

1. **Steady-state performance criteria :**

Zero error at steady-state (i.e. zero offset) is the principal steady-state performance criteria. As discussed earlier, the P-controller cannot achieve zero steady-state but as the gain k_c is increased, the offset decreases to zero. In case of PI-controller, there is no offset.

2. **Dynamic response criteria :**

Usually the dynamic performance of closed-loop system is represented by the response of a second-order system. Therefore, the controller performance can be expressed in terms of the following dynamic response criteria :

(a) The simple performance criteria : These criteria use only few points of the response, which are based on the following characteristic features of the closed-loop response : overshoot, rise time, settling time, decay ratio and frequency of oscillations. ***The controllers are designed so as to have minimum overshoot and settling time***. But one simple criteria is not sufficient to describe the desired dynamic response. The controller designs based on multiple criteria lead to conflicting response characteristics. For example, if proportional gain k_c is decreased, the overshoot decreases at the cost of increase in the settling time. ***The controller designer must achieve the compromise between such conflicting criteria***. The decay ratio is the most popular criteria for controller design. ***A decay ratio of C/A = ¼ (one quarter) gives a reasonable trade-off between a fast rise time and a reasonable settling time***. These criteria are simpler, but only approximate.

(b) Time-integral performance criteria : These criteria use entire closed-loop response from time $t = 0$ until steady-state has been reached ($t \rightarrow \infty$). The most often used time-integral performance criteria are :

(i) Integral of the square (ISE) : ISE is calculated as : $ISE = \int_0^\infty e^2(t)\, dt$.

(ii) Integral of the absolute error (IAE) : IAE is calculated as :

$$IAE = \int_0^\infty |e(t)|\, dt$$

(iii) Integral of the time-weighted absolute error (ITAE) : ITAE is calculated as :

$$\text{ITAE} = \int_0^\infty t\,|e(t)|\,dt$$

The controller having the minimum values of ISE, IAE and ITAE is considered as the best controller. The selection of criteria depends on the magnitude of error as follows :

- For suppressing large errors, ISE is better than IAE.
- For suppressing small errors, IAE is better than ISE.
- For suppressing errors which persist for longer times, the ITAE criterion is used for tuning the controller, because the presence of the large value of t amplifies the effect of even small errors in the value of the integral.

Different performance criteria lead to different controller designs.

8.6 DYNAMIC BEHAVIOUR OF FEEDBACK-CONTROLLED PROCESSES (SERVO AND REGULATOR RESPONSE)

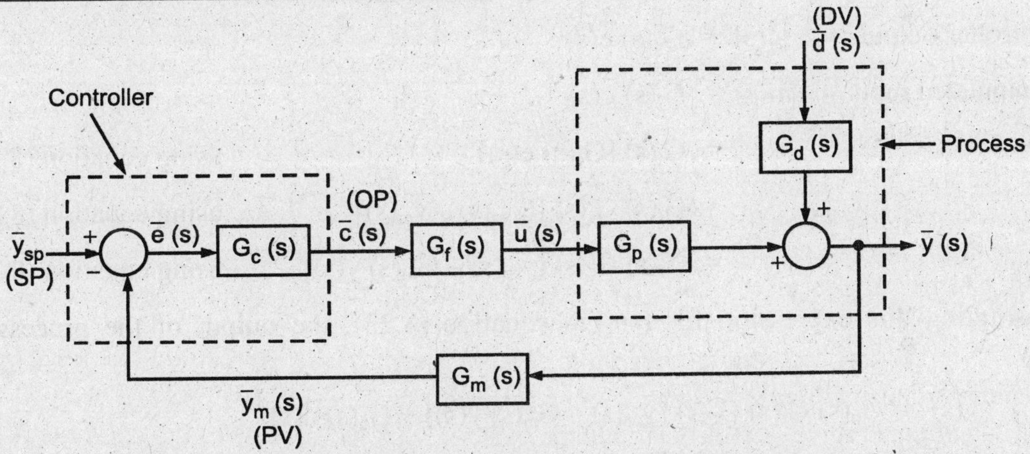

(a) Block diagram of feedback control system

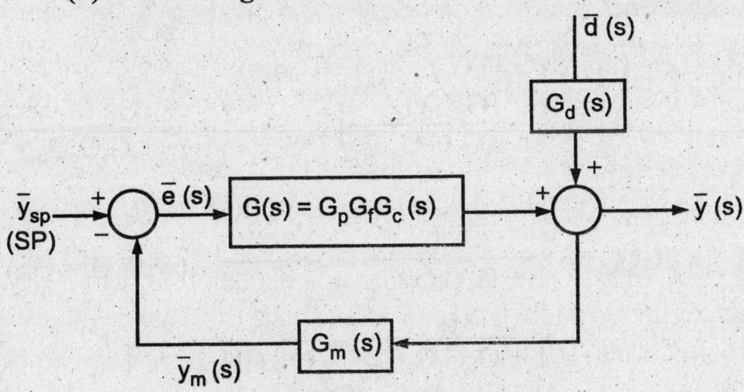

(b) Simplified block diagram

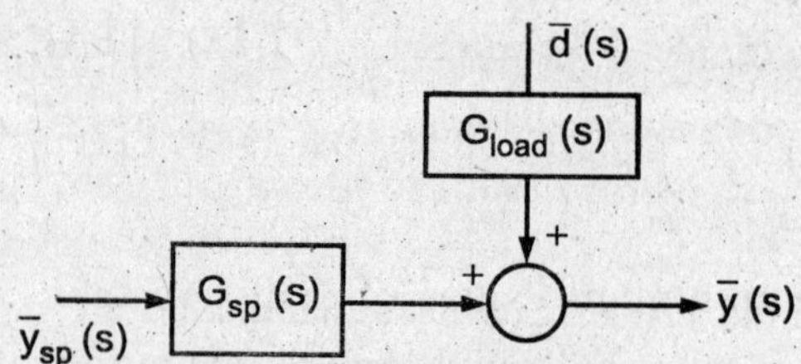

(c) Equivalent block diagram

Fig. 8.14

Fig. 8.14 (a) shows the block diagram of a feedback control or closed-loop system. The signals involved in this block diagram are expressed as

Process output (CV)

$$\bar{y}(s) = G_p(s)\,\bar{m}(s) + G_d(s)\,\bar{d}(s) \qquad \text{... (8.23)}$$

Measurement signal (PV),

$$\bar{y}_m(s) = G_m(s)\,\bar{y}(s) \qquad \text{... (8.24)}$$

Error, $\bar{e}(s) = \bar{y}_{sp}(s) - \bar{y}_m(s) = SP - PV$ ... (8.25)

Controller output $\bar{c}(s) = G_c(s)\,\bar{e}(s)$ ... (8.26)

Manipulated input,

$$\begin{aligned}\bar{m}(s) &= G_f(s)\,\bar{c}(s)\\ &= G_f(s)\,[G_c(s)\,\bar{e}(s)] && \text{... using equation (8.26)}\\ &= G_f(s)\,G_c(s)\,[(\bar{y}_{sp}(s) - \bar{y}_m(s)] && \text{... using equation (8.25)}\\ &= G_f(s)\,G_c(s)\,[\bar{y}_{sp}(s) - G_m(s)\,\bar{y}(s)] && \text{... using equation (8.24)}\end{aligned}$$

Substituting this expression for $\bar{m}(s)$ in equation (8.23), the output of the process is given by

$$\begin{aligned}\bar{y}(s) &= G_p(s)\,G_f(s)\,G_c(s)\,[\bar{y}_{sp}(s) - G_m(s)\,\bar{y}(s)] + G_d(s)\,\bar{d}(s)\\ &= G_p(s)\,G_f(s)\,G_c(s)\,\bar{y}_{sp}(s) - G_p(s)\,G_f(s)\,G_c(s)\,G_m(s)\,\bar{y}(s) + G_d(s)\,\bar{d}(s)\end{aligned}$$

Rearranging the equation

$$\begin{aligned}(1 + G_pG_fG_cG_m)\,\bar{y}(s) &= (G_pG_fG_c)\,\bar{y}_{sp}(s) + G_d\bar{d}(s)\\ \bar{y}(s) &= \left(\frac{G_pG_fG_c}{1 + G_pG_fG_cG_m}\right)\bar{y}_{sp}(s) + \left(\frac{G_d}{1 + G_pG_fG_cG_m}\right)\bar{d}(s)\\ &= G_{sp}(s)\,\bar{y}_{sp}(s) + G_{load}(s)\,\bar{d}(s) && \text{... (8.27)}\end{aligned}$$

where, $G_{sp} = \dfrac{G_pG_fG_c}{1 + G_pG_fG_cG_m} = \dfrac{G}{1 + GH}$ (with $H = G_m$)

and $G_{load} = \dfrac{G_d}{1 + G_pG_fG_cG_m} = \dfrac{G_d}{1 + GH}$

Fig. 8.14 (b) and (c) represent the equivalent block diagram of a closed-loop control system. There are two types of problems associated with a feedback control system.

1. Servo problem (response) : If the disturbance is kept constant $[\bar{d}(s) = 0]$ and set-point is changed, then the output response is known as the servo response of the closed-loop system. This response is obtained by substituting $\bar{d}(s) = 0$ in equation (8.27) to get

$$\bar{y}(s) = G_{sp}(s)\,\bar{y}_{sp}(s) = \frac{G_p G_f G_c}{1 + G_p G_f G_c G_m}\,\bar{y}_{sp}(s) \qquad \ldots (8.28)$$

2. Regulator problem (response) : If the set-point is kept constant and disturbance is changed, then the output response is known as the regulator response of the closed-loop system. This response is obtained by substituting $\bar{y}_{sp}(s) = 0$ in equation (8.27) to get

$$\bar{y}(s) = G_{load}(s)\,\bar{d}(s) = \frac{G_d}{1 + G_p G_f G_c G_m}\,\bar{d}(s) \qquad \ldots (8.29)$$

Note :

The denominators of both the transfer functions $G_{sp}(s)$ and $G_{load}(s)$ are identical i.e. $(1 + G_p G_f G_c G_m)$. Therefore, the poles of both the transfer functions are identical, which are obtained by solving the characteristic equation $1 + G_p G_f G_c G_m = 0$. ***Since the poles of both the transfer functions are same, the dynamic response characteristics of output for servo problem (change in SP) and for regulatory problem (change in DV) are identical.***

8.7 EFFECT OF DIFFERENT FEEDBACK CONTROL ACTIONS ON CLOSED-LOOP RESPONSE OF A FIRST-ORDER PROCESS

We study how the response of a normal, uncontrolled first-order process is changed when simple P, PI, PD or PID controllers are used to control the output of process at the desired value (SP).

8.7.1 Effect of P-Action

(A) Servo response :

Uncontrolled first-order process is modelled as

$$G_p(s) = \frac{\bar{y}(s)}{\bar{u}(s)} = \frac{k_p}{\tau_p s + 1} \qquad \ldots (8.30)$$

where u and y are input and output process variables respectively in deviation form,

The open-loop response parameters are

k_p = process gain, and

τ_p = process time constant

The closed-loop servo response of a feedback control process is given by equation (8.28) as :

$$\bar{y}(s) = \frac{G_p G_f G_c}{1 + G_p G_f G_c G_m}\,\bar{y}_{sp}(s) \quad [\because \bar{d}(s) = 0]$$

For a P-controller, $G_c(s) = k_c$ and

assuming $G_m(s) = G_f(s) = 1$, the output response is :

$$\bar{y}(s) = \frac{\frac{k_p}{\tau_p s + 1} \cdot k_c}{1 + \frac{k_p}{\tau_p s + 1} \cdot k_c} \bar{y}_{sp}(s)$$

$$= \frac{k_p k_c}{\tau_p s + (1 + k_p k_c)} \bar{y}_{sp}(s)$$

$$= \frac{(k_p k_c / 1 + k_p k_c)}{\left(\frac{\tau_p}{1 + k_p k_c}\right) s + 1} \bar{y}_{sp}(s)$$

$$= \frac{k_p'}{\tau_p' s + 1} \bar{y}_{sp}(s) \qquad \dots (8.31)$$

where, $$k_p' = \frac{k_p k_c}{1 + k_p k_c} = \text{closed-loop gain} \qquad \dots (8.32)$$

and $$\tau_p' = \frac{\tau_p}{1 + k_p k_c} = \text{closed-loop time constant} \qquad \dots (8.33)$$

Response characteristics :

Equation (8.31) shows that the closed-loop response transfer function for a first-order process with P-controller remains first-order but with modified parameters k_p' and τ_p'.

(i) Effect on gain : Equation (8.32) shows that the closed loop gain (k_p') is smaller than open-loop gain (k_p).

(ii) Effect on time constant : Equation (8.33) shows that the closed-loop time constant (τ_p') is smaller than open-loop time constant. This indicates that the closed-loop response is faster than open-loop response. As k_c is increased, response becomes more faster.

(iii) Unit step response : For unit step change in set-point,

$$\bar{y}_{sp}(s) = \frac{1}{s}$$

Therefore, output response is given by equation (8.31) as

$$\bar{y}(s) = \frac{k_p'}{\tau_p' s + 1} \frac{1}{s}$$

Resolving into partial fraction expansion and taking inverse Laplace transform output response is given by

$$y(t) = k_p' (1 - e^{-t/\tau_p'}) \qquad \dots (8.34)$$

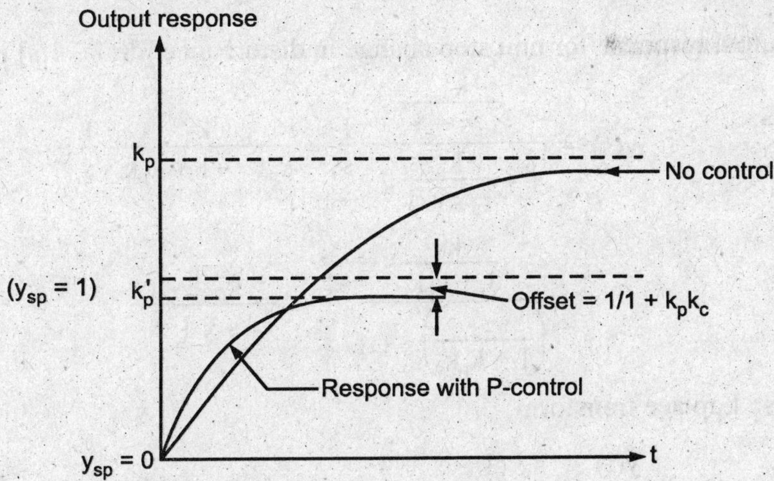

Fig. 8.15 : Closed-loop servo response of a first-order system with P-control

Fig. 8.15 shows unit step response of a first-order system with P-only control.

Ultimate response : As $t \to \infty$, $y(\infty) \to k_p'$ ($< k_p$).

Therefore, ultimate response is smaller than open-loop ultimate response.

Offset :

$$\text{Offset} = \text{(change in set point)} - \text{(ultimate response)}$$

$$= 1 - k_p' = 1 - \frac{k_pk_c}{1 + k_pk_c}$$

$$= \frac{1}{1 + k_pk_c}$$

This justifies the characteristic of P-controller that it will produce non-zero offset. As controller gain k_c is increased, offset decreases.

(B) Regulator response :

The regulator response of a first-order system is given by equation (8.29) as

$$\bar{y}(s) = \frac{G_d}{1 + G_pG_fG_cG_m}\bar{d}(s)$$

$$G_p = \frac{k_p}{\tau_p s + 1}, \quad G_c = k_c,$$

and

$$G_m = G_f = 1$$

If a disturbance transfer function is of a first-order type in the form :

$$G_d = \frac{k_d}{\tau_p s + 1}$$

(Note th[illegible]e process has same time constant for set-point change and disturbance change.)

Therefore, output response for unit step change in disturbance $[\bar{d}(s) = 1/s]$ is given by

$$\bar{y}(s) = \frac{\dfrac{k_d}{\tau_p s + 1}}{1 + \dfrac{k_p}{\tau_p s + 1} k_c} \frac{1}{s} = \frac{k_d}{\tau_p s + (1 + k_p k_c)} \frac{1}{s}$$

$$= \frac{\dfrac{k_d}{1 + k_p k_c}}{\left(\dfrac{\tau_p}{1 + k_p k_c}\right) s + 1} \frac{1}{s} = \frac{k_d'}{\tau_p' s + 1} \frac{1}{s}$$

Taking inverse Laplace transform,

$$y(t) = k_d' (1 - e^{-t/\tau_p'}) \qquad \dots (8.35)$$

Response characteristics :

(i) The closed-loop output response remains first-order with response parameters

$$k_d' = \frac{k_d}{1 + k_p k_c} \text{ and } \tau_p' = \frac{\tau_p}{1 + k_p k_c}$$

(ii) **Ultimate response :** As $t \to \infty$, $y(\infty) = k_d' = \dfrac{k_d}{1 + k_p k_c}$

(iii) **Offset :** Offset = (change in SP) – (ultimate output response)

$$= 0 - k_d' = -\frac{k_d'}{1 + k_p k_c}$$

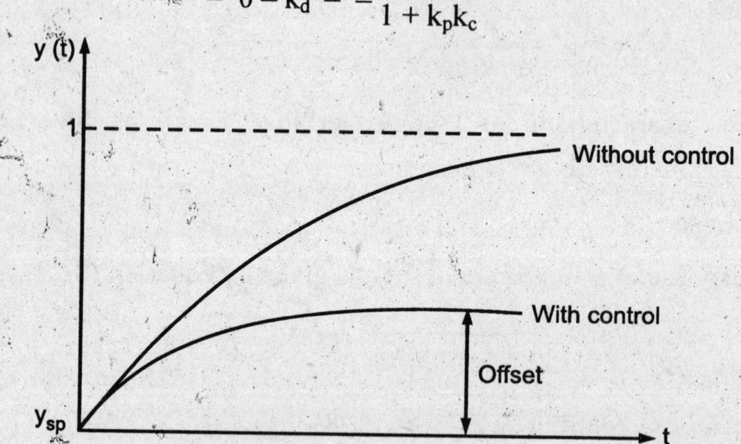

Fig. 8.16 : Regulator response of a first-order process with P-control

8.7.2 Effect of PI-Control Action

(A) Servo response :

The closed-loop servo response of a feedback control system is given by equation (8.28) as :

$$\bar{y}(s) = \frac{G_p G_f G_c}{1 + G_p G_f G_c G_m} \bar{y}_{sp}(s)$$

Substituting : $$G_p = \frac{k_p}{\tau_p s + 1},\quad G_c = k_c\left(1 + \frac{1}{\tau_I s}\right) \quad \text{... (PI controller)}$$

and $$G_m = G_f = 1$$

$$\bar{y}(s) = \frac{\dfrac{k_p}{\tau_p s + 1} k_c \left(1 + \dfrac{1}{\tau_I s}\right)}{1 + \dfrac{k_p}{\tau_p s + 1} k_c \left(1 + \dfrac{1}{\tau_I s}\right)} \bar{y}_{sp}(s)$$

$$= \frac{k_p k_c (\tau_I s + 1)}{\tau_I s (\tau_p s + 1) + k_p k_c \cdot (\tau_I s + 1)} \bar{y}_{sp}(s)$$

$$= \frac{k_p k_c (\tau_I s + 1)}{(\tau_I \tau_p) s^2 + (\tau_I + k_p k_c \tau_I) s + k_p k_c} \bar{y}_{sp}(s)$$

$$= \frac{\tau_I s + 1}{\left(\dfrac{\tau_p \tau_I}{k_p k_c}\right) s^2 + \tau_I \left(\dfrac{1 + k_p k_c}{k_p k_c}\right) s + 1} \bar{y}_{sp}(s)$$

$$= \frac{\tau_I s + 1}{\tau^2 s^2 + 2\tau\zeta s + 1} \bar{y}_{sp}(s) \quad \text{... (8.36)}$$

$$= \frac{\tau_I s + 1}{(s - p_1)(s - p_2)} \bar{y}_{sp}(s)$$

where, $$\tau = \sqrt{\frac{\tau_p \tau_I}{k_p k_c}} \quad \text{... (8.37)}$$

$$\zeta = \frac{1}{2} \frac{(1 + k_p k_c)\, \tau_I}{\sqrt{(k_p k_c)(\tau_p \tau_c)}} \quad \text{... (8.38)}$$

Response characteristics :

1. Equation (8.36) shows that the closed-loop servo transfer function of a first-order process with PI-controller is a second-order transfer function with one zero at $s = -1/\tau_I$ and two poles at p_1, p_2, which are the roots of equation

$$\tau^2 s^2 + 2\tau\zeta s + 1 = 0$$

Therefore output response is a second-order type (i.e. underdamped, overdamped or critically damped depending on the values of p_1, p_2).

2. Unit step response : For unit step change in input, the output response is given by equation (8.36) as

$$\bar{y}(s) = \frac{\tau_I s + 1}{(s - p_1)(s - p_2)} \cdot \frac{1}{s}$$

Using partial fraction expansion and taking inverse Laplace transform

$$y(t) = A_o + A_1 e^{p_1 t} + A_2 e^{p_2 t}$$

Ultimate response : Applying final value theorem, the ultimate response is

$$\lim_{t \to \infty} y(t) = \lim_{s \to 0} s\,\bar{y}(s) = 1$$

$$\therefore \quad \text{Offset} = (\text{change in SP}) - (\text{ultimate response})$$

$$= 1 - 1$$

$$= 0$$

This justifies the fact that due to addition of integral action, offset gets eliminated.

3. **Effect of k_c :** Equation (8.38) shows that value of ζ depends on the values of controller gain k_c and integral time τ_I, which in turn will decide the nature of output response, i.e. underdamped ($\zeta < 1$), overdamped ($\zeta > 1$) or critically damped ($\zeta = 1$). ***As k_c increases, damping factor ζ decreases, therefore the output response changes from sluggish overdamped ($\zeta > 1$) to faster but oscillatory, underdamped behaviour ($\zeta < 1$) as shown in Fig. 8.17.***

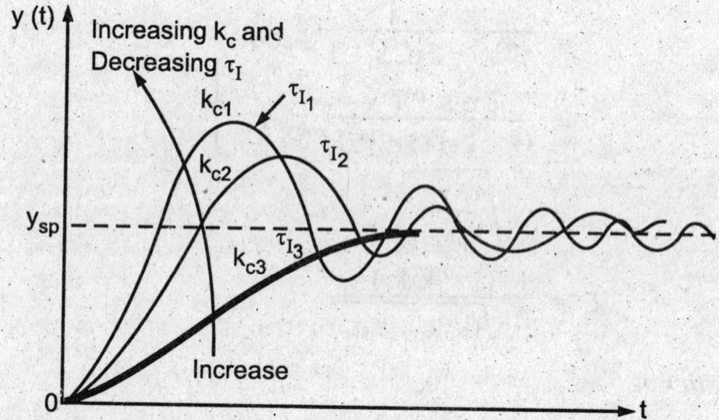

Fig. 8.17 : Effect of controller gain k_c on the closed-loop response with a PI-controller

4. **Effect of τ_I :** Equation (8.38) also shows that as τ_I decreases, ζ decreases resulting in same conclusion as that for increasing k_c values.

Thus as k_c is increased or τ_I is decreased (more reset action), the response becomes faster, but more oscillatory with higher overshoots and longer oscillations (in other words the response becomes more sensitive).

Thus when I-action is added to P-action, the response becomes sluggish and oscillatory (for increasing k_c and decreasing τ_I) but without any offset.

(B) Regulator response :

As discussed earlier, the response characteristics of a first-order system with PI-controller for change in SP are similar to those for change in disturbance.

8.7.3 Effect of PD-Control Action

(A) Servo response :

The closed-loop servo response of a feedback control system is given by equation (8.28) as :

$$\bar{y}(s) = \frac{G_pG_fG_c}{1 + G_pG_fG_c}\,\bar{y}_{sp}(s)$$

Substituting $G_p = \frac{k_p}{\tau_p s + 1}$, $G_c = k_c(1 + \tau_D s)$ (i.e. PD-control) and $G_m = G_f = 1$

$$\begin{aligned}
\bar{y}(s) &= \frac{\frac{k_p}{\tau_p s + 1} k_c (1 + \tau_D s)}{1 + \frac{k_p}{\tau_p s + 1} k_c (1 + \tau_D s)}\,\bar{y}_{sp}(s) \\
&= \frac{k_p k_c (1 + \tau_D s)}{\tau_p s + 1 + k_p k_c (1 + \tau_D s)}\,\bar{y}_{sp}(s) \\
&= \frac{k_p k_c (1 + \tau_D s)}{(\tau_p + k_p k_c \tau_D) s + (1 + k_p k_c)}\,\bar{y}_{sp}(s) \\
&= \frac{\left(\frac{k_p k_c}{1 + k_p k_c}\right)(1 + \tau_D s)}{\left(\frac{\tau_p + k_p k_c \tau_D}{1 + k_p k_c}\right) s + 1}\,\bar{y}_{sp}(s) \\
&= \frac{k_p' (1 + \tau_D s)}{\tau_p' s + 1}\,\bar{y}_{sp}(s)
\end{aligned} \quad \text{... (8.39)}$$

1. Response characteristics :

Equation (8.39) shows that the output response remains first-order, but with modified parameters

$$k_p' = \frac{k_p k_c}{1 + k_p k_c} \quad \text{... (8.40)}$$

and

$$\tau_p' = \frac{\tau_p + k_p k_c \tau_D}{1 + k_p k_c} \quad \text{... (8.41)}$$

2. Effect on gain :

Equation (8.40) shows that closed-loop gain k_p' is higher than open-loop gain.

3. Effect on time constant :

Equation (8.41) shows that closed-loop time constant τ_p' is larger than open-loop time constant τ_p. Therefore, closed-loop response is slower than the open-loop response. As k_c is increased the closed-loop time constant increases, which result in slow response.

Thus addition of D-control action to PI-control action brings stabilizing effect to the system. Due to this, comparatively higher value of k_c can be used (as compared to that for PI-controller) while maintaining moderate overshoots and decay ratio. This effect of addition of D-control action is shown in Fig. 8.18

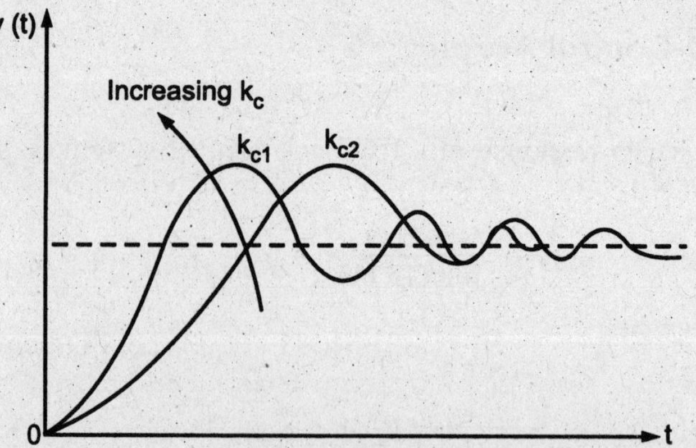

Fig. 8.18 : Effect of controller gain k_c on closed-loop response with PID-controller

8.8 EFFECT OF DIFFERENT CONTROL ACTIONS ON CLOSED-LOOP RESPONSE OF SECOND-ORDER PROCESS

8.8.1 Effect of P-Control

Uncontrolled second-order process is modelled as :

$$G(s) = \frac{\bar{y}(s)}{\bar{u}(s)} = \frac{k_p}{\tau^2 s^2 + 2\tau\zeta s + 1} \qquad \dots (8.42)$$

where, k_p = static gain

τ = natural period of oscillations = $\frac{1}{\text{natural frequency } \omega_n}$

ζ = damping ratio

The closed-loop servo response of a feedback control process is given by equation (8.28) as

$$\bar{y}(s) = \frac{G_p G_f G_c}{1 + G_p G_f G_c} \bar{y}_{sp}(s)$$

Substituting $G_p(s) = \frac{k_p}{\tau_p s + 1}$, $G_c = k_c$ (i.e. P-control) and $G_m(s) = G_f(s) = 1$,

the output response is given by

$$\bar{y}(s) = \frac{\dfrac{k_p k_c}{\tau^2 s^2 + 2\tau\zeta s + 1}}{1 + \dfrac{k_p k_c}{\tau^2 s^2 + 2\tau\zeta s + 1}} \bar{y}_{sp}(s)$$

$$= \frac{k_p k_c}{\tau^2 s^2 + 2\tau\zeta s + (1 + k_p k_c)} \bar{y}_{sp}(s)$$

$$= \frac{(k_p k_c / 1 + k_p k_c)}{\left(\dfrac{\tau}{\sqrt{1 + k_p k_c}}\right)^2 + 2\left(\dfrac{\tau}{\sqrt{1 + k_p k_c}}\right)\left(\dfrac{\zeta}{\sqrt{1 + k_p k_c}}\right) s + 1} \bar{y}_{sp}(s)$$

$$= \frac{k_p'}{\tau'^2 s^2 + 2\tau'\zeta' s + 1} \bar{y}_{sp}(s) \qquad \dots (8.43)$$

where,
$$k_p' = \frac{k_p k_c}{1 + k_p k_c} \quad \text{... (8.44)}$$

$$\tau' = \frac{\tau}{\sqrt{1 + k_p k_c}} \quad \text{... (8.45)}$$

$$\zeta' = \frac{\zeta}{\sqrt{1 + k_p k_c}} \quad \text{... (8.46)}$$

Response characteristics :

1. Equation (8.43) shows that the closed-loop response remains second-order, but with modified parameters k_p', τ' and ζ'.

2. Effect on k_p' : Equation (8.44) shows that $k_p' < k_p$, i.e. closed-loop gain is smaller than open-loop gain.

3. Effect on τ : Equation (8.45) shows that $\tau_p' < \tau_p$, i.e. closed-loop response is faster.

4. Effect on ζ : Equation (8.46) shows that $\zeta' < \zeta$, i.e. thc closed-loop response becomes faster. If $\zeta' > 1$, the response is overdamped, i.e. very sluggish. Therefore, if k_c is increased ζ' may decrease below 1 resulting in underdamped response which is faster but more oscillatory with increasing overshoot, decay ratio (as compared to that for lower values of k_c). Fig. 8.19 shows the closed-loop response of a second-order process with P-controller for increasing values of k_c.

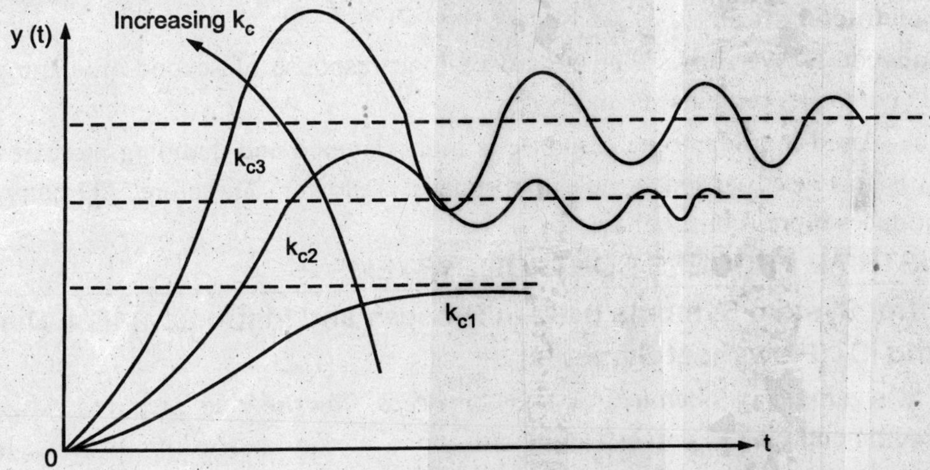

Fig. 8.19 : Closed-loop response of a second-order process with P-controller

8.8.2 Effect of PI-Control

Due to presence of integral control action, the closed-loop response of a second-order process with PI-controller shows third-order response characteristics. Such processes occur rarely in practice.

8.8.3 Effect of PD-Controller

The closed-loop servo response of a feedback control process is given by equation (8.28) as :

$$\bar{y}(s) = \frac{G_p G_f G_c}{1 + G_p G_f G_c G_m} \bar{y}_{sp}(s)$$

Substituting $G_p = \dfrac{k_p}{\tau^2 s^2 + 2\tau\zeta s + 1}$, $G_c = k_c (1 + \tau_D s)$ and $G_m = G_f = 1$

The output response is given by

$$\bar{y}(s) = \frac{\dfrac{k_p}{\tau^2 s^2 + 2\tau\zeta s + 1} k_c (1 + \tau_D s)}{1 + \dfrac{k_p}{\tau^2 s^2 + 2\tau\zeta s + 1} k_c (1 + \tau_D s)} \bar{y}_{sp}(s)$$

$$= \frac{k_p k_c (1 + \tau_D s)}{\tau^2 s^2 + (2\tau\zeta + k_p k_c \tau_D) s + (1 + k_p k_c)} \bar{y}_{sp}(s)$$

$$= \frac{\left(\dfrac{k_p k_c}{1 + k_p k_c}\right)(1 + \tau_D s)}{\left(\dfrac{\tau}{\sqrt{1 + k_p k_c}}\right)^2 s^2 + \left(\dfrac{2\tau\zeta + k_p k_c \tau_D}{1 + k_p k_c}\right) s + 1} \bar{y}_{sp}(s) \quad \ldots (8.47)$$

$$= \frac{k_p' (1 + \tau_D s)}{\tau'^2 s^2 + 2\tau\zeta' s + 1} \bar{y}_{sp}(s)$$

Response characteristics :

1. Equation (8.47) shows that the closed-loop response of second-order process with PD-controller remains second-order.
2. The closed-loop damping response is more damped and damping increases as k_c or τ_D is increased so that speed of response is slower. Therefore, PD control action produces more robust behaviour.

8.9 INDUSTRIAL PROCESS CONTROL SYSTEMS

8.9.1 Control System Symbols used in Process and Instrumentation Diagrams (P and ID) (Flowsheet Symbols)

While designing any chemical process, ***process flowsheet*** is prepared which shows different equipments in the process alongwith mass, energy and utility streams. If various process sensors, controllers and actuators are shown in correct positions on the flowsheet, it becomes the ***P and ID for*** the process. For this, instrumentation and control elements are indicated by special symbols, known as ***flow plan symbols***. These symbols are standard throughout the world so that design engineers in various disciplines can understand them.

ISA identification : The Instrumentation Society of America (ISA) has laid down a satisfactory system of symbols and identifications for industrial process instrumentation equipments. (Refer Table 8.1)

Table 8.1 : Letters of identification

Definition and permissible positions in any combination

Upper class letter	First letter (Process variable or actuation)	Second letter (Type reading or other function)	Third letter (Additional function)
A	–	Alarm	Alarm
C	Conductivity	Control	Control
D	Density	–	–
E	–	Element (primary)	–
F	Flow	–	–
G	–	Glass (no measurement)	–
H	Hand (actuated)	–	–
I	–	Indicating	–
L	Level	–	–
M	Moisture	–	–
P	Pressure	–	–
R	–	Recording (recorder)	–
S	Speed	Safety	–
T	Temperature	–	–
V	Viscosity	–	Valve
W	Weight	Well	–

Note 1 : When required, the following may be used *optionally as a first letter* for other process variables :

1. "A" may be used to cover all types of analyzing instruments.
2. Readily recognized self-defining chemical symbols such as CO_2, O_2, etc. may be used for these specific analysis instruments.
3. The self-defining symbol "pH" may be used for Hydrogen ion concentration.

Note 2 : Although not a preferred procedure, when considered necessary it is permissible to insert a lower case "r" after "F" to distinguish Flow Ratio. Likewise, lower case "d" may be inserted after "T" or "P" to distinguish Temperature Difference or Pressure Difference.

Table 8.2 gives complete general identifications of instruments and controllers on P and ID.

Table 8.2 Complete General Identifications Combination of letters)

		Recording	Indicating	Blind	Self-Actuated (Integral) Regulating Valves)	Safety (Relief) Valves	Recording	Indicating	Glass Devices for Observation only (No Measurements)	Recording	Indicating	Blind	Primary Element	Wells
		RC	IC	C	CV	SV	R	I	G	RA	IA	A	E	W
Temperature ...	T	RTC	TIC	TC	TCV	TSV	TR	TI	///	TRA	TIA	TA	TE	TW
Flow ...	F	FRC	FIG				FR	FI	FG	FRA	FIA		FE	///
Level ...	L	LRC	LIC	LC	LCV		LR	LI	LG	LRA	LIA	LA		///
Pressure ...	P	PRC	PIC	PC	PCV	PSV	PR	PI	///	PRA	PIA	PA	PE	///
Density ...	D	DRC	DIC	DC			DR	DI	///	DRA	DIA			///
Hand ...	H		HIC	HC	HCV		///	///	///	///	///		///	///
Moisture ...	M	MRC	MIC	MC			MR	MI	///	MRA	MIA	MA	ME	///
Conductivity ...	C	CRC	CIC				CR	CI	///	CRA	CIA	CA	CE	///
Speed ...	S	SRC	SIC	SC	SCV	SSV	SR	SI		SRA	SIA	SA		///
Viscosity ...	V	VRC	VIC				VR	VI	VG	VRA	VIA			///
Weight ...	W	WRC	WIC				WR	WI		WRA	WIA		WE	///

Note : The optional addition process variables given in footnotes of Table 8.1, when used, shall be combined with second and third letters as per above.

8.9.2 Surge Vessel Level Control Loop

Surge vessels are used to reduce the effect of flow rate variations between interconnected process units. Fig. 8.20 shows feedback control loop for controlling level of liquid inside a surge vessel or drum.

The control variables for this system are :

Measured variable (PV) – liquid level (h_m).

Manipulated variable (u) – outlet liquid flow rate (F_2).

Disturbance input (DV) – Inlet liquid flow rate (F_1).

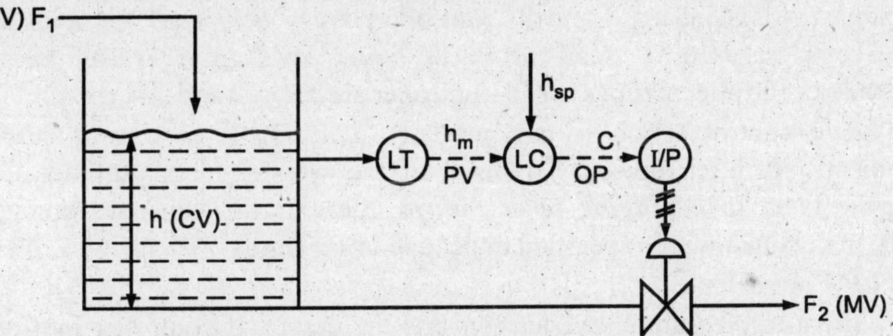

(a) Control achieved by manipulation of F_2

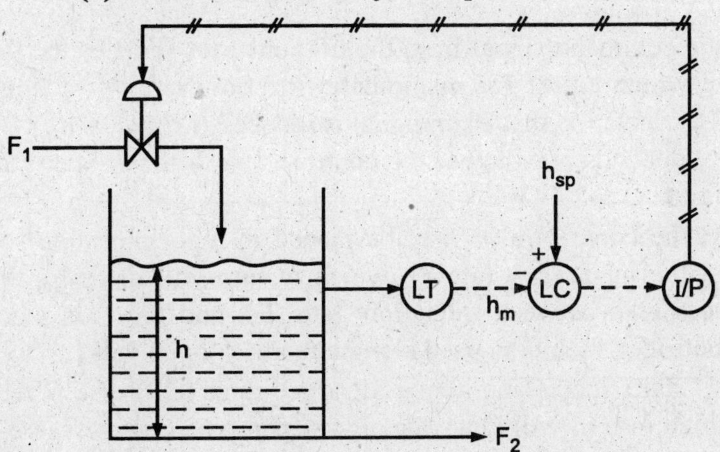

(b) Control achieved by manipulation of F_1

Fig. 8.20 : Surge vessel level control loop

The control loop consists of the following components :

1. Level Transmitter (LT) :

Level transmitter consists of a suitable level sensor (such as capacitance type, ultrasonic type or radiation type) whose output is converted by a transmitter to a measurement signal (h_m) appropriate for input to a controller, such as 4 to 20 mA. The range of transmitter can be adjusted.

2. Level Controller (LC) :

This is a simple feedback controller (P or PI-type) which compares the measurement signal (h_m) with the desired level signal (h_{sp}) and generate error signal (e) ($e = h_m - h_{sp}$).

In response to error signal, the level controller (LC) generates output (OP) or command signal (c) based on the predetermined control algorithm (P or PI). The process gain between PV (h_m) and MV (F_2) is negative, therefore direct-acting controller should be used with air-to-open control valve. As level (PV) starts increasing above PV, the output (OP) of a direct-acting controller will increase, which in turn will open the air-to-open type control valve, thereby increasing the outflow F_2, which ultimately results in decrease in level (PV) towards the set-point (h_{sp}). Standard P and PI controllers are widely used for level control. P-only controller can be used if small offset in liquid level (± 5%) can be tolerated. The recommended controller settings for PI-controller are : $k_c = 2$ and $1 < \tau_I < 5$.

Derivative control action is not normally used for level control because the level measurements are often noisy as a result of the splashing and turbulence of the liquid entering the tank. In ***averaging level control***, the exit flow changes gradually and level should be maintained within specified upper and lower limits.

3. The I/P Converter :

The current-to-pressure converter converts the output of controller into proportional air pressure (pneumatic) signal represented by (–//–//–//–) line in the range of 3 to 15 psig.

4. The Control Valve :

The pneumatic command signal from the I/P converter actuates the final control element, i.e. control valve which adjust (or manipulate) the flow rate F_2 of liquid leaving the tank (i.e. manipulated variable) so that error signal is reduced (i.e. $h_m \rightarrow h_{sp}$). The controller action (direct or reverse) depends on whether the control valve is air-to-open (fail-closed) or air-to-close (fail-open) type.

Alternatively, the control valve may be placed in input pipe line so that the command signal will adjust the input flow rate F_1, which in turn will drive h_m towards h_{sp} (i.e. zero error). The process gain between inlet flow rate (F_1) and level (h_m) is positive, therefore, reverse-acting controller should be used alongwith air-to-open valve.

As level (PV) starts increasing above SP, the output (OP) of a reverse-acting controller will decrease, which in turn will close the air-to-open type control valve, thereby decreasing the input flow rate F_1, which ultimately results in decrease in level (PV) towards the set-point (h_{sp}).

8.9.3 Temperature Control Loop

Fig. 8.21 shows a stirred tank heater in which liquid enters at a volumetric flow rate F_i at temperature T_i. The liquid is heated to temperature T by steam passing through steam coil at a flow rate F_{steam} and temperature T_{steam}. The tank is considered to be well stirred so that the temperature of the effluent is equal to the temperature of liquid inside the tank. It is desired to maintain temperature of liquid inside the tank at a desired value (set-point) T_{sp}. The control loop consists of the following components :

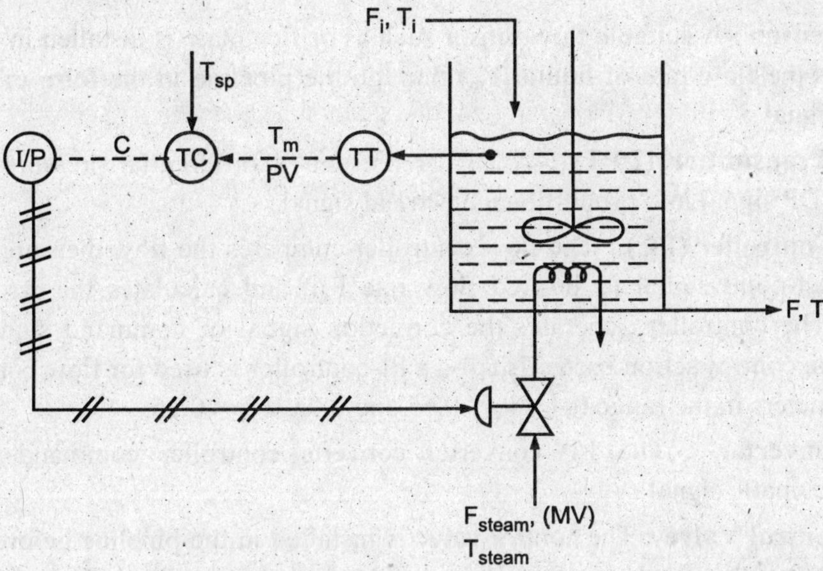

Fig. 8.21 : Feedback temperature control for a stirred tank heater

1. **Temperature Transmitter (TT)** : A suitable temperature sensor such as thermocouple is used to measure the temperature T of liquid inside the tank in terms of the measurement signal T_m.

2. **Temperature Controller (TC)** : Temperature controller compares the measured signal T_m with the set-point signal (T_{sp}) and calculate the error signal $e = T_m - T_{sp}$. In response to error signal, the controller will generate the output signal (OP) c. The I/P converter converts the correction signal (c) into proportional pneumatic signal. Usually PID-controller is used for temperature control with tuning parameters in the range

$$2 < k_c < 10, 2 < \tau_I < 10, \ 0 < \tau_D < 5$$

3. **The Steam Valve** : The steam valve acts as a final control element which is opened or closed by a pneumatic command signal from I/P converter so that steam flow rate is so adjusted (manipulated) that error is reduced or $T_m \rightarrow T_{sp}$.

8.9.4 Flow Control Loop

Fig. 8.22 shows a flow control loop used to control flow rate of liquid in the pipeline at the desired value F_{sp}. The control loop consists of the following components :

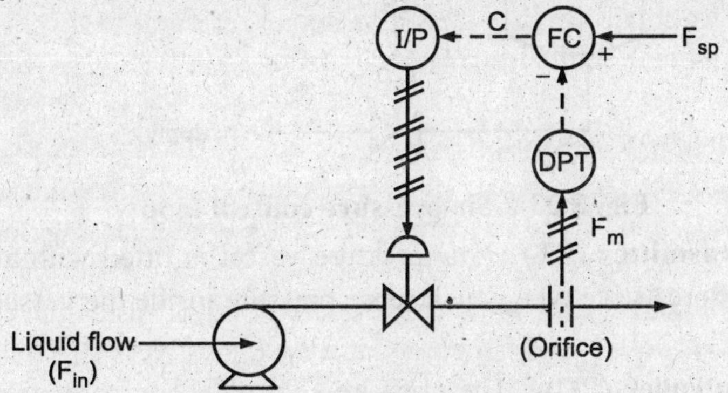

Fig. 8.22 : Flow control loop

1. **Flow sensor :** A suitable flow sensor such as orifice plate is installed in the pipeline which measures the flow rate of liquid (F_m) through the pipeline in the form of differential pressure (DP) signal.

2. **Flow Transmitter (DPT) :** A DPT represents a differential pressure transmitter which converts DP signal into proportional electrical signal.

3. **Flow Controller (FC) :** The flow controller compares the flow measurement signal (F_m) with the set-point signal (≡ desired flow rate F_{sp}) and calculates the error signal as $e = F_{sp} - F_m$. The controller generates the correction signal or command signal (c) (OP) depending on the control action used. Usually, a PI-controller is used for flow control having the tuning parameters in the range $0.4 < k_c < 0.65$ and $0.05 < \tau_I < 0.25$.

4. **I/P Converter :** The I/P converter converts controller command signal into proportional pneumatic signal.

5. **The Control Valve :** The control valve is installed in the pipeline before the orifice plate which acts as the final control element. The pneumatic signal from I/P converter changes the opening of control valve, which in turn adjust (or manipulate) the flow rate of liquid through pipeline to approach the set-point value.

8.9.5 Air Pressure Control Loop

Fig. 8.23 shows air pressure control loop used to control pressure inside the pressure vessel at the desired value P_{sp}. The control loop consists of the following components :

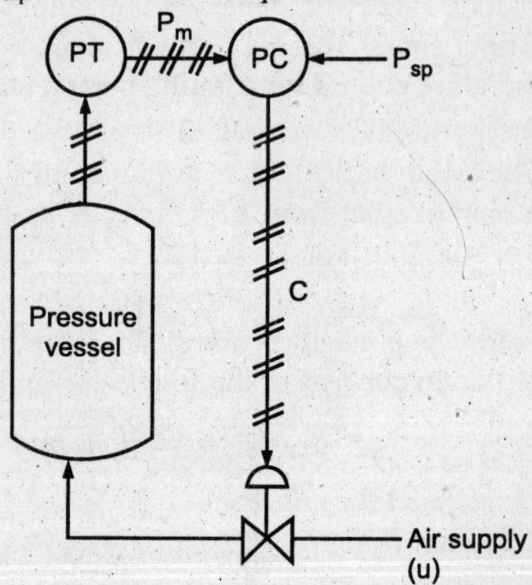

Fig. 8.23 : Air pressure control loop

1. **Pressure Transmitter (PT) :** The pressure vessel is fitted with a suitable pressure transmitter such as piezoresistive type which sense pressure inside the vessel and generate the measurement signal (P_m).

2. **Pressure Controller (PC) :** The pressure controller compares the measured signal (P_m) with the set-point pressure signal (P_{sp}) and calculates the error signal e (= $P_{sp} - P_m$). The

controller generates the correction or command signal (c) depending on the control action used. Usually, a PI-controller is used having tuning parameters in the range $0.5 < k_c < 2$ and $0.1 < \tau_I < 0.25$.

3. The Control Valve : The command signal from the controller operates the control valve which in turn adjust (or manipulate) the flow rate of air entering the vessel which affect the pressure inside the vessel to approach the set-point value.

8.9.6 Control of Continuous-Stirred Tank Reactor (CSTR)

A CSTR is used to carry out chemical reactions. These reactors have significant heat effects depending on whether the reaction carried out is exothermic or endothermic. Therefore, during the reaction, temperature inside the reactor increases (for exothermic reaction) or decreases (for endothermic reaction). It is essential to control the temperature inside the reactor so that the reaction occurs with desired yield of products. The temperature inside the reactor can be adjusted by manipulating flow rate of hot or cold liquid/stream circulated through a jacket around the reactor. Fig. 8.24 shows control loop for temperature inside a jacketed CSTR. The components of the control loop are :

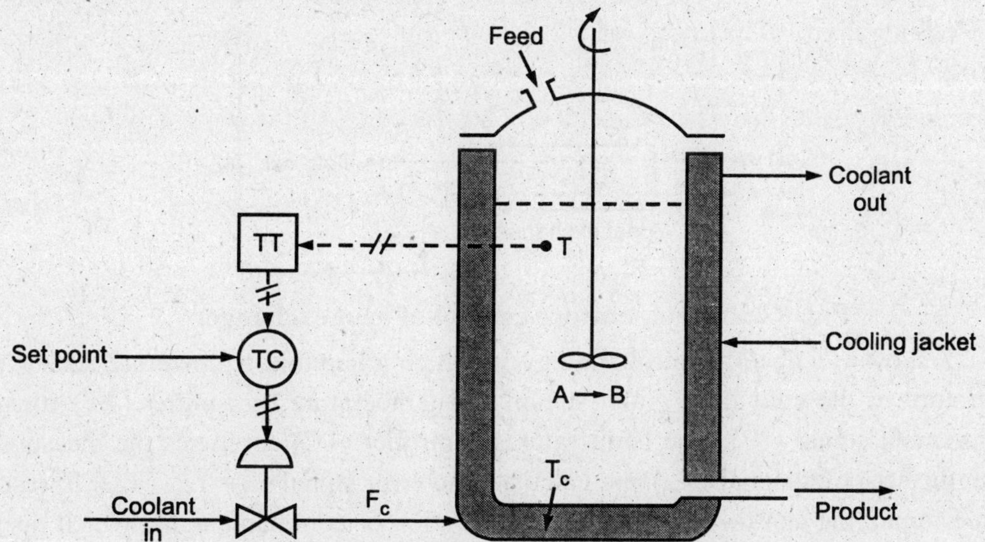

Fig. 8.24 : Temperature control of a jacketed CSTR

1. Temperature Transmitter (TT) : Temperature inside a CSTR is sensed by a suitable temperature sensor such as thermocouple as proportional e.m.f. signal which is then converted into suitable temperature measurement signal (T_m) by a transmitter.

2. Temperature Controller (TC) : Temperature controller compares the measurement signal (T_m) with the set-point signal (T_{sp}) and calculates the error signal $e = T_{sp} - T_m$. In response to this error signal, the controller generates correction or command signal (c) based on the control algorithm selected.

3. The Control Valve : The command signal opens or closes the control valve, so as to vary the flow rate of coolant (in case of exothermic reaction) or heating medium (in case of endothermic reaction), which in turn adjust the temperature inside the reactor closer to the desired set-point value T_{sp}.

8.9.7 Temperature Control of Heat Exchanger

Consider a counter-current double-pipe heat exchanger in which cold fluid at temperature T_{ci} is heated to temperature T_{co} by the hot fluid entering at higher temperature T_{hi}. The objective of control system is to maintain temperature of cold fluid outlet stream (T_{co}) inspite of the disturbances such as flow rates and temperatures of hot and cold fluids entering the heat exchanger.

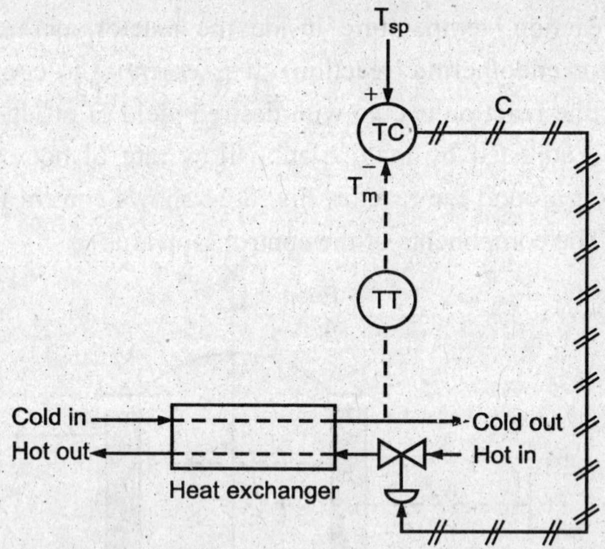

Fig. 8.25 : Temperature control of heat exchanger

Fig. 8.25 shows feedback control strategy in which a suitable temperature sensor sense the temperature of the cold fluid outlet stream and temperature transmitter (TT) convert it into measurement signal (T_m). The temperatures controller (TC) compares the measurement signal with the set-point signal (T_{sp}) and calculate the error signal e (= $T_{sp} - T_m$). In response to this error signal, the controller generate the correction or command signal which opens or closes the control valve installed in the pipe line of hot liquid entering the heat exchanger, which in turn manipulate the temperature of cold fluid outlet stream at the desired set-point value. In this feedback control strategy, controller action is based on the feedback from the temperature of cold fluid outlet stream.

8.9.8 Control of Distillation Column

Fig. 8.26 shows a binary distillation column used to separate a binary mixture (feed) A + B, where A is more volatile component than B. The feed is vaporized in the steam-heated reboiler and the vapours rise in counter contact with the fresh feed. During this intimate contact, the more volatile component A gets vaporized and rise into the column, while less volatile component B returns to the reboiler. The vapours leave from top of the column and get condensed in the water-cooled condenser, thereby giving the ***top product*** from the column which is rich in more volatile component A. The condensate is partly sent through the column as ***reflux*** which further enrich the top product. The ***bottom product*** (i.e. liquid leaving the reboiler) is rich in the less volatile product B. Thus, distillation column separates the binary feed (A + B) into top product (enriched in 'A') and bottom product (enriched in 'B').

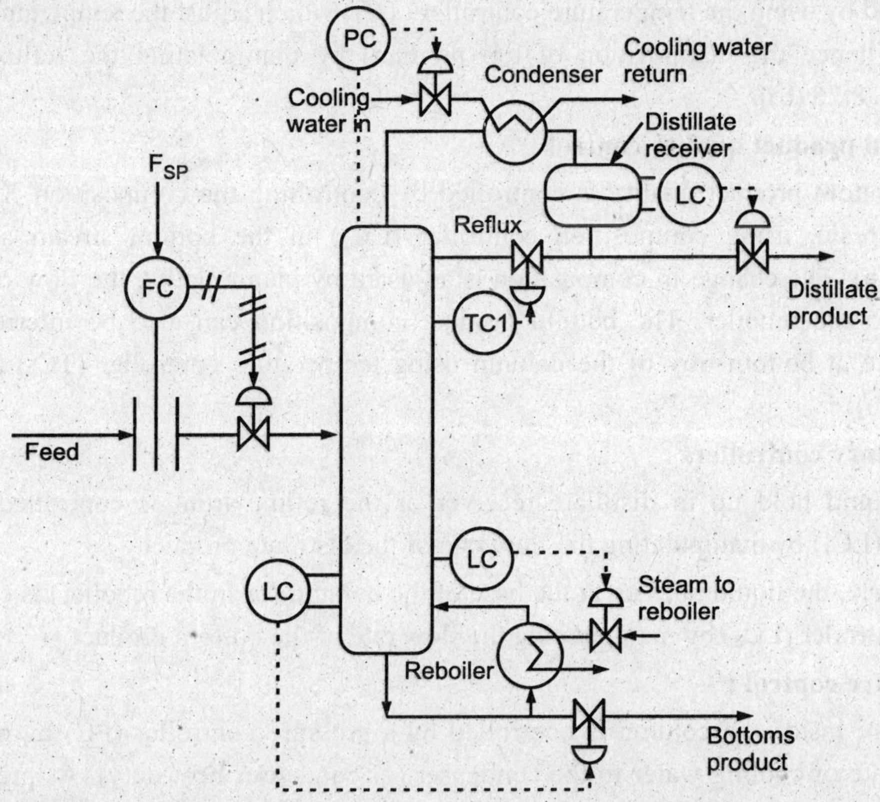

(a) Dual composition control (b) Dual temperature control

Fig. 8.26 : Control of distillation column

The objective of control system is to maintain the quality of top and bottom product (i.e. compositions) in spite of any variations in flow rate, temperature or composition of feed.

The top product quality is maintained by manipulating the flow rate of reflux stream entering the column, while the bottom product quality is maintained by manipulating the flow rate of steam supplied to the reboiler drum.

1. Top product quality control :

Fig. 8. a) shows composition control of the top product quality. In this method, the compositic he top product (X_A) is sensed using suitable analytical instrument. The composition controller (CC_1) compare the measurement signal X_{Am} with the desired value $(X_A)_{sp}$ and calculate error signal which is used to operate control valve installed in the reflux line. Thus, any change in composition of top product (X_A) is adjusted by manipulating reflux flow rate (as % of top product).

The composition controllers being costlier are not much used in practice. Instead, the top product composition can be inferred by measuring its temperature. Therefore, the quality of top product may be controlled by maintaining temperature of top tray of the column. This can be achieved by using the temperature controller (TC_1) which adjust the temperature of the top tray (and hence the composition of top product) by manipulating the reflux flow rate. [Refer Fig. 8.26 (b)].

2. Bottom product quality control :

The bottom product quality is controlled by controlling the composition X_B of bottom product stream, using composition controller (CC_2) in the bottom stream as shown in Fig. 8.26 (a). The change in composition is adjusted by manipulating the flow rate of steam supplied to the reboiler. The bottom product composition can also be inferred from the temperature at bottom tray of the column using temperature controller (TC_2) as shown in Fig. 8.26 (b).

3. Inventory controllers :

The liquid hold up in distillate receiver or the reflux drum is controlled by a level controller (LC_1) by manipulating the flow rate of the distillate product.

Similarly, the liquid hold up at the base of the column (or in the reboiler) is controlled by a level controller (LC_2) by manipulating the flow rate of the bottom product.

4. Pressure control :

Pressure inside the column is controlled by a pressure controller (PC) by manipulating the flow rate of cooling water to the condenser (or condenser heat duty). As pressure inside the column increases, the controller opens the control valve and increases the flow rate of cooling water to the condenser, thereby condensing more vapours, resulting in decrease in presence inside the column.

5. Feed control :

The flow rate of binary feed to the column is controlled by a flow controller FC.

8.9.9 Control of Compressor

Fig. 8.27 shows a reciprocating air compressor used to compress air (or any other gas) entering at atmospheric pressure P_a, which is to be compressed to higher pressure P. The pressure of compressed air can be controlled by using a pressure controller which adjust the exit pressure P near to the set value (P_{sp}) by manipulating the by-pass flow rate of air.

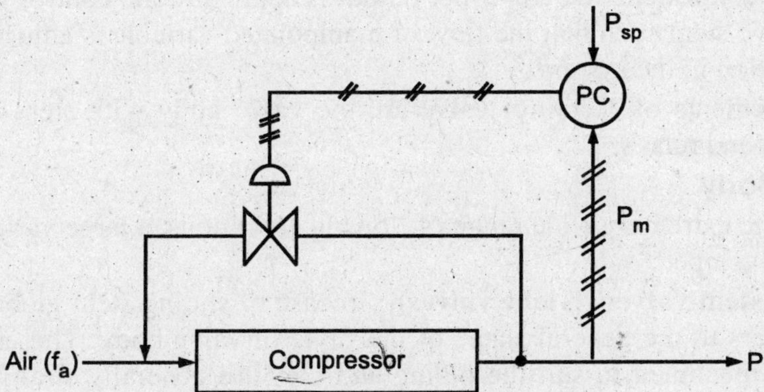

Fig. 8.27 : Control of compressor

8.9.10 Control of Adiabatic Plug Flow Reactor (PFR)

In a plug flow reactor (PFR), reactants are admitted continuously alongwith continuous product withdrawal. The reaction occurs as reaction mixture moves through the reactor. Therefore, temperature and composition of the mixture inside the reactor are functions of both, space and time. For an exothermic reaction with substantial heat effects, heat from the reactor effluent stream can be used to preheat the cold incoming feed to the reactor.

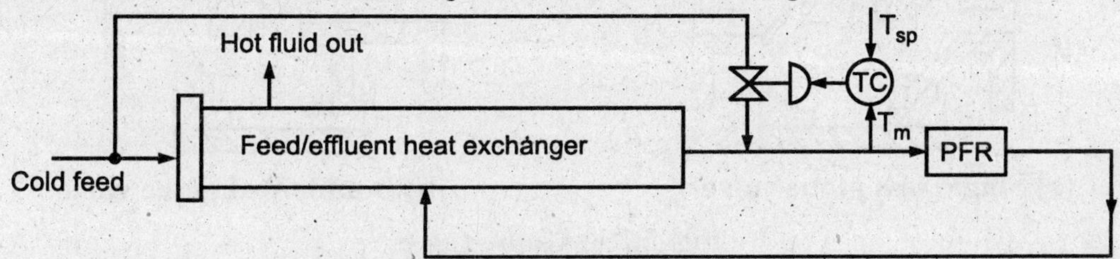

Fig. 8.28 : Control of adiabatic PFR

In adiabatic PFR, the total energy within the reactor should be maintained constant. For this temperature of the reaction mixture entering the reactor is controlled using a temperature controller (TC) by manipulating the flow rate of cold feed bypass as shown in Fig. 8.28.

8.10 CONTROL VALVES

Control valve is a valve with a pneumatic, hydraulic, electric (excluding solenoids) or other externally powered or manual actuator or that automatically fully or partially opens or closes the valve to a position dictated by signals transmitted from controlling instruments. A valve is essentially a variable orifice.

Control valves are used primarily to throttle energy in a fluid system and not for shut off purposes. The valve components should be designed to withstand high fluid velocity and turbulence for long periods without maintenance. There should be no lost motion between actuator to plug connection. Hence the internal moving parts of a control valve generally must have a heavy guiding and be more precisely aligned.

The actuator used in throttling service moves the valve stem, other sliding or rotary, to establish the desired port area through the valve. Valve positioner is used to improve the operation that also converts the controller output from electric to pneumatic or hydraulic. Thus control valve body assembly and the actuator are to be considered separately.

In automatic controllers, the controller output is applied to the control valve actuator that positions the valve stem such that the flow of manipulated variable is adjusted that brings the necessary correction in the system.

The basic elements of a control valve are the valve body with stem or plug, actuator, valve positioners and relays.

8.10.1 Valve Body

Because of the extremely wide range of flowing conditions, a large variety of valves have been specially developed.

1. Sliding stem valves (Globe valves) : In case of sliding stem globe valves, the term globe simply refers to the general shape of this style of valve body. The end connections of these valves are machined to suit the piping and they are generally straight through on the horizontal centre line, but may be offset or of angle configuration.

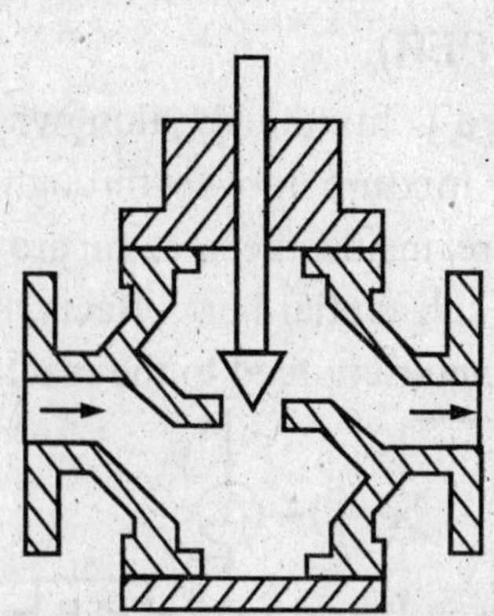

(a) Single seat globe valve

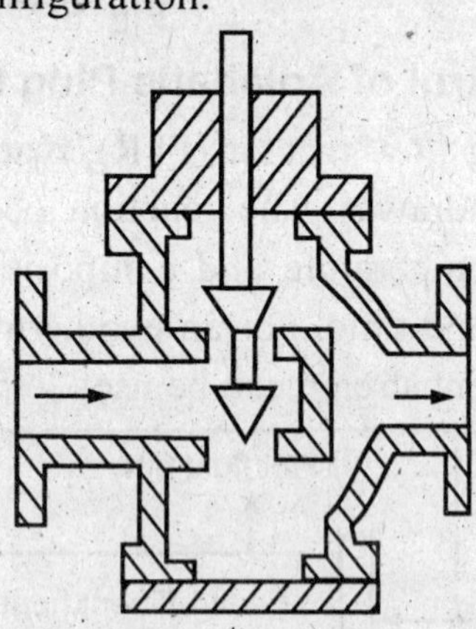

(b) Double seat globe valve

Fig. 8.29 : Globe valve

Single seat globe valve : Fig. 8.29 (a) shows a globe valve having top-guided, percentage shaped, lathe turned plug and threaded seat-ring. This valve is widely used in 3/4" and 1" sizes with full or reduced diameter trim, but the range of sizes extends to 10". For larger sizes, it is modified into quick change, cage-guided, horizontally split globe, threaded bonnet, bottom entry, top and bottom guided, designs.

Double seat globe valves : Fig. 8.29 (b) shows the double ported invertible globe body with a lathe machined parabolic shaped globe valve. Most designs have one port slightly larger than the other for ease of assembly. Skirt guided V-port plugs can be used for low pressure drop service.

Comparison between single port and double seat valves

Single seat valves	Double seat valves
1. Simple construction.	1. Complex construction.
2. Valve can be shut off to provide zero flow.	2. Valve cannot be shut off for zero flow.
3. Large thrust exerted on valve stem.	3. Comparatively little thrust exerted on stem.

2. Rotary stem valves : These valves are designed for general control service. The various designs of rotary stem valves are -

Eccentric disc globe valve : Fig. 8.30 shows a spherically faced plug segment, which is eccentrically mounted that rotates to engage the in-line seat ring. The shaft rotation is limited to 50°. A built-in rotary shaft extension for temperature dissipation and a flangeless body permit a wide range of applications with minimum design modifications.

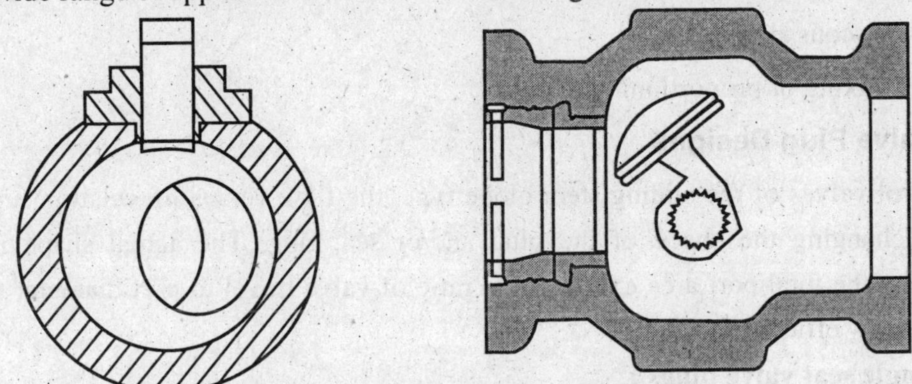

Fig. 8.30 : Eccentric disc globe valve

Advantage : The operating torque is low and the change in torque with valve opening at a constant pressure drop is small that permits flow-to-close or flow-to-open action to suit process requirements.

Butterfly valve : Fig. 8.31 shows swing-through design butterfly valve in a flangeless body designed for bolting between mating line flanges.

Fig. 8.31 : Butterfly valve

It has the metal disc pinned to a rotary shaft extending out through a stem seal assembly. Such swing-through valves are widely used for control where leakage flow between the disc and body can be tolerated, but this leakage flow should be less than 1% of maximum rating. This basic design is modified by inserting an elastomer liner in the body which may be a reinforced, molded, replaceable cylinder or it may be vulcanized directly into the body. The end corrections may be flanged, flangeless or built welded. The valves may be refractory-lined for service upto 2000°F.

3. Special valve designs : Following are the applications which demand special valve designs.

(a) Small flow measurement,

(b) Cryogenic service (for service at temperatures below – 100°C),

(c) High pressure service,

(d) For viscous slurries,

(e) For mixing or proportioning of fluids.

8.10.2 Valve Plug Designs

In control valves of the sliding stem globe type, the flow versus lift relationship may be altered by changing the shape of the plug and/or seat ring. The actual shape is greatly influenced by the total port area exposed, the ratio of valve travel to port diameter and other factors like flow efficiency.

1. Single seat valve plugs :

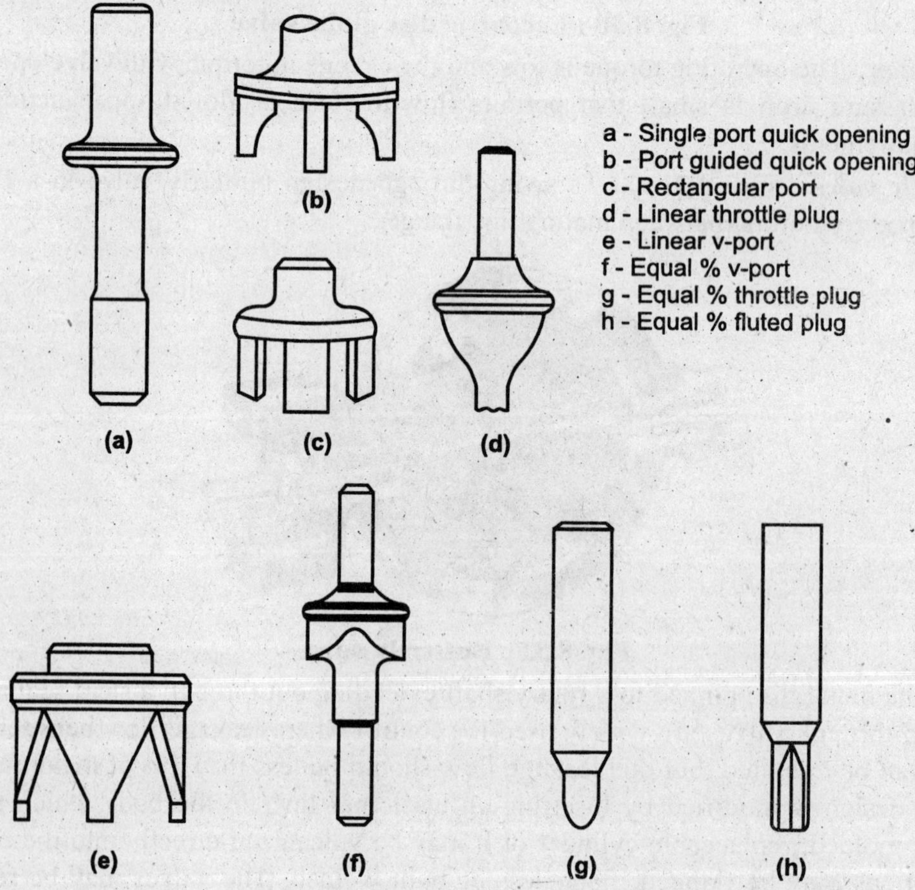

Fig. 8.32 : Single seat valve plugs

2. **Double seat valve plugs :**

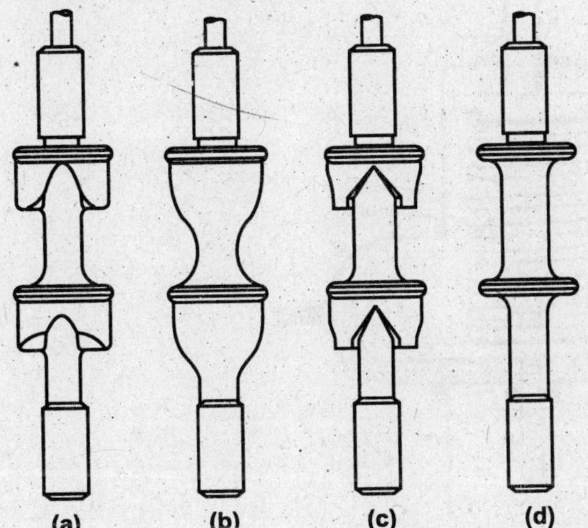

a - V-port plug with staggered ports

b - Lathe-turned valve

c - Straight-sided v-port design

d - Quick opening type

Fig. 8.33 : Double port plugs

8.10.3 Actuators

Actuator positions the valve plug in response to the controller signal. We discuss *spring-opposed diaphragm actuator* in detail.

The *direct-acting actuator* basically consists of a pressure-tight housing sealed by a flexible fabric reinforced elastomer diaphragm. A diaphragm plate is held against the diaphragm by a heavy compression spring. Signal air pressure from the controller is applied to upper diaphragm case, that exerts force on the diaphragm plate and the actuator assembly. By selecting proper spring rate or stiffness, load carrying capacity, and initial compression, desired stem displacement can be obtained for any given input signal. In case of *reverse-acting actuator* the actuator stem gets retracted with increase in pressure. The diaphragm is usually made of neoprene and a synthetic fabric reinforcement. Other actuators are - Bench range, piston actuator, motor actuator.

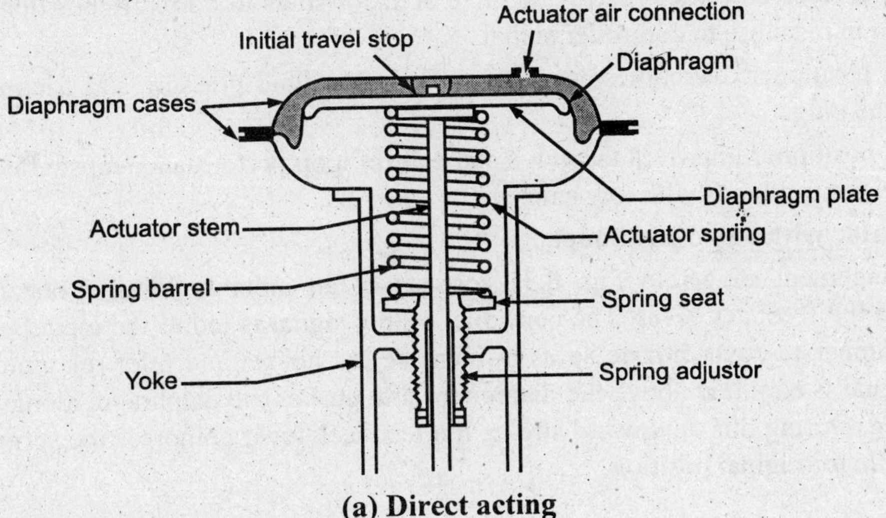

(a) Direct acting

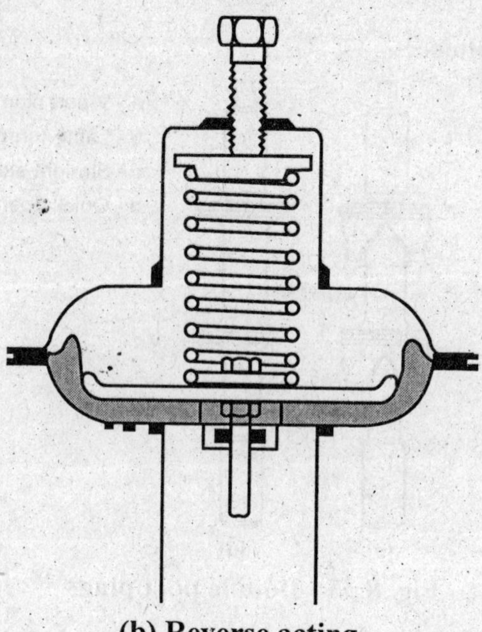

(b) Reverse acting

Fig. 8.34 : Spring diaphragm actuator

8.10.4 Valve Positioners

A valve positioner is a device designed either integrally or as an attachment to the actuator, positioners were first developed for use with spring actuators but now they are used with different actuators. When static frictional forces are large, then valve positioner is used alongwith the actuator so as to correctly position the valve stem in response to controller signal. The positioner compares the actuator stem motion with the signal from the controller and any deviation of the actual stem position from the desired position generates an error signal which activates a pneumatic relay that corrects the stem position.

Functions of valve positioner :

1. It is a servo-amplifier used with valve actuator so as to correctly position the valve stem in response to controller signal.
2. The positioner overcomes any effect of varying fluid pressure and frictional forces on the plug.
3. The positioner improves the valve and control loop performance most effectively for slow control loops with low gains.

Spring actuator with valve positioner :

The arrangement shown in Fig. 8.35 consists of an input bellows, a nozzle, a pilot amplifier and the feedback lever. The controller output signal is fed to the input bellows that causes the flapper to cover nozzle so as to increase the nozzle and pilot relay output. This amplified signal is admitted above the diaphragm that pushes the diaphragm alongwith valve stem and plug. During this downward stroke, the feedback lever compress the spring so as to bring the baffle to original position.

Finally the valve stem and plug assumes the correct position corresponding to the controller signal.

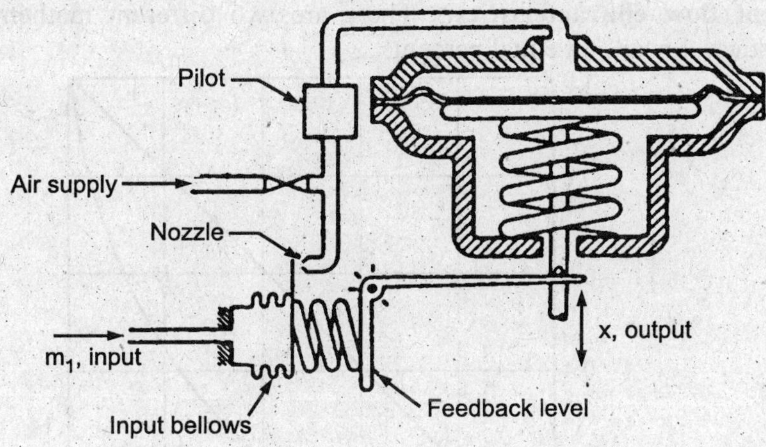

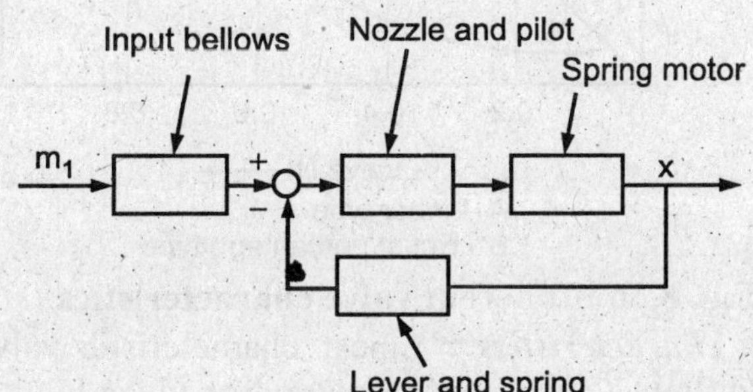

Fig. 8.35 : Spring actuator with positioner

Advantages of valve positioner :

1. When positioner is used with the actuator, it becomes power operated device. Due to this there is negligible effect of spring and diaphragm characteristics.
2. Hysteresis effect gets reduced with increase in the linearity.
3. The positioner enables the actuator to handle much higher static frictional forces.
4. Stem position is not affected much by variable thrust acting on it.
5. Since the controller signal is fed in the small area input bellows, the positioner improves the speed of response.

8.10.5 Control Valve Characteristics

The amount of fluid passing through a valve at any time depends upon the opening between the plug and seat. Hence there is a relationship between stem position, plug position and the rate of flow which is described in terms of flow characteristics of a valve. These valve characteristics are usually described graphically in terms of % flow vs. % valve lift. Two types of valve characteristics are considered viz. inherent and installed.

Inherent characteristics are plotted when constant pressure drop is maintained across the valve, while *installed characteristics* are plotted when valve is applied to particular flow system so that pressure drop across it changes with flow.

1. Inherent flow characteristics : There are two different mathematically derived flow characteristics - linear and equal percent.

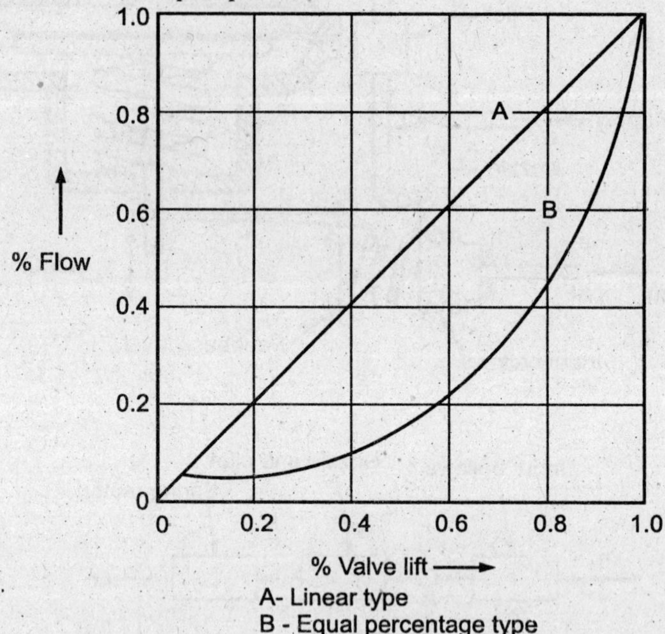

Fig. 8.36 : Inherent valve characteristics

Linear inherent flow characteristics : Linear characteristic valve has linear relation between valve opening and flow at a constant pressure drop given by -

$$\frac{Q}{Q_{max}} = \frac{S}{S_{max}}$$

where Q = Flow at constant pressure drop

S = Valve opening

For linear flow characteristic valve, for equal increments in valve travel there is equal increment of flow.

Equal percentage inherent flow characteristics : The general equation for flow vs. valve opening for equal percentage valve is

$$Q = Q_{min} \cdot R^{(S/S_{max})}$$

where Q = Flow at constant pressure drop

S = Valve opening

$$R = \text{Rangeability} = \frac{Q_{max}}{Q_{min}}$$

For equal percentage valves, equal increments in valve travel produce equal percentage changes in flow at a constant pressure drop based on the flow just before the stem position is changed. Hence the most important property of such valves is a constant percentage rate of flow change at constant pressure drop per unit change in valve opening through the major part of the stroke. When equal percentage characteristics are plotted on semilogarithmic graph, they appear linear.

The basic valve constructions give different valve characteristics as follows -

Quick-opening (or poppet type) characteristics (square root valve) : Curve 'A' of Fig. 8.37 shows inherent flow characteristic for a bevel-seated disk or plain flat disc poppet valve, which is not generally defined mathematically. For these valves the flow vs. valve lift relationship is approximately linear upto a valve opening equal to one-quarter of the port diameter or 60 to 70% of the body flow passage area. Hence the inherent characteristics may be considered so long as the valve lift is chosen to limit the maximum valve port area.

Usually for quick opening valve,

$$Q \propto \sqrt{S}$$

Straight-sided V-port or parabolic characteristics : Curve 'B' of Fig. 8.37 shows the inherent flow characteristics for a V-port valve.

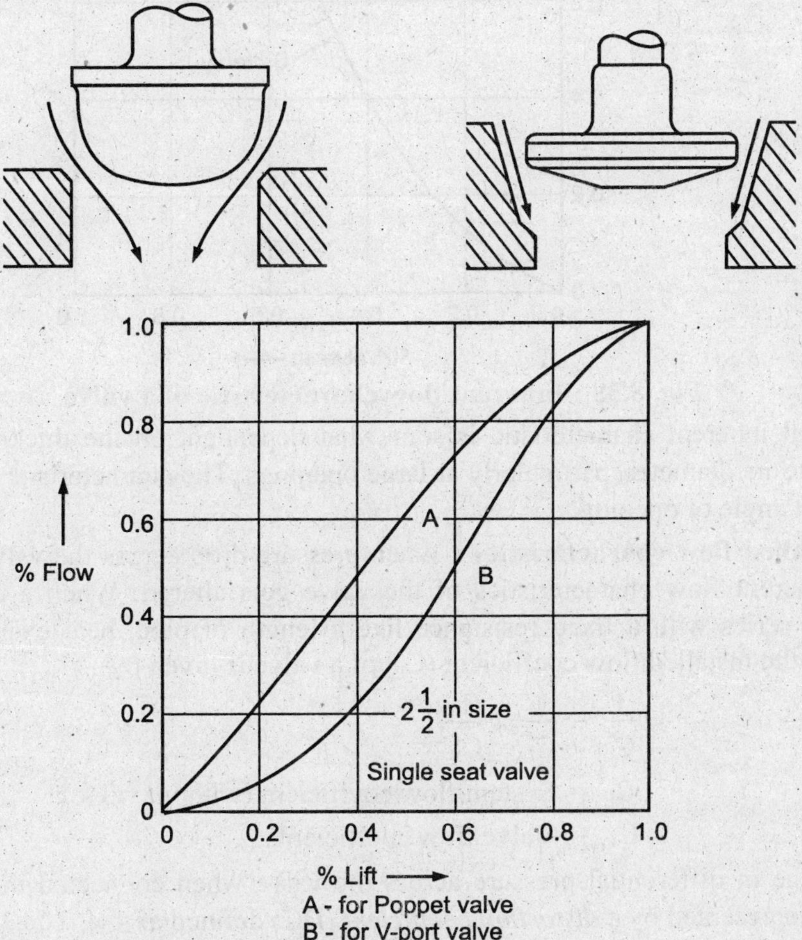

Fig. 8.37 : Plug shapes and their inherent characteristics

The flow vs. valve lift relationship of such a valve is given by

$$Q = Ky^2$$

where Q = Flow at constant pressure drop

y = Valve opening

K = Constant

For practical purposes, the characteristic approaches the equal percentage nature.

Rotary valve characteristic : Fig. 8.38 shows inherent flow characteristic of a butterfly valve which is approximately equal percentage.

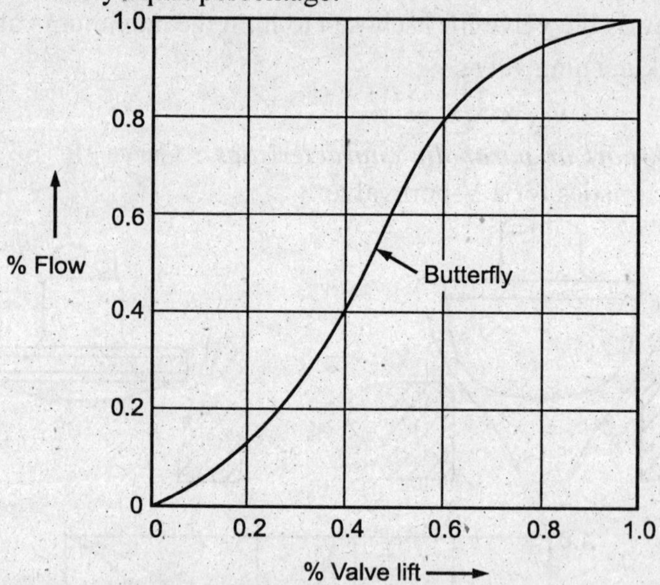

Fig. 8.38 : Inherent flow characteristic of a valve

The actual inherent characteristic is somewhat dependent on the thickness of the disk with respect to its diameter, particularly at large openings. The characteristic also varies with the maximum angle of opening.

2. Installed flow characteristics : When pressure drop across the valve changes with flow, the inherent flow characteristics of the valve gets altered. When a control valve is connected in series with a fixed resistance like a length of pipe, heat exchangers, mixing nozzles, etc., the installed flow coefficient (C_E) of a valve is given by

$$\frac{1}{C_E^2} = \frac{1}{C_L^2} + \frac{1}{C_V^2}$$

where C_L = System flow coefficient (without valve)

C_V = Valve flow coefficient

The change in differential pressure across the valve when connected in series with the resistance is represented by a *distortion coefficient* (DC) defined as -

$$DC = \frac{(\Delta P_t)_{min}}{(\Delta P_t)_{max}} \times \frac{(\Delta P)_V}{(\Delta P)_S}$$

where ΔP_t = Total pressure drop across (valve + system)

ΔP_V = Pressure drop across the valve

ΔP_S = Pressure across the system

DC is also expressed in terms of γ which represents the percentage of the total pressure drop across the valve at rated capacity. Hence for $\gamma = 100$ or DC = 1, the flow characteristic of a control valve matches with inherent nature. Fig. 8.39 shows the installed flow characteristics of a linear and equal percentage valve for different values of γ.

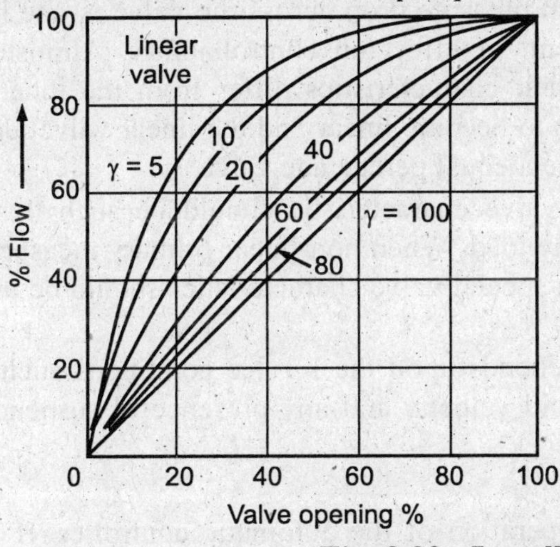

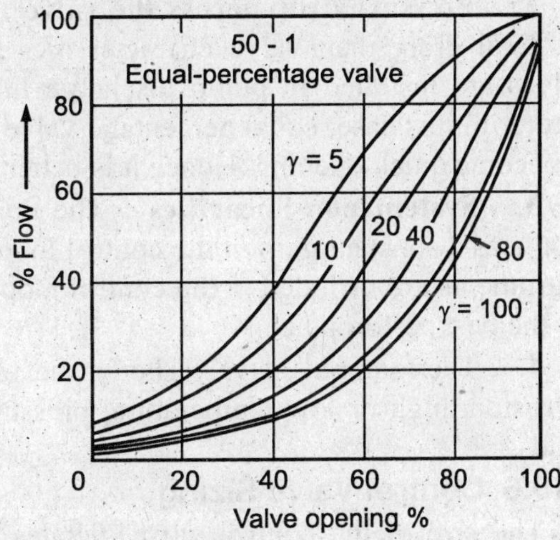

Fig. 8.39 : Installed flow characteristics

As percentage pressure loss across the valve increases, linear characteristic approaches quick opening characteristic shown in Fig. 8.39. As the percentage of system loss is reduced, equal percentage valve tends to approach a linear installed characteristic. This is the useful advantage of equal percentage valve because valves are often installed in flow systems with as little as 10 to 20% of the total drop available at the maximum rated flow.

Relation between valve gain and process gain : Control system is usually tuned or set at normal load levels, but process gain usually changes with load. Since one cannot afford to retune the controller for each new load condition, it is desirable to select the control valve that will compensate for these changes in process gain so as to maintain total gain constant.

1. If process gain decreases with increase in load, then control valve should be such that its gain increases with load. Hence for such processes equal percentage valve is used whose gain increases with load.
2. If process gain increases with load, then linear characteristic valve is used whose gain decreases with load.

Selection of control valve characteristics

There is no well defined selection procedure for the control valve characteristics that would be suitable for certain process. The selected control valve characteristics should provide equal control loop stability through full load range. Most control systems give optimum performance with linear installed characteristics. There are very few cases where the process itself will specifically indicate the use of equal percentage characteristics for optimum control. But in contrast to this, the use of equal percentage characteristic valves is greater than linear valves. The selection of control valve should be based on the process characteristics and nature of load changes. For more critical applications, the valve selection is based upon the following factors :

1. **Load variations :** At a constant pressure drop, for small load variations, the valve characteristics do not much affect the control performance. For linear load changes, linear valves are used.

2. **Pressure drop across the valve :** When pressure drop across the valve is one half the total drop, then valve characteristics have minor effect on controllability. Almost all valves are installed in pump discharge lines, their characteristics differ from the inherent nature. In this case, equal percentage valve tends to become linear and the linear valve tends to become quick opening. Hence it is better to select equal percentage valve.

3. **System non-linearities :** The control valve characteristic should be such that it produces a constant gain in the control loop at any load. When non-linear primary measuring instruments are included in the control loop, then special valve characteristics should be used for the best performance.

4. The material of valve body and plug depends upon the service conditions such as corrosion, high or low temperature, pressure, fluid velocity and any presence of suspended solids.

8.10.6 Control Valve Sizing

The size of the control valve dictates the operation of the automatic controller. If the control valve is oversize, the valve must operate at low lift and the lower part of the flow characteristic is most likely to be non-uniform in shape. On the other hand, if the control valve is undersize, the desired maximum flow demanded by the process may not be provided. The selection of proper port and body size for a control valve is based on calculation of the correct valve flow coefficient and consideration of number of factors described below :

1. **Rangeability and turndown :** *Rangeability* of a control valve is the ratio of maximum controllable flow to minimum controllable flow. *Turndown* of a control valve is the ratio of a normal maximum flow to minimum controllable flow. *Normal maximum flow* is generally taken as 70% of maximum flow. For valve sizing, the maximum flow considered should be the required maximum flow, and not the full capacity of the valve. The valve capacity is generally set 25 to 60% above the required or normal maximum flow. The maximum flow should be chosen realistically and must be carefully related to pressure drop.

2. **Pressure drop across the valve :** A control valve is essentially a variable orifice and hence its flow equation is given by -

$$Q = C_V \sqrt{\frac{\Delta P}{G}} \quad \ldots\ldots \text{(for liquids)}$$

where ΔP = Pressure drop across the valve

and C_V = Valve coefficient $= 760 \times C_V \sqrt{\frac{P_1}{RT_1}}\,(\Delta P) \quad \ldots\ldots$ (for gases)

G = Specific gravity

P_1, T_1 = Upstream absolute pressure and temperature

If the valve is installed in a long piping, then pressure drop across the valve should be estimated at maximum flow with reasonable allowances for pressure losses in series with the valve. It is assumed that one-third of the total system pressure drop should be absorbed by control valve at maximum flow. In other words, *reasonably good control can be achieved with as little as 15% of total system pressure drop across valve.*

3. **Cavitation :** This is an undesirable phenomena which can occur in control valves in liquid service. Cavitation is caused by transformation of a portion of liquid into a vapour phase during rapid acceleration of fluid as it passes through valve orifice and subsequent collapsing of these bubbles on downstream side. These collapsing vapour bubbles can cause localized pressures upto 10,000 psi that causes rapid wearing of valve body or outlet piping.

8.11 INSTRUMENTATION & CONTROL IN POLYMER PROCESSING TECHNOLOGY

8.11.1 The Extrusion Process

Introduction : Extrusion is any process in which a material is forced through a shaped orifice, with the material solidifying immediately to produce a continuous length of constant cross-section. This is very similar to squeezing toothpaste from a tube. In plastics extrusion, dry thermoplastic material is first loaded into a hopper, then fed into a long heating chamber through which it is moved by the action of continuously revolving screw. At the end of the heating chamber the molten plastic is forced out through a small opening or die with the shape desired in the finished product. As plastic extrusion comes from the die, it is fed into a conveyor belt where it is cooled by blowers or by immersion water. In large polymerization plants, extruders are fed hot melts which is then pressurized through a plate having large number of holes. Thus, 93% of the energy is required for heating and melting the feedstock into a hot viscous liquid.

Extruder control : The increasing demands of obtaining greater throughput with the increased quality from extrusion products have made accurate measurement and control of process parameters shown in Fig. 8.40.

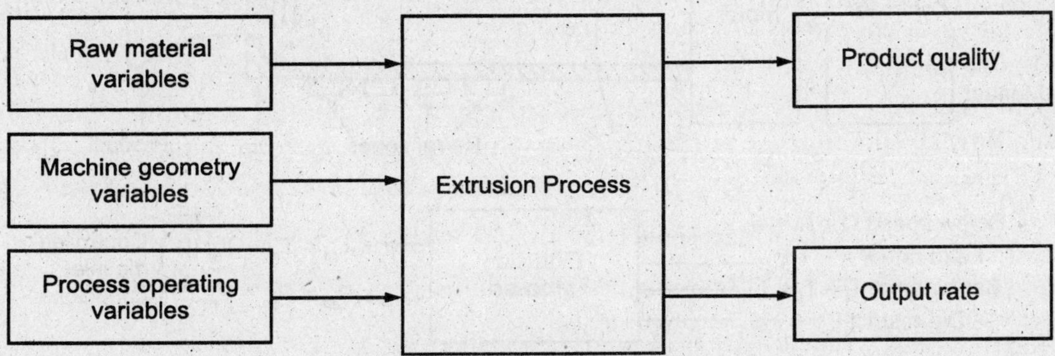

Fig. 8.40 : Extrusion process

There are different types of input variables affecting the process and causing changes in output.

(a) The machine geometry variables : They include design of screw, die, heaters, etc. which are under the control of machine manufacturer. The insufficient attention to design of machine elements affects controllability.

(b) Process operating variables : These include : (i) the machine variables like barrel and die temperature profiles, screw speed, pressure, etc. and (ii) process variables like melt temperature and pressure extending to homogeneity and viscosity.

(c) Raw material variables : These include properties as specific heat, thermal conductivity, friction characteristics and bulk density.

Every possible attempt is made to control those variables. The conflicting requirements of greater quality and higher throughputs make it essential to control all machine variables very tightly and make control of process variables more desirable. The latter part requires complex transducers and a good knowledge of machine control interrelationships.

1. Temperature control of an extruder : Fig. 8.41 shows control of die inlet conditions with transducers for melt pressure and temperature. For this the input variables like screw speed, feed rate, barrel temperature, die restrictor valve position are measured and controlled. The control scheme consists of a well insulated melt-temperature thermocouple which is properly sited with a melt pressure transducer close to it. The control system controls the barrel zone and die zone temperature as it is essential to maintain the viscosity of material constant. The deviations in viscosity cause degradation of material or produce undue stress on the screw and associated drive.

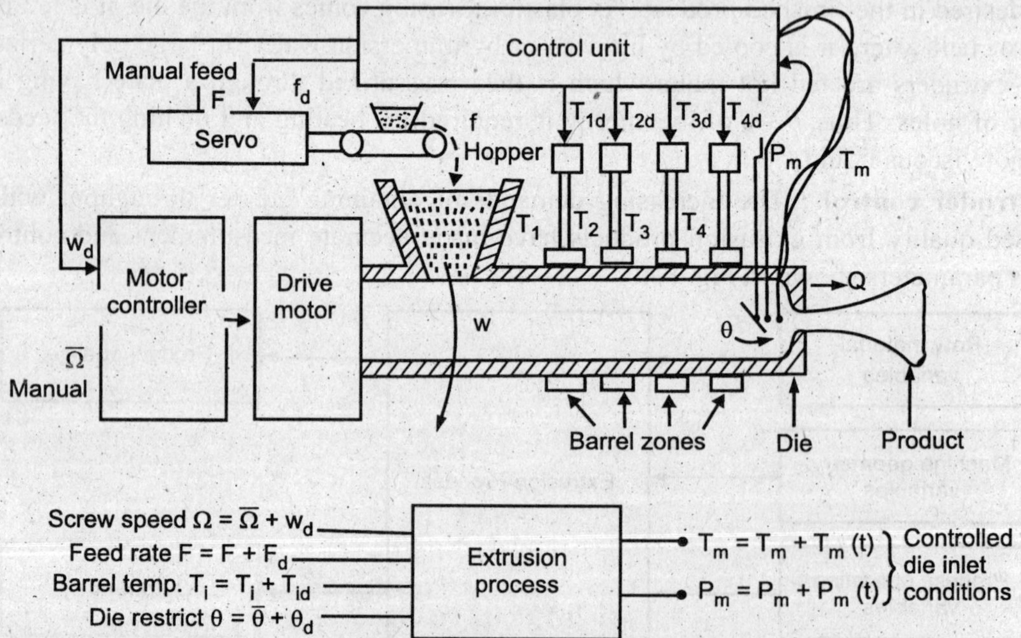

Fig. 8.41 : Extrusion process control

Temperature sensors : In plastics processing both base metal thermocouples (like nickel chrome/nickel aluminium or iron/constantan) having normal tolerance of 13°C over their working range of 0 - 400°C are used. The thermocouple is placed as close to the melt as possible (i.e. deep in the barrel) both from steady state and transient conditions. Such deep thermocouple cannot achieve good response to loop set-point changes, hence another shallow couple is used to get quick response which is in cascade with deep couple.

2. Melt pressure control : The melt pressure being the result of temperature, amount of shear history and the degree of mixing in the machine, it is difficult to control. The melt temperature and pressure are measured and controlled at the output from the extruder that ensures the melt delivery having same pressure, temperature and shear history at all times in order for the die delivery to be constant and stable. Thus machine parameters are both interdependent and strongly dependent on the machine settings and how it is operated.

3. Control of output rate : The output rate of material from an extruder can be controlled by changing the screw speed or by changing the resistance at the head end of the machine. But each of these methods has other effects like change in shear history of melt, which in turn alter the machine delivery rate. Increased screw speed alters heat-transfer conditions in the machine and the melting pattern, which also initiates the condition called surging.

4. Downstream control : The downstream units to be controlled are the die, roll stacks, vacuum sizers and the pulling system. In case of sheet lines, adjustable dies are used, that change their opening in response to signal information from a ganging system used on the sheet.

The sizers are used to fix one dimension of tubing (usually OD). Hence there is one primary dimension, namely, the wall thickness, to be controlled by control unit. The control unit may deliver information for correction of wall eccentricity. In that case, the ruler information will be derived from the wall thickness measurement. The eccentricity information can be fed back to a die adjuster to move the pin or bushing to make the inner and outer wall concentric.

The puller units have their speed varied to adjust the dimensions of the product. For this the units are equipped with drive-control systems that can vary the drive speed in conformance with a control signal. The dimensions are sensed by mechanical contact, nuclear or optical sensors using lasers.

8.11.2 Control of the Injection Moulding Process

Introduction : In this process, melted or plasticized plastic material is injected or forced into a mould where it is held until removed in a solid state, duplicating the cavity of mould. The mould may consist of a single cavity or a number of similar or dissimilar cavities, each connected to flow channels or "runners" that direct the flow of the melted plastic to the individual cavities. The injection moulding basically consists of three basic operations.

(i) **Plasticizing or plastication :** Raising the temperature of the plastic to a point where it will flow under pressure. This is usually done by simultaneously heating and masticating the granular solid until it forms a melt at an elevated and uniform temperature and uniform viscosity. This is accomplished in the cylinder of machine equipped with a reciprocating screw.

(ii) **Allowing the plastic to solidify in the mould :** The limitations of the hydraulic circuitry used in the actuation of plunger and the complicated flow paths involved in the filling of the mould and cooling action in the mould.

(iii) **Opening the mould** to eject the plastic after keeping the material confined under pressure as the heat is removed to solidify the plastic and freeze it permanently into the shape desired, for thermoplastics. The other operations involved in injection moulding are clamping the mould, ejecting the part, feeding the machine etc.

The basic components of an injection moulding systems are - blending, drying, hoppering, metering, plastication, injection, cooling and ejection. The parameters to be controlled are : (1) Temperature of barred and melt, (2) Injection pressure.

1. **Temperature control of barrel and melt :** The melt temperature depends on screw RPM, back pressure and externally applied heat. The temperature decides the viscosity of the melt and the speed and pressure of injection. It is found that one-third of the melt temperature is derived from external heat. The areas of temperature control are :

(i) **Barrel zones :** For sensing barrel temperature, thermocouples are mounted as deep in the barrel as is practical.

(ii) **Hot runners.**

(iii) **Mould :** Temperature control of both halves of the tool is essential for high quality, consistent moulding.

(iv) **Hopper :** Temperature controlled air is blown through material fed to hopper that improves the moulding consistency. The temperature maintained in hopper could be close to the plasticizing temperature of the material.

(v) **Melt temperature :** All plastic materials can be correctly processed only within a certain range of temperatures which varies from material to material. Significant material and energy savings can be achieved by correctly applying the right type of control equipment.

Control system : From a control view point, an injection moulding machine consists of a number of zones, each equipped with a temperature sensor and a controller, that regulates the heat input to the zone so as to maintain the desired temperature. A typical small machine shown in Fig. 8.42 has three or four barrel zones and a nozzle zone. The barrel zones are heated electrically using band heaters strapped around the barrel. Thermocouple must be placed as close to the melt as possible, i.e. deep in the barrel.

The on-off controller with a shallow thermocouple may give acceptable results. The P-controller cannot control the machine temperature precisely unless supply voltage is constant. A 'PD' controller may permit the use of deep thermocouples and a narrow PB that gives a tolerable control. Due to unstability problems, PI controllers are not generally applied to plastics processing equipment.

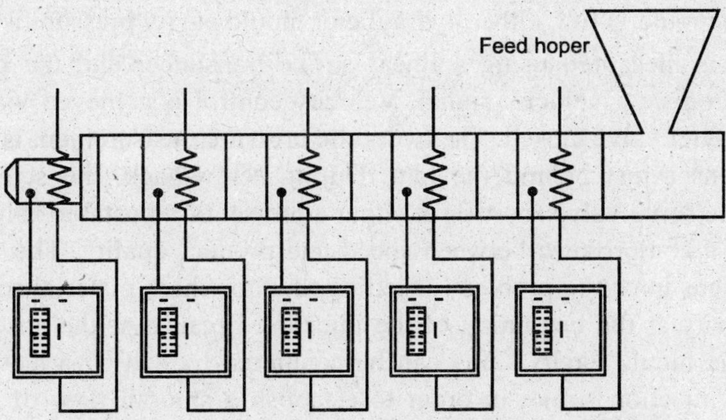

Fig. 8.42 : Temperature control of barrel zones

2. **Injection pressure and velocity control :** In order to achieve consistently good mouldings, the requirement is that the speed of plastic entering the mould is such that a constant velocity wavefront is generated until the mould is full. Once the mould is full, pressure control is required during the setting and shrinkage of the product. Correct settings ensure consistency, strength, surface finish, material savings decreased cycle times. Fig. 8.43 shows the pressure and velocity control system. During injection the actual velocity rate of the ram is under closed loop control by modulating the hydraulic oil flow to the injection ram by means of a servo valve. The hydraulic pressure will vary to achieve the desired velocity.

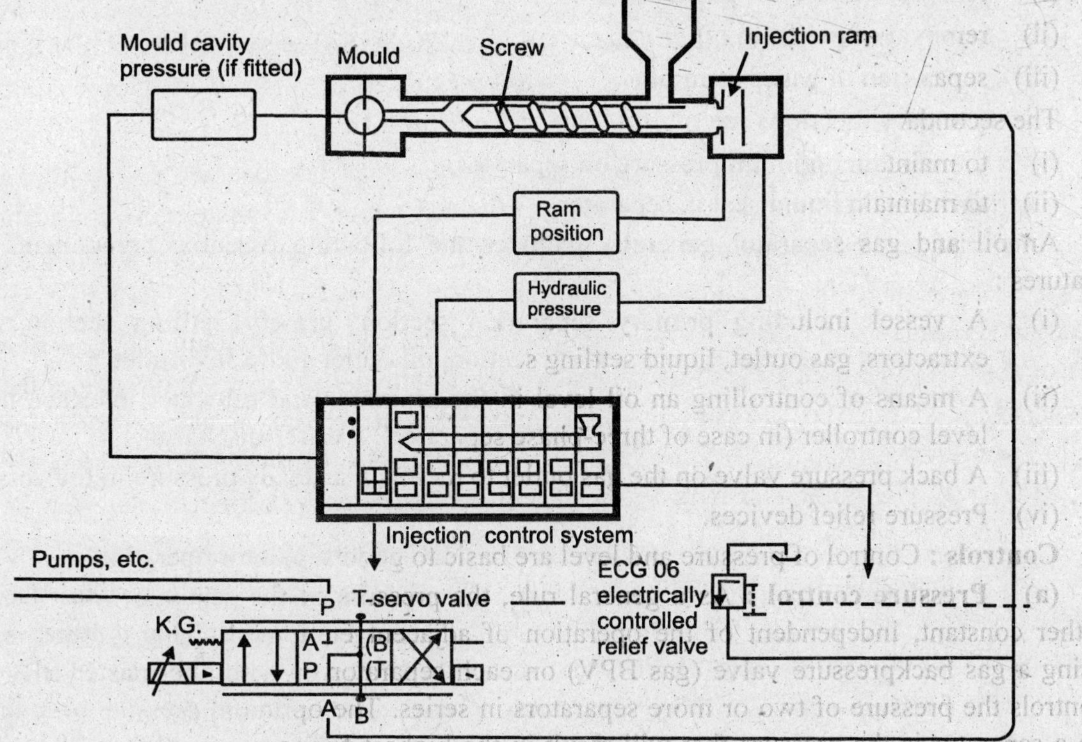

Fig. 8.43 : Velocity/pressure control system

As soon as the mould is full, either hydraulic or mould cavity pressure is controlled.

Ram position is measured using a linear stroke transducer and the position signal is differentiated to produce a velocity signal. Velocity control is achieved via the servo valve (port A) with the relief valve closed. The hydraulic pressure measurement is best achieved by positioning the sensor just behind the ram. During screw-back, the screw speed can be controlled using the servo valve (port B) at either a pre-set or adjustable value. The setting of injection speed is a compromise between speed and product quality. The moulding having narrow cross-sections have the problem of jetting, due to which material squirts, rather than flows, into the cavity at the beginning of the injection because of the absence of any back pressure within the mould cavity. This can be countered by setting a slow speed over the initial part of the injection stroke in order to establish a smooth flow of material into the mould.

8.12 INSTRUMENTATION AND CONTROL OF OPERATIONS FOR SEPARATION, TRANSPORTATION AND STORAGE OF OIL AND GAS

8.12.1 Controlling Oil and Gas Separators

Oil and gas separator is a pressure vessel used for separating well fluids produced from oil and gas wells into gaseous and liquid components. A separating vessel may be referred to as the stage separator, trap, knockout drum, flash chamber, expansion vessel, gas scrubber, filter. The primary functions of oil and gas separators are :

(i) removal of oil from gas,

(ii) removal of gas from oil,

(iii) separation of water from oil,

The secondary functions are :

(i) to maintain optimum pressure on separator,

(ii) to maintain liquid seal in separator.

An oil and gas separator generally includes the following essential components and features :

(i) A vessel including primary separation section, gravity settling section, mist extractors, gas outlet, liquid settling section, oil outlet and water outlet.

(ii) A means of controlling an oil level in the separator and oil/water interface liquid level controller (in case of three-phase separator), a water-discharge.

(iii) A back pressure valve on the gas outlet to maintain a steady pressure in the vessel.

(iv) Pressure relief devices.

Controls : Control of pressure and level are basic to good separator operation.

(a) Pressure control : As a general rule, the pressure of the separator must be held rather constant, independent of the operation of adjacent equipment. This is obtained by using a gas backpressure valve (gas BPV) on each separator or with one master BPV that controls the pressure of two or more separators in series. The optimum pressure to maintain on a separator is the pressure that will result in the highest economic yield from the sale of the liquid and gaseous hydrocarbons.

Effective pressure control can be achieved by using the proportional controller without reset. The offset due to flow rate changes normally present no problem, provided the vessel design processor and high pressure alarm or shut-down controls are consistent with the range of pressure expected for the proportional setting and offset anticipated. Fig. 8.44 (a) and (b) show the gas BPV equipped with P-controller.

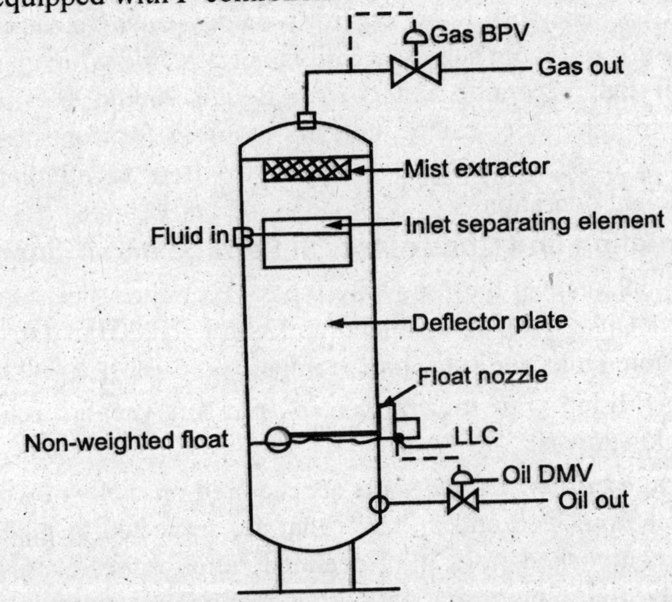

(a) Schematic of vertical two-phase oil and gas separator

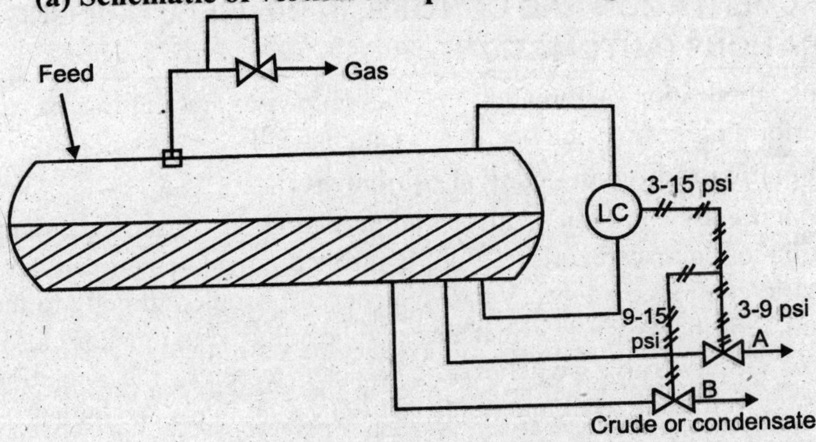

(b) Horizontal separator

Fig. 8.44 : Separator controls

(b) Liquid level control : For getting efficient vapour-liquid separation, the liquid level should be held relatively constant. Fig. 8.44 (a) shows a simple level control system which consists of a float nozzle that senses the actual level. The liquid level controller (LLC) receives this measurement signal, compares with the set point and generates correction signal in response to the deviation between actual and set value. This correction signal adjusts the opening of oil diaphragm motor valve (DMV) that discharges oil so as to maintain its level constant. Fig. 8.44 (b) shows a split-range control of horizontal separator, which has two outlet DMV's A and B. For rather steady liquid input only valve A is operating which is fully closed at pilot pressure of 3 psi and fully open at 9 psi. It would be set at a low percentage of P-control to minimize offset. If liquid level rises due to inlet fluctuations, at 9 psi valve 'B' starts to open to relieve the liquid so as to maintain the level. Once level reaches the desired value, valve 'B' closes. The split range control provides sensitive routine level control plus the added capability for relieving surges, which is not possible with a single valve system. It should be apparent that separator and control design should be compatible because a substantial portion of separator volume may be required for control purposes. Failure to properly coordinate process and control functions result in too frequent alarms and shut-downs and/or inefficient operation.

8.12.2 Instrumentation and Control for Oil Storage and Transportation

The oil storage tanks are of the following types : (i) bolted-steel tanks, (ii) welded-steel tanks, (iii) flat-sided tanks, (iv) field-welded tanks, (v) fixed roof tanks, (vi) floating roof tanks, (vii) cone-bottom tanks and (viii) pipe storage.

Storage tanks are fitted with mixers, heaters, pressure/vacuum relief devices, ganging devices, vents and blowdowns.

Venting of storage tanks : Larger vents are required on tanks in which oil is heated, on tanks that receive oil from well and on tanks that are subjected to pipeline surges. Normal venting shall be accomplished by a pilot-operated relief valve, a pressure relief valve, a pressure vacuum valve, or an open vent with or without a flame arresting device.

8.13 INSTRUMENTATION AND CONTROL IN OIL-WELL DRILLING OPERATIONS (AUTOMATION)

In a simple application, automation may be defined as linking together instruments and controls to perform predetermined operations automatically.

1. Automatic production - control equipment :

(i) Automatically controlled valves and accessories : Automatic control valves can be grouped into three major categories : fluid controlled valves, electrically controlled valves and fluid-electric-controlled valves. Valve-switches are coupled directly to the valve stem to sense the position of the valve. The switches may be adjusted to open or close a circuit as the valve opens or closes. Valve switches also indicate remotely the operational position of control valves on wellheads, well manifolds, metering tank inlets and outlets.

(ii) Automatic production programmers : These are scheduling devices that control the particular times and lengths of time that operating functions are performed. The simplest form is a time-cycle controllers, which basically consists of a clock with a timing wheels, containing a number of programming points at regular intervals around its circumference. The clock may be electrically driven, gas driven or mechanically driven.

The wellhead control can be obtained from remote location, provided all the automatic production programmers are actuated electrically.

2. Production safety controls : In some respect, virtually all automatic control equipment is also safety control equipment. This is because in case of loss of power from the controlling energy medium, the controls must return to the safest position. The safety controls involve high/low-pressure safety shut-in valves, excess flow valves, pressure and temperature switches and pump-off controls.

3. Automatic quantitative measurement : The liquid flow measurements are done with the help of positive volume meters, positive displacement meters, inferential meters.

4. Gas measurement : The primary device for gas volume measurement is the orifice meter alongwith a mercury manometer or the bellows-type chart recorder. Other types of gas measurement devices include positive-displacement meters, gas-flow computers, turbine meters and vortex meters.

5. Automatic sampler : It is a device that removes a representative volume of fluid from a moving stream and retains it in a container for later processing and analysis.

6. Automatic well-control : Wells may be controlled at the wellhead or at the well manifold.

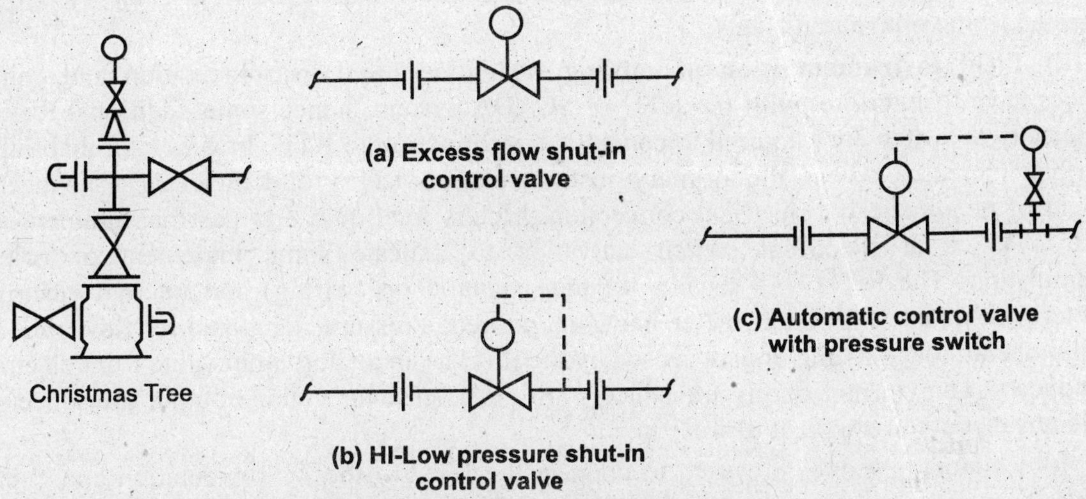

Fig. 8.45 : Wellhead safety controls

Fig. 8.45 shows three different types of automatic control valves that could be installed at the wellhead immediately adjacent to the tubing wing valve. The excess flow valve shown in Fig. 8.45 (a) is generally used only to protect against flow line breaks when the wells are chocked and controlled at the manifold. The high/low pressure shut-in valve in Fig. 8.45 (b) may be used whether the well is chocked at the wellhead or at the manifold. It gives protection against both flow line breaks and plugging.

7. Supervisory control and data acquisition systems (SCADA) : These systems can be used either to control/monitor few wells in a single field or to multiple fields that have several thousand total wells. SCADA systems consist of the basic elements : (i) SCADA equipment, (ii) field instrumentation and cabling systems, (iii) communication facilities, and (iv) digital computer systems.

(i) SCADA equipment : This equipment functions to interconnect digital computer systems and instrumentation and control devices that are related to the oil and gas producing processes. It consists of a communication adapter and the remote terminal units (RTUs). A communication adapter is directly connected to the digital computer by a high-speed data link and attached indirectly to RTUs by communication circuits. A number of RTUs generally share a common communication circuit. An RTU has the capability to store information from several input points and to transmit this information in a serial mode over a single communication circuit to a digital computer on demand. The RTU also may receive control information from the computer that it routes to a selected control point. The RTU generally is located within a few thousand feet of its connected instrumentation and control equipment but may be upto several hundred miles from the computer location. RTUs commonly sense input information related to status/alarm, gas and oil volume accumulation instantaneous analog values of temperature, pressure, flow rate, etc. Heat and electrical transients adversely affect operational reliability of RTU. Hence they are usually placed in air-conditioned buildings. All RTU input/output connections to the field cable system are protected from voltage transients.

(ii) Field instrumentation of cabling systems : Field instrumentation and control devices have to interfere with the RTU of SCADA system, hence some additional features like electrical switch are required to convey the information to RTU. In general, reliability of interface increases when the primary instrumentation has a direct electrical connection instead of pneumatic to electrical conversion. Meters for liquid and gas measurement also need to have an electrical switch activation to indicate some increment of volume accumulation. The RTU will have a separate signal loop (wiring) and internal electronic counter associated with each meter being monitored. Pressure, temperature, flow rate and similar operational parameters are sensed by the RTU as an analog input value from electrical transducers. The current output transducers are preferred over voltage output transducers to avoid any electrical transient distortion.

Multiconductor cables are used to connect the RTU to the instrumentation and control devices associated with the production process. The cables usually are buried to minimize probability of mechanical damage and electrical noise intrusion. Radio communication links between RTUs and a central location within a field can reduce overall cabling costs substantially. The low-energy signals used in the cable system require careful connection of wiring to instrumentation. Any damage to wiring insulation or collection of moisture at connection points may result in sufficient signal leakage. To avoid this alarm-signal loops are installed which are in normal condition when the sensing device has a closed electrical switch.

(iii) Communication facilities : SCADA systems require capable and reliable communication facilities to connect the communication adapters on the digital computer system with the RTUs that are located in fields being automated. Most SCADA systems used non-switched communication circuits that have a four-wire configuration. The four-wire designation provides two independent communication paths that will support simultaneous data transfer in two directions.

(iv) Digital computer systems : SCADA became possible with the development of process control type computer systems. The hardware used for a process-control computer provides direct connection to plant instrumentation and control equipment and it also provided a means to interconnect with the communication adapter of SCADA system. Process control computers had software operating systems with program execution control that was compatible with SCADA needs.

8. Measurement of bottom-hole pressures (BHP) : BHP is now-a-days determined with continuously recording pressure gauges which are either self-contained or surface-recording.

Self-contained gauges : These gauges have the pressure element and recording section which are encased and sealed against external pressure except for an opening to communicate the pressure to the element. The entire instrument is run to the depth at which the pressure is to be measured and there it is allowed to stabilize thermally, and then returned to the surface and the pressure determined from the chart. Modern pressure measuring systems incorporate force summing devices that convert pressure energy into physical displacement or deformation (elastic element gauges).

The "Amerada" type pressure gauge has a helical Bourdon tube as a pressure element that is of sufficient length to rotate the stylus over full inside circumference of the cylindrical chart holder without multiplication of movement.

The "Humble" gauge pressure element has a piston, which moves through a stuffing box against a helical spring in tension. A stylus is attached to the inner end of the piston that records longitudinally on a chart in a cylindrical holder, which is rotated by a clock.

The "Gulf" BHP gauge has a pressure element consisting of a long, metallic bellows restrained by a double helical spring in tension, alongwith cylindrical chart holder rotated by a clock.

The BHP gauges must be properly adjusted and calibrated for getting consistently reliable and accurate pressure measurements.

Surface-recording gauges : These are either permanently installed or wireline retrievable. All surface-recording gauges are run on a single-conductor armored cable that carries a direct current from the surface to the transducer in the bottom-hole instrument. Oscillating current returns through the same circuit from the transducer to surface instruments that determine and record its frequency. The pressure transducers used are capacitive, variable inductance type, piezoelectric type, potentiometric type, vibrating wire type, strain gauge type.

9. Measurement of temperature in wells : Temperature logs are used currently to identify fluid entry into the well bore, fluid migration behind the casing, tubing/casing leaks, and the extent of hydraulic fracturing and to monitor injectivity profiles. The thermometers used for sensing well temperature may be either self contained recording type or electrical surface recording type.

Self-contained recording thermometers : "Humble" gauge temperature element has a container filled with mercury, which on rise in temperature, expands into a small-diameter cylinder at the end of a piston, which extends through a packing gland against a tense helical spring. A stylus arm attached to the end of the piston extends into the cylindrical chart holder of the recording mechanism. To prevent the effect of well pressure on the temperature element, the mercury container is enclosed within an outer tube, which is filled with mercury to reduce thermal lag.

"Amerada" gauge temperature element has a bulb attached to the pressure end of the helical Bourdon tube, but internally insulated from the gauge to reduce thermal lag. The bulb contains a liquid that has a substantial vapour pressure in the temperature range of interest. The response of such liquid vapour element is not linear, hence the accuracy and sensitivity of the element depend on the temperature to be measured.

Electrical surface recording thermometers : These gauges use a thermocouple, resistance wire, or thermistor as a temperature element. They are run on armored, insulated cables and the measuring wheel is geared to drive a chart recorder, camera, or computer to record temperature against depth. Differential thermometers have been developed to record very small changes in temperature. By using these thermometers, any temperature change noted can be checked by a rerun without returning the instrument to the surface.

A temperature survey of a well is made either by running the thermometer continuously at a slow speed or by stopping it for a short time at regular intervals.

10. Measurement of mud weight : A drilling mud is used to carry out the following functions : (i) to cool the drill bit and lubricate its teeth, (ii) to lubricate and cool the drill string, (iii) to control formation pressure, (iv) to carry cuttings out of the hole, (v) to stabilize the well bore to prevent it from caving-in.

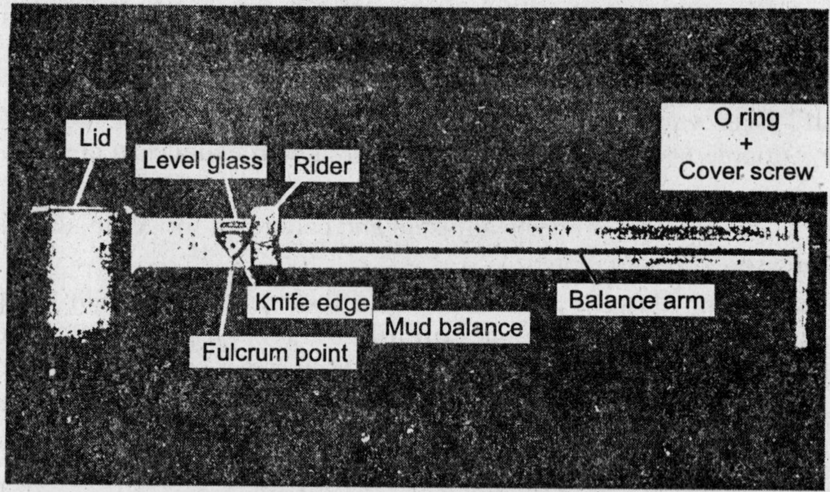

Fig. 8.46 : Mud balance

Mud weight or more precisely mud density is one of the fundamental properties of mud that is largely responsible for above functions. Mud density is defined as the mass of a given sample of mud divided by its volume, which largely depends upon the quantity of solids in liquid phase, either in solution or suspended by the particles of the liquid phase. The density of mud is given by

$$\rho_m = \frac{M_w - M_s}{V_w + V_s}$$

where M_W and M_S are masses of water (or oil) and solids, respectively, and V_W and V_S are the volumes of water (or oil) and solids, respectively. Mud weight is measured in the fields using a mud balance, shown in Fig. 8.46. For this a steel cup is filled with a freshly collected mud sample and then balanced on a knife edge, showing the reading of mud might in pcf, ppg or kg/m^3.

8.14 TELEMETRY AND TELECONTROL OF PRODUCTION OPERATIONS

The measurements taken while drilling a well are referred to as MWD. MWD allows an operator almost immediate feedback on both the geometry of the hole being drilled and the characteristics of the formations penetrated. Depending on the information obtained from MWD, the driller may take appropriate action such as changing the weight on bit (WOB), increasing the mud weight, or pulling out of the hole for a conventional logging run once the desired formation has been reached.

The MWD measuring systems have common characteristics :

(i) a downhole sensor sub,

(ii) a power source,

(iii) a telemetry system, and

(iv) surface equipment.

The downhole sensor subs may contain instrumentation capable of measuring parameters such as forque, WOB, borehole pressure, tool face angle, formation acoustic travel time, formation resistivity, hole deviation from vertical, and hole azimuth with respect to geographic co-ordinates. The sensors and the telemetry system can be activated by a surface power source, a downhole turbine or downhole batteries. The telemetry system most commonly used is that of coded mud pressure pulses.

The output from a specific sensor is converted from analog to a digital form and encoded as a series of pressure pulses, which are detected and decoded at the surface. The pressure pulses may be in the form of overpressure or underpressure anomalies introduced, respectively by either a relief valve "shorting" the mud circulation or a check valve "choking" it. The other methods used for telemetry are : (i) Electromagnetic e-mode (electric current) or h-mode (magnetic field), (ii) acoustic telemetry through drill pipe and/or tubing in straight hole, or through the earth by seismic waves, (iii) hard-wire systems, (iv) systems with self-energizing repeaters and (v) hybrid systems that combine various transmission methods.

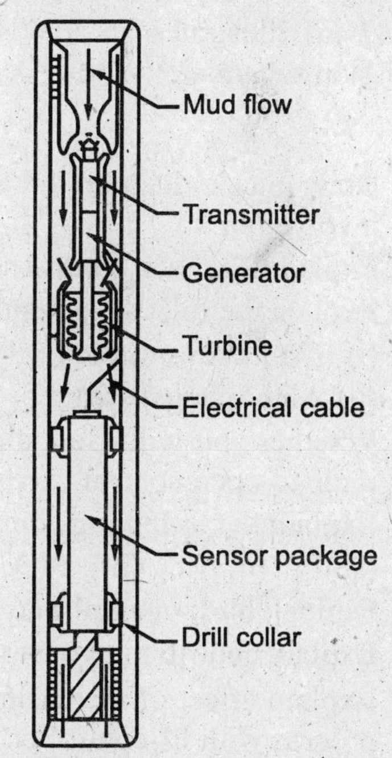

(a) MWD downhole assembly

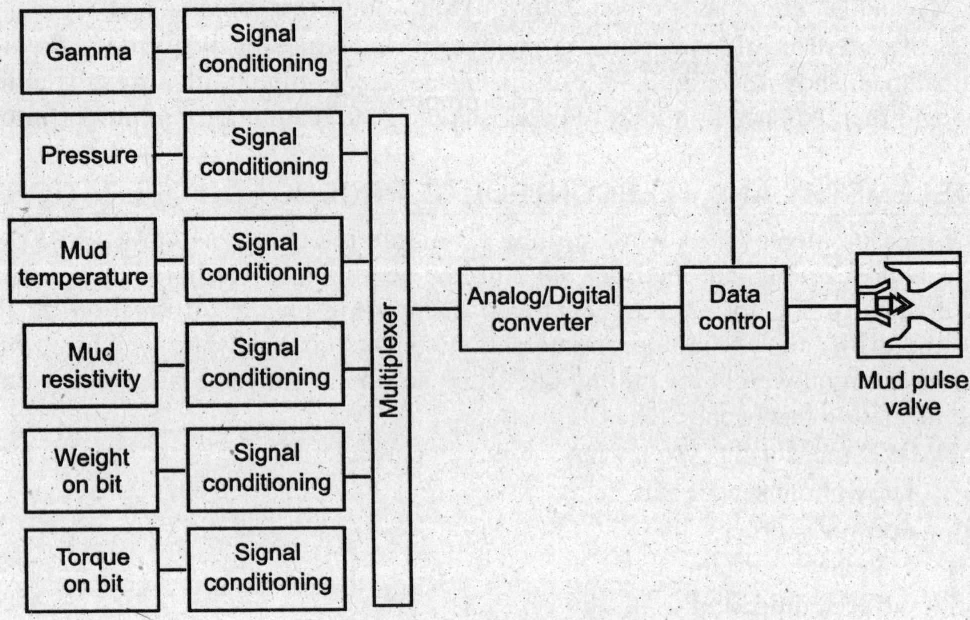

(b) MWD data transmission

Fig. 8.47 : Telemetry system

The surface equipment consists of a decoder of the parameter used in telemetering system, alongwith the signal processing hardware and software, that together produce the data that the drilling engineer needs. Output may be in the form of a visual display, either on the rig floor or at a remote site, or as a hard copy listing, or log, of the parameters recorded. Fig. 8.47 (a) illustrates an MWD downhole assembly, while Fig. 8.47 (b) shows a data transmission schematic for MWD.

EXERCISE

1. Draw block diagram of feedback control system. Explain the hardware elements involved in it.
2. Explain feedback control strategy with suitable example.
3. Explain the following features of controller action :
   (i) Direct/reverse action.
   (ii) Auto/manual switch.
4. Whether you will use a direct or reverse acting controller for a positive gain process if air-to-open control valve is used as the final control element ?
5. Explain the following control actions :
   (i) P, (ii) PI, (iii) PID.
6. Define : bias, integral time, reset rate, derivative time.
7. Explain contribution of reset action in a PI-controller.
8. Explain effect of increasing k_c and decreasing τ_I on step response characteristics of a process with PI-controller.
9. Explain the effect of derivative action when added to a PID-controller.
10. Explain working and applications of on-off controller.

11. Explain simple controller performance measures.
12. What are servo and regulator operations ?
13. Explain servo response of a first-order process with
    (a) P-only control.
    (b) PI-control.
    (c) PID-control.
14. Explain servo response of a second-order underdamped, overdamped and critically damped process with
    (a) P-only control.
15. Define offset. Explain why P-controller introduce offset ? How to remove it ?
16. Explain control loops for :
    (a) Liquid level in surge tank.
    (b) Temperature control of a steam-heated stirred tank heater.
    (c) Flow control in a pipe line. (d) Air pressure control.
    (e) CSTR control. (f) PFR control.
    (g) Distillation column control. (h) Heat exchanger control.
    (i) Compressor control.
17. How control valve works as the final control element ?
18. Describe the basic elements of a control valve.
19. Classify the control valves based on the stem movement.
20. Describe various valve plug designs.
21. Describe working of spring diaphragm actuator.
22. Describe spring actuator with valve positioner. State the functions and advantages of valve positioner.
23. Differentiate between inherent and installed flow characteristics of a control valve.
24. State the mathematical relation between the fluid flow rate through the valve and valve opening for -
    (a) Linear characteristic valve, (b) Equal percentage characteristic valve.
25. Sketch quick opening and parabolic flow characteristics.
26. Why installed flow characteristics differ from inherent characteristics ?
27. Define - (a) Distortion coefficient, (b) Rangeability.
28. What are the factors to be considered for selecting a control valve suitable for a process ?
29. What are the factors to be considered for sizing of the control valve ?
30. How valve gain affects the system gain ?
31. Describe various temperature control methods for material heated by -
    (i) steam, (ii) electricity, (iii) burning fuel.
32. How will you select the control mode suitable for controlling given process ?
33. How will you control temperature of -
    (a) heated rubber or plastic compounds, (b) melting metal,
    (c) heated glue, wax ?

34. Give reason : For temperature control of electrically heated material, the part of the heater input is uncontrolled.
35. Describe the working of spring loaded pressure regulator.
36. State applications of level control.
37. Describe various methods of liquid level control.
38. How will you control liquid level of volatile liquid in pressure vessel ?
39. Describe averaging of liquid level.
40. State applications of fluid flow rate control.
41. Flow controller using orifice requires square root extraction mechanism. Justify.
42. Describe ratio control.
43. Describe cascade control.
44. Describe control of temperature of liquid outflow from the heat exchanger based on -
    (a) product outlet temperature, (b) condensate level.
45. Distinguish between the performance oriented and inventory oriented objectives of distillation column control.
46. Describe distillation column control based on -
    (a) steam flow rate and feed flow rate, (b) distillate purity (top tray temperature), (c) reboiler level, (d) column pressure.
47. Describe the control of temperature and pressure of chemical reactor.
48. Describe alarm systems used in control room.
49. Describe construction and working of limit switches used for :
    (i) temperature control, (ii) pressure control, (iii) level control.
50. Outline the control scheme for :
    (i) batch reactor, (ii) continuous reactor.
51. Describe the factors affecting the performance of the extrusion process used in polymer processing.
52. Explain extrusion process control in detail.
53. Explain injection moulding process control.
54. What are the basic variables to be controlled in oil and gas separators ? Give the control schemes for the same.
55. Describe control of : (i) horizontal separator, (ii) vertical separator.
56. What are the instrumentation and control provisions required for safe storage and transportation of petroleum oil ?
57. Describe automatic production control equipments used in oil-well drilling operations.
58. Write a note on SCADA systems used in oil-well drilling operations.
59. How will you measure :
    (i) BHP (bottom hole pressure) and (ii) Temperature of oil wells ?
60. Describe the construction and working of mud-balance.
61. Write a note on telemetry systems used in production operations.

❑❑❑